Alessandro Cipriani • Maurizio Giri

ELECTRONIC MUSIC AND SOUND DESIGN

Theory and Practice with Max 9 - Vol. 1

Cipriani, Alessandro. Giri, Maurizio.
Electronic Music and Sound Design : theory and practice with Max 9. Vol. 1. / Alessandro Cipriani, Maurizio Giri.
Includes bibliographical references and index.
ISBN 978-88-99212-28-5
1. Computer Music - Instruction and study. 2. Computer composition.

Original Title: Musica Elettronica e Sound Design - Teoria e Pratica con Max 7

Translation by David Stutz
New sections translated by Alessandro Cipriani and Maurizio Giri

First edition 2010
Second edition 2013
Third edition 2016
Fourth edition 2019
Fifth edition 2025

Figures produced by: Gabriele Cappellani and Maurizio Refice
Index: Salvatore Mudanò
Language education consultant: Damiano De Paola

SUPPORT PAGE
The support page for this book is at: **http://www.virtual-sound.com/cmsupport**

Contemponet s.a.s., Rome (Italy)
e-mail posta@contemponet.com
URL: www.contemponet.com

CONTENTS

FOREWORD

by David Zicarelli

It might seem odd to you, but many years ago, I spent a lot of time learning about making sound with a computer by reading books and articles while trying to imagine what the synthesis techniques being described would actually sound like. While I suppose my imagination might have been stimulated by this practice, I am happy that real-time synthesis has progressed to the point where you no longer have to be deprived of the perceptual experience that is such an important part of learning the techniques of digital synthesis.

Alessandro Cipriani and Maurizio Giri's book is one of the first courses on electronic sound that explicitly integrates perception, theory, and practice using examples of real-time sound synthesis you can manipulate and experience for yourself. In my view, the manipulation aspect of learning about sound is critically important. It helps lead you to what Joel Chadabe terms "predictive knowledge" -- the ability to intuit what will happen to a sound before you take an action to change it. We all have some level of predictive knowledge. For example, most of us know that by turning a volume knob clockwise, the sound coming from our amplifier will get louder. Once we enter the realm of digital sound synthesis, things quickly get more complicated than a volume knob, and we need the first-hand experience of manipulation and perception in order to deepen our predictive knowledge.

However, to educate ourselves fully about digitally produced sound, we need more than predictive knowledge. We need to know why our manipulations make the perceptual changes we experience. This theoretical knowledge reinforces our intuitive experiential knowledge, and at the same time, our experience gives perceptual meaning to theoretical explanations.

In my opinion, Cipriani and Giri have done a masterful job of allowing experiential and theoretical knowledge to reinforce each other. This book will work either as a textbook or as a vehicle for the independent learner. As a bonus, the book includes a thorough introduction to digital signal processing with Max and serves as a wonderful introduction to the programming concepts in that software.

As you will see, the theoretical chapters are the "T" chapters, while practical and experiential knowledge is imparted by the "P" chapters. These chapters alternate, in the form of a ladder, refining the concepts at ever higher levels of sophistication.

I hope you will take advantage of the excellent Max examples the authors have created. They are simultaneously fun and enlightening, and they sound good enough to use on stage. They are also worth examining as models for your own Max patches, or for extending in new ways. But a few minutes of messing around with the examples is not the same thing as studying the concepts in the book. The book provides the language for expressing the concepts in terms of the underlying theory. Knowing the theory is essential, because presumably you're reading this book because you want to be more than someone who can turn a volume knob.

That is the authors' wish for you, and mine as well. I want to wish you good luck on this new adventure, and also thank my two Italian friends for creating such a comprehensive resource for learning about digital music – the one I wish existed when I was a student!

David Zicarelli, publisher of Max

INTRODUCTION

This is the first of a series of three volumes (now updated for Max 9) dedicated to digital synthesis and sound design. The second volume covers a range of additional topics in the realm of sound synthesis and signal processing, including dynamics processing, delay lines, digital audio and sampled sounds, the art of organizing sound, MIDI, OSC, Max for Live and realtime control. A third volume will be concerned with modulation techniques (such as AM, RM, SSB and FM synthesis), granular synthesis, GEN programming, reverberation and spatialization, analysis and resynthesis, and other topics.

PREREQUISITES

This first volume will be useful to several levels of reader. Prerequisites for its study are minimal, and include nothing more than rudimentary musical knowledge such as an understanding of notes, scales, and chords, as well as basic computer skills such as saving files, copying and pasting text.
The volume should be equally useful for self-learners and for those studying under the guidance of a teacher. It is laid out as chapters of theoretical background material that are interleaved with chapters that contain practical computer techniques. Each pair of chapters stands together as a unit. We suggest that curricula follow this structure, first touching on theory, then following up with hands-on material, including computer activities. The theoretical chapters are not intended to substitute for more expansive texts about synthesis; they provide, instead, an organic framework for learning the theory that is needed to invent sounds on the computer and to write signal processing programs.

TIME NEEDED FOR STUDY

The time needed for this material will, of course, vary from person to person. Nonetheless, here are two estimates to help in planning, one for learning under the guidance of an expert teacher, and the other for self-learners:

Self-learning
(300 total hours of individual study)

Chapters	Topic	Total hours
1T+1P+IA	Sound synthesis	100
2T+2A	Additive Synthesis	60
3T+3P+IB	Subtractive Synthesis and Filtering	110
4T+4P	Control Signals	30

Teacher-assisted learning
(60 hours of classroom-based learning + 120 hours of individual study)

Chapters	Topic	Lessons	Feedback	Studio time	Total hours
1T+1P+IA	Sound synthesis	16	4	40	60
2T+2P	Additive Synthesis	10	2	24	36
3T+3P+IB	Subtractive Synthesis	18	4	44	66
4T+4P	Control Signals	5	1	12	18

THEORY AND PRACTICE

As we just said, the teaching approach for this book is based, first and foremost, upon an interplay between theory and practice, which we believe is indispensable. One of the glaring problems in the field of digital sound processing is the knowledge gap that exists between experts in theory (who often have neither the time nor the need to tackle concrete technical problems that are so relevant to the actual practice of creating sound) and those enthusiasts, much more numerous, who love to invent and modify sounds using their computers. These enthusiasts persevere, despite gaps in their theoretical awareness and/or in their understanding of how sounds may be modified within the rigid confines forced upon them by their specific software. It is our intention help these users of music software to acquire the deeper understanding that will take them beyond the confines of specific software to access the profound power inherent in the medium.

TEACHING APPROACH AND METHOD OF THIS BOOK

On the basis of the problems and concepts described above, we have tried to fill the information gap by continuing in the direction already begun with the book titled "Virtual Sound" (Cipriani and Bianchini), also dedicated to sound synthesis and signal processing. The innovations in this new text are substantial, with regard to both the examples provided and a completely different teaching approach. Because very little academic literature is available concerning methods for teaching electronic music, we have approached the problem directly, considering various promising ways to plumb the depths of the subject material. This exercise has led us to an organic teaching method, in which we adopt various ideas and techniques from foreign language textbooks in order to develop a more context-based, open-ended and interactive concept of teaching and learning.
In addition to video examples, we have included "learning agendas" that detail the specific objectives for each chapter, that include listening and analysis activities, exercises and tests, glossaries, and suggestions for recordings to which to listen. The practical chapters of the book also include many other new features and activities, including the correction, completion, implementation, debugging, testing and analysis of algorithms, the construction of new algorithms from scratch, the replacement of parts of pre-built algorithms, and reverse engineering (in which the reader listens to a sound and then tries to invent an algorithm to create a similar sound).
These activities and tasks are intended to activate the knowledge and practical skills of the reader. When learning a foreign language, there is a gap between what one knows and what one is able to use in practice. It is common for a student's passive vocabulary (the total number of terms that the student can recognize) to be much larger than the active vocabulary that he or she can actually use while speaking or writing. The same is true of a programming language: a student can understand how algorithms work without being able to build them from scratch. The activities in this book that concentrate on replacing parts of algorithms, completing unfinished algorithms, correcting algorithms with bugs, and reverse engineering, have been included in order

to pose problems to which the reader is encouraged to find his or her own solutions, causing the learning process to become more active and creative.
When learning a foreign language, students are given replacement exercises (e.g. "replace the underlined verb in the following phrase: I wish I could go out"), correction exercises (e.g. "correct the following phrase: I want to went home"), and sentences to be completed (e.g. "I'd like to ... home"). In this context, it is vitally important for the student to work at these activities in order to avoid an excessively passive approach to learning. Our approach, likewise, not only involves interactions between the *perception* of sounds and the *knowledge* deriving from reading the book and doing the practical activities, but also interactions between these two factors and the user's own *skills* and *creativity*.

This method is not based on a rigidly linear progression, but is rather a network that enables the reader to acquire knowledge and practical skills through an interaction of four separate dimensions: learning of the theoretical concepts, learning to use the Max program, interacting with example material, and constructing algorithms.

MAX

The practical parts of this book are based on the software Max. This program, written originally by Miller Puckette, was extensively revised and expanded by David Zicarelli, and is published as a supported product by Cycling '74 (www.cycling74.com). Max is an interactive graphic environment for music, audio processing, and multimedia. It is used throughout the world by musicians, composers, sound designers, visual artists, and multimedia artists, and it has become a *de facto* standard for modern technologically-enabled creative projects in both the musical and in the visual spheres.

It is a graphic programming language, and is therefore *relatively* easy to learn, especially given its great power and expressivity. In Max one creates programs by connecting onscreen graphic objects with virtual cables. These objects can perform calculations, produce or process sounds, render visuals, or be configured as a graphical user interface. Using its sound synthesis and signal processing capabilities, one can fashion soft-synths, samplers, reverbs, signal-processing effects, and many other things.
In practice, Max adopts the metaphor of the modular synthesizer: each module handles a particular function, exchanging data with the modules to which it is connected. The difference between a traditional modular synthesizer and Max is that with Max, one can access and control a level of detail that would be inconceivable in a preconfigured synthesizer or extension module (whether hardware or software).

PRACTICAL INFORMATION

Many indispensable materials accompany this book, among them, video examples, patches (programs written in Max), sound files, programming libraries, and other materials.
These can be found at **www.virtual-sound.com/cmsupport**.

Example Files

The example files (patches), are created to be used with Max version 5 or higher, which is downloadable from the official Cycling '74 website, www.cycling74.com.

Alternating Theory and Practice

In this book, theoretical chapters alternate with chapters which are geared towards programming practice. Because of this, the reader will find himself taking on all of the theory for a given chapter before passing to the corresponding practical chapter. An alternative to this approach would be to read a single section from the theory, and then go directly to the corresponding section of the practical chapter. (For example, 1.1T and 1.1P, then 1.2T and 1.2P, etc.

The Interludes

Note that there are two "technical interludes", the first between the first and second chapters, and the second between the third and fourth chapters. These interludes, named respectively "Interlude A" and "Interlude B", are dedicated specifically to the Max language. They don't relate directly to any of the theoretical discussions, but they are very necessary for following the code traced out in the book. After having tackled the theory and practice of the first chapter, before moving on to the second chapter, it will benefit the reader to study Interlude A. Likewise, Interlude B is meant to be studied between Chapters 3 and 4.

Learning Max

Learning Max (and, in general, learning synthesis and sound processing) requires effort and concentration. In contrast to much commercial music software, Max provides flexibility to the programmer, and this design choice provides those programming with Max many alternative ways to build a given algorithm. To benefit from this freedom, however, it is advisable to consider the recommendations of the book and to code in a systematic way. Max is a true musical instrument, and learning to play it should be approached as one would approach the study of a traditional instrument (such as a violin). As with any instrument, the reader will find it necessary to practice regularly, and to stay sharp on basics while gradually acquiring more complex techniques. By approaching the software in this way, fundamental techniques and technical insights can be retained once they have been acquired.

Bibliography

The decision was made to limit the bibliography in this book to a list of only the most absolutely essential reference works, and, of course, a list of the books and articles cited in the text. A more comprehensive bibliography is available online.

Before Beginning

To begin working with this book, you will need to download the video examples, which you will find at the support page for virtual-sound.com: www.virtual-sound.com/cmsupport. While reading the theory chapters, you will find constant references to the examples contained in this downloadable archive.

To work interactively with the programming chapters of the book, you will need to download the Virtual Sound Macro Library from the support page mentioned above. It will also be necessary to install Max, which is available at the Cycling74 website: www.cycling74.com. The web page, **www.virtual-sound.com/cmsupport**, contains detailed instructions regarding how to install Max and the macro library correctly; look for the document entitled "How to Install and Configure Max". Always check the support page for patches (Max programs) related to the practice chapters of this book, as well as the audio files for the reverse engineering exercises.

Comments and Suggestions

Corrections and comments are always welcome. Please contact the authors via email at: a.cipriani@edisonstudio.it and maurizio@giri.it
http://www.edisonstudio.it/alessandro-cipriani
http://www.giri.it

THANKS

We wish to thank Gabriele Cappellani, Salvatore Mudanò and Francesco "Franz" Rosati for their patience and long hours of work, and Dario Amoroso, Joel Chadabe, Mirko Ettore D'Agostino, Luca De Siena, Eugenio Giordani, Gabriele Paolozzi, Giuseppe Emanuele Rapisarda, Fausto Sebastiani, Alvise Vidolin and David Zicarelli for their generosity.

DEDICATIONS

This text is dedicated to Riccardo Bianchini, who would have wanted to participate in the production of this teaching text, but who, unfortunately, passed away before the work began. We have collected some of his materials, revised them, and cited them in a few of the sections on theory. This seemed to be a way to have Riccardo still with us. A particular thanks goes to Ambretta Bianchini for her great generosity and sensitivity during these years of work.

Alessandro Cipriani and Maurizio Giri

1T
INTRODUCTION TO SOUND SYNTHESIS

LEARNING AGENDA

PREREQUISITES FOR THE CHAPTER

- Basic skills in using computers (operating a computer, managing files and folders, audio formats, etc.)
- Minimal knowledge of music theory (semitones, octaves, rhythms, etc.)

LEARNING OBJECTIVES

Knowledge

- To learn about the signal paths one uses in sound synthesis and signal processing
- To learn about the principal parameters of sound and their characteristics
- To learn how pitch and sound intensity are digitally encoded
- To learn about musical intervals in different tuning systems
- To learn about audio file formats

Skills

- To be able to hear changes of frequency and amplitude and to describe their characteristics
- To be able to hear the stages of the envelope of a sound or a glissando

CONTENTS

- Computer-based sound synthesis and signal processing
- Theory of timbre, pitch, and sound intensity
- Theory of glissandi and amplitude envelopes
- The relationship between frequency, pitch, and MIDI encoding
- Introduction to sampled sound
- Introduction to panning

ACTIVITIES

- Video examples

TESTING

- Questions with short answers
- Listening and analysis

SUPPORTING MATERIALS

- Fundamental concepts
- Glossary

1.1 SOUND SYNTHESIS AND SIGNAL PROCESSING

The use of computers in music has enabled composers and musicians to manage and manipulate sound with a precision and a freedom that is unthinkable with acoustic instruments. Thanks to the computer, it is now possible to model sound in every way imaginable. One might say that while the traditional composer working with traditional instruments composes *using* sounds, the electronic composer composes *the sounds themselves.*

The same thing has happened in animation graphics: thanks to the computer it is now possible to create images and film sequences that are extremely realistic, and that would have been impossible to produce by other means. Almost all cinematic special effects are now produced with computers; it is becoming commonplace to find virtual entities sharing the screen with flesh-and-blood actors.

These newfound possibilities are the result of passing from the analog world into the digital world. The digital world is a world of numbers. Once an image or a sound has been converted into a sequence of numbers, those numbers can be subjected to transformations, since numbers are easily and efficiently analyzed and manipulated by computers. The process of digitization, precisely defined as that of transforming an item of data (a text, a sound, an image) into a sequence of numbers, is the technique that makes this all possible.[1]

This text will concentrate on two subjects: sound synthesis and signal processing. **Sound synthesis** means the electronic generation of sound. In practice, you will find that the possibilities for creating sound are based largely on a few selected parameters, and that you can obtain the sonorities you seek by manipulating these parameters.

Signal processing in this context means the electronic modification of a sound, whether the sound of a recorded guitar or a sound generated by using a particular type of sound synthesis.

DIGITAL SYNTHESIS OF SOUND

When generating sound using a programming language designed for sound synthesis and signal processing, we specify a desired sound by constructing a "virtual machine" of our own design (realized as an **algorithm**[2]) , and by specifying a series of instructions which this machine will use to create the sound.

Once we have written this sequence of instructions, the programming language we're using (Max for example) will *execute* our instructions to create a *stream of digital data* in which all of the characteristics of the

---

[1] We will broaden this concept during the course of the chapter.

[2] An algorithm is a sequence of instructions, written in a programming language, that enables a computer to carry out a defined task.

sound or sounds that we have specified will be rendered.[3] Between the time that this stream of digital data is generated and the time that we actually hear the sound, another fundamental operation occurs. The computer's **audio interface** transforms the digital data into an electrical signal that, when fed to an amplifier and loudspeakers, will produce the sound. The audio interface, in other words, converts the digital data into an analog voltage (a process often abbreviated as "D/A conversion"), allowing us to hear the sounds that are represented by the stream of digital data. (fig. 1.1).

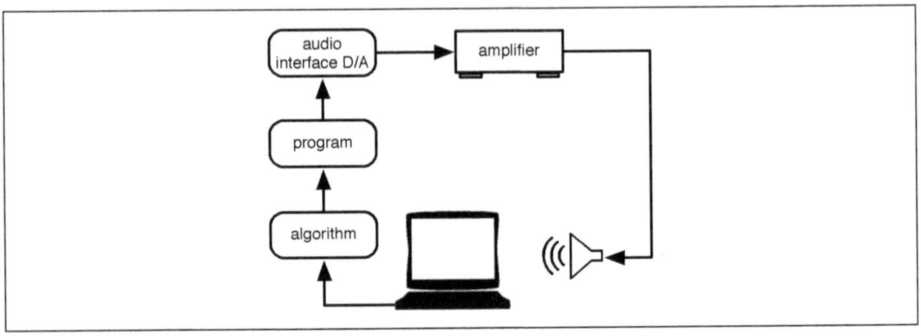

Fig. 1.1 Realtime synthesis

We can also capture the stream of data to our hard disk as an *audio file*, which will enable us to hear the result of our algorithmic processing as many times as we'd like.

When the stream of data goes directly to the audio interface as it is processed, so that there are only few milliseconds between the processing and the listening of the synthesized sound, one speaks of **realtime synthesis**. When the processing of sound is first calculated entirely and saved to an audio file (which can be listened to later) one speaks of **non-realtime** or **offline synthesis**. (In this context the latter term is not a technical one, but it is widely used.)

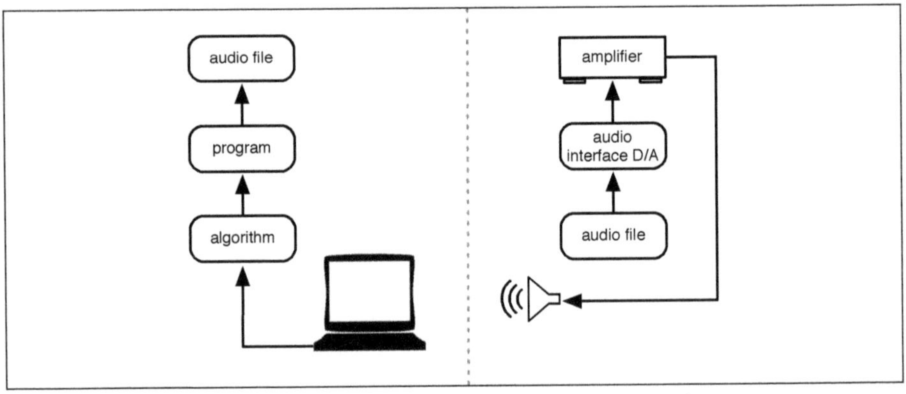

Fig. 1.2 Non-realtime synthesis and listening as separate actions

[3] In numeric form.

SIGNAL PROCESSING

Signal processing is the act of modifying a sound produced by a live source, for example through a microphone, or from a pre-existing audio file already stored in your computer. It is possible to do signal processing in various ways. We see three possibilities:

Pre-existing sound, saved separately as a sound file which is processed offline

The sound of a flute, for example, is recorded to disk using a microphone connected to the audio interface, which performs the analog-to-digital conversion.[4] We implement an algorithm in which we specify the sonic modifications to be made to the original audio file. Once executed, this program will create a new audio file containing the now-modified sound of the flute. We can then listen to the processed sound file at any time by *playing the file* (through the audio interface).

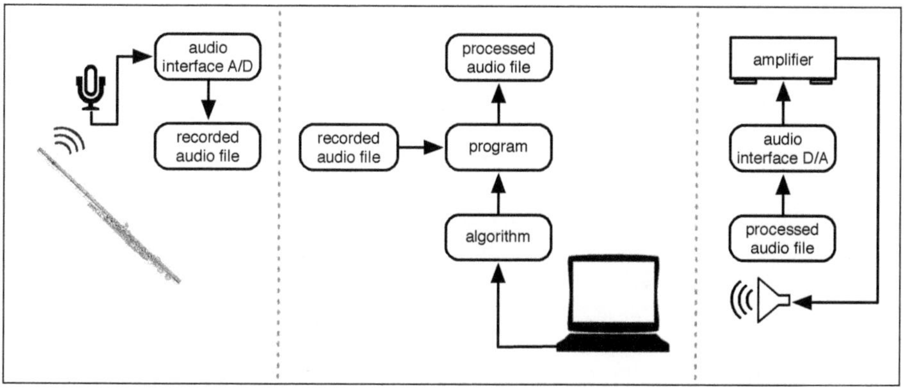

Fig. 1.3 Example of offline sound processing

Pre-recorded sound, which is then processed in realtime

A sound, already recorded in the computer as in the first example, is streamed from a pre-existing sound file. The processing program, while executing commands to modify the streamed sound file, also routes the processed sound file directly to the audio interface for listening. The program, although it is processing in real time, can also record the resulting stream into an audio file for later listening, as in fig. 1.4.

Realtime sound, processed immediately

Sound comes from a live source. As in the preceding example, the processing program, executing commands, routes the processed sound directly to the audio interface.

---

[4] A transformation of a physical sound into a sequence of numbers.

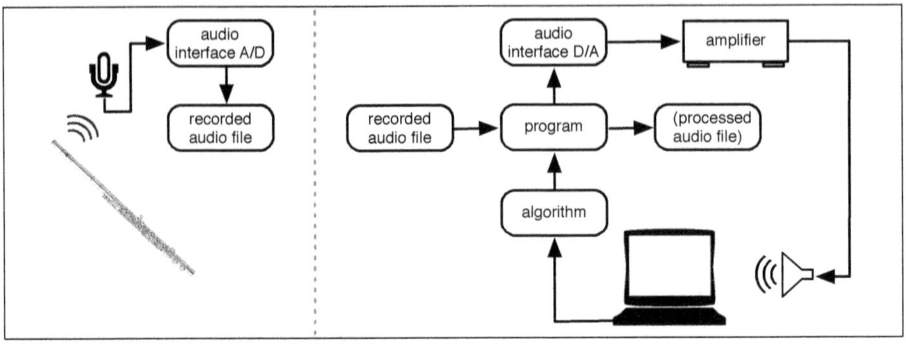

Fig. 1.4 Example of realtime sound processing on pre-existing sound

Naturally, in this case also, the program can record the processed sound as an audio file, as shown in figure 1.5.

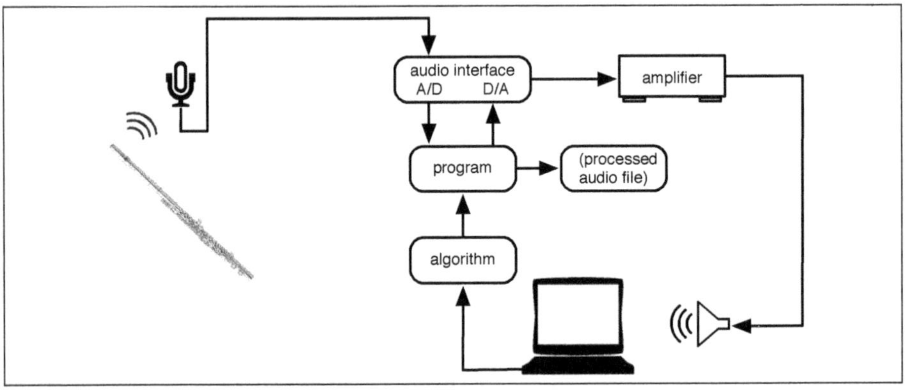

Fig. 1.5 Example of realtime sound processing on live sound

We define a **DSP system** as an integrated hardware and software system (computer, audio interface, programming language.) that enables the processing and/or synthesis of sound. The term **DSP** is an acronym for digital signal processing.

REALTIME VERSUS OFFLINE PROCESSING

We have seen that both synthesis and signal processing can occur either in realtime or offline. At first glance, the more valuable approach would seem to be realtime, because this method provides immediate feedback and an opportunity to weigh the appropriateness of the algorithm being evaluated, as well as to tune and tweak the code if necessary.

What cause is served, then, by deferring processing to offline status?

The first reason is simple: to implement algorithms that the computer cannot execute in realtime, due to their complexity. If, for example, the computer needs two minutes of time in order to synthesize or to process one minute

of sound, one has no alternative but to record the result to disk in order to be able to listen to it without interruption once the processing has finished.
At the dawn of computer music, all of the processing done for synthesis and effects was performed offline, because the processing power to do realtime calculation did not exist. With the increasing power of computers, it began to be possible to perform some processing directly in realtime, and, over time, the processing power of personal computers grew enormously, enabling them to do most synthesis and processing in realtime. But as computing power continues to grow, new possibilities are continually imagined, some of which are so complex that they can only be achieved offline. The need for offline processing will never disappear.
There also exists a second reason: a category of processing that is *conceptually* offline, independent of the power of the computer. If we want, for example, to implement an algorithm that, given a sequence of musical sounds from an instrument, will first break the sequence down into singles notes and then reorder those notes, sorting from the lowest to the highest pitch, we *must* do this processing offline. To realize this algorithm, we would first need the entire sequence, most likely recorded into an audio file in a way that the computer could analyze; the algorithm could then separate the lowest note, then the next-lowest, and so forth until finished. It should be obvious that this kind of analysis can only take place offline, only after the completion of the entire sequence; a computer that could handle this kind of algorithm in realtime (that is to say, while the instrument was playing the sequence) would be a computer so powerful that it could see into the future!
A final advantage of non-realtime processing is the prospect of *saving time*! Contrary to what one might initially think, realtime processing is not the fastest computing speed possible. We can imagine, for example, that we might modify a 10 minutes sound file using a particular type of processing. If this modification were to happen in realtime, it would obviously take 10 minutes, but we might also imagine that our computer had enough power to render this processing offline in 1 minute. In other words, the computer could render the calculations for this particular hypothetical operation at a speed 10 times faster than realtime. Offline processing, in this case, would be far more convenient than realtime processing.

1.2 FREQUENCY, AMPLITUDE, AND WAVEFORM

Frequency, amplitude and waveform are three basic parameters of sound.[5] Each one of these parameters influences how we perceive sound, and in particular:

a) our ability to distinguish a lower pitch from a higher one (frequency)
b) our ability to distinguish a loud sound from a soft sound (amplitude)
c) our ability to distinguish different timbres (waveform)

[5] We refer here to the simplest forms of sound. (i.e. we will later see how the parameter of timbre actually depends on several factors.)

Let's look at a table (taken from Bianchini, R., 2003) of the correspondences between the physical features of sound, musical parameters, and perceived sonority.

CHARACTERISTIC	PARAMETER	PERCEPTUAL SENSATION
Frequency	Pitch	High ↔ Low
Amplitude	Intensity	Forte ↔ Piano
Waveform	Timbre	Sound color

TABLE A: correspondences between sound characteristics, musical parameters and perceived sonority.

FREQUENCY

Frequency is the physical parameter that determines the pitch of a sound, that is, it is the feature that allows us to distinguish between a high-pitched sound and a low-pitched sound. The range of frequencies that is audible to humans extends from about 20 to about 20,000 hertz, that is to say, from about 20 to about 20,000 cycles per second.[6] (We'll define cycles per second in a moment.) The higher the frequency of a sound, the higher its pitch will be.
But what do we mean by hertz or "cycles per second"? To understand this, we refer to the definition of sound given by Riccardo Bianchini:

"The term 'sound' signifies a phenomenon caused by a mechanical perturbation of a transmission medium (usually air) which contains characteristics that can be perceived by the human ear.[7] Such a vibration might be transmitted to the air, for example, by a vibrating string (see fig. 1.6). The string moves back and forth, and during this movement it pushes the molecules of air together on one side, while separating them from each other on the other side. When the motion of the string is reversed, the molecules that had been pushed together are able to move away from each other, and vice versa.
The compressions and expansions (that is to say, the movements of air molecules) propagate through the air in all directions. Initially, the density of molecules in

[6] The highest frequency that someone can hear varies from individual to individual. Age is also a factor. As we get older, our ears become less sensitive to high frequencies.
[7] There are many theories about the nature of sound: Roberto Casati and Jérôme Dokic argue that the air is a medium through which the sound is transmitted, but that sound itself is a localized event that resonates in the body, or in the mechanical system that produces the vibration. (Casati, R., Dokic, J. 1994). Another point of view is expressed by Frova: "with the term 'sound', one ought to signify the sensation, as manifest in the brain, of a perturbation of a mechanical nature, of an oscillatory character, which affects the medium interposed between source and listener." (Frova, A., 1999, p.4).

air is constant; each unit of volume (for example, a cubic centimeter) contains the same number of molecules.

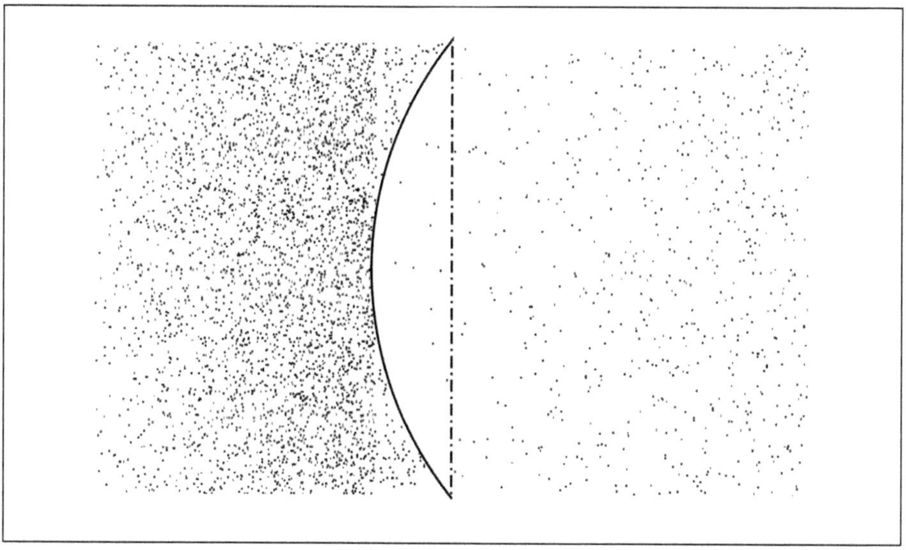

Fig. 1.6 Vibration of a string

This density can be expressed as a value called *pressure*. Once the air is disturbed, the pressure value is no longer constant, but varies from point to point, increasing where molecules are pushed together and decreasing where the density of the molecules is rarefied (see fig. 1.7).

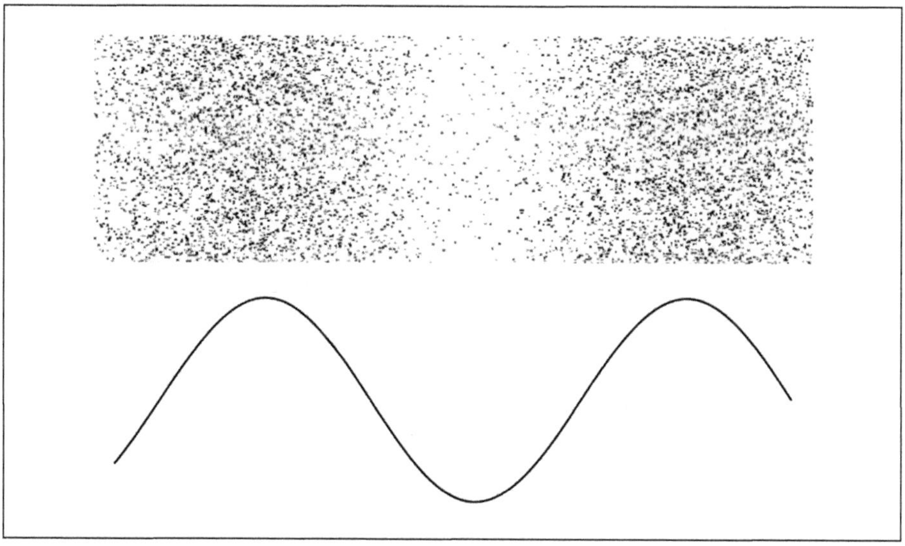

Fig.1.7 Compression and rarefaction of air molecules

Pressure can be physically studied either in terms of space (by simultaneously noting the pressure at multiple points at a given moment), or from the point of time (by measuring the pressure at a single location as a function of time). For example, we can imagine that if we were located at a specific point in space, we might observe a series of condensations and rarefactions of the air around us, as in figure 1.8.

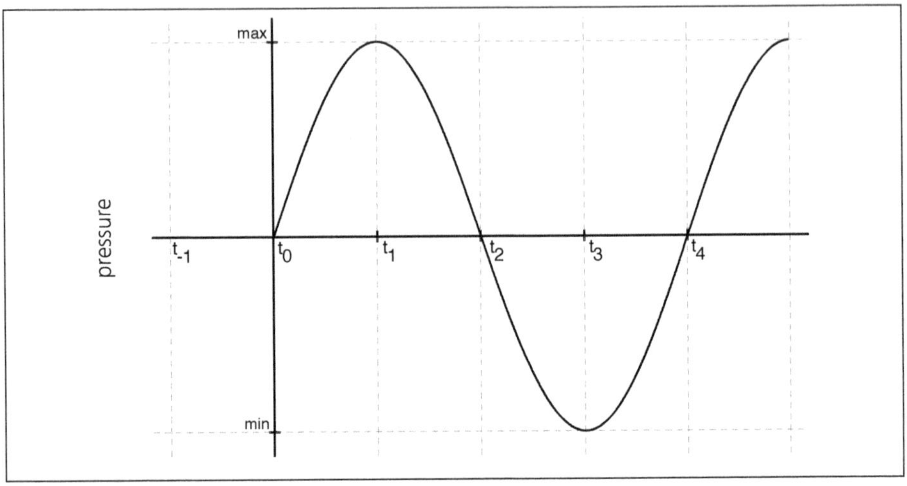

Fig.1.8 A graphical representation of compression and rarefaction

At time t_{-1}, which occurs immediately before t_0, the air pressure has its normal value, since the cyclic disturbance has not yet reached our point of observation. At instant t_0, the disturbance arrives at our observation point, pressure starts to rise, reaches a maximum value at time t_1, and then decreases until it returns to normal at time t_2. It continues to decline, reaching its minimum value at t_3, after which pressure returns to its normal value at t_4; the pattern then repeats. What has been described is a phenomenon called a **cycle**, and an event that always repeats in this way is called *periodic*.[8] The time required to complete a cycle is said to be the **period** of the wave, which is indicated by the symbol T and is measured in seconds (s) or in milliseconds (ms). The number of cycles that are completed in a second is defined as *frequency*, and is measured in hertz (Hz) or cycles per second (cps).
If, for example, a sound wave has period T = 0.01s (1/100 of a second), its frequency will be 1/T = 1/0.01 = 100 Hz (or 100 cycles per second)."(ibid)

While examining figure 1.9, listen to the sounds of Video Example 1A.[9] We can see (and hear) that increasing the number of cycles per second (Hz) corresponds to making a sound higher in pitch.

[8] Mathematically a waveform is said to be periodic if it is repeated regularly for an infinite time. In the practice of music, of course, we can satisfy ourselves with periods much shorter than infinity! We will say that a wave is "musically periodic" when it displays enough regularity to induce a perception of pitch that corresponds to the period of the wave. We'll discuss this issue in more detail in Chapter 2.

[9] Please note that video examples and other supporting materials to the book can be found on the web at http://www.virtual-sound.com/cmsupport.

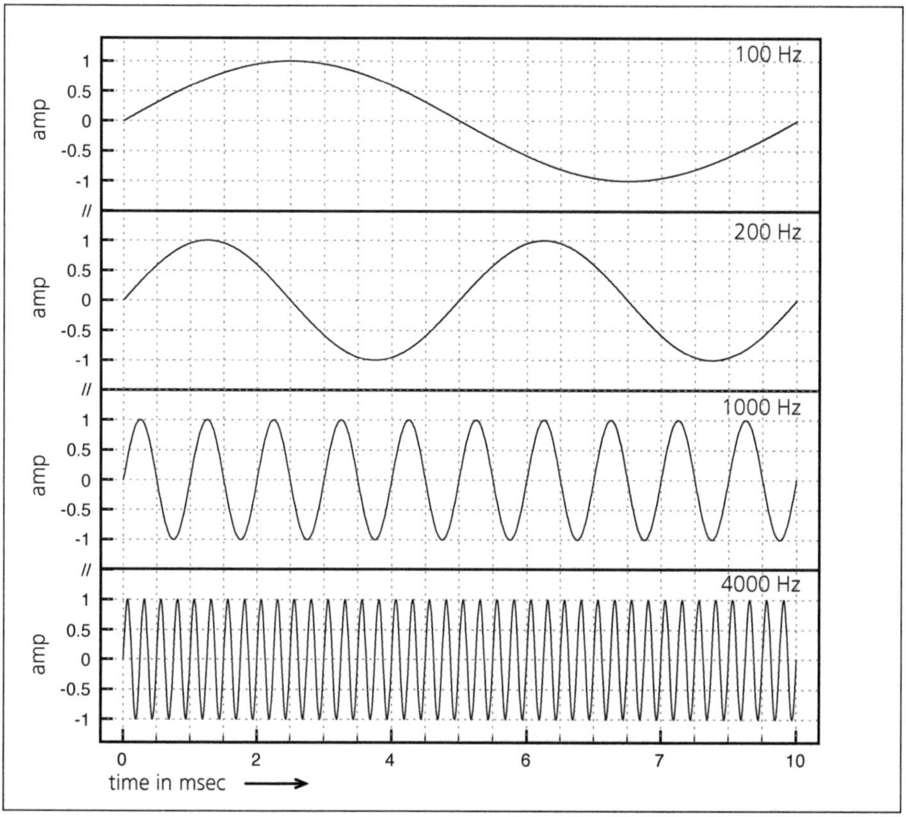

Fig.1.9 Four sounds of different frequencies

VIDEO EXAMPLE 1A • *FREQUENCY*

From the instant that it propagates in space, a wave has a length that is inversely proportional to its frequency. Let's clarify this concept: the speed of sound in air (the speed at which waves propagate from a source) is about 344 meters per second.[10] This means that a hypothetical wave of 1 Hz would have a length of about 344 meters, because when it has completed one cycle, one second will have passed, and during this second, the wavefront will have traveled 344 meters. A wave of 10 Hz, however, completes 10 cycles in a single second, which fill 344 meters with an arrangement of 10 cycles of 34.4 meters each; each cycle physically occupies a tenth of the total space available.

[10] For the record, this speed is reached when the temperature is 21°C (69,8°F). The speed of sound is, in fact, proportional to the temperature of the medium.

By the same reasoning, a 100 Hz wave has a wavelength of 3.44 meters. We see that frequency decreases with increasing wavelength, and the two quantities are, as we have said, inversely proportional.

AMPLITUDE

The second key parameter for sound is **amplitude**, which expresses information about variations in sound pressure, and which allows us to distinguish a loud sound from one of weaker intensity.

A sound pressure that is weaker than the human ear can hear is said to lie below the **threshold of hearing**, while the maximum sound pressure that can be tolerated by the human ear is defined as the **threshold of pain**. Exposure to sounds above the threshold of pain results in physical pain and permanent hearing damage.

In the wave depicted in figure 1.10, the maximum pressure value is called the **peak amplitude** of the sound wave, while the pressure at any point is called **instantaneous amplitude**.

When we generically refer to the "amplitude of a sound", we are referring to the peak amplitude for the entire sound (see figure 1.10).

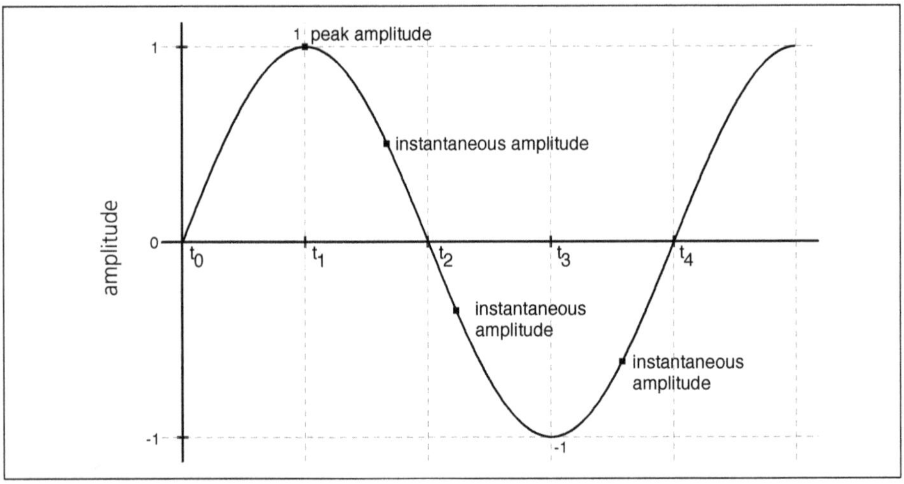

Fig.1.10 Amplitude of a sound

If we show a wave that has a peak amplitude of 1, as in the example, we will see a wave that starts from an instantaneous amplitude of 0 (at time t_0), rises to 1 at time t_1, returns to pass through 0 at time t_2, continues to drop until it reaching its minimum value of -1 at time t_3, after which it rises again to the value 0 at time t_4, and so on. When we represent amplitude this way, we are looking at it as a function of time. The process of digitization transforms such a function into a series of numbers between 1 and -1, and the values thus obtained can be used to graph the wave form (fig. 1.11). The relative position that a wave cycle occupies at a given instant is called its **phase**, and we will explore the concept of phase in more detail in Section 2.1.

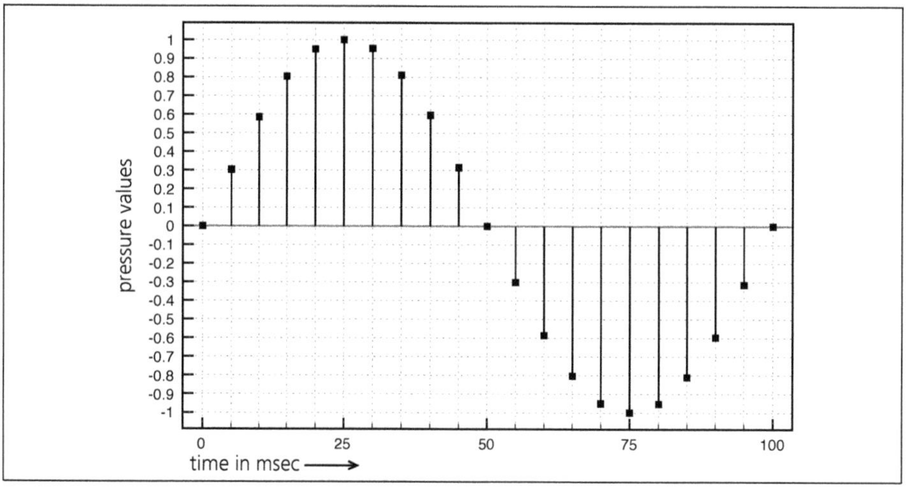

Fig. 1.11 Digital representation of a waveform

Comparing the graph to the real wave (i.e. the physical succession of air compressions and rarefactions), we can see that compression corresponds to positive numbers, rarefaction to negative numbers, and that the number 0 indicates the original stable pressure. (The absence of any signal is, in fact, digitally represented by a sequence of zeros.) Values representing **magnitude** (or amplitude values) are conventionally expressed as decimal numbers that vary between 0 and 1. If we represent the peak amplitude with a value of 1, we will have oscillations between 1 and -1 (as in the previous example), whereas if we were to use 0.5 as the peak amplitude (defined as half of the maximum possible amplitude), we would have oscillations between the numbers 0.5 and -0.5, and so on. (See figure 1.12.)

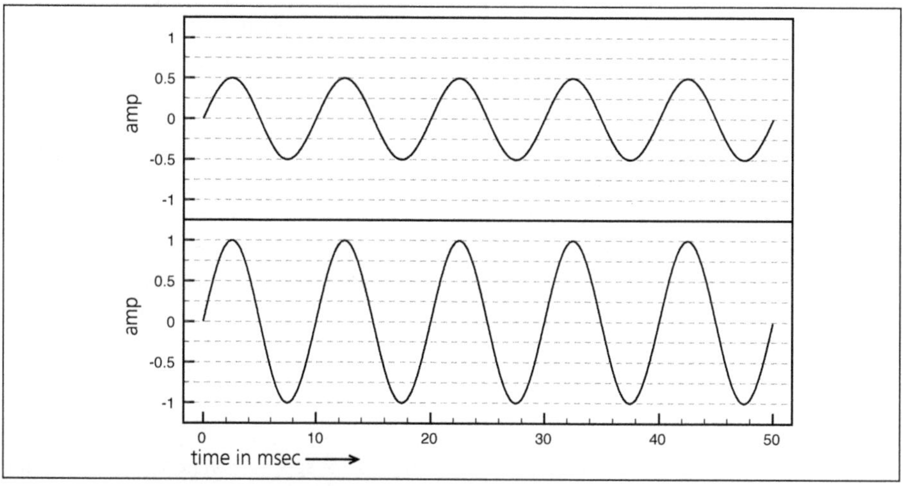

Fig.1.12 Two sounds with differing amplitudes

If the amplitude of a wave being output by an algorithm exceeds the maximum permitted by the audio interface (a wave, for example, that ranges between 1.2 and -1.2, being output by an interface that cannot accurately play values greater than 1), all of the values exceeding 1 or falling below -1 will be limited respectively to the maximum and the minimum value: offending values will be "clipped" to the values 1 or -1. Clipped waves are deformed, and because of this, their sound is distorted[11] (see fig. 1.13).

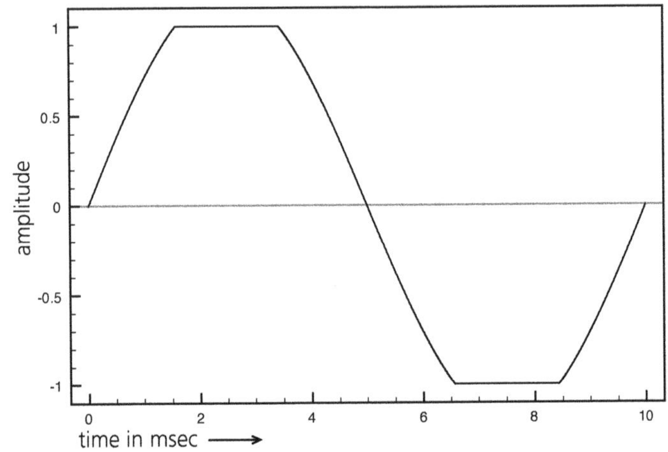

Fig.1.13 A "clipped" waveform

In most software, besides using "raw" numbers to represent amplitude, it is also possible to indicate levels by using **dBFS**: the symbol dB indicates that the level is measured in *deciBels*, and the acronym FS stands for *Full Scale* – thus the entire abbreviation can be read as *"deciBels relative to full scale"*. Whereas raw amplitude measurements represent the difference between a sound pressure measurement and some normal pressure, dBFS is instead defined as the relationship of a sound pressure at a given moment to a reference pressure (which is typically 0 dB in digital audio). 0 dBFS represents the highest level of accurately reproducible pressure (corresponding to the maximum amplitude), and lower levels are indicated by negative values.

Using this scale, the raw amplitude 1, as used in the preceding examples, would correspond to 0 dBFS, while a magnitude of 0.5 would correspond to approximately -6 dB, and an amplitude of 0.25 would fall still lower on the scale at approximately -12 dB. It follows that a reduction of 6 dB corresponds to a halving of the amplitude, whatever the level may be. This kind of relative measurement is very useful because you can use it while working with sounds of unknown loudness.

[11] As we will see in Section 5.1, harmonic distortion is the modification of a signal due to the alteration of its waveform, which results in the introduction of spectral components that are not found in the original signal.

No matter how strong the signal, we know that in order to double it, it will need to increase by 6 dB. Measurement in dB, in contrast to other measurements, is not absolute but relative; it allows us to measure and manipulate the relationship between one sound pressure level and another without knowing their absolute magnitudes.

Here is a useful rule to remember: to reduce the magnitude of a signal by a factor of 10 (in other words, to reduce it to one tenth of the original amplitude) we must reduce the signal by 20 dB. Likewise, to increase a signal tenfold, raise it by 20 dB. It follows that an increase of 40 dB would increase a signal by 100 times, 60 dB by 1000, etc. For a more detailed discussion of this, see "Technical Details" at the end of this section.

Let's look at a table relating raw amplitudes, normalized to a maximum value of 1, to amplitudes measured in dBFS.

Amplitude	dBFS
1	0
0.5	-6
0.25	-12
0.125	-18
0.1	-20
0.01	-40
0.001	-60
0.0001	-80
0	-inf

TABLE B: relationship between raw amplitude and dBFS

As we said, the deciBel is not an absolute magnitude, but is instead a relationship between two quantities, and so there is no absolute measure of 0 dB. Instead, you are free to define 0 dB as you wish, to use as a benchmark against which you will measure a given sound pressure. Unlike in digital audio, where we will usually specify that 0 dB is the *maximum* value reproducible in a given system, analog acousticians often use 0 dB to represent the *minimum* level for their amplitude scale, with *positive* numbers representing louder values.

The following list itemizes, in an approximate way, pressure levels for some common environments (measured in dB SPL at 1 meter of distance)[12] . Amplitude in this table, as you can see, is not represented using 0 dB as the maximum pressure level (as it would be in digital audio, where the amplitudes below the maximum possess negative values, such as -10 dB or -20 dB). On the contrary, these amplitudes are represented using 0 dB as a reference point for the "weakest perceptible sound," leaving all other values to be positive numbers greater than 0.

12 The acronym SPL stands for Sound Pressure Level.

140	the threshold of pain
130	a jet taking off
120	a rock concert
110	a symphony orchestra fortissimo
100	a truck engine
90	heavy traffic
80	a retail store
70	an office
60	normal conversation
50	a silent house
40	a night in the countryside
30	the rustle of leaves
20	wind
10	a light breeze
0	the weakest perceptible sound

VIDEO EXAMPLE 1B • *AMPLITUDE*

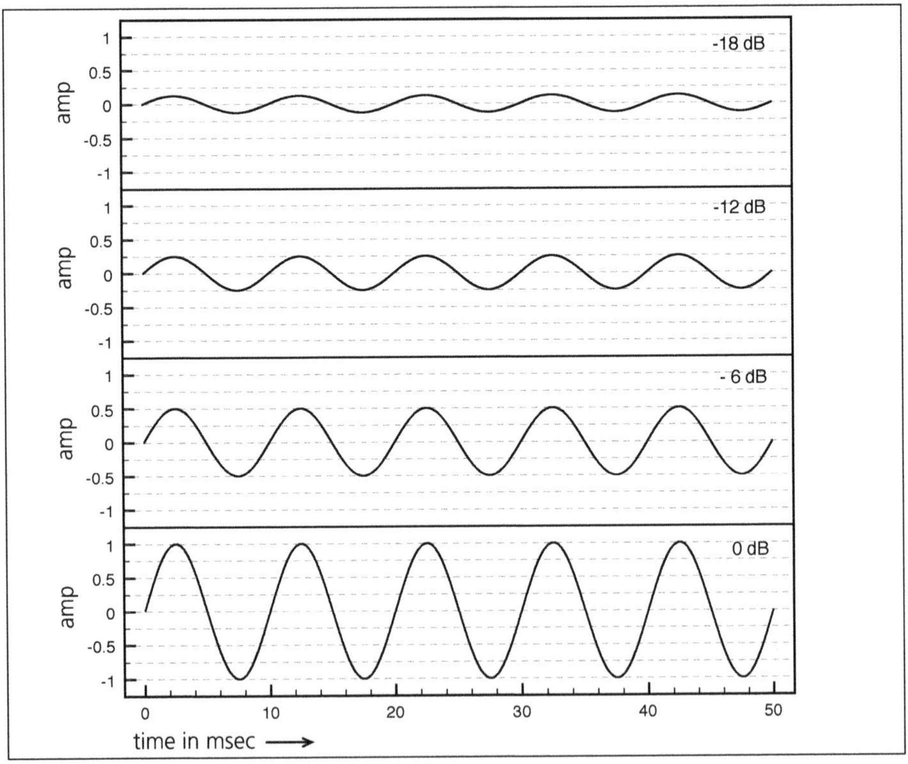

Fig.1.14 Four sounds with their amplitudes progressively doubled

From the psychoacoustic point of view, the intensity of a sound influences the perception of its pitch. Without going into too many details, it suffices to note that above 2,000 Hz, if we increase the intensity of a sound while maintaining fixed frequency, we will perceive that the pitch is rising, while below 1,000 Hz, as intensity increases, there will be a perceived drop in the pitch. On the other hand, frequency also influences our perception of its intensity: the sensitivity of the ear to volume decreases at higher frequencies, increases in the midrange, and decreases greatly at low frequencies. This means that the amplitudes of two sounds must differ, depending on their frequencies, in order to produce the same perceived sensation of intensity. A low sound needs more pressure than is required for a midrange sound to register with the same impact.
There is a graphical representation of the varying sensitivity of the ear to different frequencies and sound pressures. In figure 1.15 we see this diagram, which contains **isophonic curves** that represent contours of equal loudness. The vertical axis indicates the level of pressure in dB, while the horizontal axis represents frequency. The curves are measured using a unit called a **phon**[13] and indicate, within the audible frequency range, the sound pressure needed to produce equal impressions of loudness for a listener.[14]

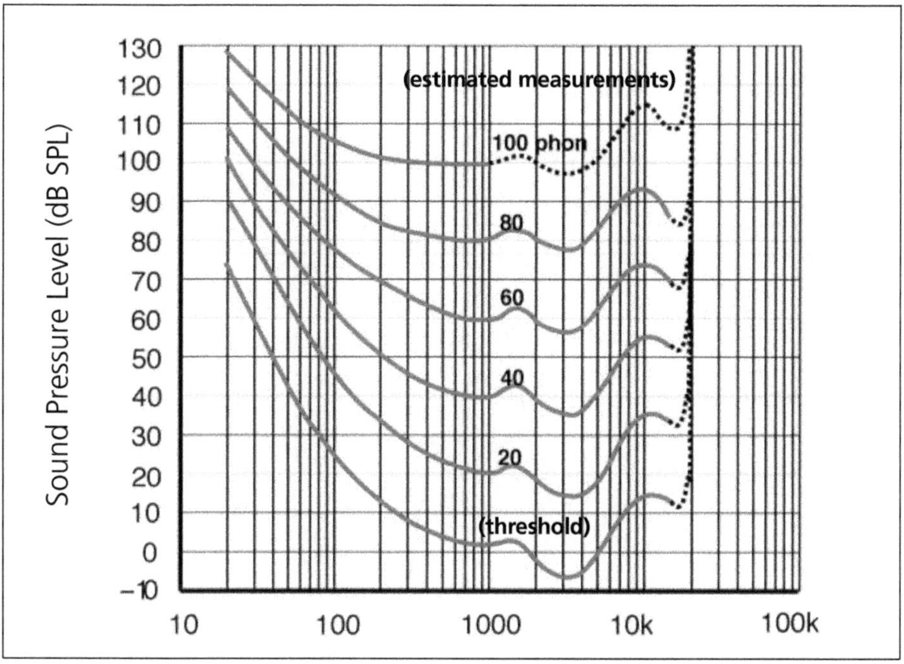

Fig. 1.15 Diagram of equal loudness contours (ISO 226:2003)

[13] The phon is a measure of perceived level of intensity which takes psychoacoustics into account. 1 phon is equal to 1 dBFS at a frequency of 1000 Hz.

[14] The diagram of equal loudness contours is named after H. Fletcher and W.A. Munson, who created the chart used for many years in psychoacoustic experiments all over the world. Recently, this diagram has been refined, and the new measures have been adopted as a standard by the International Organization for Standardization as ISO code 226:2003 (see fig. 1.15).

1000 Hz was chosen as the reference frequency for the phon, because at this frequency, a measurement in phon and one in dB often coincide. (100 dB corresponds to the feeling of 100 phon, 80 dB of 80 phon, etc.) For example, if we examine the 60 phon curve, 60 dB of pressure are necessary at 1000 Hz to produce a certain sensation, but as the pitch drops in frequency, more and more dB are required to maintain the same sensation in the listener.

WAVEFORM

The third key parameter of sound from the perceptual point of view is **timbre**. With this term, we refer broadly to various characteristics that allow us to distinguish, for example, a note played by a flute from a note played at the same frequency and with the same amplitude, by a violin. One of the most important features for defining timbre is waveform.

We'll deepen the discussion of issues relating to timbre in Chapters 2 and following. For now, we will stick to describing the main waveforms that are used in many synthesis techniques.

VIDEO EXAMPLE 1C • *TIMBRE*

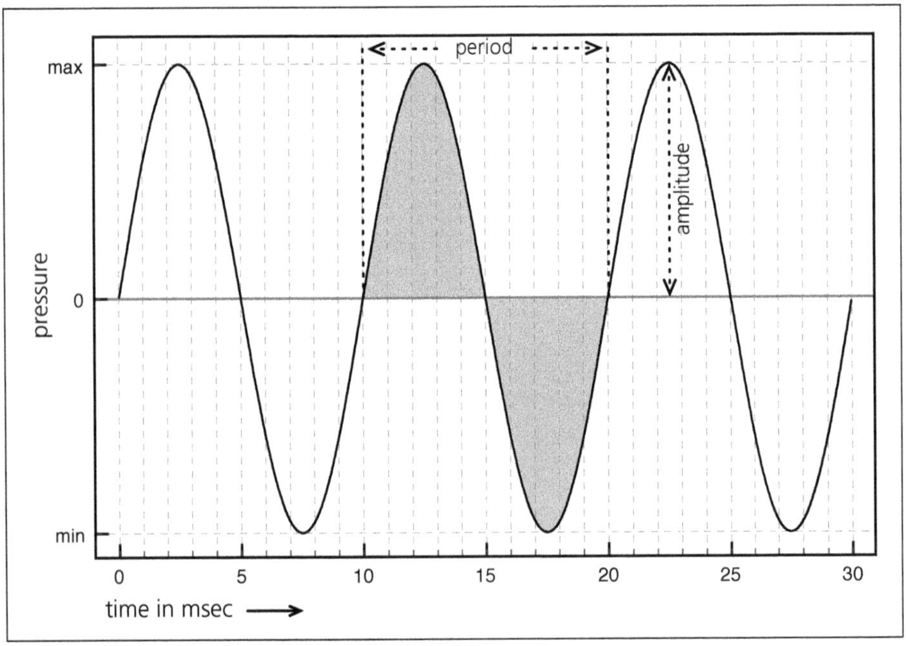

Fig.1.16 A sinusoid

THE SINUSOID

The sounds that we used in the previous section were all sinusoidal, that is to say, their waveform took the shape of a sine wave (fig. 1.16).
The **sinusoid** is both the simplest waveform and the most important one.
As we will see shortly, in the practical portion of Chapter 1, to generate a sine wave on a computer, we will use an **oscillator**: an electroacoustic device that can be simulated on the computer, generating signals with specific waveforms. The sinusoid is the building block with which it is possible to produce *all* other waveforms (just as the three primary colors can be used as building blocks when producing other colors). It is the only waveform that contains a single frequency; all other waveforms are composed of multiple frequencies, and because of this, can be decomposed into a series of sinusoids, each of which contains the energy of a single component frequency. (See Section 2.1, which is dedicated to the sound spectrum, for more details.)
The sinusoid is so named because it is the graphic representation of the trigonometric sine function. A "twin" to this waveform, which is sonically indistinguishable from the sine wave, is the cosine wave, represented graphically by the cosine function (fig. 1.17):

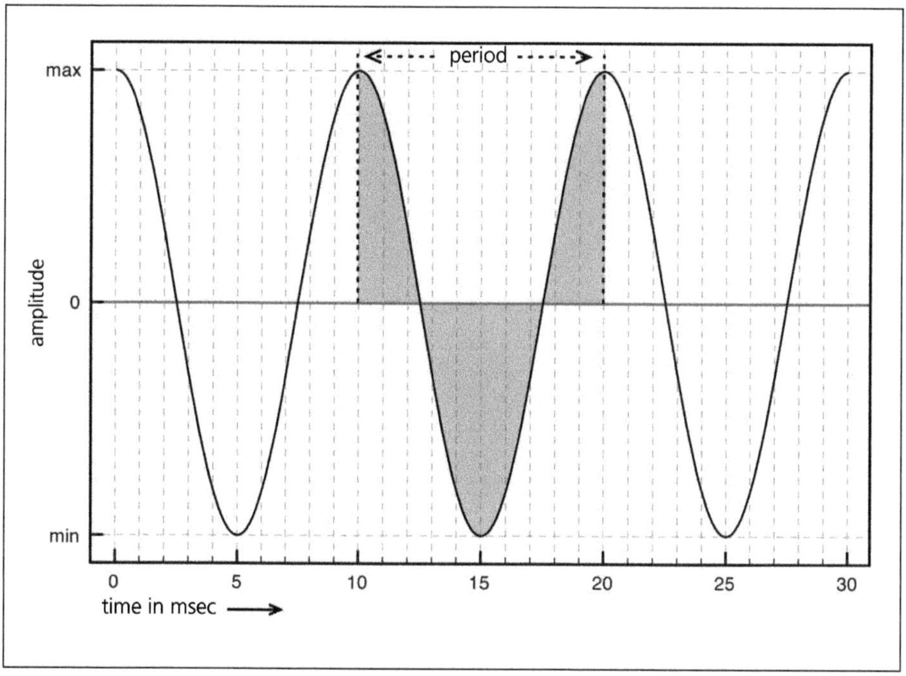

Fig.1.17 A cosine wave

As we can see, the only difference between the sine wave and the cosine wave is that the sine starts its cycle at an amplitude of 0, while the cosine starts at its maximum positive amplitude.
We'll discuss all of these topics in more detail in Chapter 2, which is devoted to additive synthesis.

OTHER WAVEFORMS

Air molecules, of course, can be set in motion by sounds that differ greatly from sine waves! In such cases, the transitions made between the compression and rarefaction phases of the wave will vary, resulting in a more complex wave form.

In figure 1.18, the four "classic" waveforms used by many synthesizers are shown: in A, a **sine wave**, in B, a **square wave**, in C, a ramp or **sawtooth wave**, and in D, a **triangle wave**.

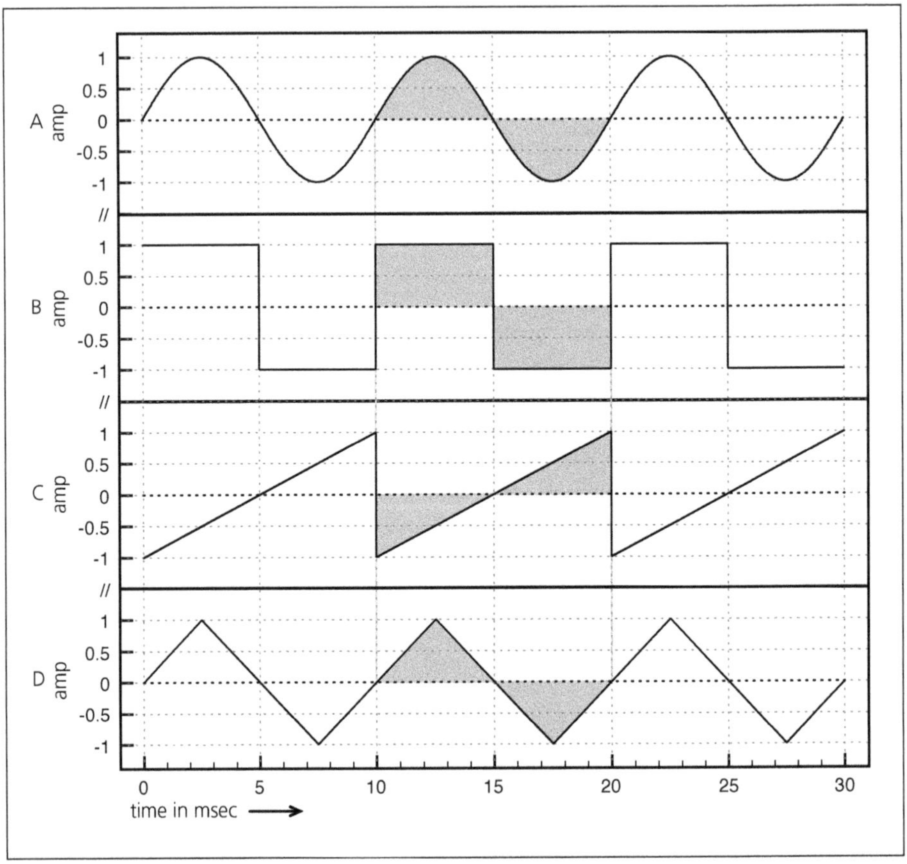

Fig.1.18 The four "classic" waveforms

These four waveforms will produce four completely distinct timbres, which we can hear in Video Example 1D.

VIDEO EXAMPLE 1D • *WAVEFORMS*

The square wave can also morph into a "rectangular" wave when the amount of time logged with positive values is varied in proportion to the amount logged with negative values. A square wave, of course, is symmetric: it spends exactly half of every cycle as negative and half as positive. If, however, the positive part were to become 1/4 of the cycle and the negative 3/4, we would have a rectangular wave. You can easily imagine an infinite number of such ratios, such as 1/5, 1/10, or 1/100.

The relationship between the two parts of such a wave is called the **duty cycle**, and it is generally indicated as a number between 0 and 1: a duty cycle of 0.5 results in a square wave, while 0.25 would result in a positive phase of 1/4 of a cycle and a negative phase of 3/4. (See figure 1.19 for several examples.)

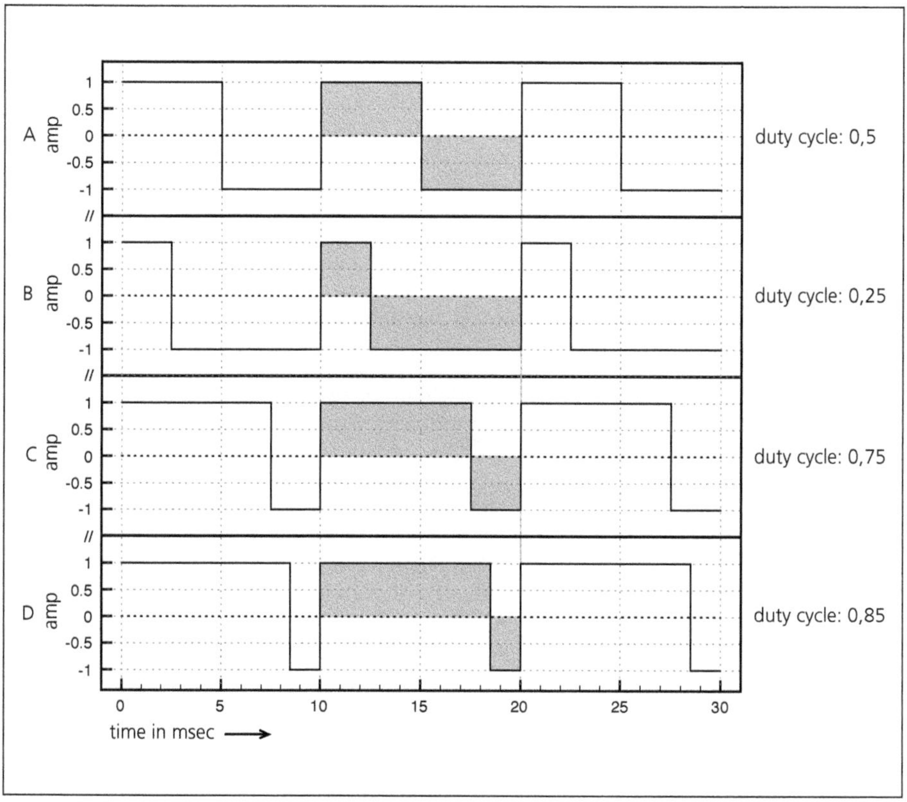

Fig. 1.19 Varying the duty cycle of a square wave

VIDEO EXAMPLE 1E • *DUTY CYCLE*

BIPOLAR AND UNIPOLAR WAVES

All of the waveforms that we have seen so far have one thing in common: they are **bipolar waves**, which have both positive and negative portions within their wave cycles. (Remember that positive amplitudes, greater than zero, correspond to compression of the molecules of the transmission medium, while negative amplitudes correspond to rarefaction.)

There are also **unipolar waves**, which lie completely above or below the value 0 (as seen in figure 1.20).

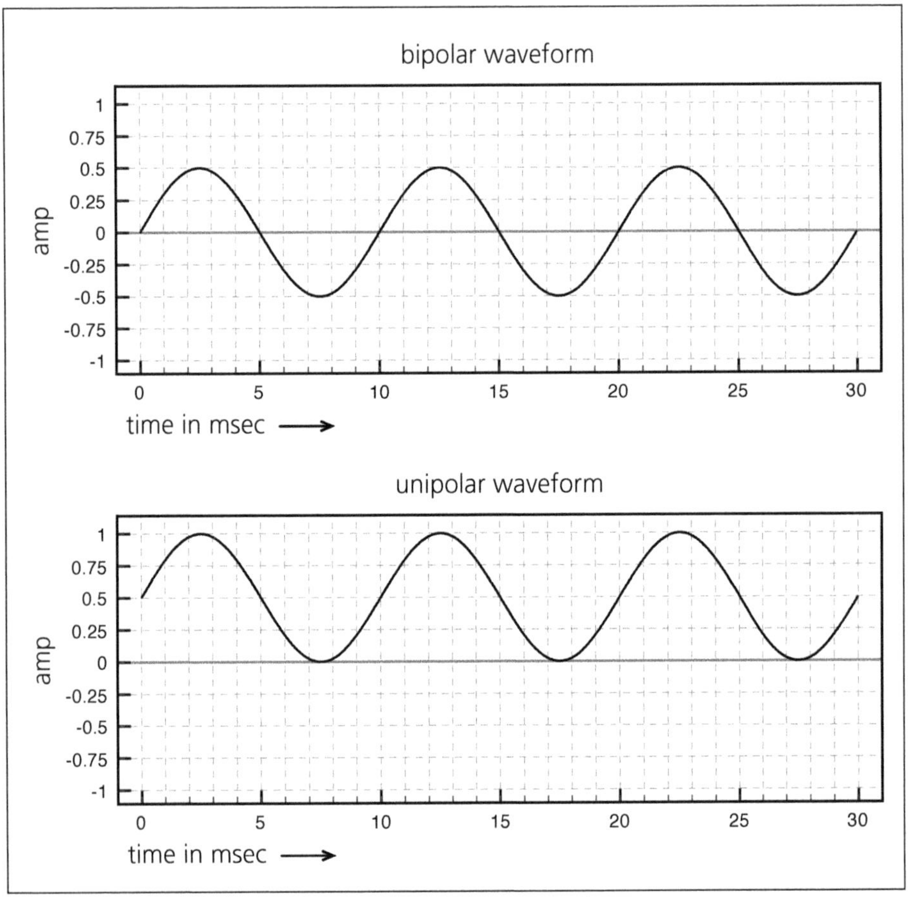

Fig. 1.20 Bipolar and unipolar waveforms

The waveforms used to produce sound are generally bipolar, because they need to alternately compress and expand a physical medium. Instead of generating audible sound, however, unipolar waveforms are often used to modify a parameter of a sound. We will discuss this topic further in Chapter 4.

TECHNICAL DETAILS • *LOGARITHMIC CALCULATION OF PRESSURE SOUNDS IN dB*

To understand how we calculate sound pressure in dB, we must introduce the concept of a *logarithm*. You may be familiar with the *power function*, in which a number is "raised" to a certain power by multiplying it by itself a specified number of times. The **logarithmic function** is simply the inverse of the power function. This means that if we have:

$a^x = y$

then we define the logarithm of y "to the base a" to equal x, as follows:

$\log_a y = x$

In other words, the logarithm tells us the power x to which we need to raise a (the *base*) to get a result of y.
By using logarithms, we can calculate the *exponent* of a. For example:

$\log_2 16 = 4$

because

$2^4 = 16.$

We return to the calculation of deciBels: from a mathematical point of view the relationship between a sound pressure level and its reference level is measured as

$dB = 20 \text{ Log}_{10} x/y$

where x / y is the ratio of the pressure of the sound (x) to the reference pressure (y).

Since the reference level in digital audio corresponds to the maximum raw amplitude, defined as 1, and since x / 1 = x, we can rewrite the equation simply as:

$dB = 20 \text{ Log}_{10} x$

Intensity in decibels is obtained by calculating the logarithm base 10 of the raw amplitude, and multiplying the result by 20.

For example, an amplitude of 0.5 will be $\log_{10} 0.5 = -0.3$ (because $10^{-0.3} = 0.5$) which when multiplied by 20 is -6 dBFS. (For the purposes of this discussion, values are approximate.)

Don't fear the math! Any programming language that is worth its salt will be able to calculate logarithms and give you results directly.

1.3 CHANGING FREQUENCY AND AMPLITUDE IN TIME: ENVELOPES AND GLISSANDI

"Any phenomenon that manipulates mechanical energy cannot switch abruptly from one energy state to the next. Thus, a sound cannot switch suddenly from silence to its maximum amplitude. A finite time, however brief, is needed, during which the sound in question can evolve to its new state. This transitional time is called the **attack transient**. By the same token, there is a **release transient** at the time during which the sound recedes back into silence.

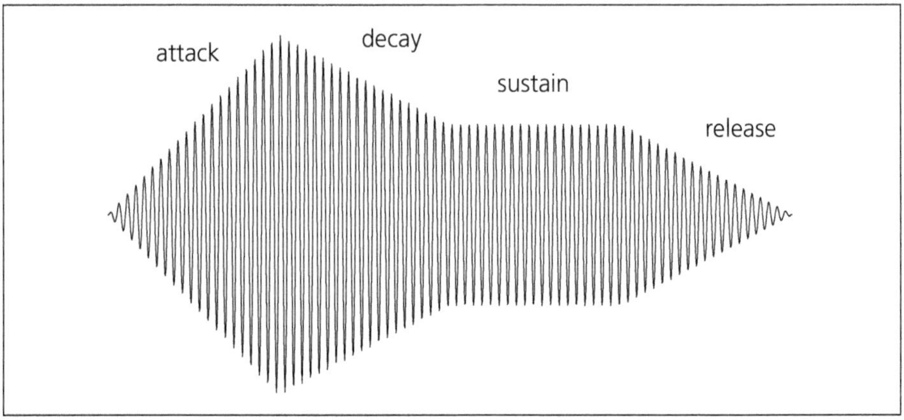

Fig. 1.21 Evolution of the amplitude of a sound in time

Figure 1.21 schematically represents the evolution of the amplitude of a sound. That evolution can be divided into four basic parts:

Attack: during which the amplitude varies gradually from zero to its maximum
Decay: during which the amplitude decreases to a certain level (in fig. 1.21, for example, it decreases to the level of the following sustain)
Sustain: during which the amplitude remains roughly constant
Release: during which the amplitude gradually recedes to zero.

The evolution of the amplitude of a sound, represented as an idealized line that links the positive peaks of its waveform, is called the **envelope** of the wave." (Bianchini, R., Cipriani, A. 2001, p.47)

An envelope represents macro-level changes in amplitude over time, presented as curves and/or straight line segments that connect the positive peaks found in the wave (see figures 1.22, 1.23 and 1.24). In contrast to waveforms, the variations in amplitude found in an envelope will not be highly detailed. In a waveform, we can trace the briefest changes in the amplitude of a sound, whereas in an envelope, we see only gradual changes.

Not all sounds follow the pattern illustrated above. Sometimes there is no *sustain* phase, (as in, for example, an unmuted piano sound) or no decay phase.

ENVELOPES OF ACOUSTIC INSTRUMENTS

In addition to waveform, "the evolution of transients plays an essential role in the definition of timbre by the listener. Sounds with different waveforms can, in some cases, be perceived to be the same (or very similar) because they have similar transients. Conversely, sounds possessing identical waveforms may be perceived to be clearly different if they have very different transients.

In figures 1.22 and 1.23, the envelopes that are characteristic for some instruments are summarized.

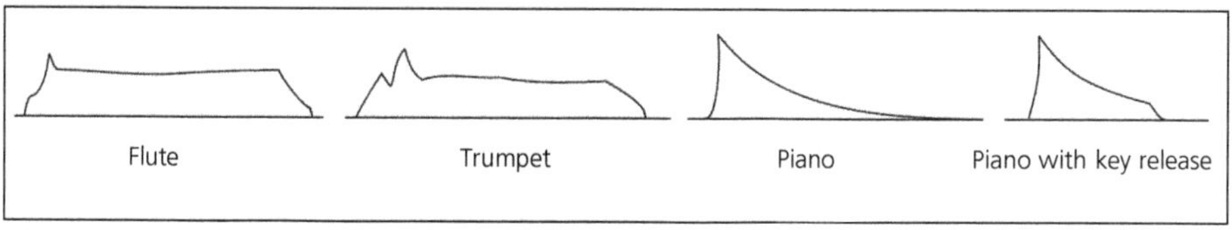

Fig. 1.22 Envelopes of flute, trumpet, unmuted piano, and piano with key release

Referring to figure 1.22, one can see how the *flute* is characterized by a fairly rapid ascent in amplitude, followed by a slight drop (an effect obtained by tonguing), a phase of constancy, and finally a fairly quick release. The attack transients of the *trumpet* display a well-known signature (and in general for all instruments with mouthpieces); we can see the characteristic "double attack" in the graph. The envelope of the *piano* has a very quick attack, followed by an exponential decay (about which we will say more shortly). This decay can be accelerated by releasing the key to apply its felt dampers to the string.

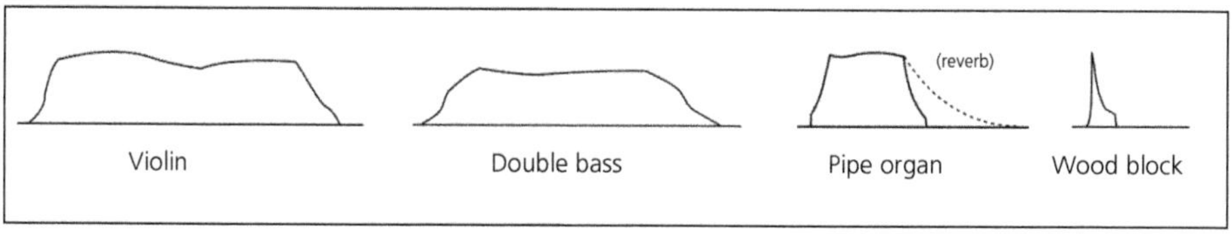

Fig. 1.23 Envelopes of violin, double bass, pipe organ and wood block

In figure 1.23, the *violin* has a fairly quick attack and release. The *double bass*, whose more massive strings resist quick changes and hence possess much greater inertia than those of a violin, are slower to vibrate during the attack and slower to stop during the release. As a consequence, the durations of both attack and release are longer than those of the violin. The *pipe organ* has very quick attack and release, but what really distinguishes its sound is the reverberation that is almost always associated with the instrument, and which has become an integral part of its timbre.

During the progression of transient changes in amplitude that occur over the lifetime of a note played on an acoustic instrument, the frequency will often vary slightly (although much less in relative terms than the amplitude). In particular, during the attack, the frequency is often initially unstable before settling upon a nominal value. This is particularly evident in the sustained notes of certain instruments and of the singing voice. Also, pitch tends to come from below and then level out during the attack of the first note of a phrase, or during a staccato section." (Bianchini, R., Cipriani, A. 2001, p.48).

ENVELOPES OF SYNTHETIC SOUNDS

To apply an envelope, using a computer, to the amplitude of a sound over time (within the lifetime of a single sound event), we need to create a form for the envelope (for example, by means of straight-line or exponential line segments), and apply it to our signal (figure 1.24).

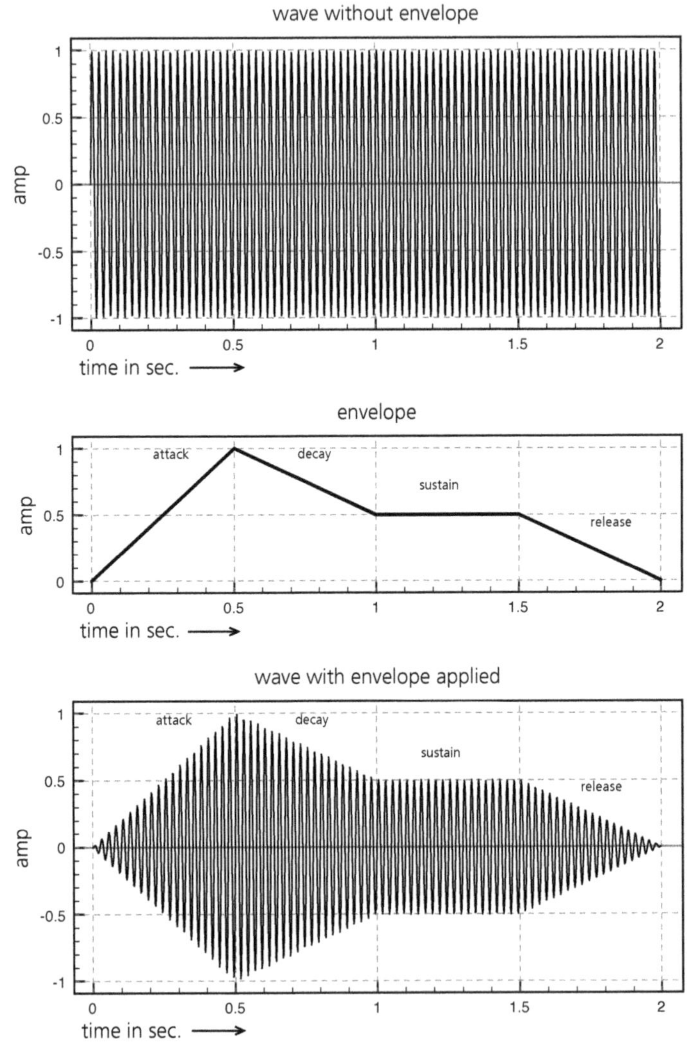

Fig. 1.24 Raw waveform without envelope, ADSR envelope, waveform with envelope applied

As shown in figure 1.24, an envelope that will be applied by a computer is usually built using a series of connected line segments. These segments are implemented as sequences of numbers (sample values) in exactly the same way that they are for digitized sounds.

To apply an envelope to a raw waveform (that is to say, a wave that has constant amplitude), we iteratively multiply, point by point, the sample values for the envelope with those of the sound itself. The values of an envelope will normally vary between 0 and 1. The envelope depicted in the figure begins and ends with the value 0, and reaches 1 at the end of its attack; the values of all of its other samples fall between 0 and 1. If we multiply, one by one, this series of values with the sample values contained in the waveform (which, remember, fall between -1 and 1), we *scale* the amplitude of the waveform by the shape of the envelope. At the beginning of the note, for example, the amplitude of the waveform will be scaled to 0 (the digital equivalent of silence), because the first value of the envelope is 0, and any number multiplied by 0 is 0. As the sample values in the envelope increase, so does the resulting product, until the maximum point is reached at the end of the attack, where the envelope will have a value of 1, and will therefore have no effect on the corresponding value in the waveform, since any number multiplied by 1 is equal to itself. Continuing with the rest of the envelope, waveform samples will always be scaled by numbers that lie between 0 and 1, which means that the waveform's amplitude will always occupy some position between silence (0) and maximum amplitude (1). Finally, at the end of the envelope's release, the waveform samples, multiplied by 0, will fall silent once again.

VIDEO EXAMPLE 1F • *LINEAR ENVELOPES*

The different phases of the ADSR envelope shown in figure 1.24 are all **linear**: each is represented by a straight-line segment, and these segments are joined at discreet points to form the envelope. An important characteristic of linear segments is that increases (or decreases) between sample values are constant for an entire segment, and because of this, an entire segment can be specified using only two points.
Often, however, using such a simplistic representation to model the evolution of sound does not permit us to fashion the envelope accurately enough, and for this reason, we will sometimes resort to segments that have exponential or logarithmic shapes.

Let's see what these two terms mean:

Exponential growth is characterized by steady growth in the changes made to sample values, and therefore takes the form of a curve that rises ever more steeply as it approaches its final point (as in figure 1.25).

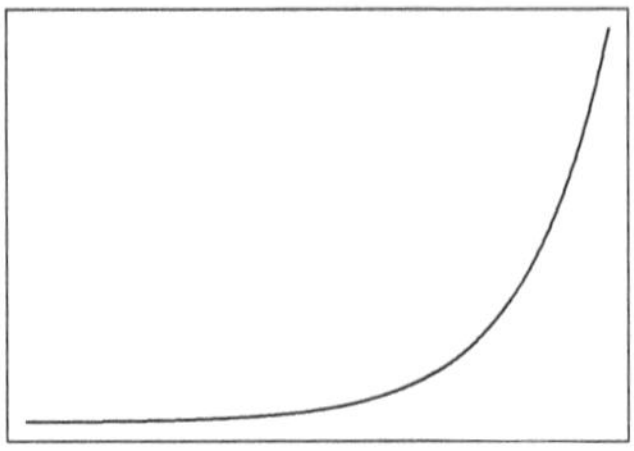

Fig. 1.25 An exponential curve

Logarithmic growth is literally the inverse of exponential growth: it is characterized by a rate of change that gradually *decreases* across successive samples, and therefore takes the form of a curve that flattens out as it approaches its final point (as in figure 1.26).

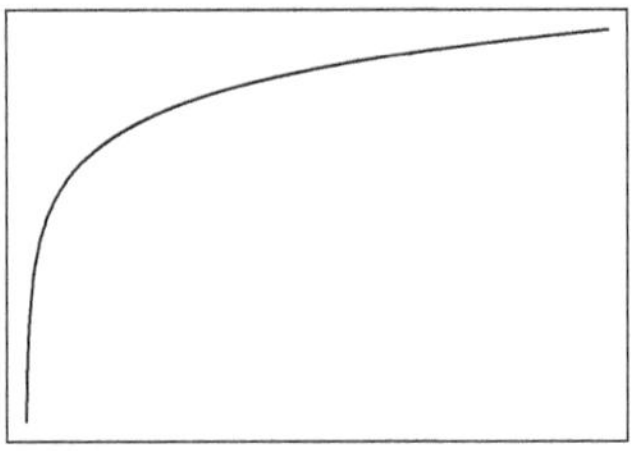

Fig. 1.26 A logarithmic curve

The envelopes of many real sounds, for example those produced by percussion instruments or by plucked strings, can be broken down into exponential and/or logarithmic segments. Many wholly synthetic sounds are also made with envelopes of this type.
Here is an example of an envelope built using exponential curves (fig. 1.27).

Fig. 1.27 An envelope built using exponential curves

VIDEO EXAMPLE 1G • *EXPONENTIAL AND LOGARITHMIC AMPLITUDE ENVELOPES*

Each phase of the envelope of a sound to be created on a computer must possess non-zero length. In addition, when fashioning an envelope on the computer, we must be careful to avoid large instantaneous changes in amplitude. Abrupt changes will result in audible clicks within the sound. A line segment for controlling an attack, for example, must occur over a non-zero length of time, however brief. The closer this time is to zero, the more you risk a nasty audible distortion of the waveform (fig. 1.28).

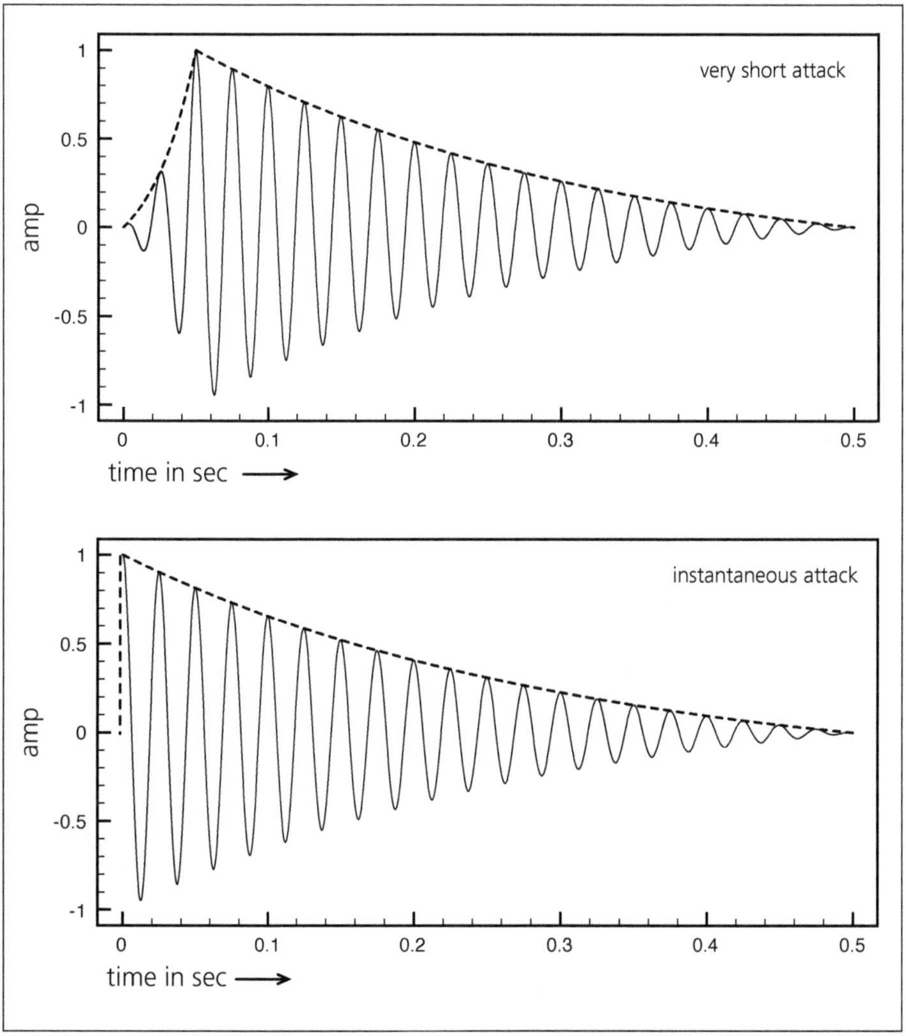

Fig. 1.28 A very short (but well-formed) attack, versus a malformed attack that will generate a click

GLISSANDI

It is also possible to create a sound that *continuously varies its frequency over time*, within the lifetime of a single sonic event. This kind of sound is called a **glissando** (plural: *glissandi*), and it may exhibit descending movement, ascending movement, or a combination of the two. To create a glissando, we once again need to create a curve using either straight-line or exponential segments, but the curve in this case will now represent the sliding movement of the pitch, and will modify the frequency of our signal rather than its amplitude. (See figure 1.29.)

As discussed in the next section, in order to adjust changes in frequency to our own psychoacoustic perceptions of pitch, more realistic glissandi are typically obtained using exponential segments.

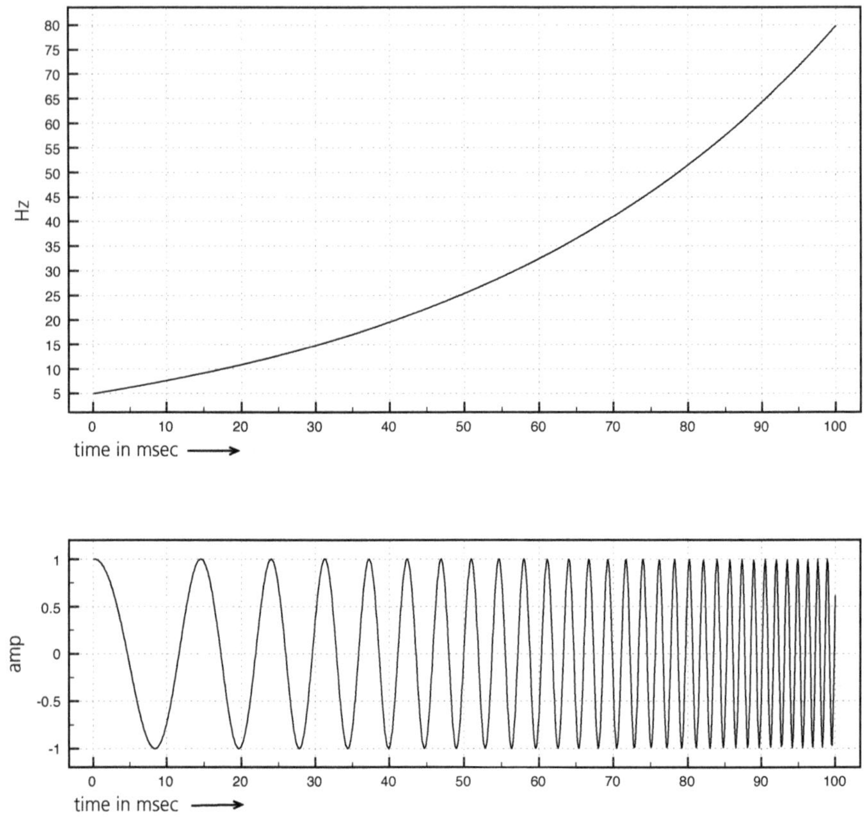

Fig. 1.29 An ascending glissando

VIDEO EXAMPLE 1H • *LINEAR LOGARITHMIC AND EXPONENTIAL GLISSANDI*

TECHNICAL DETAILS • *EXPONENTIAL AND LOGARITHMIC CURVES*

Mathematically, an **exponential curve** is defined as:

$y = a^x$

To calculate successive values of y, we must raise a positive constant *a*, also known as the base, to the power of successive values of x. Here is an example of this process, using 2 as the base:

$x = 1;\quad y = 2^1 = 2$
$x = 2;\quad y = 2^2 = 4$
$x = 3;\quad y = 2^3 = 8$
$x = 4;\quad y = 2^4 = 16$
$x = 5;\quad y = 2^5 = 32$
$x = 6;\quad y = 2^6 = 64$
$x = 7;\quad y = 2^7 = 128$
$x = 8;\quad y = 2^8 = 256$

As you can see the interval between some point y and the following y increases as x increases. (In this case, it doubles.) The resulting graph is an exponential curve (figure 1.30):

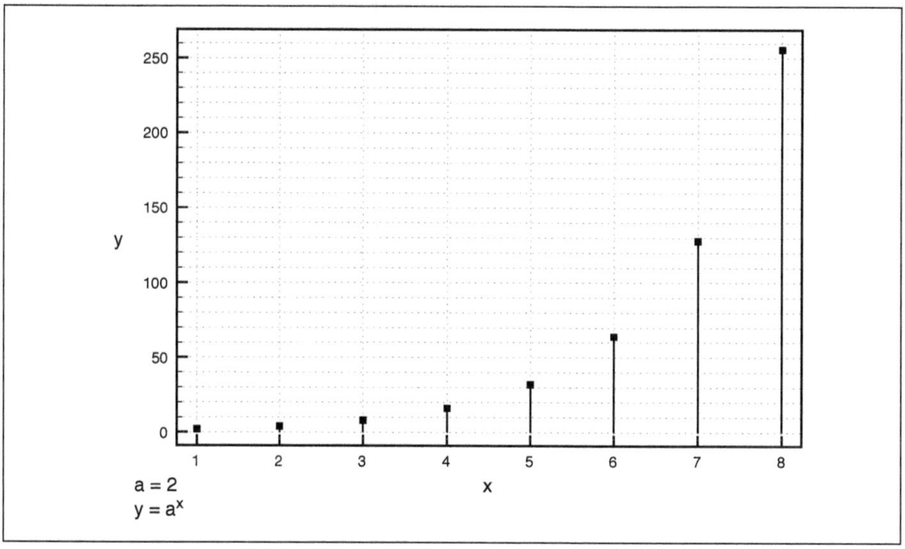

Fig. 1.30 A sequence displaying exponential growth

A **logarithmic curve** is defined, inversely, as:

$y = \log_a x$

To obtain successive values of y we simply calculate the logarithm of x, to the base *a*.

Using 2 as our example base again, we have:

$x = 1;\quad y = \log_2 1 = 0$ (because $2^0 = 1$)
$x = 2;\quad y = \log_2 2 = 1$
$x = 3;\quad y = \log_2 3 = 1.585$
$x = 4;\quad y = \log_2 4 = 2$
$x = 5;\quad y = \log_2 5 = 2.322$
$x = 6;\quad y = \log_2 6 = 2.585$
$x = 7;\quad y = \log_2 7 = 2.807$
$x = 8;\quad y = \log_2 8 = 3$

As you can see, the interval between some point y and the following y decreases[15] as x increases, and the resulting graph is a logarithmic curve (figure 1.31):

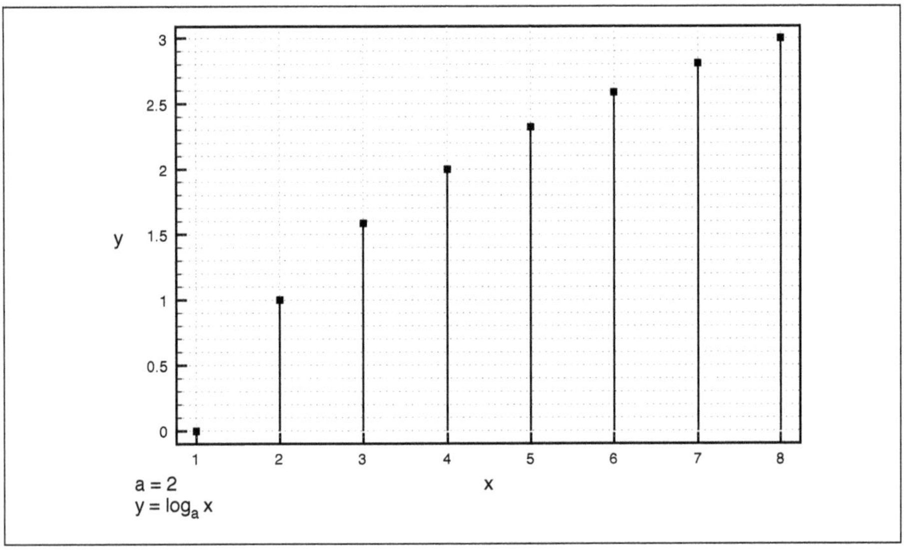

Fig. 1.31 A sequence displaying logarithmic growth

[15] The difference between the first and the second of the y values is 1, while the difference between the seventh and eighth is less than 0.2.

TEST WITH SHORT ANSWERS *(30 words maximum)*

1) What is the difference between realtime sound synthesis and realtime signal processing?

2) What is the difference between realtime sound synthesis and offline sound synthesis?

3) What type of conversion should be used if you want to digitally sample a sound?

4) What perceptual sensation corresponds to frequency?

5) What musical parameter corresponds to amplitude?

6) What are the minimum and maximum frequencies that can be heard by humans?

7) How do you measure amplitude?

8) What is the difference between peak amplitude and instantaneous amplitude?

9) What is a continuous variation of the pitch of a sound called?

10) What do you call a variation of the amplitude of a sound over time?

11) What is the name of the transition that goes from initial silence to the maximal amplitude of a sound?

12) What does the term "release" mean?

13) What happens during the sustain phase of an envelope?

14) After what stage of the envelope does decay take place?

15) Name four types of waveform.

1.4 THE RELATIONSHIP BETWEEN FREQUENCY AND MUSICAL INTERVAL

In this section we will observe the relationship that exists between frequency and musical intervals.

As a first example, if we reduce the frequency of a sound by half, we can obtain the same sound sounding an octave lower. A3 has a frequency of 440 Hz,[16] while A2, sounding an octave below, has a frequency of only 220 Hz. It is important to note that we hear the "size" of all octave intervals as equal, but that the difference in Hz between two sounds separated by an octave will vary. For the octave A3:A2 just mentioned, the ratio of the two frequencies is 2 to 1 (440 / 220), and the frequency difference between them is 220 Hz (440 - 220). Yet in another case, the octave between A7 (7040 Hz) and A6 (3520 Hz), though also having a ratio of 2 to 1 (7040 / 3520), has a difference in hertz of 3520 Hz (7040 - 3520) rather than 220 Hz! The human ear is able to recognize *intervals* between one sound and another, and in this case will easily recognize the equivalence between the two different octaves (both of which express the same ratio: 2 to 1). The ear will not, however, quantify differences in *frequency*, because such differences change depending on the frequency band.
The octave is an interval used in all musical cultures. Other intervals, however, vary from culture to culture: the intervals found in scales, in fact, can differ based on the place and time in which a piece of music was performed. Since the beginning of the eighteenth century, a scale has been used in Western music that is called the **equally tempered chromatic scale**. In this type of scale, all members of a given class of intervals share identical ratios, and in this particular scale the octave is divided into 12 equal parts, each of which corresponds to the range of a "tempered" semitone. The ratio of a semitone is approximately 1.059463 to 1: if we multiply the frequency of middle C (261.626 Hz) by 1.059463, we will obtain the frequency of the C# found a semitone above (261.626 · 1.059463 = 277.183 Hz). If we then multiply the resulting frequency by the same factor, we will obtain the frequency of D above middle C (293.665 Hz).[17] If we repeat this operation 12 times, we will obtain a note an octave above the original, possessing a frequency of 523.252 Hz, which is double the original frequency. The ratio of the equal-tempered semitone, 1.059463, is in fact the "twelfth root of 2" (up to the inevitable approximation that characterizes such numbers!) which is to say that it is the number that, when raised to the twelfth power, will results in the number 2 (the ratio of an octave). Knowing the semitone ratio, it is possible to find the frequencies for all of the notes of the equally tempered chromatic scale.

---

[16] A3 means "the A found in the third octave", which is an unfortunately ambiguous term. There are a number of conventions used for octave numbering, but none is universal. Other sources, for example, might indicate A440 as A4.

[17] Obviously, the converse is also true: dividing a frequency by 1.059463 will yield the note one semitone below.

Table C, below, shows a complete list of pitches, expressed as MIDI notes, and their corresponding frequencies. MIDI encoding assigns the value 60 to middle C (C3), and then proceeds in an upward direction, increasing the number by one for each semitone (C#3 = 61, D3 = 62, etc.). Reducing the note number by one likewise corresponds to a drop of a semitone (B2 = 59, A#2 = 58, etc.).

MIDI **Octave**	0	1	2	3
MIDI **Pitch**	from 24 (C) to 35 (B)	from 36 (C) to 47 (B)	from 48 (C) to 59 (B)	from 60 (C) to 71 (B)
C	32.7032	65.4064	130.8128	261.6256
C#	34.6478	69.2957	138.5913	277.1826
D	36.7081	73.4162	146.8324	293.6648
D#	38.8909	77.7817	155.5635	311.1270
E	41.2034	82.4069	164.8138	329.6276
F	43.6535	87.3071	174.6141	349.2282
F#	46.2493	92.4986	184.9972	369.9944
G	48.9994	97.9989	195.9977	391.9954
G#	51.9131	103.8262	207.6523	415.3047
A	55.0000	110.0000	220.0000	440.0000
A#	58.2705	116.5409	233.0819	466.1638
B	61.7354	123.4708	246.9417	493.8833

MIDI **Octave**	4	5	6	7
MIDI **Pitch**	from 72 (C) to 83 (B)	from 84 (C) to 95 (B)	from 96 (C) to 107 (B)	from 108 (C) to 119 (B)
C	523.2511	1046.5023	2093.0045	4186.0090
C#	554.3653	1108.7305	2217.4610	4434.9221
D	587.3295	1174.6591	2349.3181	4698.6363
D#	622.2540	1244.5079	2489.0159	4978.0317
E	659.2551	1318.5102	2637.0205	5274.0409
F	698.4565	1396.9129	2793.8259	5587.6517
F#	739.9888	1479.9777	2959.9554	5919.9108
G	783.9909	1567.9817	3135.9635	6271.9270
G#	830.6094	1661.2188	3322.4376	6644.8752
A	880.0000	1760.0000	3520.0000	7040.0000
A#	932.3275	1864.6550	3729.3101	7458.6202
B	987.7666	1975.5332	3951.0664	7902.1328

TABLE C: correspondences between note names, MIDI note number, and frequency

The chromatic scale that we have been discussing is said to possess intervallic equivalence, since intervals of the same type all share a constant frequency ratio. It is certainly possible to build equally tempered scales using the same principle, but that differ from the common chromatic scale: one might, for example, divide the octave into 24 steps (or any other number) rather than 12. We can also build scales that are defined by intervals that do not exhibit intervallic equivalence – in this case, frequency ratios are free to differ by scale position. In Table D we can see the differences, expressed as ratios, between the tempered scale and natural scale.[18] When we are considering an equally tempered scale, and we divide the frequency ratio of one interval by the ratio of the next-smallest interval (dividing the ratio of the fourth C to F, a ratio of 1.334840, by the major third C to E, a ratio of 1.259921, to get a cross-ratio of 1.059463, for example), we will always wind up with a number equal to the semitone ratio that is constant for this scale. This is not true of the relationships that exists between semitones of the natural scale: if we divide the ratio of the note F to its root C (1.3333) by that of E to C (1.25), we find a different ratio (1.0667) than that which exists between C and C# in this scale (1.0417). Referring now to table D, the second column gives the ratio that each scale degree in the equally tempered chromatic scale has with its root, and the third column shows the ratio that each note has with its predecessor (which you can see is always the same). The fourth and fifth columns, in contrast, show the same ratios for the natural scale. For this type of scale, the ratio that each note has with its root, and the ratios between successive notes, change continuously.

NOTE	Tempered frequency	Distances of tempered scale degree	Natural frequency	Distances of natural scale degree
C	1.0		1.0 (1/1)	
C#	1.059463	1.059463	1.0417 (25/24)	1.0417
D	1.122462	1.059463	1.125(9/8)	1.08
Eb	1.189207	1.059463	1.2 (6/5)	1.0667
E	1.259921	1.059463	1.25 (5/4)	1.0417
F	1.334840	1.059463	1.3333 (4/3)	1.0667
F#	1.414214	1.059463	1.3889 (25/18)	1.0417
G	1.498307	1.059463	1.5 (3/2)	1.08
G#	1.587401	1.059463	1.5625 (25/16)	1.0417
A	1.681793	1.059463	1.6667 (5/3)	1.0667
Bb	1.781797	1.059463	1.8 (9/5)	1.08
B	1.887749	1.059463	1.875 (15/8)	1.0417
C (upper oct.)	2.0	1.059463	2.0 (2/1)	1.0667

TABLE D: differences between the equally tempered chromatic scale and the natural scale

[18] The natural scale is defined using ratios derived from the harmonic series. (See the concept of harmonic components in Section 2.1.)

It is interesting to note that from the psychoacoustic point of view, the sensation of pitch does not follow the same rules in all frequency zones. A ratio of 2 to 1 below 600 Hz is perceived as a slightly stretched octave, while above 600 Hz the opposite is true: we will perceive such an octave as slightly squashed. The farther we stray from 600 Hz, the more this effect is accentuated.

1.5 INTRODUCTION TO WORKING WITH SAMPLED SOUND

DIGITALIZATION OF SOUND

We talked at the beginning of the chapter about the digitization (or **analog-to-digital conversion**) of a signal, which is a transformation from sound into a sequence of numbers. This is done using an **AD/DA converter** (analog-to-digital and digital-to-analog) which is generally integrated into a computer's audio interface. In Chapter 5, we will return to the subject of conversion in more depth, but meanwhile, we will give some information that may help explain some of the concepts that follow.

The computer stores sounds as a sequence of numbers. These numbers capture, instant by instant, the instantaneous amplitudes of the sound that they represent. In practice, the digital conversion of an analog sound can be considered to be a process of taking "snapshots" of the amplitude at regular intervals: each "photo" is a number. The reverse process, converting digital sound into an analog waveform, is done by re-transforming this sequence of numbers into an audible sound. (See fig. 1.32.)

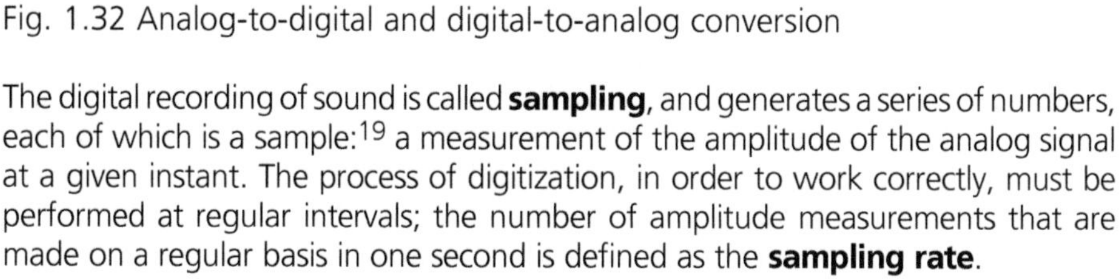

Fig. 1.32 Analog-to-digital and digital-to-analog conversion

The digital recording of sound is called **sampling**, and generates a series of numbers, each of which is a sample:[19] a measurement of the amplitude of the analog signal at a given instant. The process of digitization, in order to work correctly, must be performed at regular intervals; the number of amplitude measurements that are made on a regular basis in one second is defined as the **sampling rate**.

We can draw a parallel with film: you probably know that 24 frames, each of which consists of a fixed image, must be projected each second in order to view a movie as a continuously flowing image, rather than as a bursty series of stills.

[19] As we will see in Chapter 5, the digitization of sound actually occurs in two stages, sampling followed by sample quantization, but we will simplify the description for now as to not complicate the discussion.

In other words, there is a temporal distance of 1/24 of a second between one frame and the next, a gap of approximately 0.0417 seconds. Likewise, on a compact disc, there are 44,100 samples in each second of music. In this case, the temporal distance between one sample and the next is 1/44100th of a second, or approximately 0.000023 seconds. (The higher the sampling rate, the more accurate the representation of the stored sound. Compact Disc technology dates back to the early 80's; nowadays, one can find oneself working with sampling rates of 96,000 or even 192,000 samples per second.) This series of numbers generates motion, in the form of a wave, which ultimately produces a physical wave by moving the molecules in the air around you.
We should take a moment to clarify the distinction between the sampling frequency and the frequency of a waveform. When talking about waveform frequency, one of the three basic parameters of sound, "frequency" refers to the number of oscillations that occur per second. The term "sampling frequency," on the other hand, uses the word "frequency" to refer to the number of samples per second rather than the number of cycles per second. The more commonly used term for this concept is "sampling rate," but you will encounter both. The number of samples needed to capture one oscillation of a periodic digital waveform will change based upon the sampling frequency being used. We will return to a deeper discussion of both terms in Chapter 5.

On disk storage of sampled sounds is not restricted to sounds created using computer synthesis; it is also very common to record sound from an external source, digitally convert it, and store it to disk, or to import already recorded sound from other media, and store it to disk. There are many different formats for encoding such audio files, including:

- *Uncompressed audio formats* such as WAV, AIFF and BWF
- *Lossless formats* that compress files without sacrificing quality, such as FLAC, lossless WMA, and Apple Lossless
- Formats that use *lossy* techniques in order to achieve smaller footprints at the expense of sound quality, such as MP3, AAC, Ogg Vorbis, and standard WMA

WAV (Wave) and AIFF (Audio Interchange File Format) files, along with most of the other formats, provide a header with space for an ID, a sampling rate, the number of channels, the number of bits per sample, and the length of the audio data, along with any other metadata needed for decoding and cataloging. You can always convert a sound file from one *standard format* to another with format-specific editing programs. Many audio editors are also able to read and save audio files in different formats.
An audio file can be *monaural (mono)*, *stereo* or *multichannel*. A monaural audio file contains a single sequence of numbers that encode its digital waveform. A stereo file, on the other hand, contains two digital sequences that can be converted in parallel, one for the left channel, and right channel, each representing one speaker of a pair, or one headphone channel. A multichannel file contains a variable number of sequences (usually between 4 and 8) that can be sent to the same number of speakers. We'll talk about multi-channel sound in more detail in Chapter 5.

1.6 INTRODUCTION TO PANNING

The term **panning** refers to the placement of sound within the spatial environment created by two or more channels. We might, for example, decide to place a mono signal entirely onto the left channel of a stereo pair; by doing this, 100% of the signal would be fed into the left speaker, and nothing would be heard on the right. Conversely, if we were to listen to the same sound panned completely right, the entire signal would be sent to the right channel, leaving the left with nothing.

To implement panning, we will choose to implement an algorithm in which the measurement of position will be given by a single value, which we will call X, and which can take on values between 0 and 1. In this algorithm, when X is equal to 0, 100% of the sound will play on the left channel, when X is equal to 0.5 the sound will be located in the center, and when X is equal to 1, 100% of the sound will play on the right channel. Using the single parameter X, we can thus allow for *balance* adjustments (changes to the relative amplitudes of the right and left channels).

The procedure for panning, or balancing, using the single value X as input, consists of modifying the amplitudes found on the two channels by using X as a multiplier that is directly proportional to the amplitude of one channel, and inversely proportional to the amplitude of the other.

For example, defining the panning multiplier X as above, and the monaural sound source as amplitude A, we will:

- Multiply *A* by (1-*X*) and send the resulting signal to the left channel

- Multiply *A* by *X* and send the resulting signal to the right channel

In this way, if we want to place the signal 100% left, with no right signal at all, assign an X value of 0:

LEFT CHANNEL
$$\boldsymbol{A \cdot (1-0) = A \cdot 1 = \mathrm{A}}$$

RIGHT CHANNEL
$$\boldsymbol{A \cdot 0 = 0}$$

Conversely, if we want to place the signal 100% right, we simply assign X the value 1:

LEFT CHANNEL
$$\boldsymbol{A \cdot (1-1) = A \cdot 0 = 0}$$

RIGHT CHANNEL
$$\boldsymbol{A \cdot 1 = \mathrm{A}}$$

So far, so good. The logic, at first glance, would imply that in order to place a sound in the center, we need only to send 50% of its signal to the left and 50% to the right, using a value of X = 0.5. This is precisely what we do when we are working with an audio mixer – we center the balance control (or pan-pot), and the sound spreads itself equally across both left and right monitors. Unfortunately, in reality, things are a little more complex, and those who design mixers must take this complexity into account. Let's explore what is involved. If you listen carefully to the simple algorithm outlined above for stereo balancing, which sends 50% of the mono signal left and 50% right, you will note that when the signal is centered, the intensity is lower than when the signal is panned fully left or right.

To explain why this is happening, it is necessary to clarify the concept of signal power and signal intensity as they relate to amplitude:

The **power** of a signal is its total energy, measured at the source.
The intensity of a signal (which we have generically indicated as a parameter tied to amplitude to this point) is the energy transmitted by a sound wave through a given surface area during a given unit of time.

If, for example, you measure the intensity of a signal emitted by some source upon its arrival at the area occupied by you, the listener, you will note that by increasing the power of the signal, you obtain a proportional increase in intensity. In fact, the power of a signal varies in proportion to the *square* of its amplitude, which means that doubling the amplitude of a signal will quadruple its power.
Alternatively, halving the amplitude will reduce its power to one quarter of its original strength.

Let's lay out the case in which we have a single sound source (which, keeping our example in mind, would be the case in which a signal comes from the left or the right channel only) and that source has an amplitude (A) equal to 1. To find the power (P) of this signal, we square the amplitude, so when A = 1 the power will be:

$$\mathbf{P = 1^2 = 1}$$

Now taking the case in which there are two sound sources, one left and one right, and supposing that each of the two sources has an amplitude of 0.5, we obtain the following results:

$$\mathbf{P_{left} = A_{left}^2 = 0.5^2 = 0.25}$$
$$\mathbf{P_{right} = A_{right}^2 = 0.5^2 = 0.25}$$

If we add the power of these two sources together, we obtain the following total power:

$$\mathbf{P_{tot} = P_{left} + P_{right} = 0.25 + 0.25 = 0.5}$$

From these formulas, we can deduce that when the power of a signal is simply split arithmetically between two outputs, the resulting signals will be only half as powerful as the original signal would have been from a single source.

There are several possible solutions to this problem. One of the simplest, proposed by Dodge and Jerse (1997, p.217), is to calculate the square root of the multiplication factors for the left and right channels, and then to calculate amplitudes by using these square roots in the calculation.

For a centered sound with a position parameter of X = 0.5, we would not multiply by X directly, but rather by its square root (0.707). In this case, you will find the following:

$$P_{left} = A_{left}^2 = 0.707^2 = 0.5$$
$$P_{right} = A_{right}^2 = 0.707^2 = 0.5$$

Adding the power of the two sources together again, we obtain the following total power:

$$P_{tot} = P_{left} + P_{right} = 0.5 + 0.5 = 1$$

Adopting this new approach, we decide that we will no longer attempt to use X as a multiplication factor to keep the power readings at all panning positions in the stereo field the same, but instead we will use the square root of X to for this purpose. The factor for the left channel will be the square root of 1-X, and the factor for the right channel will be the square root of X, as follows:

LEFT CHANNEL
A · square root of (1-X)

RIGHT CHANNEL
A · square root of X

EXAMPLES:

SOUND IN THE CENTER
If we want to place the sound in the center, that is, to have 50% of the power left and 50% right, it will suffice to assign X the value of 0.5. We will then have the following: LEFT CHANNEL *A* · square root of (1-0.5) = *A* · square root of 0.5 = *A* · 0.707 RIGHT CHANNEL *A* · square root of 0.5 = *A* · 0.707

SOUND RIGHT

If we want to send 100% of the power to the right channel and no signal to the left, we need only assign X a value of 1:

LEFT CHANNEL
A · square root of (1-1) = *A* · square root of 0 = 0

RIGHT CHANNEL
A · square root of 1 = *A* · 1 = *A*

SOUND LEFT

If we want to send 100% power to the left channel and no signal on the right, we need only assign X a value of 0:

LEFT CHANNEL
A · square root of (1-0) = *A* · square root of 1 = *A* · 1 = *A*

RIGHT CHANNEL
A · square root of 0 = *A* · 0 = 0

SOUNDS WITH X = 0.25

If we want to send 25% of the power to the right channel and 75% to the left, we assign the value 0.25 to X, resulting in:

LEFT CHANNEL
A · square root of (1 - 0.25) = *A* · square root of 0.75 = *A* · 0.866

RIGHT CHANNEL
A · square root of 0.25 = *A* · 0.5

We will soon see, in the upcoming discussion of practical applications, how to use straight-line segments for panning by creating a "position envelope" for the positioning of stereo sound in space that is similar to the envelopes that we created for controlling amplitude and frequency.

COMPREHENSION • LISTENING AND ANALYSIS

In example sound AA1.1, are amplitude and frequency both fixed or do they change?

In example sound AA1.2, are amplitude and frequency both fixed or do they change?

In example sound AA1.3, are amplitude and frequency both fixed or do they change?

Which phases of the envelope does sound example AA1.1 display?

Which phases of the envelope does sound example AA1.2 display?

Which phases of the envelope does sound example AA1.3 display?

In which of the three examples there is a descending glissando?

FUNDAMENTAL CONCEPTS

1) **Sound synthesis** is the electronic production generation of sound

2) **Signal processing** is the electronic processing of sound.

3) The **characteristics of a sound** depend primarily on three basic parameters: *frequency*, *amplitude* and *waveform*. Each parameter has a subjective sensation associated with it that, unlike the parameters themselves, cannot be physically measured.

4) The range of **audible frequencies** for humans extends from about 20 to about 20,000 hertz.

5) Sound pressure weaker than the human ear can perceive is said to be below the **threshold of hearing**, while the sound pressure above which a sound becomes unbearable for a human listener is called the **threshold of pain**.

6) With the term **timbre**, we refer broadly to various characteristics that allow us to distinguish, for example, a note played by a flute from a note played at the same frequency and with the same amplitude, by a violin.

7) The **sine wave** is the only waveform that contains a single frequency. All other waveforms contain multiple frequencies, and because of this, they can be analyzed as a collection of component sine waves (a process known as Fourier analysis).

8) The idealized line joining the positive peaks found in an individual sound's waveform is called its amplitude **envelope**. It represents macro-level trends in amplitude over the lifetime of a sound. The key parts of an envelope (not necessarily present in all sounds) are: *attack*, *decay*, *sustain*, and *release*.

9) A **glissando** is a continuous variation in the frequency of a sound over time (but only within the lifetime of a single sound). A glissando can rise, fall, or move between both directions.

10) The **correspondence between frequency and musical interval** is not linear: The human ear is able to recognize *intervals* between one sound and another. The ear will not, however, quantify differences in *frequency*, because such differences are perceived to change depending on their frequency band.

GLOSSARY

AD/DA Converter
Hardware dedicated to converting signals to and from the analog and digital realms.

Algorithm
A sequence of instructions that leads to a specific result.

Amplitude
The deviation of a waveform from a zero point, representing the amount of air pressure variation in a sound.

Analog-to-digital conversion (A/D)
The act of converting an analog signal into numerical values that digitally represent the signal.

Attack
The initial portion of an envelope. Typically, the attack amplitude grows from zero to the maximum amplitude of the given sound.

Audio interface
Built-in computer hardware or a peripheral that normally possesses an AD/DA converter.

Bipolar waves
Waveforms comprised of both positive and negative portions.

Contours of equal loudness
Curves that identify the sound pressure needed at a given frequency to produce equal impressions of loudness upon a listener.

Cycle
The repeated segment of a periodic waveform.

dBFS
An abbreviation for *deciBels (dB) relative Full Scale (FS)*. dBFS is a logarithmic scale that expresses the relationship between instantaneous sound pressure and a reference pressure. In digital audio, the reference level is generally represented as 0 dBFS, meaning that 0 dBFS is the maximum amplitude that can be represented accurately; as a consequence, digital measurements in dBFS are *negative* numbers. dB is usually taken as a measure of sound intensity.

Decay
The portion of an envelope that occurs after the attack, during which amplitude decreases to the level of the following part of the envelope (usually either the sustain or the release).

Decibel (dB)
A logarithmic unit of measurement that reflects the intensity of a sound versus some reference level.

Digital-to-analog conversion (D/A)
The act of converting a digital signal (a sequence of numeric values) into an analog signal (such as an electrical signal). The digital values are converted into voltages, and when these voltages are sent to a loudspeaker, the result is audible sound.

DSP
An acronym that stands for Digital Signal Processing.

DSP system
An integrated set of hardware and software resources (computer, audio interface, programming language) that allows us to synthesize and/or process digital sounds or signals.

Duty Cycle
A parameter (expressed as a percentage) that expresses the ratio between time spent in the positive portion of a wave's cycle and the time spent in the negative portion. This is typically applied to square waves. A square wave is a special case of a rectangular waveform where the positive portion is 50% of the whole.

Envelope
A curve that outlines the evolution of a characteristic of a sound over time, e.g. an amplitude envelope, a frequency envelope.

Exponential curve
See *exponential function.*

Exponential function
A mathematical function characterized by a proportionately increasing rate of growth between successive values. When graphed, it looks like a rising curve that becomes progressively steeper.

Frequency
The rate of recurrence of the period in a periodic waveform, measured in hertz or cycles per second.

Glissando (plural: glissandi)
A sound with a continuously varying frequency.

Instantaneous amplitude
The measurement of amplitude at any instant.

Intensity
The energy transmitted by a sound wave, measured as the energy that passes through a given area in a given unit of time.

Linear function
A mathematical function defined as a steady movement between one point and another. When graphed, a linear function appears as a line segment.

Logarithmic curve
See *logarithmic function*.

Logarithmic function
A mathematical function characterized by a steadily decreasing rate of change between successive values. When graphed, it looks like an upward curve that becomes progressively flatter.

Non-realtime synthesis and processing
Synthesis or processing in which calculations are performed entirely and saved to an audio file (which can be listened to later).

Offline synthesis and processing
See *non-realtime synthesis and processing*

Oscillator
A device or software that generates a periodic waveform.

Panning
The placement and/or movement of sound within a sonic space defined by two or more channels.

Peak amplitude
The highest amplitude value in a waveform.

Period
The time required to complete one cycle of a periodic sound wave.

Phase
The position occupied by a wave cycle at a given instant in time, relative to a reference point in the cycle.

Phon
A unit used to measure perceived sound intensity, or "loudness"

Power
The total energy of an audio signal, measured at the source.

Realtime synthesis and processing
Synthesis or processing that can be heard as it is being generated.

Release
The final portion of an envelope during which amplitude gradually decreases to zero.

Sampling
Digital recording of sound, characterized by certain predefined constants, such as the sampling frequency, the number of bits, the number of channels, etc.

Sampling rate
The number of samples per second in a digital waveform. For example, the audio waveform in an audio CD is 44.1 thousand samples per second.

Signal processing
The digital processing of a sound.

Sine and cosine waves
Sine and cosine waves are waveforms that contain a single frequency. The shape of the sine wave is the graphic representation of the trigonometric sine function, while the cosine wave is based on the cosine function. Both functions are said to be sinusoidal; they differ only in phase.

Sound synthesis
The electronic generation of sound.

Sustain
The portion of an envelope during which amplitude remains roughly constant.

Threshold of hearing
The weakest sound pressure that the human ear can perceive.

Threshold of pain
The maximum sound pressure that a human listener can bear.

Unipolar waves
Waves whose sample values are all greater than or equal to 0, or whose sample values are less than or equal to 0.

Waveform
A detailed graphic representation of a signal's sound pressure levels over time.

1P
SOUND SYNTHESIS WITH MAX

LEARNING AGENDA

PREREQUISITES FOR THE CHAPTER

- Basic computer knowledge (operating a computer, managing files and folders audio formats, etc.)
- Basic knowledge of music theory (semitones, octaves, rhythm, etc.)
- Contents of the theory part of Chapter 1 (It is best to study one chapter at a time, starting with the theory and then progressing to the corresponding chapter on practical Max techniques.)

LEARNING OBJECTIVES

Skills

- To be able to use all of the basic functions of Max
- To be able to synthesize both sequenced and overlapping sounds using sine wave oscillators, as well as square wave, triangle wave, and sawtooth wave oscillators
- To be able to continuously control the amplitude, frequency, and stereo spatialization of a sound (using linear and exponential envelopes for glissandi, amplitude envelopes, and the placement of sound in a stereo image)
- To be able to generate random sequences of synthesized sound
- To be able to work with and manage elements of sampled sound

Competence

- To successfully realize a first sound study based on the techniques you have acquired in this chapter, and save your work as an audio file

CONTENTS

- Sound synthesis and signal processing
- The timbre, pitch and intensity of sound
- Glissandi and amplitude envelopes
- Relationships between frequency, pitch, and MIDI
- Introduction to working with sampled sound
- Introduction to panning
- Some basics of the Max environment

ACTIVITIES

- Substituting parts of algorithms
- Correcting algorithms
- Completing algorithms
- Analyzing algorithms
- Constructing new algorithms

TESTING

- Integrated cross-functional project: reverse engineering

SUPPORTING MATERIALS

- List of principal Max commands
- List of Max objects used in this chapter
- Messages, attributes, and parameters for specific Max objects
- Glossary of terms used in this chapter

1.1 FIRST STEPS WITH MAX

To proceed with this chapter you will need to have the Max application correctly installed on your computer. If you haven't done this, you can download it from the Cycling74 website at http://www.cycling.74.com. It will also be necessary for you to download the support materials for this book, which can be found at http://www.virtual-sound.com/cmsupport. We especially recommend that you install the *Virtual Sound Macros library*; to do this, follow the installation instructions found at the same website.

Launch Max, and select the New Patcher entry from the *File* menu (or press Command-n on the Mac or Control-n on Windows).[1] The **Patcher Window** will appear. The Patcher window is where you connect Max objects to create algorithms. Before you proceed, notice that the Patcher Window is framed by a dark border that contains a number of icons (see fig. 1.1). The four sides of this border are named *Patcher Window Toolbars*; we will explain each of the icons found in them gradually, as the need arises.

Fig.1.1 The *Patcher Window*

We will begin with the upper *Toolbar*, whose icons represent Max objects that you can use to construct "virtual machines" that embody algorithms for sound synthesis and signal processing. Max objects can be interconnected with each other: information flows (in the form of numbers, digital signals, or other kinds of data) from one object to the next through these connections. Each object is designed to perform a specific operation on the information that it receives, and each object will pass its results to any other objects that are connected to it.

---

[1] On Mac OSX, hold the Command key (⌘) down and press 'n', or on Windows, press 'n' while holding the Control key down. This will be abbreviated as <Command-n/Control-n> from this point on. Whenever you see this notation, use <Command> if you are using a Mac or use <Control> if you are using Windows.

A collection of objects that are connected together is called a **patch** (a reference to the old world of analog modular synthesizers that were programmed using physical cable connections called **patch cords**).
Let's create our first patch. If you click on the first icon on the left in the upper *Toolbar*, you will cause a new object to appear in the Patcher Window (as seen in figure 1.2).

Fig.1.2 The object box

The object that appears is a generic object called the **object box**. It is the object that we will use most often when patching. Its function depends upon the name that we give it when we type a *string*[2] into its interior.
We want to turn this object box into a sine wave oscillator; in order to accomplish this, you will need to type the word "cycle~" into the object box's interior. Try this now, and notice that as you begin to type, a menu appears that lists all of the objects whose names or whose description contain the characters which you have typed. This very useful feature, shown in figure 1.3, is called **autocompletion**.

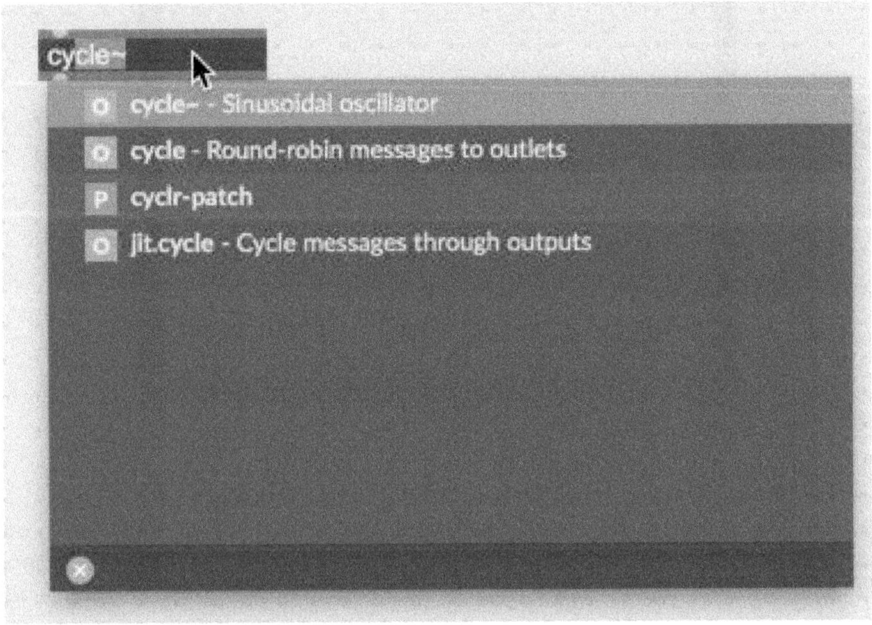

fig.1.3: the autocompletion menu

[2] The word "string" is computer programming lingo that refers to a combination of letters and numbers, such as "print", "save", "astringcontainingthenumber1", or "subsection22".

In the figure, you can see what the *autocompletion* menu looks like after typing the first two characters of "cycle~" (the 'c' and the 'y'). The stylized letter that precedes each *autocompletion* menu option specifies the type of the individual elements being suggested. In the figure, for example, we can see two letters: "o" which indicates an object and "p" which indicates an *abstraction*. (We will speak later about what *abstractions* are, and also about other types of elements that can be found within a Max patch.) Inside the object box itself, immediately following the characters that you have typed, you can see a proposed completion for the object that Max deems most likely to be used (and which is most often a name that you have typed before).

At this point, you can select the object name that you are looking for by clicking on its menu item, or by simply typing the rest of the name; for the purposes of this tutorial, make sure that you select "cycle~" and not "cycle"![3]
With "cycle~" in place, now type a space in order to see how the autocompletion menu changes depending on context. Two new categories, "Arguments" and "Attributes", appear. Without going into too much detail, the elements that populate these categories represent words that can optionally be typed in after the name of the object. Ignoring these placeholder suggestions for now, continue by typing the number 440 after the space that you have typed. (The space is very important!) After you have done this, click in an empty part of the Patcher Window[4], and the object box will now resemble figure 1.4.

Fig.1.4 The `cycle~` object

The little lighter zones that appear on the upper and lower edges of the object are the **inlets** and **outlet** for `cycle~`, respectively, which we will examine shortly. (NB: If the object doesn't display these, then you have a problem. Look for debugging tips in the FAQ at the end of this section.)

[3] Note the character '~', which is called a **tilde**, that follows the word `cycle`. The tilde character is almost always the last character in the name of objects used to process streams of digital audio; it is an important naming convention in Max. Since some external objects do not appear in the auto completion menu, you will sometimes need to type (or want to, because it is quicker!) object names directly into the object box. It will be important that you know where to find the tilde on your keyboard, especially if you have a non-English one! .

[4] Or alternatively, press <Enter> on the Mac or <Shift-Enter> on Windows.

Now we will create another object, **gain~**, which has an appearance, shown in figure 1.5, that is similar to the faders found on a mixing console.
By clicking on the seventh icon of the upper *Toolbar*, you will cause a *palette* to appear that contains all of the objects in the "Slider" category. Click on the third icon of the *palette*, or alternatively, drag this icon [directly into the Patcher Window using the mouse.]

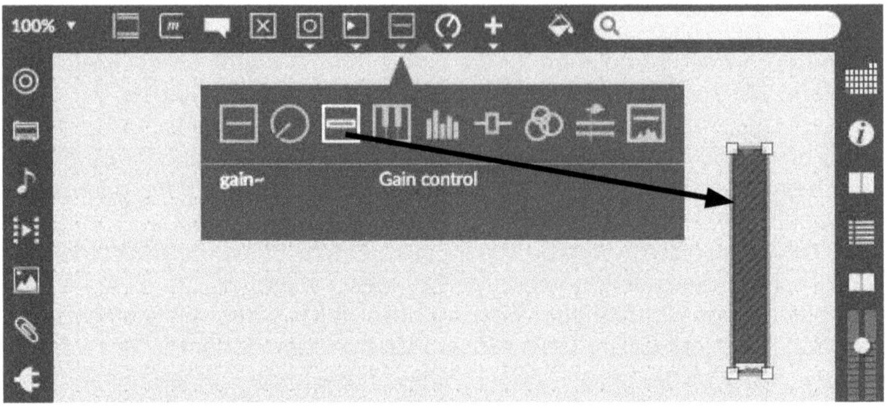

Fig.1.5 The `gain~` object

When you click on the icon, a new kind of object will appear: instead of an object box, a **new user interface object** (also known as a **ui object**) will be created. Here's a little tip: if you have a hard time finding an object in the *Top Patcher Window Toolbar*, just create an object box (the same generic object that we just used to create `cycle~`), and then type the name of the object that you want to create (such as `gain~`) into its interior. Once you've done this, click outside of the object, and the object box will immediately morph into the ui object whose name you typed.
Drag the newly created `gain~` object to a spot in the Patcher Window underneath the `cycle~` object, and connect the outlet of `cycle~` to the inlet of `gain~` in the following manner: first, bring the mouse pointer near the outlet on the lower edge of the `cycle~` object. A yellow circle, along with a box containing descriptive text (a feature officially called "*Assistance Bubble*" by Max), should appear. The circle, shown in figure 1.6a, indicates that the outlet is selected, and by clicking and dragging the mouse towards the `gain~` object, a yellow-and-black striped patch cord can be made to appear. If you drag the end of this patch cord towards the inlet of the `gain~` object (the small dark patch on its upper edge), you will see a red circle (and more descriptive text) appear, as shown in figure 1.6b. This second circle indicates that you have located an inlet that is compatible – at this point, release the mouse button, and you will have connected the two objects!

a

b

Fig. 1.6 Connecting two objects

We have connected the oscillator to the `gain~` object, which will serve to regulate the volume. We now must route the audio signal to the output: click on the next-to-last icon in the upper *Toolbar* to cause a six-category *palette* to appear[5], select the "Audio" category within this *palette*, and then click on the second icon within this category (or else drag it into the *Patcher Window*, as shown in fig. 1.7). The name of the object thus obtained is **`ezdac~`**.

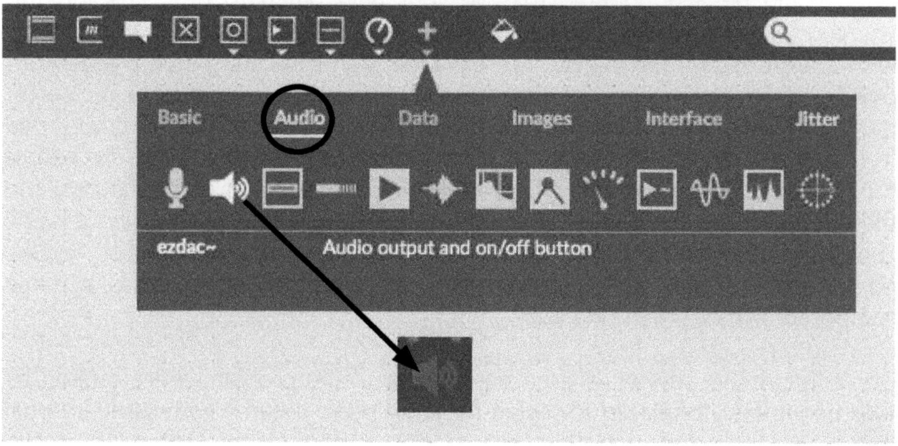

Fig.1.7 The `ezdac~` object

[5] A bit further in this same paragraph, we will better see how the upper *Toolbar* is organized.

We place the **ezdac~** under the **gain~** object and connect its left outlet to the two inlets of the **ezdac~** (as shown in figure 1.8).

Fig.1.8 Our first patch

Watch out! The **gain~** object has two outlets, which are poorly distinguished from each other. Because of this, you should verify that you've used the left outlet for making both connections. The best way to ascertain that you've used the correct outlet is to read the *Assistance Bubble* text that appears when you make the connection, and to make sure that it contains the text *gain~: (signal) Scaled Output*. If one of the two cables were to be grey rather than yellow-and-black striped as they appear in the figure above, this would indicate the you've mistakenly used the right outlet, in which case you would need to cancel the patch cord by selecting the cord with a click (causing it to appear fatter) and pressing the <Delete> key (which is the same key that you press to delete text). The cord would disappear, and you could then reconnect the objects, using the correct inlet/outlet pair.
Now would be a good time to save your new patch to disk, keeping this warning in mind: DON'T EVER save your patches to a file that shares a name with a pre-existing Max object! For example, don't call this patch **cycle~** (or **cycle** without the tilde, for that matter!) Doing this would be a recipe for confusing Max, and for causing unexpected results the first time that you tried to reload your patch. Given that it is impossible to remember all of the names for Max objects, a good technique for avoiding the use of object names, and therefore averting the danger of a confusing name, is to give your files a name composed of more than one word: "test oscillator", for example, or "cycle~ object test", or any other combination. No Max object possesses a name composed of more than one word.

Don't forget this advice! A large percentage of the problems encountered by Max beginners are related to saving files that share a name with some internal object. We will return to this topic and explain the logic behind it in the interlude that follows this chapter.

Good! We've finished implementing our first patch, and we are ready to make it run. It lacks one more touch, however: up till now we've been in **edit mode**, in which we assemble patches by inserting, moving and connecting objects together, and now we need to make the transition into **performance mode**, where we will be able to hear and test our patch. To do this, click on the small padlock that appears at the bottom left of the Patcher Window, or else press <Command-e/Control-e>.[6] Once we are in performance mode, the padlock at the bottom left will appear to be locked. (If it appears to be open, you are still in edit mode!)

Having switched to performance mode, click on the `ezdac~` object (the small loudspeaker), and then slowly raise the level of the `gain~` slider. You should hear a sound, pitched at A above middle C. By clicking repeatedly on the `ezdac~` loudspeaker, it is possible to alternately disable and enable sound output for the patch. (If you are not hearing any sound at all, you should try consulting the FAQ at the end of this section.)

Now that we've built a patch and seen it work, let's revisit what we did:

The `cycle~` object is an oscillator (a sound generator that produces a periodic waveform, in this case, a sine wave), and the number '440' that we typed into its interior indicates the frequency that we want it to produce; in this case, we specified that the sine wave[7] should repeat itself 440 times per second.[8]

In more formal terms, `cycle~` was the name of the object, and 440 was the **argument**; a value used by the object to specify its operation. In this case, the argument 440 caused `cycle~` to produce a tone at 440 Hz.

The signal outlet of the `cycle~` object was connected to the inlet of the `gain~` object, which caused the signal generated by `cycle~` to be passed on to the `gain~` object, where it could be modified, as we have seen, by moving the volume fader. The modified signal was then passed on to the `ezdac~` object (the little loudspeaker), which attenuated the signal and routed it to the sound driver,[9] which managed a digital-to-analog conversion that transformed the numeric representation of the sound into an audio wave that you could hear on your headphones or speakers. (This conversion, by the way, is where `ezdac~` got its name; it is a quasi-acronym for EaZy Digital-to-Analog Converter.)

Let's now broaden the function of this patch. Let's make it possible to actually see what is happening in addition to hearing the sound. Save the current patch (which you will need again in the next section) into an appropriate folder, for example "My Patches", and close the Patcher Window. If you haven't already downloaded and unpacked the "Max Chapter Materials Vol 1" archive that can be found at www.virtual-sound.com/cmsupport, do this now.

---

[6] Alternatively, you can move back and forth between edit and performance modes by holding down the <Command> key (on the Mac) or the <Control> key (on Windows) and clicking the left mouse button on an empty part of the Patcher Window.

[7] In this case, it is actually a cosine wave, as we will see in the next chapter.

[8] All of these concepts were laid out in Theory Section 1.2.

[9] A sound driver is a piece of system software that enables programs such as Max to manage incoming as well as outbound audio signals.

Open the file **01_01.maxpat**, which you will find in the *"Max Chapter Materials Vol 1/Max Patches Vol 1/Chapter 01 Patch"* folder (see figure 1.9).

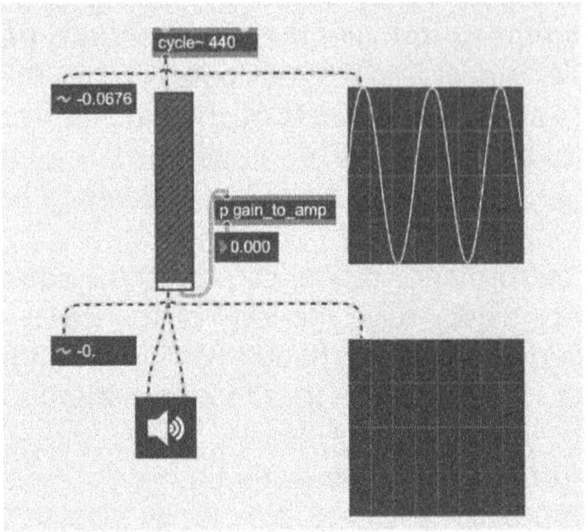

Fig.1.9 The file 01_01.maxpat

When this file opens, you will see that we have added new objects to the original patch. The new objects on the left, in which you can see numerical values, are called **number~** objects, and they show, via the value that they display, a snapshot of the signal that they are receiving. The larger rectangular objects on the right are called **scope~** objects,[10] which act as oscilloscopes on which it is possible to view an incoming signal as graphic waveform. The object [p gain_to_amp] and the object that is connected to its outlet (which is called a **flonum** or a float number box) are used to view exactly how much **gain~** is being applied to amplify or attenuate the signal.

Once again, start the patch by clicking on the **ezdac~**, and observe the numbers changing in the **number~** object high on the left. These numbers are being produced by the **cycle~** object and, if we observe them for a bit, we can see that their values, both positive and negative, fall between 1 and -1. On the upper right side we can see the **scope~** object displaying the same numbers in graphical form; the upper half of its panel corresponds to positive numbers, and the lower half to negative numbers. In the **scope~** panel, hundreds of different elements are shown, visualized as a sequence of points, rather than the single number shown by the **number~** object. The points fall very close to each other on the screen, and so they appear as a solid curve. The elements that they represent, the numbers themselves, are called *samples* in the terminology of digital music. And the line made from these sample values, as they undulate high and low across the oscilloscope panel, is precisely the sinusoidal wave produced by the **cycle~** object.

[10] The **number~** and **scope~** objects can be found in the upper *Toolbar* in the previously described "Audio" category, which you will remember can be accessed by clicking on the next-to-last icon and selecting "Audio". Also remember that if you can't find an object here, you can always use the trick that we demonstrated above: take an object box and type the name of the desired object into its interior.

The patch also contains a second **number~** and a second **scope~**, each connected to the **gain~** object. These objects should be displaying the number 0 and a flat line (which is, of course, a sequence of zeros), because the volume fader is at its lowest setting, resulting in a volume of 0. If we move the **gain~** fader upwards, we should see **number~** begin to display values that start out very small and gradually grow larger as the volume rises, and at the same time, the flat line of the lower **scope~** should begin its undulation and assume the same look as the other **scope~**. We can infer from this that **gain~** is controlling the amplitude of the signal– the more we raise the fader, the greater the amplitude of the oscillations becomes. If we go too far, and raise the value of the **gain~** fader to be close to its maximum setting, we see **number~** begin to exceed the amplitude limits of 1 and -1, and the waveform on the oscilloscope becomes clipped. More important than these visual clues, you should be able to actually *hear* the sound change, as it becomes distorted.

We can draw some conclusions from what we've seen:
1) The **cycle~** object produces a sequence of digital values that follow the pattern of a (co)sine wave.
2) The numerical limits for samples in this sine wave are 1 and -1. The actual sequence that these values follow can be seen on the upper **scope~**, which shows the waveform at its maximum amplitude, above which the quality of the sound would be distorted.
3) The **gain~** object modifies the amplitude of the sine wave, causing the sample values at its outlet to be different than the corresponding sample values received on its inlet. How does it do this? By multiplying the values that it receives by a quantity that depends upon the position of the fader. When the fader is in its lowest position, the signal is multiplied by 0, and the result is a stream of zeros (because any number multiplied by 0 is 0). One can see that as we raise the fader, the multiplication factor rises. If, for example, we move it to 0.5, the amplitudes of the samples that enter the **gain~** object are diminished (because multiplying a number by 0.5 is the same as dividing by 2).[11]

As we move it to 1.0 (which is about 3/4 of the way up the fader), the sample values entering the object are identical to those leaving. Finally, if we raise the fader all of the way, the most extreme of the sample values will exceed the limits of 1 and -1, although these samples will then be brought back into line during the digital-to-analog conversion. When that happens, however, the waveform will no longer be a sine wave. Instead, it will be clipped (as we can see in the lower oscilloscope). Sample values that fall outside of the -1 to 1 range are

[11] To adjust the fader to a position that corresponds to a multiplication factor of 0.5, watch the number box that is connected to the [**p** gain_to_amp] object, which is set up precisely for the purpose of displaying the value of the multiplication factor. The fader is actually divided into logarithmic increments, and using a formula that we'll explain later, the [**p** gain_to_amp] object converts these fader positions (which can be read from one of the outlets of the **gain~** object) into an amplitude level. We will return to this topic in Interlude A, which follows this chapter. One thing to note is that when the multiplication factor is near 0.5, the sine wave takes up about half of the oscilloscope screen.

actually simply reassigned the maximum possible amplitude during conversion, and the distorted sound that we hear reflects the resulting truncated waveform. We have continued the exploration of the concepts of frequency, amplitude, and waveform, which we began in Section 1.2 of the theory chapter. Let's recap some practical aspects of these basic concepts:

- Amplitude is the physical parameter that corresponds to the intensity of a sound; it is the parameter that controls the perception of whether a given sonic event is *forte* or *piano*. In Max, the absolute value of amplitude (that is, the value of the parameter, independent of its sign) always lies between 0 and a maximum of 1.
- Frequency is the physical parameter that relates to pitch; it is the parameter that controls the perception of whether a given sonic event is high or low in pitch. The values are expressed in hertz (Hz), and we need to keep in mind that sounds audible to humans fall in the range between 20 and around 20,000 Hz.
- Waveform is a fundamental element of timbre, which we define as the overall quality of a sound. Timbre enables us to perceive, for example, the difference between the middle C played on a guitar and the same note played on a saxophone. We have seen and heard the timbre of the sine wave produced by `cycle~`.

FAQ (Frequently Asked Questions)

In this section, we will try to give answers to some of the more common problems that are encountered by new users of Max. You should probably read these carefully even if you have not experienced a problem, since they contain information that you will use in the following sections of the book.

Question: I created an object called "cycle~440", as instructed in this section, but the object has no inlets or outlets. What went wrong?

Answer: Be sure that you typed a space between "cycle~" and "440", because the first is the name of the object, while the second is an argument, which in this case represents the frequency of the sound. If the two words are run together, Max will search for a non-existent object named "cycle~440", and when nothing is found, Max will have no inlet or outlet information with which to work.

Q: Very good. Why, then, didn't Max give me an error message?

A: There *is* an error message, which can be found in the **Max Console**, which is a window that the program uses to communicate with you. To call it from the keyboard, use <Command-m / Control-m>, or click on the fourth icon of the right *Toolbar*[12]: a window will appear on the right of the Patcher Window.

12 When there is an error in the Max Console, but the window is hidden, the icon in the Toolbar displays a red dot.

In the window, you will probably find a message such as *"cycle~440: No such object"*. If you double-click on the error message, the object that caused it (in this case, the bogus "cycle~440" object) will be highlighted in the Patcher Window.

Q: I inserted a space between "cycle~" and "440", but the object has no inlets or outlets just the same!

A: There is a more subtle error that often turns up for some new users when using objects that have a tilde ('~') at the end of their name. If you have a keyboard on which there is no tilde key, and so you need to press a combination of keys in order to produce the character (for example, <Alt-5> on some Macs), you may have continued pressing one of the modifier keys when typing the space (for example, <Alt-Space> on the Mac). The resulting combination is not recognized by Max, and Max is not able to separate the object name from its argument. Delete the space and re-insert it, avoiding pressing modifier keys at the same time.

Q: There is no sound.
A: Have you clicked on the **ezdac~** object (which is the loudspeaker icon)? Have you raised the volume fader above zero? Are you sure that sound on your computer is not muted, or that you are able to produce sound by using a program other than Max? Have you checked the Audio Status window (which you can find in the *Options* menu), to see that the correct sound driver is selected?

A COMPACT "SURVIVAL MANUAL" FOR MAX

In this section, we will give some essential information for easily navigating the Max environment.

BASIC KEYBOARD COMMANDS
Mac <Command-n> or Windows <Control-n> will create a new Patcher Window, which is the workspace for implementing patches.

Mac <Command-e> or Windows <Control-e> will toggle between edit mode and performance mode in the Patcher Window. In edit mode, we assemble patches by creating objects using the Top Patcher Window Toolbar; in performance mode we can activate patches and interact with their graphical user interface objects (such as float number boxes or the **gain~** object).

Mac <Command-m> or Windows <Control-m> will call up the Max Console if it is not already visible. The Max Console is a window used by the Max environment to communicate, using brief text messages, with its user. We will learn more about this window shortly.

Instead of using the Patcher Window, it is possible to create some common objects by typing simple one-character commands, without having to use <Command> or <Control> keys. The character 'n', for example, will create (when your Patcher is in edit mode) an empty object box at the position of the mouse pointer. There are other keys that also enable object creation: in edit mode, try positioning the mouse pointer and pressing 'f', 'i', 't', and 'b', and observe the various objects (which probably mean nothing to you at the moment!) that are created. We will use these objects frequently in the course of the following chapters.

SELECTION, DELETION, AND COPYING

To delete a patch cord or an object, you need to insure that you are in edit mode,[13] select the patch cord or object with the mouse, and then press the <Delete> key (which may also be referred to as the <Backspace> key). We can select multiple objects at a time by clicking on a blank spot in the Patcher Window and dragging a rectangle that "touches" the objects to be selected (see fig 1.10).

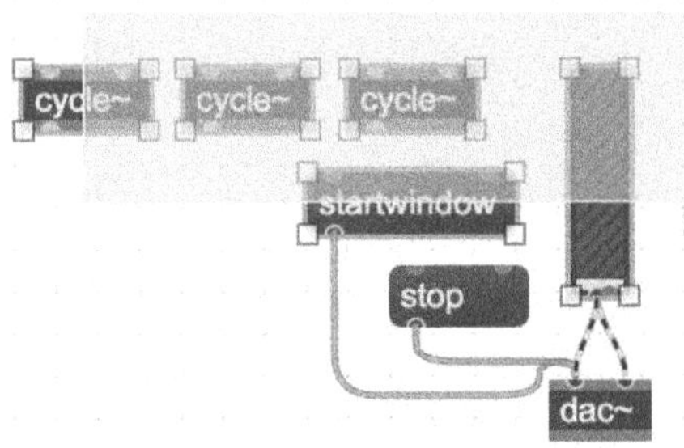

Fig. 1.10 Selecting objects

At this point, if we move one of the selected objects, all of them will move; likewise, if we press the <Delete> key, all of the selected objects will vanish. Using this selection technique, objects will be selected but not patch cords. If we need to select the patch cords at the same time we are selecting objects (for example, to delete them) we need to hold the <Alt> key down while dragging the selection rectangle, and make sure that we "touch" the cables that interest us (as seen in figure 1.11).

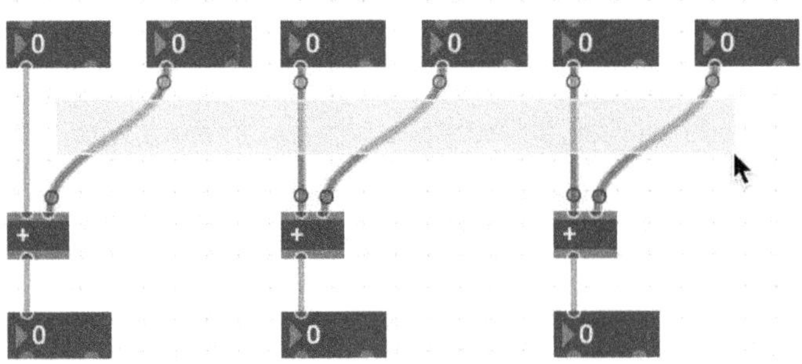

Fig. 1.11 Selecting patch cords

[13] Check to make sure the padlock at the bottom left of the window containing the patch is open.

With the <Alt> key held, we can also copy an object. Simply click-and-drag to tear off a copy. If you first select multiple objects and then drag them using <Alt-Click>, you can copy them all (as in figure 1.12).

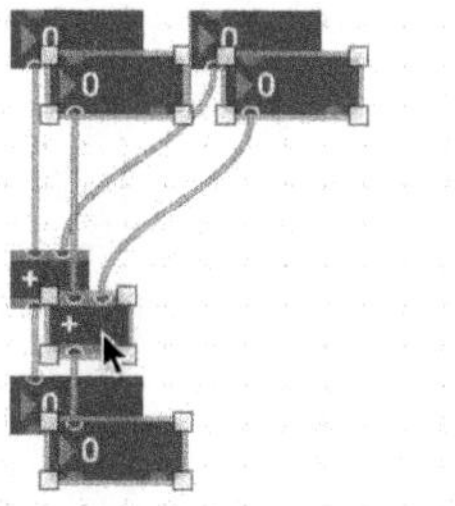

Fig. 1.12 Copying multiple objects at once

If you make a mistake (for example, you delete one object rather than another), you can undo the action by selecting the Undo command from the *Edit* menu. Repeatedly selecting Undo can cancel an entire sequence of commands and return the patch to the state that preceded those actions. If, after undoing one or more actions, you decide that there wasn't actually an error (for example, you wanted to delete the object after all), you can restore actions by using the Redo command, which is also found in the Edit menu.
The command equivalents of undo and redo are <Command-z> and <Shift-Command-z> on the Mac and <Control-z> and <Shift-Control-z> on Windows.[14]

DOCUMENTATION AND HELP
This book is self-contained: within it you will find all that you need for understanding and using the patches with which we illustrate Max synthesis and signal processing techniques. But the Max environment also provides extensive illustrative materials that can be accessed by selecting the **Max Documentation** item from the ***Help*** menu.

[14] <Shift> is the modifier key used to type capital letters.

When you select this item, you will obtain the window shown in figure 1.13 (which may be quite different looking in different versions of Max).

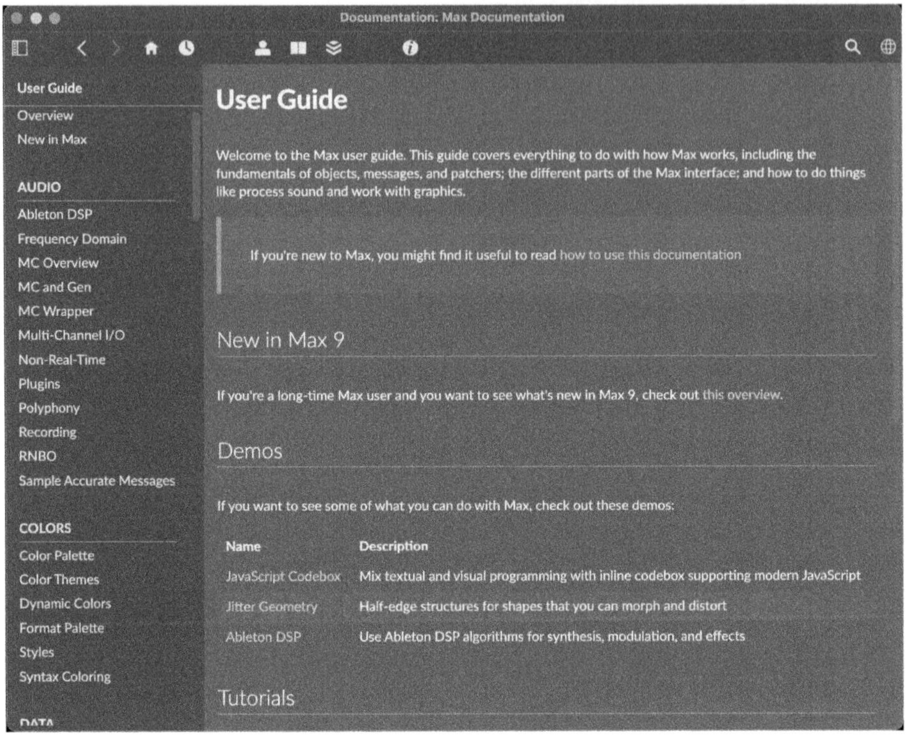

Fig. 1.13 The Documentation window

In the figure we see a part of the *Documentation* window for Max. The initial screen shows the User Guide: the left column lists the different topics divided into categories (Audio, Colors, etc.). Browse through the topics, for example in the Audio category, and don't worry if you don't understand everything right away. For a guide on how to use the documentation, click on the icon at the top, which is an 'i' in a white circle, and select 'How to Use the Documentation' from the pop-up menu.

There are also help patches for all of the individual objects found in Max. When you are in edit mode, <Alt-Click> on an object (without dragging), and a help patch relevant to the clicked object will open. This patch will be fully functional, and will summarize the principal characteristics of the object. <Alt-Click> while in edit mode on the `cycle~` object, for example, will bring up the **help patch** seen in figure 1.14 (which again may be quite different in different versions of Max).

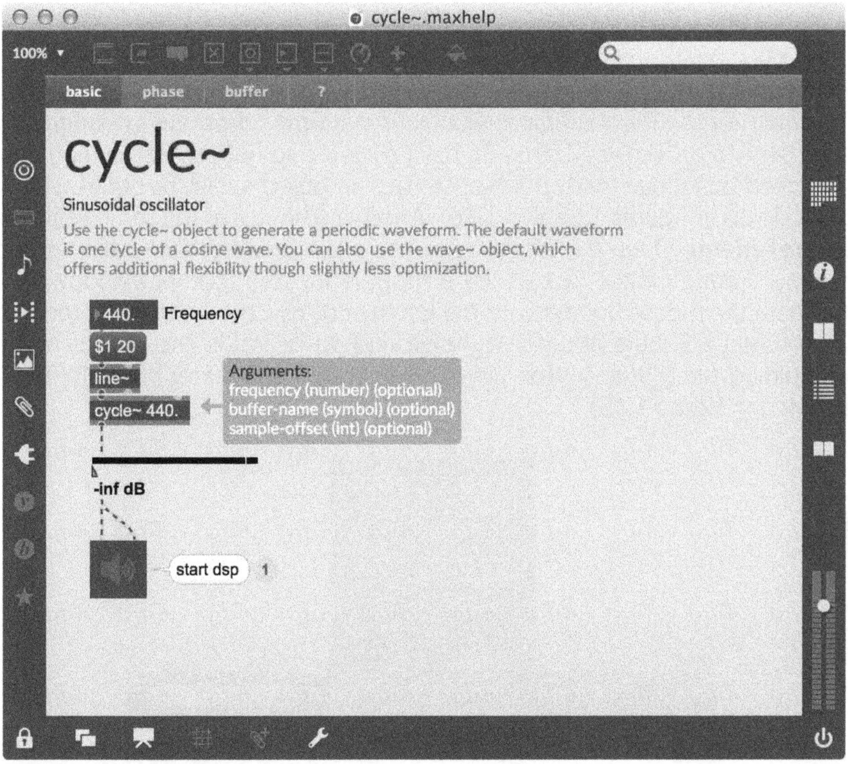

Fig. 1.14 A help patch

Help patches all share a very specific structure: they are divided into panes that can be displayed by clicking on tabs that are visible in the upper left part of the window: each individual pane explains some specific characteristics or behaviors for the object in question. The number of tabs and the names on these tabs will vary from object to object, with the exception of the first and last tabs, which are shared by all objects and are labeled consistently. The first of these shared tabs, labeled "basic", highlights the fundamental features of the object being examined, while the last shared tab, labeled with a question mark, contains a menu whose first item, "Open Reference", can be used to call up a detailed page from the reference manual, and whose succeeding menu items lead to help patches for related objects, to objects that are similar to the object in question, and finally, to tutorials illustrating the use of the object. Whether or not you read the deeper explanatory material contained in a help patch such as this one, we still recommend that you take a peek! They are working patches that can teach a great deal about the practical techniques and specialized vocabulary used in Max.

Another source of information is the **Clue Bar**, which appears on the right side of the lower Toolbar when you hover the mouse pointer over an object. The Clue Bar consists of text with the name of the object and a brief description. Clicking on the name of the object brings up a menu with links to the help patch, the reference page, and a few objects related to that object.

The comprehensive help system is undoubtedly one of the strongest points of the Max environment. We have already encountered other aspects of it: remember the Assistance Bubble text, which we see every time that we work with patch cords. The Assistance Bubble dynamically describes messages that can be sent to or received from an object's inlets and outlets. Recall that to see it, we need only hover with the mouse over an object's inlet or outlet when in edit mode (as in figures 1.6a and 1.6b). Another resource in the same vein is the **Quickref menu**. Open 01_01.maxpat once again, and put the patch into edit mode by clicking on the lock at the bottom left of the Patcher Window. Now hover with the mouse pointer over the left inlet of **cycle~** so that the red circle and Assistance Bubble appear. Right-clicking while inside the red circle, and then holding the mouse button down, will cause the *Quickref* menu to appear (as shown in figure 1.15).

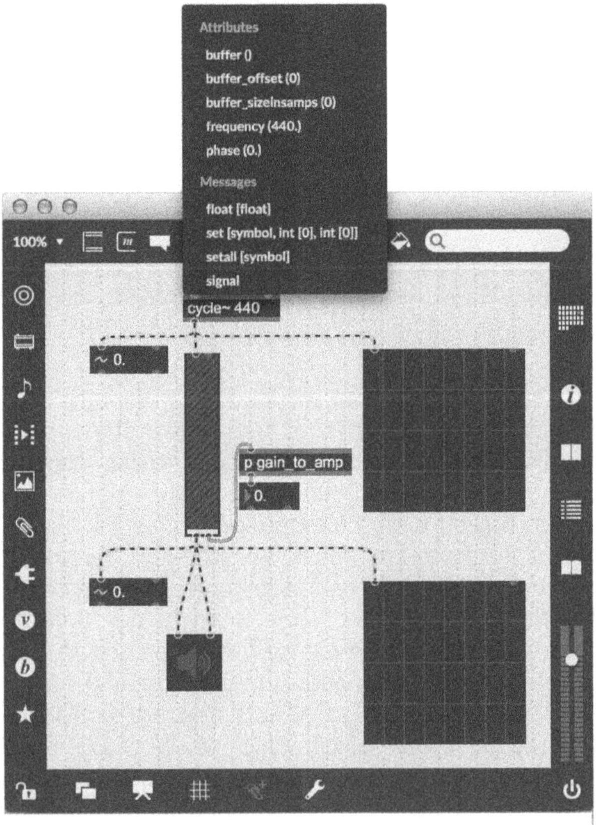

Fig. 1.15 The Quickref menu

This menu is categorized into two types of elements: **Attributes**, about which we will speak more in a bit, and **Messages** which correspond to the messages that a given object is able to "understand" and use. By selecting a message from the list, it is possible to create a new object that is automatically connected to the target object (in this case, **cycle~**). Click, for example, on the float [float] item, and a new object will appear, already connected to **cycle~**, as in figure 1.16.

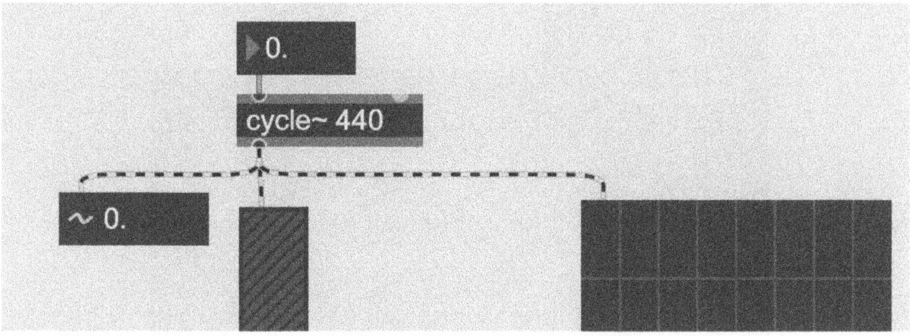

Fig. 1.16 Connecting an object by means of Quickref

If you now put the Patcher into performance mode (by closing the lock in the lower left with <Click>), and make vertical sliding strokes of the mouse over the new object while holding the mouse button down, you will see the numbers change in the object's UI. This object's purpose is, in fact, to store and enter numeric values; it is named **number**, or *number box*. Numbers that we generate by sliding the mouse over this object are sent to **cycle~** to modify its frequency. (You will note, however, that the argument of 440 that you can see inside of the **cycle~** object doesn't change. Instead, the frequency is overridden invisibly by the newly transmitted values.) Run the patch by clicking on the loudspeaker icon and raising the fader to about 3/4 of its range, and then set the number in the number box to values between 500 and 1000 by sliding the mouse. You will hear the oscillator change pitch, driven by the frequencies being output by the number box. We will speak at much greater length about the number box in following sections of this chapter.
If you now move the mouse pointer to the left side of an object (in *edit* mode, of course) you will see a circle appear, containing a small triangle (fig. 1.16b). Click on this icon, and a new context menu will appear, called the *Object Action Menu*.

Fig. 1.16b The *Object Action* icon

This menu (fig 1.16c) contains the most useful elements for managing, transforming, and finding information about an object. In practice, all of the items found in this menu are also reachable in other ways (and we will progressively find out what use they serve); this menu has the advantage of placing them all where they can be invoked with a single click.

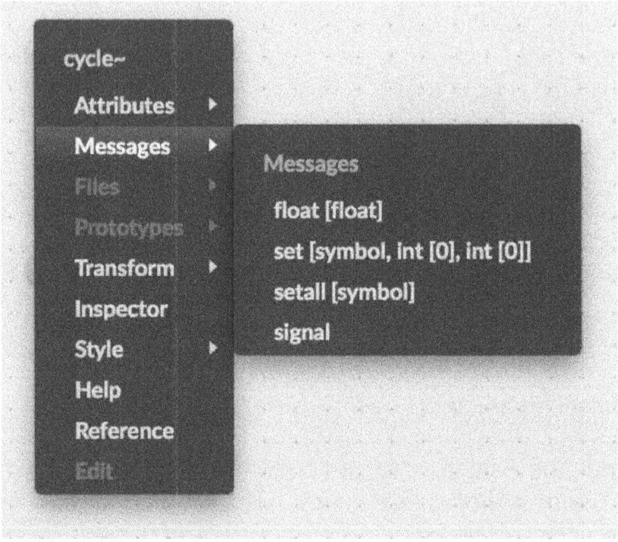

fig. 1.16c The Object Action Menu

PATCHER WINDOW TOOLBARS

We will now examine in more detail the four *Toolbars*, which, as we have said, surround the *Patcher Window* (which is, to say, the window in which we write our Max programs). The **Upper Toolbar** contains the interface objects available in Max, grouped into categories (see 1.17), as well as a Zoom menu in the upper left, by which it is possible to enlarge or shrink the view of the *patch*.

The first four icons after the Zoom menu correspond to four frequently used objects: the *object box* (which you already are familiar with), the *message box*, the *comment box*, and the `toggle` object, whose acquaintance we will make in a bit. Five icons follow, from which it is possible to open the same number of *palettes*, each containing objects from a pre-determined category:

Buttons: this *palette* contains interface objects that act like buttons.
Numbers: this *palette* contains interface objects that display and generate values (such as the *number box* that we already encountered in fig. 1.16).
Sliders: this *palette* contains interface objects that function as cursors; in other words, they produce ranged values when you drag them using the mouse.
Max for Live: this *palette* contains the interface objects for Max for Live (which we will discuss in the second volume).
Add (other objects): this *palette* contains all of the other relevant objects, and is sub-divided into the sub-categories *Basic, Audio, Data, Images, Interface*, and *Jitter*.

We have already seen the *Audio* sub-category in fig. 1.7, and we will explore the contents of the other categories as we find the need.

After the icons used to create the different Max objects, there is one representing a can of paint. This icon doesn't serve to create objects, but rather, it is used to configure the graphical appearance of the *Patcher Window* and of the Max objects contained in the *Patcher Window*: a click on the icon brings up the *Format Palette*. We will not occupy ourselves with details of appearance during this first section, but you should explore the icon anyway: select (in *edit* mode) an object box within patch 01_01.maxpat and, after bringing up the *Format Palette*, try modifying its color, or the size and type of font that it exhibits, for example.

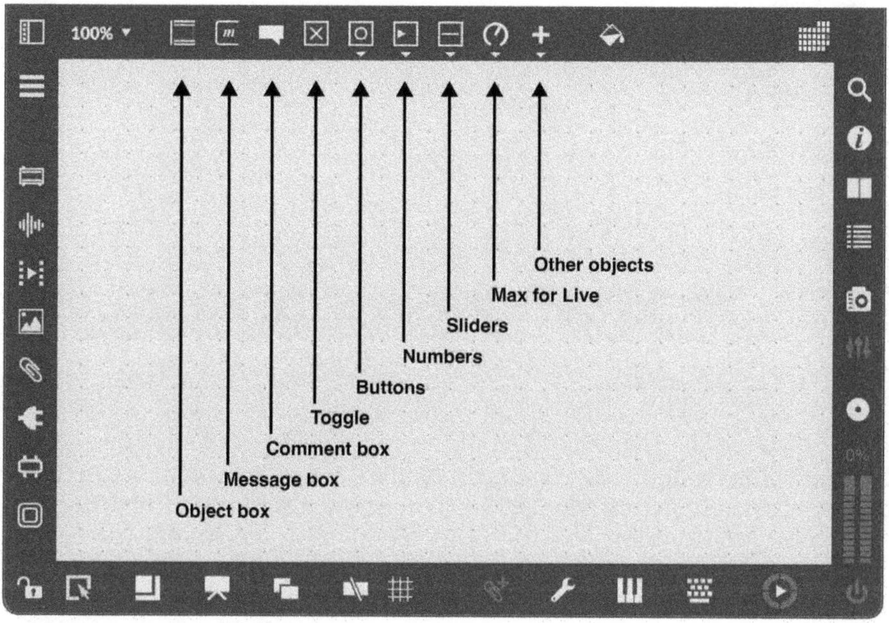

fig 1.17 the upper *Toolbar*

The right side of the upper *Toolbar* contains a last icon which opens a calendar showing, in chronological order, the names of the patches we worked on.

By using the **Left Toolbar**, it is possible to access any or all of the many types of files used when programming Max (fig. 1.17b).

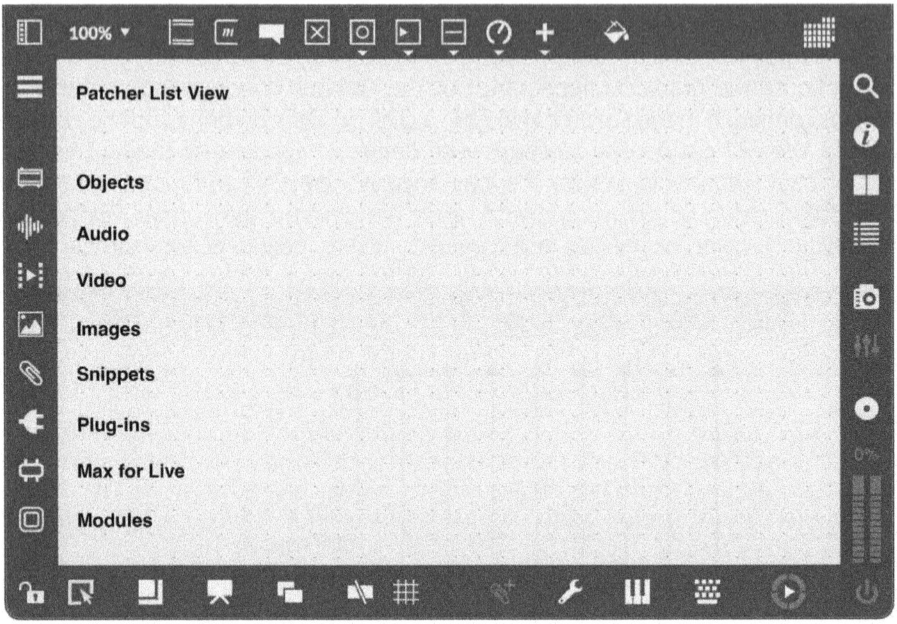

fig 1.17b The left *Toolbar*

The first icon at the top, to the left of the Zoom menu, is used to open a side browser showing items corresponding to the various file categories accessed by the subsequent icons in the left Toolbar. Below this is the Patcher List View: clicking on this icon displays a list of all the items in the current patch. Now click on the third icon: a slide-out menu appears that contains all of the objects available in Max (not only interface objects, reachable from the upper *Toolbar*). Objects in this menu are divided into categories and sub-categories, and a double-click on the name of an object will cause it to appear within the patch. Alternatively, you can also drag a name into the *Patcher Window,* causing an instance of the object to appear. (These two alternative approaches to creating objects are consistently available from the *Toolbar* menus.)

The fourth icon enables us to locate and use audio files within a *patch*, the fifth, video files and the sixth, images. Note that to be visible in these menus, a file must be found in Max' *File Search Path*, which we will revisit later. As long as you are here, try, with the padlock icon open, dragging some files from the audio menu into the patching area and observe what happens; we will revisit this menu in Section 1.5. The seventh icon, shown as a paper clip, enables us to access *Snippets*, which are reusable fragments of code captured using the lower *Toolbar* (see below). The eighth icon gives us access to Max for Live plug-ins, VSTs, and Audio Units that are installed on our computer. Just for the moment, we will ignore the remaining icons and move on.

The **Lower Toolbar** contains tools used while programming Max. The first icon is the padlock, which, as you already know, enables us to transition from edit mode into *performance* mode, and vice-versa. We will discuss each of the other icons contained in this *Toolbar* at the appropriate time, and for the moment occupy ourselves with the eight icon, which is a paper clip embellished with a plus sign that closely resembles the paper clip found in the left Toolbar. This icon enables us to create *new snippets*. To understand the *snippet* feature, open the patch file named 01_01.maxpat (fig. 1.9), put the *Patcher Window* into *edit* mode, and select the **gain~** objects (the vertical faders), the **ezdac~** object (the little speaker), and the **[p gain_to_amp]** object[15]. At this point, click on the paper clip icon in the lower *Toolbar* and a small window will appear in which we can name the snippet being saved: type "audiostart" and hit enter. Next, create a new patch and click on the sixth icon of the left *Toolbar* (the other paper clip). A menu will appear that, among its other entries, now contains an item called "audiostart". Drag this element into the Patcher Window, and you will see the snippet that you previously saved appear. Using this technique, it is possible to capture frequently needed pieces of code for reuse. As you can see, the menu already contains some pre-defined snippets for you to use; you can easily create more while you work with Max.

We now move to the **Right Toolbar**: almost all the icons contained in this *Toolbar* display some form of the **Sidebar**, which is a drawer-like window that opens on the right side of the *Patcher Window* and which contains a variety of useful tools and information. Open, for example, patch 01_01.maxpat (fig. 1.9), put it into edit mode, select the **ezdac~** object (the little speaker), and click on the second icon (shown as the letter "i" inscribed in a circle). This will open the *Sidebar* and display the *inspector* for the selected object. (The *inspector* contains all of the attributes that define the appearance and the behavior of an object, and we will speak about it in great detail later in the book.) The third icon enables quick access to documentation about the selected object, while the fourth opens the Max Console, a window through which, as we have already learned, Max displays error messages and other useful information.
We will talk about the other icons at the appropriate time.
At the bottom of this Toolbar, the combined Audio Meter/Gain controls can be seen, which display and control the global audio volume of the patch, as well as an Audio On/Off button, which can be used to activate or disable the production of audio signals in the patch (in exactly the same way as the **ezdac~** object can).

---

[15] To select multiple objects, you can use the technique shown in fig. 1.10 or else click on the objects, one after another, while holding the shift key down.

SOME ORDER FOR A CHAOTIC WORLD

You probably noticed that some of the patch cords in patch 01_01.maxpat (figure 1.9) had angles in them which divided their connections into tidy segments. How was this done? The answer is simple: by selecting **Segmented Patch Cords** from the *Options* menu.

If you use this option, the procedure for connecting two objects will be slightly different than what we've seen already: begin connecting with a click on the outlet that will form the source of the connection, and then pull the patch cord out from the object *without holding the mouse button down*. (The cable will remain hooked to the mouse pointer.) Segments can be created at any time with a click of the mouse at the point at which you want to change direction; for every click, there is a new segment. The final click should be made on the inlet of the object to which you wish to connect.

If you make an error and want to release the cable without connecting, you need to <Command-Click> on the Mac or <Control-Click> on Windows, or else hit the escape key (<Esc>).

If you select some objects that are lined up roughly horizontally, and then press <Command-y/Control-Shift-a>, the objects will become perfectly aligned. The same command works to create vertical columns of objects one over the other. (The two `scope~` objects and the two `number~` objects in 01_01.maxpat were aligned in this way.) Objects can also easily be aligned using the **Snap to Object** function (which is active by default). Every time that you position an object in a patch, this function will align that object with other nearby objects. Another related function is **Distribute**, which can be found in the *Arrange* menu; this function makes it possible to distribute a group of selected objects at equal intervals horizontally or vertically.

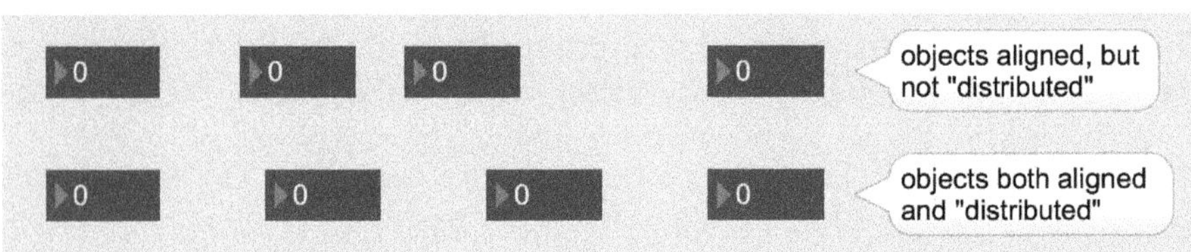

fig. 1.18: the *Distribute* function

A complex patch can be very crowded, with dozens of objects and patch cords stretched between them. In this case, it is possible to render a set of the objects and cords invisible when in performance mode, but still visible while in edit mode, so that they can do their work behind the scenes. To hide one or more objects and patch cords, select them while in edit mode and press <Command-k/Control-k>. When the Patcher is put into performance mode, the objects will vanish. To reverse this action, and make the objects reappear during performance mode, use <Command-l/Control-l> (lower key "el") in edit mode. By selecting multiple objects, it is possible to hide multiple objects at once using these commands. An alternative to the keystroke commands is found in the *Object* menu, where **Hide on Lock** and **Show on Lock** can be found. Play with 01_01.maxpat, making various objects and patch cords in the patch appear and disappear.

There is yet a still more efficient way to put order into patches, which is to use a feature called presentation mode. We will explain this mode once we find ourselves building a more complex patch.

EXERCISE

Create a new Patcher Window and attempt to reproduce the patch contained in the file **01_01.maxpat**.
Use the snippet that you saved in the preceding paragraph (if you haven't yet done this, make it now!), because otherwise it will be impossible for you to create the `[p` gain_to_amp`]` object.
Pay careful attention that you don't confuse the **`number~`** object with the number box! If you don't succeed in finding **`scope~`** and **`number~`** in the Top Patcher Window Toolbar, remember that you can always take an object box, type the name of the object into its interior, and morph the object box into the graphic object that you seek. Note that the displayed waveform on the oscilloscope created by you is different from that in the original file. We will see why in the following section.

1.2 FREQUENCY, AMPLITUDE AND WAVEFORM

In the previous section, we gave **cycle~** a frequency by typing the number 440 as a fixed argument into the inside of the object box. We then discovered, through the actions of a number box, that it is also possible to vary the frequency at any time by sending numbers to the left inlet of the object. In figure 1.19 we see another type of object that can be used to modify the frequency of **cycle~**.

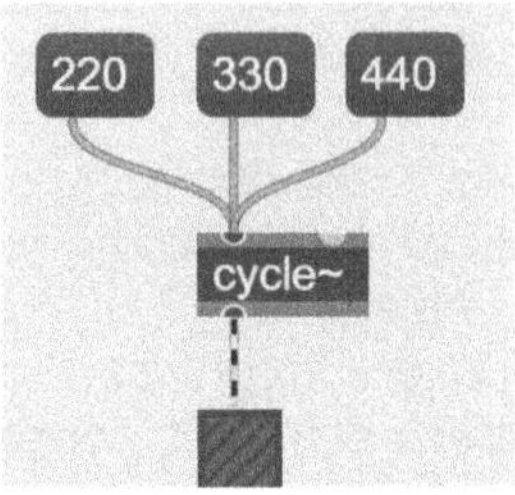

Fig. 1.19 Use of the *message box*

Here we have added three new *message boxes* to the previous patch. (The message box is the second icon in the Top Patcher Window Toolbar.) The ***message box*** can be distinguished from the *object box*, since an *object box* has small gray bars on its upper and lower edges, while a *message box* has a uniform background color and rounded corners. A message box can contain any message that you type into it (a message being some amalgam of characters, phrases, words, numbers, and other symbols), and its stored message is sent whenever it is clicked in performance mode. It is a very important object, so commonly used that it can be created by just typing the letter 'm'.

Try modifying the patch from the previous section[16] in the way that we just suggested, by adding some message boxes, filling them with numbers, and then clicking on them to vary the frequency of the **cycle~** (after, of course, following what should now be a familiar startup procedure: enter performance mode, click the **ezdac~** loudspeaker to enable the digital-to-analog converter, and raise the level of the volume fader). Note that the "440" argument that follows the word "**cycle~**" doesn't change when we click on a message box. The argument to **cycle~** is replaced by the message box value, which is immediately copied into an internal storage slot (that has no visual representation) in the object. The frequency that we hear from **cycle~** while the patch is running is based on this internal value rather than the onscreen characters.

With the message box mechanism, we can only send pre-defined values that we have placed into message boxes ahead of time. If we wish to change numbers arbitrarily while a patch is running, we need to use a number box for integer values or a **flonum** (or *float number box*) for floating point values.

[16] If you didn't save the patch from the previous section, modify the file 01_01.maxpat and save it using another name. (One that doesn't correspond to a Max object name! See Section 1.1 for advice on this.)

These objects are in the Numbers *palette* (sixth icon in the Top Patcher Window Toolbar, fig. 1.20) and can be created instantly by typing the single character 'i' (for the integer number box) or 'f' (for the floating point number box).

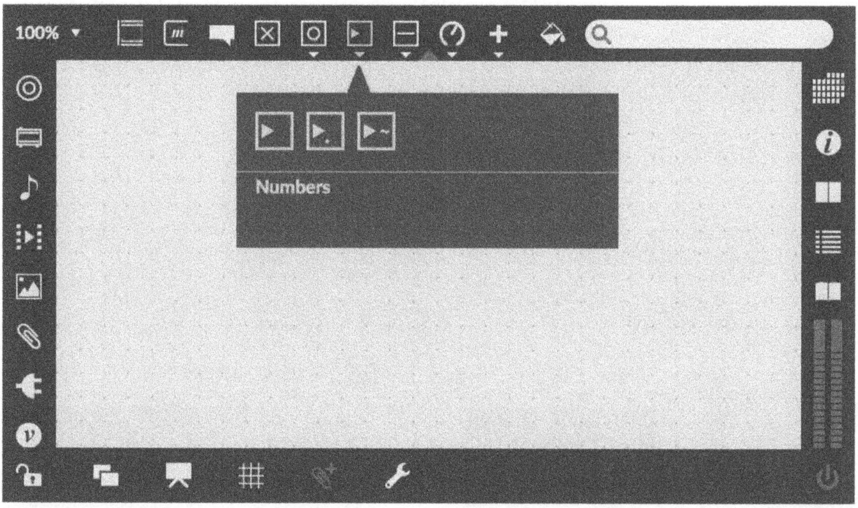

Fig. 1.20 The icons for **flonum** and **number** as they appear in the Numbers *Palette*

Add a **flonum** to the patch (the icon with the triangle and the little decimal point), switch to performance mode, activate **ezdac~**, and vary the frequency in the following way: click on the float number box, and, holding the mouse button down, slide the mouse up to raise the frequency or down to lower it. If you click on the left part of the float number box, you will be incrementing or decrementing the integer part of the number, while if you click on the right part, you will be changing the fractional part of the number. A different way to modify the number in the **flonum** is to select the object with a click and then to type numbers directly into it; when you then type <Enter> or click away from the object,[17] the number you typed will be input (figure 1.21).

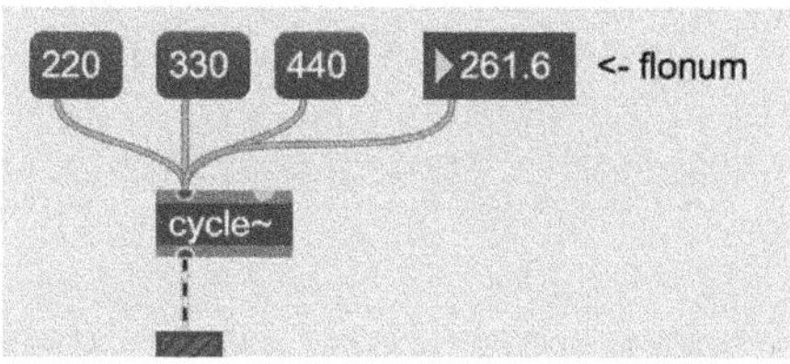

Fig. 1.21 The **flonum** object

[17] When you are in performance mode and the object is selected, the triangle will be yellow.

A sine wave, having no harmonics,[18] is scarcely audible at low frequencies, and because of this, you will hear frequencies below 100 Hz only if you are using a good sound system or headphones. If you are using the speakers built into a laptop, you will only hear frequencies above 100 Hz. To input accurate frequencies quickly, and to avoid out-of-range numbers, click on the `flonum` object to select it (the triangle on the left will change to yellow to indicate that it is selected) and then type directly with the keyboard.

Now open the file **01_02.maxpat** (shown in figure 1.22).

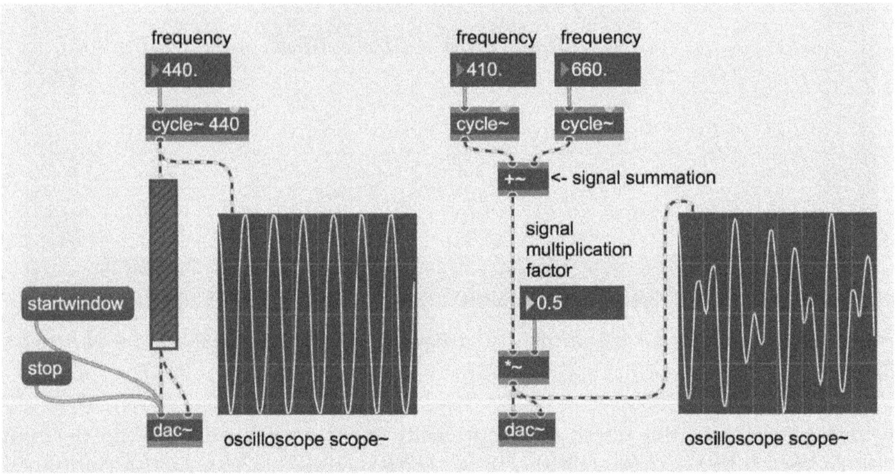

Fig. 1.22 The file 01_02.maxpat

In this patch, there are two modules for generating sound, and a **dac~** has been substituted for the **ezdac~** used previously. The **dac~** is another object for doing digital-to-analog conversion. It starts and stops MSP upon receiving the "***startwindow***" and "***stop***" messages, respectively. (Remember that you can send messages using a message box.) The advantage to using the "*startwindow*" message instead of simply clicking on the loudspeaker of the **ezdac~** is that **dac~** activates audio processing exclusively for the window that contains the patch. If we have many patches open and we click on an **ezdac~** to activate processing, all of the patches start up at the same time, because **ezdac~**, by default, activates processing for all open windows.[19] Consequently, from now on, we will use the "*startwindow*" message.[20]

Another new feature of this patch can be seen in the labels that we have added to various objects (for example, the "frequency" label over the float number

---

18 For the theory behind harmonics, see Theory Chapter 2.

19 Actually, it is possible to reduce the effective range of an **ezdac~** to a single window by using the *Inspector*, which is a window for changing the characteristics of an object. We will discuss this very soon.

20 Besides "*startwindow*", there is also a message named "***start***" that, if sent to the **dac~**, will activate audio processing for all open windows.

box that is connected to the oscillator). It will become extremely useful to be able to add such comments to our patches once they begin to become very complex. You can insert comments into your patches using the **comment box**, which is the third object of the Top Patcher Window Toolbar. A comment box can also be inserted by typing the single character 'c'.
If we activate the patch and vary the frequency of the first **cycle~**, we notice that the waveform shown on the **scope~** becomes narrower when the frequency is higher. This occurs because, as we have already learned, the period of the wave (that is to say, the duration of one cycle) is inversely proportional to frequency.

Moving on, we now will see that it is possible to hear many sounds at once. Drop the level of the fader on the left and then adjust the frequencies of the two **cycle~** oscillators on the right (to, say, 330 and 420 Hz). The sound of these two oscillators will be summed by the **+~** object, an object that performs signal summing. (Summing two signals simply means overlapping them, as we would on a mixer.) We have removed the **gain~** fader from this patch, and have substituted a multiplication operation, which uses the ***~** object, to adjust the volume. To hear the sound of the two oscillators, we must multiply by an object that is not zero (as we first saw in Section 1.1).[21]

Increment, with caution, the float number box connected to the right inlet of the multiplier. We need to raise only the fractional part of the number, and so we click on the right side of the object, after the decimal point, and drag the number higher. We see that if the multiplier exceeds the value 0.5, the sound acquires a distorted waveform. Why? Because numbers that exceed the range between -1 and 1 are clipped to either -1 or 1 by the digital-to-analog converter, as we have seen before. When we are summing two arbitrary sine waves together, each of which has an amplitude that varies between -1 and 1, the resulting wave will most likely have amplitude values that span the interval -2 to 2, and therefore, any multiplication factor greater than 0.5 will exceed the limits of the converter. An example: if we have an amplitude equal to 2 and a multiplication factor of 0.6, the result of the multiplication will be 1.2, which is greater than 1. If we were now to raise the fader connected to the left oscillator, the limit for distortion would change to an even lower number, because of the addition of the new signal: we would now be summing three different signals at the same time. (All of the signals sent to the two **dac~** objects are summed, of course, because they are all being routed to the same D/A converter!)

Try implementing a patch that sums two sine waves, by recreating the right part of file 01_02.maxpat in a new Patcher Window (if you like, use some of the segmented patch cords that you will recall you activate by selecting Segmented Patch Cord from the Options menu). Don't forget to connect the "startwindow" and "stop" message boxes to the **dac~** . Remember also that you need to transition from edit mode into performance mode (using

[21] If you have clicked on the "*stop*" message to stop audio processing for the patch, you need to remember to restart it with a click on "*startwindow*".

<Command-e/Control-e> or the lock icon at the bottom left) in order to use your patch. Above all, don't forget that, to hear something, you need to click on the "startwindow" message, to choose frequencies using the float number boxes connected to the oscillators, and to choose a number between 0 and 0.5 in the float number box connected to the multiplier ***~**.
If you've created your patch from scratch (rather than copying and pasting from the last patch) note that the waveform seen in your **scope~** is much more crowded than the one that you see in file 01_02.maxpat. To obtain a closer match, take a number box (the one without the decimal point, first of the Numbers *palette* shown on figure 1.20) and connect to it to the left inlet of the oscilloscope (the same inlet that you have used to connect the multiplier ***~**), and then vary the number in the box while the patch is running. You will see that this number is clearly linked to the overall amount of signal that is shown in the oscilloscope. It behaves like a kind of zoom: the lower the number that we enter, the larger the image of the signal becomes. In reality this is not a zoom function, but rather a slightly different concept, and to understand it, we need to drop into edit mode, select the **scope~**, and either press <Command-i/ Control-i> or click on the icon that contains an 'i' that you can find in the right *Toolbar*. As we have already discussed, this will open a slide-out window attached to the right side of the Patcher Window (fig. 1.23).

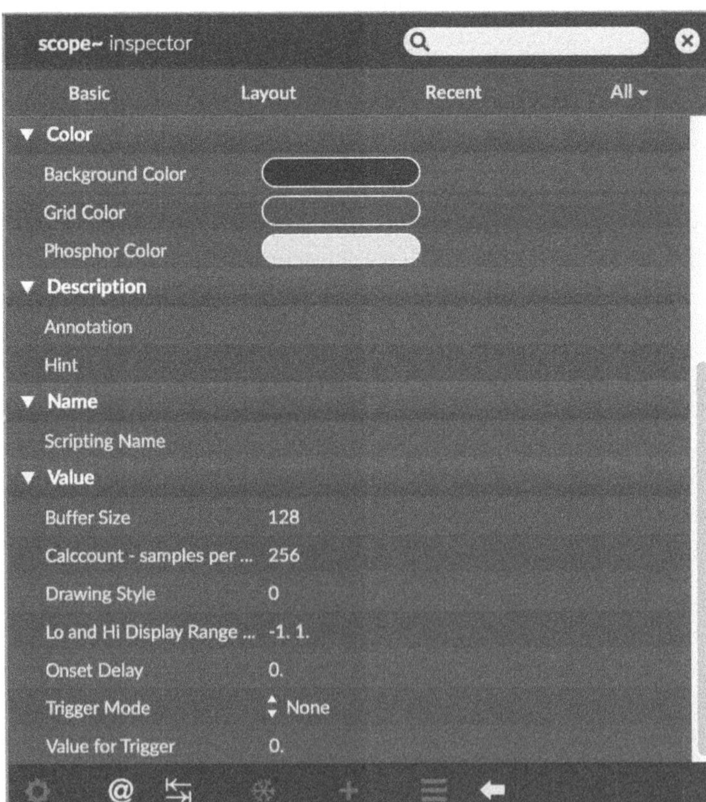

Fig. 1.23 The inspector for the **scope~** object

What we see is the **inspector** for the `scope~` object, a window through which it is possible to configure various properties of an object. All objects in Max have an inspector, and we will see many of them in the course of this book. The properties of an object (called **attributes** in Max) are subdivided into categories in the inspector, and these categories can vary from object to object. The inspector for a `scope~` object has the categories "Appearance", "Behavior", "Color", "Description", "Name", and "Value". We will look at the use of some of these categories during the course of this book, but for now, let's look only at the attributes found in the "Value" category for `scope~`.
The first attributes that we see are ***Buffer Size*** and ***Calccount - samples per pixel***. The waveform that we see on the screen doesn't display a point for every sample, but instead, each pixel drawn represents a fixed number of samples. Samples to be displayed, therefore, are divided into groups of data, and the size of each of these chunks can be configured using the *Calccount* attribute. It is also possible to set how many of these groups you want to display on the screen of the oscilloscope, and therefore how many pixels will be drawn, by using the *Buffer Size* attribute. The attribute that we modified with the number box connected to the left inlet of the `scope~` is *Calccount*, or the number of samples displayed per pixel. As we now understand, we can modify that attribute when in edit mode using the inspector, but dragging the numeric value higher or lower with the mouse in performance mode also works!
There are other interesting attributes that we can modify by using the oscilloscope's inspector. For example, the *Lo and Hi Display Range* are numbers that represent the minimum and maximum sample values that can be displayed. These limits are initially set to -1 and 1, and knowing this, we can now understand why samples that have a value larger than 1 or less than -1 are not visible on the display: they fall off of the edge, so to speak. By modifying the limits, we could see whatever values we chose to onscreen (but for the moment don't do this, because it might confuse things).
By manipulating the "Color" category attributes we can modify colors for elements such as the signal trace or the background. The procedure is fairly intuitive: click on a color bar, and a window will appear in which it is possible to change the color of the selected element. Besides color, there are numerous other attributes, many of which we will eventually touch upon as we proceed. Objects are not the only thing that can be modified in this way: it is also possible to modify the attributes of the Patcher Window itself by using the **patcher inspector**: to see this, deselect the `scope~` object (and any other selected objects) and then click on the small diamond-shaped icon containing the letter "P" which can be found in the upper part of the *inspector* window. We will return to the Patcher Inspector in Section 1.3.

Before illustrating some non-sine waveform generators, let's introduce a new object that will be very useful for routing and comparing signals: **`selector~`**. You'll use an object box to create it, because it requires a numeric argument when it is created – the number indicates the number of signal inlets that the object must have. To each inlet it is possible to connect a different signal. There is one further inlet, on the left, that establishes which signal will be handed to the outlet of the object. Using this object, it is possible to choose one signal at a time from among many.

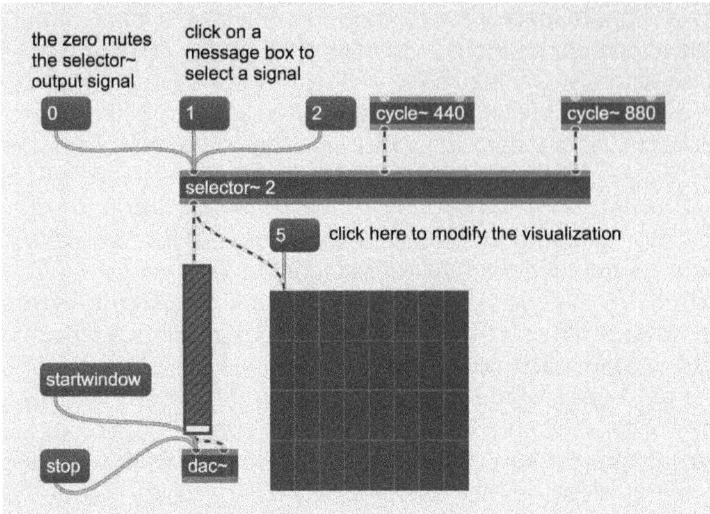

Fig. 1.24 The **selector~** object

Figure 1.24 shows a patch that clarifies the operation of **selector~**. Try to implement it;[22] it will be a good exercise. Open a new Patcher Window and reconstruct the patch, remembering that the rounded boxes on which are written "startwindow", "stop", and those that contain numbers, are message boxes, while those on which are written "**cycle~ 440**", "**cycle~ 880**", "**selector~ 2**" and "**dac~**", are object boxes.

You are probably wondering how to make the **selector~** object as long as is shown in the figure. In edit mode, you need to select the object, and then drag one of the four small squares that appear at its corners horizontally with the mouse.

Now that you've reconstructed the patch, check to make sure that it works: put the patcher into performance mode, start audio processing by clicking on "*startwindow*", and raise the **gain~**. If you then click on message '*1*', the signal on the first signal inlet will be routed through the **selector~**, and so you should hear the A440 generated by the first **cycle~** object. Likewise, clicking on '*2*' will route the second inlet, producing the octave above (880 Hz). If instead you click on '*0*', the **selector~** will be closed and you will hear nothing. If you want to change the number of oscillators that are active, say to 4, change the argument of **selector~** from 2 to 4 and you will see two new **selector~** inlets become active, to which you can connect additional signals.

Now let's explore how to generate waveforms that differ from sine waves. We begin with a sawtooth wave: in this waveform, as we discussed in Section 1.2 of the theory part of this chapter, the signal amplitude grows linearly from -1 to 1, at which point it returns immediately to -1 and begins the cycle again.

---

22 Remember to insert a space between the name of the object and the first argument for **cycle~** and **selector~**.

Open the file **01_03_sawtooth.maxpat** (seen in figure 1.25).

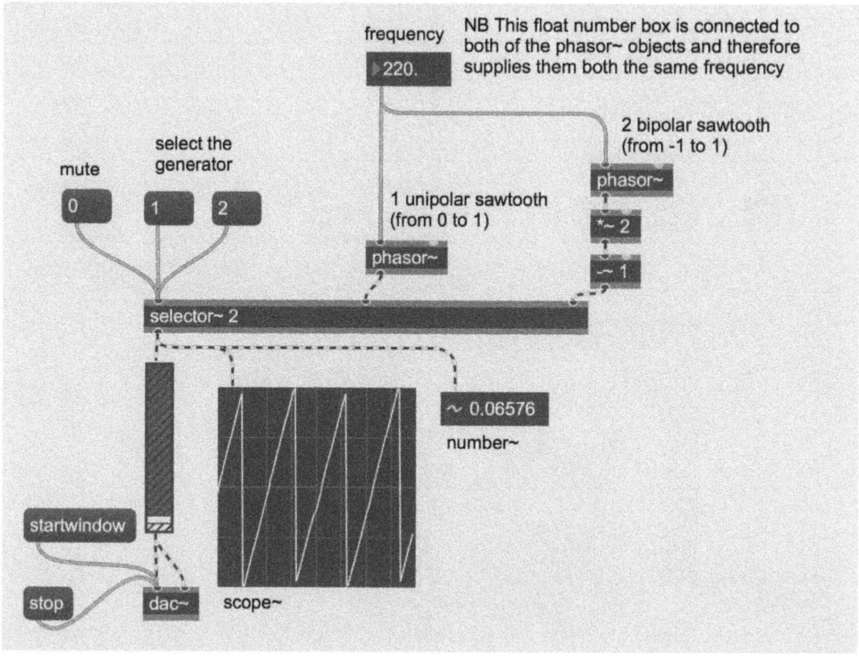

Fig. 1.25 The file 01_03_sawtooth.maxpat

Here we again encounter the **selector~** object that we just learned how to use, which will allow us to compare two different signals. We activate the patch, clicking on the "*startwindow*" message and hearing the first signal (after setting whatever frequency we'd like in the float number box) when we click on the message box that contains the number 1, and raise the fader. We see in the **scope~** rectangle the sawtooth waveform. The **phasor~** object is an oscillator that generates a ramp that goes from 0 to 1, and cyclicly repeats at a frequency that we can adjust exactly as we did with **cycle~**. The **phasor~** object produces a sawtooth waveform that is "cut in half", so to speak, because it goes from 0 to 1, instead of from -1 to 1, oscillating only in the positive range.[23] Since digital signals are nothing but numbers, we can change this "half" sawtooth into a "whole" by applying a pair of arithmetic operations: first multiply the output of **phasor~** by 2, resulting in a ramp running from 0 to 2, and then subtract 1 from this ramp, resulting in a new ramp that runs from -1 to 1. We see these operations rendered in the second signal of the patch, and by clicking on '*2*', we can hear the "whole" sawtooth; we see on the oscilloscope that it is bipolar, crossing into both positive and negative territory.

[23] This kind of oscillation is named unipolar oscillation, as we saw in Section 1.2 in the theory chapter.

Now open the file **01_04_triangle_square.maxpat**.

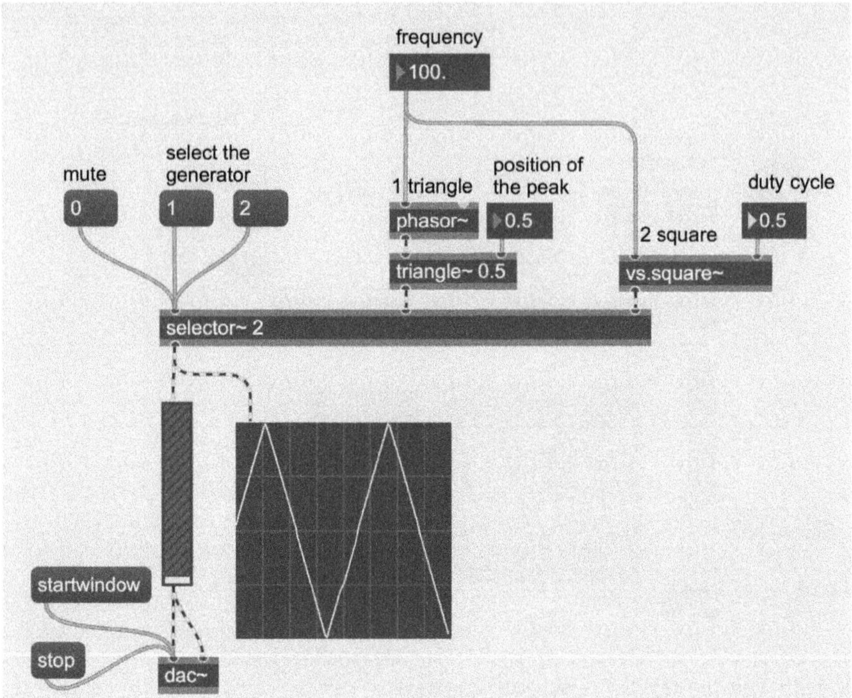

Fig. 1.26 The file 01_04_triangle_square.maxpat

This patch contains an object, part of the Virtual Sound Macros library, which you first see evidence of in the Max Console (<Command-m/Control-m>): if you see the message *"vs.square~: No such object"*, you have not installed the library containing the **Virtual Sound Macros**[24] and this library cannot be found in Max' search path.
Remember that you will find complete instructions for this at www.virtual-sound.com/cmsupport. In any case, here is what to do:

1) Copy the file "Virtual Sound Macros.zip" onto your computer and unarchive it. It can be found at www.virtual-sound.com/cmsupport in the "Virtual Sound Macros" folder.
2) Locate the folder "{User Name}/Documents/Max 9/Packages" (substituting your own computer account name for {User Name}).
3) Put the "Virtual Sound Macros" folder from step 1 into the Packages folder that you located in step 2.
4) Restart Max.

[24] The Virtual Sound Library is a library of objects created especially for this book that augments the standard objects found in Max. You will find more detail on this library and on external libraries in general in Interlude A, which follows this chapter.

Let's return to our patch, where we again find a **selector~** object used to compare two signals. The first is a triangle wave: click on the message box containing '*1*' and activate the audio by clicking on the "*startwindow*" message to see it. The **triangle~** object that we see being used is not an oscillator; it is more like a "factory" that can produce triangle signals, and which is designed to produce a single cycle every time that it receives a ramp that runs from 0 to 1. As we saw above, the **phasor~** object conveniently produces a ramp from '0' to '1'. To produce a triangle wave, therefore, we need only hook **triangle~** up to a **phasor~**, and to set the number box connected to the **phasor~** to the frequency that we wish to hear. Listen to the timbre of the triangle wave by raising the fader.

The argument of the object, '0.5', indicates the point at which the peak of the triangle will occur in the cycle. The value '0.5' indicates that the peak will come exactly half-way through the cycle. It is possible to modify this point by means of the right inlet to the object. If you modify the number in the float number box that you see connected to the **triangle~**, the triangle skews left or right, depending on the number selected. In fact, when the value is 1, the wave becomes a sawtooth. As you will note, changing the shape of the triangle changes the timbre of the sound.

The second oscillator, **vs.square~** (selected by clicking on message box '*2*'), generates a square wave. This generator is part of the Virtual Sound Macros library which we will discuss in more detail in Interlude A. The float number box connected to the right inlet of the object controls the **duty cycle** for the wave, which you will remember is a ratio between positively-valued cycle time and negatively-valued cycle time. It is expressed as a decimal number that varies between 0 and 1; the value indicates the point in the cycle where the part of the wave with positive amplitude passes to the part of the wave that has negative amplitude. When the duty cycle is equal, indicated by the value 0.5, the two regions of the wave each take up half of the cycle, and we have a square wave. If we change the duty cycle to 0.25, the positive part of the wave will occupy a quarter of the cycle and the negative part three quarters; if we change it to 0.75, the positive portion will now take up three quarters of the cycle and the negative portion will fill the remaining quarter. Try varying the duty cycle by manipulating the float number box: the waveform, and naturally, the timbre, will change as a result.

BAND-LIMITED GENERATORS

You probably noticed, in the last patches, that the **phasor~**, **triangle~** and **vs.square~** objects generated sounds that sometimes seemed distorted,[25] particularly when you changed the frequency to very high values. This happens because the frequencies generated by these objects can exceed the capabilities of the driver's digital-to-analog conversion. We will discuss this in more detail (and using correct terminology) in the next chapter, which is devoted to additive synthesis, and also in Chapter 5, which is dedicated to digital audio.

25 To be precise, "distortion" isn't the word used, but rather "foldover". We will explain this in detail in the theory part of Chapter 5.

In general use, the generators that we have used so far are rarely used to generate sound, but instead, to generate signals for control and modulation (and we will address these uses in Chapter 4).
Do generators for triangle waves, square waves, and sawtooth waves exist that sound good and that don't produce spurious frequency components? The answer, of course, is yes; these objects are named **tri~**, **rect~**, and **saw~** respectively,[26] and they are generically referred to as **band-limited oscillators** (figure 1.27).

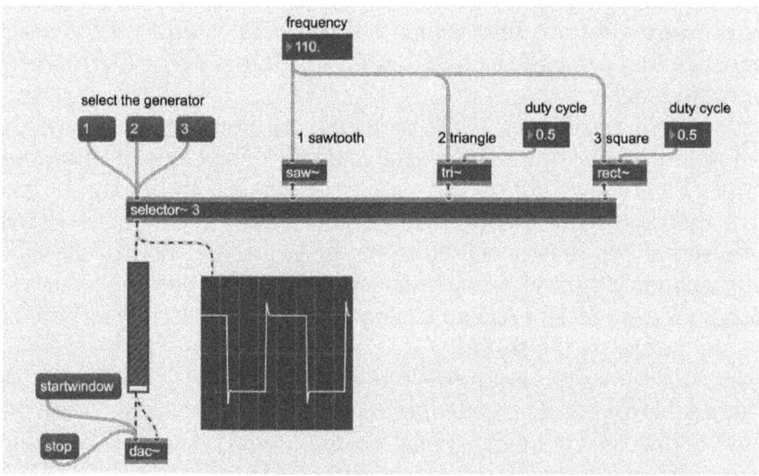

Fig. 1.27 The file 01_05_band_limited.maxpat

In the 01_05_band_limited.maxpat patch, the **selector~** object can be used to compare the timbre of these three oscillators. Also try comparing these oscillators to their corresponding non-band-limited cousins. Spurious components are not present in the three new generators, and by using them, it is possible to render high-frequency sounds that are both pleasing and accurate. Note that the waveforms produced by these oscillators are not perfectly square, or triangular, or sawtooth: they contain frequency components that differ from those of corresponding non-band-limited oscillators, and because of this, their waveforms differ.

ACTIVITY

Create a patch to compare the timbres of seven waveforms: the sine wave, the sawtooth, the triangle wave, and the square wave, including both band-limited and non-band-limited versions of the last three. Use the **selector~** object for the comparison, and use a single float number box to set the frequency of all of the seven generators.

[26] Note that all of the oscillators, and in general, all of the objects that work directly with sound, are characterized by a tilde at the end of their name. We will return to this topic in Section 1.7.

1.3 VARIATIONS OF FREQUENCY AND AMPLITUDE IN TIME: ENVELOPES AND GLISSANDI

To continuously vary sound parameters in time, we need to introduce the concept of lists, plus a few other miscellaneous new objects and concepts. Let's make a small digression to discuss some of the functions of Max.
A **list** is a set of numbers, and/or words, and/or other character combinations, which is considered to be a unified whole. Here are some examples of lists:

"1 2 3 4 3 2 1"
"2 3.14 5 333"
"0 stop 1 start"
"time 120"

There are many objects that use lists as input, and one very common object that is used to contain and build them is the message box, which you already know well. (figure 1.28.)

Fig. 1.28 A message box that contains a list

The **print** object will display whatever it receives in the Max Console; the object is created by using an object box in which you type the word "print". The Max Console, as you already know, is used by programs for communication. If you can't see the Max Console, you can call it up by typing <Command-m/Control-m>, and it is a good idea to have this window always visible, especially when the patch that you are constructing is not working as you expect: all error messages are sent to the Max Console.
Try connecting a message box to a **print** object; open a new patcher window with <Command-n/Control-n> and create two objects as in figure 1.29.

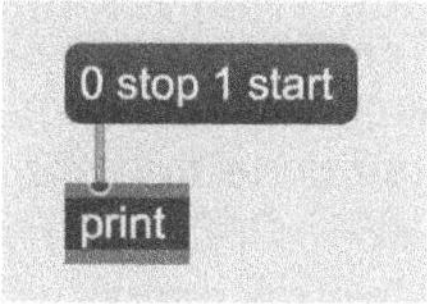

Fig. 1.29 Visualizing a message

Write a message such as is in the message box in the figure, and then switch into performance mode using <Command-e/Control-e>. If you click on the message box, you should see the message output in the Max Console. If you now double click on the message that appeared in the Max Console, the print object that produced it will become selected in the Patcher Window, in exactly the same way that double-clicking error messages was seen to select the objects that generated them. (See question 2 of the FAQ in Section 1.1.)
Try connecting a number box to **print**, and, returning to performance mode, clicking inside the number box and sliding the mouse while holding down the

button: numbers will appear in the Max Console. Note that the contents of the message box, unified as a list, appear on a single line in the Max Console, while the numbers, being separate elements, each appear on their own lines.

We now turn to one of the most important objects, **button**, which appears in the Buttons *palette* and which can also be created by typing the single letter 'b' (as seen in figure 1.30).

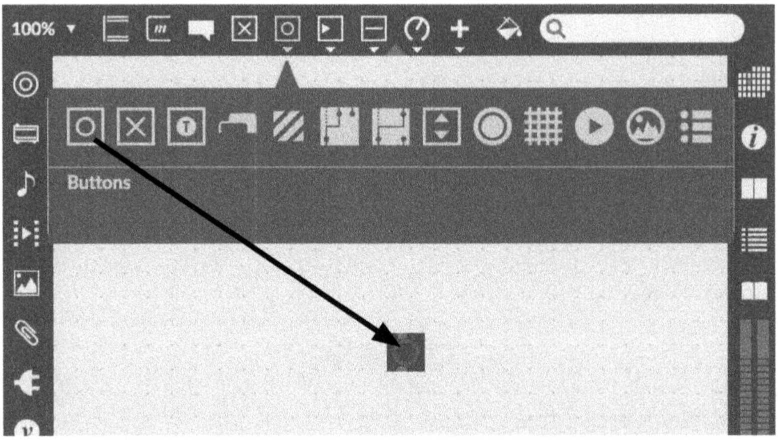

Fig. 1.30 The button object

The button object produces the message "***bang***". What does "*bang*" mean in the language of Max? It is a trigger. It means "go", or "begin", or "execute", or "trigger the action that you were told to do", and it is recognized by the majority of objects. It is a little like the pistol shot that signals the beginning of an athletic event. Try connecting a button to the message box that we have already connected to print: every time the we click on the button, a bang is received by the message box, which then sends its message to the print object, causing the message to appear in the Max Console. The same thing happens if we connect the button to the number box, and indeed for most other objects as well: when they receive a bang, they perform their principal action. Connect a button directly to print (disconnecting the other objects). What happens when you click? Try it. The button object also has an inlet, and when messages are sent to it, the object reacts "with a bang".

To conclude this brief digression, let's discuss the object **line~**. This object is a generator of signal segments that move from value to value over specified time intervals. To create a segment, the object needs a starting value and a list containing pairs of values: a value to be reached, coupled with a time in milliseconds. The list can contain one or more pairs; each indicating a value and a time. The following list, for example, specifies two segments:

"440 5000 110 3000"

and will be interpreted by **line~** as instructions to reach the value 440 in 5 seconds (5000 milliseconds) and to then drop to the value 110 in 3 seconds (3000 milliseconds). Try this out by creating a patch like the one shown in figure 1.31:

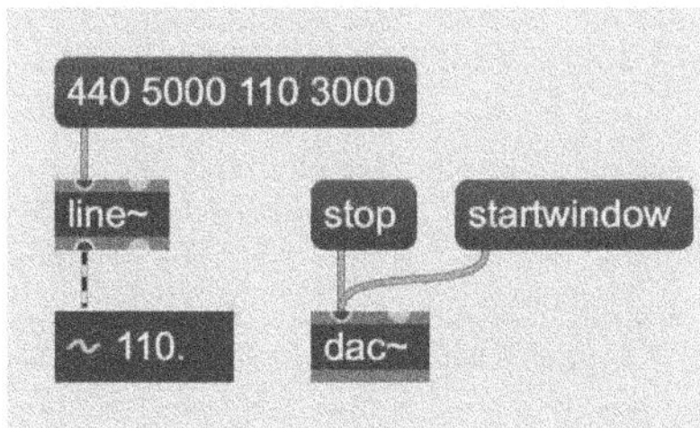

Fig. 1.31 The **line~** object

As you see, there is a message box connected to the **line~** object, which in turn is connected to a **number~**.[27] On the right is the **dac~** object: it is necessary to turn on audio processing in order to activate **line~** (which is, after all, an object that generates signals, even though they are not audible). After clicking on "*startwindow*", click on the message box connected to **line~** and observe the numerical values displayed by **number~**, which start at 0 (the default initial value for **line~** if no other value is specified as an argument), grow to 440, and then drop to 110, where they stay. If you click again on the message box, the values will begin from the last value specified, 110, and move up to 440 and then back to 110. Try changing the list contained in the message box and try different combinations of segments, remembering to always pair a value to reach with a time in milliseconds. If **line~** receives a single value rather than a list, it moves to this value instantly (that is to say, in 0 milliseconds). Connect a number box to the **line~** object, input some single numbers, and watch the signal jump immediately to the numbers received, without passing through intermediate values. A single number can therefore be used to set the point of departure for a **line~** in the following way: format a message box with a single value, a comma, and then a list of pairs, as in figure 1.32.

Fig. 1.32 This message box contains both a single element and a list

If we send this message to the **line~** object, the **line~** will immediately take on the value 220, after which it will climb to 440 in 5 seconds, and finally drop to 110 in an additional 3 seconds, remaining at 110 afterwards. Type the message "220, 440 5000 110 3000" (remembering the comma, which is important!) into the message box in your own patch and verify that the course taken by the **line~** is as we have described.

[27] Can you find **number~**? It is the third icon in the Numbers *palette*. If you still can't find it, use the technique we have already seen: take an object box, type **number~** into it followed by <Enter>, and the object will appear.

GLISSANDI

You ought to be able to use a "route" composed of line segments, such as we have just seen, to control the frequency of an oscillator, creating glissandi. And this is exactly what we will do in the patch contained in **01_06_glissandi.maxpat** (shown in figure 1.33).

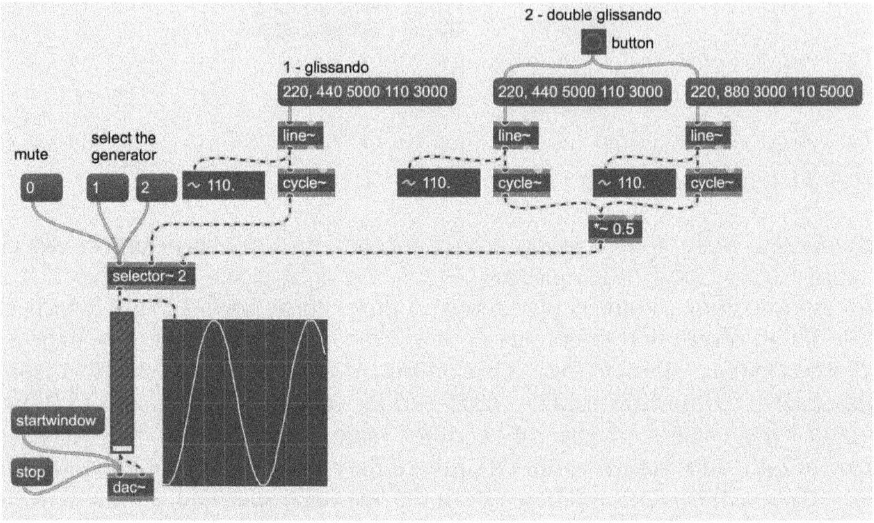

Fig. 1.33 The file 01_06_glissandi.maxpat

In this patch, along with a brief recap of objects that we have already presented, we find two algorithms that generate glissandi. By connecting a **line~** to an oscillator, it becomes possible to vary the frequency of that oscillator continuously.
Activate the patch with a click on *"startwindow"*, and listen to the first glissando by raising the **gain~** fader, clicking on the *'1'* message connected to **selector~**, and finally on the message box connected to the first **line~**. The **number~** object permits you to see how the frequency is changing: it departs from 220 Hz and arrives at 440 Hz in 5 seconds, as an ascending glissando, after which the pitch descends to 110 Hz over 3 seconds, where it rests "forever". Or at least as long as we don't click on the message box connected to **line~** again (and hear once again the same sequence of ascending and descending glissandi), or click on the *'0'* message that is connected to **selector~** (thereby telling the object to stop passing any signal through), or perhaps click on *"stop"*.
By dropping into edit mode and modifying the message, it is possible to implement whatever "frequency routes" you like. Try substituting, for example, these lists, or others of your own invention:

"2000, 1500 3000 80 100 440 5000"
"880, 880 3000 110 1000"

The second of these departs from 880 Hz and then "arrives" at 880 Hz after 3 seconds. What does this mean? It is a way that we can dictate that pitch will stay still for 3 seconds, since the pitch for departure matches that for arrival.
Try implementing the following route: leave from 400 Hz, arrive at 500 Hz after 1 second, then descend to 300 Hz in 0.1 seconds, rest at 300 Hz for 4 seconds, and then climb to 1000 Hz over 0.5 seconds.
The second algorithm in the patch implements simultaneous glissandi using two oscillators. We have connected a **button** to two message boxes, each of which specifies how to produce a glissando on one of the two **line~** objects. As we know, when we click on the **button**, it will produce a bang, which in this case, will be sent to the two message boxes, which will then send their messages at the same time. After selecting message '2', connected to **selector~**, click on the **button** and hear the two glissandi, which depart from the frequency 220 Hz and separate, one heading for 440 Hz and the other for 880 Hz (with different arrival times). After they arrive, both oscillators drop to 110 Hz.
As you see, the **line~** object has a second outlet on its right, from which a bang emerges when it has finished executing its commands. If we connect this outlet back to the **button** that sends the messages to the two **line~** objects in the right part of the patch in figure 1.33, we will obtain a glissando that repeats itself periodically. (See figure 1.34: to kick off the loop, you need to click at least one time on the **button**.)

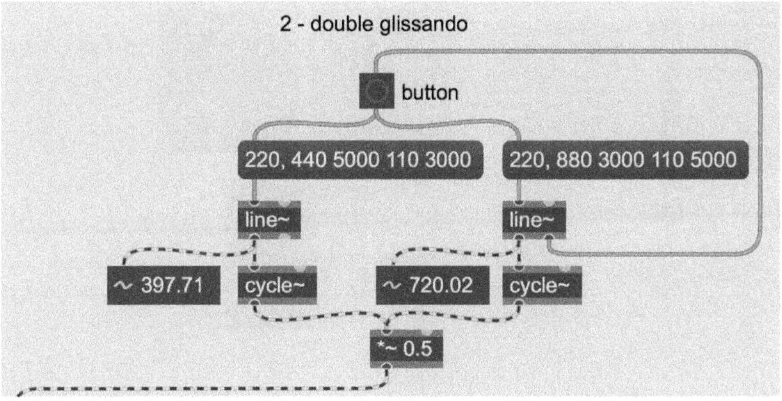

Fig. 1.34 A looped double glissando, which continuously repeats

Notice that the outlets of the oscillators enter the left inlet of the multiplier simultaneously. This works because all signals entering an inlet are automatically summed; it is therefore not always necessary to use a summation object as we did to illustrate the object in patch 01_02.maxpat.
The object *~ multiplies by 0.5, halving the amplitude of the signal that it received in order to avoid distortion. Try changing the two glissando specifications, and try adding a third oscillator, connected again to the left inlet of the multiplier: what must you type in place of 0.5 in this case to avoid distortion?

ENVELOPES

The oscillators that we have used until now produce continuous sounds, generating their signals at maximum amplitude whenever the patch is active. If we want to work with sounds that evolve over time, however, we need to begin working with sounds that have envelopes.
As we already know (see figure 1.22: the file 01_02.maxpat), we can modify the amplitude of an oscillator by using multiplication: if we multiply the signal by 1.0, the amplitude doesn't change, if we multiply by 0.5, the amplitude is halved, and if we multiply by 0, the amplitude changes to 0, which means that we can no longer hear the sound or how it changes. To use an envelope, that is, to change the amplitude of a sound over time, we connect an oscillator to a multiplier, and we connect a signal to the other inlet of the multiplier that varies in time, following the shape of the envelope that we wish to use. The object that we use to generate this signal is the `line~` object that we now know well. Open the file named **01_07_envelopes_1.maxpat** (see figure 1.35).

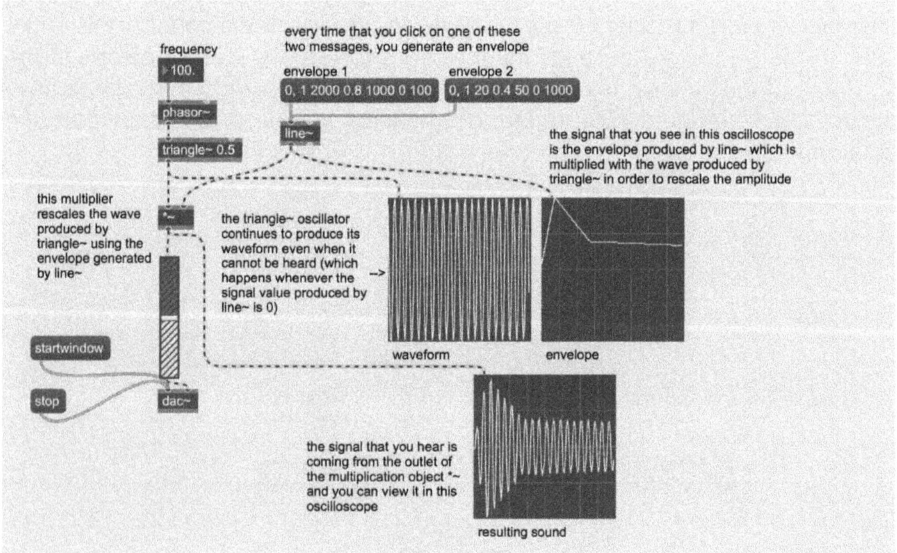

Fig. 1.35 The file 01_07_envelopes_1.maxpat

Here we have a `*~` object that multiplies the signal from the oscillator together with the envelope generated by `line~`. The values that `line~` generates in this case vary between 0 and 1 – these numbers indicate that we intend to dynamically modify the amplitude of the sound from some maximum (when the signal produced by `line~` will be 1.0) to silence (when the signal produced by `line~` will be 0). On the upper left `scope~`, we can see the waveform produced by the oscillator, on the right we can see the envelope being generated by `line~`, and on the lower `scope~` we can see the result of multiplying the oscillator signal by the envelope generated by `line~`. We say that the envelope of the sound has been shaped using multiplication, or more commonly, that the envelope has been *applied* to the sound.

Observe the patch, turning it on and reflecting carefully on the relationship between the signals produced by the objects connected to the three `scope~` objects. Enter edit mode and try to create some other envelopes. Remember that the values produced by `line~` must lie between 0 and 1. What happens if the final value of the envelope is non-zero? Try it! It is also possible to graphically modify envelopes; let's open **01_08_envelopes_2.maxpat** (seen in figure 1.36) to see this.

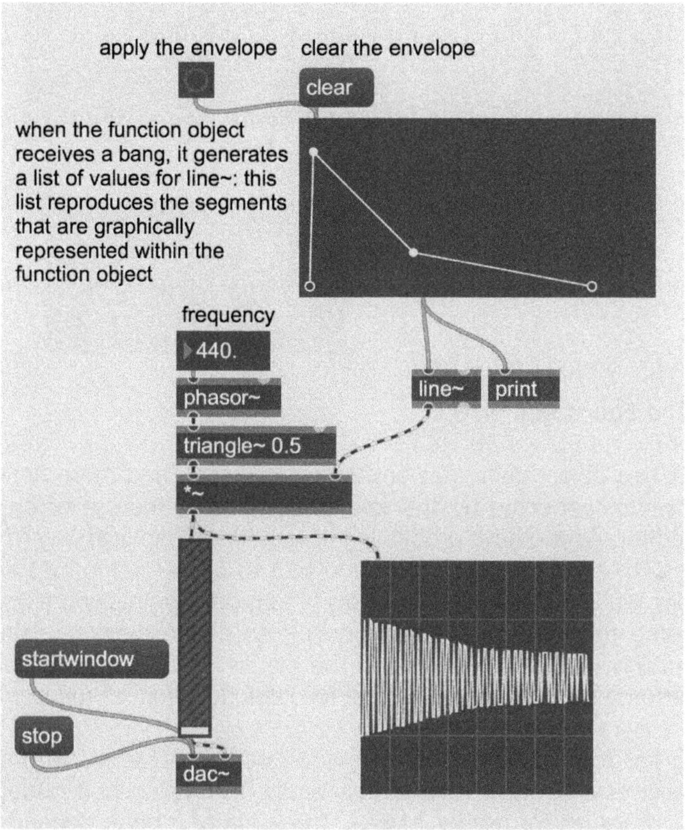

Fig. 1.36 The file 01_08_envelopes_2.maxpat

In the upper part we see a new graphic object: **`function`** (figure 1.37) which can be found in the Audio sub-category of the Add *palette*..

Fig. 1.37 The `function` object

The `function` object generates envelopes, glissandi, and more generally any series of points connected by line segments, through the use of an onscreen graphical editor. As you have probably guessed, it is a graphical way to construct the "routes" that we previously built and sent to `line~` using message boxes. It is possible, while in performance mode,[28] to modify points and to create new ones by using the mouse. It is also possible to delete them by using <Shift-Click> (pressing <Shift> while clicking the mouse on the point to delete). The "*clear*" message (sent using a message box) will delete all of the points.

This object has four outlets (which we won't occupy ourselves with now), and when it receives a bang, it immediately emits from its second outlet (not the first!) a list of values for use by `line~`. The value of a point depends upon its vertical position, and varies between 0 (when it is at the bottom) and 1 (when it is at the top). The horizontal distance between points represents the time needed to travel the segment that connects them in milliseconds. If we create or move a point, we see a legend appear inside the `function` object that indicates the new value of the point: the letter 'X' designates the horizontal position, and the letter 'Y' designates the vertical position.

[28] It is often difficult for new users to understand which operations must be performed in edit mode, and which in performance mode. Remember that edit mode is for creating, adjusting, and deleting objects, and also for connecting them using patch cords. It is, in other words, the mode to use when assembling patches. On the other hand, all operations that manipulate data, such as modifying numbers by sliding the mouse over a number box, or moving a signal level fader, or even creating and modifying points within a function object, are done in performance mode.

Try modifying the envelope and listen to its actions on the sound. It is very important that the last point be in the lowest position, corresponding to 0 (you will know when it is there, because the appearance of the point changes from a solid disc into an empty circle), or else the sound will not fade away. We've connected a print object to the second outlet of **`function`**, in order to see the list that is generated.
In the patch, the list generated by **`function`** for **`line~`** is set to have a maximum duration of one second. Is it possible to change this duration? Of course!
The inspector, which as we know is the window for examining and tweaking the attribute values of objects, can be used to modify the **`function`** object. Remember that to open the inspector for an object, we need to be in edit mode, where we select the object with the mouse and press <Command-i/ Control-i>. There are other ways to invoke the inspector; as long as you are in edit mode, you can, for example, select the *Object Action Menu* for the object (as seen in fig. 1.16b) and click on its "Inspector" item (as in fig. 1.38).

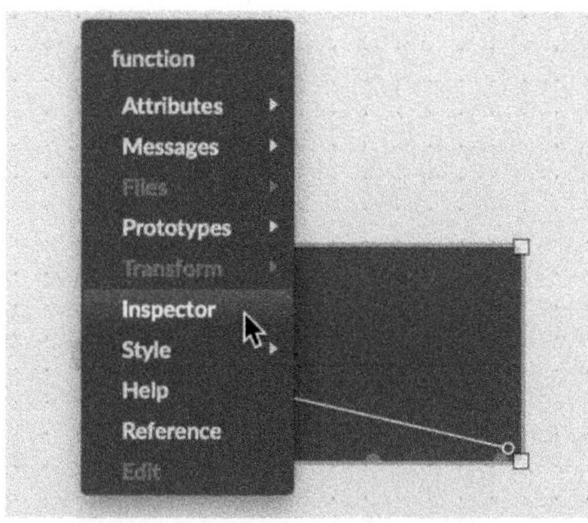

Fig. 1.38: Opening the *Inspector* via the *Object Action Menu*

Alternatively, as you already know, you can click on the "i" in the right Toolbar in order to activate the window.

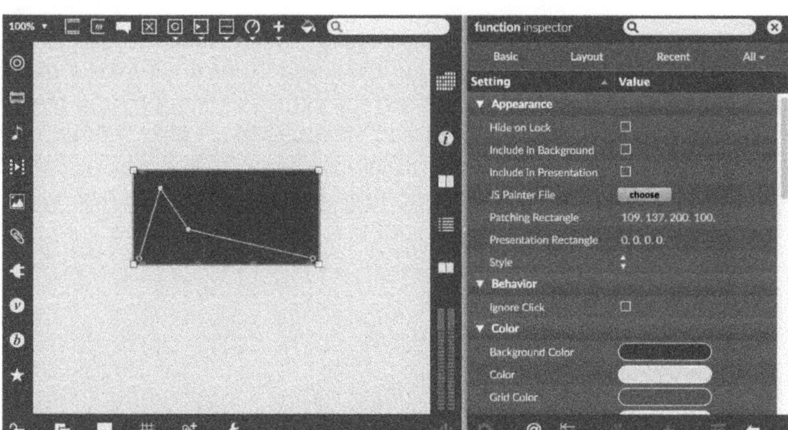

fig. 1.39: the *inspector* as it appears within the *sidebar*

In figure 1.40 we can see the collection of "Behavior" attributes that are shown for the `function` object in the *inspector*.

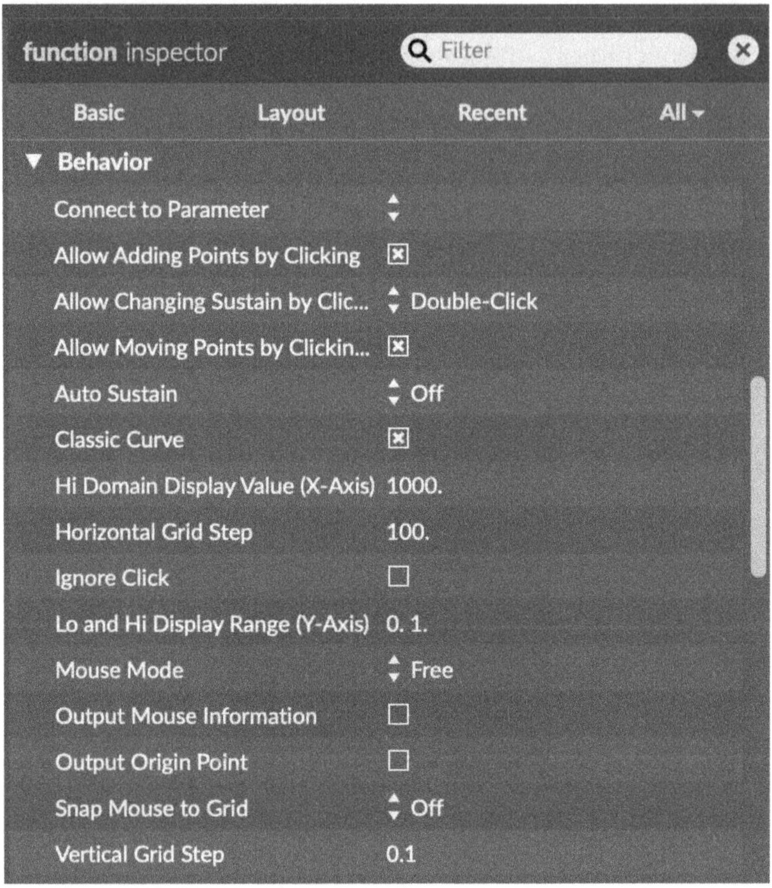

Fig. 1.40: the inspector's "Behavior" category for the `function` object

There are numerous attributes in this category, but fortunately they are listed in alphabetical order, making them easy to locate. First of all, take a glance at ***Lo and Hi Display Range*** (which we can translate as minimum and maximum values for the graph's y-axis). These can be used to modify the values that correspond vertically to the highest and lowest points in the graph. To modify the values, simply select them with a double-click and overwrite new values.

Another interesting item can be found nearby, the ***Hi Domain Display Value*** (with which you can adjust the graph's "domain", or x-axis values). This attribute specifies the overall duration of the envelope in milliseconds. Type 5000 into the cell, which designates a 5 second envelope, and then close the inspector. Envelopes plotted on the **function** object will now have a duration of 5 seconds, which we can test by placing a first point all the way to the left and a last point all the way to the right. Try other durations for the envelope.

You can discover the purpose of other attributes in the inspector by passing the mouse over them and watching the text that appears in the Clue Bar (we remind you that this is a text that appears on the right side of the lower Toolbar.)
Naturally, it is possible to play more than one note at the same time, using the same envelope, as in the file **01_09_envelopes_3.maxpat** (seen in figure 1.41).

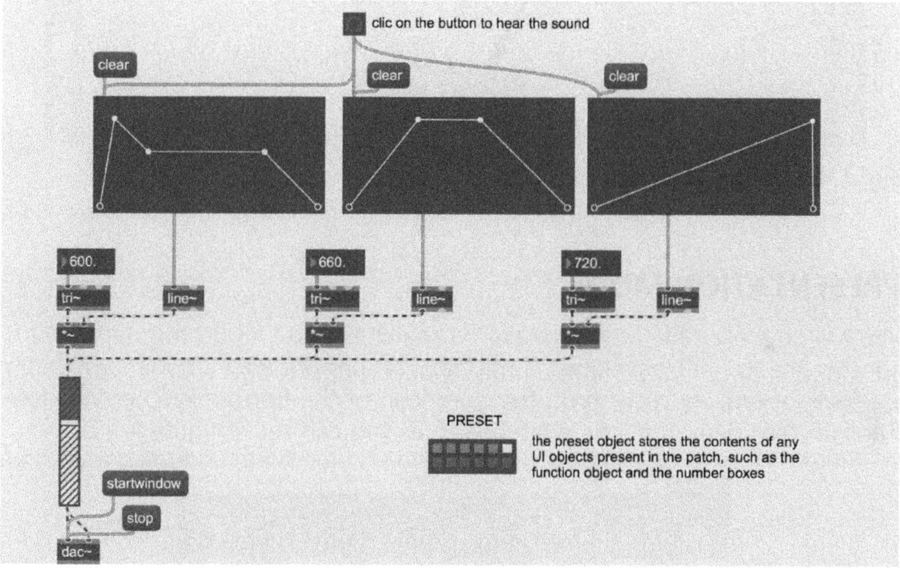

Fig. 1.41 The file 01_09_envelopes_3.maxpat

Here there are three oscillators, each possessing their own envelope.[29] If we set three distinct frequencies, draw an envelope for each using the mouse as we have just seen, and then fire up the patch using the "*startwindow*" message and click on the button at the top, we will hear three sounds play, each evolving differently.
The small grid that can be found in this patch is a **preset** object, which is very convenient to use when we have an algorithm that has many parameters (as in this case). As you have certainly noticed, Max does not save the values contained in number boxes or other interface objects when we save a patch.

[29] Again in this case, the **function** objects are connected to their **line~** objects by means of the second outlet. We will discuss the characteristics of the first outlet in Section 2.4.

However, using the **preset** object, it becomes possible to remember these values. By clicking on one of the lighter squares, you recall a configuration that was previously saved into that slot in the object. Shift-clicking on a square will record a new configuration into it using current values. In figure 1.42, we see the icon for the **preset** object as it appears in the Top Patcher Window Toolbar.

Fig. 1.42 The **preset** object

PRESENTATION MODE

We will now examine how to make our patches tidier; to do this, let's return to the file 01_09_envelopes_3.maxpat. In *performance* mode (with the padlock locked) try clicking on the third icon of the Bottom Patcher Window Toolbar, that depicts a little whiteboard (as you can see in figure 1.43).

Fig. 1.43 The presentation mode icon

We see that the patch is completely changed: what remains visible are only comments and interface objects (which are objects, in performance mode, that you can interact using the mouse or the keyboard, or which display dynamic data). The other objects and patch cords have vanished, and if that isn't enough, all of the remaining elements have changed their position, and in some cases, their dimensions!
We have, in fact, moved into **presentation mode**, a mode in which only objects that have been explicitly chosen to appear are visible; furthermore, their positions and dimensions are completely independent from what they were in the patch that we just left. If we click once again on the chalkboard icon, we will return to "normal" **patching mode**, and all of the objects will return to their original positions and sizes. At this point, click on the padlock to go into edit mode: we see that some of the objects have a subtle pink halo around

them, and this halo designates them as objects that will be part of presentation mode. To add an object to presentation mode, you can, while in edit mode, select it and press <Command-Shift-p/Control-Shift-p>, or else you can click on the object with the right mouse button and then select *Add to Presentation Mode* from the context menu that appears at the mouse pointer. Presentation mode can be exploited from both edit and performance mode (accessible, as always, from the padlock icon): edit-presentation mode is when you can change settings and adjust the presentation positions of objects, while performance-presentation is when you can start up a patch and modify its parameters.
To make a patch appear in presentation mode by default, every time that it is loaded, you need to bring up the *Inspector Window* from within the *View* menu: the menu item will open a window displaying the inspector for the *Patcher Window*, in which you can then check the "**Open in Presentation**" attribute that is found in the *View* category.

ACTIVITY

Using the file 01_09_envelopes_3.maxpat, create your own envelopes and save them as presets. Add one or two oscillators with different timbres, such as a square wave and a sawtooth wave, for example, each with its own envelope. Remember that new **function** objects should be connected to their **line~** objects using the second outlet rather than the first. Add the interface objects (the number box and **function** objects) for the new oscillators to the set of objects visible in Presentation Mode.

EXPONENTIAL AND LOGARITHMIC CURVES

The **line~** object connects points using linear line segments, which means that it moves from one value to the next over a given time by applying constant increments (or decrements). Movement between frequencies, however, is exponential: for every rise of an octave, the value of the underlying frequency parameter doubles. (The note A, for example, written in bass clef between the first two lines of the staff, has a frequency of 110 Hz. Moving upward from that note, the successive octaves are 220 Hz, 440 Hz, 880 Hz, etc., as shown in figure 1.44.)

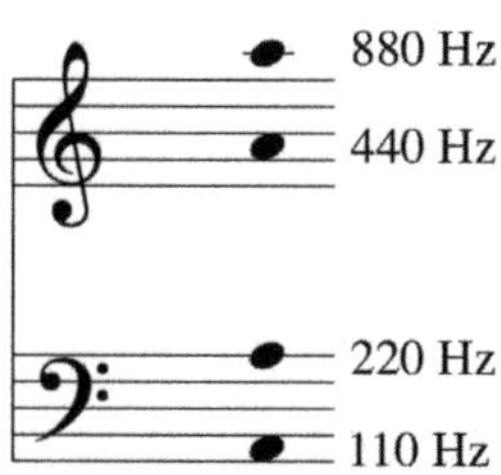

Fig. 1.44 Successive octaves double their frequencies

If we calculate the ratio between the frequencies that define an octave, rather than taking their difference, we realize that this ratio remains constant between one octave and another; the difference measured in frequency, however, is not constant – it is larger at high frequencies than it is at low frequencies. Because of this, the glissandi that we implemented in the first part of this section, using linear parameter changes, are quicker at low frequencies than they are at high frequencies. A four-octave linear glissando that extends, for example, from 110 Hz to 880 Hz, will travel across its lowest octave, between 110 Hz and 220 Hz, four times faster than it travels across its highest, that of 440 Hz to 880 Hz. As we mentioned earlier in Section 1.3 of the theory part of this chapter, the way to create an evenly moving glissando is to use an exponential curve.[30]

In Max, it is possible to move between two values described on an exponential or logarithmic[31] curve by using an object named, appropriately enough, **`curve~`**. This object functions much like `line~`, but it needs a third parameter in addition to value and time interval, which is called the **curve parameter** or **curve factor**, and which varies between -1 and 1. Positive values for this parameter will yield exponential curves, with different curve factors zero will generate linear segments exactly like `line~`, and negative numbers will yield logarithmic curves.[32] With this object we can create more "natural" glissandi. For example, an acceptable[33] glissando between 220 Hz and 880 Hz can be obtained using a curve parameter of 0.5, and the message box connected to the `curve~` object would contain a list like this:

"220, 880 4000 0.5"

which says "go from the value 220 to the value 880 in 4 seconds using an exponential curve with a curve factor of 0.5".

Open the file **01_10_env_gliss.maxpat** (seen in figure 1.45). Here we have two algorithms: the first generating the glissando in the manner just described, and the second using `curve~` not only to construct the glissando, but also to implement an amplitude envelope with exponential attack and decay. The values in this envelope go from 0 to 1 in 5 milliseconds with a curve factor of 0.5, afterwards they remain at 1 for 200 milliseconds with a factor of 1 (even if the region remains stable), and finally they return to 0 over four seconds with a factor of -0.85. Activate the patch and listen to the sounds produced, and afterwards, try changing various parameters, especially the curve factor.

---

[30] Remember that exponential growth is characterized by constantly increasing growth between successive points, and it appears graphically as a line that rises ever more rapidly towards its final value.

[31] For exponential growth, see Section 1.3 in the theory half of this chapter.

[32] The algorithm used in the `curve~` object is distinctive, and its author, Richard Dudas, has said that he found it using trial and error. It doesn't correspond directly to the logarithmic and exponential equations shown in Section 1.3 of the theory section, but it approximates their growth well enough to be useful.

[33] This glissando is still not perfect (every arbitrary octave is not traversed in exactly the same time interval), but it is a much better approximation. We will return after a little while to this discussion.

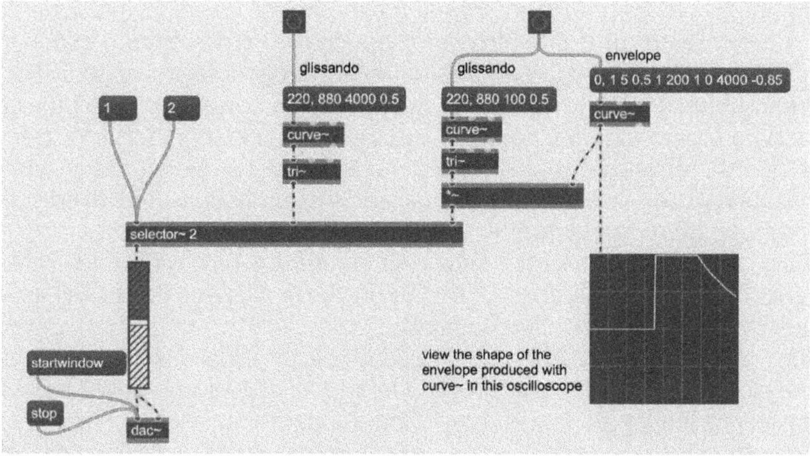

Fig. 1.45 The file 01_10_env_gliss.maxpat

It is also possible to use the **function** object to manage a **curve~** object. To do this, you need to open the inspector for a **function** object and change the value of its *Mode* attribute (found in the "Appearance" attribute category) to "curve". Once you have done this, when the patch is in run mode you can change the curve parameters used for any given segment by holding the <Alt> key down and grabbing and dragging the desired segment with the mouse.

Let's examine one aspect of **curve~** more closely: we have already noted that when the curve factor is positive we have an exponential curve and when it is negative we have a logarithmic curve. When, however, the point of departure is greater than the point of arrival, and therefore the values found in the curve decrease rather than increase, we have to change the sign of the curve factor to obtain matching growth patterns, as can be seen in figure 1.46.

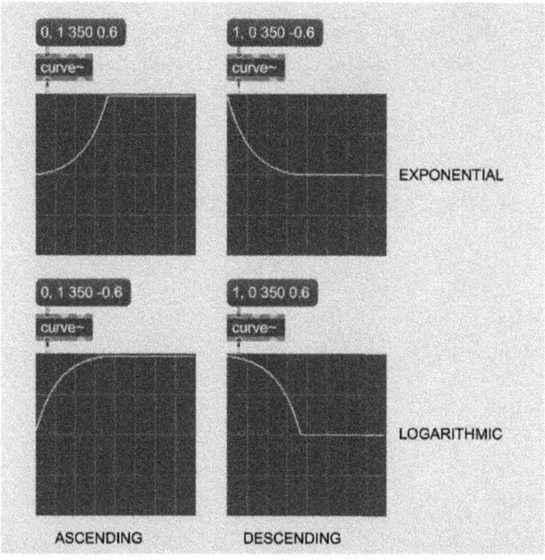

Fig. 1.46 Building exponential and logarithmic curves using **curve~**

In the figure, we see that the ascending exponential curve (at the upper left), uses a curve factor of 0.6, which corresponds to the descending exponential curve (in the upper right), that uses an inverted curve factor of -0.6. For the logarithmic case (in the lower half of the figure), you must also invert the curve factor when reversing direction. The **curve~** object is very useful for creating more realistic envelopes than those generated by **line~** for some types of sounds: percussion instruments, pianos, and instruments with plucked strings, for example, all have logarithmic attacks and exponential decays.
Now try duplicating the patch shown in figure 1.47, copying with care the contents of the message boxes. Clicking on these message boxes will activate various types of envelopes for comparison.
The first envelope, which has a short logarithmic attack and a long exponential release, sounds like a little bell struck with a stick. The second envelope, which has instead a long exponential attack and a logarithmic release, has the same growth as the first sound, but in reverse (as though you were playing a magnetic tape backwards). The last two envelopes are classic ADSR (Attack Decay Sustain Release) envelopes, the first of which uses exponential segments, and the second, logarithmic segments. In the **scope~** rectangle, you can observe the shape of the active envelope when you click on a message box. Add your own message boxes using envelope variations, and watch them as well.

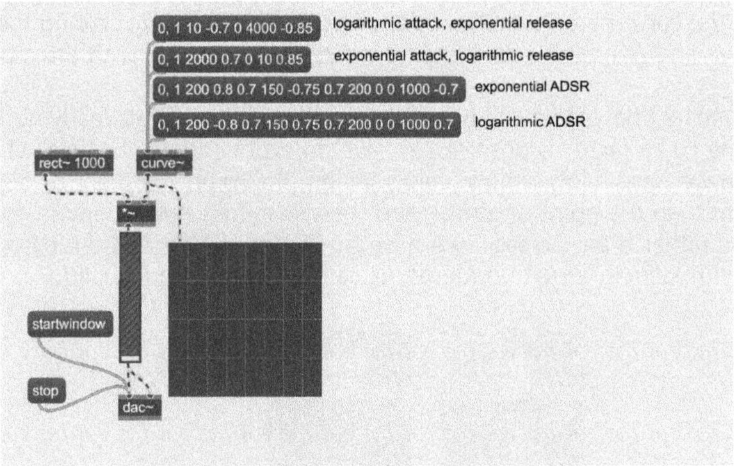

Fig. 1.47 Exponential and logarithmic envelopes

ACTIVITY

Create a patch with three sawtooth oscillators (using **saw~**) and connect two **curve~** objects to each of these objects, one to create a glissando, and the other to create an amplitude envelope. Adjust the curve factor for the pitch **curve~** to produce the most natural glissando. Make it possible to start all three sounds at the same time using a bang.

To create natural glissandi, as you found out while doing the previous activity, is not easy to do using **curve~**, because a single curve factor has different effects when we change the frequency interval for the glissandi. That means that a factor of 0.5 functions well enough for a glissando between 220 Hz and 880 Hz, but not as much is needed for a glissando, for example, between 220 Hz and 3520 Hz (in which case it would be too fast in the bass register, and because of this, you use a higher factor). There exists, therefore, an even better method for producing realistic frequency glissandi, and we will visit this technique in the following section. Of course, if we are actually after a less "real-world" glissando, with unexpected speed-ups and slow-downs, the **curve~** object, with its curve factor, can be perfect!

1.4 THE RELATIONSHIP OF FREQUENCIES TO MUSICAL INTERVALS AND OF AMPLITUDES TO SOUND PRESSURE LEVELS

Up until now, we've supplied oscillators with their frequencies in hertz, but wouldn't it be nice to be able to supply the note that we want (for example, middle C) and let Max calculate the frequency for us? This is possible using the **mtof** object, which converts a MIDI-encoded note value into a frequency ("mtof" stands for "MIDI-to-frequency").
MIDI is an acronym that stands for Musical Instrument Digital Interface, which is a protocol (that is, a set of rules for controlled interaction) for communication between electronic musical instruments, and between instruments and a computer. MIDI encodes notes as successive integers that run from 0 to 127. Middle C is 60, the C# above it 61, the D 62, and so on. Likewise, the B below middle C is 59, and descending semitones drop the value by 1. Just because the MIDI protocol was designed for communications between instruments and computers doesn't mean that we need connect an instrument to our computer in order to use it. The conversion of musical notes to frequencies is done using MIDI note numbers in Max; it made sense to reuse this widely implemented encoding rather than invent a new one for the same purpose.
MIDI also encodes octaves: the octave of middle C is 3, the octave above is 4, and so on (see Table C in Section 1.4 of the theory chapter). Middle C, therefore, is notated as C3, while the B immediately below is B2 (because, by definition, octaves run C to B, and thus it belongs to the lower octave).

We can see all of this summarized in the file **01_11_conv_midifreq.maxpat** (shown in figure 1.48).

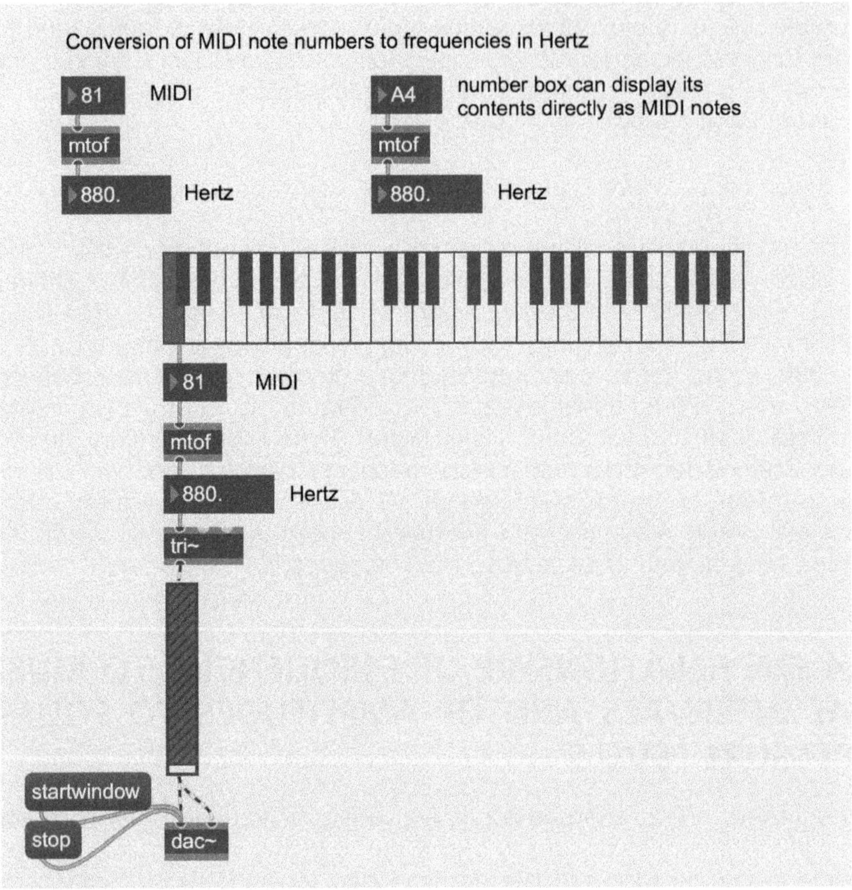

Fig. 1.48 The file 01_11_conv_midifreq.maxpat

In the upper part of this patch, we see how the `mtof` object works: if the object receives numbers, they will be interpreted as being MIDI note numbers, and converted into frequencies. An integer number box (which has a triangle without a decimal point in it), besides being capable of displaying MIDI notes as numbers, can be specially configured to display notes as note names plus octave numbers (C3, C#3, D3, etc.). To do this, go into edit mode, select the number box, and call up the inspector using <Command-i/Control-i>. By locating the "Appearance" category and selecting the MIDI option in the pop-up menu that can be found to the right of the "Display Format" item, you can activate this option. Returning to the patch that we just opened, at the top right, we can see what this looks like, since the number box is using MIDI formatting for its output. If you want to change the notes step-by-step, you can select the number box in performance mode, and then use the <UpArrow> and <DownArrow> keys (that you will most likely find at the bottom of your keyboard).

The lower part of the same patch applies the resulting conversion to the frequency of an oscillator, and also introduces a new graphical object, the **kslider** (seen in figure 1.49).

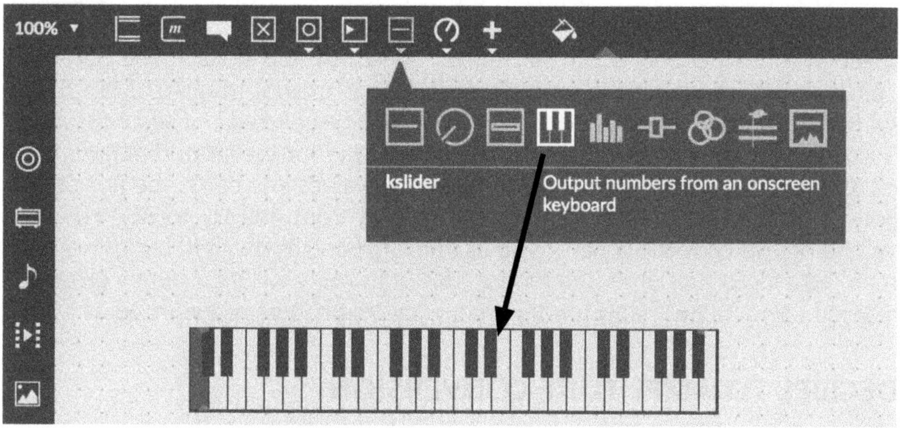

Fig. 1.49 The **kslider** object

Note that this object is found in the "Sliders" *palette*. This object depicts a musical keyboard, and clicking on a key will cause the related MIDI note number to be emitted from its left outlet. Try playing some note sequences using the **kslider**.

NATURAL GLISSANDI

Thanks to the **mtof** object, or better, thanks to the analogous object **mtof~** (with a tilde) which generates a signal rather than a single number, it is possible to implement glissandi that have constant velocity throughout the entire MIDI range. To see how, build the patch shown in figure 1.50.

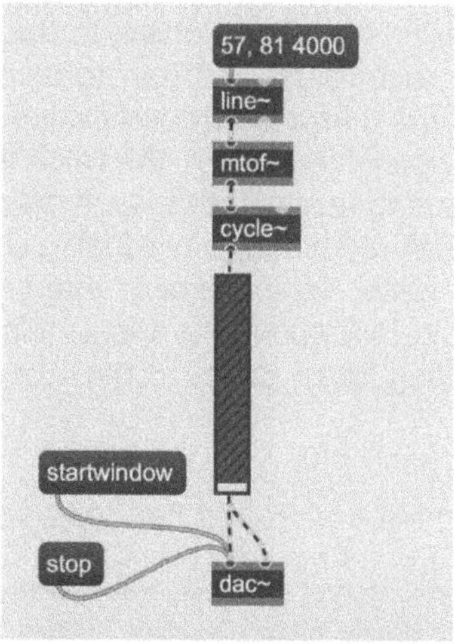

Fig. 1.50 How to obtain a much better natural glissando

The `line~` object illustrated in the figure generates a segment[34] that goes from 57 to 81 in 4 seconds. The generated numbers are routed to an `mtof~` object, which interprets the values as fractional MIDI note numbers and converts them into hertz, transforming, essentially, a glissando of note values into a glissando of frequencies. The resulting glissando will be perceived as uniform, and its speed will not depend upon the register in which it is occurs. The particular "pitch route" shown in the example covers two octaves, from A2 (MIDI 57) to A4 (MIDI 81): the first octave, from 57 to 69, will be covered in 2 seconds, which is exactly the same amount of time that it will take for the second octave, from 69 to 81. When `mtof~` converts the MIDI note values into hertz, the first octave goes from 220 Hz to 440 Hz, and the second from 440 Hz to 880 Hz - the second octave correctly covers twice as much ground as the first, but as we have seen, adjusts for the time differential. This uniformity will exist in any glissando realized using `line~`, and for any frequency that can be represented as MIDI.

DECIBEL TO AMPLITUDE CONVERSION

Another useful object converts sound pressure level, expressed as deciBels (see Section 1.2 of the theory part of this chapter), into amplitude: **`dbtoa`**.
As in most digital systems, in Max deciBels are expressed as negative numbers and the value of 0 dB represents the maximum amplitude with which the system is capable of working. A drop of 6 dB in amplitude is roughly half the loudness of the original signal. Therefore, if 0 dB corresponds to an amplitude of 1.0, -6 dB corresponds to roughly 0.5, -12 dB to about 0.25, and so forth. Glance at the file **01_12_conv_dbamp.maxpat** (seen in figure 1.51) for more. Using this patch, we can control the volume of an oscillator by entering a level for it in dB. The outlet of the oscillator is passed to a new graphical object, the **`levelmeter~`**, which confirms the sound pressure level in dB for the signal produced. As we can see, not surprisingly, the signal level output corresponds closely to that the original number that we entered into the float number box on the right. While varying dB values in this patch, you probably noticed an annoying noise that occurred when the input value jumped too much at one time. We can eliminate this artifact by using the `line~` object to smooth any unruly sequence of values, interpolating[35] such values and transforming them into a smoothed signal. To accomplish this, we must convert every value that we want to dispatch to `line~` into a pair of two elements: first, the value that we want to move to, and second, the time to spend reaching this value. When processed in this way using `line~`, values will always change gradually, eliminating gaps between values and the resulting noise. To implement interpolation in the patch, we must append a duration in milliseconds to the amplitude values produced by dbtoa, and pass the resulting list of values to the `line~` object.

---

[34] Note that the numbers generated are not simply the integers between 57 and 81, but include intermediate decimal numbers.

[35] The technique of interpolation consists of estimating intermediate values between two successive values. We will tackle this more deeply in our discussion entitled "Interpolation in wave tables" found in Theory Section 2.1.

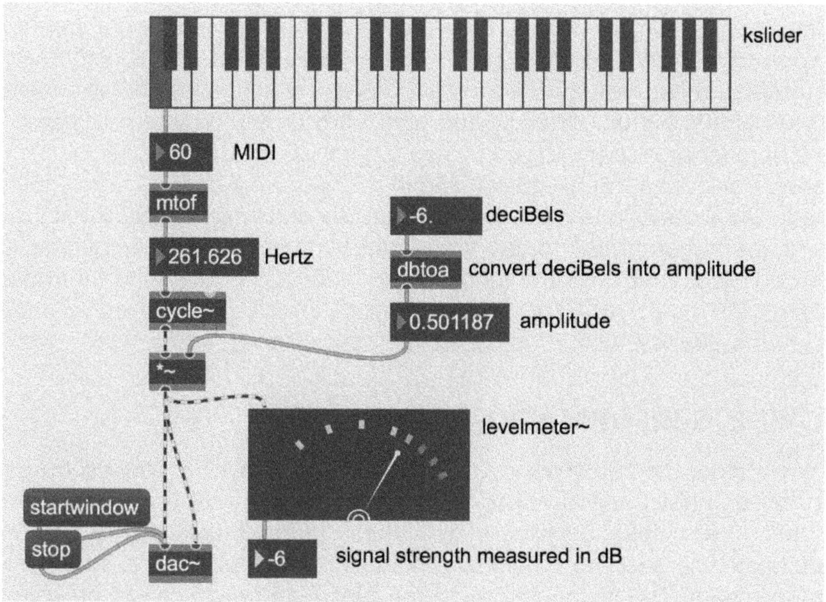

Fig. 1.51 The file 01_12_conv_dbamp.maxpat

In Max there are a zillion ways to do this, and what we see here is one of the simplest. There is an object named **append** that adds its argument to whatever message it receives. To see it in action, take a look at **01_13_conv_interp.maxpat** (seen in figure 1.52):

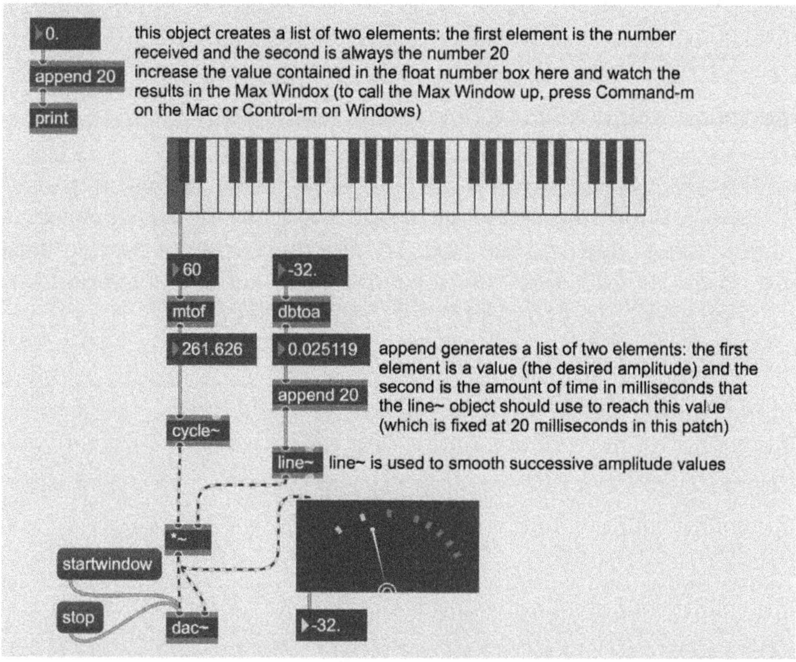

Fig. 1.52 The file 01_13_conv_interp.maxpat

In the upper left part of the patch, we've now connected a float number box to an **append** with an argument of 20. The **append** object adds its argument to any message it receives, and because of this, every time a number is generated by the float number box, the **append** object produces a two-item list consisting of the number received followed by the number 20. Below this, we connect the **append** object to a **line~** object, and in this way we pass from one amplitude value to its successor gradually, over a 20 millisecond interval. Recall that **line~** expects the first argument to be a value (which in this case is an amplitude value furnished by **dbtoa**) and the second (the value "20", furnished by **append**) indicates the time spent to reach the value. In this patch, every change in amplitude value will take 20 milliseconds to be reached.

PROVIDING INFORMATION FOR USERS

If you compare the patches shown in figures 1.51 and 1.52, you will note that in the second patch we have removed the comments near the number boxes, but that if you pass the mouse over these number boxes in performance mode, you will see the same commentary text appear in a small yellow floating square. This is done by using the **hint** feature, which can be accessed from the inspector. In edit mode, call up the inspector for one of the number boxes, and find its Hint attribute in the "Description" category. Edit the text field in the box next to the attribute name in order to provide the text that will be shown in the yellow rectangle. If, on the other hand, you'd like to provide a comment that will appear in the Clue Bar when the mouse passes over your object, you can type this message into the item named "Info View Text" on the same inspector panel.

ACTIVITY

Modify the patch contained in file 01_13_conv_interp.maxpat in a way that also interpolates the frequency, and creates a glissando between one note generated by **kslider** and the next. Try different times for moving between the two notes (20, 200, 2000 milliseconds). You must use an **append** object and a **line~** object, and connect them to the oscillator.

1.5 INTRODUCTION TO WORKING WITH SAMPLED SOUND

We'll now take a brief look at some of the objects that allow you to manipulate sampled sound. The easiest way to bring up an audio file while working with Max is to click (while in *edit* mode) on the fourth icon of the left *Toolbar*, which will cause a slide-out menu to appear with a list of all of the audio files available. If you drag one of these list elements to the inside of the Patcher Window, an object called a **playlist~** will be created (as shown in fig. 1.53a).

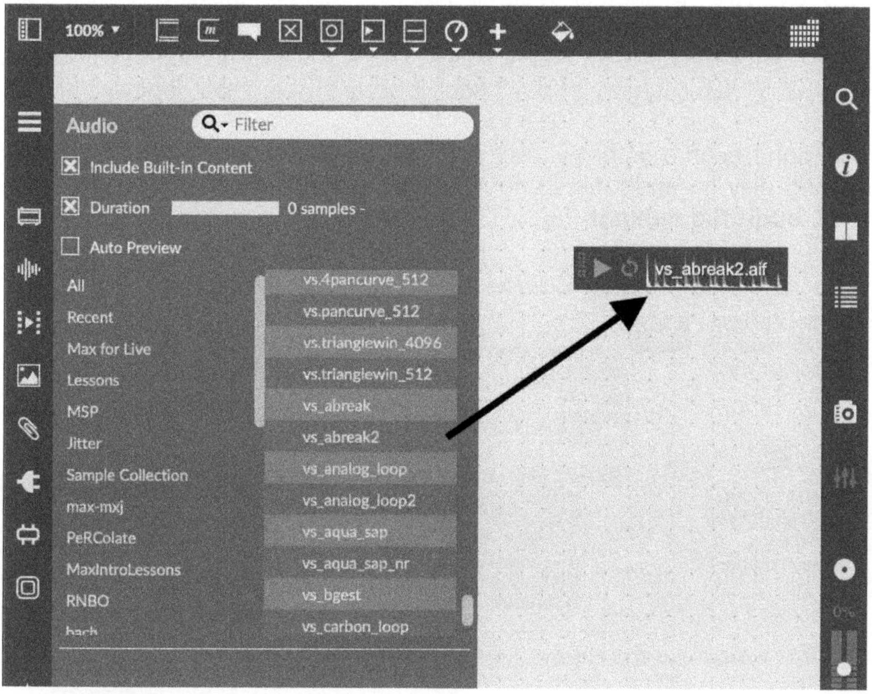

Fig. 1.53a The `playlist~` object

As you can see, this is an interface object that contains several elements: a triangular button for playing the audio file, a button shown as a circular double arrow which enables "looping" the sound (the *loop* function continuously repeats playback), and finally a graphical representation of the waveform of the sound, over which is superimposed the name of the audio file. The first two outlets of the object are the right and the left channels of its audio signal, so connect the leftmost outlet of the object to a **gain~** that is in turn connected to a **dac~** and use the relevant commands (startwindow and stop) to listen to the sound produced by the object. (You might want to activate the *loop* function in order to play sound continuously.)

You can add new audio files, whether in edit mode or in *performance* mode, by dragging them over the **playlist~** object. If you position the mouse pointer over the central part of the object, a red frame will appear and the new file will be substituted for the old when you release the mouse button.

If, however, you move the mouse pointer over the upper or lower edges of the **playlist~**, a red line will appear (at the top or bottom, respectively), and the new file will be added to the list before or after the current file.

To create a new **playlist~** object, you don't have to use an audio file from Max' search path, as we just did. You can actually drag any audio file, whether it is found on your computer's desktop or in an arbitrary folder, into the Patcher Window. It should also be noted that it is possible to move an audio file from one **playlist~** to another by clicking and dragging on the area at the left side of the sample that is covered with small dots (called the *handle*). Of course, If you just want to create an empty **playlist~**, this can be done by accessing the "Audio" sub-category of the "Add" *palette* in the upper *Toolbar*.

If you don't need a graphical user interface object for your program, you can load and play an audio file using the **sfplay~** object: open the file named **01_14_audiofile.maxpat** (fig. 1.53b) to see this.

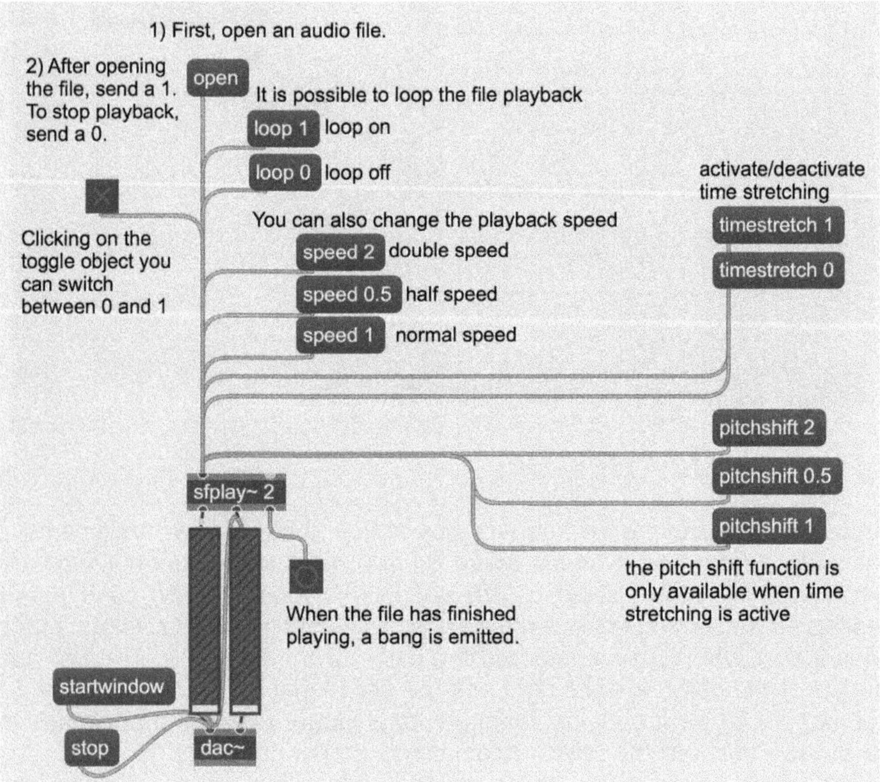

Fig. 1.53b The file 01_14_audiofile.maxpat

This object can have a numeric argument to indicate the number of channels in the file (for example, '2' for a stereo file). To open a file, send the message "***open***" by means of a message box, and select the file that you want. (Legal file types include AIFF, NeXT/Sun, WAVE, and Raw Data Files.)

You could also drag an audio file onto the object from the left *Toolbar* or directly from any folder, in the same manner as shown for the **playlist~** object.
To play a file, send the number 1, to stop it send the number 0. The graphical **toggle** object (which is the little square marked with the number 2 in the patch, and which is the fourth object in the Top Patcher Window Toolbar) enables you to send exactly these two numbers; by clicking on the object, you toggle the two object on and off (which is shown by the presence or absence of an X inside the object), and you cause the object to send the values 1 and 0, respectively. By using the message "***loop*** *1*", it is also possible to play the file as a loop (during which the file repeats indefinitely); to deactivate looping, send the message "*loop 0*". Finally, the message "*speed*", followed by a number, enables you to change the speed at which the file is played. '1' mean normal velocity, '2' double velocity, '0.5' half-speed, and so forth.
When playback speed is anything but 1, the pitch of the original sound will be altered as a consequence. For example, with "speed 2" the sound will be played an octave higher, while "speed 0.5" will cause playback to sound an octave lower. If, however, we activate the time stretch feature by sending the message "timestretch 1" (which is visible in the right part of fig. 1.53b), the pitch and the speed of playback become independent. The "speed" command, in this case, will alter playback speed without affecting the pitch of the sound. To change the pitch when time stretch is active, you can use the "pitchshift" message (again visible in the right side of fig. 1.53b). The message "pitchshift 2", for example, will raise playback pitch by an octave, while "pitchshift 0.5" will drop the pitch by an octave. In both of these cases, the speed of playback will remain unchanged[36].
In the patch, two **gain~** objects are connected to control the volume of a stereophonic sound. Note that there is a patch cord cross-connecting the two **gain~** objects; in this mode the **gain~** object on the left controls that on the right. If you modify the fader position of the left-hand **gain~**, you will see the right fader change itself to the same value. If, however, you change the right fader directly, the left fader doesn't move, because there is only a patch cord going from left to the right, but not vice versa. This commonly used technique makes it convenient to change the volume using a single fader, but allows the faders to differ when they need to.

[36] **sfplay~** recognizes many other commands. Call up the help file for **sfplay~** (<Alt-click> on the object in edit mode) to scope out all of the possibilities.

MANAGING FILES WITH THE FILE BROWSER

A very convenient system for opening files from **`sfplay~`** is provided by the **File Browser** (as seen in figure 1.54). This is a panel (that can be called up from the *File* menu, or by typing <Command-b / Control-b>) that enables you to view, open, or drag any files into your patches that are contained in Max' search path[37].

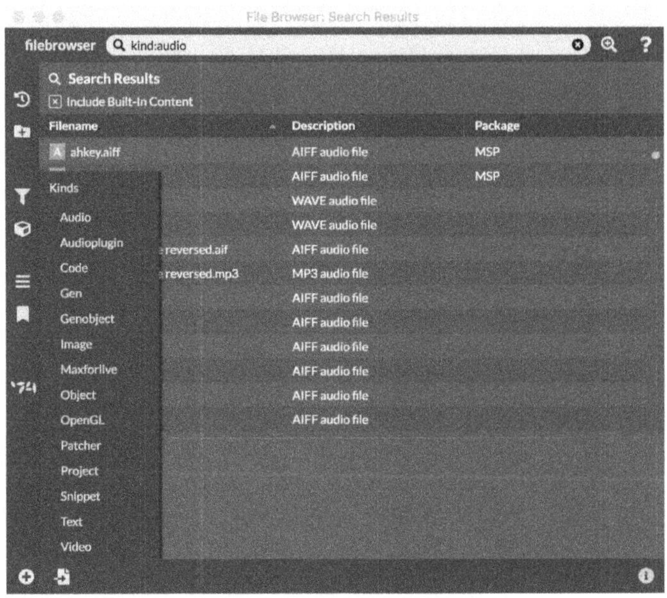

Fig. 1.54 The *File* Browser

In figure 1.54, we can see the File Browser. Notice that a few icons are visible on the left: the first two at the top are used to show recently used files and recently added files respectively. The third icon, a stylized funnel, opens a pop-up menu with which you can specify the type of file to show (for example, audio files, images, video files, etc.), while the rectangle on the right lists files of the type selected that you can find in the search path. (In the image shown, "audio files" is the type selected.) To load a new sound into a **`sfplay~`** object while in performance mode, you can drag the sound from the File Browser directly onto the object. (In figure 1.55, the file anton.aif is being dragged onto the **`sfplay~`** object.) It is also possible to open images and videos using the same technique in many other Max objects.

[37] Max' search path is a combination of folders that are used by the program to find the elements needed to complete a patch. For example, you have installed the Virtual Sound Macros in the Packages folder, which is part of this search path. It is possible to add new folders to the search path by using the File Preferences window, which can be invoked from the Options menu. Alternatively, you can add a subfolder or a file to the user library folder, which is named "{User Name/Documents/Max 9/Library" (substituting the account name you use on your computer for {User Name}). All documents and folders placed in this user library folder automatically become part of the search path.

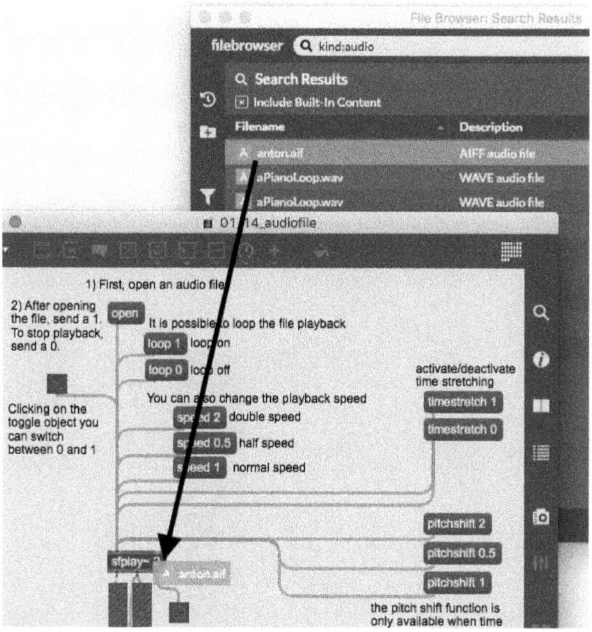

Fig. 1.55 Dragging an audio file from the File Browser into the **sfplay~** object

RECORDING AN AUDIO FILE

The object that enables us to record sounds to disk is called **sfrecord~**. Open the file **01_15_audiofile_record.maxpat** (seen in figure 1.56) to try it.

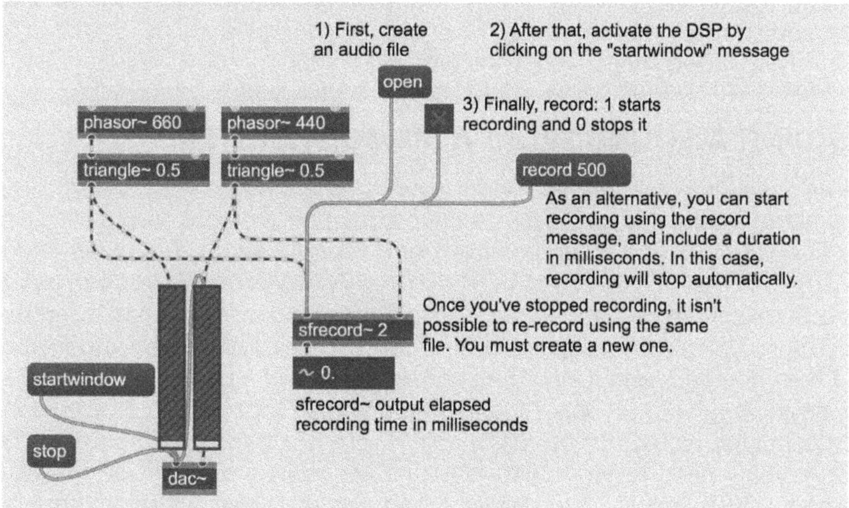

Fig. 1.56 The file 01_15_audiofile_record.maxpat

We can create an audio file on disk by sending the message *"open"* to the **sfrecord~** object. It is also possible to select the format to be used for the file at this point: the possible choices match those that can be read by **sfplay~**.

Once we've created the audio file that will soon hold our sound, we still have two steps to complete: first, we must click on *"startwindow"* to activate the two triangle wave oscillators that will produce the signal that flows into the two channels of the **sfrecord~** object, and secondly, we must activate recording with the **toggle**. (We can both start and stop the recording using this control.) Recording can also be activated by providing a duration in milliseconds when you send the *"record"* message. (This method circumvents the need to manually stop recording.)
Alternatively, we can use the Global Record button found at the bottom of the right Toolbar (fig. 1.56b).

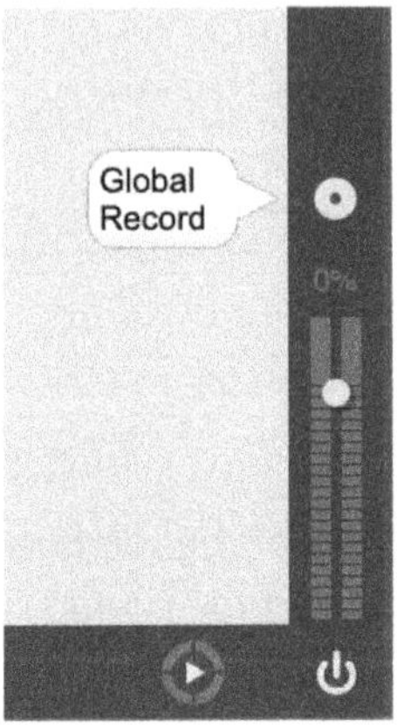

fig. 1.56b: the Global Record button

Clicking this button starts recording the sound produced by all active patches. A second click will stop recording. The resulting sound file will be located in the "{User Name}/Documents/Max 9/Recordings" folder.

READING A SOUND FROM A MEMORY BUFFER

We've seen how to read and write sounds to and from disk, but it is also possible to load a sound file directly into computer memory, in order to have faster access than would be possible from disk. (Access to disk drives is slow because mechanical movement must occur whenever reading files from a disk.) For example, if we wanted to load many different sounds into a patch and then move quickly between them, it would be fastest to load all of them into memory and then hop back and forth. The internal memory of a computer, however, is always more limited for space than its disk, and so for files that are very long, this technique would not be reasonable. There is a tradeoff: if you want fast access, you'll need to work with files that are short enough to be loaded in memory, but if you want to use very long files (files that occupy more space than you may have available in memory, or which would occupy the major part of your memory) you will have to compromise, and include the time needed to read the disk as part of the design of your algorithm.
When loading a sound into memory, you will need to use an object named **buffer~**, which has the job of allocating a chunk of memory that can contain

the sound. The object's name is based on the word **buffer** that refers to a section of computer memory used to store data temporarily. Besides the `buffer~` object, you will also need an object to read the buffered sound; a number of them exist, but one of the most useful is **`groove~`**, whose operations we will examine shortly. Open the file **01_16_buffergroove.maxpat** (seen in figure 1.57):

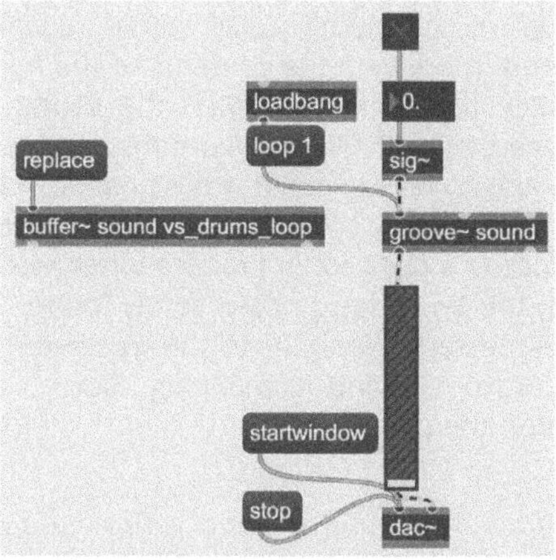

Fig. 1.57 The file 01_16_buffergroove.maxpat

There is a `buffer~` in the upper left of this patch that has two arguments: a name by which other objects can refer to it, and a name for the file to be loaded into it. We have given this `buffer~` the name "sound" and loaded the file vs_drums_loop.aif into its memory (which is a drum riff that you can find included as part of the Virtual Sound Macros)[38] If we want to load a different sound, we can do this by clicking on the message box "***replace***", or by dragging an audio file onto the `buffer~` from the File Browser (as we saw in figure 1.55). Double-clicking on `buffer~` while in performance mode will open a window that shows the waveform for the sound loaded (as seen in figure 1.58).

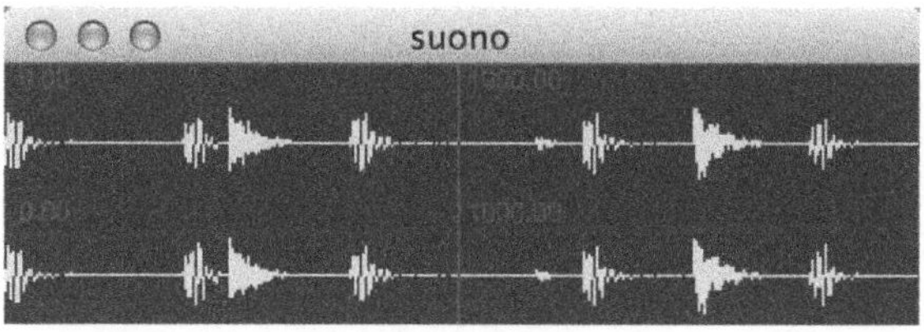

Fig. 1.58 The contents of the buffer "sound"

[38] If you followed the installation instructions for the Virtual Sound Macros library that were listed at the end of Section 1.2, that library should now be part of Max' search path, which means that the `buffer~` should be able to load the "vs_drums_loop" sound without needing to specify which folder to search.

Returning to the patch, on the right is a **groove~** object with the argument "sound", which refers to the name of the buffer for it to read. Clicking on the **toggle** at the top will activate this object; note that the values 0 and 1 generated by this **toggle** are converted into a signal by the **sig~** object,[39] because the **groove~** object, unlike **sfplay~**, needs a signal on its left inlet in order to read its sound file. The *"loop 1"* message puts the sound into loop mode, in which the file will continuously play, starting again from the beginning when it reaches the end. Modifying the contents of the number box connected to **toggle** will modify the speed at which the sound is read (0.5 is half speed, 2 is double speed, etc.).[40] We will learn much more about **groove~** in Chapter 5. What remains to be explained is the final object, **loadbang**, which is connected to the message box containing *"loop 1"*. This object generates a bang every time the patch is opened; in practice when we load the file 01_16_buffergroove.maxpat, the **loadbang** object sends *"bang"* to the message box, which then sends the message *"loop 1"* to the **groove~** object. This cascade of messages saves you from having to manually click on the startup message box whenever you open the patch.

[39] We will speak of the differences between signals and Max messages in the first section of Interlude A.

[40] The **groove~** object, like **sfplay~**, also has "timestretch" and "pitchshift" attributes that allow you to change the reading speed without changing the pitch, and vice versa.

1.6 INTRODUCTION TO PANNING

As we saw in Section 1.6 of the theory, to position a sound in a stereophonic field, we need to calculate a multiplication factor for the volume of the two channels, taking into account that the perceived intensity of the sound will be proportional to the power of its signal[41].
First, we must calculate a multiplication factor for the relative volumes of the two channels. If for example, we want a sound panned fully to the left, the multiplication factor for the left channel will be 1, and 0 for the right. If we want a centered sound, the factor for both channels will be 0.5. If we want the sound to be panned fully right, the factor for the right channel will be 1, and 0 for the left. Intermediate positions can be captured by using appropriate intermediate values.
You should be able to see that the multiplication factors for the right and left channels are complementary. When one goes up, the other goes down. We can simulate, for example, moving sound from the left channel to the right, in order to see how the multiplication factors for the two channels will change:

Sound position	**left channel factor**	**right channel factor**
Fully left	1	0
Partially left	.75	.25
Centered	.5	.5
Partially right	.25	.75
Fully right	0	1

Table A

As the multiplication factor for the left diminishes (because the sound is moving to the right), the multiplication factor for the right increases. Note that the sum of the two factors, right and left, is always 1. The values for the two factors are therefore linked, and can not assume arbitrary values. They cannot, for example, both have the value 1, or both 0. This means that we can control their position in the stereo field using just one of the factors, for example the right channel, and we can extract the other factor using a calculation: in this case, the left factor will always be equal to 1 minus the right factor (because, as we know, the sum of the two factors will always be 1).
Having picked a multiplication factor, we also need to take psychoacoustics into account: the perceived intensity of the sound will be proportional to the square of its amplitude (as you remember from Theory Section 1.6). This means that before using the amplitude multiplication factor, we must calculate its square root as a final step.
These dangerously mathematical details can be clarified by looking at the algorithm implemented in **01_17_pan.maxpat** (seen in figure 1.59).

41 As we will see in chapter 4, thanks to the multi-channel system it's possible to perform a panning with two or more channels in a simple way. However, we believe it's important to show the calculations required to perform the stereo panning.

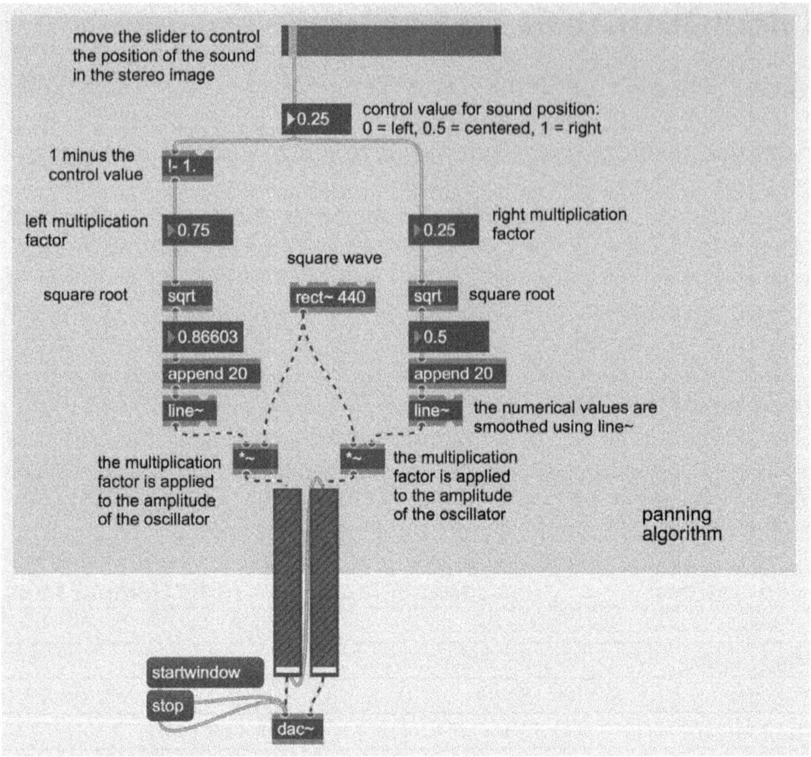

Fig. 1.59 The file 01_17_pan.maxpat

First off, we introduce a new graphical object, **slider**, which is a UI slider that produces a stream of integers when it is moved. This object can be either vertical (appearing similar to the `gain~` fader) or horizontal, as you see in the figure. If you resize the `slider`, rendering it longer than it is wide, it will change orientation automatically.

In this patch, the slider is configured (via the inspector) to produce decimal values that run from 0.0 to 1.0; with these values we will control the position of the sound. For the left channel, the values are subtracted from the number 1 using the object `!-`, which subtracts the number that it receives on its left inlet from its argument. (We will have more detail about this object in Interlude A). For the right channel, the value doesn't need modification. The higher the output on the left, the lower the output on the right, and vice versa. If the left is 0.75, for example, we will have 1-0.75=0.25 on the right; if the value on the right is 0.15, the left will be 1-0.15=0.85.

Next, we calculate the square root of the number using the **sqrt** object, specifically designed to perform square roots, and the results of this calculation is placed into lists using `append` (which was already seen in Section 1.4) and passed to the `line~` object, which smooths the gaps between one value and the next using a 20 millisecond "slew value" furnished by the `append` object. Finally, the values output by `line~` are used to multiply the amplitudes of the signals on both channels. Moving the slider, either left or right, will move the sound in the corresponding direction.

It is also possible to automatically move a sound along a stereo field under the control of an algorithm, as we now see in the file **01_18_pan_function.maxpat** (shown in figure 1.60):

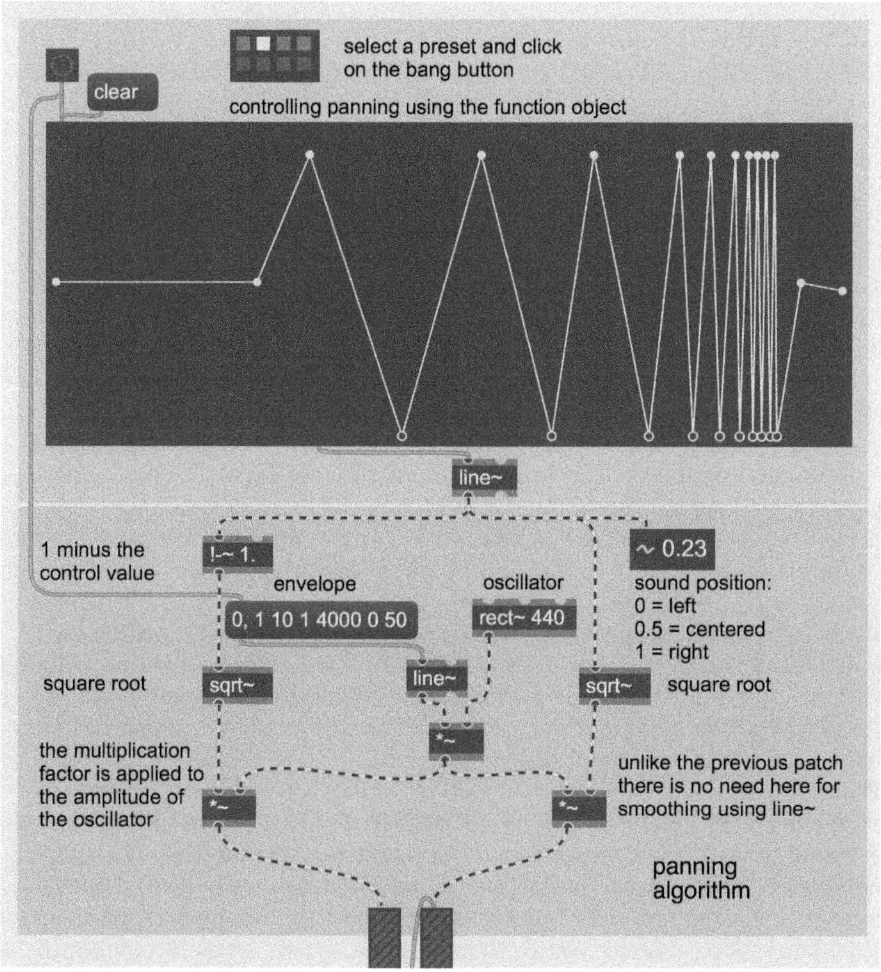

Fig. 1.60 The file 01_18_pan_function.maxpat

In this case, we control the position of the sound by using the `function` object, which we have already used to generate, together with `line~`, the envelope of a sound. The envelope generated by `function` and `line~` in this patch, unlike envelopes that we've used before, controls the movement of the sound in time rather than its pitch or amplitude; as long as the values stay between 0 and 1 (which will be true if we leave the default values for `function` untouched), we can use them to control the trajectory of the moving sound. We have recorded some easy-to-follow examples in the `preset`; you should also try to create some of your own. Note also that in this patch, unlike the preceding one, we have also added an amplitude envelope to give an attack to the sound at the beginning of its trajectory and to silence it at the end.

1.7 SOME MAX BASICS

To conclude this first chapter, we'll take a look at some basic properties of the Max environment.

GREY OR YELLOW-AND-BLACK PATCH CORDS? MAX VS. MSP

You have certainly noticed that the patch cords between objects are shown as either grey or as striped yellow-and-black. What is the difference? Across grey patch cords pass **messages**, consisting of numbers, alphanumeric strings, or lists, while across yellow-and-black cords pass **signals**, or constant-rate sample flows that are a digital representation for sound.
Originally, Max was a system very similar to the one that we are learning, except that it could only generate messages to control external devices. Max was not able to generate or manipulate audio signals; in essence, only grey patch cords were available. Later, when the production of faster chips introduced the possibility for realtime synthesis and signal processing on small computer systems without dedicated hardware, MSP was introduced in order to take advantage of these new capabilities and to produce and process signals. Yellow-and-black cords were added to extend the capabilities of the existing system.
MSP is an extension of Max that enables sound synthesis and signal processing. It is not a stand-alone program, but instead, a series of objects (both of the object box and of the graphical variety) that extend those found in Max, and which can generally be distinguished by a name that ends with a **tilde** ('~').
With MSP objects, you can implement all of the functions typical of sound synthesis and signal processing; there are oscillators, envelopes, filters, delay lines, etc. The characteristic that unites all of these functions is, as we have said, that they operate on signals, or digital sound.
What is digital sound? It is the numerical representation of physical sound waves. Inside a digital system, sounds (whether electronic or natural) are saved as a series of numbers. With the computer (and with a system such as MSP) it is possible, for example, to transform an acoustic sound into numbers by using an analog-to-digital converter, to carry out operations upon the resulting numbers using signal processing, and afterwards, to play back the new series of numbers on a loudspeaker using digital-to-analog conversion. Alternatively, a series of numbers can be directly generated using sound synthesis and transformed into audible sound using digital-to-analog conversion (as we saw in the first section of the theory half of this chapter).
Someone might object to the need for MSP, pointing out that Max objects (those without the tilde) already possess the ability to operate on numbers. We have, after all, already seen that it is possible to perform addition and subtraction, to calculate square roots, and presumably all other mathematical operations. Likewise, we have seen that it is possible to convert MIDI note values into their corresponding frequencies by means of `mtof`, which is a Max object that has no tilde.[42] What is the true difference between Max and MSP?

[42] But, remember, there is also the `mtof~` object!

Generally speaking, numbers are passed around by Max objects more slowly than those passed between MSP objects. Max objects are used to manage control parameters like the pitch of a note or its intensity, which can easily be passed around as small, easily managed, packets of data, while in the case of MSP objects, the digital signals with which they communicate must be continuously generated, point by point, at all times that a patch is active. If we modify the spatial position of a sound by using the horizontal slider in the patch 01_17_pan.maxpat, for example, the slider generates at the most a few dozen or so "Max numbers" per second (which we can watch in the number box below it). The digital oscillator that does the work of generating the sound, however, must generate at least 44,100 "MSP numbers" per second (the standard sampling rate for a CD) in order to have good sound quality. (For a deeper discussion of this topic, see theory Section 5.1.)
A second related, and perhaps more important, difference is that Max, unlike MSP, processes its messages at a variable speed. Returning to the slider example, the quantity of numbers generated per second by the slider depends upon the speed with which it is moved. In MSP, however, signals always operate at a constant speed, which as we know is called the sample rate. Signal data is passed, in our example, at the above-quoted 44,100 "MSP numbers" (samples) per second, and interrupting the flow of this data would result in clicks, undesirable digital noise, and general chaos. In our patches, when we click on the "*startwindow*" message connected to the **dac~**, we start this flow; when we click on "*stop*", we halt it.[43] As before, a deeper discussion of these topics will be found in Chapter 5, which is dedicated to digital audio.

ORDER OF EXECUTION IN MAX

We now touch upon a very important topic: the order in which operations are executed in Max.
In the Max environment, there is a general rule that says that objects exchange their messages in an ordered right-to-left sequence. This means that if a set of messages is generated at the same instant, the message generated by the right-most object (and within a single object, the message which is generated at the right-most outlet) precedes all other messages. It follows that the last message to be generated is the left-most. Try implementing the patch shown in figure 1.61.

From what we learned in Chapter 1, when we click on the button, the message "*bang*" will be sent to the three message boxes, which will in turn send their own messages to the **print** object, which will output the results onto the Max

[43] It is important to underscore the fact that the flow of data continues whenever a patch is active, even when it is not producing audible sound. If we reduce the amplitude of a signal to 0, for example, it will still consist of an uninterrupted flow of zeros, and if we set the frequency of an oscillator to 0 Hz, the oscillator will simply spit out a single repeated sample value (the value of which will depend upon which waveform is being generated and also upon the location in the cycle being produced by the oscillator when it is set to 0 Hz).

Console. In what order will the text for the three messages appear? If you try this out, you will see this sequence of messages in the Max Console:

print: three
print: two
print: one

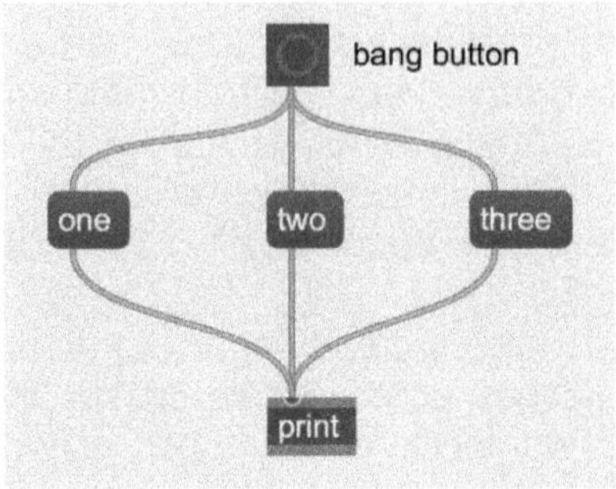

Fig. 1.61 Order of execution

As we might have anticipated, the order of execution goes from the right to the left. This goes for all Max objects.
This leads to a question that is very important and which has a profound influence on more complex patches. Patches will often not behave as we expect them to, because we have not constructed them taking the order of execution into account. Try to move the message boxes, changing their order (without unhooking the **button** and the **print** object), and observe the consequences on the order in which things are printed in the Max Console.

Caution! All that we have said about order of execution is in regard to Max messages (with their grey patch cords) and not to MSP signals (with their yellow-and-black cords). MSP signals, as we have seen, are generated as an uninterrupted flow and follow, therefore, an alternate rule, which we will examine in detail in Chapter 5.
If an object has multiple outlets, these will also follow the right-to-left rule of precedence. Construct the patch in figure 1.62:

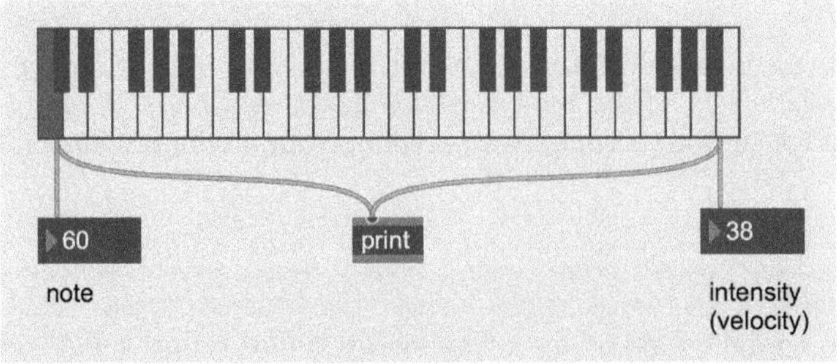

Fig. 1.62 The rule of precedence for outlets of an object

As we see, the **kslider** object (represented by the musical keyboard) has an outlet on the right in addition to the left outlet that we used before. The right outlet simulates intensity for the note played, and the higher up you click on the key, the greater will be the intensity reported (for which values range from 0 to 127). As above, the first value to be printed is that from the right outlet, which is the velocity value.[44]

THE PANEL OBJECT AND BACKGROUND LEVELS

During your perusal of the previous section, you probably wondered, when opening the files 01_17_pan.maxpat and 01_18_pan_function.maxpat, how the colored rectangles that contain the various parts of these patches were created. This rectangles were made with a graphical object named **panel** (seen in figure 1.63), whose look you can change using the inspector.

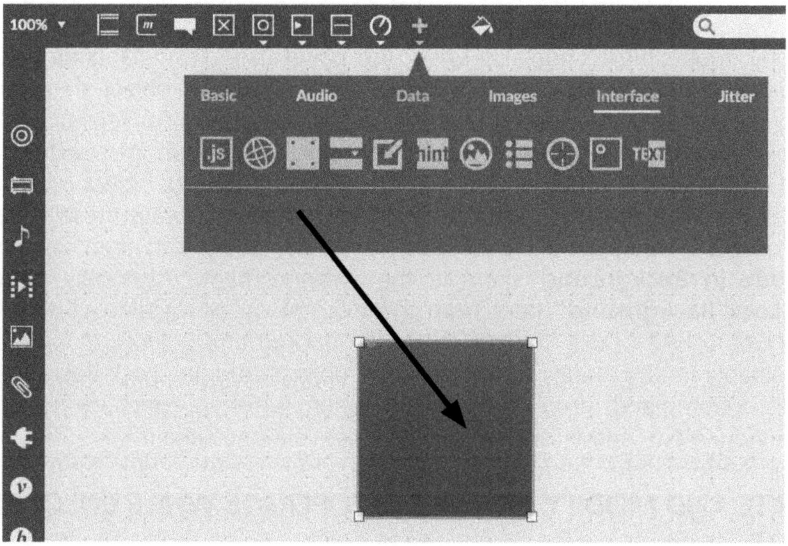

Fig. 1.63 The **panel** object in the Add *palette*, "Interface" category

Open a new patch and create a panel object, and then call up the inspector (<Command-i / Control-i>, or click on the 'i' icon at the bottom of the Patcher Window). By using the *Appearance* category attributes, we can decide, among other things, the thickness of the border ("Border Size", which defaults to 0, which is invisible), and the dimensions ("Patching Rectangle", which we know can also be changed by dragging the lower right corner of the object). There are many other possibilities which we will not discuss here (but which you should certainly experiment with!).
Switching to the *Color* category, you can modify the color of the background

[44] In MIDI lingo, the term velocity refers to the **velocity** with which the key is pressed. For questions regarding MIDI, we point you at Chapter 9. In Section 1.1 of Interlude B we will return to more on the topic.

("Interior Color"), and the color of the border ("Border Color"); this is also where you can create a gradient (using "Gradient Color").
After modifying the properties of a panel to your liking, create one or more number boxes and place them inside the panel: the boxes remain visible. If, however, you create the panel *after* having creating the number boxes, the boxes will be covered by the new panel. (Try this!) This happens because when we place objects over other objects, those created more recently will cover the older ones. In other words, every new object is created with a higher level than those before it. It is, however, possible to change this order. An object can be sent to the lowest level of all by means of the "**Send to Back**" command in the **Arrange menu**. Try this with the panel that you created to cover the number boxes: select it and then invoke "Send to Back". Now all of the covered boxes will be visible above the panel.

If you try, while in edit mode, to select all of the objects lying above a panel using the technique illustrated earlier in figure 1.10,[45] you will notice that it is nearly impossible to not also select the panel itself. This happens because the panel, although located at a lower level, is still an object that can be dragged, modified, or deleted like the others. Another inconvenience is that patch cords are hidden by the `panel` object when you go into performance mode. To solve this problem, we need to push the `panel` object to an even lower level – the so-called "background level" which is always present behind the "normal" foreground. To do this, select the panel and then invoke the "**Include in Background**" item in the *Arrange* menu. After this, toggling the "**Lock Background**" item from the *View* menu or pressing <Command-Alt-l / Control-Alt-l> will "freeze" all of the background objects, making them unselectable in any mode. To unfreeze the objects, toggle "Lock Background" or press <Command-Alt-l / Control-Alt-l> again, which will uncheck the option in the *View* menu and leave the objects accessible once again.

CREATE AND MODIFY PATCHES IN "OPERATE WHILE UNLOCKED" MODE

In addition to the normal edit mode, it's possible to use a mode that allows the user to edit a patch and operate on the patch itself at the same time: in other words, it's like being in edit mode and performance mode at the same time.
This mode is called Operate While Unlocked (OWU) and can be activated by opening the padlock at the bottom left of the patch and selecting the icon next to it, showing a box with a pointer inside (figure 1.64).

fig. 1.64: activate OWU (Operate While Unlocked) mode

When we are in this mode, the interface objects (like the number box or the

[45] Remember that this technique for multi-selecting objects consists of clicking and dragging the selection rectangle across all objects to be selected.

gain~ object) are all active: this means that if we drag the mouse pointer inside a number box, for example, we do not move the object (as if we were in "simple" edit mode), but we modify its value (as if we were in performance mode). The same thing happens for all the plain interface objects. On the other hand, the object boxes (such as **cycle~** or **mtof**) behave like in edit mode, i.e. they are moved by dragging the mouse.
If we are in OWU mode and we want to move an interface object (and not interact with it) we must place the mouse on the edge of the object, which will automatically highlight: clicking on the highlighted border and dragging the mouse will move the object.
In OWU mode, a click inside a message box causes the object to transmit the message it contains. If, on the other hand, we want to modify the message, we must first select the object (with shift-click, or with a simple click on the border) and then hit return.

ACTIVITY - *CORRECTING ALGORITHMS*

If you haven't already downloaded "Max Chapter Materials Vol 1" from www.virtual-sound.com/cmsupport, do it now.
Open the file **01_correction.maxpat**, which can be found in the folder "*Max Chapter Materials Vol 1/Activities and Tests Vol 1/01 Patching Activities*".

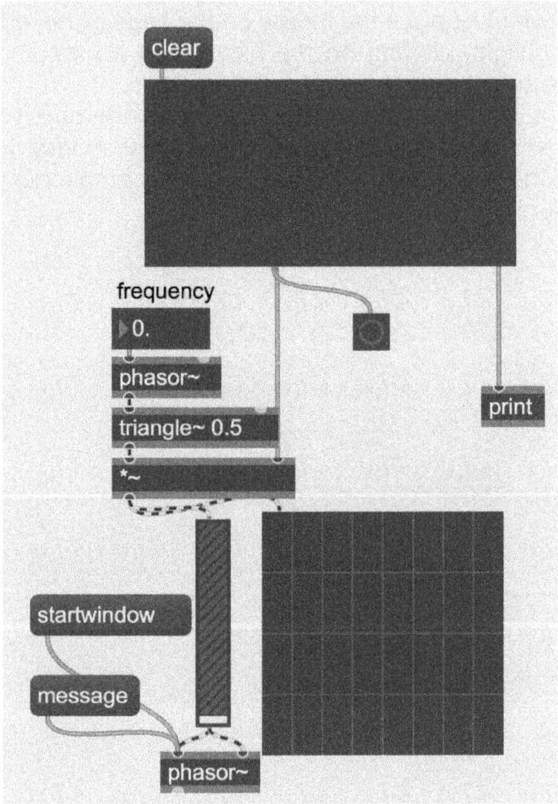

Fig. 1.65

Find the errors and the positional mistakes in the objects: there are two objects to move, one to substitute, one object in which there is an error, and one missing object. Correct the patch so that it will generate a triangle wave at 221 Hz using an envelope with a slow attack, a brief sustain, and an immediate decay. Make sure so that the patch displays the values generated by the `function` object in the Max Console.

ACTIVITY – *COMPLETING ALGORITHMS*

Open the patch **01_completion.maxpat**.

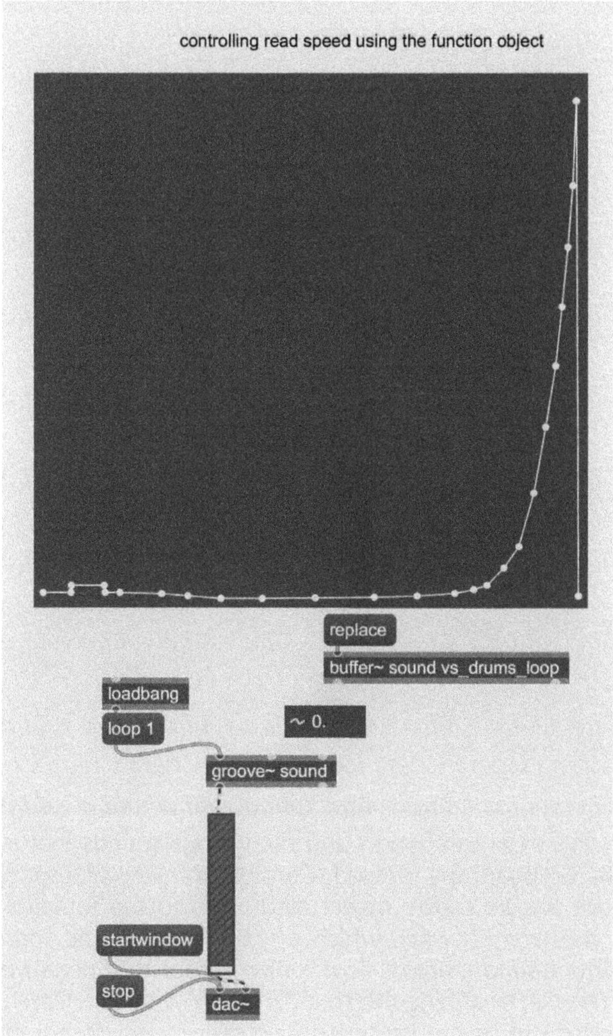

Fig. 1.66

This patch is incomplete. You can see a graphical **`function`** object that contains an envelope for controlling the playback speed of the "vs_drums_loop" sound, but this object has nothing to activate it, and is not connected to any other object! Considering that **`groove~`** accepts on its left inlet a signal to be interpreted as playback speed (1 = normal speed, 0.5 = half speed, etc.), try to complete this patch by making **`groove~`** utilize the existing but unused playback envelope, and then listen to how many variations can be made by simply tweaking this single parameter. Also find a solution for using **`number~`** to visualize the values being output by the **`function`** object in real time

ACTIVITY – *ANALYZING ALGORITHMS (ACTIVITY A)*

Open the patch **01_analysis_A.maxpat**:

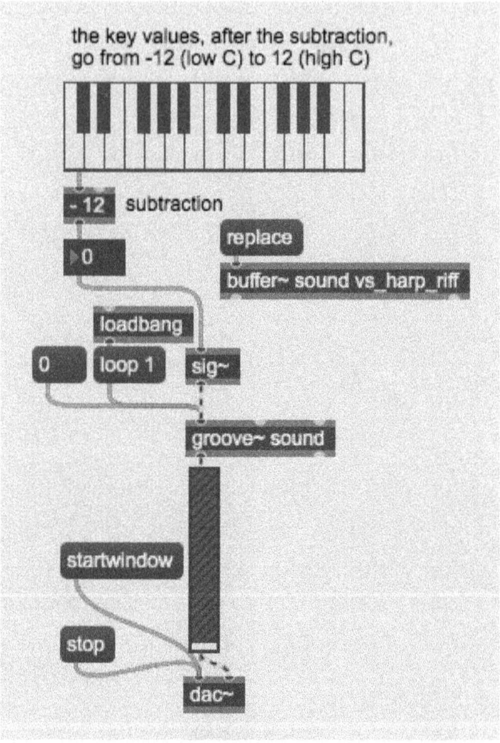

Fig. 1.67

Describe how this algorithm works and the various sounds that it emits when the keys of the keyboard are pressed. Consider the key values indicated in the comment above the `kslider` object, and listen to the sampled sound used in this patch (vs_harp_riff.wav), which can be found in the *soundfiles* folder inside the "*virtualsound macros*" folder. Remember that negative values read the sound in reverse, swapping the sound's attack with its release in time. Note the non-standard use of the keyboard: successive keys do not correspond to semi-tones, but to something else. What is it? If you can't find the answer, it may help to consult the ratios for natural frequencies in Table D of Section 1.4 in the theory chapter.

ACTIVITY – *ANALYZING ALGORITHMS (ACTIVITY B)*

Open the patch **01_analysis_B.maxpat**, and see a variation of the algorithm used in Activity A:

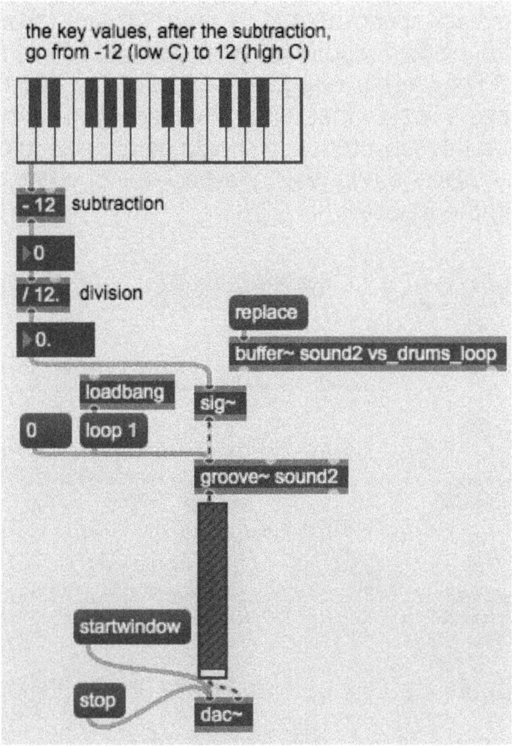

Fig. 1.68

Describe how this algorithm works, and the various sounds that it emits when the keys of the keyboard are pressed.

ACTIVITY – *SUBSTITUTING PARTS OF ALGORITHMS*

Open the patch **01_17_pan.maxpat** (seen in figure 1.68), and delete the **rect~** object. In its place, insert a sampled sound using **sfplay~** (without an argument, in a manner that uses only the left channel), with control over looping, three different playback speeds (0.125, 1, and 50), an "*open*" command for opening the file "*vs_piano_tango.wav*" (that you will find in the "*virtualsound macros/soundfiles*"[46] folder), a **toggle** to activate and deactivate the reading of the audio file, and a button that will signal reading the end of the file. Once you have completed this substitution, it should be possible to control the stereo position of the "*vs_piano_tango.wav*" playback (or of whatever audio file has been loaded) using the **slider**.

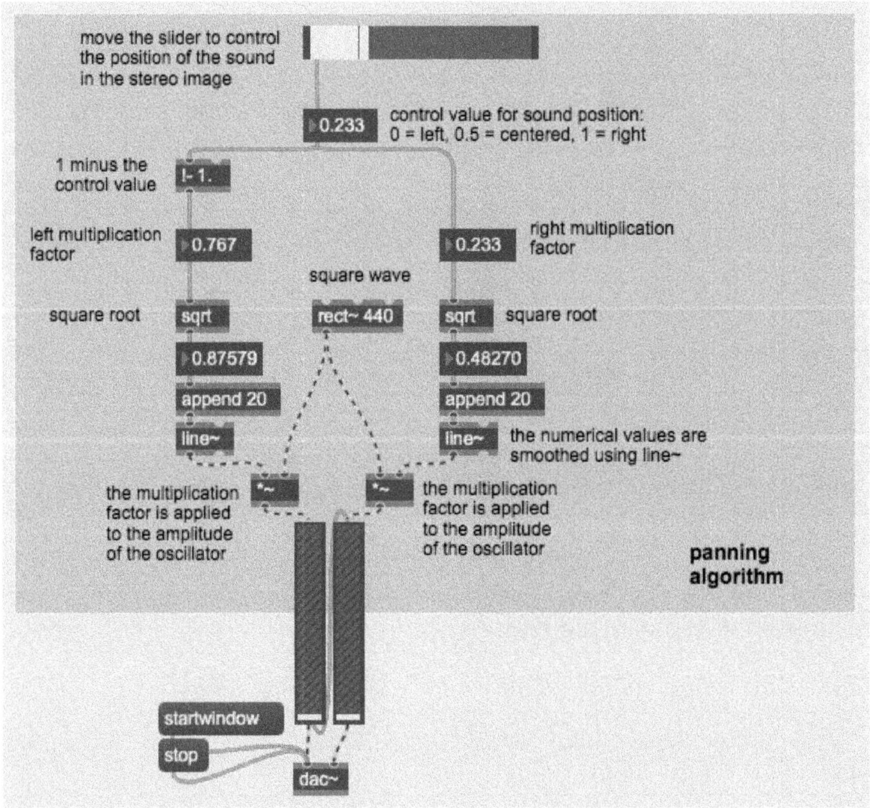

Fig. 1.69

[46] Remember that you can find the Virtual Sound Macros folder (if it has been correctly installed) in the "{User Name}/Documents/Max 9/Packages" folder. For further details, see the support page at www.virtual-sound.com/cmsupport.

INTEGRATED CROSS-FUNCTIONAL PROJECT – REVERSE ENGINEERING A

Listen carefully and analyze the sound *"01_reverse_engine_A.aif"*, and describe the properties of its amplitude and frequency envelopes. Implement an algorithm from scratch that allows you to recreate a similar type of sound.

Time for completion: 2 hours.

INTEGRATED CROSS-FUNCTIONAL PROJECT – REVERSE ENGINEERING B

Listen carefully and analyze the sound *"01_reverse_engine_B.aif"*, in which you will find a variation of the file *"vs_harp_riff.wav"*. Describe the differences between one and the other, and in particular, the behavior of pitch over time (the frequency envelope). Afterwards, make an algorithm that allows you to recreate a similar kind of sound, considering that, among the files in *"virtualsound macros/soundfiles"*, you have at your disposal the file *"vs_harp_riff.wav"*, and that you can use the **`function`** object to control the **`groove~`** object (as you have seen in the preceding activities).

Time for completion: 1 hour.

LIST OF PRINCIPAL COMMANDS

Open a new Max document
<Command-n/Control-n>

Switch between edit mode and performance mode
<Command-e/Control-e>

View the Max Console
<Command-m/Control-m>

Cancel an in-progress patch cord when "Segmented Patch Cords" is selected
<Command-click/Control-click>

Align the objects in a patcher window
Select + <Command-y/Control-Shift-a>

Open the inspector for an object
Select + <Command-i/Control-i> OR
Select + click on the icon containing an 'i' which is in the Right Patcher Window Toolbar.

Make floating yellow hints appear when you pass the mouse over an object
Hints are entered via the inspector: in the Hint attribute of the inspector, enter hint text

Make annotations appear in the Clue Bar when you pass the mouse over an object
Annotations are entered via the inspector: in the Annotation attribute of the inspector, enter annotation text

Copy objects or groups of objects from one patcher to another
Select + <Command-c/Control-c> + click on second patcher + <Command-v/Control-v>

Select multiple patch cords at once
<Alt-drag> across patch cords to be selected

Copy an object
Holding the <Alt> key down, click on an object and drag the "tear-off" copy to a new location.

Select and copy a group of objects
<Alt-drag> across the group to select it + restrike <Alt> and drag, "tearing off" new copies

Select an audio driver
Options->Audio Status

Turn on segmented patch cords
Options->Segmented Patch Cords
Every click creates a new segment, with the final click falling on the inlet to be connected

Create new objects with the press of a key
Within a patcher:
n = new object box
b = new button
t = new toggle
i = new integer number box
f = new float number box
m = new message box
c = new comment box

Open the online Max documentation
Select *Reference* from the Help menu.

Open the help patch for a single object
In edit mode, Alt-click on an object

Search for objects possessing analogous or complementary functions
In edit mode, select object + <Alt-click> on the object to obtain its help patch. In the upper left of the help patch there is a row of tabs; the last of these, labeled with a question mark, will lead to a menu from which it is possible to open the help patch for objects that either similar to or that are often used together with the selected object.

View the reference page from the manual for an object
In edit mode, select object + <Alt-click> on the object to obtain its help patch. In the upper left of the help patch there is a row of tabs; the last of these, labeled with a question mark, will lead to a menu, and the first item in this menu, "Open Reference", will open a page from the reference manual that contains detailed information about all of the characteristics of the selected object.

Open a FIle Browser
File->Show File Browser
<Command-b/Control-b>

Hide (or unhide) an object or a patch cord when it is in performance mode
In edit mode, select objects by clicking or using <Alt-click> + <Command-k/Control-k> to hide, or <Command-l/Control-l> to unhide selected objects

LIST OF MAX OBJECTS

Max arithmetic operators

* Multiply numbers on the inlets of the object
/ Divide numbers on the inlets of the object
+ Sum numbers on the inlets of the object
- Subtract numbers on the inlets of the object

For all of these operators, the first operand is the number on the left inlet, while the second operand is the argument (or else the number on the right inlet). These objects are listed among the math operators in the *Math menu* of the object list.

MSP arithmetic operators

*~ Signal multiplication
/~ Signal division
+~ Signal addition
-~ Signal subtraction

In all of these operators, the first operand is the signal, which enters via the left inlet, while the second operand is the argument (or the number or signal on the right inlet). These objects are listed among the math operators in the *MSP Operators* menu of the object list.

`append`

The `append` object adds its argument to whatever message it receives. Its outlet produces a list composed of a received number or list, followed by its argument, which is always at the end of the list on the outlet.

`buffer~`

This object allocates memory that can contain a sound. See also glossary 2P.

`button`

Generates a bang on every click of the mouse, and transforms all messages that it receives into a bang on its own outlet, flashing to indicate this.

`comment`
(comment box)

Allows the addition of captions to a patch. The object doesn't carry out any functions other than commenting upon the program.

`curve~`

Functions like `line~`, but requires a third parameter called the "curve parameter" which is sent along with a value and a time to be spent reaching the value, and which varies between -1 and 1. The curve parameter indicates different gradations of curvature: positive values indicate an exponential curve, negative values a logarithmic curve, and the value 0 will generate lines that are identical to those produced by `line~`.

`cycle~`

An oscillator which produces a wave that is by default sinusoidal.

`dac~`
A digital-to-analog converter that routes its signal inlets to the current sound driver, and which can activate and stop MSP when it receives the messages "*startwindow*" and "*stop*", respectively.

`dbtoa`
Convert the amplitude of a sound expressed in deciBels into amplitude. In Max, dB are expressed as negative numbers, with the value 0 dB designating the maximum possible amplitude.

`ezdac~`
A digital-to-analog converter that can start and stop MSP.

`flonum`
(float number box)
Stores, displays, modifies, and/or transmits the value of a floating point number.

`function`
Generates, through its graphical editor, envelopes, glissandi, or more generically, a series of points connected by line segments. It is possible to adjust existing points, create new ones, or delete points by using the mouse. The "*clear*" message deletes all points. The maximum and minimum values for the envelope can be changed by setting the Graph Range attribute in the inspector, and the duration of the envelope in milliseconds can be changed via the Graph Domain attribute.

`gain~`
Rescale the amplitude of the signal on its inlet as a function of fader position, and pass the resulting signal to its own outlet.

`groove~`
Plays sounds loaded in a `buffer~`.

`kslider`
Emits, on its left outlet, the MIDI note number for the key pressed on its keyboard. (The name is an abbreviation for "keyboard slider".)

`levelmeter~`
Measure the intensity of a received signal.

`line~`
Signal generator that produces linear segments (that move from one value to the next at a given time). To create a segment, the object takes a departure value plus a list containing one or more pairs of target values and times in milliseconds.

`loadbang`
Generates a bang every time that the patch is opened (loaded).

message
(message box)
An object that contains a message constructed of characters and/or numbers. The message can be sent to its outlet by clicking on the message box.

mtof
Converts a MIDI note value received on its inlet to a frequency value in hertz on its outlet. ("mtof" stands for "MIDI to frequency".)

mtof~
Signal version of `mtof`, which also generates a signal.

number
(number box)
Stores, displays, modifies, and/or transmits the value of an integer. Can display its contents as either a number or as a MIDI note.

number~
This MSP object has a dual role: it can monitor a signal, displaying as a number the current sample value of the signal it is receiving without sending it to its outlet; it can also be used to generate a signal based on the number that it contains. Clicking on the left part of the object toggles it between these roles.

(object box)
A "container" that is capable of morphing into any Max object when provided with its name. Inserting an object that has no graphical representation, such as `cycle~`, `print`, `line~`, `mtof` etc. (a large majority of Max objects), will cause appropriate inlets and outlets to appear on the object box, while a graphical object will replace the box with its own visualization.

panel
Graphical object, used normally to provide a background color, which can be modified via the inspector.

phasor~
Oscillator that generates a ramp that moves from 0 to 1, repeating this cycle at a configurable frequency.

playlist~
An object that can play a list of audio files (one at a time).

preset
Allows for recording and recalling specific configurations of patch parameters (presets).

print
The `print` object displays whatever message it receives in the Max Console. Double-clicking on the printed message from within the Max Console will select the object that generated the message in its Patcher Window.

rect~
Oscillator for generating band-limited square waves.

saw~
Oscillator for generating band-limited sawtooth waves.

scope~
Oscilloscope: the signal on its inlet can be seen moving on its screen.

selector~
Receives multiple signals and routes only one (or none), dynamically designated, to its outlet.

sfplay~
Read an audio file already saved on disk. To open a file, send the command "*open*" and choose the desired file. To play the file, send '1' as a command, to stop the file, send '0', to loop the file send "*loop 1*", and to stop looping, send "*loop 0*". The "*speed*" command, together with a multiplier, changes the speed at which the file is played back.

sfrecord~
Enables recording sound to disk. The command "*open*" creates a file on disk, while recording can be started and stopped using `toggle`.

sig~
Converts Max numbers into MSP signals.

slider
Graphical object that produces a stream of integers at its outlet. These objects can be configured for either vertical or horizontal display.

sqrt
Mathematical operator that calculates the square root of the value on its inlet.

toggle
Graphical object that, on every click, sends either a 1 or a 0 on its outlet, in alternation.

tri~
Oscillator for generating band-limited triangle waves.

triangle~
A "container" for producing triangular signals, which generates one cycle of a triangle wave every time it receives a ramp signal going from 0 to 1 on its signal inlet (which can be, for example, produced by a `phasor~`).

vs.square~
Oscillator that generates a non-band-limited square wave. This oscillator is part of the Virtual Sound Macros library.

MESSAGES, ATTRIBUTES, AND PARAMETERS FOR SPECIFIC MAX OBJECTS

buffer~
- Replace (message)
Message for loading a new file into a buffer~, which reallocates memory according to the size of the new file.

curve~
- Curve Parameter or Curve Factor (parameter)
A factor that ranges between -1 and 1, that controls the curvature of an envelope segment. Positive values generate exponential curve, negative values a logarithmic curve, and zero generates a straight-line segment.

function
- Hi Domain Display Value (attribute)
Attribute of function that sets the maximum display value for the x-axis, which corresponds to the total duration of the envelope in milliseconds.

- Lo and Hi Display range (attribute)
Sets the minimum and maximum display range for y-axis values.

patcher inspector
- Open in Presentation
Activation option, which when set causes a patch to *open in presentation* mode rather than patching mode.

scope~
- Buffer size (attribute)
Attribute of scope~ used to set the number of "sample packets" in its buffer, that is the number of pixels displayed in the oscilloscope.

- Calccount – Samples per pixel (attribute)
Attribute of scope~ used to set the samples-per-pixel for the oscilloscope trace.

- Lo and Hi Display range (attribute)
Attribute of scope~ that sets the minimum and maximum sample values displayed. These limits are initially set to -1 and 1, but can be modified to any value.

sfplay~
- Loop (message)
Command that, with a '1' (loop 1) activates, and with a '0' (loop 0) disables, the looping of an audio file.

- Open (message)
Command used to select an audio file to be played.

GLOSSARY

Arguments
Parameter values that follow the name of an object inside an object box, which initialize the characteristics and internal variables of the object.

Autocompletion
Feature of the Max environment (for example, in the Object List) that causes a menu to appear containing all of the objects whose names begin with characters already typed.

Band-limited oscillators
Oscillators that do not generate frequencies that exceed the conversion limits of the sound driver.

Bang
A message that triggers an action in a Max object. When an object receives a bang, it performs its principal action.

Buffer
A region of memory, created to contain ephemeral data. In Max, such a region can be given a name so that other objects can access and refer to it.

Clue Bar
Information text that appears on the lower Toolbar when you hover the mouse over an object.

Edit mode/Performance mode
The two working modes of the Max environment. Edit mode is used to assemble patches by inserting, modifying, deleting, and connecting objects. Performance mode is used to execute such patches; while in performance mode, objects are "active", and can receive and act upon parameter values.

File browser
A UI panel that displays and categorizes the files that populate Max' search path and from which files can be browsed, opened, and dragged into patchers.

Grid
A lattice that can be switched on and off in the Patcher Window which restricts the placement of objects and which facilitates the accurate alignment of objects.

Help (menu)
The menu through which it is possible to call up the many different help components in the Max environment.

Hide on lock / Show on lock
Items in the *Object* menu that allow objects and patch cords to be hidden (or shown) when in performance mode.

Hint
A suggestion that pops up in a yellow rectangle, triggered by hovering with the mouse pointer over an object. In edit mode, an object's hint can be edited via the inspector's Hint tab.

Inlet
One of the inputs for an object, represented graphically as a small dark rectangle on the upper edge of the object when in edit mode.

Inspector
A window used to set object attributes while in edit mode.

Left toolbar
Enables access to all files used while programming Max.

List
A set of numbers, and/or words, and/or arbitrary combinations of characters, which taken together form a whole.

Lower toolbar
Enables dynamic control of the Max programming environment.

Max help
The principal help window in the Max environment.

Max console
A window used by Max to communicate with its user using short blurbs such as error messages, printed lists, etc.
Double-clicking on such a message within the Max Console causes the object that produced the message to be highlighted in its Patcher Window.

Message (Max)
Packets of information, consisting of numerical values, strings, or lists of the same, which are passed between objects without regard for the sampling rate that is in effect within the environment.

Object action menu
A menu that can be accessed while in edit mode by hovering with the mouse pointer over the left side of an object and clicking on the circular icon containing a triangle that appears. This menu provides access to all of the elements needed to manage, transform, and graphically format the object.

Operate While Unlocked (OWU)
Allows the user to adjust the interface objects while patching.

Outlet
One of the outputs for an object.

Patch
A set of connected objects that implements some pre-determined function or algorithm.

Patch cords
The cords used to connect objects within a patch.

Patcher inspector
A window through which it is possible to set various properties of a Patcher Window.

Patcher window
A window in which you assemble an algorithm (or a "virtual machine") by using "patching" objects together via patch cords.

Patching mode
See Presentation Mode / Patching Mode

Performance mode
See Edit Mode / Performance Mode

Presentation mode / Patching mode
A display mode for patchers in which only objects that have been explicitly chosen to be visible appear. The positions and dimensions for these objects are independent from the positions and dimensions that the same objects occupy while in *patching mode* (non-presentation mode). To cause a patcher to automatically *open in presentation* mode when it is loaded, activate the *Open in Presentation* option in the patcher inspector (which can be called up via the *View* menu).

Quickref menu
A comprehensive menu that can be called up while in edit mode with a click on an object outlet. The menu is subdivided into two categories of elements: Messages, and Attributes. Messages correspond to the types of data that the object "understands"; by selecting a message, it is possible to automatically create and connect new objects related to the data type of the selected outlet. Finally, Attributes correspond to the properties that can be set in the object's inspector.

Right toolbar
Activates the **Sidebar**, a slide-out window that appears beside the Patcher Window, which contains a variety of documentation and useful tools.

Segmented patch cords
An option for the Max environment that can be set via the *Options* menu, which allows you to lay out patch cords that have multiple segments. At each click, a new segment is created.

Signal (MSP)
A constant-rate flow of samples that represent sound in the digital domain.

Upper toolbar
Contains the interface objects available in Max, organized into categories.

Virtual sound macros
A library of objects and abstractions created to accompany this book, which extends the set of standard Max objects.

Interlude A
PROGRAMMING WITH MAX

LEARNING AGENDA

PREREQUISITES FOR THE CHAPTER

- Contents of Chapter 1 (Theory and Practice)

LEARNING OBJECTIVES

Skills

- To learn how to use the basic features of Max that pertain to integers and floating point numbers
- To learn how to generate and control sequences of random numbers, optionally with the use of a metronome
- To learn how to construct embedded objects and abstractions
- To learn how to repeat messages across multiple object outlets
- To learn how to assemble and manipulate lists, using both non-graphic and graphic methods
- To learn how to use variable arguments
- To learn how to manage communication between objects without the use of patch cords

CONTENTS

- Integers and floating point numbers in Max
- Generating and controlling random numbers with the objects `random`, `drunk`, etc.
- Generating regular rhythmic events using the `metro` object
- Constructing subpatches and abstractions
- Managing list and variable arguments
- Using the `send` and `receive` objects for wireless communication between objects

ACTIVITIES

- Analyzing algorithms
- Completing algorithms
- Replacing parts of algorithms
- Correcting algorithms

TESTING

- Integrated cross-functional project: reverse engineering

SUPPORTING MATERIALS

- List of Max objects
- Messages, attributes, and parameters for specific Max objects
- Glossary

In this first "Interlude" we will examine a few aspects of programming Max in more depth, so to provide useful information to you. Because of the essential nature of this information, we encourage you to not skip over this section unless you are already truly expert in Max. It is important that you implement all of the tutorial patches that we propose in the text, as these small efforts yield the biggest results.

IA.1 MAX AND THE NUMBERS: THE BINARY OPERATORS

Like any respectable programming language, Max can do many things with numbers. We will begin this chapter by looking at the simplest operators, those for addition, subtraction, multiplication, and division.

INTEGER ADDITION

Recreate the simple patch shown in figure IA.1 (and make sure that there is a space between '+' and '5'!).

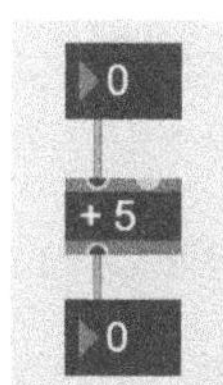

Fig. IA.1 Addition

The **+** object adds its argument (which is, in this case, 5) to whatever number it receives on its left inlet. If we feed some numbers to the object via the number box above it (by selecting it, for example, in performance mode and then using the arrow keys on the keyboard to change its value), we can track the results of the operation in the lower number box.
The right inlet of + changes the argument, and if we enter a number on this inlet by using another number box, the number will be substituted for the argument of the + object in the sum that will be produced when new numbers are input via the left inlet.
Try this by adding a number box on the right, as shown in figure IA.2:

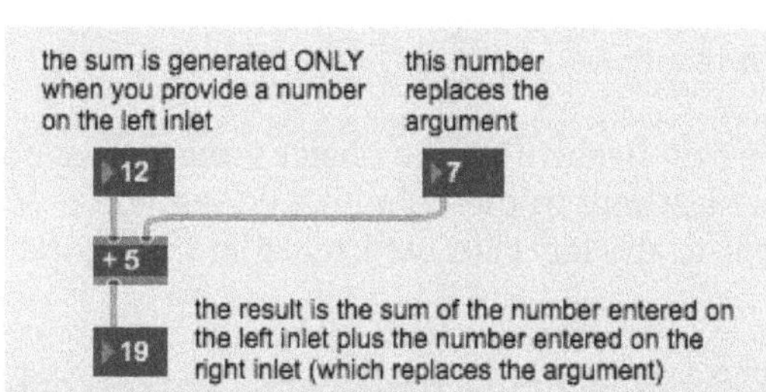

Fig. IA2 Addition with a changeable argument

When you play with this patch, note that the + operation is executed only when a number is sent to its left inlet, and never when a number is sent to its right inlet. Every time a new number is sent to one of the two inlets, an internal variable corresponding to that inlet is updated. The old contents of the variable are deleted, and replaced by the new value. In addition, a number sent to the left inlet triggers the + operation, summing the contents of the two internal variables and emitting the result. This is a common pattern: a large majority of Max object execute their functions and emit results only when a message is received on their left inlet. Messages that enter other inlets either modify arguments by updating internal data structures or else modify the behavior of the objects without causing visible results.

In the lexicon of Max objects, the left inlet is defined as a "**hot**" **inlet**, one that causes the operation to be carried out on the object in addition to updating the inlet's corresponding internal values. Most other inlets are defined as "**cold**" **inlets**, which update internal variables without producing output. Note that the circle that appears around the inlet of an object when you hover above it with the mouse in edit mode is red for the "hot" inlets and blue for the "cold" inlets.

Is there a way to update the value of the sum when we send a number to the right inlet of an addition object? In other words, is there a way to convert a "cold" inlet into one that behaves like a "hot" one? Of course there is, and we can examine the technique in figure IA.3:

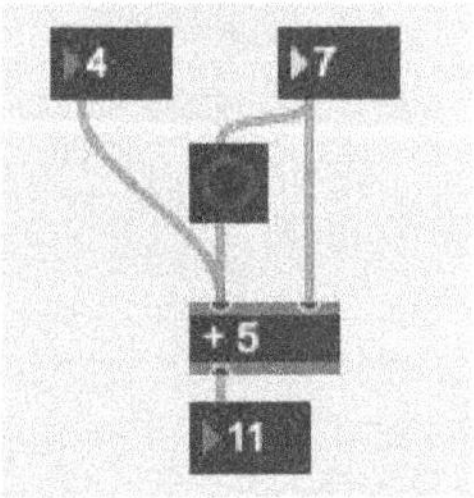

Fig. IA.3 How to make a "cold" inlet behave like a "hot" one

In this patch, we first send a number to the right inlet, and then a bang to the left inlet (remembering the right-to-left order for Max messages). Since `button` transforms anything that it receives into a bang, inputting a number on the right inlet produces this bang message, which, as you know, will force the receiving object to produce a result, which, in this case, is our sum.

What is added? The numbers within the object's internal variables, which in this case are the number last sent to the right inlet (in the figure, the number 7) and the last number sent to the left inlet (which is 4 in the figure).[1]

[1] Recall that in this figure, just as in the next, the original argument '5' is replaced by any numbers sent to the right inlet.

In this style of patch, the "cold" inlet of the addition object behaves as though it were a "hot" inlet. Try building it, and verifying that the number box on the right triggers a result every time that its value is changed.

It is essential that the positions of the objects in your patch are absolutely the same as the positions in the figure. Placing the `button` to the right of the + object, for example, will produce undesired results, since the bang will fire before the new value is stored, causing the addition object to use the old value that had been copied into the internal variable previously in its calculation rather than the new value (as shown in figure IA.4).

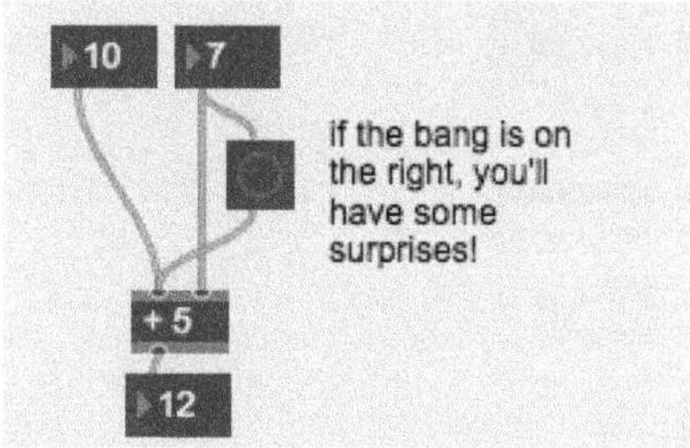

Fig. IA.4 Buggy results produced by an error in the order of execution

Delete the two number boxes above the + object and connect a message box to its left inlet. After this is done, type two numbers (separated by a space) inside the message box, as in figure IA.5:

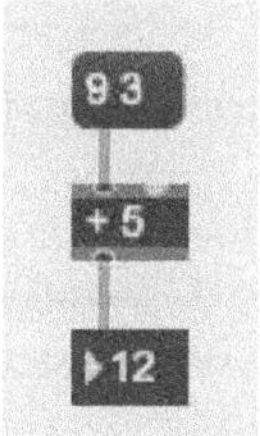

Fig. IA.5 Summing a list

If you now click on the message box in performance mode, the + object will sum its values; the operator behaves as though it had received the second number on the right inlet (and, as usual, the argument 5 inside the object box is replaced by that new value). This behavior (the ability to accept lists of two or more elements on their left inlet and then route the individual list items to the other inlets) is also a common feature of many Max objects, and works not only with binary operators, but often with objects that have three or more inlets.

To see a simple musical application of Max's addition object, open the file **IA_01_transposition.maxpat** (seen in figure IA.6).

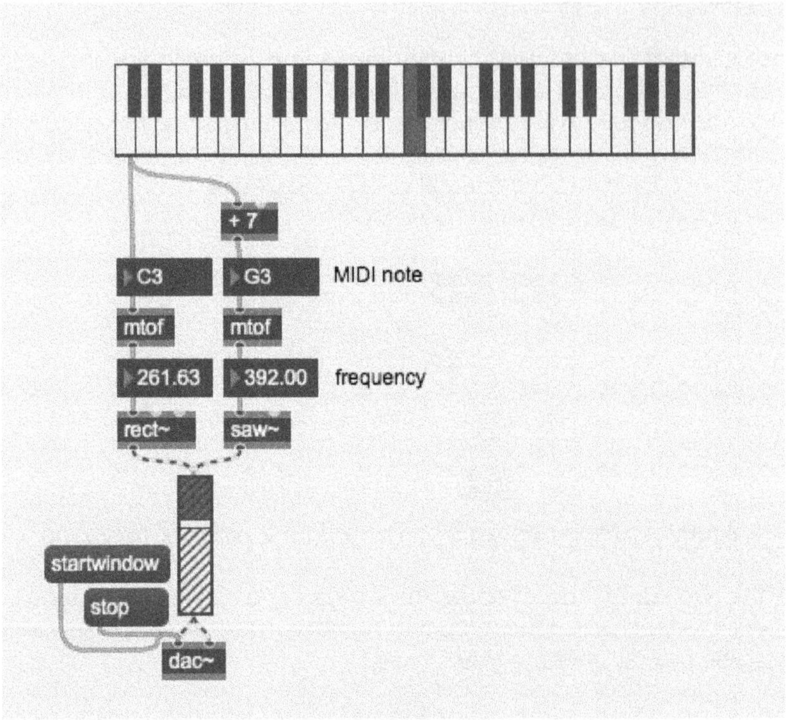

Fig. IA.6 The file IA_01_transposition.maxpat

Every time a key is pressed on the **kslider** object in this patch, two notes are generated, the second of which is 7 semitones above the first – the musical distance of a fifth. Every time that we press a key on the **kslider**, the value of the corresponding MIDI note number (a C in figure IA.6, for example) is sent to the **mtof** object on the left, which converts it into a frequency value. At the same time, the note number is also sent to a + object that adds 7 (producing the MIDI note number for a G in the example). The resulting sum is sent to the **mtof** object on the right side of the patch.
By using an addition object in this way, it is possible to transpose MIDI notes by arbitrary intervals of our own choosing. In this example, after the MIDI values of the two notes are converted into frequencies, they are sent to two oscillators, **rect~** and **saw~**, which sound at the interval of a fifth. Try modifying the patch to use other intervals (a third, or 4 semitones; a fourth, or 5 semitones; an octave, or 12 semitones, etc.). After this, try adding another addition object, connected to another dedicated **mtof** object and oscillator, so that every **kslider** keypress produces a three note major chord. For example, if the C2 key were pressed (the key that corresponds to the note one octave below middle C), a chord of C E G in the second octave (C2 E2 G2) would be produced.

NUMBERS WITH A DECIMAL POINT, AND OTHER OPERATIONS

Up until now we've used only integers. When the + object is given an integer as its argument (or has no argument at all), Max will assume that you would like to perform integer math. To make the object work with floating point numbers, as shown in figure IA.7, we need to connect float number boxes to its inlets, and, as you can see, to provide an argument of "0.". (The decimal point is important, but it is not necessary to put any numbers after the decimal point.) The decimal point in the argument declares to the + object that we intend to use non-integer numbers on its inlets, or in other words, that we intend to use floating point math. Duplicate the patch yourself and do some sums using floating point numbers (remembering that the "hot" inlet is on the left).

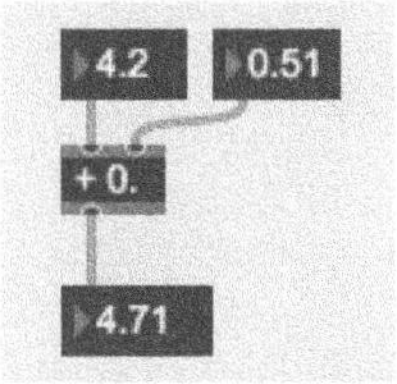

Fig. IA.7 Summing numbers that contain decimal points

Everything that we have covered to this point about addition also applies to subtraction, multiplication, and division. Try building the patch shown in figure IA.8 to verify that this is the case:

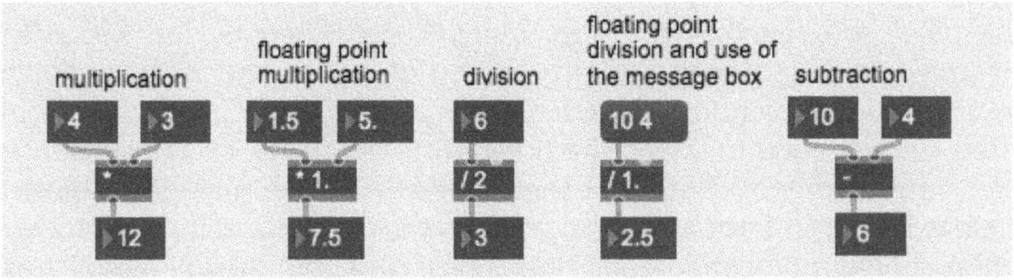

Fig. IA.8 Other mathematical operators

A brief piece of advice is in order at this point: do these exercises! Although they may seem trivial, doing them will help you to notice the details and the quirks of the Max environment, details whose importance will be revealed in the patches that we will pursue in the following chapters. For example, in the test case with the comment "floating point division and the use of the message box", you see that we are submitting a list of *integers* ("10 4") for evaluation. Despite the fact that integers are submitted, the operator was already declared to represent a floating point operation, thanks to the floating point argument provided in its object box, and as a consequence, the result emitted will be a floating point number.

Let's again use some of these simple operations in a musical context. You'll remember how the distance between two notes, an interval, can be expressed as a ratio between the two frequencies. For example, the interval of a fifth, corresponding to 7 semitones, can be expressed using the ratio 3/2.

Given a frequency (let's say 261.63 Hz, which is middle C), if we multiply the frequency by 3 and then divide by 2, we will obtain the frequency for the note a fifth above (which in this case would turn out to be 392.44 Hz, a G). To see this in action, open the file **IA_02_fifth.maxpat** (shown in figure IA.9):

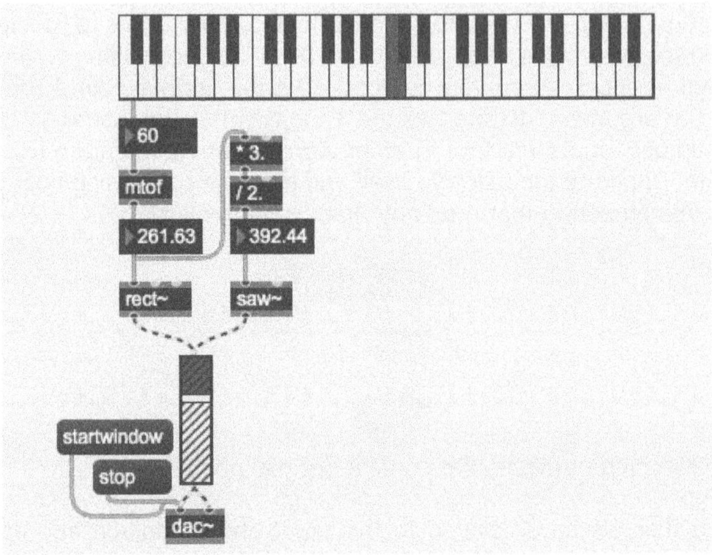

Fig. IA.9 The file IA_02_fifth.maxpat

In the patch we see that the note number generated by the **`kslider`** is transformed into frequency though the use of **`mtof`**, and is then sent to a **`saw~`** oscillator. The output of **`mtof`** is also multiplied by 3/2, in order to obtain the frequency needed to sound the note a fifth above, which is then sent to a second **`saw~`** oscillator. Note that the arguments to the multiplier object and to the divider object have a decimal point as their last character, which declare that Max should use floating point operations. Also note the routing of the two patch cords that exit the float number box under the **`mtof`** object: one cord is connected directly to the **`saw~`** object below it, but the second heads off to the right, heads upwards, and finally winds up connected to the multiplier object that has the argument 3.

If you compare figures IA.6 and IA.9, notice that the frequencies calculated for the note a fifth above are different. By using two distinct **`mtof`** objects in the first patch, we calculated a *tempered* fifth (the fifth normally found in western music), which is defined as the interval formed by combining 7 tempered semitones. When we used the ratio 3/2 on the output of a single **`mtof`**, however, we calculated a *natural* fifth, which is slightly wider that a tempered fifth. The difference is around 2 *cents* (which is a unit defined to be 1/100 of a tempered semitone).

OPERATIONS THAT USE THE EXCLAMATION POINT

All of the operators spoken of so far are *binary operators*, so called because they need two inputs (also called operands in computer lingo) to produce their output. In the objects that we have already seen, the first operand is the number that is input on the left inlet and which triggers the operation, while the second operand is the argument (or else the number on the right inlet).
For subtraction and division, however, there also exist two objects for which the operands are reversed. Their second operand is input on the left inlet and triggers the operation, while the first operand is the object's argument.
The name for these "reversed" objects is made up of an exclamation point plus the character for the underlying operation: **!-** for subtraction (which we have already encountered in patch 01_17_pan.maxpat), and **!/** for division.
See figure IA.10 for examples:

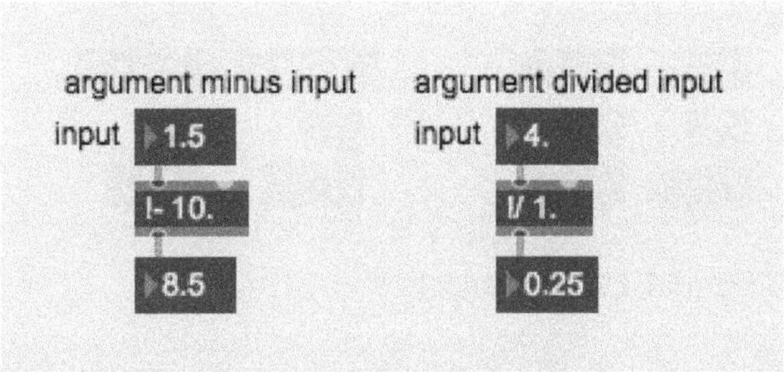

Fig. IA.10 Operators that contain the exclamation point

In the first case, the value being input (1.5) is subtracted from the argument (10), and the result is 8.5 (10 - 1.5). In the second case, the argument (1) is divided by the value being input, which results in 0.25, since 1/4 = 0.25.
The operands are reversed with respect to the normal order for subtraction and division. Build this patch and compare these operations with their analogs that lack an exclamation point. We already encountered the **!-** operator in action in Section 1.6, in the patch 01_17_pan.maxpat.

All of these operators also exist in MSP versions that generates a signal (**+~**, **-~**, ***~**, **/~**), which we have already used a few times in the previous chapter. MSP operators require a signal to be present on one of the two inlets (usually the left), and can receive either a signal or numeric values on their other inlet. (They can also use a single value provided as an argument.) For more information about operators and objects, remember that <Alt-Click> will bring up help patches when in edit mode.

THE INT AND FLOAT OBJECTS

Two objects exist that allow you to store values and recall these values later using a bang. They are **int** (for the storage of integers) and **float** (for floating point numbers).
In figure IA.11, we see that these objects possess two inlets; if a value is sent to the "hot" left inlet, the value is both stored and also immediately transmitted on the outlet, while if a value is sent to the "cold" right inlet, it is stored but not transmitted. To retrieve the stored value at any time from either of these objects, a bang can be sent to their left inlet, which will cause the value to be transmitted. In both cases, incoming values are copied into the object's memory (and can therefore be recalled with a bang whenever we'd like) until new values take their place.

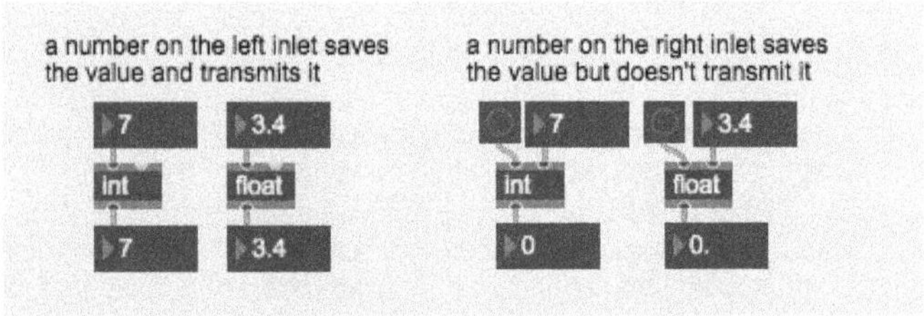

Fig. IA.11 The **int** and **float** objects

IA.2 GENERATING RANDOM NUMBERS

A random number generator is another feature that is seldom lacking in programming languages. Such a generator is particularly useful in an environment such as Max for creating scenarios that are not rigidly pre-determined. For example, we might want to be able to "humanize" the envelope of a series of sounds by adding a small but random quantity of time to every attack, or to "warm" a sound by lightly varying its frequencies with a small, indeterminate, offset, or even to "randomize" a phrase by probabilistically generating a set of notes within an interval. The object that generates random numbers in Max is called **random**, and it produces a new number every time it receives a bang. Build the patch in figure IA.12 to try it:

Fig. IA.12 A **random** number generator

The **random** object takes a numeric argument that indicates the range of numbers to be generated: if we call the argument 'n', the generated numbers will fall between 0 and n-1. In the case illustrated in the figure, the argument is 100, which means that the object will produce values between 0 and 99. Click a few times to verify this. (If we want numbers between 0 and 100, we would obviously type 101 as the argument.) If the range of numbers generated by **random** always starts (apparently) at 0, how can we generate numbers within some other range, say between 50 and 60? Based on what we know so far, a first, simple solution might be to generate random numbers for an equivalently-sized range starting at 0 (from 0 to 10 for this example, which implies an argument of 11), and then shift the range by adding an offset (in this case, 50) to the resulting numbers using the + object. Modify the patch as demonstrated in figure IA.13 to try this out.

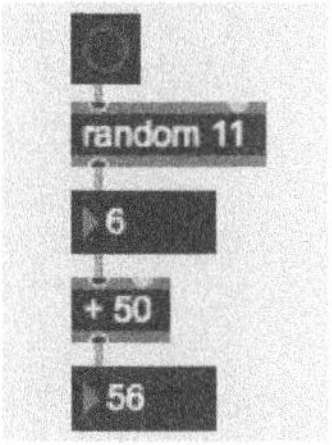

Fig. IA.13 Generating random numbers between 50 and 60

The **random** object has a right inlet that changes the value of its argument. If you connect a number box to this inlet, it is possible to modify the range of numbers being produced. For example, add a number box to the last patch, and use it to send the number 30 to **random**. Now the random numbers produced will vary between 0 and 29, and the addition object, by adding 50, will transform the numbers produced into values lying between 50 and 79.
If you also add a number box to the right inlet of the addition operator, you will be able to modify both the range and the base number from which it departs (as shown in figure IA.14).

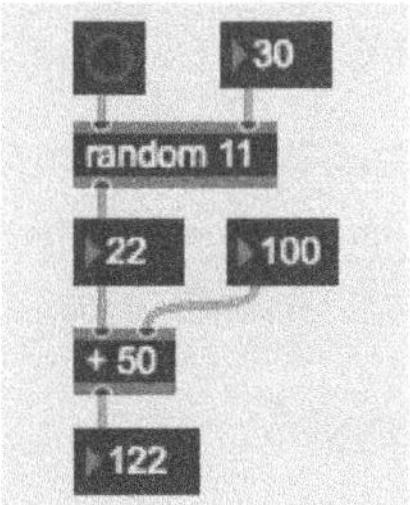

Fig. IA.14 Random numbers with a variable range

In the example shown in figure IA.14, we see that the new arguments sent from the number boxes are 30 for **random** (resulting in random numbers between 0 and 29) and 100 for the addition object. The results will be therefore numbers between 100 and 129.
Actually, if we send a list of two integer values to the right input of the **random** object, these values will be considered as the minimum and maximum random value (minus 1) that can be generated. But how can we send a list to the **random** object? We could use a message box, but the values entered into the object would not be editable in performance mode. It would be more interesting to have, for example, two number boxes with which we could vary the minimum and maximum values of the generated random numbers at will.

We will discuss the treatment of lists in depth in section IA.7, and for now let us introduce an object that, in its default configuration, combines two input numeric values into a list. This object is called **pak**: reconstruct the patch in Figure IA.15.

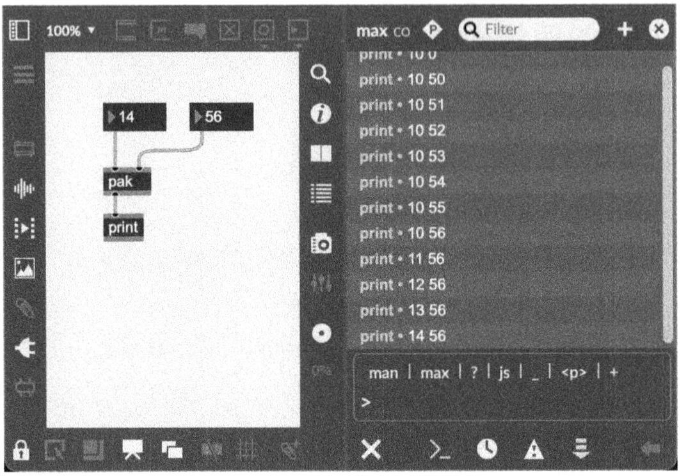

fig. IA.15: the **pak** object

We have connected two number boxes to the inputs of **pak** and a **print** object to its output. As you can see in the Max Console on the right, whenever a value is changed in the number boxes, the **pak** object generates a list of two elements.
If we connect the **pak** object to the right input of **random**, we can then define a range for the random numbers. Open the patch **IA_03_random_min_max.maxpat** (Figure IA.16).

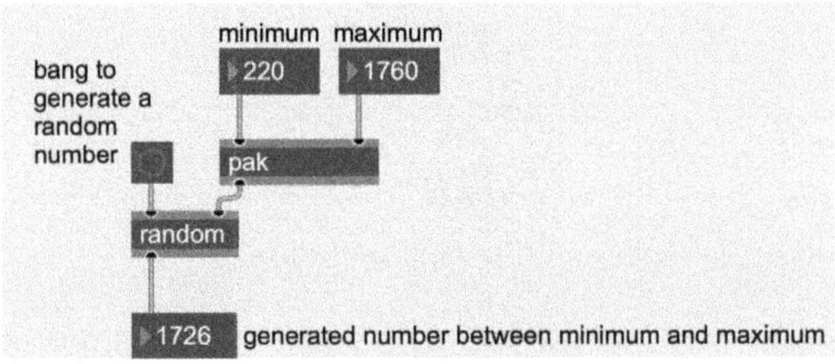

fig. IA.16: file **IA_03_random_min_max.maxpat**

In the example shown in the figure, the interval used lies between 220 and 1760. These two values correspond to frequencies in hertz for A below middle C and the A three octaves higher.
The values used in the example above suggest that we could use this patch to generate random frequencies to be sent to an oscillator, and this is exactly what we've done in the patch shown in figure IA.17, which we invite you to construct on your own using the previous file **IA_03_random_min_max.maxpat** as a

start. We have simply patched a **rect~** oscillator into the algorithm, as well as the few objects that are needed to hear generated sound. Using this simple modification, we can produce sounds at various integer frequencies[2] in the interval between 220 Hz and 1760 Hz.

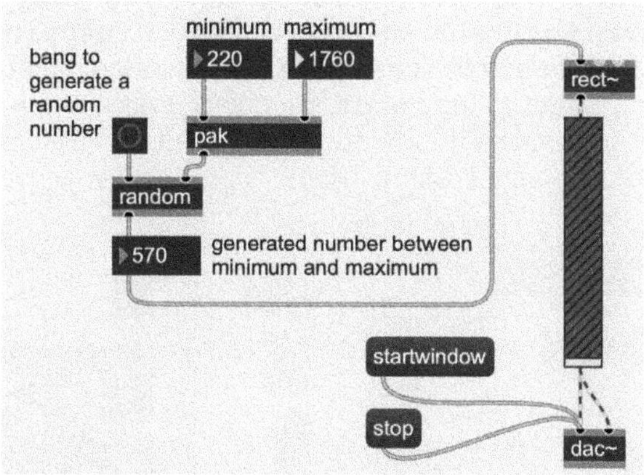

Fig. IA.17 Generating random frequencies between a minimum and a maximum

What if we want to generate only notes that are part of the chromatic scale? To generate frequencies that correspond only to tempered notes of the chromatic scale, we would need to first generate MIDI note numbers using **random**, and then afterwards convert these note numbers to frequency values using the **mtof** object. Here is a patch similar to the previous one that does this (see figure IA.18). Try patching this on your own.

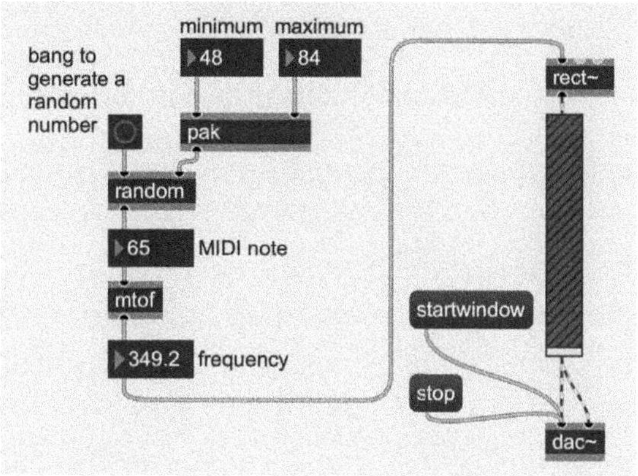

Fig. IA.18 Generating random MIDI notes between a minimum and a maximum pitch

[2] We use the term "integer frequencies" because by default the **random** object generates integers.

The maximum and minimum pitches are represented as MIDI note numbers, and these values are then converted into frequencies and sent to the **rect~** object. Let's add an envelope to this patch by using the **line~** and **function** objects as we did in Section 1.3 (see figure IA.19). The patch cord that leaves the + object at the bottom left is now connected to a number box labelled "MIDI note" and to a **button** that is itself connected to a **function** object. Every time that we send a bang to the **random** object, a random number is generated and another bang is sent to the **function** object, which in turn furnishes a list to a **line~** that generates an envelope that is used to scale the output of the **rect~** oscillator[3] via multiplication. Try it!

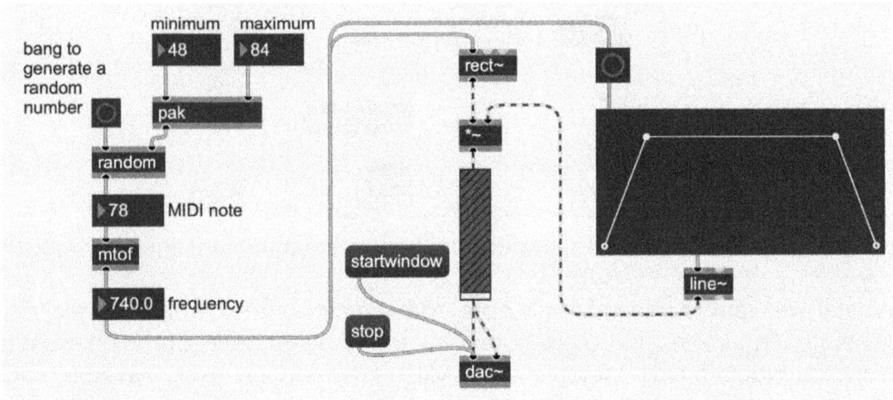

Fig. IA.19 Random notes, each with an envelope

[3] These are all things that we have already examined in detail in Section 1.3. If the function of the patch is not clear, try reviewing that section of the book.

IA.3 MANAGING TIME: THE METRO OBJECT

Until now, in order to produce an event we have had to click on some graphical element of a patch. This, however, is not always convenient, and so it is probable that someone out there is asking whether it is possible to create a series of events in Max (such as a phrase built out of notes) without having to start every single event "by hand". Naturally, the answer is yes: there are innumerable ways to produce more or less complex musical structures "programmatically" in Max.

We will demonstrate by starting with one of the most important objects for this purpose, the **metro** object, which represents a metronome that generates an endless sequence of bangs, each separated from its predecessor by a fixed time interval in milliseconds, given as the argument to the object. Make the patch shown in figure IA.20:

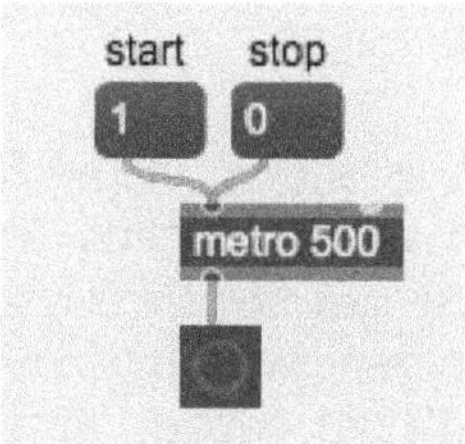

Fig. IA.20 The `metro` object

The two message boxes contain the numbers 1 and 0, which serve respectively to activate and stop the metronome. The argument of the `metro` is "500", which means that the object will produce a bang every half second (500 milliseconds). The button connected to the object gives us an easy way to actually see the generated sequence of bangs. If you would like to change the time between events, connect a number box to the right inlet of the `metro`. To start and stop the metronome, we can use a `toggle` object (which we first encountered in file 01_14_audiofile.maxpat); the `toggle` object is the fourth icon in the Top Patcher Window Toolbar. Every time that it receives a click, `toggle` alternates between a 1 and a 0, which is very useful in cases such as the current start/stop scenario. To try these changes out, modify the preceding patch in the manner shown in figure IA.21 and then click on the `toggle`.

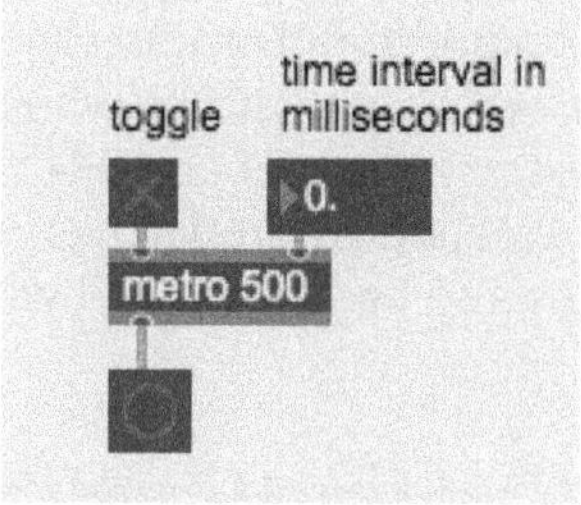

Fig. IA.21 Varying the time interval for a `metro`

We can use the **metro** object to generate a sequence of random notes, by applying it to the example patch that we implemented in figure IA.19. (The modifications can be seen in figure IA.22.)

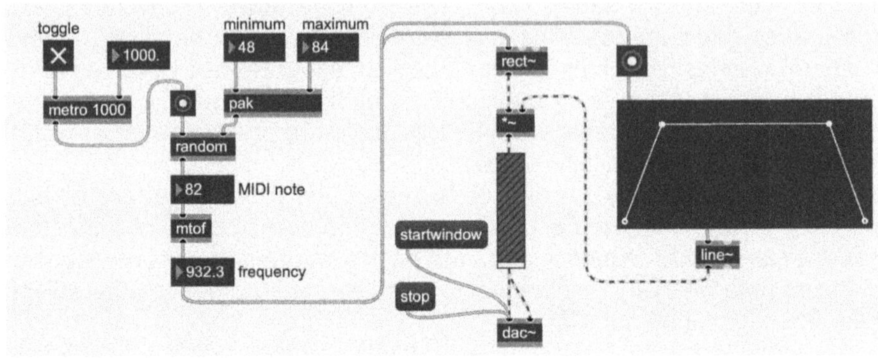

Fig. IA.22 A stream of random notes

Add the **metro** to the patch as shown in the figure, and you can use it to generate streams of notes at various speeds. You will notice a flaw in the patch: clicks are generated if the **metro** rate is less than 1000 milliseconds. This happens because the envelope generated by **line~** (which is defined as being 1000 milliseconds long) doesn't get enough time to terminate properly when the rate of the **metro** is less than 1000, and consequently the envelope jumps suddenly to 0 at the beginning of each new note. This can be heard as a click at the end of every note under 1000 milliseconds long. We will see soon how to link the duration of the envelope to the rate of the **metro**. Meanwhile, save the patch to disk; we will return to it shortly.[4]

IA.4 SUBPATCHES AND ABSTRACTIONS

THE SUBPATCH

Little by little, as our understanding of Max has grown, the complexity of our patches created has also grown. Sooner or later, the day will come when we need to implement an algorithm that will be too big for the computer screen! Even at our current level, tracing the path of data and understanding the behavior of an algorithm is starting to become difficult within the sea of little object boxes that defines a complex Max algorithm. Fortunately, the Max language permits the creation of **subpatches**, which are patches wholly contained within a single object box, which take the external form of an object box with inlets and outlets. The object that enables the creation of subpatches is called **patcher**, and it is so commonly used that it can also be abbreviated with just the letter '**p**'.

[4] As we already pointed out in Section 1.1, it would a very bad idea to save this patch using a name that happens to match an existing Max object. Therefore, don't call this patch *"random.maxpat"*, for example, or *"metro.maxpat"*. The better way to go would be to use a name composed of multiple words with spaces between them, such as *"random sequence.maxpat"*.

Reopen the patch from figure IA.22 (which we suggested that you save), go into edit mode, and create an object box in which you type "p random-minmax" (as shown in figure IA.23).

Fig. IA.23 The **patcher** object

Now press <Enter> or click in an empty spot in the Patcher Window. An empty window will appear, in edit mode, which has the title *[random-minmax]*.
The title of the window corresponds to the argument that we gave to the **patcher**, and is typed in brackets to indicate that it is not a free-standing Patcher Window, but instead, a patch that is contained within another patch. Arrange the windows in a way that you can see them both (that is to say, in a way that you can see both the window entitled *[random-minmax]* and the main window that contains the random-minmax **patcher** that we just created).
The argument given isn't used in any special way by the **patcher**, but it is always a good idea to name any **patcher** in a way that suggests the behavior that it implements. In the current example, we are about to create a random number generator that will generate numbers that span an interval ranging from some minimum to some maximum, and so we name it "random-minmax".
The *[random-minmax]* window shows the internal implementation of this **patcher**, and inside the window we will implement the patch, putting it in contact with the "outside world" (defined, in this case, as the Patcher Window containing the subpatch) by using inlets and outlets. To clarify how this is done, let's construct the subpatch, step-by-step.
Before anything else, we create some inlets; we will use the **inlet** object, which is in the "Basic" sub-category of the "Add" *palette* in the upper Toolbar, for this purpose (as seen in figure IA.24).

Fig. IA.24 The **inlet** object

After creating an **inlet** object on the inside of the *[random-minmax]* window, an inlet appears on the **patcher** in the main window (as shown in figure IA.25).

Fig. IA.25 A **patcher** object displaying an internal **inlet**

We add two more **inlet** objects at the top of the *[random-minmax]* window, and also an **outlet** (which is also available in the "Basic" sub-category of the "Add" *palette* in the upper Toolbar) at the bottom, and then we verify that the **patcher** object box in the main window now has three inlets and an outlet (as in figure IA.26). Note that **inlet** and **outlet** objects, as we add them, display numerical labels that correspond to a progressive order.

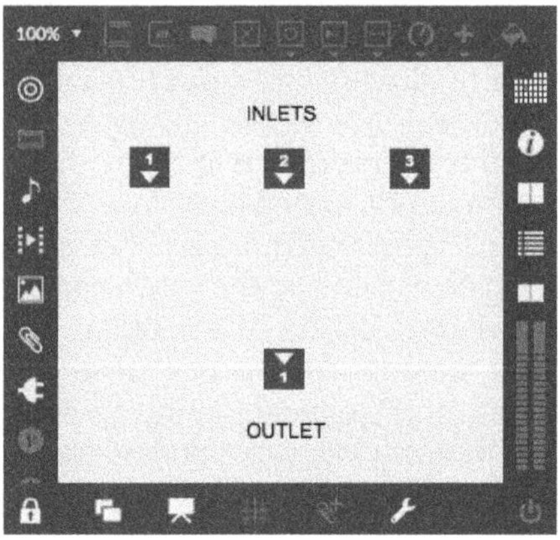

Fig. IA.26 The **inlet** objects and an **outlet** in a subpatch

We next need to copy the section of the main patch that generates random numbers between a minimum and a maximum. Select the relevant objects and press <Command-c/Control-c> to copy them, as in figure IA.27.

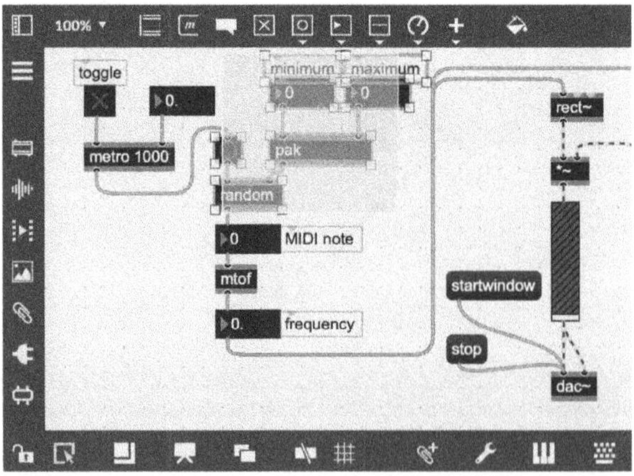

Fig. IA.27 Selecting the random generator portion of the patch

Now bring the *[random-minmax]* window to the front and paste the copied objects by pressing <Command-v/Control-v>. After this, connect the three **inlet** objects respectively to the button and to the two number boxes, and then connect the outlet of the + object to the **outlet** object, as in figure IA.28:

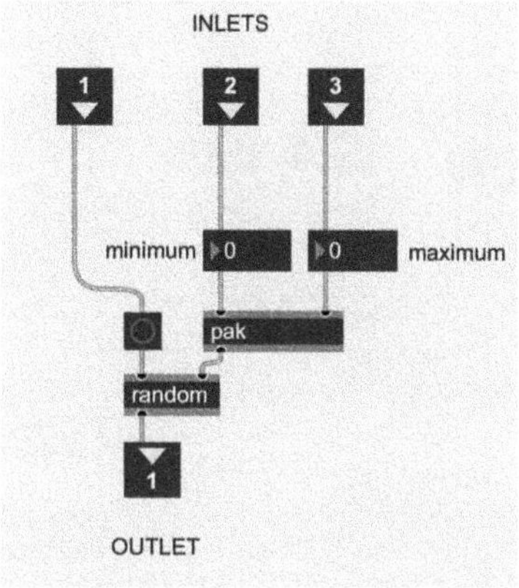

Fig. IA.28 Connecting the **inlet** and **outlet** objects of a subpatch

Next, return to the main window and delete the part of the algorithm that we just copied to the internal subpatch, taking care to preserve the two number boxes used to display the minimum and maximum limits for the random interval. Finally, connect the **patcher** object to the surrounding patch as illustrated in figure IA.29:

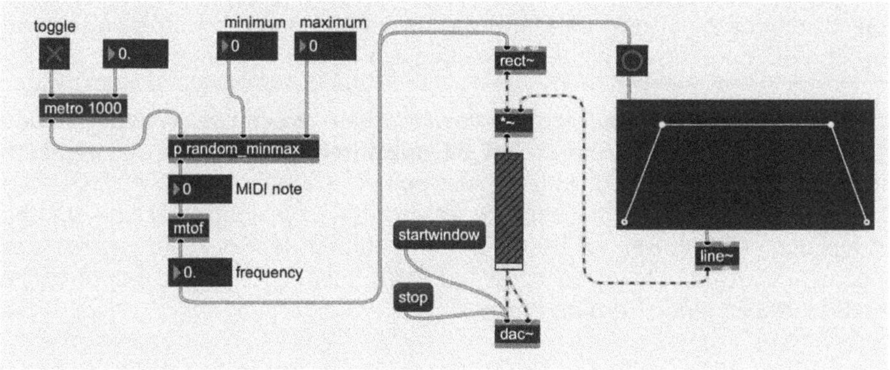

Fig. IA.29 The operational subpatch

The **patcher** now contains the algorithm for generating random numbers, and this algorithm can be used in Max like any other little box. Put both Patcher Windows into performance mode and make sure that the patch behaves in the same way that it did before by generating a random stream of notes and varying the parameters. It is possible to close the *[random-minmax]* window and then reopen it by double-clicking (in performance mode) on the **patcher** object.

Another way to create a subpatch is to select a group of objects that you would like to insert into a new object and then choose the ***Encapsulate*** item from the *Edit* menu. Try, for example, to change the oscillator section into a subpatch that takes a MIDI note number on its inlet, and that produces a signal outlet. To do this, first, select the section of the patch that is relevant, that is, from the number box "MIDI note" to the multiplier connected to the **gain~** object. (as in figure IA.30):

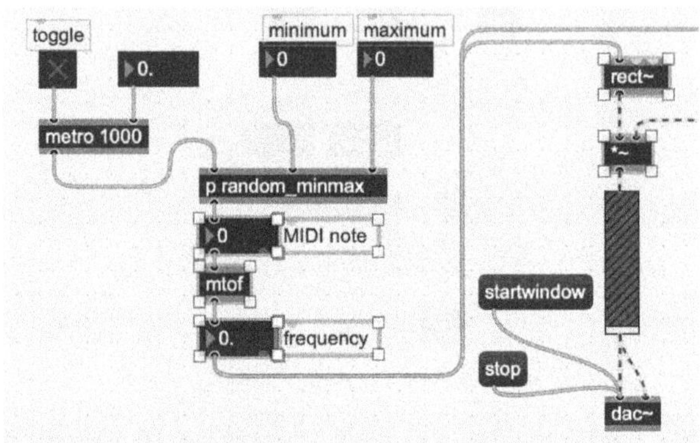

Fig. IA.30 Selecting the oscillator block

After this, select the *Encapsulate* item from the *Edit* menu[5] and the group of objects will "magically" reappear in a **patcher** that has no arguments. Type in a name argument to illuminate the function of the object, perhaps, for example, "oscillator", and then clean up and compact the patch so that it occupies less space. In figure IA.31 we see how this might finally look: note that, to accommodate our user interface, the **button** connected to the **function** object must now receive its bang directly from the **metro** object.

If you have had any problems following these examples, we've included the completed patch in the file **IA_04_subpatch.maxpat**. We recommend, however, that you try to build it on your own.
It is possible to modify a subpatch at any time by double-clicking on the corresponding **patcher** and putting it into edit mode. Note that patches and subpatches are able to move back and forth between edit and performance modes independently from each other.

[5] You can also use the keyboard shortcut <Mac: Shift-Command–e>, <Win: Shift-Control–e>.

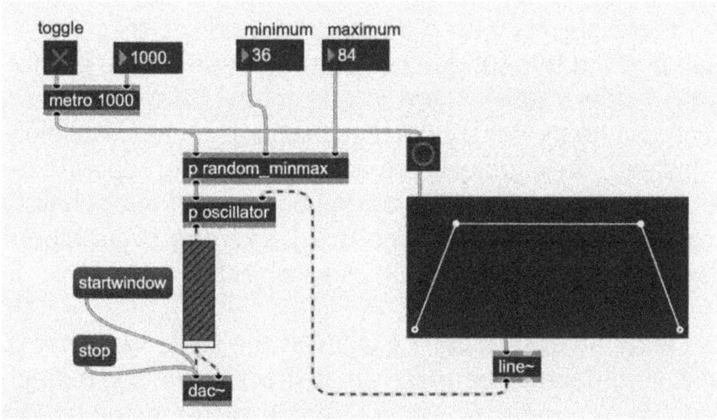

Fig. IA.31 Adding a second subpatch

ABSTRACTIONS

The **`patcher`** object is useful, as we have seen, for collapsing and hiding the interconnected objects of an algorithm in a single object box that performs the algorithm. But if we decide that we want to use this algorithm in a different patch than the one in which it was created, we have a problem: the only way to use it in a different patch is to copy and paste it into the new Patcher Window. Wouldn't it be nicer to be able to pack an algorithm into a "real" object that we could reuse simply by typing its name into an object box, exactly as we do with standard Max objects? The good news is that some patches *can* be reused in this way, as though they were objects. Key to this usage is that Max knows where to find them.

Look for the file **IA_05_abstraction.maxpat** to see a completed example (shown in figure IA.32).

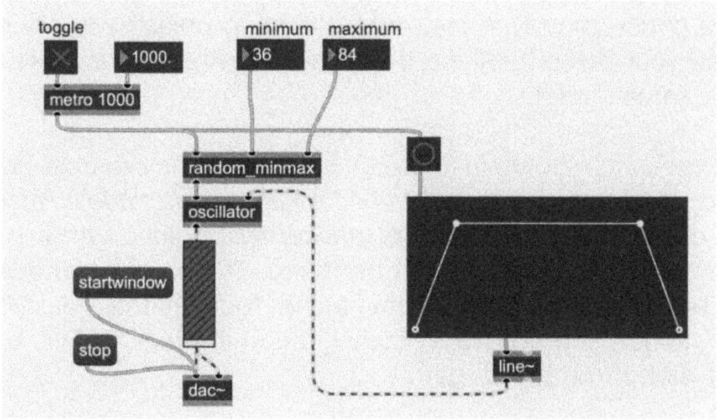

Fig. IA.32 The file IA_05_abstraction.maxpat

This patch is almost the same as the preceding one, the only difference being that in place of the two **`patcher`** objects that had as their arguments "random-minmax" and "oscillator", there are now two external objects whose names are **`random-minmax`** and **`oscillator`**.

We can open these objects with a double-click and see that their internals are exactly the same as the two subpatches that we made for the previous example, but we can no longer modify them in edit mode. This difference isn't trivial: the two objects are no longer subpatches that are stored completely within the main patch. Instead, these objects are actually stored in separate external files, and Max has loaded these files into the subpatches on our behalf. This kind of Max file is called an **abstraction**, and is a packaging of an algorithm that is meant to be used over and over again as an object.

How do you create an abstraction? Exactly in the same way that you create a patch. There is no difference between an abstraction file and a patch file; when we create a patch or an abstraction and save it with a name (among files that we've already used, for example, names might be *01_06_glissandi* or *oscillator*), Max creates a file that can be loaded as either an autonomous patch or as an abstraction that is usable as an object from any Patcher Window.
An abstraction can be used simply by typing the name without its extension (for example, *oscillator* rather than *oscillator.maxpat*) into an object box. You need to pay a little attention to managing your file locations on disk, of course, to be sure that everything will work. Returning to the two external objects named `random-minmax` and `oscillator`, for example, where are their abstraction files located? In the folder *"MaxMSP Patches/Interlude A Patches"* – if you look at the contents of this folder, you will find two files called, respectively, **random-minmax.maxpat** and **oscillator.maxpat**. Whenever Max opens or creates a patch, it recursively loads any external objects that it needs into memory, first searching for them in the folder that contains the patch being loaded, and, if they are not found, then stepping through the folders of the search path. (These folders are partially pre-defined and partially user-specified within the File Preferences window, which you remember can be called up from the *Options* menu.
This discussion should have now clearly revealed why it is important that you never save a patch using the name of an existing object: you are risking that Max will load your patch (thinking that it is an abstraction) in place of the real object of the same name!

Referring to the patch shown in figure IA.32, the objects `random-minmax` and `oscillator` load from the folder *"MaxMSP Patches/Interlude A Patches"*, while the `line~` object loads from the *"msp-externals"* folder, which is the folder where the standard MSP objects can be found. The objects `random-minmax` and `oscillator` are visible only from patches found in the *"MaxMSP Patches/ Interlude A"* folder, and not from patches found in other folders, because this folder is not part of the search path.

To make a non standard object (such as the abstractions that we have been discussing) visible from other any other patch, you need to put it into a folder that is already part of the search path, or else add the folder containing it to the search path by using the File Preferences[6] window or, as we touched on in Section 1.5, we can place the object in the user library folder "{User Name}/ Documents/Max 9/Library" (substituting, as always, the account name you use on your computer for {User Name}). We could, for example, create a folder named "my abstractions" and then include it by using the File Preferences window to add its path; alternatively, we could place it into the user library folder. In this way, every patch saved in the "my abstractions" folder (or in any of its subfolders) will be usable as an abstraction within other Max patches, independent of where it is located.
Recapping these rules for clarity:

- If you want your abstractions to be visible only to the patches found in a specific folder, place the abstractions in that specific folder. When this technique is used, patches in other folders will know nothing about the existence of these abstractions.
- If, however, you want your abstractions to be visible to any and all Max patches, place these abstractions into a folder that is already part of the Max search path, or else into a folder that you will add to the search path by using the File Preferences window.

Returning for a moment to the *Virtual Sound Macros* library, this folder and its subfolders contains dozens of objects that will be used during the course of this book. You will remember that we have already encountered one of these objects: `vs.square~`. We can now see that this object is, in fact, just another abstraction. If you create an instance of it in an empty patcher, and then double click on it this object in performance mode, it will open into a window that reveals the internals of the patch.

Besides abstractions, it is also possible to create external objects using programming languages such as C and Java. There are dozens of object libraries containing externals and abstractions available on the web, some freely downloadable, and some available for purchase. You can also install the libraries (Packages) that Cycling '74 makes available directly from Max through the **Package Manager**: select the *Show Package Manager* item from the File menu. The Package Manager window will appear; we can use it to install dozens of very useful extensions.

One last tip: you have seen that by double-clicking on a `patcher` object that contains a subpatch, you can open a window in which you can view the contents of the object and modify them in edit mode. In the case of an abstraction, you

---

[6] To include a new folder in the File Preferences window, click on the "+" symbol at the bottom left of the window. This will create a new path that contains a "choose" button in place of a file path. Click on this button to select the folder that you would like to include.

have found that you can view its contents with a double-click, but you cannot modify them by switching to edit mode.

How then, can you work on abstractions? You know that these objects are backed by files on disk, and it turns out that these files can be loaded directly from disk and edited like any other patch. To load the file for an abstraction once you've got it open, you can click on the third icon in the Bottom Patcher Window Toolbar at the bottom of the relevant Patcher Window. (The icon depicting two overlapping white rectangles.) This button will open a menu from which you can select an item labeled "Open Original", which is exactly what you are trying to do. Once the abstraction is modified and saved to disk, all of the patches that contain it will immediately use the new version.

To conclude this section, we will reiterate the various types of objects that can be used in Max:

1) Standard objects: these are part of the "standard distribution" of Max and are found in a folder named "*externals*" that is installed along with the program.

2) Subpatches: these are Max patches that are stored internally within another patch. As we have seen, it is possible to create subpatches by using the **`patcher`** object.

3) Abstractions: these are Max patches that are used as objects in other patches. To be "seen" by applications, they must be put into folders that are part of Max's search path (see above). There are many abstractions implemented by the Max user community which are available on the web. Additionally, the Virtual Sound Macros library is made up almost entirely of abstractions created specifically for this book.

4) Third party externals: these are written by programmers using programming languages other than Max, and are available on the Web either for sale or as freely downloadable libraries. These objects add to the capabilities of Max, and most are written in C. Like abstractions, third party externals must be put into a folder that is part of Max's search path. We don't discuss this kind of external in the course of this text, be we do indicate some of the most interesting libraries on the "Useful Max Links" page that can be found on www.virtual-sound.com/cmsupport.

5) Java and Javascript objects: it is possible to write code using the Java and Javascript languages, and to store this code within Max objects specifically designed contain such code, such as **`mxj`**, **`js`**, and **`jsui`**. We will not discuss these objects, because programming in Java and Javascript is far beyond the scope of this book.

IA.5 OTHER RANDOM NUMBER GENERATORS

So far, we have used the **random** object to generate integer random numbers. If we want to generate floating-point numbers, we need to write a numeric argument with a decimal point (as we have already seen for mathematical operators): see Figure IA.33.

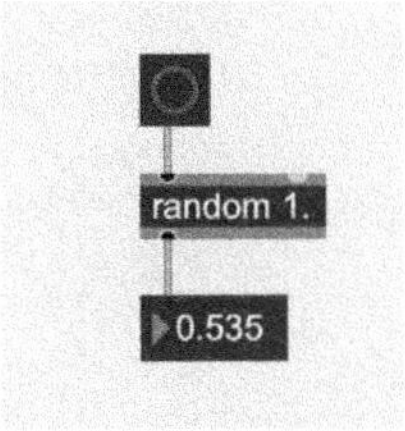

fig. IA.33: generating decimal numbers between 0 and 1

If we do not want to add an argument to the object, or if for any reason we want to alternate between floats and integers, we can turn on (or off) the "floatoutput" attribute.
To change attribute values directly in the patch in performance mode (i.e. without using the inspector), we can use the **attrui** object (the name stands for ATTRibute User Interface). This object, connected to any other object, allows us to view and modify its attributes (see Fig. IA.34a).

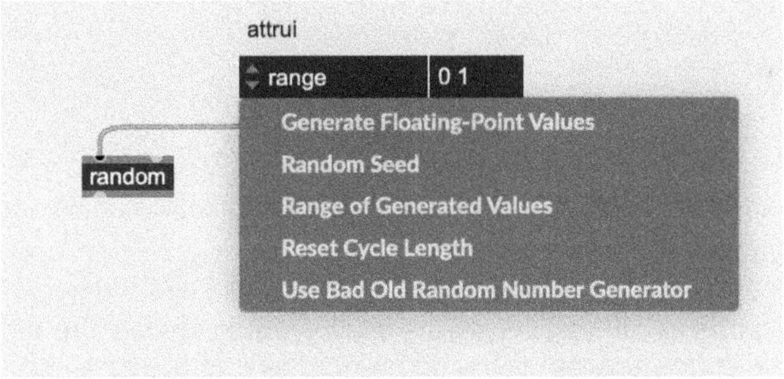

fig. IA.34a: the **attrui** object connected to the **random** object

In the figure we see an **attrui** object linked to the **random** object: on the left you can see the name of the attribute ("range") and on the right the relative value ("0 1"). If you click on the attribute name, a drop-down menu appears with a list of all attributes of the linked object.
The **attrui** object can be created as usual by calling (with the 'n' key) a generic object box and writing the name "attrui" into it.

Another, faster method is to select an attribute of the object we are interested in from the Object Action Menu[7] (see Figs. 1.16b and 1.16c in Section 1.1): an **attrui** linked to the object with the selected attribute will appear (see Fig. IA.34b).

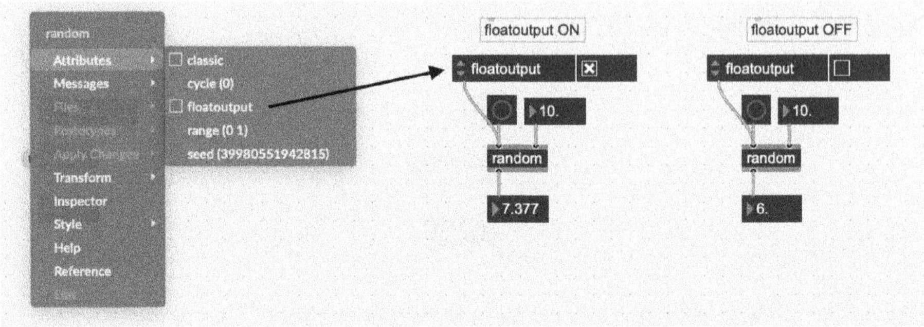

fig. IA.34b: **attrui** created with the Object Action Menu

As we saw in Section IA.2, if we want to generate random numbers between a minimum and a maximum, we have to send a list of two elements to the **random** object via a message box or objects that handle lists, such as **pak**.
If we want the same functionality using a single object, we can use the **vs.between** object from the Virtual Sound Macros library: this object generates integer or floating point numbers between a given minimum and maximum[8] (as seen in figure IA.35).

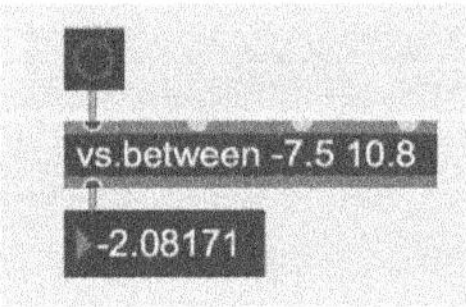

Fig. IA.35 The **vs.between** object

The two arguments of **vs.between** allow you to define the limits of the interval in which to generate the random numbers; in the case shown, we are generating numbers between -7.5 and 10.8.
The second and third inlets of **vs.between** enable you to modify these limits on the fly. Let's look at an application of this object: build the patch shown in figure IA.36 to try it out. The generator on the left produces MIDI note numbers between 36 and 95,[9] while the generator on the right produces intensity values in deciBels between -20 and 0. The MIDI note numbers are converted into frequencies, while

[7] We remind you that the Object Action icon (a triangle in a circle) appears when you move the mouse to the left side of the object.
[8] Note that this object is simply an abstraction that contains the **random** and **pak** objects. You can verify this by opening it with a double-click (in performance mode).
[9] When **vs.between** generates integers, these will be found between the minimum value and the maximum value minus 1.

the deciBel values are converted into raw amplitude values using **dbtoa**. Note that the object **vs.between** on the right has two arguments: "0." and "0." (both using a decimal point). These arguments are present only to tell the object to generate floating point numbers; in their absence, or with integer arguments given, **vs.between** would generate integer values only for the dB values, and we would therefore have had less fidelity in the amplitude dimension.

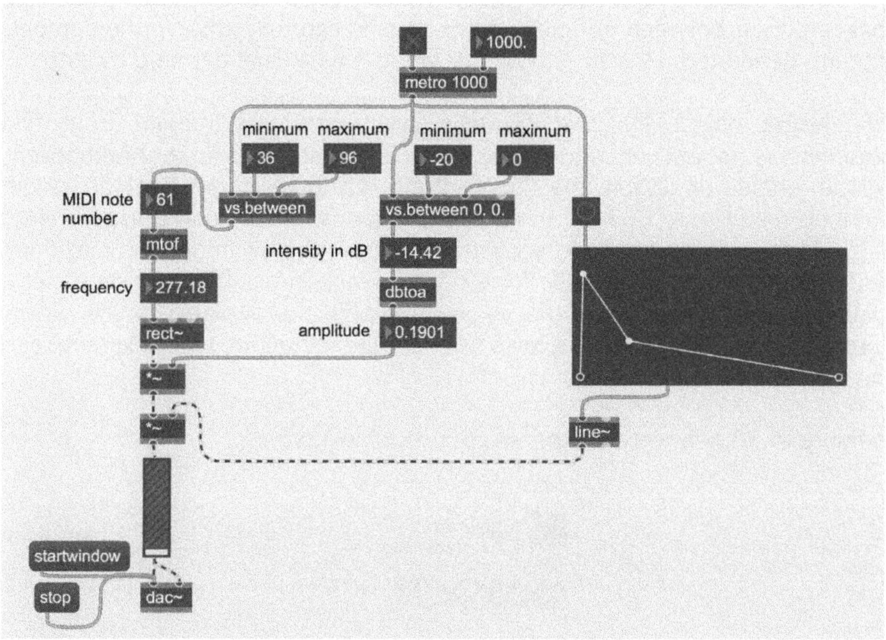

Fig. IA.36 An application of **vs.between**

There is another interesting random number generator that is part of the standard Max library: **drunk**. This object accepts two arguments and generates random numbers in the interval between 0 and the first argument. However, any two values generated in succession are guaranteed to diverge by no more than a value (called step size) that is defined by the interval between 0 and the second argument.

Observe the patch shown in figure IA.37, which we invite you to try yourself:

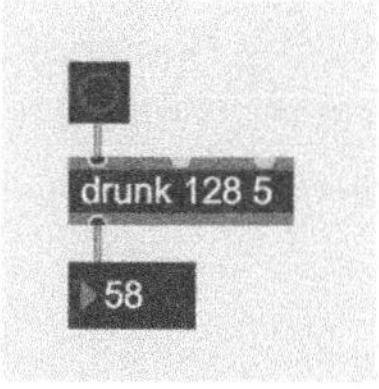

Fig. IA.37 The **drunk** random number generator

In this case, **drunk** generates random integers between 0 and 128, moving between succeeding values by adding a number between -4 and 4.
Try generating a series of numbers and you will see that between one number and the next there is a jump that is always less than 5 – the object implements what is called a "random walk" (or a "drunkard's walk"). Add a number box to its center inlet (which corresponds to the maximum number that can be generated) and also to the right inlet (which corresponds to the maximum leap that can occur between numbers, minus 1), and carefully observe the numbers that are generated, as well as how the random walk changes step by step.

The **drunk** object, like the **random** object, produces integers if its first argument is an integer, and floats if the argument is a float. Alternatively, we can enable or disable the "floatoutput" attribute to get float or integer numbers (see Figure IA.34b). In addition, it is possible to send a list of values (e.g., via the **pak** object) to its second input to set the minimum and maximum values of the "random walk". If we do not want to use two objects to set a minimum and a maximum, the **vs.drunk** object is available in the Virtual Sound Macros library, which allows us to set the minimum, the maximum, and the step size as arguments.

In figure IA.38, we see how the **vs.drunk** object works:

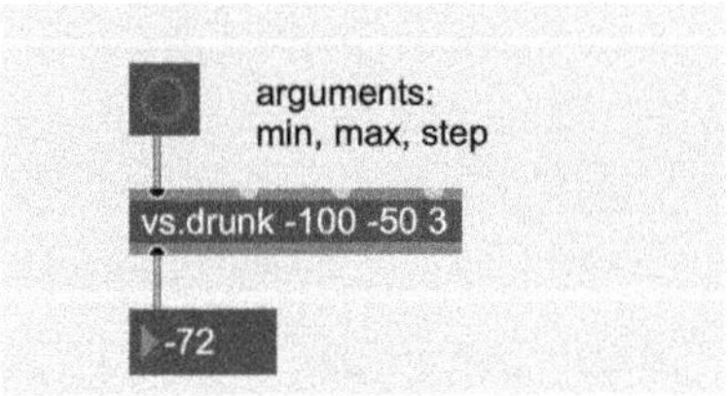

Fig. IA.38 the **vs.drunk** object

The object can take three arguments that set the minimum, maximum, and step size, that is, the random distance between one number and the next. If at least one of the minimum and maximum arguments is a float, we will have floating point values in the output, otherwise we will have integer values. Inlets number 2, 3, and 4 are used to modify these arguments. Now let us see the object in action, open the file **IA_06_random_walk.maxpat** (as shown in figure IA.39).

This patch is a modified version of the one shown in Fig. IA.36. The **vs.drunk** object is used to generate MIDI values, while **vs.between** adjusts the intensity similarly to the same object in Fig. IA.36.

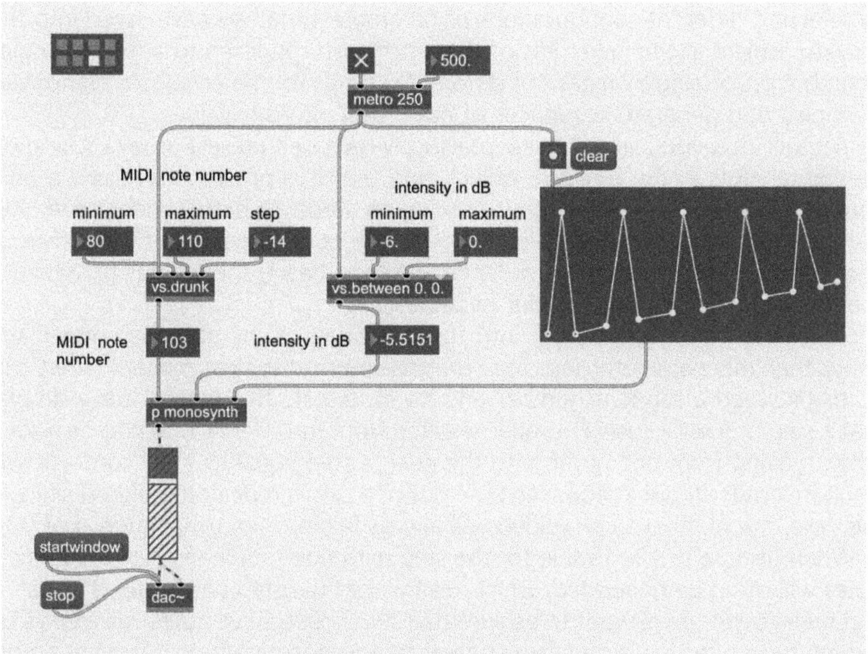

Fig. IA.39 The file **IA_06_random_walk.maxpat**

The lower subpatch, named **monosynth**, contains the now familiar **rect~** generator, and a **line~** object to implement its envelope. You can see the subpatch in figure IA.40.

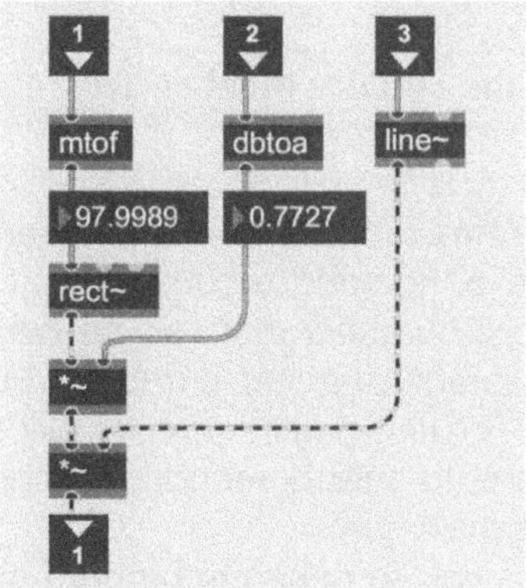

Fig. IA.40 Internals of the **monosynth** subpatch

As you can see, the first **inlet** of the subpatch is connected to an **mtof** converter, which converts MIDI note numbers to frequency in hertz, while the second is connected to a **dbtoa** object, which converts values in deciBels into raw amplitude values. The last **inlet** is connected to the **line~** object, which, as we have seen, is used for the envelope.

By selecting different configurations of parameters that we have saved into the `preset` object at the lower left of the patch, you can listen to a few examples of timbre processing by means of different settings for the envelope, along with examples that generate sequences of notes and intensity values.
Remember that you can call these previously recorded presets up by clicking on the lighter dots in the `preset` object, and that it is possible to record a new configuration into a preset by shift-clicking on a dot. To better understand how note sequence are generated, let's look at the values produced by `vs.drunk` and select different presets in order to see (and hear!) the various possibilities produced by the random number generator.
Let's delve a little more deeply into the operation of the **step** parameter: we know that this parameter indicates the maximum distance, minus 1, that can occur between a random number and its successor. This means, for example, that a step of 5 will cause a number selected from the interval 0 to 4 to be added when moving from one number to the next; a step equal to 1, by contrast, will result in a monotonous sequence built out of a single repeated number, since in this case, the number to be added will always fall into the trivial interval of 0 to 0. When using a smallish value for the step parameter, perhaps 2 or 3, identical notes will often be generated, which means that the step parameter is equal to 0 in many cases; if we want to be sure that two consecutive notes will always be different, we need use a *negative* number for the step parameter (which is simply a convention established by the programmer who created the `drunk` object). A negative step size sent to the object will select an interval between 1 and the absolute value of the step parameter, minus 1. This guarantees that the distance between one number and the next will not be 0; a step of -2, for example, will ensure that the notes will always move chromatically (all with a distance of 1), while a step of -3 generates movement by either a whole step or a half step.

Finally, let us summarize the random number generators we have discussed in this section:

`random`	Generates random numbers whenever it receives a bang. It has a numeric argument that specifies the range of random numbers that can be generated: if the argument is an integer, integer numbers will be generated; if it is a float, floating-point numbers will be generated. A list can be used to specify random numbers between a minimum and a maximum.
`vs.between`	Allows you to generate random numbers, integer or float, between a minimum and a maximum.
`drunk`	Takes two arguments and generates random numbers (integer or float) between 0 and the first argument. However, two successively generated values can only differ by a distance (step) between 0 and the second argument minus 1. If the step is a negative value, the same random number will not be generated twice in a row.
`vs.drunk`	Generates random walks between a minimum and a maximum (integer or float).

IA.6 MESSAGE ORDERING WITH TRIGGER

Continuing our presentation of fundamental Max objects, let's discuss **`trigger`**, an object that enables you to repeat an incoming message on multiple outlets. This object accepts a variable number of arguments; these arguments indicate the type and the number of outlets to be created. Build the patch shown in figure IA.41:

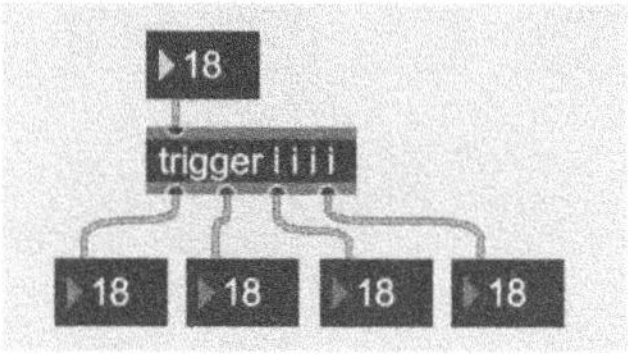

Fig. IA.41 The `trigger` object

We have given the object 4 'i' arguments, which cause the object to have 4 outlets of integer type. The 'i' is an argument that specifies a type for a corresponding outlet of `trigger`. If we connect four number boxes to the resulting outlets, we will see four copies of the number on the inlet produced. To what purpose are four copies of the same number? To control the order in which the copies are delivered! You already know that the order of execution of Max objects goes from right to left, which means that the first message to be delivered from this particular `trigger` object will be from its fourth outlet, the one farthest to the right. If we need to be sure that some object receives a number before others do, it will suffice to connect it to the farthest right outlet of `trigger`.
We see an example of message delivery order in the following patch, figure IA.42, which doesn't use `trigger`. (Remember that if you want to align the objects in columns as shown, select the row or column of objects in question a press <Command-y/Control-Shift-a>.)

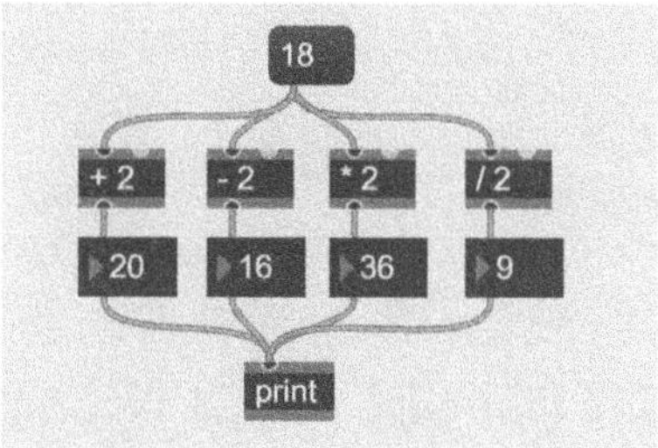

Fig. IA.42 Simultaneous operations

If you click on the message box that contains the number 18, you will see the results of the four operations show up in the Max window in the following order: 9, 36, 16, 20. As we already know, this shows that the first operation to be executed is the farthest to the right, and the last is the farthest to the left.

Now, let's change the order of division and multiplication to that shown in figure IA.43:

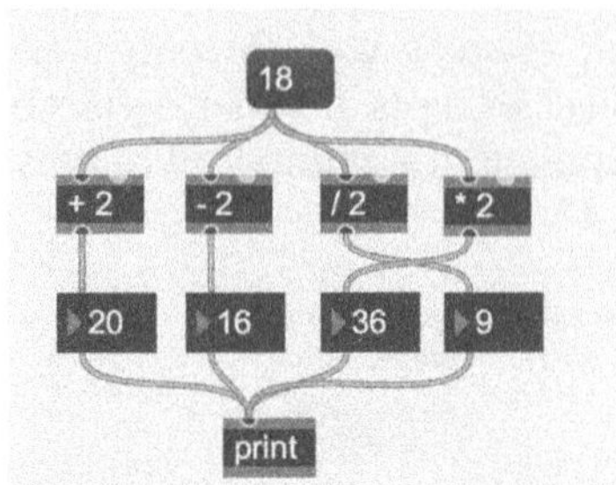

Fig. IA.43 Crossed messages

This time, when you click on the message box, the results in the Max window are 36, 9, 16, 20, showing that the multiplication is executed first. We can begin to understand Max's implementation of messaging better: the number box that is connected to the multiplication object is found to the left of the one connected to the division object (meaning that you might think that it would execute after the number box on its right). Yet the result of the multiplication is the first thing to be shown by `print`. This happens because the result of the multiplication, the number 36, is free to propagate all of the way to the `print` object at the bottom of the patch, without having to wait for any other results. Only at this point does message flow need to return to the top of the patch, where the number 18 in the message box is routed to the division object, the second operation from the right. Again the result flows all of the way to the `print` object, after which control passes to subtraction, and then finally to addition.
Try now to apply a `trigger` to this patch, as shown in figure IA.44. Note that we have used the abbreviated name '`t`' for the object. Like `patcher` objects, `trigger` objects are used very frequently, and so they can be abbreviated by their first letter.

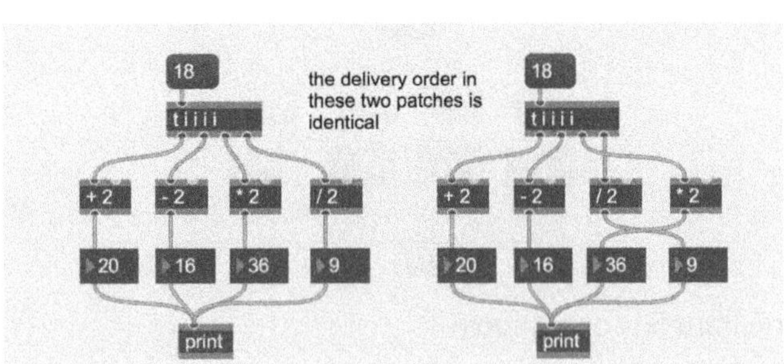

Fig. IA.44 Crossed messages with a `trigger` object

When we now swap the positions of the multiplication object and the division object (as in the right part of the figure), the resulting order printed in the Max window doesn't change, because the division operation is always performed first. This is due to the fact that the / object is connected to the rightmost outlet of trigger. Try this out!

The **trigger** object is not restricted to integers. It can also produce other kinds of messages, as shown in figure IA.45:

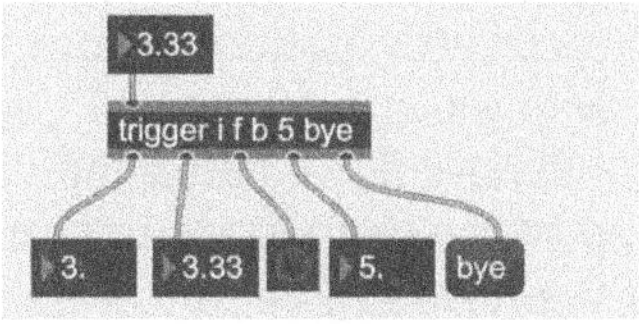

Fig. IA.45 Different arguments to **trigger**

In this patch (which we encourage you to try), we have provided 5 different arguments: '**i**' is an integer, '**f**' is a floating point number, '**b**' is a bang, '5' is a constant, and "bye" is a constant string. When given a number at the input, the first two arguments ('i' and 'f') will convert it into an integer and a floating point number (the integer will be truncated, as we see where 3.33 becomes 3), while the other three arguments are changed into a bang, a constant number 5, and a constant string "bye". Note that to be able to display the string "bye" within the message box, we have connected the trigger outlet to the right inlet of the message box, not the left! The left inlet is reserved for some commands that we will encounter later on in this interlude.[10]

So the **trigger** object, as you can see, does more than order messages: it can also change the type of a message or transform it into a constant. This characteristic is very useful, for example, when we want to obtain a result when sending a message to an operator's "cold" inlet, as seen in figure IA.46.

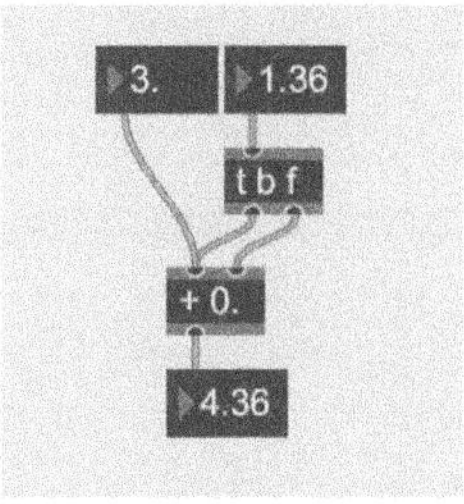

Fig. IA.46 Another way to make a cold inlet hot

With this approach, every time that we update the float number box on the right, the **trigger** first sends the number on its right outlet, followed by a bang on its left outlet which forces the + object to perform its calculation. Try using this technique in the "drunk-between" patcher in file IA_06_random_walk.maxpat, substituting **trigger** for the **button**, and verify that the patch's function doesn't change.

---

[10] This is clearly an exception to the rule that the "hot" inlet of an object is on the left. The right inlet of message box was added in Version 5 of Max, to make it easier to use. In earlier versions, it was necessary to use the left inlet to carry out a more complicated operation in order to display a message in a message box, which we will discuss fully in Section IA.8.

In more complex patches, it is often difficult to set the order of execution between elements based solely on the positions of the objects in their patcher. In these cases, `trigger` is an invaluable object. Return, for example, to the patch in figure IA.4, in Section IA.1, where the incorrectly positioned `button` caused an erroneous result. By using a `trigger` with the arguments "*b i*", we could have ensured that the bang to the left inlet would have arrived after the numeric value on the right.
In conclusion, here is a recap of the various arguments for the `trigger` object, as well as a few more that we have not yet encountered:

i integer
f floating point number
b bang
l list (a message composed of elements, discussed in Section 1.3 and IA.7)
s symbol (also known as a string – for example "open", "close", "johnny" etc.)

Any other arguments are interpreted as constants; for example, if you use "55" as the first argument, trigger will generate the value 55 on the first outlet whenever it receives a message on its inlet.

IA.7 OBJECTS FOR MANAGING LISTS

You have already learned about lists in Section 1.3, where we used them to create segments for the `line~` object. Let's look at some of the other ways in which they are useful.

THE UNPACK AND UNJOIN OBJECTS

A list, as you know, is a message composed of multiple elements, which can be unpacked using the **unpack** object, which needs as many arguments as there are elements in the list. Each argument serves to specify the type of an element. In figure IA.47a, we see an example (which you should build, as usual).

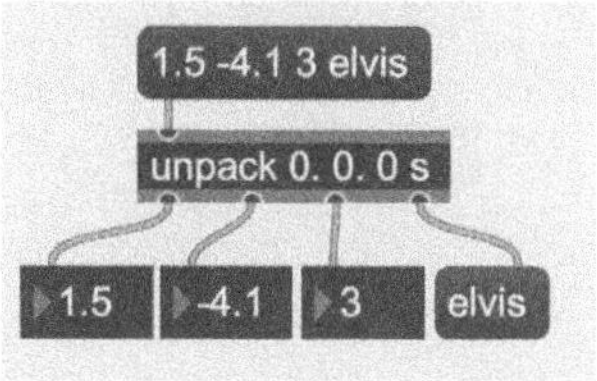

Fig. IA.47a The `unpack` object

In this example, a message box containing a list of four elements is connected to an `unpack` object which has four arguments: the first two are floating point numbers, the third is an integer, and the fourth is a string or a symbol (represented by the letter 's'). Clicking on the message box, the four elements are separated and sent to number and message boxes connected to `unpack`. (As we saw in the preceding section, to display a message sent to a message box, we must send it to the right inlet.)
Another object that breaks lists into pieces is the **unjoin** object, which takes a numeric argument that specifies how many elements it should extract from any list that arrives on its inlet. (See fig. IA 47b.)

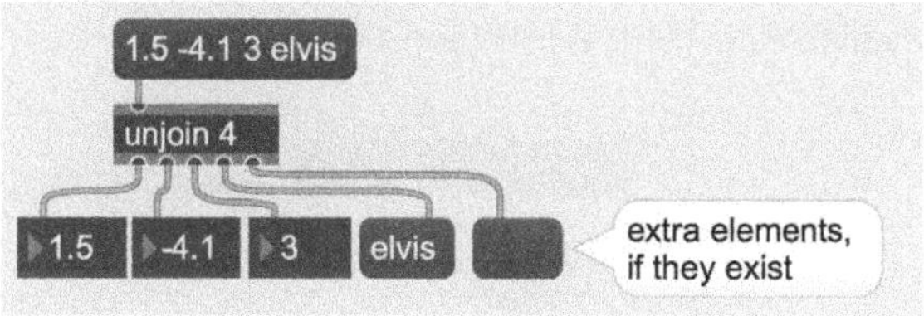

fig. IA.47b: the `unjoin` object

In this case, it isn't necessary to specify the types of the list items being unpacked (whether they are numbers, integers, floats, or strings). As you can see, the argument for the object in the example is 4, which signifies that the object will be able to break a list arriving on its inlet into four parts. But notice that the `unjoin` object in the figure has five outlets rather than four; the final outlet is there to handle the possibility that there might be more elements in the list than specified by the argument. If, for example, we send the list [1 2 3 4 5 6 7] to the object in the figure, the first four list elements will be unpacked and passed to the first four outlets, while the remaining elements will be passed as a list [5 6 7] to the fifth and final outlet. (Build this patch to try this out.)

THE PACK AND JOIN OBJECTS

A series of independent elements can be packed together into a list by using the **pack** object, which takes as many arguments as there are elements in the list. Each arguments specifies the type of the element and its initial value. In figure IA.48a, we see an example (which you should recreate!):

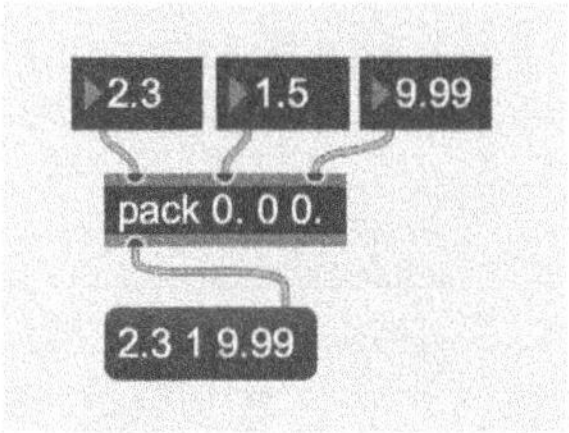

Fig. IA.48a The `pack` object

Here, three number boxes are connected to a **pack** object that has three arguments: a floating point number, an integer, and another floating point number. The object gathers the three numbers together into a list, which we can inspect by sending it to the right inlet of a message box. If you try modifying the number boxes, note that the message box updates only when the number on the left is modified, exactly like most other Max objects. Note also that since the second argument of **pack** is an integer, if you send a floating point number to the second inlet, it will be truncated and transformed into an integer. Referring to figure IA.48 we see that sending the second inlet the number 1.5, the second element of the list is the integer 1.

A second object that can be used to construct lists from individual elements is the **join** object, which takes a numeric argument that specifies the number of inlets to make available to form a list. (See fig. IA.48b.)

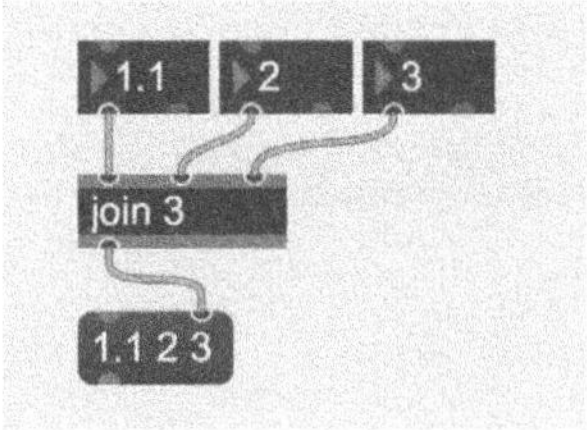

fig. IA.48b: the `join` object

In this figure, which we encourage you to build yourself, you will see a **join** object being used to create a list that contains three elements. Each inlet can receive messages of any type: integers, floats, strings, or more interestingly, lists. What this means is that it is possible to build lists with more elements than were originally specified by the numeric argument of the **join** object.

Try this by building the example patch shown in figure IA.48c.

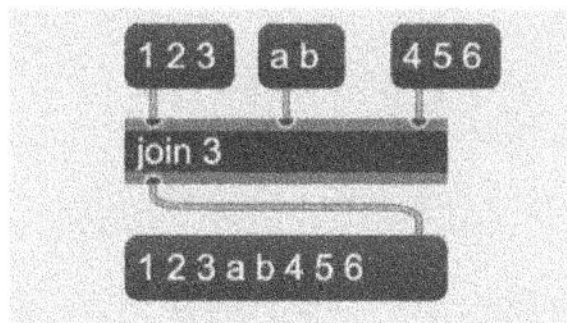

fig. IA.48c: sending lists to a **join** object

In this example, we have formed a list containing eight elements by sending lists on each of its three inlets.
Based on this capability, the **join** object might seem to be more flexible than **pack**, but in some cases, **pack** is indispensable. For example, the arguments of **pack** actually specify the initial value of an element in addition to its type, a feature that is unavailable in **join**.
Figure IA.49 demonstrates this by adding a fourth argument to our **pack** object, without necessitating another number box for updating its value.

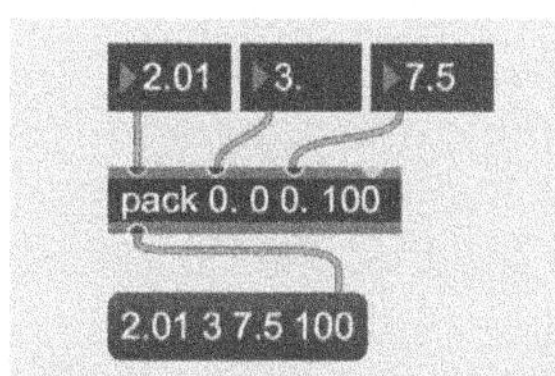

Fig. IA.49 Passing an argument as an element of a list

The list produced is made up of four elements, and the last element maintains the value that we gave it as an argument (100 in this case). Thanks to this behavior, we can, for example, send lists that contain fixed values by setting those values using arguments, and then updating only those arguments that need to change. In Section 1.4, for example, we saw that to pass a list to a **line~** object consisting of two elements (a value to reach and a fixed time in milliseconds in which to reach this value), we could use the **append** object to append a constant time in milliseconds (see Section 1.4, figure 1.52, file 01_13_conv_interp.maxpat).[11]

[11] If you don't remember any of this, this is a good opportunity to turn back to Section 1.4 to the section entitled "Conversion of deciBels to Amplitude" to review to discussion, since it used one of the fundamental techniques for interpolating numerical values, and consequently for smoothing and transforming MSP signals.

Using the **pack** object, we can obtain the same result, as seen in figure IA.50.

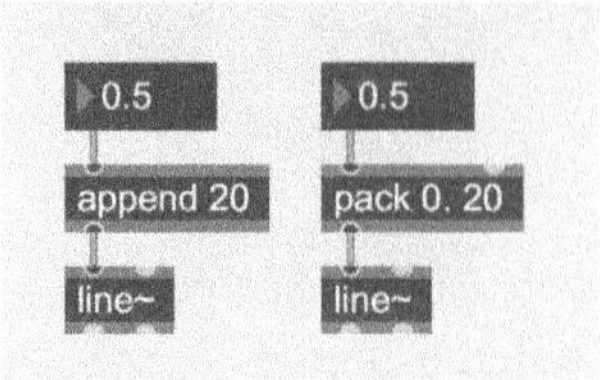

Fig. IA.50 Two ways to create lists of elements for the **line~** object

In both cases illustrated in the figure, we send the **line~** object a list of two elements, 0.5 and 20, which "instruct" the **line~** to reach the number 0.5 in 20 milliseconds.

THE ZL OBJECT

There are naturally other object that enable us to work with lists. One of the most important is the **zl** object, which is really more like a group of objects, or better yet, an object whose functionality morphs based on the arguments that we give it. As a first example, the argument "***len***" tells the object to return a number that reflects how many elements are contained in any list that it receives. In figure IA.51, we see that the object returning the number 4 upon receiving a list of 4 elements.

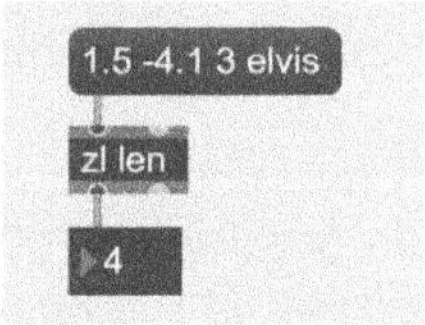

Fig. IA.51 The "*len*" function of the **zl** object

If, rather than "*len*", the argument to **zl** is "***group***" followed by a second numeric argument, the object regroups elements that it receives into lists which take the length given by the second argument (as seen in figure IA.52).

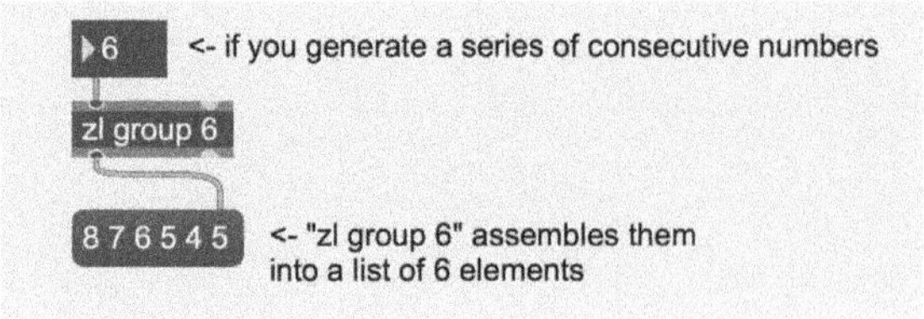

Fig IA.52 The "*group*" function of the **zl** object

Build a copy of figure IA.52 (remembering to connect the right inlet of the message box) and generate a series of numbers by clicking and sliding the mouse over the number box. The numbers, that initially arrive in dribs and drabs, are assembled into tidy lists of 6 elements each by **zl**. Every time that a list is completed, it is sent to the outlet of **zl** and displayed in the message box.

There are many other variants of the `zl` object: with the "***join***" argument, for example, the object combines two lists, with the "***slice***" argument followed by a numeric second argument, it divides a list into two parts, the first being a list whose length is specified by the second argument, and the second being a list that contains any remaining elements. These two functions are shown in figure IA.53.

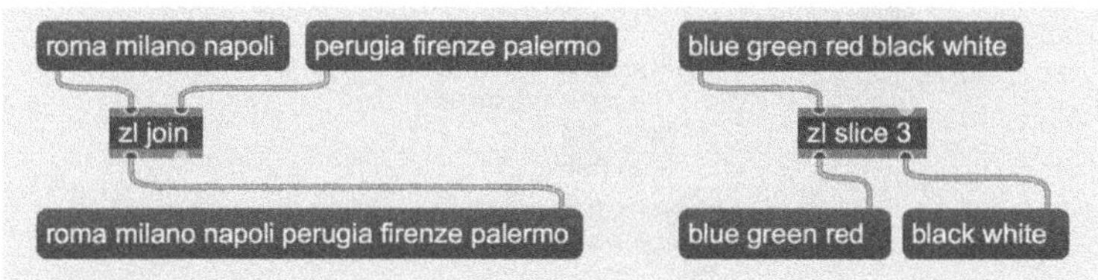

Fig. IA.53 Some other functions of the `zl` object

To see the numerous functions implemented by the `zl` object, take a look at its help file. (<Alt-click> on the object in edit mode.)
The objects in the "zl" group can also be created by using the syntax "zl. function_name". For example, [`zl` len] using this convention becomes **`zl.len`**, [`zl` slice] becomes **`zl.slice`**, and so forth.

THE APPEND AND PREPEND OBJECTS

We will now briefly delve into the characteristics of two other objects that are very useful for building lists: **`append`** and **`prepend`**. The **`append`** object (which, you will remember, we already used in the patch 01_13_conv_interp.maxpat) adds its argument to the end of any list that it receives, while the **`prepend`** object adds its argument to the beginning of any list it receives (as in figure IA.54).

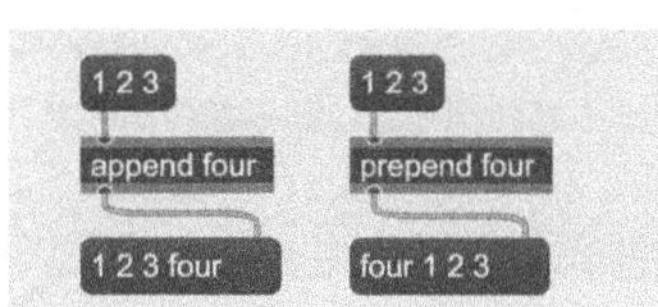

Fig. IA.54 **`append`** and **`prepend`**

You have already seen one possible use for **`append`**, but what might **`prepend`** be useful for? As one example, it can be useful in cases in which we need to send a (fixed) command to an object followed by a (variable) numerical value. Reopen the file 01_14_audiofile.maxpat (Section 1.5, figure 1.53); this patch demonstrates the function of the **`sfplay~`** object, which reads an audio file from disk and can vary the speed at which it is read by sending the "***speed***" command, "*speed 1*" signifying normal speed, "*speed 0.5*" half speed, etc.

Connecting a float number box to a **`prepend`** object with "*speed*" as its argument, and then connecting this object to **`sfplay~`**, enables us to obtain a continuous variation in the playback speed, as you see in figure IA.55. Try this modification of file 01_14_audiofile.maxpat yourself.

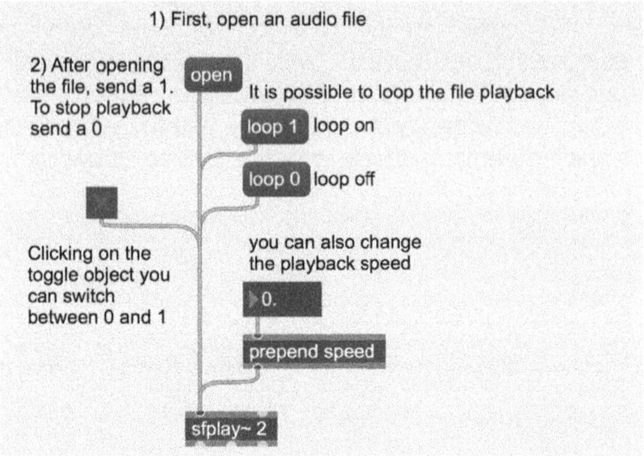

Fig. IA.55 One possible use of **`prepend`**

Analogously, it is possible to manage the commands "*loop 1*" and "*loop 0*", found in the upper right of the figure, by connecting a **`toggle`** to a **`prepend`** object taking "*loop*" as an argument. Try this!

THE MULTISLIDER OBJECT

Let's move now to a graphic object that generates lists of numbers: **`multislider`** (seen in figure IA.56). This object can be found in the "Sliders" *palette* (Top Patcher Window Toolbar).

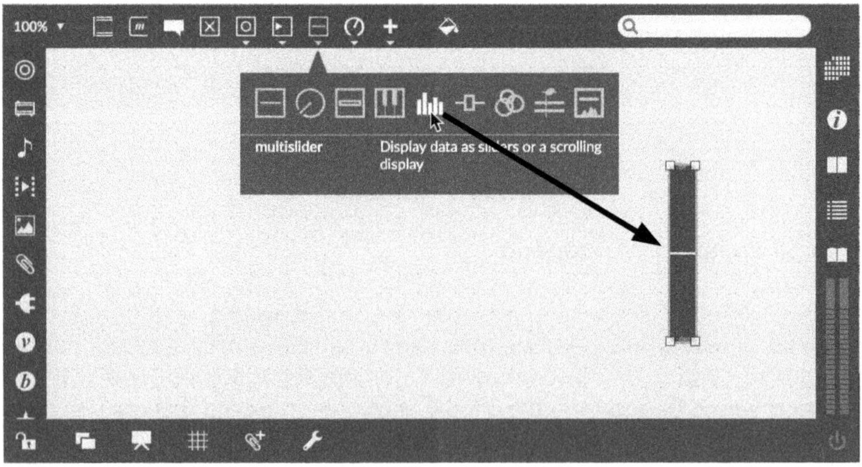

Fig. IA.56 The **`multislider`**

The first thing to do once you've inserted this object in the Patcher Window is to widen it by clicking and dragging on its lower right corner. Hover over the lower right part of the object, and when the icon changes into a double-ended arrow, you can click and drag to the right, until you obtain a rectangle with a width about twice its height (as shown in figure IA.57).

Having done this, now call up the inspector for the `multislider`: locate the "Sliders" category and type 16 into the field containing a 1, next to the ***Number of Sliders*** label. After this, type "0 100" into the spot that contains the value "-1. 1.", next to the ***Range*** label. Now locate the "Style" category, and select **Integer** in the menu found for the "**Sliders Output Value**" property (which is the lowest property on the page). Finally, you can close the inspector window: through these actions, you have created an object with which it is possible to graphically generate lists of 16 integer elements with values between 0 and 100. Add a wide message box to the patch, as in figure IA.57, and try it out.

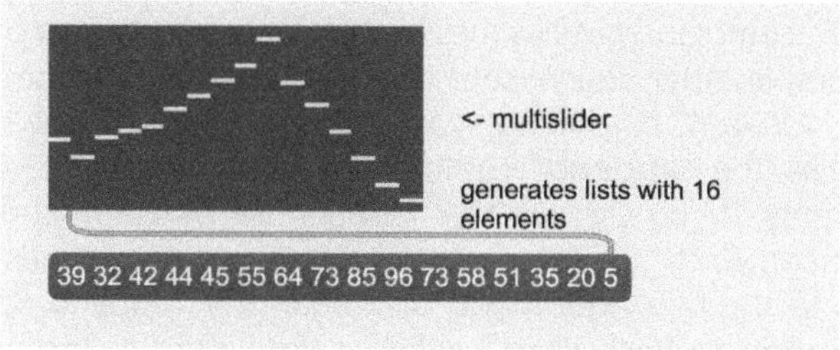

Fig. IA.57 Lists of numbers generated by the `multislider` object

Every time that you modify the position of the 16 sliders within the `multislider`, a list of 16 elements is generated, whose values can be seen within the message box. In the course of this book we will have many different occasions to use this exceedingly useful UI object.

IA.8 THE MESSAGE BOX AND VARIABLE ARGUMENTS

COMMANDS FOR MESSAGE BOX OBJECTS

Until now, we have used the right inlet of the message box to directly display messages within it, but as we have already intimated, there is also a left inlet through which we can send commands to the object and update its internal variables. The possible command messages are illustrated in figure IA.58; as you see, they are contained in various message boxes that send them to another message box acting as a "receiver". Try building this patch.

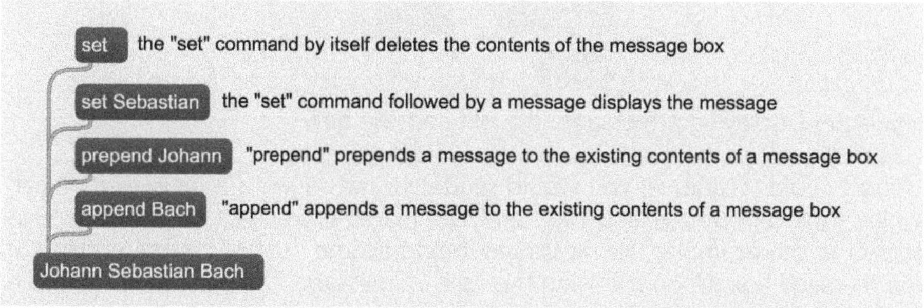

Fig. IA.58 Commands for the message box object

Let's examine these command messages one by one. The first is "***set***", which deletes the contents of the message box and replaces them with the message following the command text "*set*". The command "*set Sebastian*", for example, which we see in the figure, will make the word "Sebastian" appear inside the message box. (Try this.) Before Max 5, it was always necessary to use the "*set*" command to display a message inside a message box, but now, as we know, we can use the right inlet for this purpose. The "*set*" command without any message following it simply deletes whatever contents are in the message box.

The "***prepend***" command puts its message before the contents of the message box; if, for example, after you've sent the "*set Sebastian*" command you send the "*prepend Johann*" command, you will see "Johann Sebastian" in the receiver. Likewise, the "***append***" command adds its message to the end of the receiver's contents; if you click on the "*append Bach*" command, you will see "Johann Sebastian Bach". If we repeat the last two commands, we will add new elements to the message. If you click again on "*append Bach*", you will see "Johann Sebastian Bach Bach", while if you click on "*prepend Johann*", you'll get "Johann Johann Sebastian Bach Bach" and so on. Be careful not to confuse the command messages "*append*" and "*prepend*" with the **append** and **prepend** objects! These objects add their argument to whatever message they receive on their inlets, and emit the resulting messages from their outlets, while the commands simply add elements to the contents of the message box that receives them.
In versions of Max earlier than Version 5, as we have said, there was no right inlet on the message box, and it was therefore necessary to prepend the "*set*" command to whatever message you wanted to see in the message box.
The simplest way to do this was to use the **prepend** object (NOT the "*prepend*" command!) with an argument of "*set*". In figure IA.59, we see this old method and the new method, side by side.

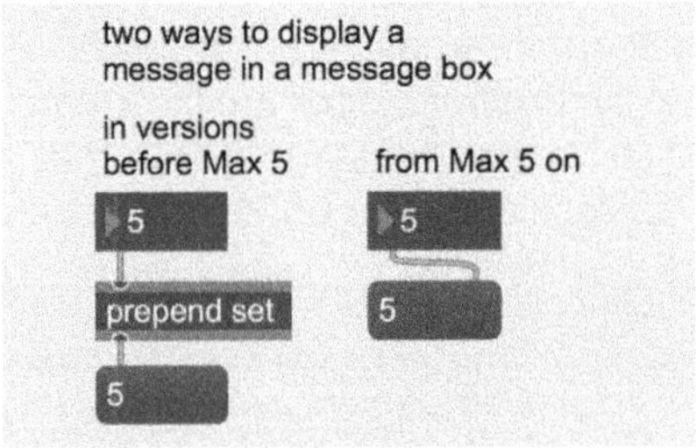

Fig. IA.59 Displaying a message: the old and the new

Using the old technique, you would send your message via a **prepend** object, which took care of inserting the "*set*" command: if you sent the number 5, as shown in the example, the message would become "*set 5*" before arriving at the message box. Upon receiving the "*set 5*" message, the message box would delete its previous contents and display the new message "5". Naturally, this old way still works alongside the new, since without it, many older patches would no longer function.

VARIABLE ARGUMENTS: THE DOLLAR SIGN ($)

We now move to an important and useful feature of the message box: its capacity for **variable arguments**. The dollar sign ('**$**') in a message box represents a variable argument, and when we have one or more elements in a message box that consist of a dollar sign followed by an integer (such as $1, $2, etc.), such elements will be replaced by the corresponding elements of incoming messages. Here is a series of examples that clarifies how this mechanism works. Build the patch shown in figure IA.60, which uses a single dollar sign argument:

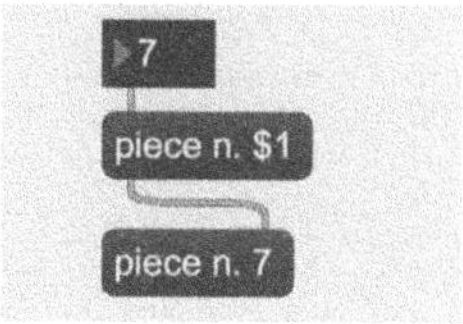

Fig. IA.60 Use of a variable argument in a message box

In the message box in the middle of the patch, we have two strings, "piece" and "n.". There is also a variable argument, "$1", which will take on the value of the first element in any message that it receives. We connect a number box, which sends messages consisting of a single number at a time, to the message box. When one of these message is received, the "$1" element is replaced by the incoming number and the transformed message that results is sent to the lower message box for display. In practice, the upper message box has an internal variable (corresponding to the "$1") that is updated by incoming messages on the left inlet. This technique provides us with a third way to construct a list of two values for use by the `line~` object when performing an interpolation (for the first two, see Section IA.7, figure IA.50). We see it in figure IA.61.

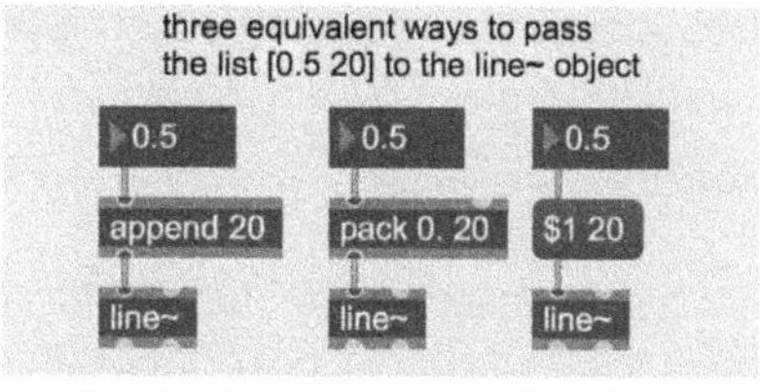

Fig. IA.61 Three ways to obtain the same result with Max

The next example (as shown in figure IA.62, and which you should build, as usual) uses two variable arguments:

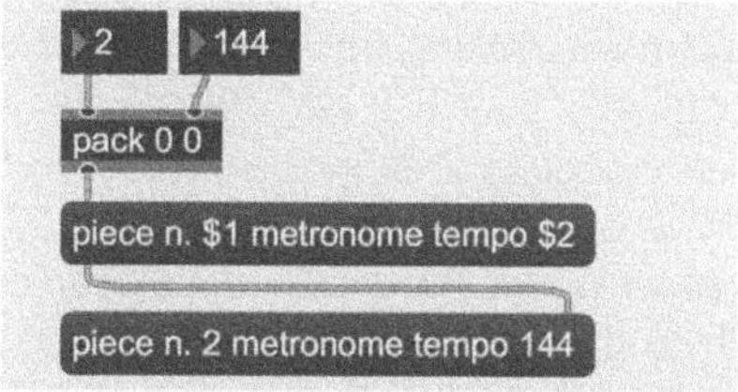

Fig. IA.62 How to use two dollar variables

Here, the variable arguments are "$1" and "$2", which means that the first and second elements of the list received on the message box will be used as replacement values. To pass two numerical arguments to the message box in the form of a list, we "pack" them together using the **pack** object (remembering that this list will be sent to the message box only when we update the "hot" inlet of **pack**). It isn't possible to simply give the first element to the left inlet and the second element to the right inlet, because anything sent to the right inlet will become the new contents of the message box!
In figure IA.63 we illustrate a patch that generates random glissandi: try building it.

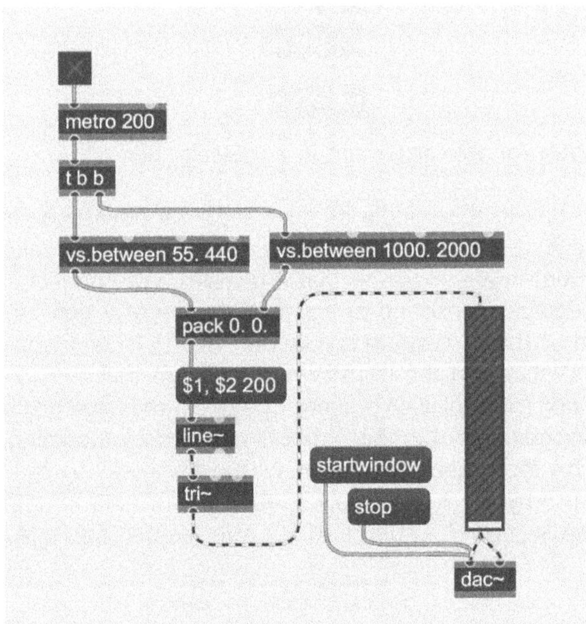

Fig. IA.63 A stream of random glissandi

For every bang generated by the metronome, two random numbers are created, the first between 55 and 440, and the second between 1000 and 2000. These two numbers are joined into a list and passed to a message box.
Inside the message box is a message consisting of two dollar variables: "$1, $2 200". If, for example, the two **vs.between** generators produce the numbers 400 and 1500, the message generated in the message box would be "400, 1500 200". This message is sent to **line~**, which generates a segment that goes from 400 to 1500 in 200 milliseconds; the **tri~** oscillator connected to **line~** produces a glissando from 400 to 1500 Hz. (Remember that a comma inside a message box separates messages.) In figure IA.63, therefore, the message box connected to **line~** contains two messages: "$1" and "$2 200". To change the points of departure and of arrival for the glissandi, you can create four float number boxes and connect them to the second and third inlets of the two **vs.between** objects. Once you have done this, you will be able to create descending glissandi, for example, by giving frequency values that have a higher point of departure than

point of arrival. For example, you could give the values 1000 and 2000 to the float number boxes for the left **vs.between** object, and the values 55 and 440 to the float number box of the **vs.between** object on the right. Give it a listen!

VARIABLE ARGUMENTS: SETDOMAIN

We now move on to another practical use of variable arguments in the message box. You will recall a problem that we encountered when building the patch that created a sequence of articulated notes using a **metro** and an envelope generated by a **function** object connected to a **line~**. The duration of the envelope was always the same, even when we sped up or slowed down the rate of the metronome, and because of this, whenever the duration of the envelope became greater than the time between successive bangs from the metro, we heard an undesirable clicking noise.
The duration of the envelope generated by the **function** object can be changed, as we learned in Section 1.3, by using the Hi Domain Display Value (x-Axis) attribute, which can be modified within the inspector, but which can also be modified by sending the object a "***setdomain***" message followed by a duration in milliseconds. (In a mathematical graph of a function, the values for the x axis – the horizontal axis – are called the "domain" of the function, and this is where the name of the "*setdomain*" command comes from.) Let's try using this message on a **function** object in the patch contained in the file IA_06_random_walk.maxpat (as seen in figure IA.64).

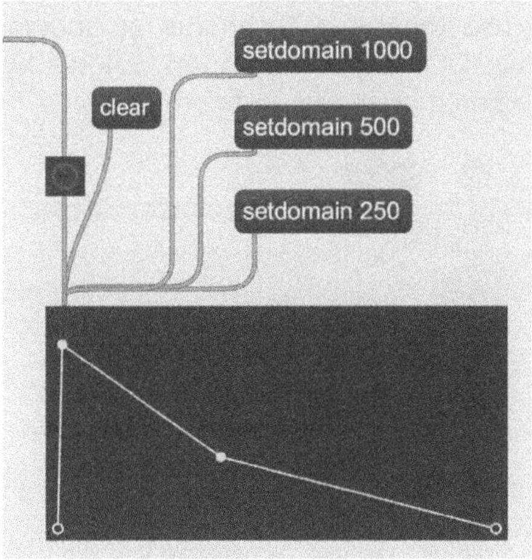

Fig. IA.64 Changing the duration of an envelope

By clicking on the various message boxes while the patch is executing, you will hear that the duration of the envelope changes (with the values in the figure we can have an envelope that lasts for 1, 0.5, or .025 seconds). Thanks to the use of a variable argument "$1" we are able to bind the duration of the envelope to the duration of the metronome pulse.

Try changing the patch to do this, in the way shown in figure IA.65:

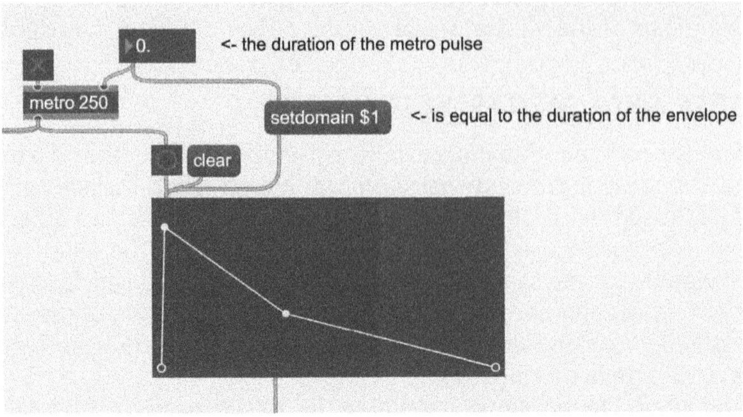

Fig. IA.65 The duration of the envelope is bound to the rate of the **metro**

The float number box that regulates the rate of the **metro** also now modifies the message *"setdomain $1"*, which is sent to **function**, and if we slow down or speed up the metronome rate, the duration of the envelope will change to match. Naturally *"setdomain"* is not the only message that can be sent to the **function** object; we encourage you to glance at the help file to learn more about the various properties of this object.

We will be able to use the same technique as shown in figure IA.65 to synchronize the duration of the glissandi found in figure IA.63 to a metronome rate. Try adapting the patch as shown in figure IA.66:

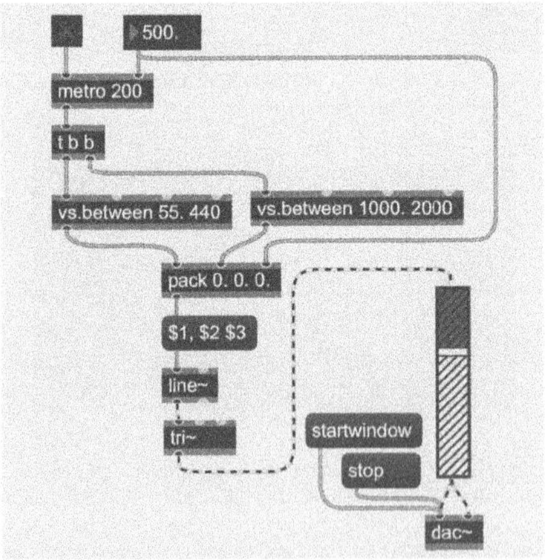

Fig. IA.66 A stream of random glissandi with variable tempo

As you see, we have furnished a variable rate to the **metro** object by using a float number box connected to its right inlet. The same value is also given to the last inlet of the **pack** object, which constructs lists consisting of three glissando parameters: a departure frequency, an arrival frequency, and a duration.

These lists are passed to the message box that contains the message "$1, $2 $3"; the three parameter values are plugged into the three variable arguments and the resulting list is sent to **line~**. The value used for the rate of the **metro** object is put into variable "$3", and therefore specifies the duration of the glissando as well.

IA.9 SENDING SEQUENCES OF BANGS: THE UZI OBJECT

The creatively named **uzi** object will show up on many occasions, as soon as the next chapter. This object fires a variable-length sequence of bangs at its target as fast as possible, regulating the number of bangs fired using the argument passed to it. (See figure IA.67 for a simple case.)

Fig. IA.67 The uzi object

In the sample case shown, every time the object receives a bang, 4 additional bangs are generated in succession (and can be seen in the Max window).
Parallel to this, the right outlet of uzi generates a numerical sequence (always at the maximum speed possible) that starts at 1 by default and ends at the number given by the argument. Try moving the **print** patch cord to the third outlet of uzi to verify this result in the Max window. It is also possible to change the number of bangs generated by uzi by using the right inlet of the object. (Try this by connecting a number box to the second inlet.)

IA.10 SEND AND RECEIVE

Let's see now two objects that are very useful for simplifying complex patches, and that enable you to use "wireless communication" within your Max patches. They are the **send** and **receive** objects.
The **send** object is able to transmit messages to the **receive** object without the use of patch cords. To do this, the objects must have matching string arguments which give a name to the "channel" over which they communicate.

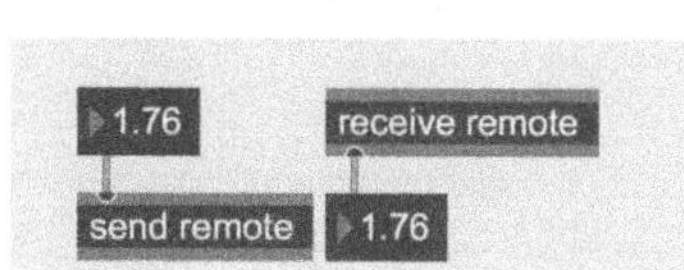

Fig. IA.68 Wireless connections

In figure IA.68, (which you should construct yourself in an empty Patcher Window), we see a **send** object that has as its argument the word "remote", and also a **receive** object with the same argument.

This argument can be any string, and what is important is that objects must share the same argument string in order to communicate. A float number box is connected to the **send** object in this patch, and every time the number changes, it will be transmitted to the **receive** object. **Send** and **receive** are very important, and are used so often that they can be abbreviated simply by using their initials '**s**' and '**r**'. It is possible to transmit any message whatsoever, and if there are more than one **receive** objects with the same argument, the **send** object will fan the same message out to all receivers (as shown in figure IA.69).

Fig. IA.69 The same message received by two **receive** objects

Naturally, it is also possible to have multiple **send** objects that share the same argument, and each will transmit its message to all **receive** objects that possess this argument. The pair of objects becomes indispensable when making complicated patches, because it enables you to eliminate, for example, the patch cords between objects that are far apart that would in the end be graphically confusing. On the other hand, if there are too many **send** and **receive** objects in a patch, it becomes difficult to follow the routing of messages. You must, therefore, carefully balance the use of patch cords with the use of wireless communication!
It is important to emphasize that **send** and **receive** objects fully replace direct connection by patch cords. Two or more objects connected via **send** and **receive** behave exactly as though they were connected directly by patch cords. This means, for example, that MSP signals connected to **send** objects with the same arguments sum their incoming signals in exactly the same way that signals connected to the same inlet with patch cords are summed.[12]
Open the file **IA_07_multisend.maxpat** (shown in figure IA.70).

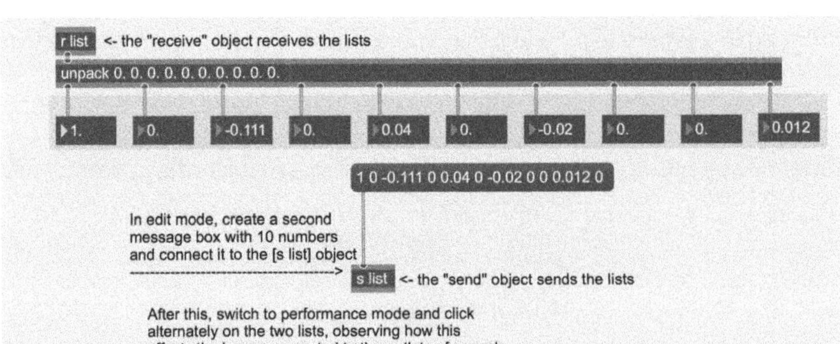

Fig. IA.70 The file IA_07_multisend.maxpat

[12] We spoke about this property of MSP signals when discussing the file 01_06_glissandi.maxpat. See figures 1.33 and 1.34 in Section 1.3.

This patch shows a scenario in which a list of numbers is being transmitted. Make the suggested changes to the patch, and then save it using a different name. As you can observe, the list of numbers is sent using **send**, [**s** list], to a corresponding **receive**, [**r** list]. The **receive** is connected to an **unpack** which distributes the single values to ten number boxes below it. Now open the file **IA_08_multislidersend.maxpat** (shown in figure IA.71).

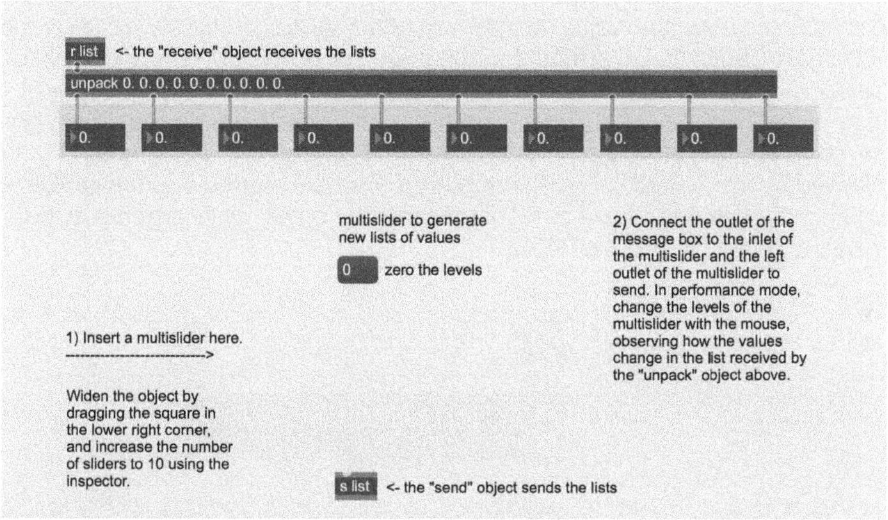

Fig. IA.71 The file IA_08_multislidersend.maxpat

This patch shows a similar scenario, in which the list of numbers to send is controlled by a **multislider**. Insert the **multislider** as described by the comments in the patch. After you have tested all of its behaviors, save the patch. In this scenario, as in the last, the list of numbers is sent using a **send** object [**s** list], to the corresponding **receive** [**r** list].[13]

[13] If you left open the preceding patch (IA_07_multisend.maxpat) note that the number boxes are updated in both. This happens because the **send** and **receive** of both patches share the same argument ("*list*") and the messages are therefore transmitted from one patch to the other. This is very helpful when we need to pass a message from one patch to another, but on the other hand, we want to avoid passing messages inadvertently between different patches, so we need to ensure that we don't have **send** and **receive** objects sharing arguments by mistake.

IA.11 USE OF ATTRIBUTES INSIDE THE OBJECT BOX

As we know, the arguments are parameters that we can set by writing their value inside the objects, so if, for example, we create the object [**cycle~** 440] we get a sinusoidal oscillator whose argument (440) specifies the initial frequency.
Attributes, on the other hand, are parameters that we set inside an object's inspector, or by sending a message to the object itself. For example, if we want to change the maximum value on the x-axis of a **function** object we can set the Hi Domain Display Value attribute in the inspector or directly send the message "setdomain", followed by the desired value, to the object (see paragraph IA.8).
There is another way to set the attributes: write directly inside the object box the name of the attribute preceded (without spaces) by the symbol @ and followed by the desired value. The attributes must be inserted after any possible arguments; they don't have to follow a particular order, while arguments do.
Recreate the patch in Figure IA.72.

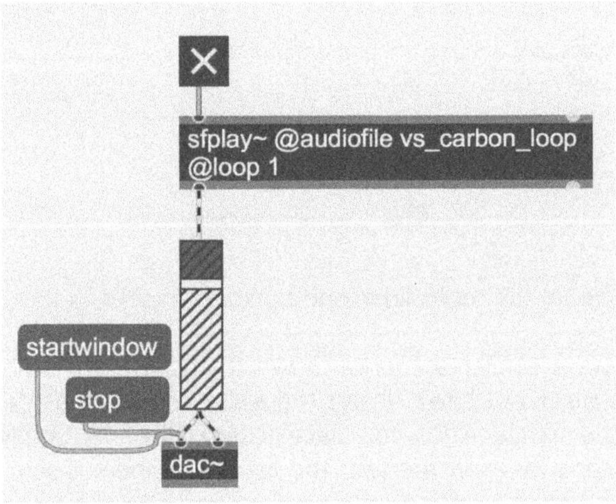

fig. IA.72: **sfplay~** with attributes

In this patch we can see the **sfplay~** object in which the "audiofile" and "loop" attributes have been set directly inside the object. If you activate the patch, you will hear a looped vs_carbon_loop[14] drum pattern looped. Open the object inspector and check that the attributes have actually been set (they are in the last category "sfplay~").
As we said, the order of the attributes doesn't matter (because the name of the desired attribute is specified): try, for example, to reverse the order of "audiofile" and "loop" within **sfplay~**; the result will be the same.

[14] The audio file vs_carbon_loop.aif is part of the Virtual Sound Macros library: in order for the patch in figure IA.72 to produce a sound, it is necessary to have that library installed. Refer to the indications given at the beginning of chapter 1P for correct installation of the library.

IA.12 MULTICHANNEL AUDIO

Let's now discuss an important feature of Max: the possibility to manage multiple audio signals using a single patch cord. This greatly simplifies the control of signals that must be processed in parallel, such as the signals produced by the oscillators in additive synthesis (see chapter 2) or the signals that are used for the spatialization of the sound made with several speakers (we will discuss this in chapter 4 and, more extensively, in the third volume). As we will see, the possible applications are manifold and we will use the multichannel features of Max whenever necessary.
Multichannel objects are characterized by the prefix "mc" added to their name: almost all MSP objects have a multichannel version (**mc.cycle~**, **mc.line~**, etc.). There are also several other objects, designed expressly for the management of multiple signals, which we will see in the course of this and the next volumes.
Let's see a patch that uses the multichannel functions of Max: load the file **IA_09_multichannel.maxpat** (figure IA.73).

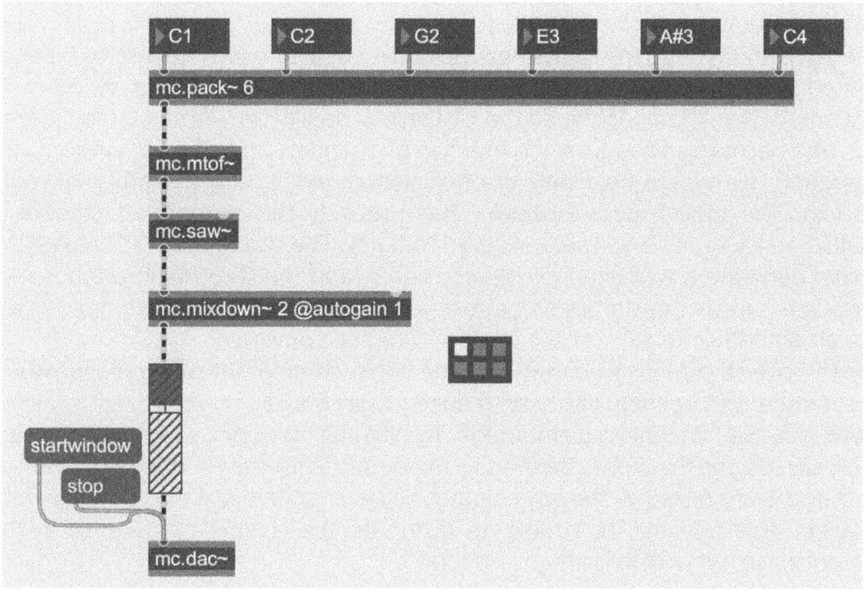

fig. IA.73: file IA_09_multichannel.maxpat

In this patch, we have the multichannel version of some objects we already know (**mc.saw~**, **mc.mtof~** and **mc.dac~**) and a couple of new multichannel objects (**mc.pack~** and **mc.mixdown~**.) In addition to the new names, you will surely notice the different appearance of the patch cords that connect multichannel objects: they have black and blue stripes and are thicker than the normal MSP "audio cables".
First, listen to the various presets: you'll hear several chords made with 6 band-limited oscillators. Note that the output signal is stereo and you can hear three oscillators on the left channel and three on the right.

Let's analyze the patch: the first object at the top, **mc.pack~**, is used to assemble multichannel signals; the argument indicates the number of the object inputs. Each input can receive an audio signal or a numerical value that is converted internally into a constant signal (as does the **sig~** object we saw in section 1.5, figure 1.57). At the output we have a multichannel signal that contains all the input signals: these signals are not added or mixed, but simply grouped, and can be separated again, for example with the **mc.unpack~** object or with other multichannel operators. It is possible to know how many signals there are in a multichannel patch cord by hovering over the patch cord with the mouse pointer: if you do it with the cable coming out of **mc.pack~**, a small blue box containing the number 6 should appear.
The next object, **mc.mtof~**, converts the MIDI note values to the corresponding frequency: at the output of the object we will then have a multichannel signal which groups 6 frequency values. Note that the **mc.mtof~** object has no arguments or attributes to determine how many channels it should handle, because in this case it is not necessary. If we do not specify otherwise, in fact, multichannel objects adapt themselves to the number of audio channels they receive: therefore when the **mc.mtof~** object receives a 6-channel signal, in turn it generates a 6-channel signal.
The same thing happens to the next **mc.saw~** object, which generates 6 band-limited sawtooth oscillators, each with a frequency received by **mc.mtof~**.
If we now want to hear the sound of these 6 oscillators with a stereo system, it is first necessary to reduce the number of channels from 6 to 2: without this operation, we would hear only the first two channels, and the other 4 would be lost. The object **mc.mixdown~** has precisely this purpose: it receives a multichannel signal and mixes its components. The argument "2" makes the object generate a two-channel (stereo) signal, and the @autogain attribute we have set, causes the signals to be rescaled so that their sum does not exceed the amplitude limits -1,1 of the analog to digital converter.
Try to hover the mouse pointer over the cable coming out of **mc.mixdown~**; the number of channels has been reduced from 6 to 2.
How are the channels distributed? By default the **mc.mixdown~** object cyclically assigns the input channels to the output channels: in our case channels 1, 3 and 5 are mixed in the left channel, while channels 2, 4 and 6 in the right channel. It is possible, of course, to distribute the channels differently in the stereo space: we will talk about this later.
The stereo signal is passed to the object **mc.gain~** (the multichannel version of **gain~**)[15] and from here to **mc.dac~** which sends the signal to the sound card.

[15] If you look closely at the **mc.gain~** object, you will notice that the fader is divided into two parts: this indicates that the received signal has two channels. Try to copy the object and connect it directly to the output of **mc.saw~**: the fader will now be divided into 6 parts, corresponding to the 6 channels generated by the connected object.

Let's make a clarification: the multichannel version of MSP objects (**mc.mtof~**, **mc.saw~** etc.) is obtained through an "invisible" wrapper which creates a number of MSP objects equal to the number of channels required. The object **mc.saw~** in figure IA.73, therefore, is not really a single object, but a wrapper containing 6 copies (also called instances) of the **saw~** object. For simplicity, however, we will call "objects" all multichannel versions of common MSP objects.
Let's now see another feature of the multichannel system: if we perform an operation (for example a mathematical process) between two multiple signals, the operation is performed between pairs of channels, and a multichannel signal is generated that contains the result of all the operations.
The patch of figure IA.74 shows us how we can rescale the signal of four oscillators with a single multichannel operation: try to reconstruct it.

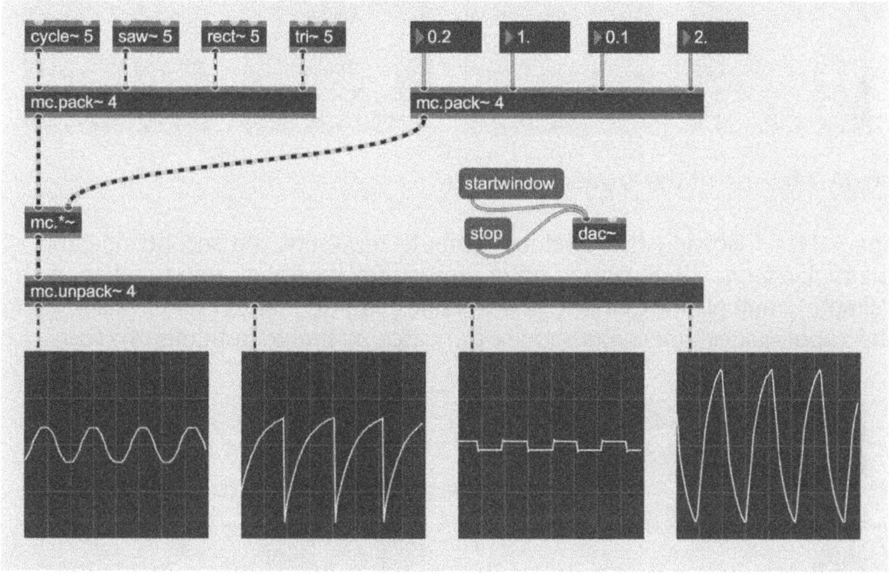

fig. IA.74: multichannel multiplication

First of all, note that this patch does not produce sounds, because the **dac~** object and the connected message boxes have the sole purpose of activating the DSP "engine."
Through two **mc.pack~** objects we have created a multichannel signal that groups the outputs of four oscillators and a second multichannel signal containing four rescaling factors; the two signals are sent to a multichannel multiplier **mc.*~** which performs the four multiplications two by two. After that, we send the multichannel signal to the **mc.unpack~** object which separates the rescaled oscillators.

You can set the rescaling factors directly within the **mc.*~** object using the @ values attribute: modify the patch of figure IA.74 as shown in figure IA.74b.

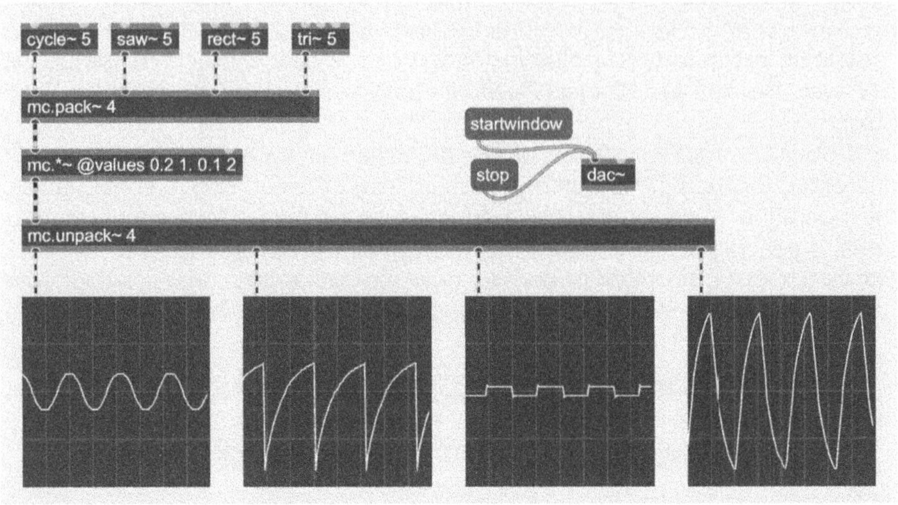

fig. IA.74b: use of the @values attribute

The values following the @values attribute represent the second operand of the multichannel multiplier; in other words they have the same function as the "simple" multiplier argument. These values can also be set dynamically using the "applyvalues" message: modify the patch as shown in figure IA.74c.

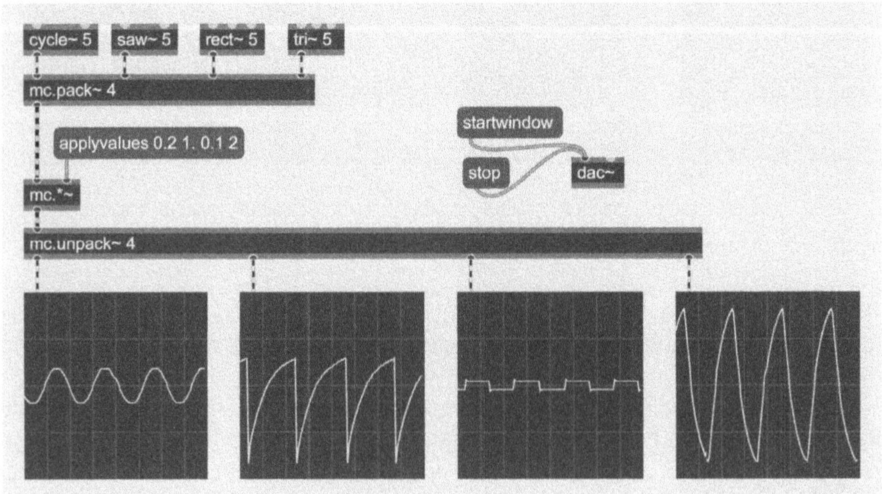

fig. IA.74c: use of the applyvalues message

After creating the message box containing the "applyvalues" message, it is of course necessary to click inside it (in performance mode).

The **scope~** object too can handle multichannel signals: starting from figure IA.74c, create a new **scope~**[16] and connect it to the output of **mc.*~** (Figure IA.74d).

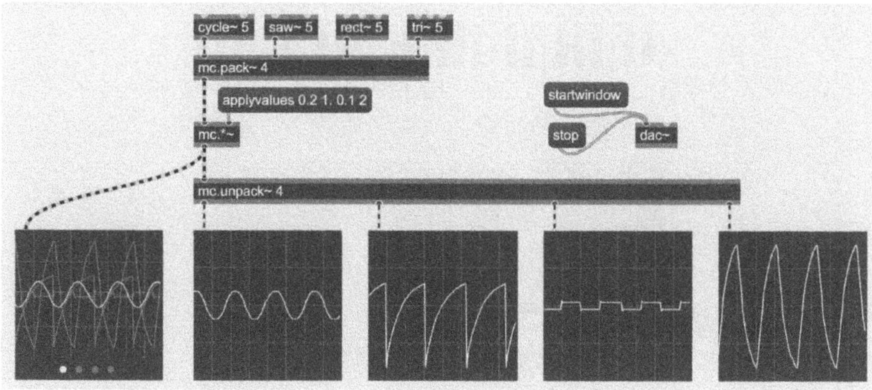

fig. IA.74d: use of **scope~** with multichannel signals

As you can see, the new **scope~** (on the left) displays all the signals it receives: one of these is highlighted (the sinusoid, in the figure) while the others, with a darker color, are in the background. The four dots in the lower part of the object panel are used to select the signal to be highlighted. The number of dots present depends, of course, on the number of channels received by the object.

During the next chapters, we will examine other characteristics of the multichannel system which, as we have said, will be useful in many situations.

[16] It is not necessary to create the object using the name **mc.scope~** (although it can be done), the oscilloscope automatically adapts itself to the number of received channels.

ACTIVITY– *ANALYZING ALGORITHMS*

Examine this patch:

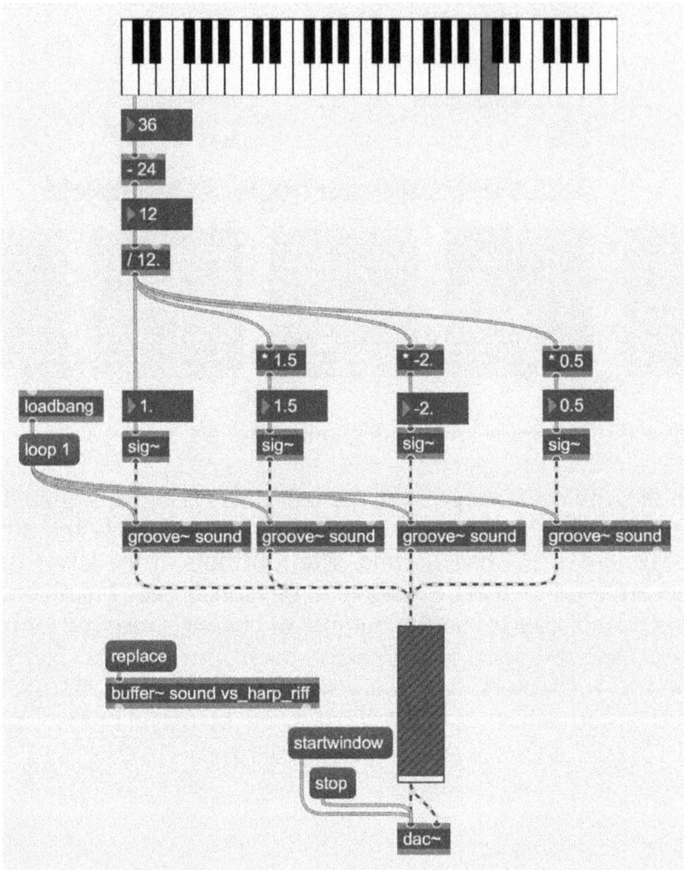

Fig. IA.75

Now construct this algorithm on your computer and describe its function, detailing the various sets of sounds that are emitted by key presses and multiplication factors. To obtain a clearer understanding of what is happening in the patch, think about the values of the multipliers while reviewing Table D of Theory Section 1.4T. Note that the values of the `kslider` keys in this algorithm go from -24 to 24, (this means that the first C of the kslider must be 0, the following subtraction brings the value down to -24.). Consider the result of using this non-standard keyboard: successive keys do not correspond to successive semitones. For example, the factor 2, triggered by the highest C, transposes up one octave and doubles the speed of the sound played from an audio file. Which key halves the frequency? Which takes it to 1/4 of the original?

ACTIVITY – *COMPLETING ALGORITHMS (ACTIVITY A)*

Open the patch **IA_Completion.maxpat**.

This patch is incomplete. There are four objects that can be found on the right that have no connections. Move these into functional positions based on the following hint: the output of the patch "random-minmax" is a message, not a signal, while `groove~` accepts only signals, used as a stream of multiplication factors, on its inlet. How can we resolve this problem? For what purpose can the `*~` object be used? What signal should the `number~` object monitor? What does `sig~` do?

Complete the patch and experiment with various changes to minimum and maximum values, using both positive and negative numbers. (Of course, the minimum value should always be less than the maximum value!)

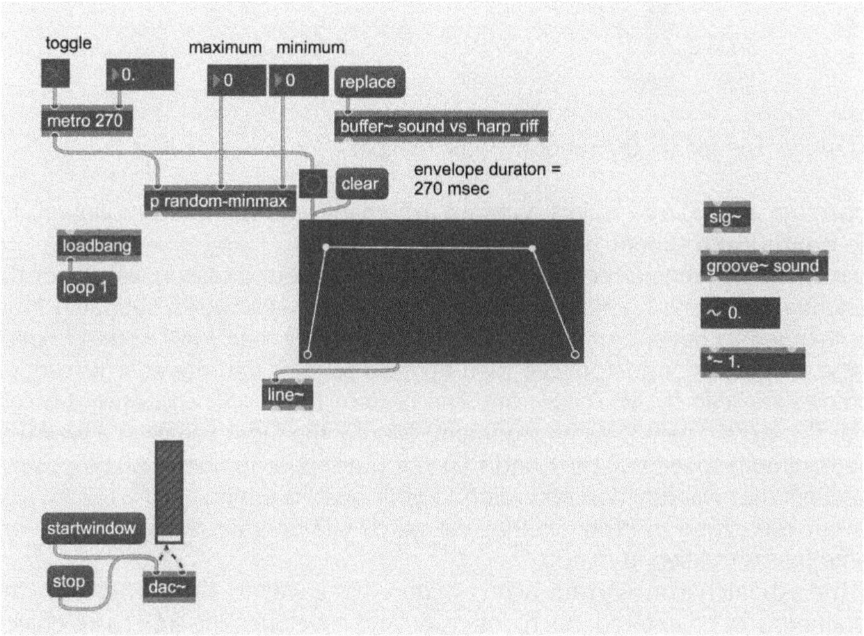

Fig. IA.76 The file IA_Completion.maxpat

ACTIVITY – *COMPLETING ALGORITHMS (ACTIVITY B)*

In figure IA.76, we see that the duration value for the `metro` object in milliseconds is equal to that of the `function` object: this equality is regulated manually, simply by entering the same values in the right inlet of `metro` and in the inspector of `function`. What must we add to the patch in order to control both durations from a single number box?

ACTIVITY– *REPLACING PARTS OF ALGORITHMS*

Open the file **IA_06_random_walk.maxpat** (as seen in figure IA.77).

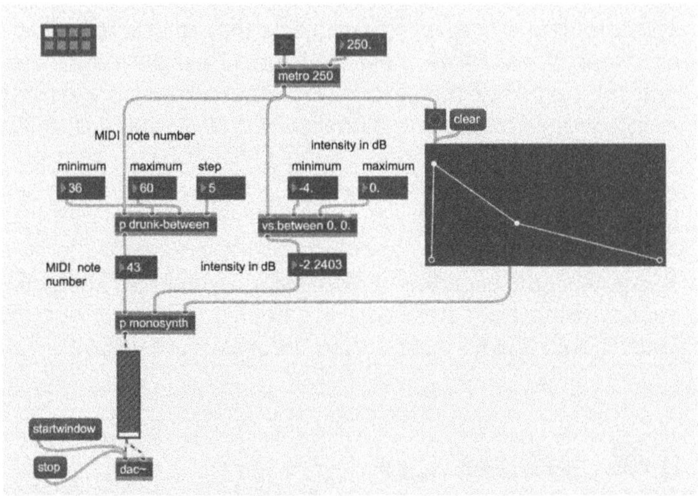

Fig. IA.77 The file IA_06_random_walk.maxpat

Substitute a `sfplay~` object, without argument (and therefore monaural) for the `monosynth` subpatch.
To make this change effective, the number boxes used to capture values for the minimum, maximum, and step inlets of the `drunk-between` subpatch must be changed to generate multiplication factors rather than MIDI note numbers. These multiplication factors can then be used to alter the rate at which sound samples are read by `sfplay~`, and can be sent to it using a `prepend` object with the word "speed" as its argument. Modify the input values in a way that the minimum speed will be 1 and that the other two numbers will be positive numbers that will function according to your own invention.
To put everything in order so that the patch will operate correctly, there are some things to keep in mind:
1) The subpatch `monosynth` was configured in a way to allow three separate parameters to be entered: pitch, intensity, and envelope. The `sfplay~` object, on the other hand, will need a new multiplier connected to its outlet, which will be used modify the output, applying intensity and envelope processing.
2) The "`monosynth`" subpatch has an internal `line~` object that receives values from `function`. In the new situation, how will we send data from `function` to the multiplier that we have placed between `sfplay~` and `gain~`?
3) We want to use the audio file vs_harp_riff.wav, and so how will we load it into `sfplay~`? How will we put the object into a loop? How will we activate and deactivate it? Remember, once we are in performance mode, we will need to first open the audio file, then activate the loop, and then send a message to start the object.
4) Make sure to synchronize the duration of the metronome interval with the duration of the envelope by using the "*setdomain*" message.

ACTIVITY – *CORRECTING ALGORITHMS (ACTIVITY A)*

Open the patch **IA_Correction_A.maxpat** (as seen in figure IA.78):

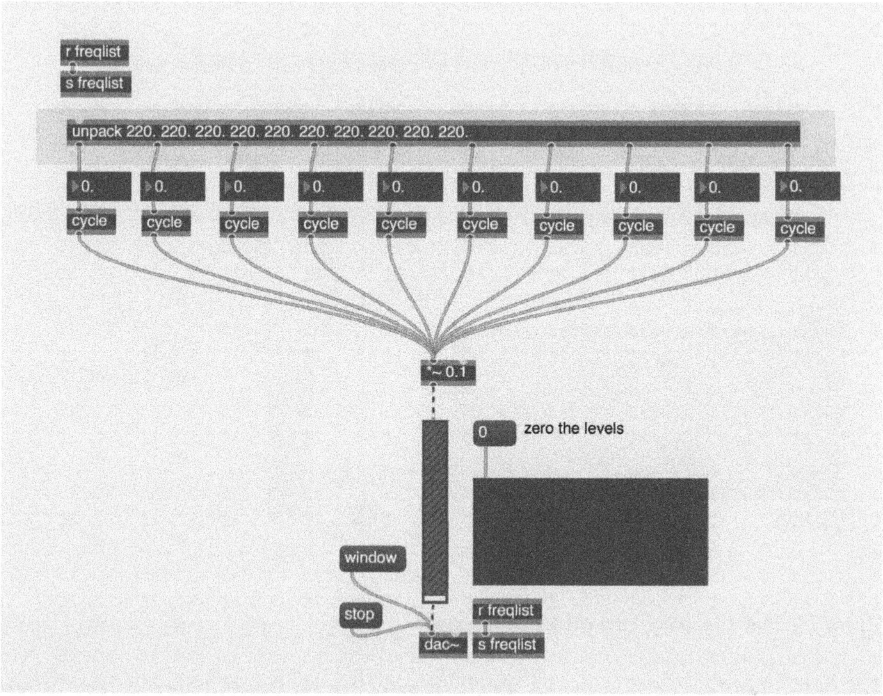

Fig IA.78 The file IA_Correction_A.maxpat

This patch contains some errors, each of which may be repeated a few times. The goal of the patch, when corrected, is to generate ten sine waves with frequencies that are controlled by the `multislider`, and to sum these waves before they are output. Find and fix the errors, and then experiment with different frequencies for the oscillators by working with the `multislider`.

ACTIVITY – *CORRECTING ALGORITHMS (ACTIVITY B)*

Open the patch **IA_Correction_B.maxpat** (as seen in figure IA.79):

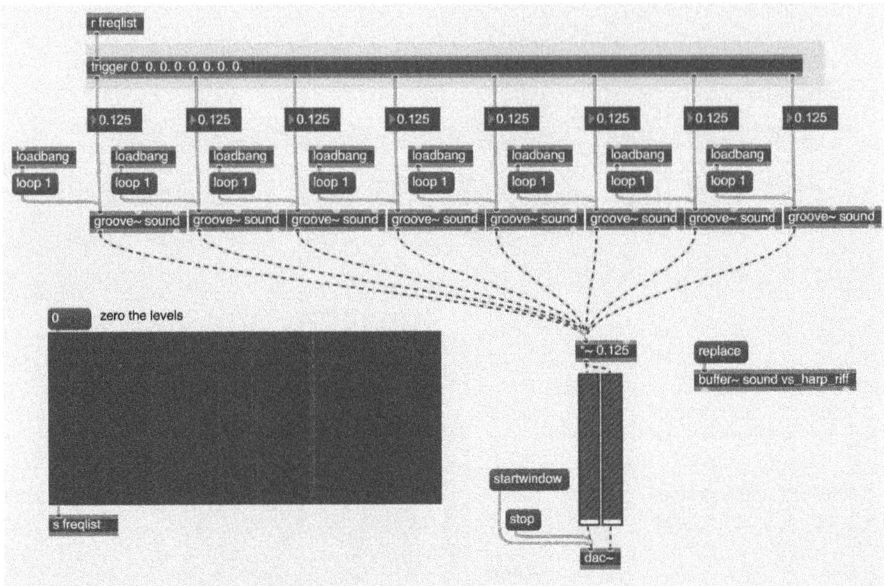

Fig IA.79 The file IA_Correction_B.maxpat

This patch contains some errors, each of which may be repeated a few times. The goal of this patch, once corrected, is to generate 8 concurrent instances of the audio file vs_harp_riff.wav with different read speeds, controlled by the `multislider`, and to sum these sounds before they are output. Find and fix the errors, and then experiment with various combinations of the 8 speeds by working with the `multislider`.

INTEGRATED CROSS-FUNCTIONAL PROJECT – *REVERSE ENGINEERING*

Open the algorithm that you prepared as a solution to the "Replacing Parts of Algorithms" exercise (figure IA.77). Now listen to the following 3 sounds:

IA_reverse_engine_A.aif
IA_reverse_engine_B.aif
IA_reverse_engine_C.aif

Listen carefully to them, one sound at a time, and then use your patch to replicate the sound as closely as possible, by modifying the read speed parameter and the envelope (via the `function` object). All three of the sounds can be made using this patch, using vs_harp_riff.wav as their underlying audio file, and without altering the programming details of the algorithm (except for changing the parameter values, of course).

Completion time: 1 hour.

LIST OF MAX OBJECTS

!-

Performs a subtraction in which the *second* operator is entered on the left inlet (and consequently triggers the operation), while the *first* operator is entered as the argument.

!/

Performs a division in which the *second* operator is entered on the left inlet (and consequently triggers the operation), while the *first* operator is entered as the argument.

attrui

This object, connected to any other object, allows us to view and modify its attributes.

drunk

Generates random numbers between 0 and the first argument, minus 1, using a drunkard's walk algorithm. Two successive numbers can vary by no more than a value between 0 and the second argument, minus 1.

float

An object that stores floating point values and recalls them upon receiving a bang.

inlet

An object that, when inserted in a subpatch, creates an inlet on the patcher object that corresponds to the subpatch in the main window.

int

An object that stores integer values and recalls them upon receiving a bang.

join

An object that can be used to construct lists from messages received on its inlets.

mc.mixdown~

Mixes multichannel signals.

mc.pack~

Groups the individual signals into a multichannel signal.

mc.unpack~

Separates the individual signals contained in a multichannel signal.

metro

Generates a sequence of bangs, spaced evenly in time using an interval specified in milliseconds as the object's argument.

multislider
A graphical object that represents a group of sliders, and which generates lists of numbers.

outlet
An object that, when inserted into a subpatch, creates an outlet on the patcher object that corresponds to the subpatch in the main window.

p
See the **patcher** object.

pack
Enables bundling a series of independent elements into a list.

patcher
An object that contains subpatches.

prepend
An object that prepends its argument to any message that it receives.

r
See the **receive** object.

random
An object that generates random numbers.

receive
An object that can receive messages from **send** objects without the use of patch cords.

s
See the **send** object.

send
An object that can send messages to **receive** objects without the use of patch cords.

t
See the **trigger** object.

trigger
Repeats received messages across multiple outlets, the number of which is determined by the number of its arguments.

unjoin
An object that will break lists received on its inlet into single elements.

unpack
Enables breaking a list down into a series of independent elements.

uzi
An object that sends a specified number of bangs to its outlet as quickly as possible.

vs.between
An object in the *Virtual Sound Macros* library that generates random numbers between a given minimum and maximum.

vs.drunk
An object in the Virtual Sound Macros library that generates a "random walk" between a minimum and a maximum.

zl
A multi-function object that manages lists: its function changes according to the argument given.

MESSAGES, ATTRIBUTES, AND PARAMETERS FOR SPECIFIC MAX OBJECTS

a group of objects
Encapsulate (message)
Message that enables you to easily create a subpatch, moving a selected group of objects to the inside of a new patcher window.

arguments
`trigger`

b: convert the input message into a bang
f: convert the input message into a floating point number
i: convert the input message into an integer
l: convert the input message into a list
s: convert the input message into a symbol

`zl`

group: group the input values into a list of determined length
join: combine the two input lists
len: return the length of a list
slice: divide the input list into two parts

`drunk`
- Step
Value that determines the maximum difference between one random number generated by `drunk` and the next. It must be set using the third inlet to the object.

`function`
- Setdomain (message)
Message that enables setting the size of the domain of a `function` object.

message box
- Append (message)
The message "*append*", followed by a message, adds the message to the end of the contents of the message box. It is important not to confuse this command with the object of the same name! (See `append` in the "List of Max Objects" in Chapter 1P.)

- Prepend (message)
The message "*prepend*", followed by a message, inserts the message at the beginning of the contents of the message box. It is important to not confuse this command with the object of the same name. (See prepend in the "List of Max Objects" above.)

- Set (message)
This message deletes the contents of a message box and substitutes the message following the command word "*set*". The message "*set*" without any message simply deletes the contents of a message box.

Multichannel Objects
- @values (attribute)
Sets the values for the individual instances of a multichannel object
- applyvalues (message)
Dynamically sets the values for the individual instances of a multichannel object

`multislider`
- Number of sliders (attribute)
Attribute that sets the number of sliders contained in a **`multislider`**.

- Range (attribute)
Attribute that sets the minimum and maximum values to be generated by a **`multislider`**.

`sfplay~`
- Speed (message)
Message that varies the speed at which **`sfplay~`** reads an audio file.

GLOSSARY

$
Variable argument: when we have one or more elements in a message box consisting of a dollar sign followed by an integer (such as $1, $2, etc.), these elements are replaced by the corresponding elements of messages that arrive on the inlet of the message box.

Abstraction
An object that contains a patch that is usable from within another patch. If the file containing an abstraction is found in Max's search path, the abstraction is available to any patch.

Subpatch
Patches that are contained within a patcher object and which are visually represented by a single object box with inlets and outlets. Subpatches are available only within the patch in which they were created, unless they are manually copied and pasted into some other patch.

2T
ADDITIVE AND VECTOR SYNTHESIS

LEARNING AGENDA

PREREQUISITES FOR THE CHAPTER
- Contents of Chapter 1 (Theory)

LEARNING OBJECTIVES
Knowledge
- To learn about the theory behind adding waveforms (phase, constructive interference, destructive interference)
- To learn about the theory and use of basic additive synthesis, using both fixed and variable spectra to produce both harmonic and non-harmonic sounds
- To learn about the relationship between phase and beats
- To learn how to use wavetables, and how interpolation is implemented
- To learn some theory to support basic vector synthesis

Skills
- To be able to differentiate between harmonic and non-harmonic sounds
- To be able to recognize beats upon hearing them
- To identify the different segments of a sound envelope, and to describe their characteristics

CONTENTS
- Additive synthesis using both fixed and variable spectra
- Harmonic and non-harmonic sounds
- Phase and beats
- Interpolation
- Vector synthesis

ACTIVITIES
- Video examples

TESTING
- Questions with short answers
- Listening and analysis

SUPPORTING MATERIALS
- Fundamental concepts
- Glossary
- Discography

2.1 FIXED SPECTRUM ADDITIVE SYNTHESIS

A sound produced by an acoustic instrument, any sound at all, is a set of complex oscillations, all produced simultaneously by the instrument in question. Each oscillation contributes a piece of the overall timbre of the sound, and their sum wholly determines the resulting waveform. However, this summed set of oscillations, this complex waveform, can also be described as a group of more elementary vibrations: sine waves.
Sine waves are the basic building blocks with which it is possible to construct all other waveforms. When used in this way, we call the sine waves frequency components, and each frequency component in the composite wave has its own frequency, amplitude, and phase. The set of frequencies, amplitudes, and phases that completely define a given sound is called its **sound spectrum**. Any sound, natural or synthesized, can be decomposed into a group of frequency components. Synthesized waveforms such as we described in Section 1.2 are no exception; each has its own unique sound spectrum, and can be built up from a mixture of sine waves. (Sine waves themselves are self-describing – they contain only themselves as components!).

SPECTRUM AND WAVEFORM

Spectrum and waveform are two different ways to describe a single sound. Waveform is the graphical representation of amplitude as a function of time.[1] In figure 2.1, we consider the waveform of a complex sound in which the x-axis is time and the y-axis amplitude. We note that the waveform of this sound is bipolar, meaning that the values representing its amplitude oscillate above and below zero. A waveform graph is portrayed in the **time domain**, a representation in which instantaneous amplitudes are recorded, instant by instant, as they trace out the shape of the complex sound.

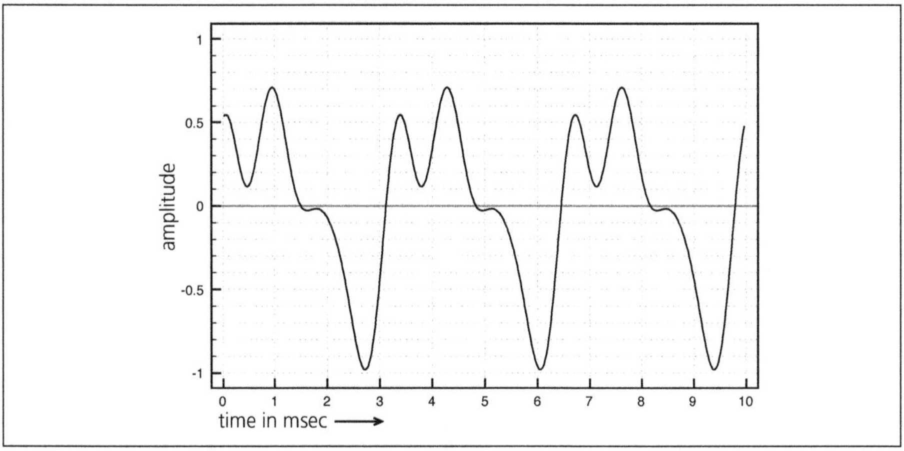

Fig. 2.1 The waveform of a complex sound

[1] In the case of periodic sounds, the waveform can be fully represented by a single cycle.

In figure 2.2, we see the same complex sound broken into frequency components. Four distinct sine waves, when their frequencies and amplitudes are summed, constitute the complex sound shown in the preceding figure.

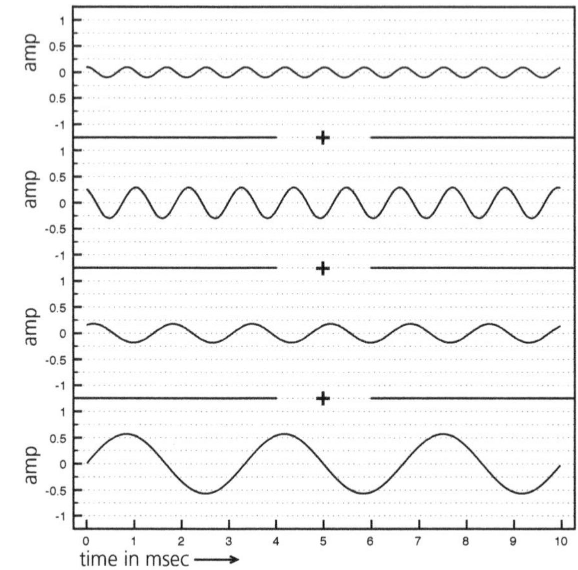

Fig.2.2 Decomposition of a complex sound into sinusoidal components

A clearer way to show a "snapshot" of a collection of frequencies and amplitudes such as this might be to use a graph in which the amplitude of the components is shown as a function of frequency, an approach known as **frequency domain** representation. Using this approach, the x-axis represents frequency values, while the y-axis represents amplitude. Figure 2.2b shows our example in this format: a graph displaying peak amplitudes for each component present in the signal.

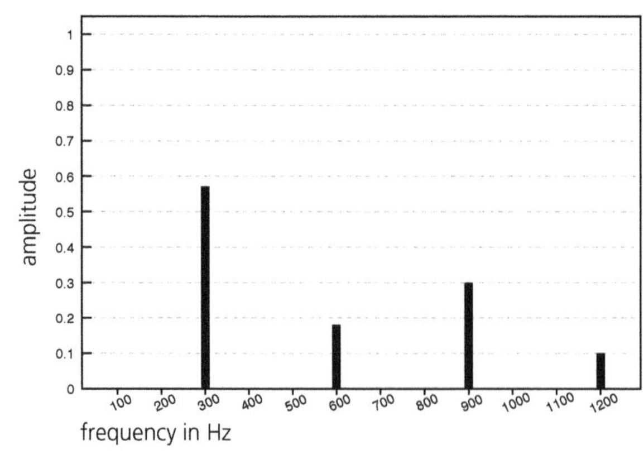

Fig. 2.2b A sound spectrum

In order to see the evolution of components over time, we can use a graph called a **sonogram** (which is also sometimes called a spectrogram), in which frequencies are shown on the y-axis and time is shown on the x-axis (as demonstrated in figure 2.2c). The lines corresponding to frequency components become darker or lighter as their amplitude changes in intensity. In this particular example, there are only four lines, since it is a sound with a simple fixed spectrum.

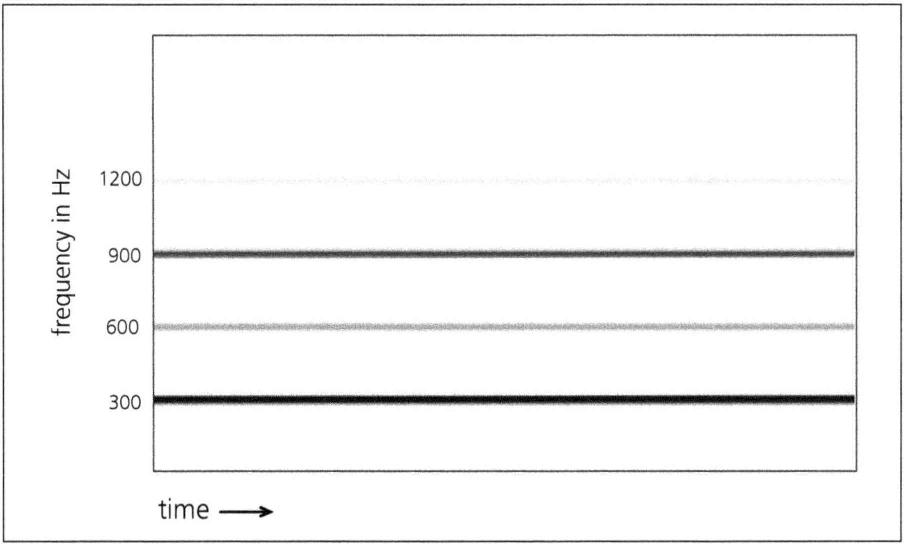

Fig. 2.2c A sonogram (also called a spectrogram)

Now we will consider a process in which, instead of decomposing a complex sound into sine waves, we aim to do the opposite: to fashion a complex sound out of a set of sine waves.

This technique, which should in theory enable us to create any waveform at all by building up a sum of sine waves, is called **additive synthesis**, and is shown in diagrammatic form in figure 2.3.

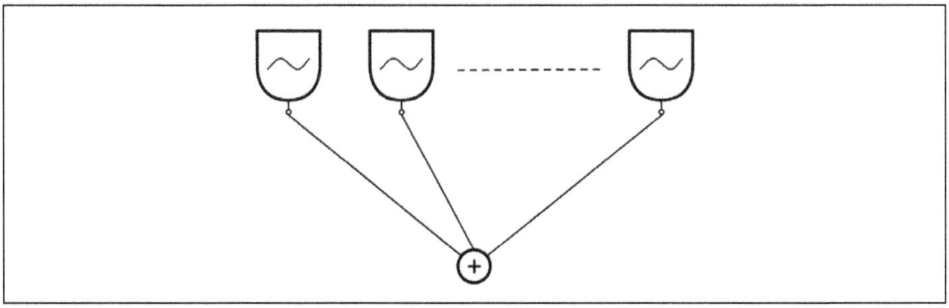

Fig. 2.3 A sum of signals output by sine wave oscillators

In figure 2.4, two waves, A and B, and their sum, C, are shown in the time domain.

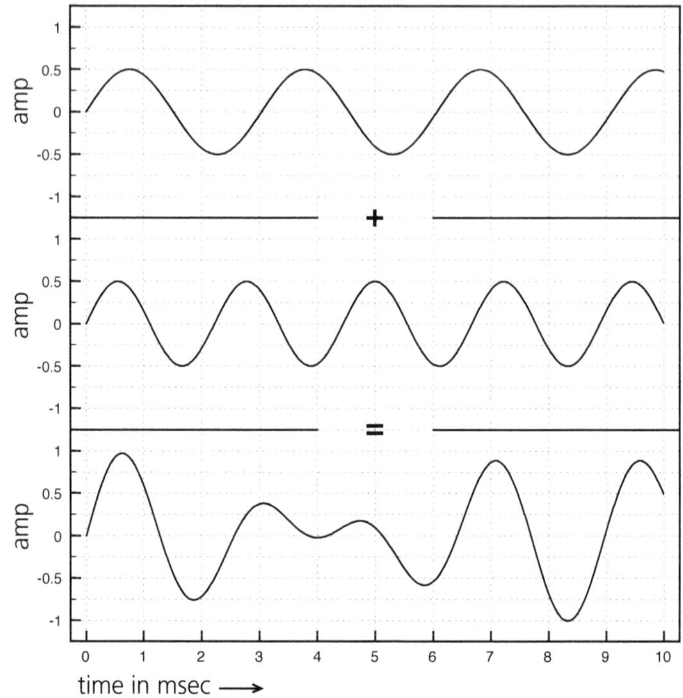

Fig.2.4 A graphical representation of a sum of sine waves

As you can easily verify by inspection, instantaneous amplitudes for wave C are obtained by summing the instantaneous amplitudes of the individual waves A and B. These amplitude values are summed point-by-point, taking their sign, positive or negative, into consideration. Whenever the amplitudes of A and B are both positive or both negative, the absolute value of the amplitude of C will be larger than that of either of the component, resulting in **constructive interference**, such as displayed by the following values:

A = -0.3
B = -0.2
C = -0.5

Whenever the amplitudes of A and B differ in their signs, one being positive and the other negative, the absolute value of their sum C will be less than either one or both components, resulting in **destructive interference**, as shown in the following example:

A = 0.3
B = -0.1
C = 0.2

"The largest part, indeed nearly the entirety, of sounds that we hear in the real world are not *pure* sounds, but rather, **complex sounds**; sounds that can be

resolved into bigger or smaller quantities of pure sound, which are then said to be the components of the complex sound. To better understand this phenomenon, we can establish an analogy with optics. It is noted that some colors are *pure*, which is to say that they cannot be further decomposed into other colors (red, orange, yellow, and down the spectrum to violet). Corresponding to each of these pure colors is a certain wavelength of light. If only one of the pure colors is present, a prism, which decomposes white light into the seven colors of the spectrum, will show only the single color component. The same thing happens with sound. A certain perceived pitch corresponds to a certain **wavelength**[2] of sound. If no other frequency is present at the same moment, the sound will be *pure*. A pure sound, as we know, has a *sine* waveform."
(Bianchini, R., Cipriani, A., 2001, pp. 69-70)

The components of a complex sound sometimes have frequencies that are integer multiples of the lowest component frequency in the sound. In this case the lowest component frequency is called the **fundamental**, and the other components are called **harmonics**. (A fundamental of 100 Hz, for example, might have harmonics at 200 Hz, 300 Hz, 400 Hz, etc.) The specific component that has a frequency that is twice that of its fundamental is called the *second harmonic*, the component that has a frequency that is three times that of the fundamental is called the *third harmonic*, and so on. When, as in the case we are illustrating, the components of a sound are integer multiples of the fundamental, the sound is called a *harmonic sound*. We note that in a harmonic sound the frequency of the fundamental represents the greatest common divisor of the frequencies of all of the components. It is, by definition, the maximum number that exactly divides all of the frequencies without leaving a remainder.

VIDEO EXAMPLE 2A – *HARMONIC COMPONENTS*

If the pure sounds composing a complex sound are not integer multiples of the lowest frequency component, we have a non-harmonic sound and the components are called **non-harmonic components**, or **partials**.

VIDEO EXAMPLE 2B – *NON-HARMONIC COMPONENTS*

2 "The length of a cycle is called its **wavelength** and is measured in meters or in centimeters. This is the space that a cycle physically occupies in the air, and were sound actually visible, it would be easy to measure, for example, with a tape measure." (Bianchini, R. 2003)

TECHNICAL DETAILS – PHASE

We already pointed out, in the previous chapter, the trigonometric functions **sine** and **cosine**, which respectively generate sine waves and cosine waves. These functions are very important because they describe simple harmonic motion, which is the fundamental movement of all vibrating bodies (and therefore of all bodies that produce sounds).

In more general terms, the sine function describes the motion of an object that is subject to a force displacing it from a position of equilibrium. The magnitude of this force is proportional to the distance of the object from the point of equilibrium. Many real world phenomena trace their progress in such a sinusoidal form, including the movement of a swinging pendulum, the changes in length of the day during the course of a year, and the motion of a piston in a car engine.

From the trigonometric point of view, if we construct a unit circle (a circle with a radius of 1) whose center we place at the origin of a Cartesian coordinate system, we can define sine and cosine as a projection of an arbitrary ray onto the y-axis and onto the x-axis, respectively (as shown in figure 2.5).

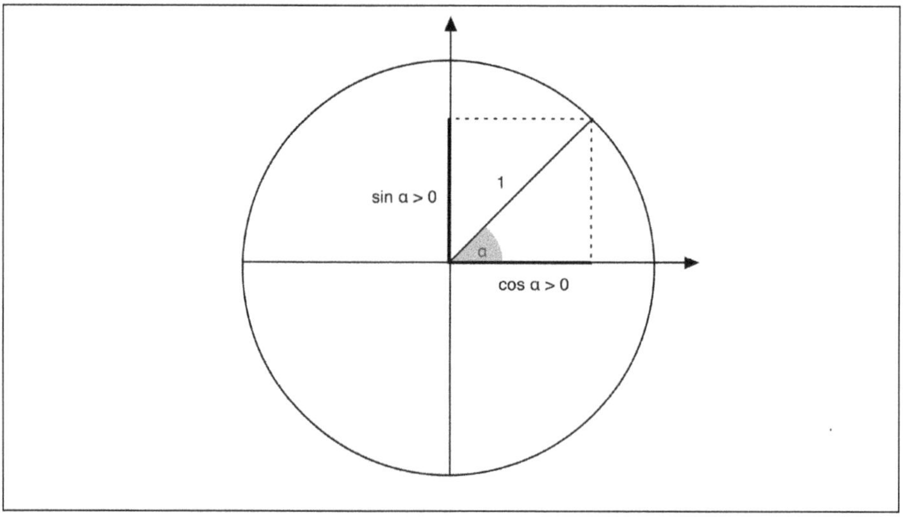

Fig. 2.5 Sine and cosine of the angle α

As you can see in figure 2.5, if we rotate the ray counterclockwise around the circumference of the circle and track the angle α formed between the ray and the x-axis, the projected lengths of the ray onto the coordinate axes will equal the values of $\sin(\alpha)$ and $\cos(\alpha)$. When the angle α has swept the entire circumference, forming angles of 0 to 360 degrees (or from 0 to 2π radians), we will have finished a complete cycle of the sine and cosine functions. As you can see in figure 2.6, a sine wave can be thought of as a graphical display of the changing length of the projection onto the y-axis while the value of the underlying angle varies over time.

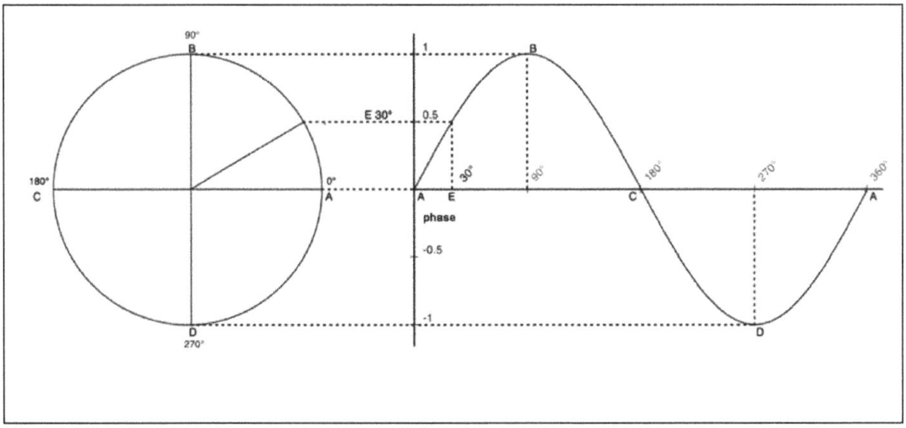

Fig. 2.6 Graphical representation of a sine wave with regard to phase

The angle α can also be defined as the phase of a waveform. As the phase passes from 0 degrees to 360 degrees (or from 0 radians to 2π radians), the waveform, as we have already seen, completes one cycle.

Often in programming languages for computer music one finds "normalized" phase: a phase value that, instead of being represented in degrees or radians, is represented as decimal values between 0 and 1. To clarify the equivalence relationships that exist for these different representations of phase, the following figure shows some common phase values in degrees, radians, and normalized decimal values, along with related values of the sine function. Verify these relationships visually by following the progression shown in figure 2.7.

PHASE			VALUE
Degrees	Radians	Normalized	
0°	(0)	0	0
45°	(π/4)	0.125	0.707
90°	(π/2)	0.25	1
135°	(3π/4)	0.375	0.707
180°	(π)	0.5	0
225°	(5π/4)	0.625	-0.707
270°	(3π/2)	0.75	-1
315°	(7π/4)	0.875	-0.707
360°	(2π)	1	0

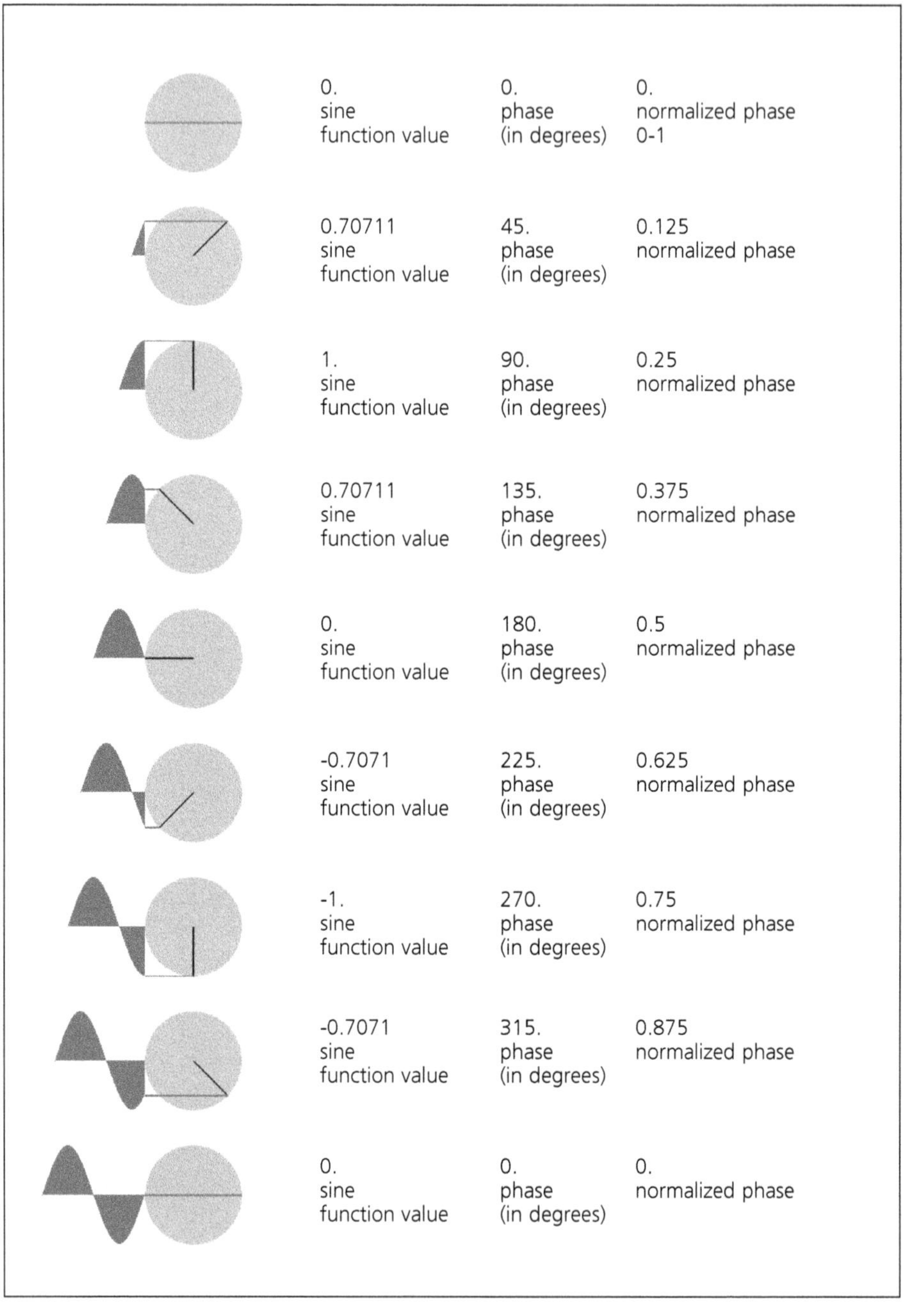

Fig. 2.7 Construction of a sine wave

VIDEO EXAMPLE 2C – *PHASE AND SINE WAVES*

A phase of 360 degrees is equivalent to a phase of 0 degrees. Because of this, the cycle wraps around endlessly, beginning anew whenever we increment phase values beyond the basic range.
In figure 2.8, we have graphed the projection of our ray onto the x-axis rather than the y-axis, producing a graph that is otherwise known as the cosine function.

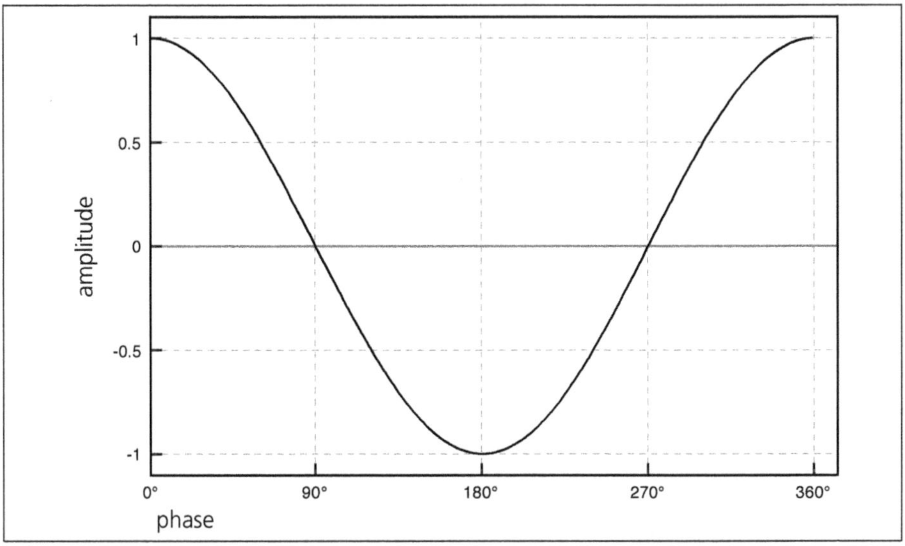

Fig. 2.8 The cosine function

The two waveforms are identical. The cosine wave is simply a sine wave whose phase is shifted by 90 degrees, as you can see in figure 2.9.

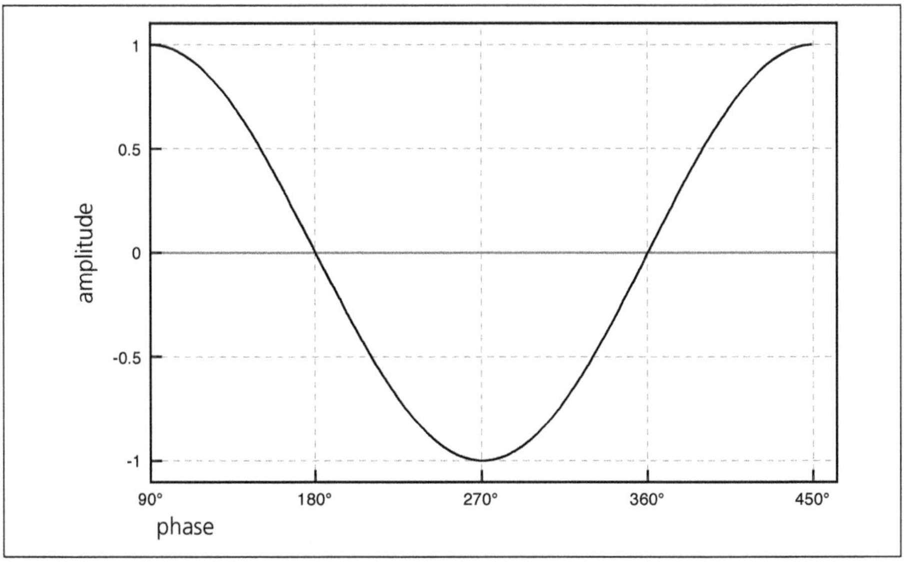

Fig. 2.9 A sine wave, phase shifted by 90 degrees

If we go further and shift the phase of a sine or a cosine wave by a full 180 degrees, we obtain a waveform that has *reversed polarity* with respect to the original waveform (which had a phase angle of 0 degrees). For every positive value in one of these waves, there is a corresponding negative value in the other. In such a case, the two waves are said to be **in antiphase** (as shown in figure 2.10).

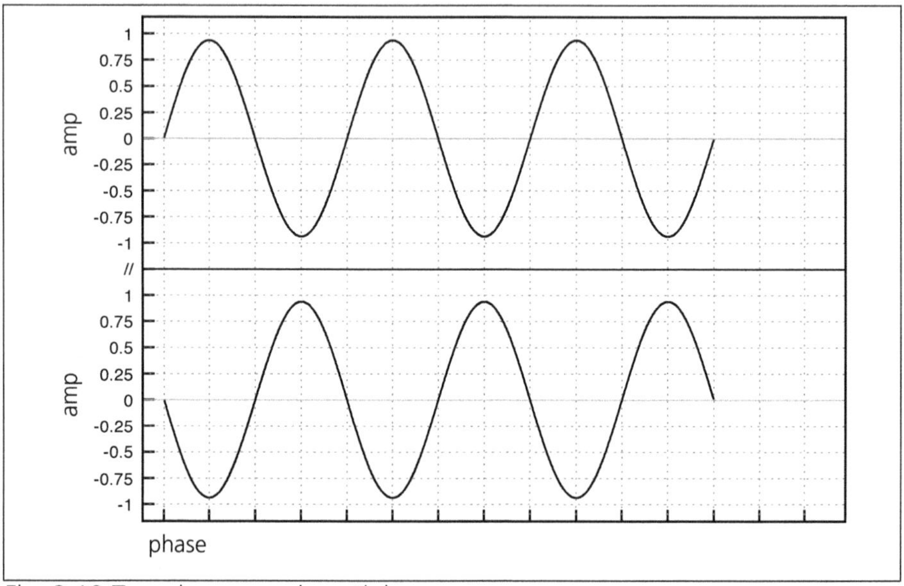

Fig. 2.10 Two sine waves in antiphase

If we sum the two waveforms in figure 2.10, destructive interference will completely eliminate the sound, since the sum of every sample from the first waveform with its corresponding sample in the second waveform will always yield 0.

An easy way to obtain a polarity-reversed waveform consists of multiplying every sample value by -1. Using this method, positive values are transformed into negative, and negative into positive.

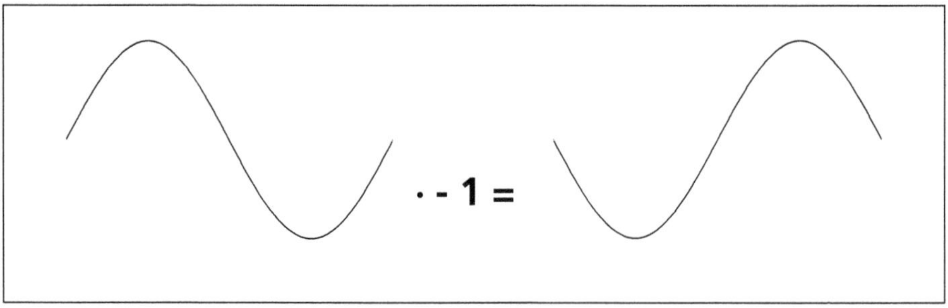

Fig. 2.11 Multiplication of a sampled signal by a negative constant

We will revisit this discussion in Section 2.2, entitled "Beats".

HARMONIC AND NON-HARMONIC SPECTRA

We can obtain sounds with either a **harmonic spectrum** or a **non-harmonic spectrum** by using additive synthesis.

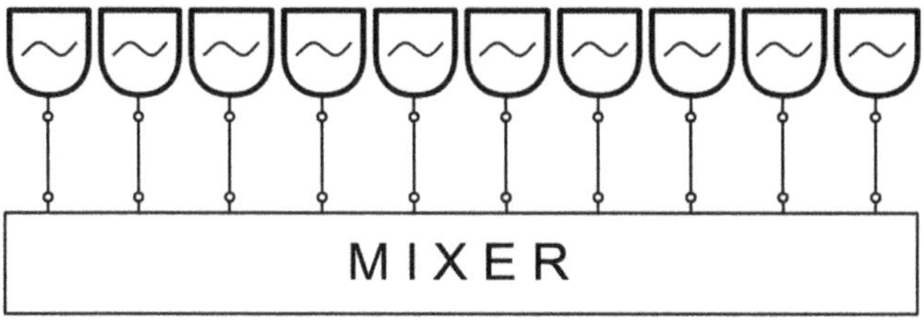

Fig. 2.12 Summing oscillators

In the diagram in figure 2.12, we see sine wave oscillators, whose outlets are summed together using a mixer.
In figure 2.13 we show four examples of additive synthesis that produce harmonic spectra.

arm	amp
1	1
2	0
3	.33
4	0
5	.2
6	0
7	.14
8	0
9	.11
10	0

arm	amp
1	1
2	.5
3	.33
4	.25
5	.2
6	.16
7	.14
8	.12
9	.11
10	.1

arm	amp
1	.5
2	1
3	0
4	0
5	0
6	0
7	0
8	0
9	0
10	0

arm	amp
1	1
2	0
3	0
4	0
5	0
6	0
7	0
8	0
9	0
10	0

Fig. 2.13 Waveforms constructed from summed sine waves

When defining the spectrum of an harmonic sound, it is sufficient to provide the amplitudes of the non-zero components, using a table such as the following:

HARMONIC	I	II	III	IV	V	VI	VII	VIII	IX	X
FREQ. (Hz)	100	200	300	400	500	600	700	800	900	1000
AMPLITUDE	1	.8	.6	.75	.4	.3	.2	.28	.26	.18

In this table, all of the upper components have an amplitude near 0. The table can be graphed as shown in figure 2.14, where we see the spectrum of a sound: the horizontal axis shows frequencies by harmonic number, and the vertical axis shows amplitude. This spectrum is clearly harmonic, since the frequencies are equidistant from each other; all of the components have a harmonic relationship with the fundamental. The line traced over the spectrum is called the **spectral envelope**: it is a curve that connects the tops of the bars that represent the amplitude of the harmonics.[3]

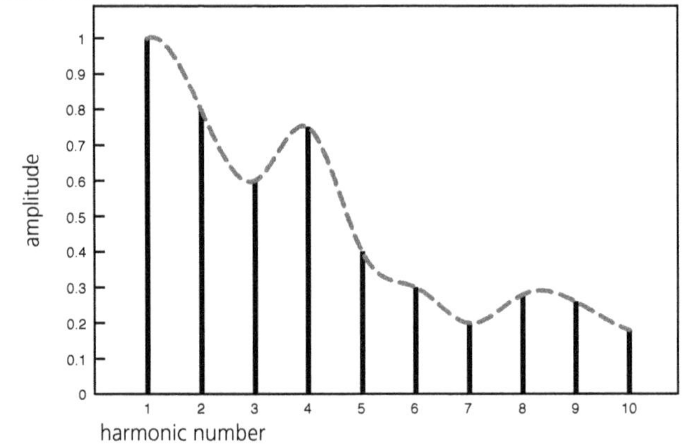

Fig. 2.14 Spectral envelope

In figure 2.15 the waveform produced by the spectrum pictured in figure 2.14 is shown. As you see, it is a periodic waveform: a wave whose shape repeats once per period without changing.

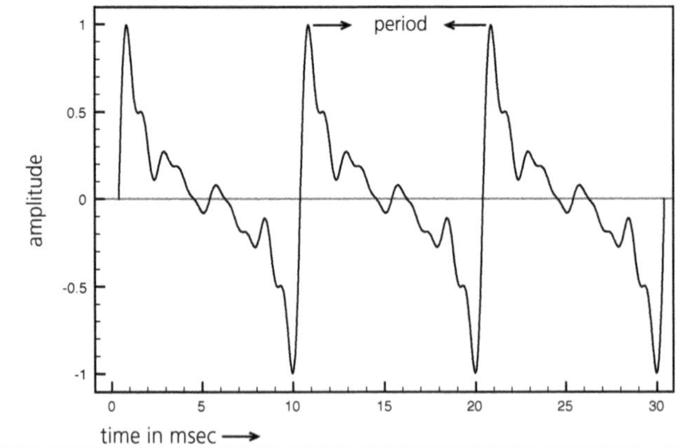

Fig. 2.15 Periodic waveform

[3] It is possible, by means of this envelope, to apply the spectral profile of one sound to another completely unrelated sound, independent of the frequency content of the components (see Section 2.4, and especially Chapter 12).

Some waveforms, very common in the production of analog and digital electronic music, can be approximated by a series of harmonics whose amplitudes are expressed by convenient formulas.

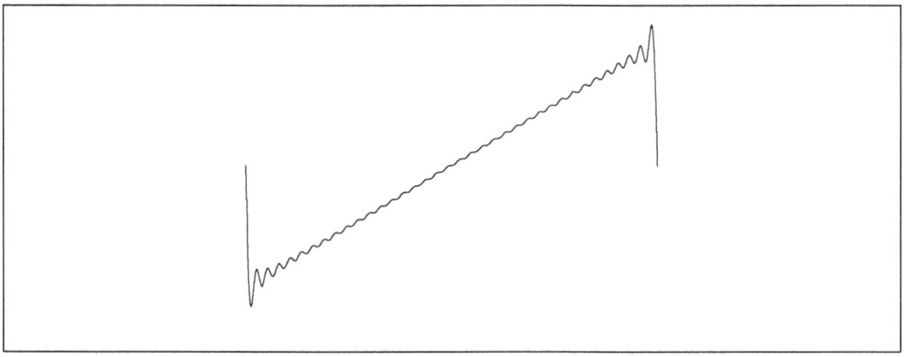

Fig. 2.16 Sawtooth wave

For example, the **sawtooth wave**, as seen in figure 2.16, can be approximated by a series of harmonically linked sine waves that all have a phase of 180 degrees (like the wave in the lower part of figure 2.10), and whose amplitudes are:

fundamental	1/1
second harmonic	1/2
third harmonic	1/3
fourth harmonic	1/4
fifth harmonic	1/5
sixth harmonic	1/6
...	

As you can see, for the nth given harmonic, the amplitude will be 1/n. The more harmonics are present, the more the resulting waveform will resemble that in figure 2.16.

Of course, a "perfect" sawtooth wave could only be produced using an infinite series of harmonics. (See figure 2.17.)

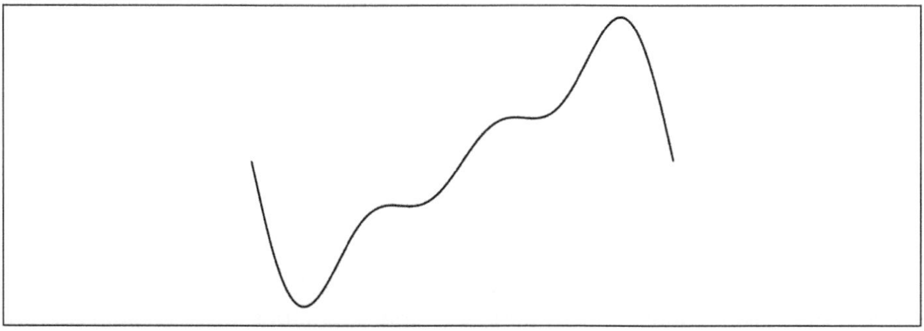

Fig. 2.17a Sawtooth wave with 3 harmonics

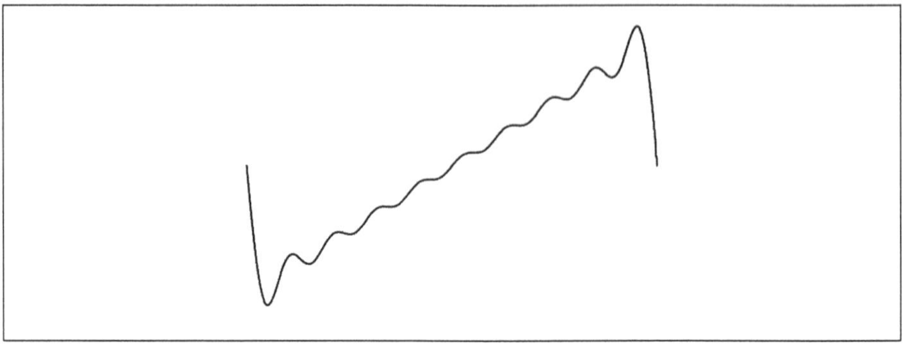

Fig. 2.17b Sawtooth wave with 9 harmonics

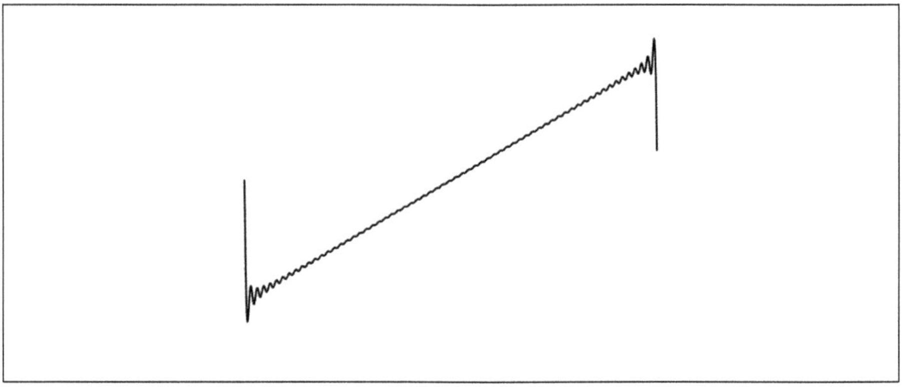

Fig. 2.17c Sawtooth wave with 64 harmonics

Another very common waveform is the **square wave**.

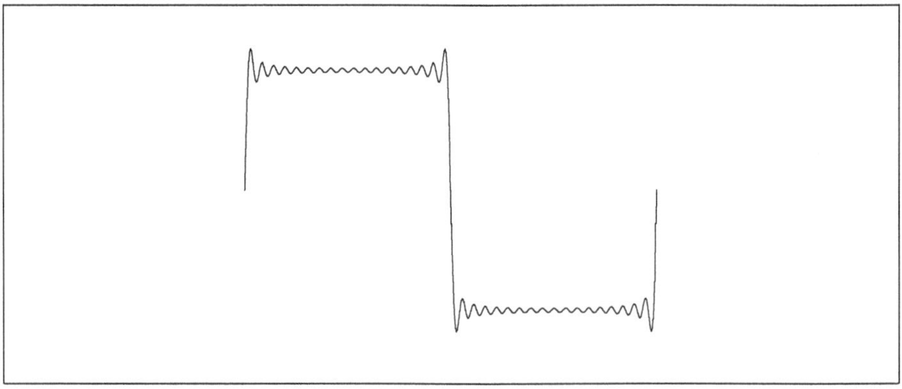

Fig. 2.18 Square wave

The series of components used for the approximation of the square wave is similar to that of the sawtooth wave, but consists of only odd-numbered components with phase of 0 degrees. The amplitude of even-numbered components in this waveform is always 0.

fundamental	1/1
second harmonic	0
third harmonic	1/3
fourth harmonic	0
fifth harmonic	1/5
sixth harmonic	0
seventh harmonic	1/7
...	

The shape of the **triangle wave** is shown in figure 2.19.

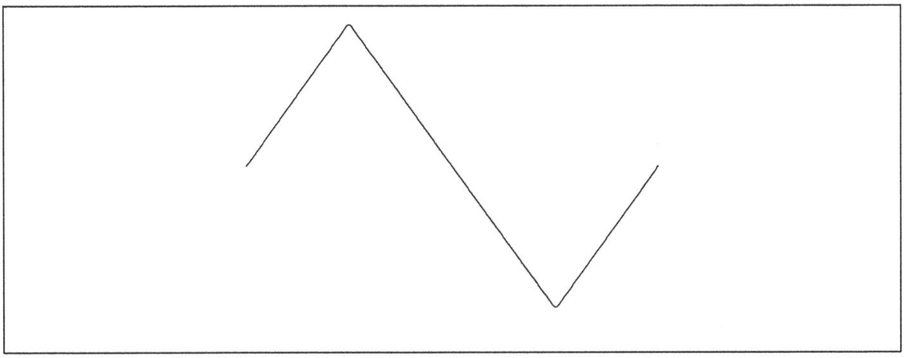

Fig. 2.19 Triangle wave

You can approximate the triangle wave by using an amplitude factor of $1/n^2$, for odd n only, and by multiplying the series of odd numbers alternately by 1 and by -1 (or by alternating the phase of the sine waves between 0 degrees and 180 degrees).

Here are the resulting factors:

fundamental	1/1
second harmonic	0
third harmonic	-1/9
fourth harmonic	0
fifth harmonic	1/25
sixth harmonic	0
seventh harmonic	-1/49
...	

As we learned in the earlier section dedicated to phase, multiplying a digital sine wave by a negative number will give you a "reversed" form of the wave, out of phase by 180 degrees. The negative values in this table should be thought of as being 180 degrees out of phase with the positive values.

As a final wave to consider, examine the **impulse** (shown in figure 2.20), which is a signal that contains energy at all frequencies (for a deeper definition of the impulse, see Section 3.9).

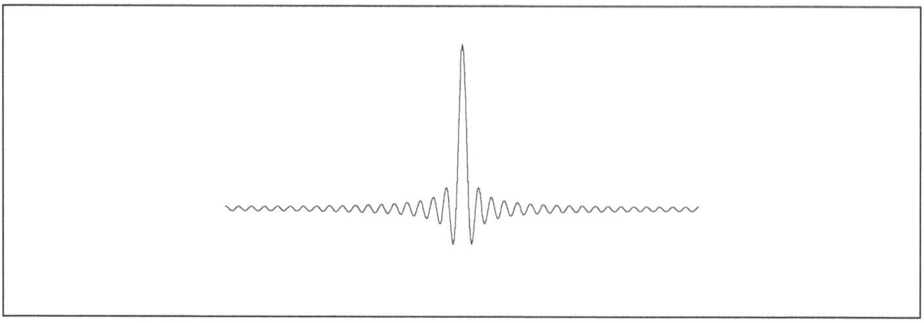

Fig. 2.20 Impulse

The impulse can be approximated by using an identical amplitude for all harmonics.

1 1 1 1 1 ...

When approximating an impulse, the components should all be cosine waves rather than sine waves. The cosine function is, as we know, identical to the sine function, but out of phase by $\pi/2$ (or 90 degrees). See the discussion of phase above for more details.

VIDEO EXAMPLE 2D – *CLASSIC WAVEFORMS*

Normally, in the presence of a harmonic sound, we perceive a single pitch, which is almost always the pitch of the fundamental. There are cases, however, in which a fundamental is not present in a sound, but the sound still possesses harmonic structure. In this case, the **missing fundamental**, sometimes called the phantom fundamental, can still be identified by our brain. We encounter telephones and radios every day which have speakers that cannot accurately reproduce bass frequencies. Despite these limitations, we are able to infer the fundamental frequencies of the sounds we hear on these devices by listening to upper harmonics alone.

Let's look at two examples of this phenomenon, both of which begin with a fundamental frequency of 100 Hz:

> The first sound is composed of all harmonics from the first through the seventh. (See figure 2.21.)

> The second sound has only the fourth through seventh harmonics (400 Hz, 500 Hz, 600 Hz, 700 Hz, as shown in figure 2.22).

As you can see, the period of the two waveforms is the same. The greatest common divisor (100 Hz) shared by these components is the same, and because of this, their perceived pitches will also be the same, even when the frequency of this 100 Hz component is absent.

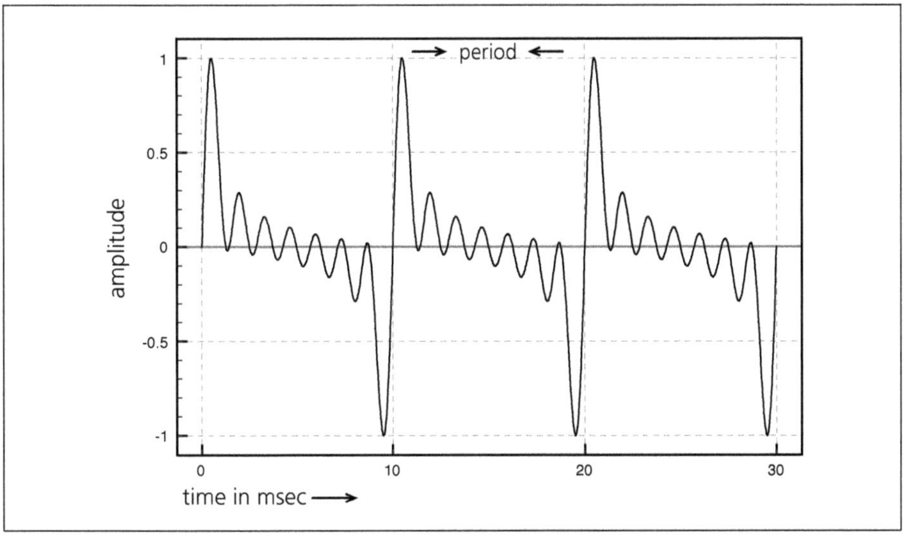

Fig. 2.21 Periodic sound composed of the first through seventh harmonics

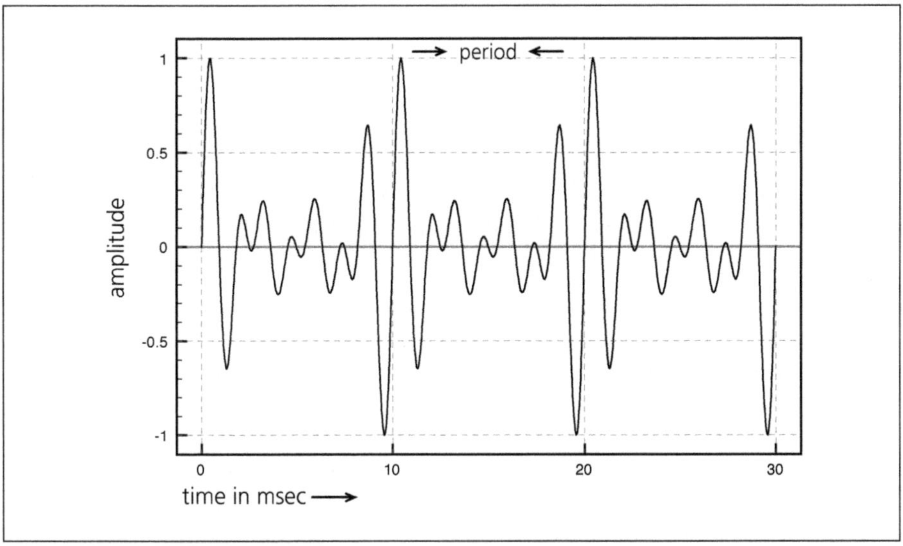

Fig. 2.22 Periodic sound composed of the fourth through seventh harmonics

If, however, too many components are missing in the lower portion of the spectrum, we can no longer perceive the fundamental, leaving such a sound devoid of definite pitch.

VIDEO EXAMPLE 2E – *MISSING FUNDAMENTAL*

There is, of course, a second kind of sound: spectral components can have *non-harmonic* relationships, resulting in non-harmonic sounds. If you compare the upper portion of figure 2.23 with figure 2.14, you will quickly observe that the frequencies in figure 2.23 do not exhibit the same kind of equal spacing; it is easy to suppose that a greatest common divisor does not exist for these component frequencies. This means that a fundamental frequency, from which the frequencies for all other components can be derived as integer multiples, does not exist. In this case, the relationships between the frequencies are irrational.[4] In the lower portion of figure 2.23, we can see that the resulting waveform is non-periodic. It does not repeat cyclically.

VIDEO EXAMPLE 2F – *NON-HARMONIC SOUNDS*

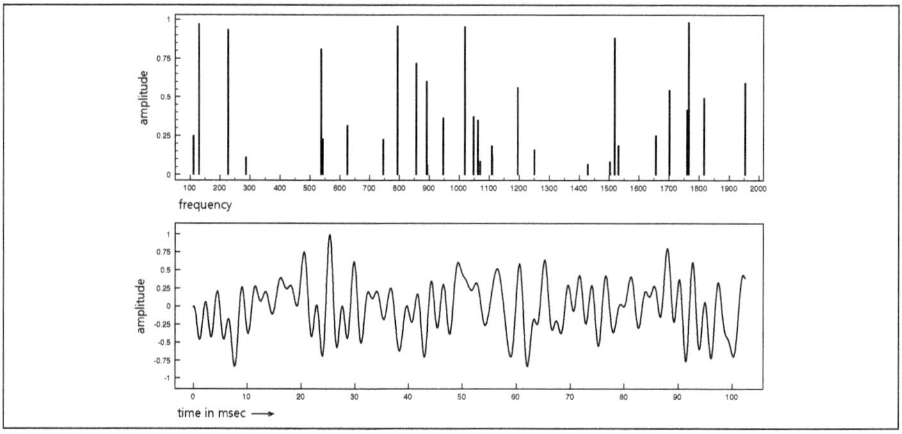

Fig. 2.23 The spectrum and waveform of a non-harmonic sound

"Periodic sounds, such as the pitched sounds made by musical instruments, or the vowel sounds of the human voice, are perceived as being equipped with a definite pitch.[5] (A better term might be quasi-periodic sounds, since physics defines periodic phenomena as being infinite.) Non-periodic sounds, such as the sounds made by musical instruments of indeterminate pitch like cymbals, gongs, and triangles, or consonants produced by the human voice, are not perceived to have definite pitch. The closest we can come to pitch identification for such sounds is to perceive a frequency band in which the density of components is thick enough to bestow a relevant amplitude."
(Bianchini, R., Cipriani, A., 2001, pp. 71-72)

[4] An irrational number is a number that cannot be expressed exactly as an integer fraction with a non-zero denominator. Some famous irrational numbers are the square root of 2 and π.

[5] Assuming that the fundamental frequency falls within the audible band of frequencies, of course.

Sounds can contain both harmonic and non-harmonic components; this is true in particular for musical instruments and naturally occurring sounds. A flute sound, for example, contains harmonic frequencies that give the note played its pitch, but it also contains non-harmonic elements that are tied to the breath of the player. Another example is the sound of a piano, which has non-harmonic components during its attack that are tied to the action of the hammers on the strings; to make the sound even more complicated, the string vibrations of the piano don't produce mathematically perfect harmonic partials, but instead produce partials that are stretched apart by a very small amount.[6]
An interesting experience, which should stimulate discussion about the concepts of harmonicity and non-harmonicity, is to try constructing periodic sounds that have fundamental frequencies that fall below the audible frequency range. By cleverly choosing a set of irregularly spaced harmonics, we can easily hear that the resulting sound is non-harmonic and has no definite pitch, even though it is periodic by definition (meaning that all of its components are related to its infrasonic fundamental via integer ratios). For example, let's hypothesize a sound that has components at 113 Hz, 151 Hz, 257 Hz, 331 Hz, 577 Hz, 811 Hz, 1009 Hz, and 1237 Hz. This sound is non-harmonic to the ear, despite the fact that it is periodic and has a fundamental of 1 Hz, of which all of the components are integral multiples. The implied fundamental of which we spoke earlier cannot be identified, not only because the ear can't hear a frequency of 1 Hz, but also because the components in question are very distant from their fundamental, being the 113th harmonic, the 151st, and so on.

VIDEO EXAMPLE 2G – *PRESET 1 – Non-harmonic periodic sound with an infrasonic fundamental*

It is also possible to construct a non-harmonic, yet periodic, sound that possesses components whose frequencies form integer ratios with some theoretically audible fundamental, but that does not cause our brains to hear its fundamental. For example, a fundamental of 35 Hz forms a basis for harmonic frequencies of 455 Hz, 665 Hz, 735 Hz, 945 Hz, 1085 Hz, 1295 Hz, 1695 Hz, and 1995 Hz, and yet it is simply not possible for our brain to re-create the lost fundamental and to attach a definite pitch to the sound since so many of the lower harmonics are lacking.

VIDEO EXAMPLE 2G – *PRESET 2 – Non-harmonic periodic sound with a missing fundamental of 35 Hz*

[6] Piano tuners know this phenomenon well, since they need to tune slightly low in the bass octaves and then gradually higher as they move towards the upper range to ensure that the higher harmonics of the low notes are in tune with the fundamentals of high notes.

PERIODIC VERSUS APERIODIC, AND HARMONIC VERSUS NON-HARMONIC

Let's systematize and clarify the concepts that we have introduced in this chapter.

The cycle is the smallest portion of a wave that repeats over time.

The fundamental of a harmonic sound is the component with the lowest frequency, and generally also the highest amplitude. The frequencies of all of the other components are integer multiples of this frequency.
If the lowest component in a harmonic sound is missing, but the immediately succeeding components are present, the sound will be heard as having a pitch equal to the missing fundamental. One way of understanding this is that the period of the waveform (the duration of the wave portion that repeats periodically) corresponds to the inverse of the frequency of the missing fundamental.

If, in addition to the fundamental, we start to remove other lower harmonics, we hear the gradual loss of its harmonicity, because at some point, our brain is no longer able to reconstruct the fundamental. A sound thus obtained is non-harmonic, but at the same time periodic, because its period is still the inverse of the frequency of its "virtual" fundamental.

The fundamental of a **periodic sound** is the frequency of which all components are integral multiples. It follows that the fundamental frequency of such a sound, whether real or virtual, is the greatest common divisor of the component frequencies that are present. A non-harmonic sound composed of partials at 100, 205, 290, 425, and 460 hertz, for example, has a fundamental of 5 Hz, and is therefore a periodic sound that repeats 5 time per second (although it is not possible to hear this fundamental).

A **non-periodic sound** is, by contrast, a sound for which it is not possible to identify a portion that repeats in time. An example of non-periodic sound is white noise,[7] or the sound made by a percussion instrument that has no definite pitch such as a cymbal.

We've seen that you can have a periodic sound that has no definite pitch. On the other hand, is it possible to have a non-periodic sound that does have a definite pitch? Certainly. It is enough to have components whose frequencies are close to being integral multiples of some audible fundamental. The partials 110, 220.009, 329.999, 439.991, and 550.007 hertz, for example can be heard unequivocally as an A, even though their period doesn't correspond to the perceived fundamental, but rather to the greatest common divisor of the components, which is 0.001 hertz. To be precise about this, the period of this waveform is 1000 seconds, and a sound with a period as long as this is psychoacoustically equivalent to a non-periodic sound.

[7] For a definition of white noise, see Section 3.1.

To have a truly non-periodic sound with a fixed spectrum, the spectrum must include irrational frequencies, such as the following: 100, 200+π/5, 300+π/4, 400+π/3, 500+π/2. A sound such as this would be impossible to reproduce on a computer, of course, because of numerical compromises that are imposed by the CPU when performing calculations. Nonetheless, for the example cited, we could still obtain a sound with such a long period that we could consider it, for all practical purposes, to be non-periodic.

We define sounds such as those found in the last two examples, which have a perceptible pitch and a series of components that are almost multiples of the fundamental, as **quasi-harmonic sounds**.

Sounds with variable spectra (which we will speak more about in Section 2.4) can easily be non-periodic. (Sounds, for example, in which components slide irregularly from one frequency to another.) Real-world, non-electronic, sounds are almost never periodic. It is simply impossible, even for the most precise clarinettist in the world, to emit a sound in which successive periods of the waveform are perfectly identical (not counting the fact that the poor clarinettist would need to produce such a sound for an infinite amount of time...)

In the case of natural sounds that are harmonic and have definite pitch (such as the clarinet), we speak of such sound as being "quasi-periodic" or "pseudo-periodic".

The fundamental

It is exceedingly difficult to give a definition for the **fundamental** that admits all cases. For a periodic sound with a given pitch, the fundamental is easily defined as the frequency that forms integer ratios with all other components. The pitch that we perceive for such a sound corresponds to the pitch of this fundamental. We can also say that in the case of the "quasi-harmonic" sounds that we saw above, the fundamental ought to be the lowest component, since this component also happens to be the frequency that we perceive to be the pitch of such sounds.

But what about the case of non-harmonic sounds? If a sound is still periodic, we could say that the fundamental is the component that corresponds to the greatest common divisor of the components, such as in the case that we examined above that had an implied fundamental of 5 Hz. But such a "fundamental" is not audible, since its frequency is well below the audio band. Likewise, we could designate the lowest component of a non-harmonic sound as its fundamental (which would be the 100 Hz component in the example above), but such a component turns out to be not very important. In many percussive sounds, for example, the lowest components turn out to be almost inaudible, while those with higher frequencies almost completely characterize the timbre; removing the "fundamental" from such a sound doesn't change its timbre in the least. Because of this, in the cases of non-harmonic sounds, we will simply choose to say that no fundamental exists. We will use the term only for sounds that have definite pitch, whether periodic, quasi-periodic, harmonic, or quasi-harmonic.

INTERPOLATION

In the preceding section we spoke of **digital oscillators** without clarifying how they function. Referring to figure 2.24, we construct a **wavetable** (or array[8]) of 20 elements, and fill it with values taken from a sine wave moving between amplitudes of -1 and 1.

indices	0	1	2	3	4	5	6	7	8	9	10	11	12	13	14	15	16	17	18	19
values	0	.31	.60	.83	.97	1	.92	.74	.48	.17	-.16	-.47	-.73	-.91	-1	-.97	-.84	-.61	-.32	0

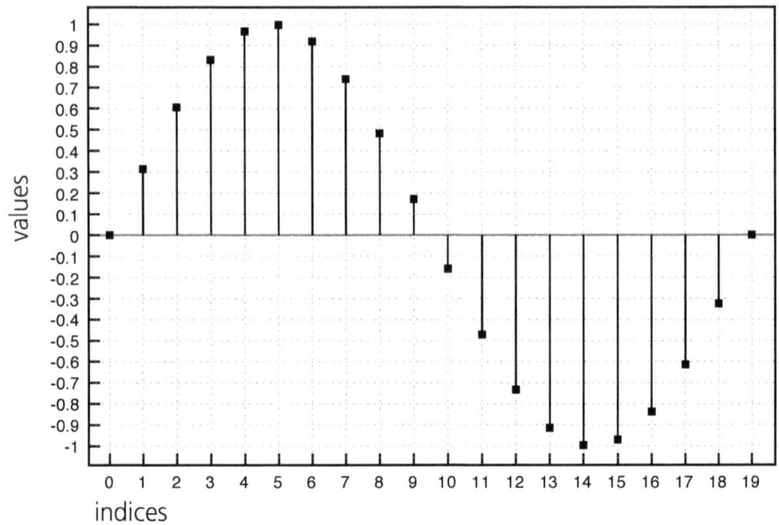

Fig. 2.24 A wavetable containing values taken from a sine wave

Every element is identified with an index or phase,[9] which are numbered from 0 to 19 in the example. Each index refers to a value, which is indicated in the upper portion of the figure. The set of values in this example wavetable sketch the outline of a sine wave when taken consecutively (or more accurately, a few points that roughly approximate a sine wave).

To generate a sine wave, you need to do nothing more than read one value after another from the wavetable and, when you have reached the end, start again from the beginning. Don't be deceived, however: it almost never works to simply read the values that *exactly* correspond to the indices of the wavetable. In the case shown, for example, reading the 20 elements one after the other at a sampling frequency of 44,100 Hz would result in reading the table 2,205 times in one second, generating 2,205 cycles of a sine wave (since 44,100/20 = 2,205).

8 We will define an **array** as an ordered series of values in which each value is assigned a numerical index, drawn from the consecutive integers beginning with 0. For example, the index 0 in the array (2, 3.5, 6, 1, -12) refers to the value 2, the index 1 refers to the value 3.5, the index 2 refers to 6, and so on.

9 See the "phase" section above. The concept here is similar, but in this case the indices or phase values indicate a position within the cycle of a waveform.

If we want to produce a frequency different than 2,205 Hz, say perhaps 441 Hz, every cycle would need to be 100 elements long (since 44,100/100 = 441). This means that, given a wavetable of 20 elements, we would need to read more intermediate elements than actually exist. The indices to consider would not be 0, 1, 2, 3, 4, etc., as in the last example, but rather 0, 0.2, 0.4, 0.6, 0.8, 1.0, etc. Such fractional indices might serve to help us arrive at 100 elements, but what values would they take on? We might, for example, use the value 0 (which is the value associated with the index 0 in figure 2.24) for *any* fractional index lying on the interval between 0 and 1. For the indices between 1 and 2, we might use the value 0.31 (associated with index 1), and so forth. Another possibility would be to *round* the index values, assigning the value 0 (the value for index 0) to 0.2 and 0.4, while assigning 0.31 (the value for index 1) to the indices 0.6 and 0.8. Both cases, however, would result in distortion, due to the stepped nature of the signal (shown in figure 2.25).

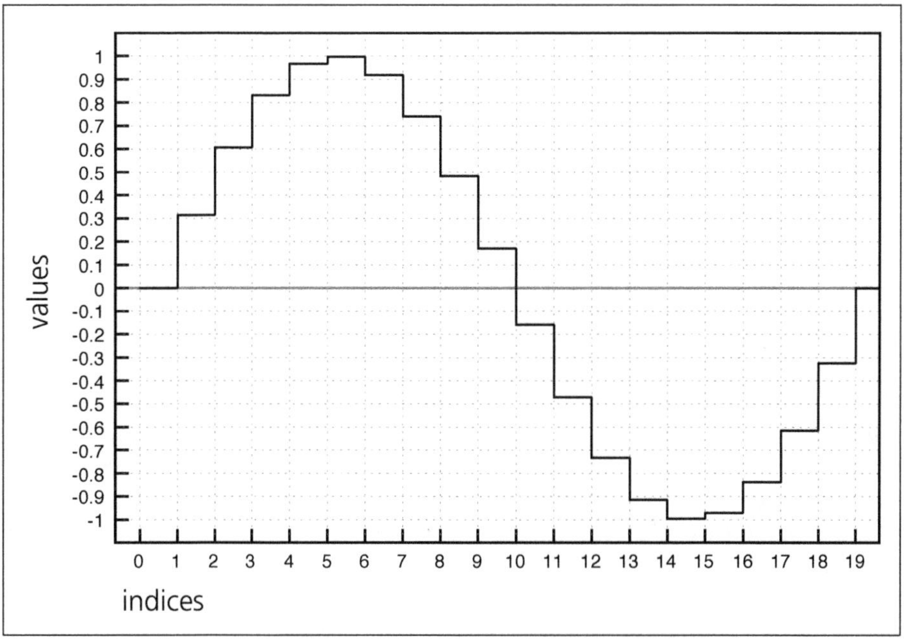

Fig. 2.25 A stepped waveform

The distortion problems in this example are caused by the differences between the values that ought to be found in a sine wave and those obtained by truncating decimal places using the methods that we have been experimenting with. The amount of error contained in the truncated values varies continuously, resulting in an imprecise digital signal whose stepped appearance will be heard as distortion. To obtain better results, we could instead use a technique for defining intermediate values called **interpolation**, which consists of estimating intermediate values between points in a wavetable using a calculation. The example of this technique shown in figure 2.26 is called **linear interpolation**; the figure shows how an intermediate value could be calculated between a point, designated as k, and its successor, designated as k+1.

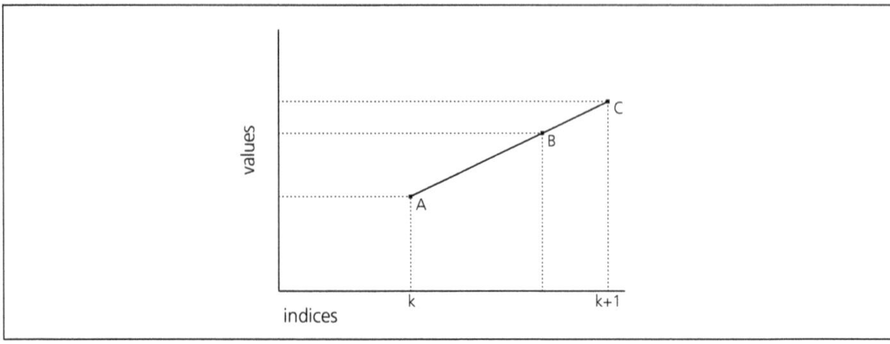

Fig. 2.26a Linear interpolation

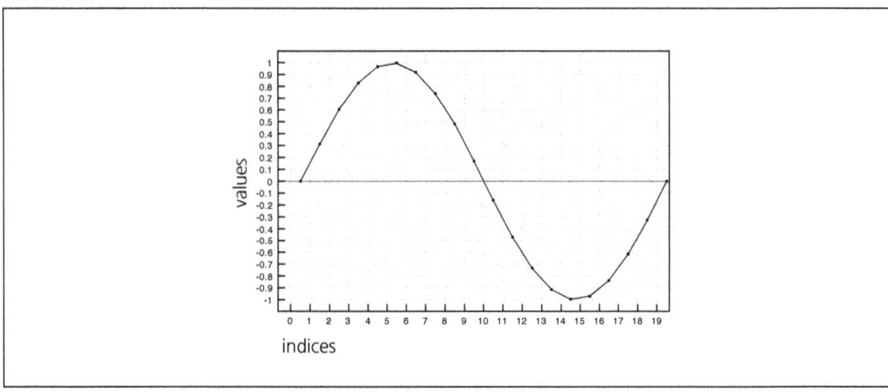

Fig. 2.26b Graph of an interpolated waveform

Using linear interpolation, the value for an intermediate index, designated as B in the figure, is calculated as lying on a line between the values for the two known indices A and C. Using such interpolation to insert values between every point in the table enables us to appreciably reduce the distortion associated with the previous jagged waveform. The improvement in terms of sound quality is huge (due to a big reduction in harmonic distortion[10]), but there is a tradeoff: the time needed to calculate every value is now much greater. The technique yields the following values (graphed in figure 2.26b) for the fractional indices between 0 and 1 of the sine wave shown in figure 2.24.

Indices	Values
0.0	0.0
0.2	0.062
0.4	0.124
0.6	0.186
0.8	0.248
1.0	0.31

[10] Harmonic distortion is changes in a signal's spectrum that can be attributed to alterations of its waveform. See Section 5.1 for more details.

There are other kinds of interpolation. Besides the very simple, but not very efficient, linear interpolation, polynomial interpolation (quadratic, cubic, or even higher degrees) is widely used, and allows for a major reduction in harmonic distortion. It is, however, also computationally expensive. Given its complexity, we will not expand upon its internals, but be aware that many programming languages for sound synthesis make it possible for you to use polynomial interpolation in their oscillators.

Computer music programming languages often use "normalized" indices or phases when working with wavetables (see the discussion of the term *phase* above), in which the indices are always a decimal number between 0 and 1, independent of how many elements are in the wavetable. 0 corresponds to the first value in the table, 0.5 to the central element, and so forth. In the case of the table shown in figure 2.24, for example, the relationship between integer indices and normalized indices would be as follows:

Integer Index	Normalized Index
0	0
1	0.05
2	0.1
3	0.15
4	0.2
...	...
10	0.5
...	...
18	0.9
19	0.95

As you can see, the normalized value 1 never occurs, because it coincides with the beginning of a new cycle (just as a phase of 360 degrees is equivalent to 0 degrees).

When we want to construct a sound using **fixed spectrum additive synthesis**, in which neither the frequency nor the amplitudes of the components vary over time, we can work in one of two ways. The more typical and simpler method is to sum the outputs of multiple sine wave oscillators, each of which generates a frequency component of the sound. The second, more efficient method consists of summing all of the sine wave components directly within a single wavetable, which contains as a result one complete cycle of the waveform. We then use a single oscillator to read this wavetable and generate the complex sound. This second method optimizes the use of computer resources; to realize the sound shown in figure 2.14, for example, we would need only a single oscillator, rather than the 10 sine wave oscillators that would be needed for the first method.

Technically, we shouldn't call the second method additive synthesis, since there is no realtime addition of signals going on. You might instead think of it as a simple form of wavetable synthesis that loads a complete wave cycle, containing all of the necessary sine wave components, into an oscillator for playback.[11] However you think of it, the results obtained using either method, as well as the principles that stand behind the techniques, are the same.

TEST WITH SHORT ANSWERS *(30 words maximum)*

1) What can you do using additive synthesis?

2) When does one encounter constructive interference? Destructive interference?

3) What relationship must the fundamental have with one of its components to be defined as harmonic?

4) If a sound has a harmonic type of spectrum, does this imply a periodic or a non-periodic wave form? Why?

5) If it is impossible to hear a definite pitch for a sound, is that sound harmonic or non-harmonic?

2.2 BEATS

If two waves have the same frequency, but not necessarily the same amplitude, and if their positive and negative peaks coincide, we say that they are **in phase**. Summing waves that are in phase will never result in destructive interference, and the amplitude of the summed wave can be calculated as a point-by-point sum of the two waves. Figure 2.27a shows two waves with the same frequency that are in phase. Due to the constructive interference that is always present when waves are in phase, it is easy to see that their sum is simply the sum of the amplitudes.

On the other hand, if the two waves are in antiphase (out of phase by 180 degrees, as shown in figure 2.27b), the point-by-point sum will yield a wave that has a peak amplitude that is equal to the difference between the peak amplitudes of the two constituent waves. At the limit, if two waves are out of

[11] The wavetable synthesis that is used in many commercial synthesizers almost always uses multiple wavetables, along with a mechanism for morphing from one table to the other in order to obtain complex sounds that evolve in time. By contrast, the simple fixed spectrum case that we illustrate here requires only a single table. In Section 2.3, we will examine a variation on this technique.

phase and their amplitudes are equal, as shown in figure 2.27c, the result of summing them will be 0 at all points; the two waves will cancel themselves out. In example 2.27d, two waves of equal frequency and amplitude are shown out of phase by 90 degrees (in the same relationship that sine waves have to cosine waves). In this case, positive and negative peaks no longer coincide, and because of this, we observe both constructive and destructive interference in action. The resulting sine wave has the same frequency as the original waves, but its phase and amplitude differ from those of the originals.

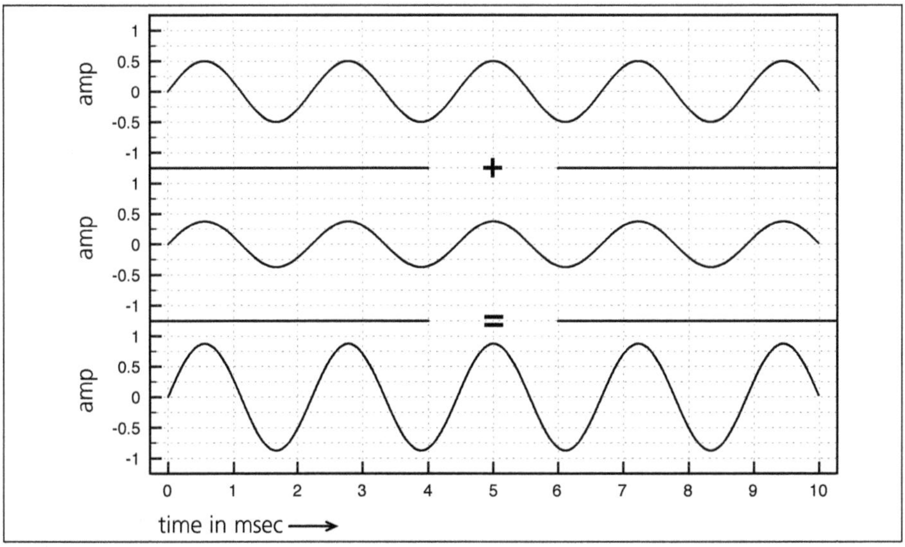

Fig. 2.27a Sum of two in-phase waves

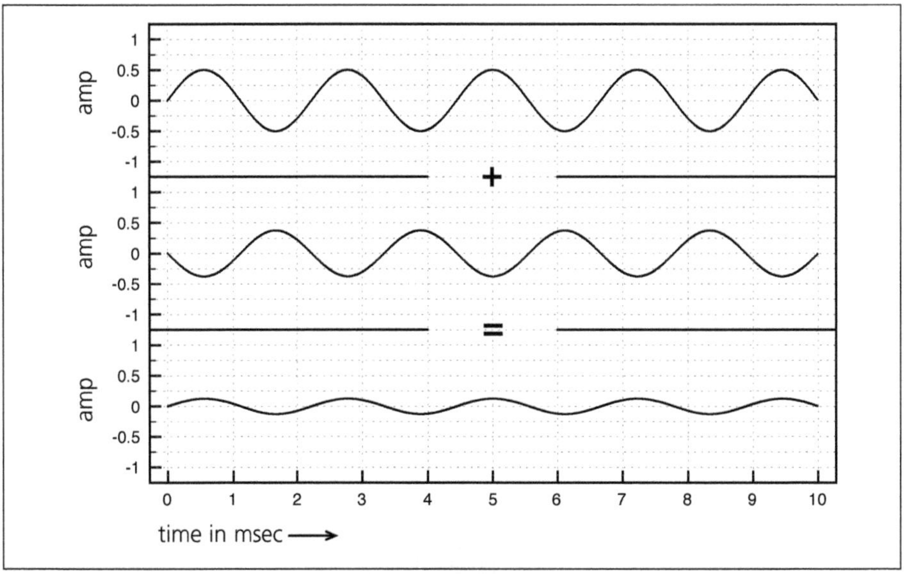

Fig. 2.27b Sum of two waves in antiphase

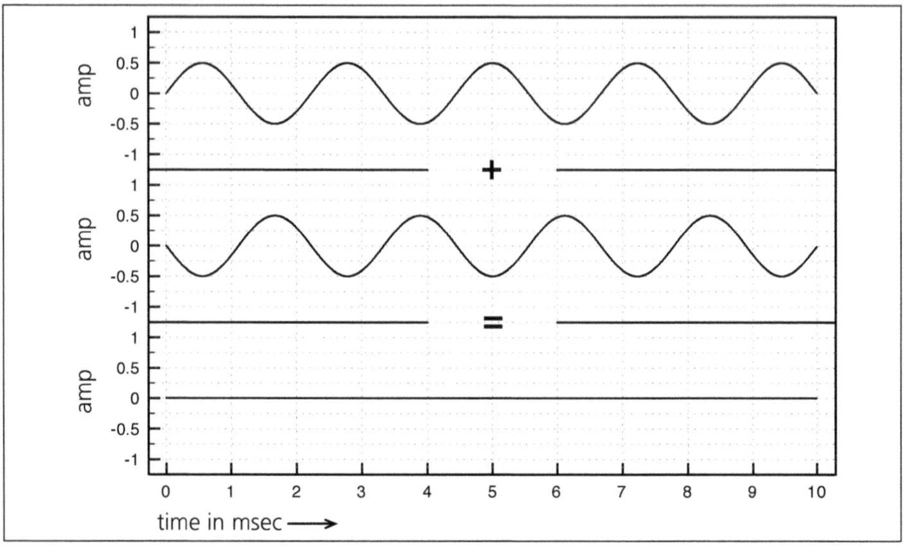

Fig. 2.27c Sum of two waves of equal amplitude in antiphase

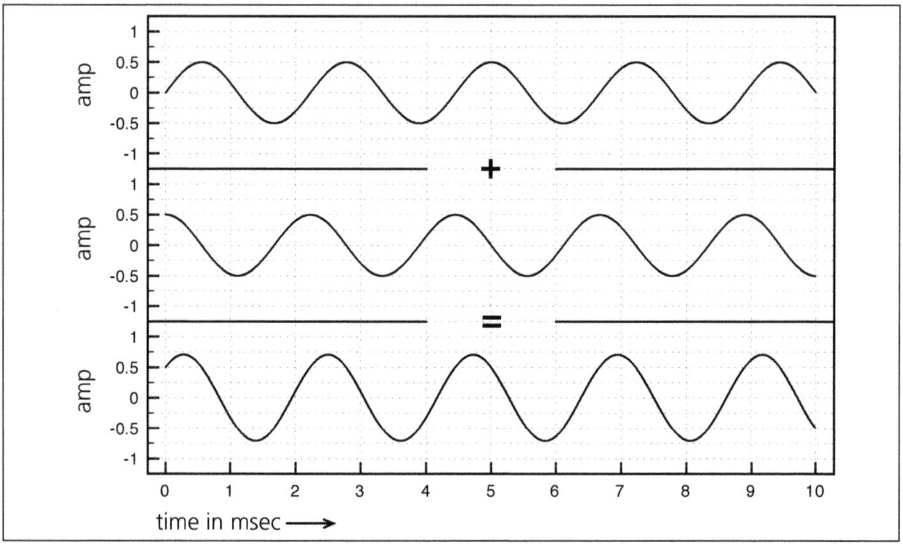

Fig. 2.27d Sum of two waves whose phase differs by 90 degrees (sine and cosine waves)

Now let's consider the sum of two sine waves with frequencies that differ slightly from each other, as shown in figure 2.28.

The two waves start out in phase, with the resulting constructive interference causing the overall amplitude to grow, but after a certain number of oscillations, they gradually shift to being maximally out of phase with each other, which causes the overall amplitude to be reduced.

After a certain number of oscillations, the waves are once again in phase, and the cycle repeats. The amplitude of the resulting wave will alternately rise and fall, causing a phenomenon known as **beats**.

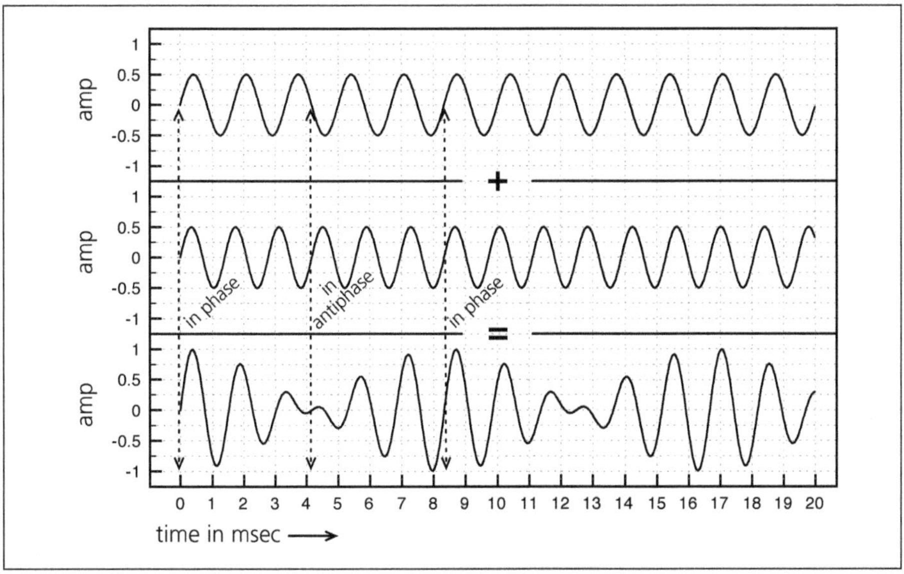

Fig. 2.28 Sum of two waves with slightly different frequencies

Such a periodic oscillation in amplitude will itself have a frequency equal to the *difference in frequency* between the two interfering waves. For example, if the frequency of the first sine wave is 220 Hz and the second is 222 Hz, the oscillation in amplitude that will be heard in the resulting wave will be 2 cycles per second. (We will say "2 beats per second"). Besides this beat frequency, the audible frequency of the resulting wave will lie between the two original frequencies; if we represent the frequencies as f1 and f2, the perceived frequency will be (f1 + f2) / 2, which, in the example given, would be 221 Hz.

VIDEO EXAMPLE 2H – *PRESET 1 – Beats caused by sounds of 220 and 222 Hz*

By the same method, if the frequency of the first wave were to be 439 Hz and the frequency of the second 435 Hz, the resulting wave would have 4 beats per second, and its frequency would be heard as 437 Hz.[12]

[12] If the difference between the two frequencies becomes larger than the minimum audible frequency (around 30 Hz), beats become inaudible and give rise under certain conditions to so-called *difference tones* or *Tartini tones*.

VIDEO EXAMPLE 2H – *PRESET 2 – Beats caused by sounds of 439 and 435 Hz*

The beats phenomenon is caused by the small difference in frequency between the two summed waves, which results in the cyclical variation in the amplitude of the resulting wave. If we slowly increase the difference between the two frequencies, the frequency of the beats will increase as well. As we go farther, continuing to increase the difference between the frequencies, at some point we will no longer perceive single beats, but instead we will hear the interference between the two waves as a sort of "roughness" in the sound. Increasing the difference even further, we will ultimately hear two distinct sounds. When two interfering sounds create beats or the sensation of roughness rather than two distinct sounds, we say that the respective frequencies lie within a "critical band"; when we hear two distinct frequencies instead, these frequencies are said to fall outside of the critical band. In other words, the **critical band** delineates boundaries within which our ears cannot separate individual sounds; instead, we resolve the complexity of such a signal with a sensation of roughness or by hearing beats.

The width of the critical band, established experimentally, varies with changes in the intermediate frequency between the two frequencies in play. Above 200 Hz, the width of the critical band increases as the intermediate frequency increases, corresponding to an interval that lies somewhere between a whole tone and a minor third. This interval may explain why we hear the intervals of a whole tone and semitone as dissonant, while intervals larger than the critical band seem more consonant.[13] Below 200 Hz, on the other hand, the width of the critical band remains a constant width, and because of this, it occupies an interval (in semitones) that steadily increases as the pitch descends. This means that at lower frequencies, only very wide intervals are perceived of as consonant. This phenomenon is well known to composers of all periods – examine any score, perhaps one written for piano, for example, and it is probable that the intervals between notes sounding simultaneously in the low register will be wider than the intervals between notes in the middle and higher registers.[14]

[13] We are speaking of pure sounds, devoid of harmonics. In more complex sounds, such as the sounds of acoustic musical instruments, we need to also consider the strongest components of the spectrum, which are in general the first harmonics. An interval of a seventh, formed by complex sounds, will be heard as dissonant, because the second harmonic of the lower sound and the fundamental of the higher sound, fall within the critical band. The intervals considered dissonant can be heard as such by a musician even if they are played with pure sounds, because an educated musical ear is habituated to associate certain intervals with the sensation of dissonance. On the other hand, it is definitely possible for a non-musician to perceive any interval outside of the critical band as being consonant, or non-rough.

[14] Unless, of course, the composer is purposefully exploiting dissonance by using small intervals in the lower range!

In the following table (taken from Rossing, T. 1990, p. 74) we see the relationship between intermediate frequencies and the width of the critical band. As you can see, when the intermediate frequency is around 100 Hz, the critical band is 90 Hz, or 90% of the intermediate frequency. At the extreme opposite, for an intermediate frequency of 10,000 Hz, we find a critical band of 1200 Hz, which is equal to only 12% of the intermediate frequency.

Intermediate Frequency	Width of the Critical Band
100	90
200	90
500	110
1,000	150
2,000	280
5,000	700
10,000	1,200

VIDEO EXAMPLE 2H – *PRESET 3 – Gradual passage from beats to two distinct tones*

When we sum three or more sine waves whose frequencies differ only slightly, beats result between each pair of waves. For example, if we have three sine waves with frequencies of 200, 201, and 202.5 Hz, we will have the following combinations:

1) 200 Hz + 201 Hz 1 beat per second
2) 201 Hz + 202.5 Hz 1.5 beats per second
3) 200 Hz + 202.5 Hz 2.5 beats per second

Besides the beats produced by each of the three combinations, the beats themselves will also interact in a periodic fashion, both in pairs and as three sounds together, resulting in accented beats that repeat regularly. In our case, the rhythmic cycle will repeat itself every 2 seconds. In 2 seconds, the first pair of sounds will have produced 2 complete beats, the second pair 3 complete beats, and the third pair 5 complete beats.

VIDEO EXAMPLE 2H – *PRESET 4 – Multiple beats: combinations of three sine waves*

Dodge and Jerse (1985, p. 37) assert that the phenomenon of beats can also be heard, although in a less marked way, between two frequencies that nearly form an octave, such as the frequencies 220 and 443 Hz. These are beats of the second order, with a ratio of 2:1, and the beat frequency in this case is equal to the difference between the frequency of the higher sound minus the frequency of the lower sound transposed upwards by exactly an octave (443 - 440 = 3 beats per second, in our example). Beats of this type vanish above about 1500 Hz.[15]

VIDEO EXAMPLE 2H – *PRESET 5 – Beats among tones forming a near-octave*

If instead of summing two sine waves, we sum two complex sounds whose frequencies differ by only a small amount, we can create beats between the upper components of the first sound and the upper components of the second. For example, if we have a first sound that contains frequency components at 100, 202.5, and 750 Hz and a second sound that contains components at 101, 220.5, and 753.5 Hz, we will obtain 1 beat per second between the components of 100 and 101 Hz, 2 beats per second between 200.5 and 202.5 Hz, and 3 beats and a half per second between 750 and 753.5 Hz (ignoring any beats at the octave which in this case will be almost imperceptible). In figure 2.29, we present the sonogram of this combination. You can see the beats appear as dark zones at regular intervals.

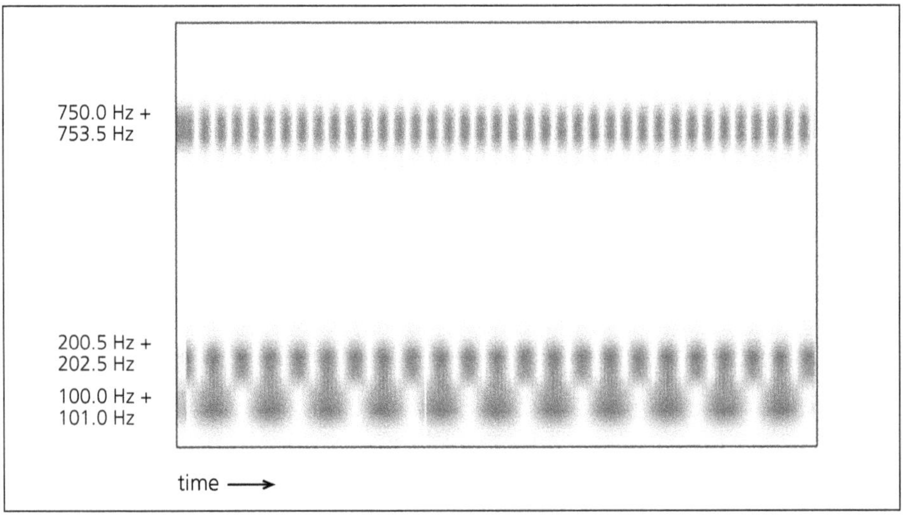

Fig. 2.29 Beats between two complex sounds

[15] In the text of Dodge and Jerse, beats at the fourth and at the fifth are also cited, although they are scarcely audible.

VIDEO EXAMPLE 2H – *PRESET 6 – Multiple beats: combinations of two complex sounds*

If a number of oscillators generate complex sounds by sharing the same wavetable, and if the frequencies of these sounds differ only slightly from each other, it is possible to obtain interesting pulsing patterns that are produced by the beats between the harmonics of the sounds. It is often possible to hear "internal melodies" or even glissandi between harmonics in these patterns. To achieve this, it is necessary to ensure that the beat rates differ for each harmonic. Two complex sounds that share the same waveform, with fundamentals of 110 and 111 Hz, for example, will pulsate once per second at the fundamental, twice per second at the second harmonic (where the frequencies are 220 and 222 Hz), three times per second at the third, and so on. The interactions between these pulses create a movement within the sound. If after this we add a third sound at 112 Hz, there will now be 2 pulses per second at the fundamental, 4 per second at the second harmonic, 6 at the third, etc., and these pulsations will be more or less strong depending upon whether all three components, or only two, are in phase at a given moment. Increasing the number of oscillators will increase the complexity of the rhythmic pulsations. In figure 2.30 we show the sonogram of a sum of 7 sounds (each of which has 24 harmonics) whose frequencies fall near 110 Hz. The frequencies of the individual oscillators for this example are spaced at intervals of 0.07 Hz (110.07, 110.14, etc.)

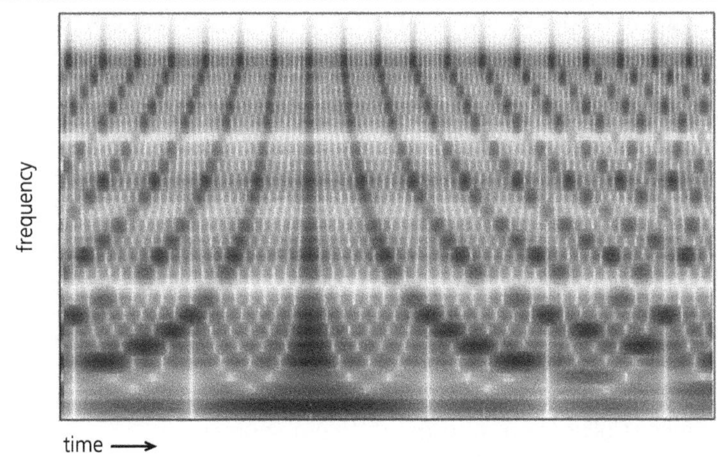

Fig. 2.30 Beats between 7 complex sounds each of which has 24 harmonics

VIDEO EXAMPLE 2I – *Multiple beats: combination of 7 complex sounds*

2.3 CROSSFADING BETWEEN WAVETABLES: VECTOR SYNTHESIS

The sounds that we have created to this point through the use of wavetables have all been obtained using one table alone. In this section, we will relax this limitation and discuss a technique that involves crossfading between tables, which will enable us to generate sounds whose spectra vary. We have thus far used single timbres, contained in single tables, but if we build several tables, each containing a different timbre, we can crossfade between them in time, dissolving from one timbre to another and thereby changing the spectrum. For example, we might use the attack of a lute to model the beginning of a sound, and move from the lute to the decay of an electric guitar at the end of the same sound.
For our current discussion we will limit ourselves to using tables that contain single wave cycles, each differing from the others purely in terms of waveform (since we haven't yet touched on other synthesis techniques that might be relevant). During the course of a musical event (a single note), we will generate a sound that changes in time simply by dissolving from one table to another. You may hear this technique described using many different names – wavetable crossfading, **vector synthesis**, and linear algorithmic synthesis are all valid.
The implementation details of this type of synthesis are rather simple, since one can sum any number of different sounds by using the correct envelopes. You need only to organize a few things in the right way, including the sounds to be used, their durations, the length of the crossfades, and so forth. In the simple case of two sounds, for example, we would use one envelope segment to take the first sound from the maximum amplitude to 0, while taking the second sound from 0 to the maximum using a second envelope. Generally, however, such a simple case can be implemented using a single segment for both purposes, by applying the envelope directly to the first sound's amplitude, and reversing it[16] to control the second sound.

We see in figure 2.31 an example of a crossfade: given two waveforms, the mixed signal passes from the first to the second timbre over a span of 10 cycles. For two sound sources, the passage from one to the other can be described by a line segment, but when there are more than two sources the movement is better described by using a geometric plane or a three-dimensional space. When vector synthesis is implemented in hardware, in fact, a joystick is often used as the controller for mixing the different sources.
It is interesting to note that a sound effect known as *infinite glissando* or **Shepard tone** can be generated by using vector synthesis. The sound generated by this particular effect seems to slide endlessly, without ever arriving at a final pitch or passing beyond hearing. The effect can be obtained by crossfading sounds in which glissandi are slightly out-of-phase in time between themselves, and we will examine how to do this in more detail in Interlude B of this book.

---

[16] We will see in the practical portion of this chapter how to actually accomplish this.

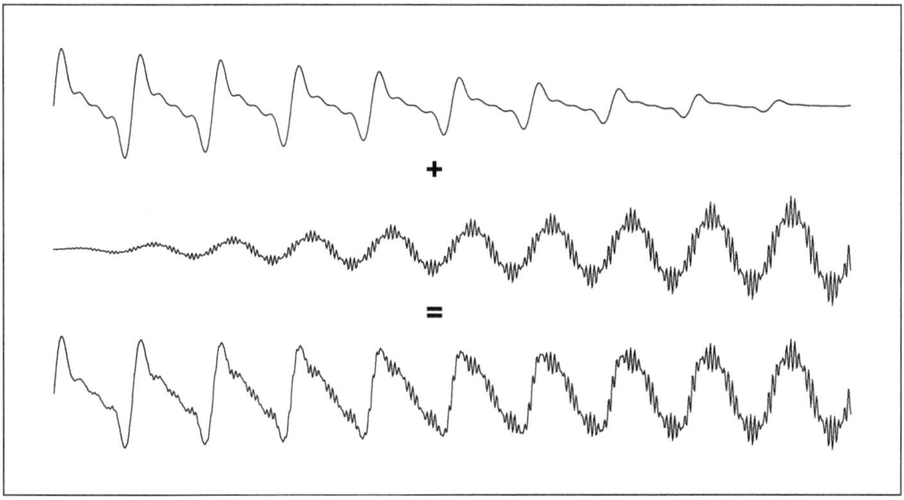

Fig. 2.31 Crossfading between two waveforms

VIDEO EXAMPLE 2J – *VECTOR SYNTHESIS ON A SEGMENT*
VIDEO EXAMPLE 2K – *VECTOR SYNTHESIS ON A PLANE*
VIDEO EXAMPLE 2L – *INFINITE GLISSANDO, OR SHEPARD TONE*

2.4 VARIABLE SPECTRUM ADDITIVE SYNTHESIS

This section will discuss how to overcome some of the synthesis limitations imposed by fixed spectra.

Sounds, of course, are not static phenomena; they are dynamic and variable to the extreme. Over the evolutionary course of a note played by an acoustic instrument, for example, all three of the basic parameters (frequency, amplitude, and spectrum) vary continuously.

"The independent temporal evolution of all frequency components is a basic characteristic of natural sounds, and for this reason it is important to learn how to manage such changes in order to produce a 'living' sound." (Ibid, p. 55.) Not only the amplitude and the frequency of the fundamental of a particular complex sound possess "signature" variations that make them unique to us. The amplitudes and frequencies of each and every spectral component also change over time. From this, we might deduce that additive synthesis using a fixed spectrum, as demonstrated in Section 2.1, is unlikely to be very interesting. Let's search, therefore, in order to find a way to implement a richer model that includes the possibility for spectral variation.

In figure 2.32, we see how a spectrum of a sound can be made to vary by applying various envelopes to each of the sound's components.

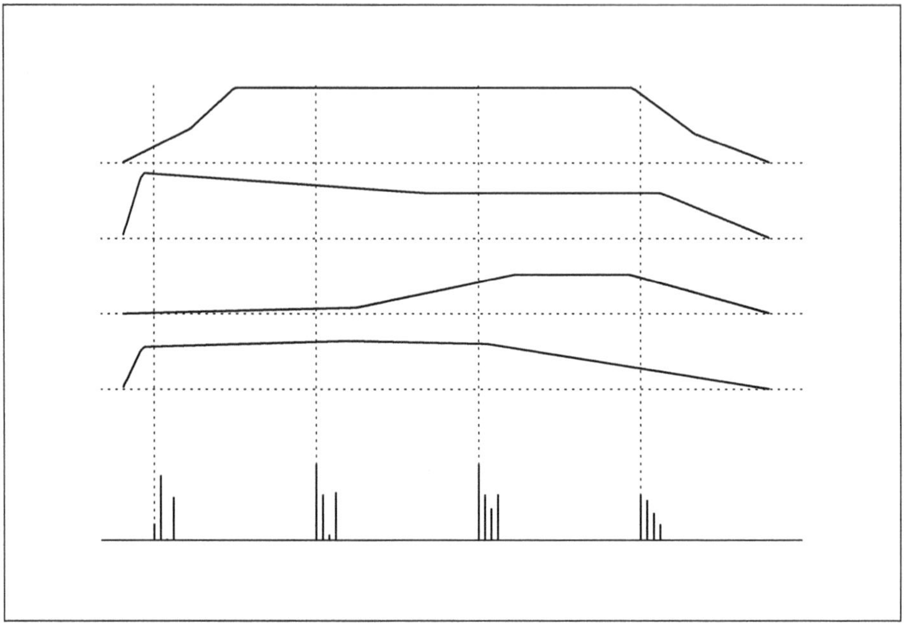

Fig. 2.32 Variable spectrum

During a single event, every single component can vary in both amplitude and frequency. In the practical part of this chapter, we will create components that are initially harmonic and that change to being non-harmonic (and vice versa), keeping their fundamentals fixed while modifying the frequencies of their components by using glissandi. This method will enable us to generate variable spectra, or sounds whose timbre changes in time, by modeling changing frequency and/or amplitude ratios between components.

From what we have said, it should be evident that the spectrum parameter is very different from the parameters of frequency and amplitude. The latter parameters are one dimensional quantities (which is a way to say that a single number can completely capture their state – the values of those parameters can be represented as points on a line). Because these units are one dimensional, it is easy to compare them. We can confirm, for example, that a certain frequency's relationship to another by using simple operations such as "less than" or "greater than" to compare the numbers.

On the other hand, timbre (or even better, spectrum), is a multi-dimensional quantity, whose definition requires capturing a whole series of numbers expressing the amplitude, the frequency, and the phase for each component. Because of this, it is not possible to define an absolute scale for timbre. (It is not possible to say that one timbre is "higher" than another, for example.) It certainly *is* possible to identify characteristics of timbre, such as brilliance, harmonicity, roughness, or denseness, that can be used to order sounds, but these characteristics are difficult to characterize with numerical precision.[17]

Variable spectrum additive synthesis is clearly a very powerful technique, enabling variations in time for every single component of a sound. Using it, it would be theoretically possible to completely describe any timbre, or any sound! In practice, however, creating such descriptions would not be easy. Every sound would be defined by dozens or even hundreds of components, and for each of these components it would be necessary to specify separate amplitude and frequency envelopes (or perhaps a series of glissandi from one to another). It is easy to imagine that each sound in a score of medium complexity (containing hundreds of sounds) would require summing dozens of components along with numerous other parameter specifications. From a practical point of view, we might hypothesize that when the components of a sound are few (no more than 8, or perhaps 16) it ought to be possible to fully create such a specification in a relatively efficient way, but that sounds beyond that level of complexity ought to be realized using a different strategy.

An example of such an alternate strategy might be the use of the so-called **masking** method, which is a method that consists of defining a "mask" of two envelopes that trace the progress of the lowest and the highest frequencies, and automatically reconstructing all frequencies for the other components by subdividing the space between the two extremes into equal or unequal parts, as shown in figure 2.33.[18]

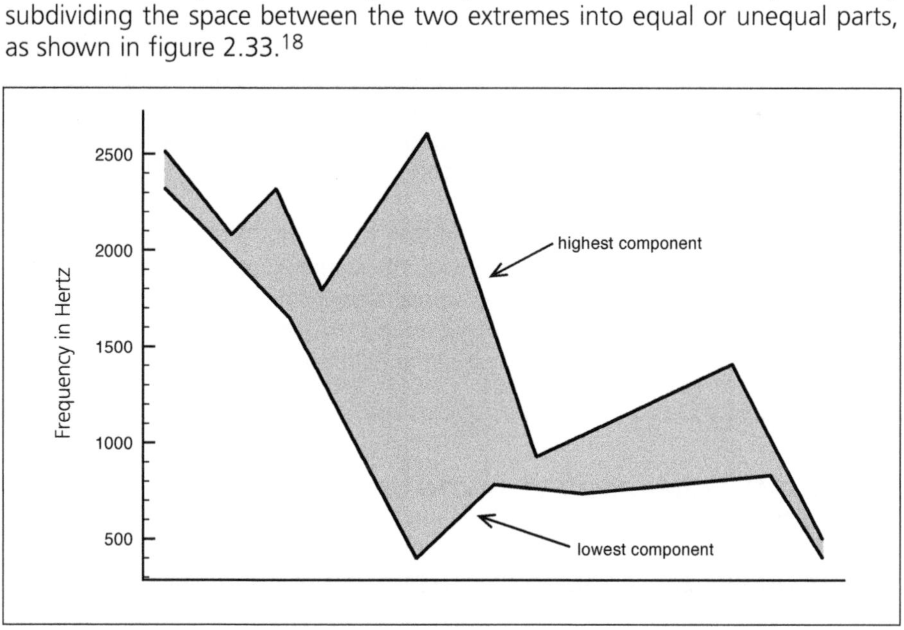

Fig. 2.33 Frequency masking for a complex sound

[17] Some interesting articles with regard to the multi-dimensional representation of sound timbre were written by J. Grey. (1975 and 1977)

[18] The masking technique can also be applied, obviously, to other parameters than frequency.

In figure 2.34 we see the sonogram (partial) resulting from the masking operation of figure 2.33, applied to a sound with 10 partials.

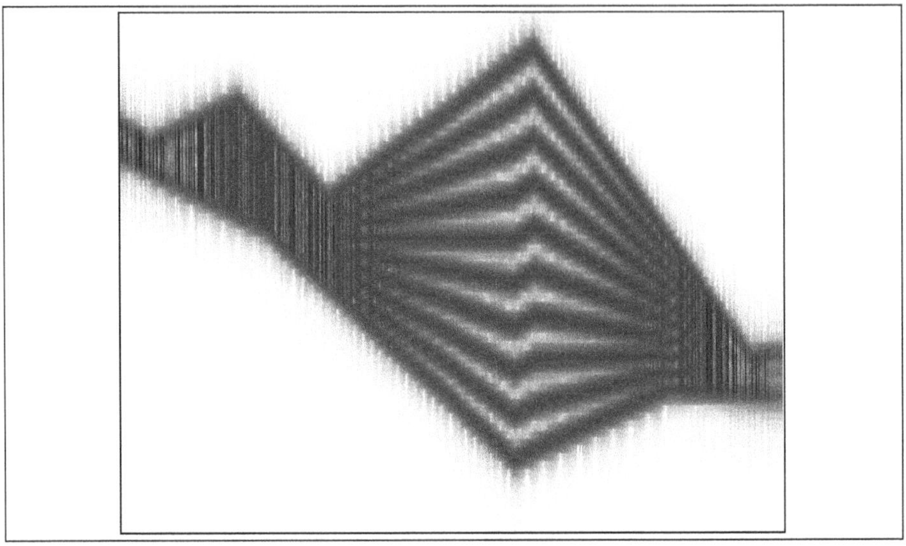

Fig. 2.34 Spectrum resulting from a masking operation

Another possibility would be to define two or more spectral envelopes and to interpolate from one to the other during the evolution of a sound. Such interpolation would be similar to vector synthesis, which we discussed in Section 2.3, but in the case of vector synthesis, the frequencies of the components were fixed. Here, the frequencies of the components might differ, enabling them to slide from one spectral envelope to another.

Other possibilities include defining control functions, either graphically or mathematically, that govern the behavior of synthesis parameters, or to use random numbers, or to build special-purpose algorithms for the generation and control of the components in a complex sound. In Section 2.4 of the practical chapter we will see how to implement some of these techniques.

VIDEO EXAMPLE 2M – *ADDITIVE SYNTHESIS USING A VARIABLE SPECTRUM - EFFICIENT CONTROL*

VIDEO EXAMPLE 2N – *ADDITIVE SYNTHESIS USING A VARIABLE SPECTRUM CONTROLLED – MASKING*

The most practical method for managing large numbers of timbral parameters is to perform *analysis* of a pre-existing sound followed by its *re-synthesis* through additive synthesis with a variable spectrum. So far, we have constructed complex sounds using sums of simple sounds; we have developed a *synthesis* process. But it is also possible to take the other road, that of *analysis*, by decomposing a complex sound into its simple components. The **Fourier theorem** (developed by the French mathematician and physicist Joseph Fourier, who was active in the eighteenth and early nineteenth centuries) confirms that "any periodic waveform can be represented by a series of harmonics, or sine wave components, each with a particular amplitude and phase. It is therefore possible to reconstruct the *spectrum* of any periodic sound." (Ibid, p. 72.) Systems for the analysis of sound, even non-periodic sound, are manifold. We will speak of them in a future volume, where we will discuss the concepts of re-synthesis in detail. For now, it is simply useful to know that the data needed to specify the evolution of amplitude and frequency, which we have already referred to repeatedly, can also be reconstructed from the analysis of any complex sound.

TESTING – *TEST WITH SHORT ANSWERS*

1) Under what conditions can we say that two sounds are in phase?

2) Under what conditions can we say that two sounds are in antiphase?

3) If two sine waves are summed, one of 5,600 Hz and the other of 5,595 Hz, how many beats per second will they produce?

4) What is the difference between fixed spectrum additive synthesis and variable spectrum additive synthesis?

5) If you modify the frequencies and the amplitudes of the components of a complex sound, will you encounter variations of timbre?

TESTING – *TEST WITH LISTENING AND ANALYSIS*

6) Is the sound in Example AA2.1 harmonic or non-harmonic? Explain your answer.

7) Does the sound in Example AA2.2 move from harmonic to non-harmonic, or vice versa? Explain your answer.

8) Is the attack of the sound in Example AA2.3 harmonic or non-harmonic? Explain your answer.

9) Is the decay of the sound in Example AA2.4 harmonic or non-harmonic? Explain your answer.

FUNDAMENTAL CONCEPTS

1) In additive synthesis, the amplitude values of a set of different waves are added together, sample by sample, taking into account the signs of the samples.

2) In a complex sound **harmonic components** are those whose frequencies form integer ratios with some fundamental. In the absence of such ratios, we speak of **non-harmonic components**.

3) If two waves have the same frequency, and their positive and negative peaks coincide, we speak of them as being **in phase**. If the waves are exactly half of a period out of phase, we speak of them as being in **antiphase**.

4) The phenomenon known as **beats** is caused by a slight difference in frequency between two summed waves. It has the effect of periodically varying the amplitude of the resulting wave. If instead of summing pure sine waves, we sum two complex sounds of slightly varying frequency, beats are not only created between the fundamentals, but also between every component of the first sound and the corresponding component of the second sound.

5) In natural sounds, the values of all basic musical parameters change in time.

GLOSSARY

Array
(See *Wavetable*)

Beats
Cyclic variations in the amplitude of a sound, caused by summing two sounds whose frequencies differ slightly.

Complex sound
A sound formed by frequency components (sine waves).

Constructive interference
A condition determined by summing two wave whose amplitudes, at a given instant, are either both positive or both negative.

Destructive interference
A condition determined by summing two waves whose amplitudes, at a given instant, are of opposite sign.

Fixed spectrum additive synthesis
Additive synthesis in which the summed components vary neither their amplitudes nor their frequencies in time.

Fourier theorem
A theorem proposed by Joseph Fourier that states that every periodic waveform is representable as the sum of sine waves.

Frequency domain (representation in the)
Graphical representation of the amplitudes of all of the components in a sound, in which frequency values are shown on the x-axis, and amplitude values are shown on the y-axis.

Fundamental
The lowest frequency component of a harmonic spectrum.

Harmonic components
The higher components in a complex sound whose frequencies are integer multiples of the frequency of the fundamental.

In antiphase
A condition in which two waves of the same frequency are combined with each other 180 degrees out of phase, causing destructive interference.

In phase
A condition in which two waves of the same frequency, whose cycles exactly coincide, are combined with each other, causing constructive interference.

Infinite glissando
See *Shepard tone*

Masking
A technique for establishing parameter boundaries by limiting the range of an upper and a lower parameter as they change over time. The upper and lower limits of the mask can be either constant values and/or envelopes.

Missing fundamental
A sonic phenomenon in which a sound possesses definite pitch, but the pitch, which by definition is the fundamental of the sound, is missing as a component, having an amplitude of 0.

Non-harmonic components
The higher components of a complex sound whose frequencies do not form integer ratios with the lowest frequency in the sound.

Partials
See *Components* (of various types)

Periodic wave
A waveform that repeats itself exactly, once per period.

Periodic sound / non-periodic sound
A periodic sound is a sound produced by a wave form that repeats periodically. A non-periodic sound, on the other hand, is a sound for which it is not possible to differentiate a wave form that repeats cyclically in time.

Phase
The relative position that the wave cycle of a sound occupies at a given instant in time.

Quasi-harmonic components
The higher components of a complex sound whose frequencies come very close to forming integer ratios with the fundamental.

Shepard tone
An effect in which a sound seems to slide endlessly without concluding. It can be obtained by crossfading between instances of a wavetable that are slightly out of phase with each other.

Sonogram (Spectrogram)
A representation of spectral evolution as a function of time. The frequencies of the components are shown using one axis (usually the y-axis) and time is indicated using the other axis. The amplitude of every frequency component is shown, quantized by the units of the chromatic scale.

Sound spectrum
A representation of the amplitudes of the components of a sound as a function of frequency. (See *Frequency domain*.)

Spectral envelope
Considering the graph of a spectrum, a spectral envelope is a curve that outlines the components shown in the graph, pulling the amplitude bars of all of the components into a single entity.

Time domain (representation in the)
A graphical representation of instantaneous changes in the amplitude of a sound, in which time is shown on the x-axis and amplitude is shown on the y-axis.

Variable spectrum additive synthesis
Additive synthesis in which the summed components vary their amplitudes and/or their frequencies in time.

Vector
(See *Wavetable*)

Vector synthesis (Wavetable crossfading)
Crossfading between wavetables, used as a method for generating a variable spectrum.

Wavetable
A wavetable, or vector, or array, is an ordered series of values, each of which is associated with a numerical index value.

Wavetable synthesis
A synthesis technique that in its simplest form consists of playing a table that contains a single cycle of a complex waveform with an oscillator. In addition to this simple definition,

there is also a table-based technique that goes by the same name, which involves dynamically modifying a complex waveform in realtime by evolving multiple wavetables (in a manner similar to vector synthesis).

DISCOGRAPHY

Karlheinz Stockhausen, Studie I and Studie II, Stockhausen Verlag, CD ST100-3
Franco Evangelisti, Incontri di Fasce sonore, ed RZ 1011-12
Walter Branchi, Alba Plena, www.walter-branchi.com
David Wessel, Antony, Wergo, WER 20302

2P
ADDITIVE AND VECTOR SYNTHESIS

LEARNING AGENDA

PREREQUISITES FOR THE CHAPTER
- Contents of Chapter 1 (Theory and Practice), Chapter 2 (Theory), Interlude A

LEARNING OBJECTIVES
Skills
- To learn how to synthesize a complex sound from simple sine waves
- To learn how to synthesize harmonic and non-harmonic sounds using additive synthesis and wavetables, and to transform one into the other (and vice versa) by using amplitude and frequency control
- To learn how to implement triangle waves, square waves, and sawtooth waves approximately by adding component harmonic sine waves together
- To learn how to control beats between two sine waves or harmonics
- To learn how to synthesize sounds using vector synthesis

Competence
- To successfully realize a sound study based on additive synthesis and save it to an audio file

CONTENTS
- Additive synthesis using both fixed and variable spectra
- Harmonic and non-harmonic sounds
- Phase and beats
- Interpolation
- Vector synthesis

ACTIVITIES
- Correcting algorithms
- Completing algorithms
- Replacing parts of algorithms
- Analyzing algorithms

TESTING
- Integrated cross-functional project: reverse engineering
- Integrated cross-functional project: composing a brief sound study

SUPPORTING MATERIALS
- List of principal Max commands
- List of Max objects
- Messages, attributes, and parameters for specific Max objects
- Glossary

2.1 FIXED SPECTRUM ADDITIVE SYNTHESIS

To start things off, let's create a patch for producing harmonic sounds in Max using additive synthesis, with figure 2.12 of the theory chapter as our implementation guide. The diagram in that figure shows 10 oscillators, all summed using a mixer, and so we will begin with 10 **cycle~** objects that will furnish the 10 sine waves, each producing a frequency which is an integer multiple of the fundamental (in order to be harmonic). To calculate the frequency values needed, we will simply multiply the frequency of the fundamental by the first 10 integers. The resulting patch is shown in figure 2.1 (**02_01a_additive.maxpat**).

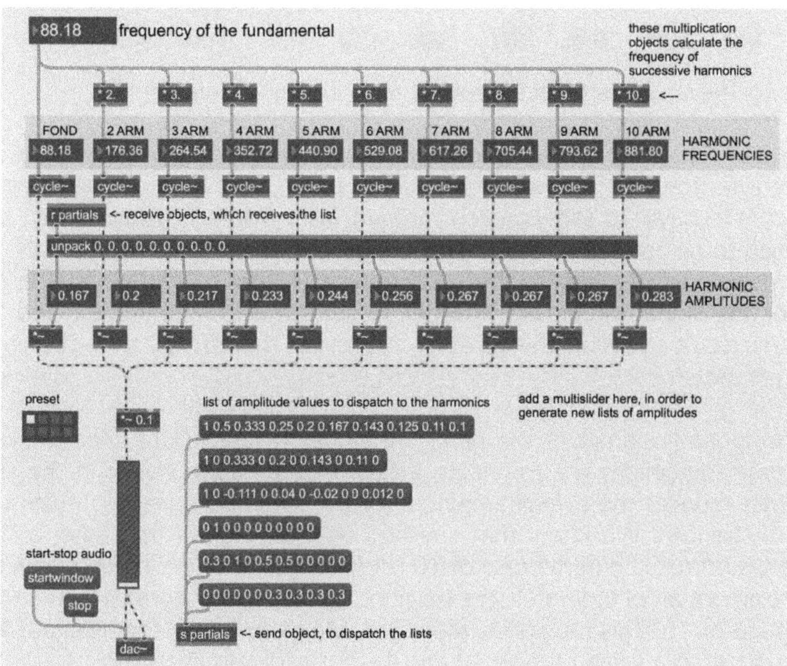

Fig. 2.1 02_01a_additive.maxpat

The number box at the top of the patch is used to set the fundamental frequency for the entire patch, which is then passed to the 9 * operators using successive integers to produce harmonic frequencies that are multiples of the fundamental. The frequency of the fundamental and of the frequencies being produced by these multipliers can be viewed in the 10 number boxes below, which are themselves connected to as many **cycle~** objects. These, in turn, are connected to signal multipliers (*~) that rescale their outputs. Normally the amplitude of a signal produced by **cycle~** will have a peak value of 1, and for this reason the value given to each multiplier serves to directly reflect the relative amplitude of each harmonic (for example, 1.0 · 0.5 = 0.5). The signal multipliers enable each harmonic to have its own distinct amplitude, determined by the value fed into its multiplier. Given that we have 10 oscillators, 10 values completely specify the amplitudes to be used.

As we learned in Section IA.10 of Interlude A, we can create a list of numbers by using either a message box or a **multislider**. The first technique is immediately obvious in this patch: desired amplitudes are grouped into lists within message boxes, and then dispatched to the 10 multipliers by using a send object ([s partials]). The corresponding **receive** object is connected to an **unpack** object that takes care of distributing single values to appropriate multipliers (as seen in figure 2.1b).

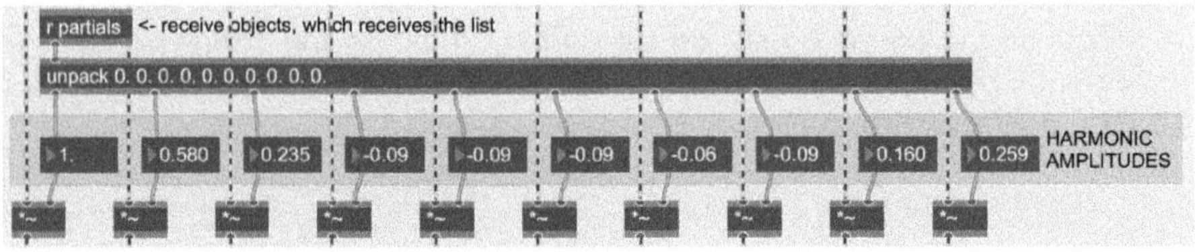

Fig. 2.1b The **unpack** object breaking a list into single elements

Amplitude lists might also, however, be created using a **multislider**. Create one now in the lower right of the patch, and configure it using the Inspector to have 10 sliders, each ranging from 0 to 1. This **multislider** will need to be connected to a **send** object with the argument "partials". It's also possible to manipulate the float number boxes connected to the right inlet of the signal multipliers in order to set different amplitudes, and then save the result by using the **preset** object on the left (by shift-clicking on the small dots).

The component signals in the patch, after being rescaled by their individual amplitude multipliers, are routed to a final multiplication object in the signal path that reduces the overall amplitude of the summed signal to 1/10th of its original strength. We know that any two or more signals that enter a single inlet are summed. So in the case of 10 oscillators, if all of the components have the maximum amplitude of 1, the resulting summed waveform would have an amplitude of 10. This multiplier, therefore, serves to return the absolute value of the signal to a value between 0 and 1, thus avoiding distortion.[1]

The amplitude **multislider** must dispatch data continuously, since we would like variations to be sent out as they are made, even while the value of a slider is being changed. By default, however, **multislider** updates the list of values that it outputs only when the mouse is released, at the end of an edit. To enable continuous updating, open the object's inspector, look for the "Mouse Output Mode" attribute (under the Style category), and in the attribute's menu, select the option "Mouse Down + Continuous Data".

As we said, thanks to the ability to manage multiple audio channels, it becomes very easy to create patches in which different signals are processed in parallel: the patch of figure 2.1 does not yet take advantage of this possibility because

[1] For a discussion of distortion due to excessive amplitude see Section 1.2 of Chapter 1T.

we first wanted to show the complete algorithm, to better understand the path of the individual signals.
Now we can see how the same algorithm can be realized using multichannel signals: load the patch **02_01b_multichannel_additive.maxpat** (figure 2.1c).

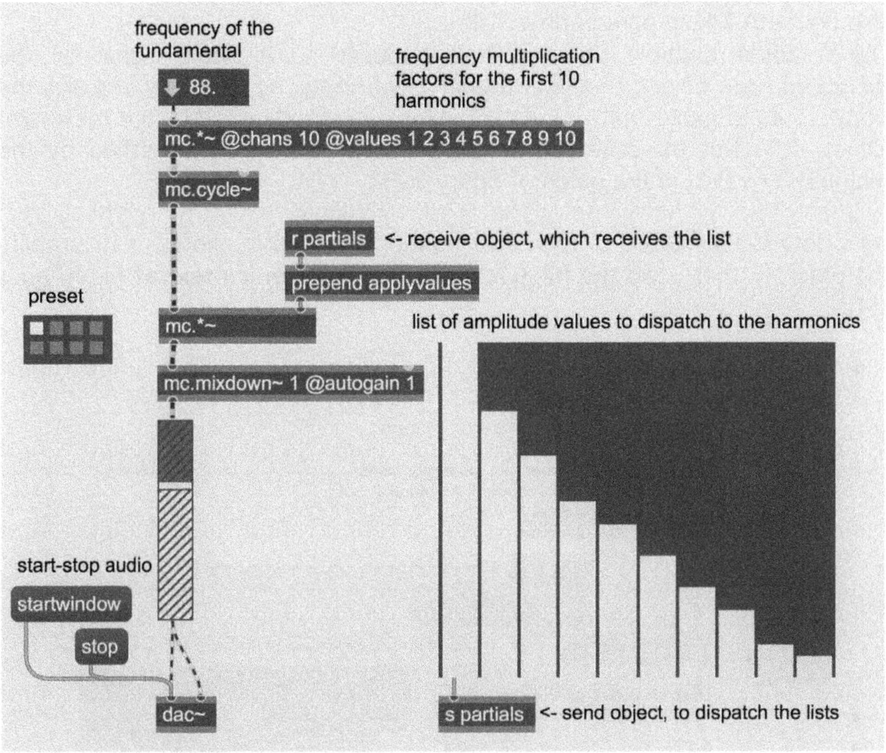

fig. 2.1c: file **02_01b_multichannel_additive.maxpat**

Let's analyze the patch starting from the top: the first object is a `number~` in "signal generator" mode; note that the small wave that usually appears on the left side has been replaced by an arrow pointing downwards. In this modality the `number~` object generates a constant signal corresponding to the value shown. To switch from one modality to another; you need to click on the icon (wave or arrow) on the left of the object.
The value generated by `number~` (88, in the figure) is passed to the multichannel multiplier `mc.*~`: Note that "@chans 10" has been set as the first attribute. This attribute determines the number of audio channels we want (i.e. the number of copies, or instances, of the signal multiplier): the (single) signal transmitted by the `number~` object is sent to all channels of the object `mc.*~`. The second attribute is "@values 1 2 3 4 5 6 7 8 9 10", which sets the multiplication factors for each instance (see also figure IA.74b in paragraph IA.12).
The values generated by the multiplier are passed to the multiple oscillator `mc.cycle~` which, when receiving a 10-channel signal, generates 10 sinusoidal oscillators (in this case there is no need for the @chans attribute because the object `mc.cycle~` internally generates a number of oscillators equal to the

number of channels it receives. The amplitude of each oscillator is then rescaled by another multiplier **mc.*~**, which receives, through a couple of objects [**s** partials] and [**r** partials], the list of amplitudes generated by the **multislider**. Before being passed to the multiplier, the "applyvalues" message is prefixed to the list (via **prepend**), so that each value is assigned to a different channel (see also figure IA.74c in paragraph IA.12).
The resulting multiple signal is then reduced to a single signal by the **mc.mixdown~** object: the "@autogain 1" attribute, as we know, rescales the signal so as to avoid that the instantaneous amplitude exceeds the maximum values -1,1 (This attribute carries out the same function performed by the multiplier [*~ 0.1] in the patch of figure 2.1).

Let's now see a feature of the multichannel system that allows us to simplify the patch further: load the **02_01c_additive_harmonic.maxpat** file. (figure 2.1d).

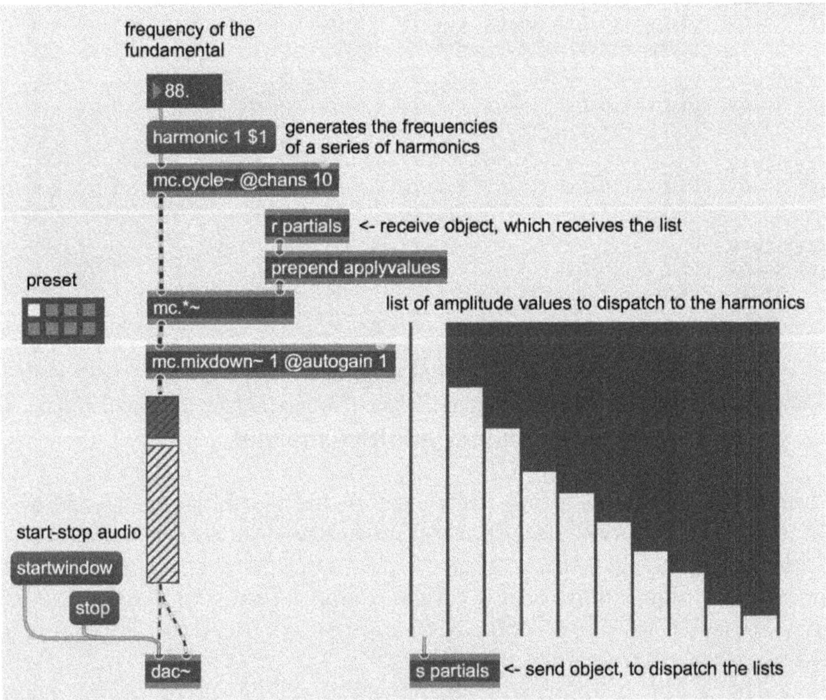

fig. 2.1d: *patch* **02_01c_additive_harmonic.maxpat**

As you can see we replaced the multiplier at the top of the previous patch with the message [harmonic $1]. This message is part of a series of "generator" messages that set, according to certain functions, the values of the instances contained in a multichannel wrapper[2]. The word "harmonic" is the name

---

[2] We remind you that the wrapper contains the instances (copies) of the MSP objects necessary to generate the multiple signal: see paragraph IA.12.

of the generator, the following value, 1, indicates a normal sequence of harmonics (we will see later what is generated with different values) and the last value determines the fundamental frequency of the harmonic series. The series generated in the patch in the figure will, therefore, be 88, 176, 264 etc. Each of these values is sent to a different oscillator. This is just one of the messages available to generate values in the multichannel system: we will see other messages soon. Notice that we added to the **`mc.cycle~`** object the attribute "@chans 10" (which in the previous patch was in the top multiplier, now deleted) so that the wrapper knows how many copies (or instances) of the oscillator we want.

The patch of figure 2.1d is much more "slim" than the equivalent patch of figure 2.1, and it makes us understand the utility of the multichannel system. However we must not think that the second patch, having so fewer objects, is lighter for the CPU: in reality, as we said, the multichannel wrapper creates "behind the scenes" the number of objects needed to manage all the signals; this means that even in the patch of figure 2.1d there are 10 **`cycle~`** oscillators and 10 multiplier MSPs, although invisible.

Using this patch, create various spectral profiles, saving them as presets and changing between them to compare the differences in timbre made by lower, middle, and upper components, as we covered in the theory chapter.

ACTIVITIES

Using the patch **02_01c_additive_harmonic.maxpat**, create two presets, one that has the amplitudes of the odd harmonics set to 1, and those of the even harmonics set to 0. Apart from timbre, what is the obvious difference? Why?

Continuing to use **02_01c_additive_harmonic.maxpat** (and referring to the discussion of missing fundamentals in Section 2.1T), begin with a spectrum in which the amplitudes of all harmonics are 1, and then zero out the amplitude of the fundamental. Listen for the illusion that the zeroed fundamental appears to be present. Try reducing the amplitude of successive harmonics, one by one. At what point can you no longer perceive the fundamental?

PHASE

We now take on a topic discussed at length in Section 2.1T (Section 2.1 of Chapter 2T), the phase of a periodic waveform. It is a basic concept that will develop over many chapters; because of this, it is important to understand how phase is managed using Max. Probably you have noticed that the **cycle~** object has two inlets: the left, as we already know, allows us to set the frequency, and the right allows us to set the normalized phase, a phase that is expressed as a value between 0 and 1 (rather than a value between 0 and 360 degrees or between 0 and 2π radians, both of which we encountered in the box dedicated to phase in Section 2.1T).
Build the patch shown in figure 2.2 in a new Patcher Window.

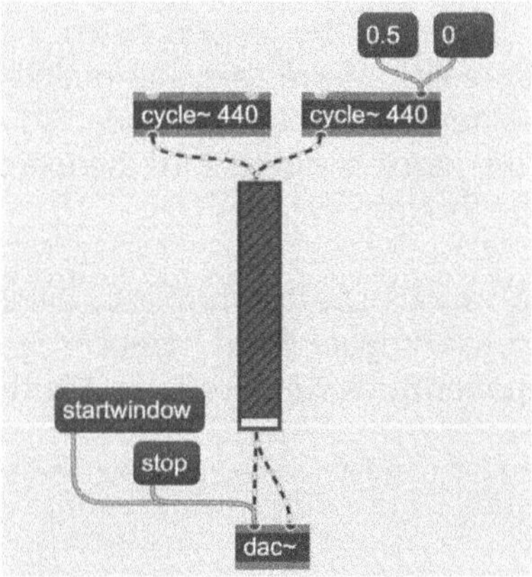

Fig. 2.2 Constructive and destructive interference

We have two **cycle~** objects at 440 Hz, the second of which has two message boxes, containing the numbers 0.5 and 0, connected to its right inlet (its phase inlet, as we just learned). Start the patch by clicking on "startwindow" and raising the **gain~** fader: you will hear a perfectly in-phase A440 generated by the two oscillators.
Clicking on the message box that contains 0.5, the sound vanishes. What has happened? We've set the phase of the second oscillator to 0.5, which is exactly half a cycle (180 degrees). The two oscillators become polarity-reversed[3] and because of this, their sum is always zero. Clicking on the message box that contains the number 0 will reset the two oscillators to being in-phase, enabling us to hear the sound once again.
To better understand the phase combinations, modify the patch to look like figure 2.3.
We've now replaced the two message boxes connected to the right inlet of the second oscillator with a float number box, and we've added three **send** objects to route the signals produced by the oscillators and their sum to three **scope~** objects.

[3] See the box dedicated to phase in Section 2.1T.

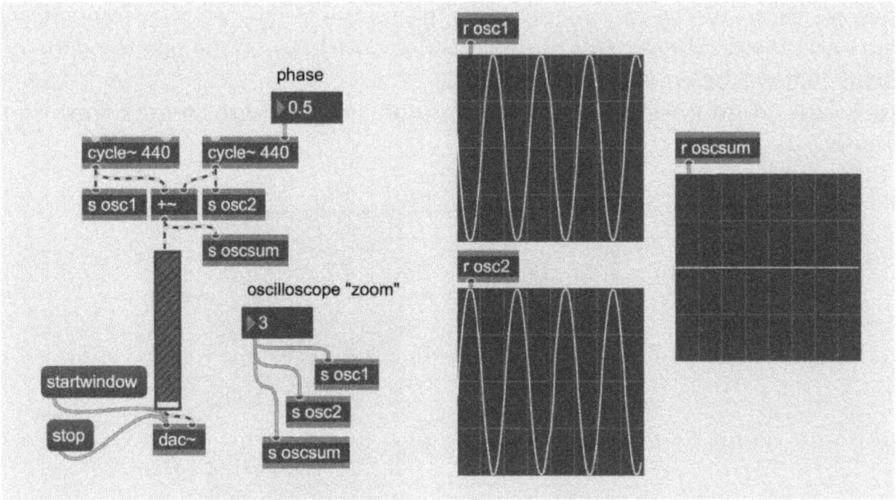

Fig. 2.3 Variations of phase

Besides this, we now vary the "Samples per Pixel" attribute[4] of the three oscilloscopes to control their displays. This is done by using three additional **send** objects, all connected to an integer number box. You will note that both signals and numerical values are sent to the oscilloscopes using the same name ("osc1", "osc2", and "oscsum") – recall that the **scope~** object accepts both the signals to be displayed and the parameter values to control that display on the same inlet.
After setting the number boxes to the values shown in the figure and clicking on "startwindow", you should see polarity-reversed sine waves displayed in the first two oscilloscopes, and a "null" waveform (a flat line) in the third. Click on "stop" and check that the two sine waves actually have opposite phase, as we have done in the figure. Now, after clicking "startwindow" again, modify the value in the float number box to control the phase of the second oscillator.
When it begins to drop from 0.5 towards 0, the oscillators are no longer in antiphase, and you hear a sound growing progressively in amplitude until the two oscillators are completely in phase and their summed amplitude ranges between -2 and 2.[5] Try using phase values larger than 1, and note that whenever the phase is equal to an integer, the sound reaches its maximum amplitude, and whenever the phase is exactly halfway between two integer values (such as 1.5, 2.5, 3.5, etc.), the sound is cancelled out. Phase values larger than 1 (larger than 360 degrees) cause the cycle to wrap around, beginning anew, as we explained in the box dedicated to phase in Section 2.1T. Of course, all of these observations hold true only if the two generators share exactly the same frequency. If they don't, the ratio between the phases of the

[4] See Section 1.2, where we demonstrated that this attribute can be considered, only a little inappropriately, as a kind of "zoom factor" for the oscilloscope.

[5] The resulting wave oscillates between -2 and 2 because it is the sum of two cosine waves (more on this shortly) that oscillate between -1 and 1 and are perfectly in phase

two oscillators would vary continuously, giving rise in the case that frequencies are only slightly different (for example 440 and 441 Hz), to the phenomenon of beats that will be covered in Section 2.2.
Let's look at another possibility for the right inlet of **cycle~** (as shown in figure 2.4).

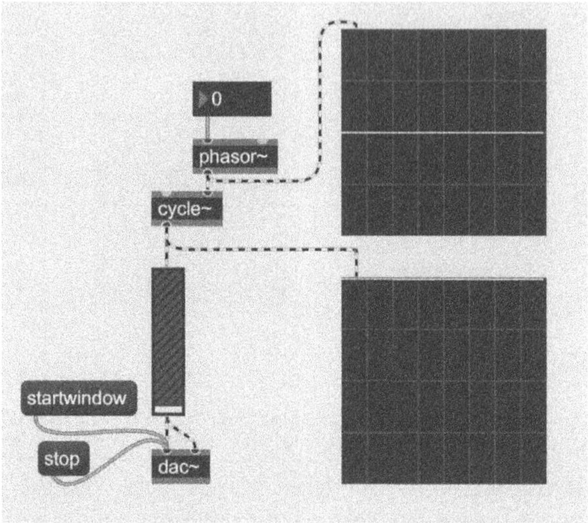

Fig. 2.4 Oscillator controlled by a **phasor~**

Here we have a **cycle~** set to 0 Hz, since it has neither an argument nor has it received a numeric message on its left inlet. The phase of this **cycle~** is set to be modified by a **phasor~**, which in the figure also has a frequency of 0 Hz, so to remain still. Looking at the oscilloscopes, we see that the **phasor~** generates a stream of zero-valued samples, which implies that it is frozen at the beginning of its cycle, and **cycle~** generates a stream of ones, which means that it too is frozen at the beginning of its cycle. It is important to stress that the cycle of a waveform generated by **cycle~** begins with the value 1; **cycle~** generates a cosine wave, as we pointed out in Section 1.1, which explains why the cycle starts at 1, its maximum positive value.[6] This is not a general rule: **phasor~**, for example, begins its cycle at 0.
Now we will give **phasor~** a frequency higher than 0 Hz; we set it to 5 Hz in the example shown in figure 2.5.

Build this patch yourself. The phase of the **cycle~** object is slaved to the **phasor~** object, causing it to oscillate at the same frequency and with the same phase as the **phasor~**. As you will recall from Section 1.2, **phasor~** generates a ramp from 0 to 1, and this ramp, when applied to the phase inlet of **cycle~**, produces the oscillation. (This explains the motivation behind the name **phasor~**: one of its main functions is to control the phase of other objects.)

[6] For a definition of the cosine function, see theory sections 1.2 and 2.1.

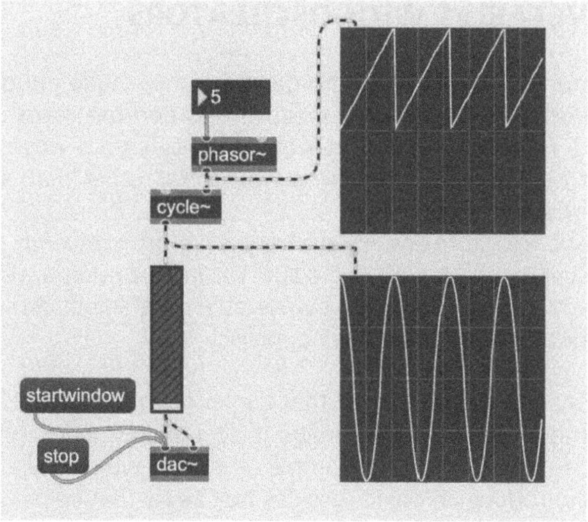

Fig. 2.5 **phasor~** set to 5 Hz

As we see in figure 2.5, every ramp generated by **phasor~** results in one complete oscillation of **cycle~**, which is running at 5 Hz in this example. If we were to eliminate the **phasor~** and give **cycle~** a frequency of 5 Hz by sending it a message on its inlet, or by providing an argument, we would obtain an identical oscillation. In other words, **cycle~** behaves as though it has an "internal phasor". Such an "internal phasor", interestingly, is lacking in the **triangle~** object (encountered in Section 1.2), which can only oscillate when controlled by an external **phasor~**. Yet in the case of the **triangle~** object, we still speak about its phase (or index), thinking of this as the indexed absolute position within the waveform cycle (see Section 2.1T). And **triangle~** is not alone; we will see shortly another important example of an object that produces oscillations when connected to a **phasor~**.

One might ask what would happen if the **cycle~** object in figure 2.5 were to have its own frequency in addition to the frequency being provided by **phasor~**? The answer is: nothing particularly interesting. The two frequency values (that of the **cycle~** and that of the **phasor~**) are simply summed. Try this, by giving an argument of 440 to **cycle~**, for example, and then setting the frequency of **phasor~** to 220 Hz. The result will be a (co)sine wave with a frequency of 660 Hz.

USING WAVETABLES WITH OSCILLATORS

Using a large number of oscillators to generate the simple periodic waveform that accompanies a fixed harmonic spectrum, as demonstrated in the patches of figure 2.1, 2.1c and 2.1d[7], might well be considered a waste of resources. We know that oscillators can generate waveforms other than sine waves, as we discussed briefly in Chapter 1.
Indeed, it is possible to store entirely arbitrary waveforms into wavetable memory for the use of such oscillators. Saving a sum of sine waves as a wavetable in this way, and then supplying this stored wavetable to a single oscillator, is much more "economical" than the additive approach.

In MSP the managed memory array that can contain such waveforms is called a buffer, and the object used to manage it, first encountered in Section 1.5, is called `buffer~`. Let's look at an example of its use, which will also give us the opportunity to introduce an object besides `buffer~` that helps with wavetable synthesis.
Open the file **02_02_buffer.maxpat** (shown in figure 2.6).

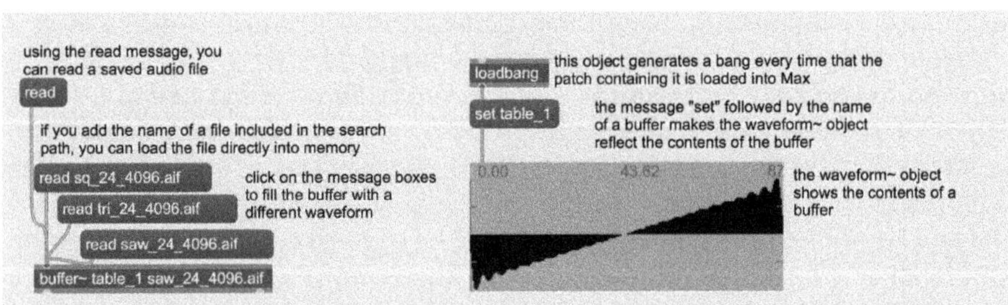

fig. 2.6: file **02_02_buffer.maxpat**

For now, let's only look at the left part of the patch, where we see the `buffer~` object with its two arguments: "tabella_1" and "saw_24_4096.aif". The first argument is a name for the buffer (we will see after a short while why it is useful to give a name to a buffer), and the second is the name of the audio file that is to be loaded into the buffer. To be found by Max, the audio file must be somewhere within the search path.[8] It is also possible to load an audio file into a buffer by means of the "**read**" command, usually followed by the name of the file, as shown in the figure[9]; you may also choose to drag the name of an audio file from the File Browser directly onto the `buffer~` object, as we did with the `sfplay~` object in Section 1.5.[10]

[7] We remind you that, although in Figures 2.1c and 2.1d there is only one multichannel oscillator, Max actually uses multiple copies of single oscillators behind the scenes.

[8] The file saw_24_4096.aif can be found in the Virtual Sound Macros library. You'll recall that we introduced the search path in Sections 1.2 and IA.4, when talking about subpatches and abstractions.

[9] The waveform that it is loaded in this patch can also be found in the Virtual Sound Macros library, in a folder named "virtualsound waves".

[10] Recall that the File Browser is called up via the File menu or by pressing <Command-b/Control-b>.

Returning to the patch, the **buffer~** object in the left part of the patch manages a buffer that we have named "table_1", which contains a waveform that had already been saved into the file "saw_24_4096".
The strange name for the file simply indicates the form of the wave, "sawtooth", and tells us that it contains 24 component harmonics and is 4096 samples long. Double-clicking on the **buffer~** object will open a window that shows the contents of the buffer.
Moving to the right of the patch, we see a **waveform~** object, which is new to us. This graphical object can be used to show the contents of a **buffer~** graphically within a Patcher Window. It is in the "Audio" category of the Add palette. As soon as you find yourself needing to use multiple **buffer~** objects in a patch, you will also need a way of indicating which buffer you wish to display in a given **waveform~** object; to do this, you simply send the object a "set" message followed by the name of the **buffer~** that you wish to display using a message box.
The "**set**" message, in fact, merits a brief digression, since it has so many applications. We saw in Section IA.8 of Interlude A, dedicated to the message box, that when "set" precedes another message, that message will be displayed directly within the target message box. In our current case, "set" indicates the buffer to be displayed by waveform~. The "set" message (recalling that this is a message we're talking about, not an object!) is used by many other Max and MSP objects, and is generally used to set parameter values for properties that vary from object to object. We will encounter this message over and over again during the course of the following chapters.

Returning to the patch, note that the name that we pass to **waveform~** is the name of the buffer ("table_1"), and not the name of the file (saw_24_4096.aif), and that every time that we load a new waveform into this buffer, it will be displayed by the **waveform~** object. The numbers in the upper part of the object indicate the length of the buffer in milliseconds: an audio file with 4096 samples, played using a sampling rate of 44,100 Hz, is around 93 milliseconds long. As we already know, the **loadbang** object connected to the message box generates a bang every time that the patch containing it is loaded into Max. In this case, the bang is used to send the "set table_1" message to initialize the **waveform~** without requiring a click on the message box.
The **buffer~** object is in the patch to hold the wavetable, of course, but in order to actually hear its contents as a waveform, we will need an oscillator. Among the many possibilities offered by MSP, we have chosen to use the **wave~** object.

Close the patch that had been open, and open in its place the file **02_03_wave.maxpat** (as shown in figure 2.7).

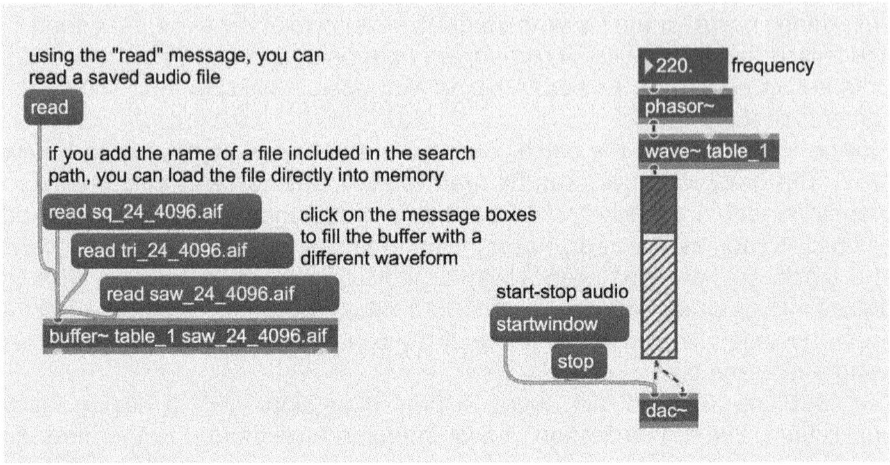

fig. 2.7: file 02_03_wave.maxpat

The **wave~** object isn't really an oscillator; it is more like an object that specializes in reading wavetables. It needs a connection to a **phasor~** in order to function, which serves to indicate the current phase of the wavetable, or the point in the table from which to read the next sample, exactly as it did for the **triangle~** object that we encountered in Section 1.2.[11] As you can see, the object requires an argument, that provides the name of the buffer to be used. In this case, it is "table_1", which refers to the contents of the **buffer~** on the left. The name also indicates which buffer to use; were you to use different **wave~** objects, each with its own buffer, you would refer to them by using the name of their backing wavetable.

Activate the patch and click on the various message boxes connected to the **buffer~** in order to hear the timbre change; each message loads a different waveform into the wavetable.[12] Each of these waveforms contains up to 24 components, and so they are equivalent to summing up to 24 sine wave oscillators in various harmonic relationships.
There is no standard Max object that permits you to compile wavetables by providing component amplitudes levels, although other programming environments have such objects, such as the GEN10 generator in CSound. Fortunately, however, Max is a language that is versatile enough to allow us to construct and use such an object. We have constructed an algorithm to do this that can be found in our Virtual Sound Macros library.

[11] See also the section dedicated to phase in Section 2.1T..
[12] We should point out that also the **cycle~** object can use waveforms other than cosine waves through the use of **buffer~** objects.

Look for the file **02_04_gen10.maxpat**, which is shown below in figure 2.8.

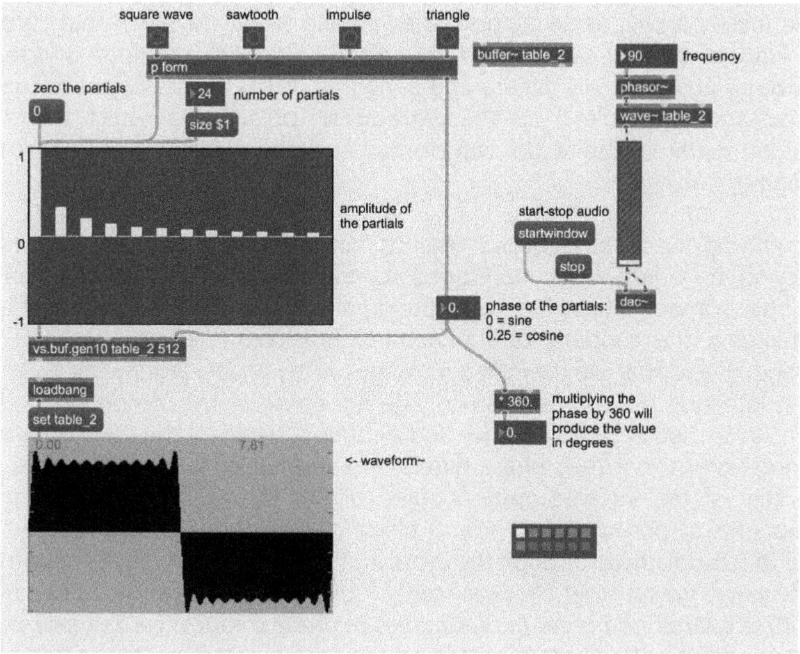

fig. 2.8: file 02_04_gen10.maxpat

In this patch, the **buffer~** object uses a buffer named "table_2", which isn't loaded with a file, but rather, with a waveform compiled using the **vs.buf.gen10** object, which can be seen in the left part of the patch under the **multislider**. This object (which is an abstraction constructed using standard Max objects) is part of the previously mentioned Virtual Sound Macros library; it loads a given buffer with a waveform calculated as the sum of harmonic components.[13]

The object accepts two arguments, the name of the buffer to be compiled, and its length in samples, which can be changed using the center inlet. The amplitude values of the harmonic components are furnished to **vs.buf.gen10** as a numeric list; in the patch we see a **multislider** that generates lists with a variable number of elements, each representing the amplitude of one component.

[13] Recall, as we showed in Section 2.1T, that this case isn't properly additive synthesis, but rather wavetable synthesis. For fixed harmonic spectra, the results are identical.

Once it is filled, we can see the contents of the buffer thanks to the graphical **waveform~** object that lies at the lower left. The **loadbang** object connected to the message box, as usual, generates a bang when the patch that contains it is loaded. In this case, when the file 02_04_gen10.maxpat is opened, **loadbang** automatically generates a bang that forces the message box to send the message "set table_2" to the **waveform~** object, after which the object will stand ready to display the waveform associated with the **buffer~** object managing "table_2".

By modifying the **multislider** settings, you can create different timbres; try modifying the sliders, which represent component amplitude values. You can add or remove components by modifying the number of sliders in the **multislider** by changing the contents of the number box connected to the "size $1" message. (Recall that we examined messages with variable arguments in Section IA.8 in Interlude A.) You can also change the phase of the components; as we learned in Section 2.1T, a sine wave and a cosine wave share the same waveform, differing only in that their phase differs by a quarter cycle, or 90 degrees. The right inlet of the **vs.buf.gen10** object allows for setting the phase of the components as portions of a cycle: a phase of 0 is the beginning of a cycle, a phase of 0.5 is halfway through the cycle, and so forth. If we want to have a sum of sine waves we must set the phase to 0, a sum of cosine waves requires a phase of 0.25 (a quarter of a cycle, or 90 degrees of phase shift relative to a sine wave), etc. If you modify the phase by acting on the float number box connected to the right inlet of **vs.buf.gen10**, you will see a change in the waveform shown in the **waveform~** object.[14] First, zero all of the components by clicking on the message box containing the '0' that can be found over the **multislider** (to which it is connected). After this, give a positive value to the first component (by raising the first slider in the **multislider**). You will obtain a sine wave that can made to "flow" through the **waveform~** object by gradually varying the phase. Note that if you set the phase to 0.5 (to half a cycle, equivalent to 180 degrees), the sine wave will appear reversed (in antiphase), as we saw in the part of Section 2.1T dedicated to phase. Another way to obtain a reversed sine wave in this patch is to provide negative values for the fundamental amplitude by setting the first slider below the 0 line (returning the phase setting to 0, of course).

In the other part of the patch is the [**p** form] subpatch, which generates a few of the classic waveforms: square, sawtooth, and triangle waves, as well as an impulse. (For a reminder on any of these, see Section 2.1T.)
Clicking on any of the four buttons generates lists of harmonics (to 24 components) that approximate the related waveform. You can see how these lists are generated by opening the subpatch with a double click. Analyzing all of the algorithms used in this subpatch would take too long, and be too complex; instead of this, we will limit ourselves to a discussion of the sawtooth section (shown in figure 2.9).

[14] Recall that to modify the fractional part of a value, you need to place the mouse pointer over the right side of the float number box.

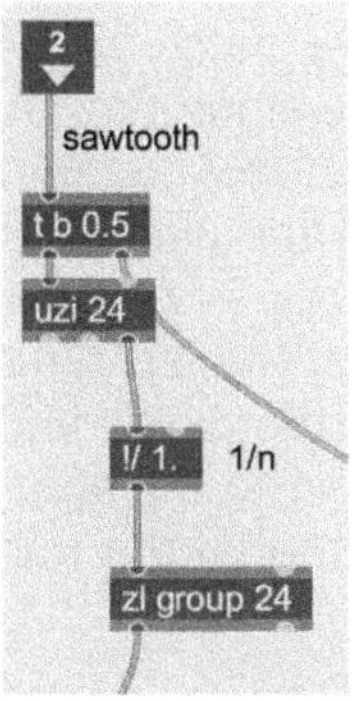

Fig. 2.9 Calculating components for the sawtooth wave

In Section 2.1T, we learned that a sawtooth wave can be approximated by summing harmonics, each with a phase of 180 degrees and an amplitude factor of 1/n (with n being the number of the harmonic):

1/1 1/2 1/3 1/4 1/5 1/6 1/7...

Our algorithm generates this series of amplitude factors and collects them into a list that is formatted for the external **multislider**. When a bang arrives on the **inlet**, trigger is fired, which sends a value of 0.5 to the right **outlet**[15] as its first action; this value represents phase, and rotates all of the components by 180 degrees. The trigger then generates a bang that is passed to the **uzi** object, which fires 24 bangs from its left **outlet** while sending a consecutive series of numbers (from 1 to 24) from its right. The numbers are passed to the **!/** object, and are used as the denominators for the 1/n calculation. (Recall that we introduced the "exclamation point" arithmetic operators in Section IA.1 of Interlude A.) The result of each calculation is passed to the [**zl** group 24] object, which aggregates the elements that it receives into groups of 24. Once it has received 24 items, as specified by the argument, it sends the entire group as a list to its left **outlet**. The list is returned by the subpatch and arrives at the **multislider**.

ACTIVITIES

Using the patch 02_04_gen10.maxpat, and exploiting the phenomenon of the "phantom fundamental" that was covered in Section 2.1T, make a spectrum in which all of the amplitudes of the harmonics are 1, but the amplitude of the fundamental is 0. For comparison purposes, listen to a spectrum in which the fundamental is equal to the zeroed frequency. Try reducing the amplitude of successive harmonics to 0, one by one. At what point can you no longer hear the phantom fundamental?

15 Recall that Max objects follow right-to-left precedence. (See Section 1.7.)

Open the subpatch [p form] in the patch 02_04_gen10.maxpat and tinker with it in order to understand how the algorithms that generate the components for the square wave and for the impulse work. Reread the help files for the objects used, and study the workings of the patch. (The object **vs.even-odd** is part of the Virtual Sound Macros library. It sorts the numbers that it receives: if the number is even, it is output from the left outlet, and if odd, it is output from the right outlet.) The first object that you'll find in all of the patch's algorithms is a `trigger` that sends a number to the right outlet and a bang to the rest of the algorithm. Do you remember what this number does?

FIXED NON-HARMONIC SPECTRA

The components of a fixed non-harmonic spectrum can be set at will, since their frequencies need not maintain integer ratios with some fundamental. Because we can't use **vs.buf.gen10** to generate such components, we'll need to build another patch with an oscillator for every partial, and we will do it using the multichannel system: open the file **02_05a_nonharmonic_mc.maxpat** (figure 2.10a).

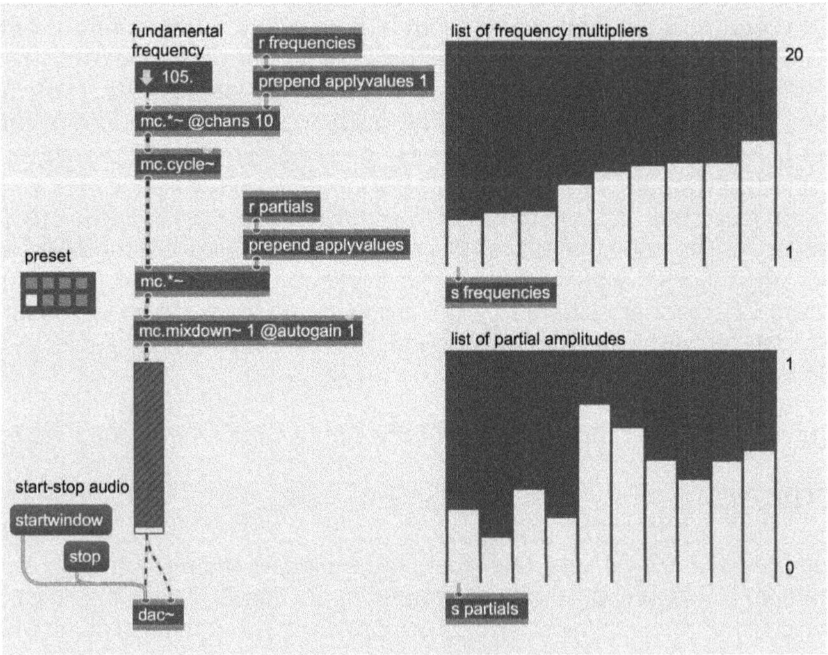

fig. 2.10a: file **02_05a_nonharmonic_mc.maxpat**

This patch is very similar to that of figure 2.1c (02_01b_multichannel_additive.maxpat), the difference is that the multipliers of the fundamental frequency (at the top of the patch) are not consecutive integer values, but arbitrary values, between 1 and 20, set with the **multislider** at the top.

Note that this **multislider** has 9 sliders, one for each component, excluding the fundamental. The generated list arrives, through [**r** frequencies], to the object [**prepend** applyvalues 1] visible at the top: the numerical value 1 immediately after the "applyvalues" message represents the multiplication factor of the fundamental, the other 9 multiplication factors are set, as we have said, from the **multislider**. At the bottom we have a second **multislider** (with 10 elements) that generates a list of amplitudes for the partials, with a mechanism identical to that of figure 2.1c.
With the message for the generation of harmonic series that we have seen in figure 2.1d (patch 02_01c_additive_harmonic.maxpat) it is also possible to create some kind of inharmonic series: load the patch **02_05b_nonharmonic_series.maxpat** (figure 2.10b).

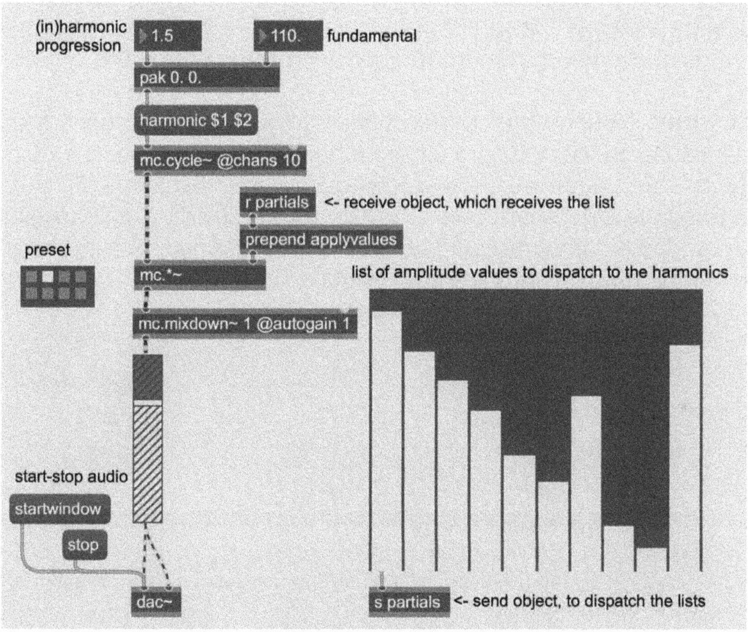

fig. 2.10b: patch **02_05b_nonharmonic_series.maxpat**

As we know the syntax to generate, for example, a harmonic series with fundamental 100 Hz is "harmonic 1 100": the first argument, 1, represents the multiplication factor of the harmonic series. How does this multiplication factor work? First of all, let's note that the interval in hertz between one component and the next, in a harmonic series, is always the same, and is equal to the frequency of the fundamental. For example, the harmonic series built on a fundamental of 100 Hz is 100, 200, 300, 400, 500, etc. The interval between each component is 100, equal to the frequency of the fundamental. As we have just said, the first argument of the "harmonic" generator is the multiplication factor of this interval; therefore, for example, the message "harmonic 0.9 100" rescales by a factor of 0.9 the interval between one component and the other, reducing it to 90 (i.e., 100 * 0.9), and the series then becomes 100, 190 (100 + 90), 280 (100 + 90 * 2), 370 (100 + 90 * 3) and so on. In other words, with

the compression or the expansion of the interval between the components, the series becomes inharmonic.
The two number boxes at the top of the patch are used respectively to set the compression/expansion factor of the harmonic series and the fundamental frequency: before being sent to the message box [harmonic $ 1 $ 2], the two values are sent to the **pak** object which transforms them in a list of two elements. Note that the object is called **pak** and not **pack**: it is not a typo; this object differs from the one we already know because it generates a list every time one of its elements is modified (not only the one on the left). In this way we are sure that the list is sent every time we update one of the two values. The **pak** object is therefore a builder of lists similar to **pack**, but unlike the latter all its inputs are "hot".
Listen to all the presets and try to create new ones: pay attention to the multiplication factor of the series! A high value is likely to quickly bring the last components above the maximum frequency reproducible by the system.[16]

We said, at the beginning of this section, that we could not generate a non-harmonic sound by compiling a table using the **vs.buf.gen10** object, but in reality, this isn't quite true. As we demonstrated in Section 2.1T, it is in fact possible to create a non-harmonic sound by using the very high harmonics of a very low fundamental, whose amplitude is set to 0, along with the amplitudes of the lower harmonics. Let's see how to make a sound of this type by opening the file **02_06_nonharm_gen10.maxpat** (shown in figure 2.11).

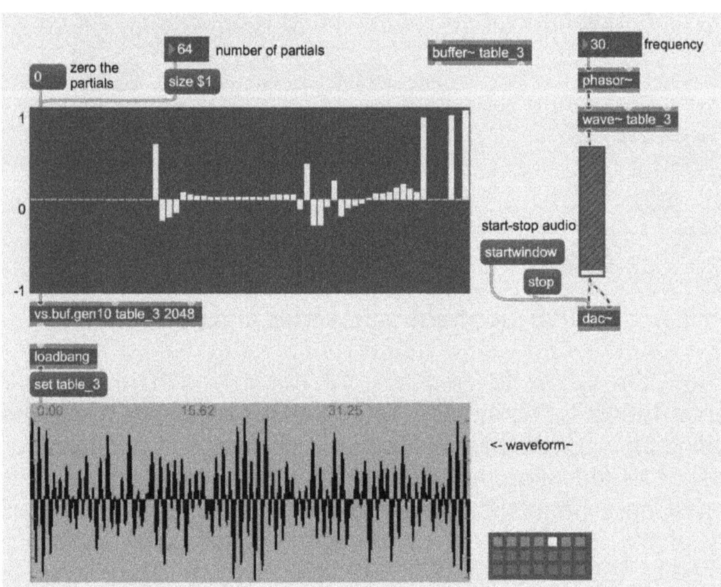

fig. 2.11: file **02_06_nonharm_gen10.maxpat**

[16] For example with the message "harmonic 10 300" the ninth component would be at 24300 Hz, above the maximum reproducible frequency with a sampling frequency of 44100 or 48000 Hz.

This patch is very similar to that of figure 2.8, and so in this case we will again compile a buffer to be read by **wave~** by using **vs.buf.gen10**. The buffer will contain a waveform built strictly from high harmonics; the fundamental and any harmonics near the fundamental have no significance and have amplitudes of 0. The oscillation frequency of the waveform will be set to a very low value, often below the audible frequency band; that which we hear will therefore be equivalent to partials that our brain cannot relate to a common fundamental (both because the components fall below the threshold of audibility and because the low harmonics have a null amplitude). The resulting sound is definitely non-harmonic. By the way, this trick isn't necessary for the amplitudes: can you understand why? (Hint: what difference is there, in the patch shown in the figure, between the multiplication operators used for frequencies and those used for amplitude?)

Try the various presets and observe how the examples use irregularly-spaced components by preference. After this, create some new presets, paying careful attention to keep the non-harmonicity of your sounds! It is necessary, from the moment that we start using upper harmonics, to increment the dimensions of the array in the **buffer~**[17] (which in this patch has 2048 elements).

ACTIVITIES

Using 02_05a_nonharmonic.maxpat as a start, try to create spectra with partials very close to each other; change the range of the **multislider**[18] for the frequency multipliers in a way that their sliders have a minimum of 1 and a maximum of 1.05, and after modifying its value range, set a frequency for the lowest component between 50 and 400 Hz. Is a non-harmonic spectrum still generated? How would you define what you hear? We will revisit this in Section 2.2.

[17] Owing to the fact that, for example, the 64th harmonic repeats its cycle 64 times in the buffer; we need enough points in such a table to avoid a distortion of the 64 cycles of this waveform. The **wave~** object, in fact, implements a simple linear interpolation (see the section on interpolation of tables in 2.1T) and because of this, a sine wave sampled with too few points starts to resemble a triangle wave, or at least a jagged line.

[18] In edit mode, select the **multislider** and open the Inspector by pressing <Command-i/ Control-i>. Select the Sliders tab, and set the high and low values for Slider Range to 1 and 1.05.

2.2 BEATS

Producing the phenomenon of beats within Max is trivial: summing two **cycle~** oscillators whose frequencies are slightly different, perhaps 440 and 441 Hz, is all that it takes. As you know, a sum such as this will produce a wave whose perceived frequency will be 440.5 Hz and whose amplitude will oscillate once per second (as shown in figure 2.12).

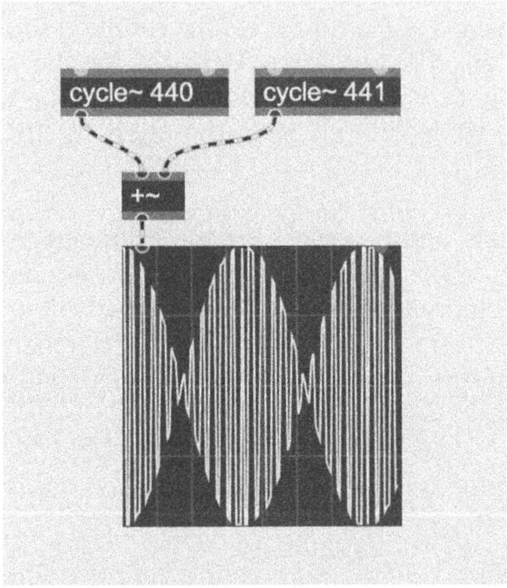

fig. 2.12: beats

Construct the patch shown in figure 2.12. Set the number of "Samples per Pixel" for **scope~** so that you see one, two, or three complete cycles inside the oscilloscope window. (Try starting with the value 256.) Increasing the frequency of the second oscillator to increase the frequency of the beats will also raise the resulting frequency. If, for example, the second **cycle~** is increased to 450 Hz, you will hear 10 beats per second and a frequency of 445 Hz for the resulting wave. Try this: construct a patch that simply sums two sine waves as in figure 2.12 (remembering to connect everything to a **gain~** and a **dac~**, of course!). Starting at the same frequency, try varying the frequency of one of the oscillators to create beats. Note that, as a side-effect, the perceived frequency moves up and down depending on the distance in Hz between the oscillator frequencies.
Let's examine how we might build a patch that allows us to vary the number of beats without changing the perceived frequency of the resulting wave.

The solution is shown in the patch found in **02_07_beats.maxpat**, displayed in figure 2.13, which has one number box for the central frequency, and another for the number of beats per second. The number of beats is divided by 2 and the result is then both added to and subtracted from the central frequency, a calculation that results in two frequencies with a distance between them equal to the number of beats desired in Hz, and a central frequency that matches the specified one. Try varying the number of beats in order to hear that the central frequency now remains fixed, thanks to the symmetric separation of pitches that occurs simultaneously.

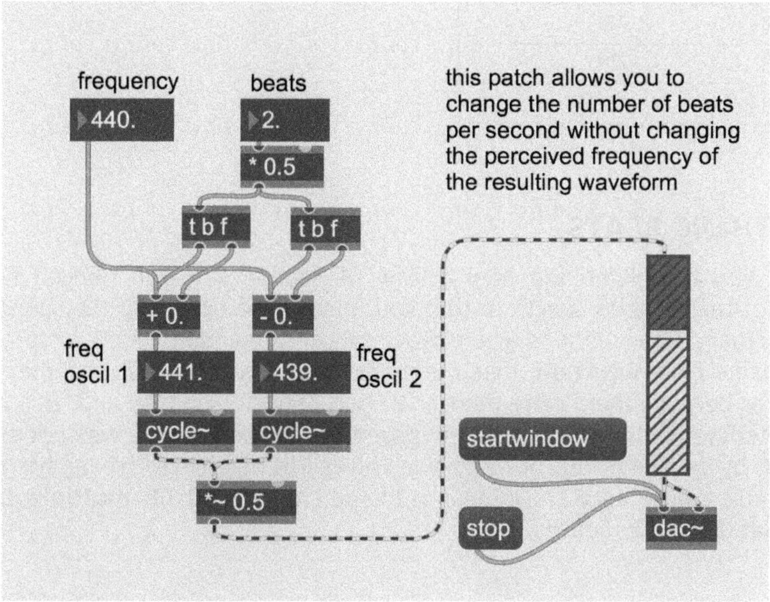

fig. 2.13: file **02_07_beats.maxpat**

Do you recall what purpose the two trigger arguments 'b' and 'f' serve in the upper part of the patch? Refer to Section IA.6 if you need a refresher.

In Section 2.2T, we learned that when increasing the number of beats (by increasing the frequency difference between two sounds), there is a point where the sound becomes "rough," after which it is no longer possible to distinguish single beats. After this point, if you continue to increase the difference, the rough sound will eventually separate into the two distinct pitched sounds that are its constituents. Referring to the table published by Thomas D. Rossing (previously cited as Rossing, T., 1990, p. 74, and duplicated here as Table A) and using the patch in figure 2.13, try setting the intermediate frequency to match the values in the table, and then increasing the distance between the two sounds until you can hear two distinct sounds.

Are there differences between the values that you find and those outlined in Table A?

Intermediate Frequency	Critical Band
100	90
200	90
500	110
1000	150
2000	280
5000	700
10000	1200

table A

RHYTHMIC BEATS

When you completed the final activity of Section 2.1, you noticed that in place of the complex spectrum that you might have expected, the sound that was actually obtained was a sine wave whose amplitude varied more or less irregularly. Now we know that these oscillations were beats, and they were irregular because there were more than two oscillators in play and, as a result, the interference between all of the superimposed sine waves was not simple. In fact, by summing four or more sine waves it is possible to create interesting "rhythmic beats," as you can hear in the patch in file **02_08_multiple_beats.maxpat** (shown in figure 2.14).

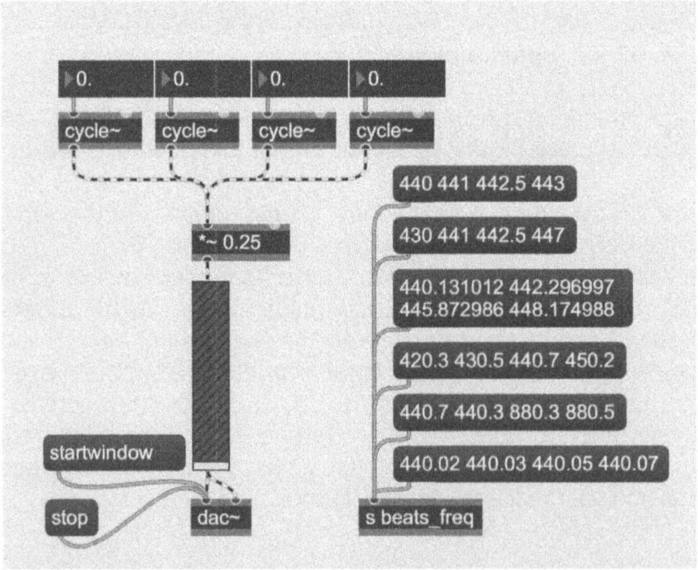

fig. 2.14: file **02_08_multiple_beats.maxpat**

The patch in figure 2.14 is incomplete. There are two objects to add that will ensure that the four float number boxes connected to the oscillators in the upper part of the patch receive the values sent by the message boxes in the right part of the figure. Before continuing, add these objects, making all of the connections necessary.
In this patch, there are four sine wave oscillators that are summed. Click on the message boxes to hear examples of rhythmic patterns generated by beats. Try to obtain other interesting rhythmic variations by changing the frequencies of the oscillators.

Question: why are the four oscillators sent to a multiplier that scales them by 0.25? If you don't know how to answer this, review the beginning of Section 2.1T. Try to describe, listening to the final example in the patch, what is happening from an amplitude point of view. Also, notice that the variations in intensity in this example become more evident after a few minutes; can you explain why?

You can easily create a multichannel version of the previous patch: transform it as shown in figure 2.14b.

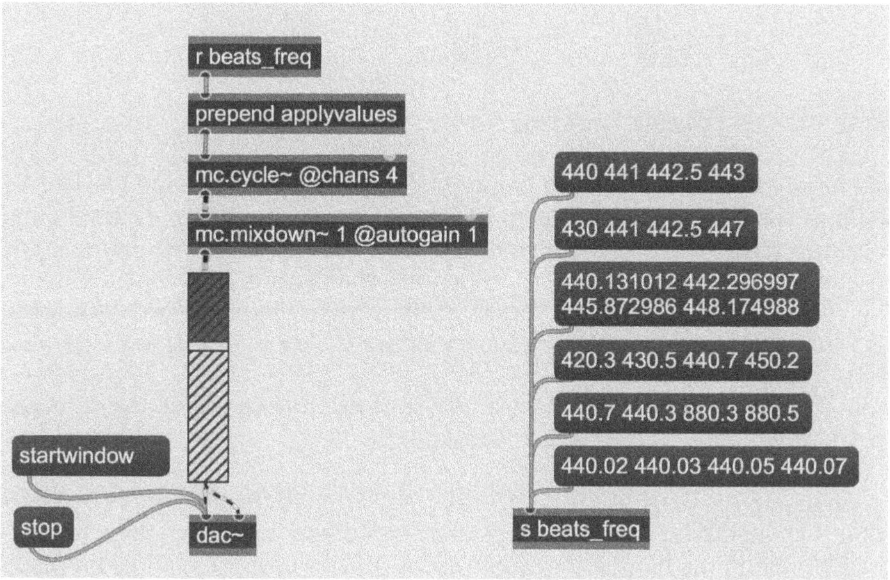

fig. 2.14b: multichannel version of the patch 02_08_multiple_beats.maxpat

The beat lists are sent (preceded by the "applyvalues" message) directly to the **mc.cycle~** object which, thanks to the attribute "@chans 4", generates 4 sinusoidal oscillators. The **mc.mixdown~** object with argument "1" transforms the multichannel signal into a single signal.

As we have said, there are several messages that generate series of values for the multichannel system. We have already seen the message "harmonic", we will now take a look at "deviate", which creates a random series of values around a central value. Change the previous patch as shown in figure 2.14c.

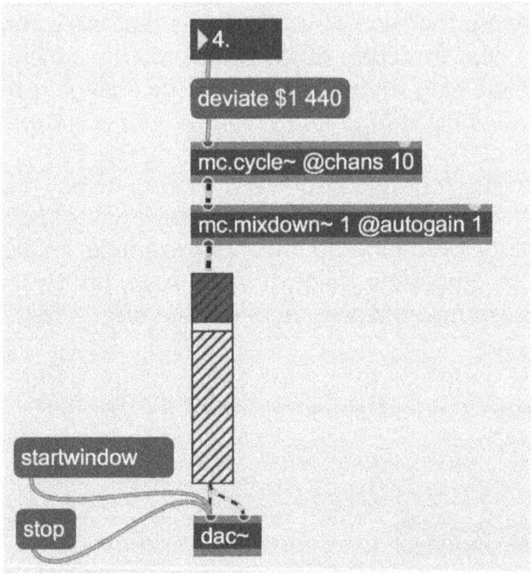

fig. 2.14c: the "deviate" message

We have connected a floating point number box to the message [deviate $1 440]: as we said, this allows us to generate a series of random values around a central value. The first argument represents the maximum random quantity to add or remove to the central value, and the second argument represents the central value: in the case shown in the figure, therefore, each sinusoidal oscillator will have a random frequency between 436 (440 - 4) and 444 (440 + 4).
Note that the value of the @chans attribute of `mc.cycle~` has been increased to 10, so we have 10 parallel oscillators.

Try changing the value of the number box and listen to the differences between sounds created with very low values (between 0 and 1) and very high (greater than 10). Bring the number box value above 10 and hear the gradual transition between multiple beats, "rough" sound and inharmonic frequency band.

BEATS OF THE HARMONIC COMPONENTS

Naturally, it is also possible to sum complex sounds whose frequencies are close to the same value.In combinations of complex sounds, every harmonic present will generate beats (as we learned in Section 2.2T).

By summing larger numbers of complex sounds, it is possible to generate polyrhythms from their beats; one example that is truly a "dance of the harmonics" can be heard in the patch found in **02_09_beats_harm_comp.maxpat**.

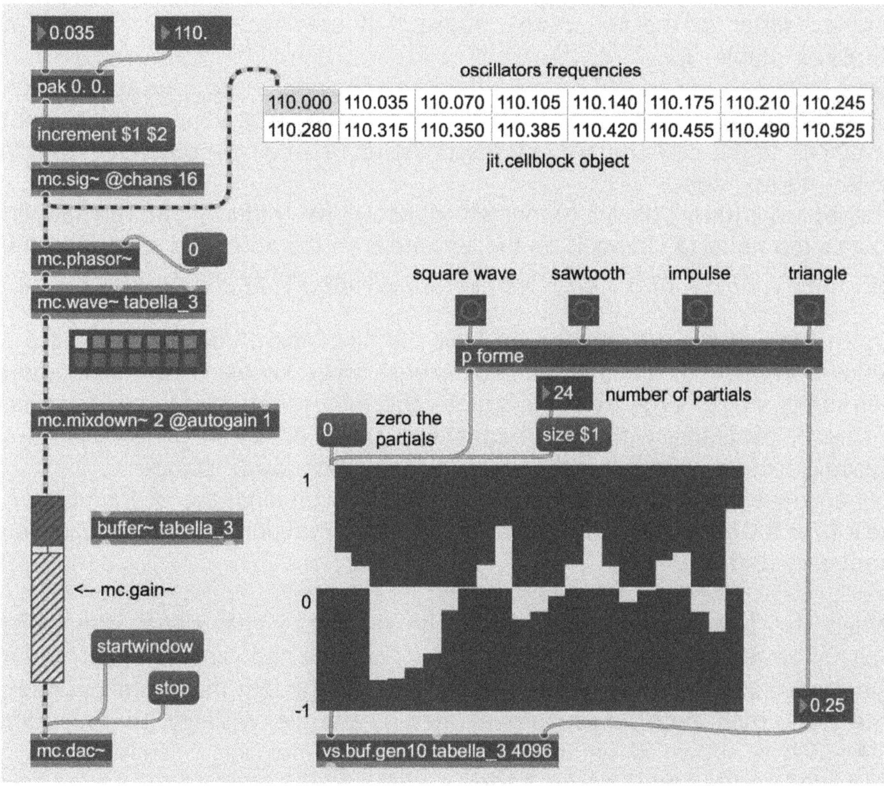

fig. 2.15: The file **02_09_beats_harm_comp.maxpat**

Thanks to the multichannel system, this patch generates 16 oscillators, all using the same waveform that is compiled by `vs.buf.gen10` and stored in [`buffer~` table_3]; it is also possible to generate the "classic" waveforms with the subpatch [`p` form] (see paragraph 2.1).

The patch presents some new features. First of all, on the top left we see a new message that generates values for the multichannel system: "increment" which creates a series of numerical values with a constant increase. The first argument is the value of the increment, and the second is the initial value of the series: for example the message "increment 2 100" produces the series of values 100, 102, 104, 106 etc.

The message is sent to the object `mc.sig~`, multichannel version of `sig~` (see paragraph 1.5P), which produces a multichannel signal composed of 16 channels, each of which transmits one of the values created by the "increment" generator.

The multichannel signal is sent to a new object, **jit.cellblock**, visible at the top of the patch. This object shows the values of a multichannel signal connected to it.[19]
The same signal is also passed to the **mc.phasor~** object (which, when receiving a 16-channel signal, generates 16 instances of the **phasor~** object) and the latter to the **mc.wave~** object that uses the waveform stored in [**buffer~** table_3].
Notice the message box [0] connected to the right input of **mc.phasor~**: when a single value is sent to a multichannel object, this value reaches all the present instances. In this case, the value 0 resets the phase of all the **phasor~** objects to the starting point.
The **mc.mixdown~** object connected to **mc.wave~** reduces the 16 channels to a stereo signal (8 channels on the left and 8 on the right) and sends it to the **mc.gain~** object, which we know is the multichannel version of **gain~**.

Try the various presets, and notice how the "increment" generator creates a series of frequencies that are very close to each other. You can hear the different harmonics that emerge from the sound, and then vanish. It is interesting that a sum of oscillators with fixed frequencies and spectra can generate such a dynamic texture, with internal pulsations that continuously change.
We encourage you to experiment with different combinations of frequencies; hear how the behavior of the beats changes when you increase or decrease the frequency distance.

When the frequency distribution of the oscillators is irregular, the beats polyrhythms disappear, because the sounds emerge and vanish randomly, but the sound nevertheless acquires a depth and density that make it much more interesting than the fixed sound generated by a single oscillator. Try to modify the patch as shown in figure 2.15b (replace the message "increment" with "deviate", as we saw in figure 2.14c).

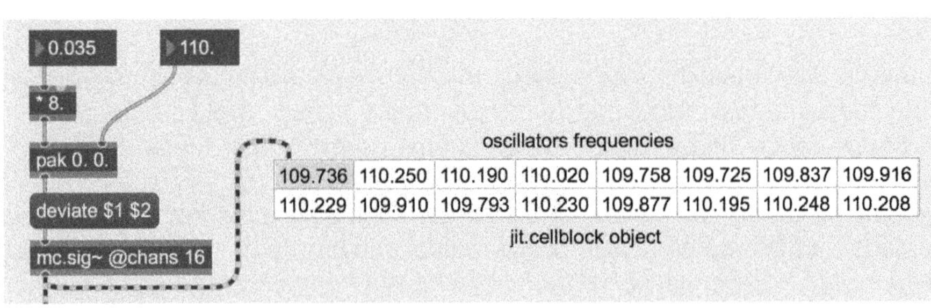

fig. 2.15b: modification of the patch 02_09_beats_harm_comp.maxpat

[19] The prefix "jit" at the beginning of the name indicates that the object is part of the Jitter library, dedicated to the processing of video, graphics, and management of matrices. Over time this object has "evolved" and now performs different functions, such as the display of multichannel signals.

Note that we have multiplied the first argument (top left) by 8, to make sure that the difference between the frequencies generated by "deviate" is comparable to that of the frequencies generated by "increment" (could you explain why? What function has the first argument in the two generators?).
Listen to all the presets again and note the differences with the previous version.

ACTIVITIES

Sum the output of a sine wave oscillator with a complex sound (created using `vs.buf.gen10`) and try to create beats between the sine wave and one of the components of the complex sound.

Using the paired objects `function` and `line~`, create some glissandi for an oscillator (as done originally in Section 1.3) that are summed with the output of a fixed pitch oscillator so as to obtain beats that accelerate and slow down. Try this with additional sliding pitch oscillators, in order to obtain "beat rhythms" that can be modified.

Repeat the preceding exercise using complex waveforms (as in the 02_09_beats_harm_comp.maxpat patch). Try to understand which frequency values are the most effective.

Create a patch similar to 02_07_beats.maxpat, that uses complex wave forms in place of sine waves.

SUPERSAW

In the modified patch in Figure 2.15b, if we replace the `mc.wave~` object with the `mc.saw~` object, we get a "supersaw". This term is used to define the rich, deep sound of a series of parallel sawtooth oscillators that are slightly out of tune, usually by a few Hz.[20]
Let's look at a multichannel implementation of this technique, load the file **02_09b_supersaw.maxpat** (Fig. 2.15c).

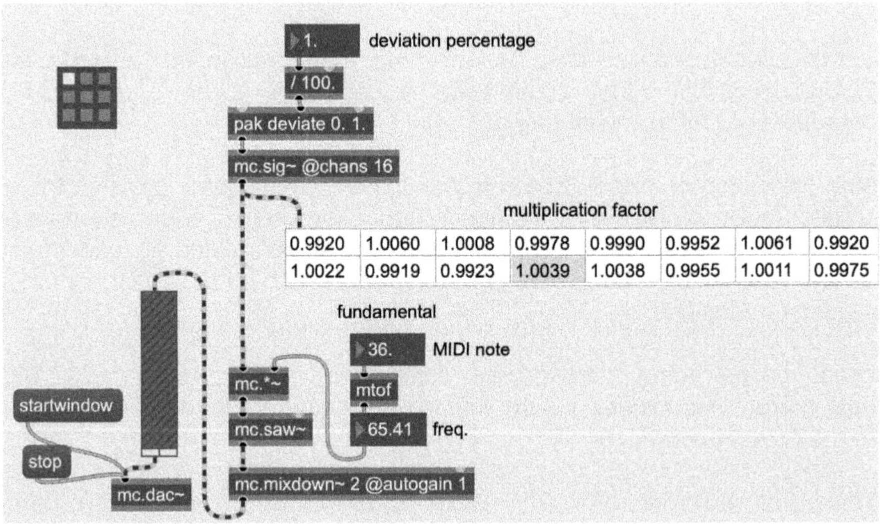

fig. 2.15c: file **02_09b_supersaw.maxpat**

Compared to the previous patch, we have made one change: the previous "deviate" message in Figure 2.15b, in fact, added or removed absolute values to the frequency. This means that, for the same deviation, at lower frequencies the sound is more out of tune than at higher frequencies, because the same deviation in Hz has a more effect at lower fundamental frequencies.
To solve this problem in the implementation of Figure 2.15c, we apply the "deviate" message to a multiplication factor of the fundamental, rather than directly to the frequency. As can be seen in the figure, this multiplication factor varies slightly above and below 1. If we then apply the multiplication factor to the fundamental of the sound, the deviation in Hz will increase as the frequency of the fundamental increases, and this will keep the sensation of detuning constant.
Listen to the presets and try to create new ones. Also try replacing the `mc.saw~` oscillator with the other band-limited oscillators `mc.rect~` and `mc.tri~`.

The "Ableton DSP Objects" library contains interesting modules from Ableton Live's native devices. In this library, there are several sound synthesis and

[20] The first commercial synth that introduced this technique was the Roland JP-8000.

processing algorithms in the form of Max objects. These objects have the advantage of being ready-to-use, saving us the trouble of having to program the corresponding algorithms from scratch. On the other hand, they have the limitation of being "black boxes" about which we do not know the details, and often, as we will see, the parameters have a normalized range from 0 to 1, which gives us no information about the actual value of the parameter itself. Another limitation is that the algorithm is not modifiable (the objects are compiled and therefore closed): this means that if we need an implementation other than the one proposed by the library objects, we have no choice but to program the algorithms we need in Max (which is the purpose of this series of books anyway).
However, some of these objects are very effective, and as we explore the various techniques, we will present their characteristics.

Let's start with the **abl.dsp.swarm~** object, which simulates the supersaw sound (with some differences) and allows us to choose from four different waveforms. Open the patch **02_09c_abl.dsp.swarm.maxpat** (Figure 2.15d).

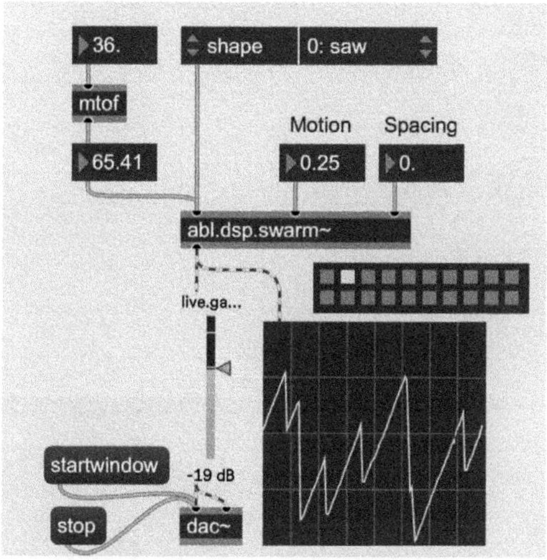

Fig. 2.15d: patch **02_09c_abl.dsp.swarm.maxpat**

The object receives at the first input the fundamental frequency of the group of oscillators, at the second input a "motion" parameter that determines the movement of the individual oscillators (the frequency of each oscillator varies randomly over time), and at the third input a "spacing" parameter that arranges the oscillators at frequencies at different intervals that give more or less harmonicity to the result. Both parameters are normalized between 0 and 1. A final parameter is "shape", which allows us to choose a waveform between "saw", "sine", "square" and "triangle". To change this parameter we used an **attrui** object.
Try out the different presets and experiment with new ones. With the 10 presets in the second row, we tried to identify the different frequency distributions given by the "spacing" parameter.

2.3 CROSSFADING BETWEEN WAVETABLES: VECTOR SYNTHESIS

To implement crossfade, or vector, synthesis in Max, we will need to have two waveforms and a way of moving from one to the other. First of all, let's see how to combine the sounds of two oscillators that have different waveforms, but that are oscillating at the same frequency, by opening the patch **02_10_two_wavetables.maxpat** (shown in figure 2.16).

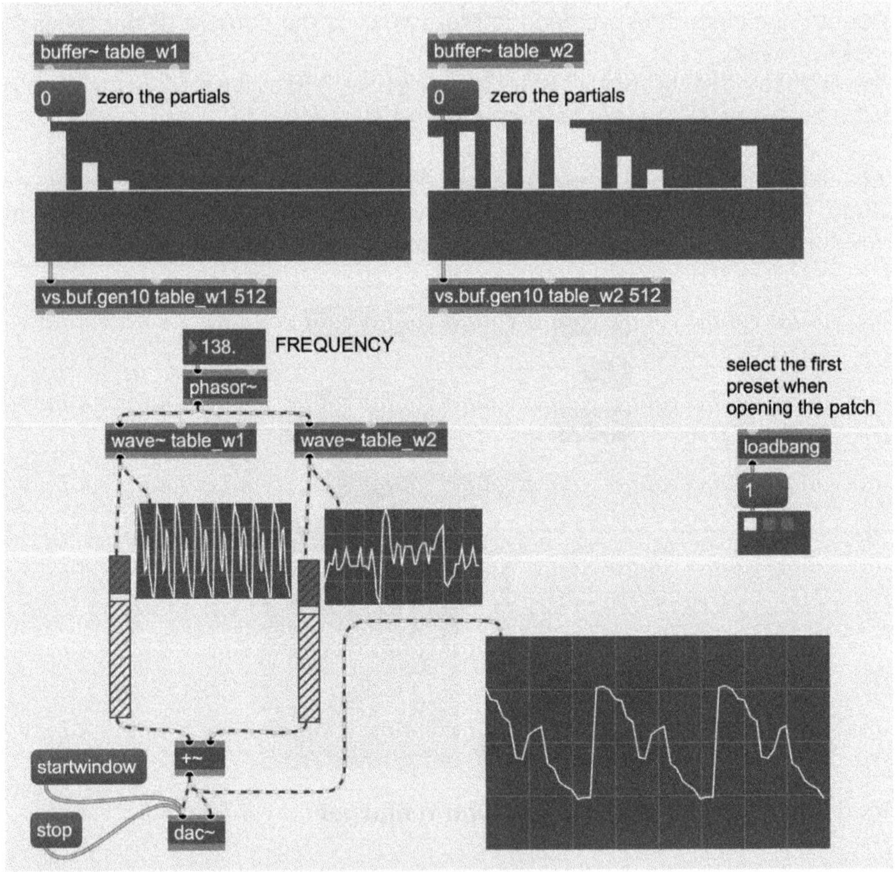

fig. 2.16 : file **02_10_two_wavetables.maxpat**

The two waveforms are loaded into two `wave~` objects, both of which are slaved to a single `phasor~` object since they need to share the same frequency. Their two outlets are controlled separately by `gain~` faders, which are summed before the output is sent to the `dac~`.

Watch the oscilloscope, noticing that as soon as we take the left fader higher than the right (or vice versa), the resulting waveform is more similar to the left wavetable (or to the right).

Furthermore, it is also possible to modify the values for the partials of each wavetable; try this, and then open the patch named **02_11_crossfading.maxpat** (shown in figure 2.17).

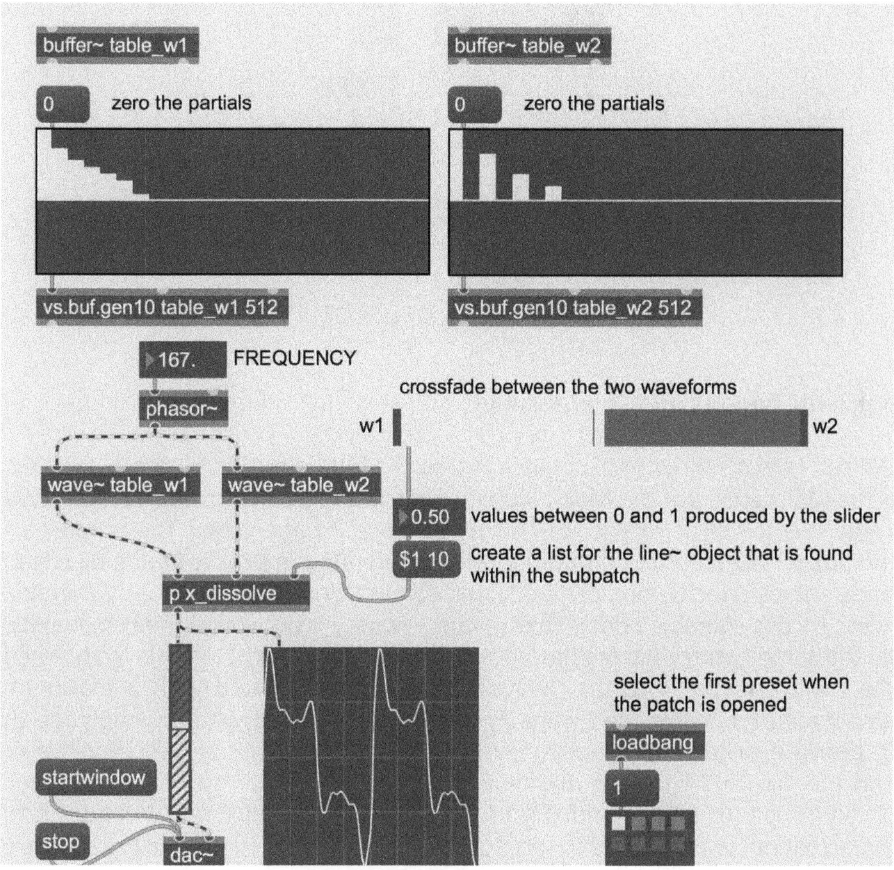

fig. 2.17: The file **02_11_crossfading.maxpat**

In this patch, like the last one, we have two waveforms loaded into two **wave~** objects that share a single **phasor~**. The two signals output by these objects enter into a subpatch [**p** x_dissolve] that actually implements the crossfade. The control of the crossfade is accomplished by means of the slider (which we saw first in Section 1.6); its attributes have been modified using the Inspector to put it into a mode that produces decimal numbers in the range of 0 to 1. The values output by the slider are sent to the **inlet** of the subpatch [**p** x_dissolve] in the form of lists for input to the **line~** object that it contains. Remember that the first element of a list (that here is set up by the variable $1) indicates to **line~** the value to be reached, while the second element of the list indicates how much time to take to reach that value (which is, in this case, is always 10 milliseconds). Whenever the value of the slider is 0, we will hear the sound from table_w1 exclusively, and whenever the value is 1, we will hear the sound from table_w2; intermediate values will yield various mixtures of the two sounds.

The contents of the subpatch [p x_dissolve] are shown in figure 2.18.

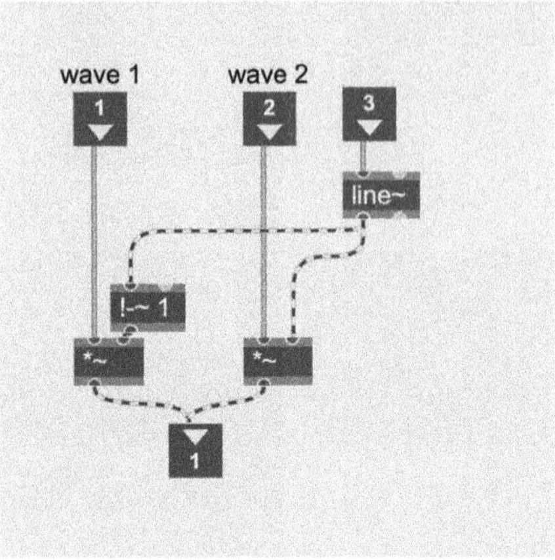

fig. 2.18: The subpatch [p x_dissolve]

We can now see how this subpatch works in a little more detail: the **!-~** object is the MSP version of the Max **!-** object that was explained in Section IA.1. (We know it is the MSP version, of course, because it has a tilde.) The purpose of the **line~** object is to smooth the values generated externally by the **slider**; these values directly multiply the signal coming from the "wave 2" wavetable inlet. To this signal is added that of the "wave 1" wavetable inlet, multiplied by the same control factors, but inverted using the object [**!-~** 1]. Thus, when the control factor is 0, the "wave 1" wavetable is heard with a maximum amplitude of 1, while the "wave 2" wavetable is muted with an amplitude of 0. Likewise, when the factor is 1, the "wave 1" table has an amplitude of 0, and the "wave 2" table a maximal amplitude of 1. The rest of the subpatch is very simple to understand. Try to implement a few mixtures of the sounds, first creating waveforms by setting the components in the **multislider** objects that are connected to the **vs.buf.gen10** objects, and then setting the frequency and varying the timbre by moving the **slider** horizontally to interpolate between the two wavetables. Don't forget to start up the DSP by clicking on the "startwindow" message, of course!

The next patch that we will look at, **02_12_autodissolve.maxpat** (shown in figure 2.19), enables automatic dissolves that can be used to play a sequence of notes whose timbre varies continuously.

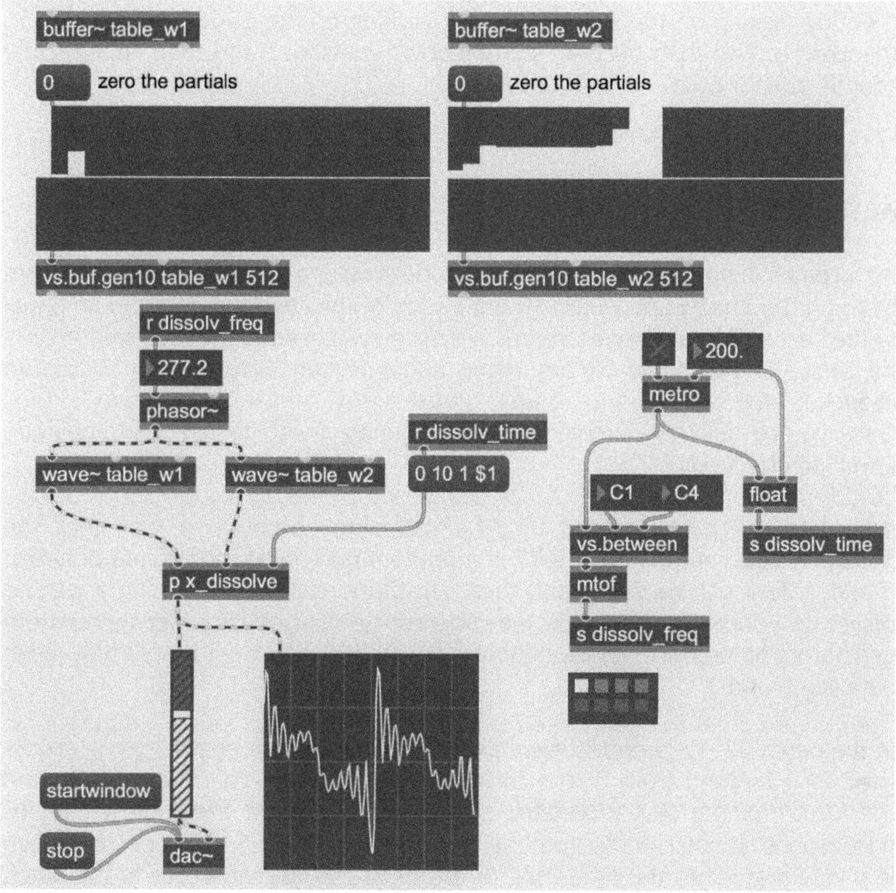

fig. 2.19: file **02_12_autodissolve.maxpat**

On the right, we have a metro connected to a **vs.between** object, which generates a random series of values within the interval given (and which we first encountered in Section IA.5). These values, interpreted as MIDI notes, are transformed into frequencies and sent, using [s dissolv_freq], to a the **phasor~** that controls the two **wave~** objects. The beat duration of the metronome is saved into the **float** object (in other words, it is sent to its "cold" inlet).
On every bang produced by the metronome, the time interval to be used for the crossfade between the first and second waveforms is sent using [s dissolv_time] to a list that is used by the [p x_dissolve] subpatch that we examined in the previous section.

This simple patch, judging from its results, is somewhat interesting. It yields the same kind of sounds that can be obtained using subtractive synthesis, (although using filters, which we will learn about in Chapter 3), and it shows that the crossfade technique can be very efficient. Try the various presets (recalling them by clicking on the **preset** object, clicking on the **toggle** connected to the **metro**, and then on the "startwindow" message), and then create some sounds of your own.

ACTIVITIES

In the patch in figure 2.19, add an amplitude envelope to the resulting waveform by using the **function** object. The duration of the envelope needs to be equal to the beat length of the **metro**, for which you will need to use the "setdomain" message along with variable arguments and a message box, as originally shown in Section IA.8.
Once you've built this, implement new sounds, trying to use the amplitude envelope effectively.

Automate the patch named 02_11_crossfading.maxpat in a way that the horizontal slider moves "by itself" in a random way, producing values between 0 and 1. First use **random**, and then substitute **drunk** (both using a **metro** object, of course), and analyze the different results obtained. Set the random generators to produce values between 0 and 100 and then rescale the result between 0 and 1.

In the patch 02_12_autodissolve.maxpat, the metronome beat length is always used for dissolving from 0 to 1 (from the first to the second wavetable), and the return to the first wavetable always occurs over a fixed interval of 10 milliseconds (as you can see from the message box [0 10 1 $1]). Modify the patch in a way that varies the time used to return to the first table. Still in the patch 02_12_autodissolve.maxpat, use a **function** object in place of the message box to implement a dissolve with multiple segments. The duration of the envelope created with function must be equal to the beat length of the **metro**, necessitating the use of the "setdomain" message and variable arguments for message box (again, as seen in Section IA.8).

Before moving ahead, allow us present a new object to you, a two-dimensional slider named **pictslider**, in the "Sliders" palette in the Top Patcher Window Toolbar[21], and which looks as shown in figure 2.20.

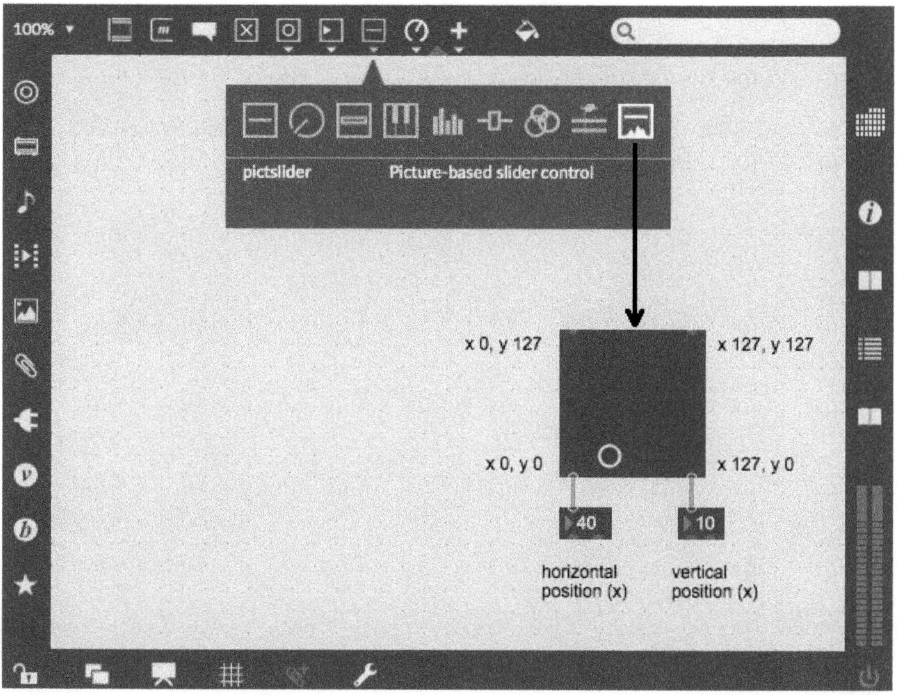

fig. 2.20: the **pictslider** object

This object has a handle that can be moved in two dimensions. The left outlet reflects the horizontal position, and the right reflects the vertical position. By default, the range of values generated by **pictslider** runs from 0 to 127 in both directions, but this can, of course, be modified by using the *Inspector*. Construct the patch shown in figure 2.20 in order to understand this object's functionality.

It is also possible to send numerical values to the two inlets of the object in order to set the location of the handle by means of these values; the value sent to the left inlet controls horizontal movement, and the inlet on the right, vertical movement.

We now enter the specific territory of vector synthesis, and will construct an interpolation between four wavetables by using the two-dimensional **pictslider** object along with three instances of the [**p** x_dissolve] subpatch, ganged together.

21 If you can't locate the object, you can narrow down your choices by typing pictslider into an empty object box

Open the file **02_13_vectors.maxpat** to see this configuration in action (shown in figure 2.21).

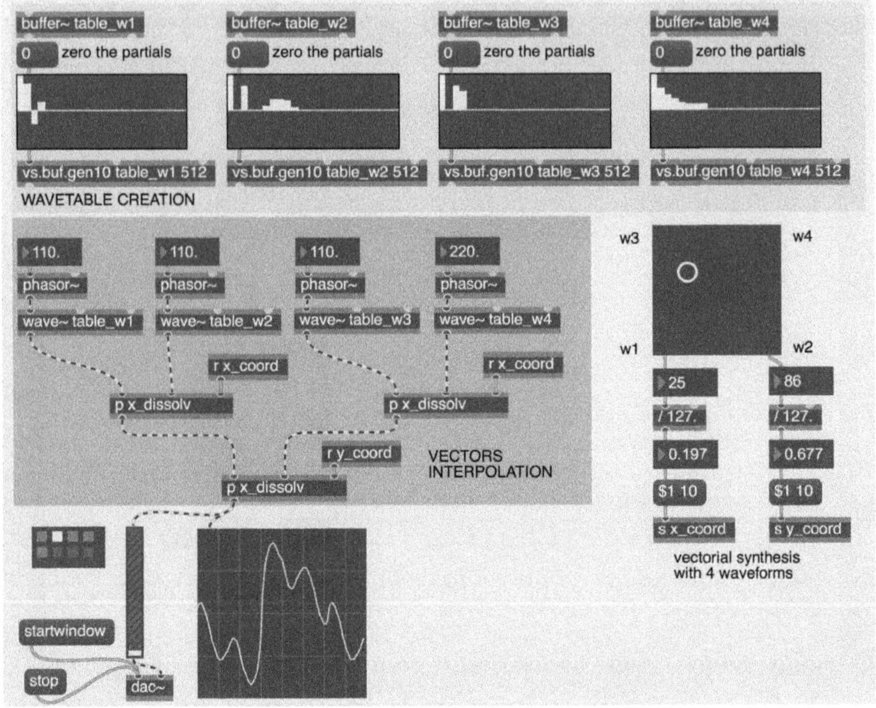

fig. 2.21: The file **02_13_vectors.maxpat**

You have an extensive timbral palette to work with in this example, because you can move freely within the mixing plane of the **pictslider** towards any of the corners, where the pure waveforms are found. We have used 4 different **phasor~** objects, each of which is connected to its own **wave~** in a way that allows its oscillator to have an independent frequency; this allows us to create interesting effects with beats and/or with changing pitches. Notice that the four signals produced by the oscillators are fed into two [p x_dissolv] subpatches that are identical to the equivalently named subpatch in figure 2.18, and the outputs of these subpatches are then fed again in series into a third [p x_dissolv] subpatch.

On the right of the patch, we have a **pictslider** that generates, by default, values between 0 and 127; the values are divided by 127 and thus transformed into decimal values in the range of 0 to 1. (It isn't possible to set a range of 0 to 1 in the Inspector, because **pictslider** generates only integers.) We can see now the path followed by the generated values: the values produced on the left outlet, after being reduced into decimal form, are associated with the value 10 in a message box, using dollar variables, and sent, using [s x_coord], to the two [p x_dissolv] subpatches to which the four oscillators are connected.

The horizontal movement of the **pictslider**, therefore, controls the mixture of the pair of oscillators containing the wavetables table_w1/table_w2 and the mixture of the pair of oscillators containing the wavetables table_w3/table_w4. The two signals leaving the upper [p x_dissolv] subpatches are then sent, as we have already pointed out, to the lower [p x_dissolv] subpatch.

Returning to the **pictslider**, we see that the values produced on the right outlet (after undergoing the same transformations as the values on the left) are sent, by means of [s y_coord], to the lower [p x_dissolv] subpatch. The vertical movement of the **pictslider**, therefore, controls the mixture between the two signals received by the lower [p x_dissolv] that are, as we have already pointed out, the signals produced from the two upper [p x_dissolv] subpatches. When the handle is exactly in one of the corners, the play of messages produces one waveform by itself, using the scheme shown in figure 2.21. Try it, and then explain how it works.

ACTIVITIES

Automate the patch 02_13_vectors.maxpat with a **metro** to generate random notes and two **functions** to create a constantly changing route between the 4 waveforms.

Let us now look at another Ableton library object, **abl.dsp.basicshapes~**: load the file **02_13b_abl.dsp.basicshapes.maxpat** (fig. 2.21b).

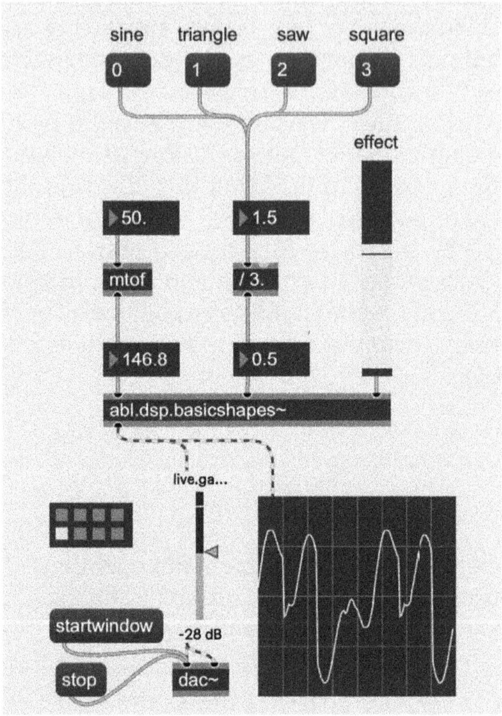

fig. 2.21b: file **02_13b_abl.dsp.basicshapes.maxpat**

The first object input is for the frequency value, the other two are for two parameters called "shape" and "effect" respectively. The "shape" parameter is used to interpolate between sine, triangle, sawtooth, and square waveforms. Since the parameter is normalized between 0 and 1, it is difficult to select an exact waveform directly, so we extended the range from 0 to 3 so that the 4 waveforms correspond to the integers 0, 1, 2, and 3, and then before passing the parameter to the second input, we divided the value by 3 to get the original range from 0 to 1.
The "effect" parameter is also normalized between 0 and 1, and it performs a different transformation for each waveform: try to see how it works by selecting each waveform in turn and moving the slider along the length.[22]
We can control the "shape" and "effect" parameters simultaneously with a pictslider and realize a vector synthesis with the object. Modify the patch as shown in Figure 2.21c.

[22] There is also the **abl.dsp.dualbasicshapes~** object that contains two copies of the oscillators and a "detune" parameter.

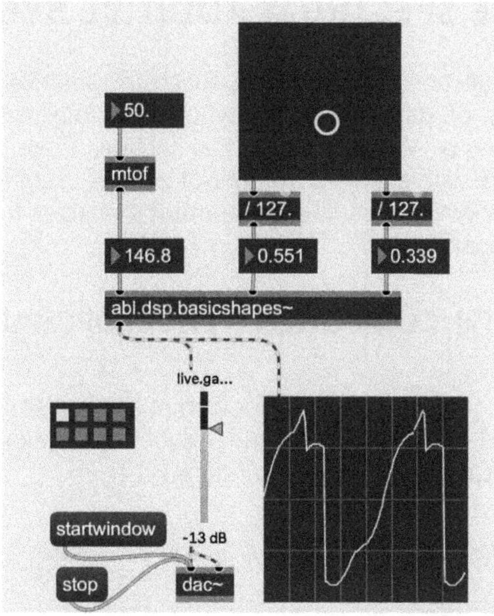

fig. 2.21c: vector synthesis with **abl.dsp.basicshapes~**

By default, the **pictslider** object produces values between 0 and 127, so we need to divide the outputs by 127 to get values between 0 and 1. Try moving around the sound space of the **abl.dsp.basicshapes~** object by continuously varying the **pictslider** slider.

In Section 2.3 of the theory chapter we spoke of Shepard Tone; in Interlude B, we will return to this particular effect, once we have acquired some skills that we will need for its implementation.

2.4 VARIABLE SPECTRUM ADDITIVE SYNTHESIS

As we learned in Section 2.4T, variable spectrum additive synthesis requires a notable quantity of data, especially when it is implemented using many frequency components. We will begin this section, therefore, by examining how we might work with a limited number of partials using techniques that we already know, after which we will explore other strategies for managing larger numbers of components.

WORKING WITH COMPONENT ENVELOPES USING A USER INTERFACE

Let's proceed by degree, and begin by looking at the implementation of a single oscillator, equipped with amplitude and frequency envelopes. Open the file **02_14a_oscil_func.maxpat** (shown in figure 2.22)

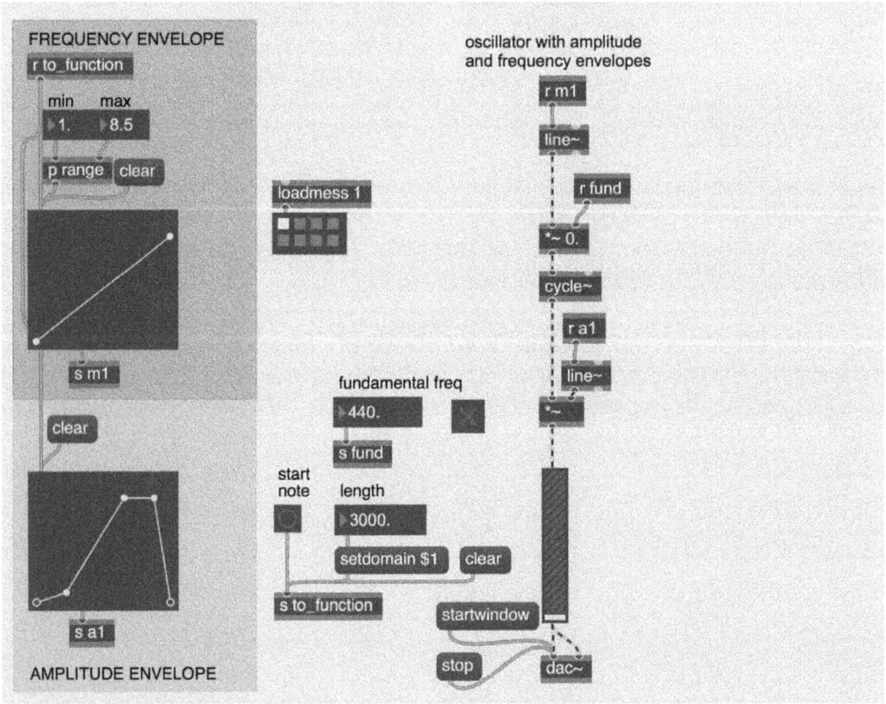

fig. 2.22: The file 02_14a_oscil_func.maxpat

Before analyzing the details of the patch, let's try to identify its function: click on the various presets stored in the `preset` object towards the center of the window and observe the changes to the two `function` objects within the colored regions. These two objects define amplitude and frequency envelopes for a single sine wave.
Now click on the message box that contains the message "*startwindow*" and then on the bang button that is labeled "start note"; you will hear a sound

whose amplitude and frequency follow the shapes of the envelopes defined in the two **function** objects. Note that the **preset** object is connected to a **loadmess** object, which is very similar to a **loadbang** object, but instead of generating a bang when the patch that contains it is loaded, it sends its argument as a message ('1' in this case, which selects the first preset).

Try all of the presets, noticing that the length of the sound (and of the corresponding glissando) is given by the value that can be found in the number box labeled "length". The range in which the glissando can move, on the other hand, is given by the combination of the value contained in the number box labeled "fundamental freq" and the values contained in the number boxes found in the upper left of the patch and marked "min" and "max". (If we refer to the printed example, the value "fundamental freq" is 440, while "min" and "max" are respectively 1 and 8.5. The glissando therefore goes from 440 · 1 = 440 Hz to 440 · 8.5 = 3,740 Hz.)

Commencing our analysis, you can see that there are two **function** objects, through which amplitude and frequency envelopes can be defined in the lower left of the patch. These two objects transmit, using **send** and **receive** objects, the envelope lists for the **line~** objects that can be found in the right part of the patch.
Every time that we click on the bang button found in the middle of the patch and labeled "start note", we send a bang to the [**s** to_function] object, which transmits to the corresponding [**r** to_function], from which a bang arrives at the two **function** objects, which each send lists that define frequency and the amplitude envelopes for their matching **line~** objects.

The frequency and amplitude envelopes have the same length; the length value, in milliseconds, is sent to both the **function** objects by the float number box found under the "length" label and that is connected to the message box that contains the message "*setdomain $1*". The "*setdomain*" command, as we learned in Section IA.8 of Interlude A, sets the maximum value of the x-axis (horizontal axis) of function, and therefore determines the maximum length of the envelope.

Let's now examine the range of the y-axis (vertical axis), which represents the interval across which the values of the envelope can move. The upper **function** object, as we said, outlines the frequency envelope, and as we also mentioned, it is possible to define minimum and maximum factors for this envelope, using the [**p** range] subpatch (that we will examine in a moment), each of will be multiplied by the value of the fundamental frequency. These two values represent the limits that can be reached by the envelope factors. For example, in figure 2.22 we have a fundamental frequency of 440 Hz, and the multiplication has 1 as its minimum limit and 8.5 as its maximum, which enables the frequency range of the oscillator to vary between 440 Hz (440 · 1) and 3740 Hz (8.5 · 440). The values given to the multiplier (in this case 1 and 8.5) correspond to the "Lo and High Display Range" items found in the Inspector for the **function** object. Opening the [**p** range] subpatch with a double click, let's see how they are packaged (as shown in figure 2.23).

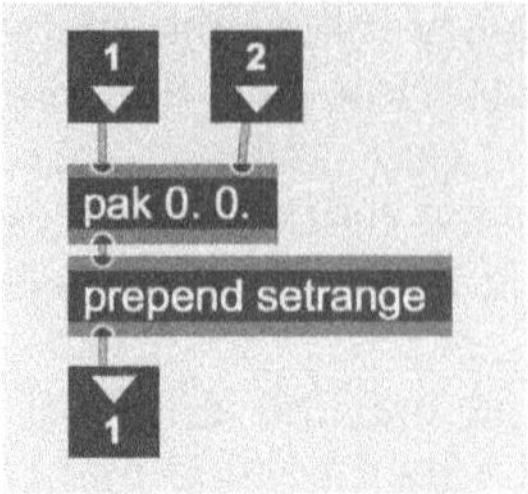

fig. 2.23: The contents of the [p range] subpatch

The two values, minimum and maximum, enter a **pak** object, which transforms them into a list of two elements.[23] This list enters a **prepend** object, which prepends the word "**setrange**" and sends it on to the outlet. The message that exits the subpatch and reaches the frequency envelope is therefore a list of three elements, of which the first is the word "setrange", which is then followed by the two numeric values. The two values don't represent the effective frequency, rather, they are multipliers of the fundamental frequency; in the example shown in figure 2.22, it can be varied between the fundamental frequency (set with the float number box labeled "fundamental freq") and a frequency 8.5 times higher.
The amplitude envelope isn't sent a similar "setrange" command because amplitude always falls into a range between 0 and 1.

Proceeding with our analysis of the patch, we see that the lists generated by the **function** objects are passed along to the oscillator via the **send** objects [s m1] and [s a1], and likewise, the fundamental is passed along by [s fund]. The oscillator that receives these values can be found in the right part of the patch; the envelope for the frequency multiplier is received by [r m1] and immediately sent along to a **line~** object, whose output is multiplied by the value of the fundamental received by [r fund]. The signal output by this multiplier is then sent to the frequency inlet of **cycle~**, which produces a signal that is rescaled by the amplitude envelope (which is received on [r a1] and passed to the second **line~** object) by means of the now familiar multiplier, which combines the values produced by the oscillator with those produced at the same time by **line~**.

Starting from this patch, we will see shortly how to create a variable spectrum additive synthesis algorithm using the multichannel system.
First we have to talk about a message that allows us to send values to the individual instances of a multichannel object: "setvalue". This message needs two parameters; the first indicates the instance to be modified, the second the value (or values) to be sent[24].

[23] We remind you that the **pak** object performs a function similar to that of the **pack** object, but unlike the latter, all its inlets are "hot"..
[24] As we will see later, via "setvalue" we can also send messages or change the attributes of individual instances of a multichannel object.

Recreate the patch of figure 2.24a.

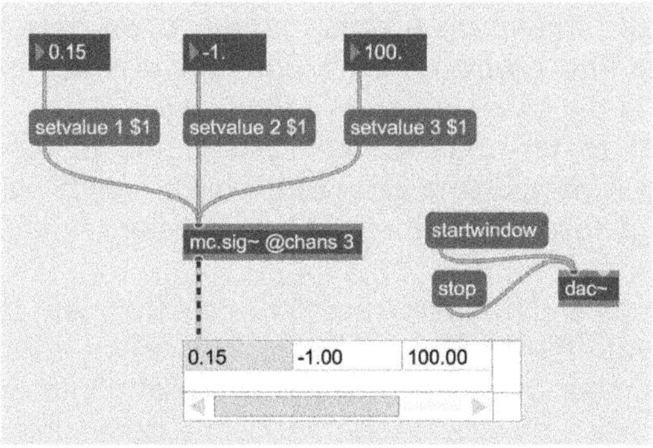

fig. 2.24a: the "setvalue" message

We have a three-channel **mc.sig~** object, and through three "setvalue" messages we can modify the value of individual instances, as we can see in the **jit.cellblock** object located at the bottom of the patch.
Thanks to this message we can independently modify the frequency and amplitude envelopes of the components of a variable spectrum. Load the patch **02_14_addvar_func.maxpat** (figure 2.24b).

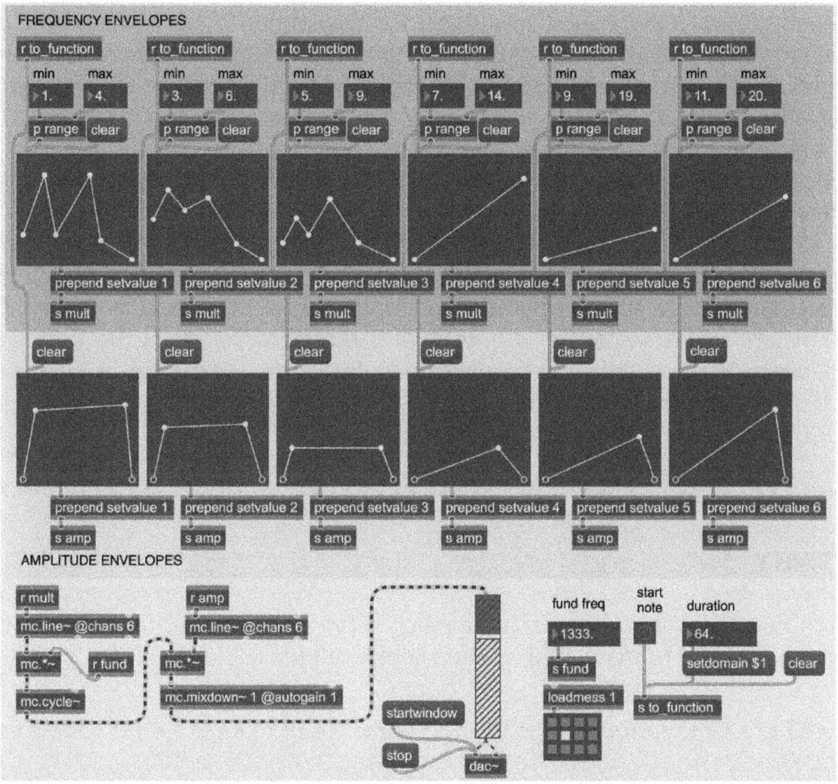

fig. 2.24b: The file **02_14_addvar_func.maxpat**

Listen to the different presets first.
In this patch we can specify the frequency and amplitude envelopes of 6 sinusoidal oscillators. There are 6 pairs of **function** objects each of which sends the lists for the envelopes to a different instance of a multichannel algorithm (visible in the lower left part of the image).
Before being sent to the multichannel system, the list generated by each **function** object is passed to a **prepend** object, which places before it the "setvalue" message followed by the destination instance number (a value from 1 to 6).
The lists of amplitude and frequency envelopes are then sent to two **mc.line~** objects that generate the relative envelopes. Notice the attribute "@chans 6" which sets the number of desired instances: the attribute was specified only in the two **mc.line~** objects; as we know the other objects, receiving the multichannel signal, are set automatically.
The duration and the fundamental frequency, provided by the two float number boxes visible in the lower part of the patch, are common to all of the oscillators. The pairs of multipliers for the fundamental frequency, defined by means of the two float number boxes connected to each [**p** range] subpatch, are unique to each oscillator. In this patch, the "*setdomain*" command is used to set up a single value for duration that is sent to all of the **receive** objects [**r** to_function] from the single **send** object [**s** to_function]. All of the **receive** objects then pass the command along to both to the **function** object for frequency and to the **function** object for amplitude.
Now let's review the 12 presets stored: the first row of presets contains brief sounds with recognizable fundamentals and with "pseudo-instrumental" envelopes, the second row is characterized by glissandi, and the third row features non-harmonic sounds.
Study carefully the various parameters that define the sounds: the ranges of the different amplitude envelopes, the frequency of the fundamental, the length of the sound, and the shapes of the envelopes all contribute to the character of the sound that we hear. Try making variations of the presets, first by altering global parameters, such as duration or fundamental frequency, and then the parameters that are specific to individual components, such as the frequency multipliers or the shapes of the envelopes. Strive to understand in what way each of these parameters influences the resulting sound. Finally, try making your own new sounds entirely from scratch.

ACTIVITY

Add a **kslider** (a keyboard) to the patch shown in figure 2.24a to modify the frequency of the fundamental, using a tempered scale.

WORKING WITH ENVELOPES OF SINGLE COMPONENTS USING TEXT DESCRIPTIONS

We have seen that by working with envelopes in a graphical user interface, we can realize interesting sounds, as long as they only require a reasonably small numbers of oscillators for which we can interactively chart parameter paths for individual components. The UI-based technique does a good job of establishing an immediate relationship between that which you see on screen and that which you hear.

If, however, we need to define similar "parameter paths" very precisely (if, for example, we want the attack for the first component to be 5 milliseconds, that of the second component to be 7.5 milliseconds, and so on) we will probably need to give up on the graphical interface and, instead, use something like text-based lists to describe the envelopes. Although a text-based approach gives up some of the immediacy of UI-based interaction, a line of text occupies less space than UI objects, and it also allows for great precision when managing larger numbers of oscillators. We are still talking about a limited number of components, in any case, since even text descriptions of envelopes would be extremely laborious and tedious to write out for tens or hundreds of oscillators. Before studying a patch in which you manage envelopes using lines of text, we need to present an aspect of the message box that we have not yet exploited: its ability to connect "remotely" with other objects. We know already that clicking on a message box will cause its contents to be emitted from its outlet and therefore transmitted to objects to which it is connected. It is also, however, possible to send messages to objects that are not directly connected by using a semicolon '**;**', which is a character of special significance for the message box. Interestingly, the message box considers the first element after a semicolon to be the name of a `receive` object, and the elements following this name as the message to be sent to this `receive` object. To clarify this mechanism, open the file **02_15_message_send.maxpat** (shown in figure 2.25).

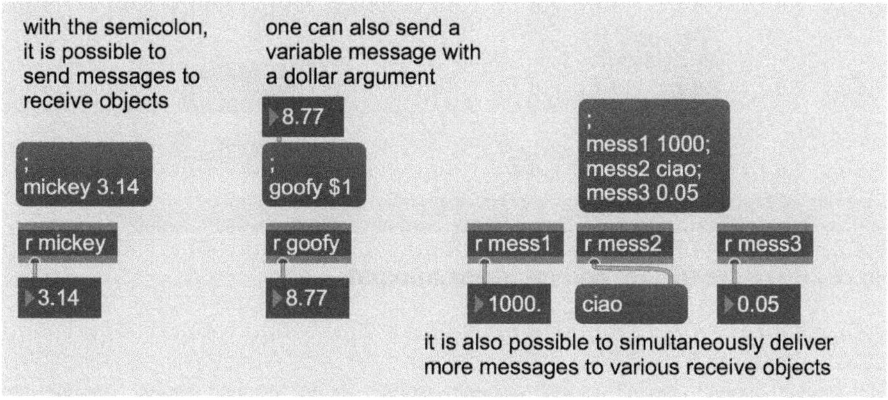

Fig. 2.25 The file **02_15_message_send.maxpat**

If you click on the [; mickey 3.14] message in the patch, you'll see the [**r** mickey] object receive the message "3.14", exactly as though you had issued the numeric message using a [**send** mickey] object. The first word after the semicolon is equivalent to the argument passed to **send** and **receive** objects, and the elements that follow it represent the actual message to be sent. It is also possible to use variable messages with $ arguments, as we see in the next example. Most interesting of all, we can send multiple messages at a time to multiple destinations within a single message box; click on the message box on the right side of the patch to dispatch three different messages to three distinct receive objects.[25]

Thanks to the semicolon, we can create message boxes that contain all of the parameters for a sound to be created using variable spectrum additive synthesis, and send them simultaneously with a single click. Let's see how: open the file **02_16_addvar_mess.maxpat** (shown in figure 2.26).

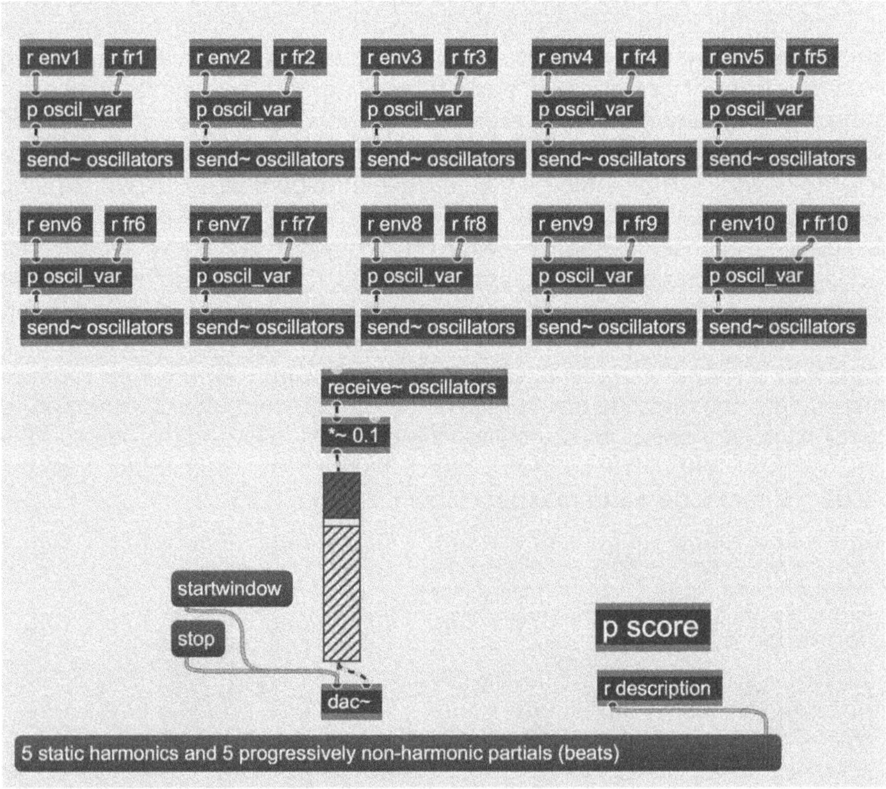

Fig. 2.26 The file **02_16_addvar_mess.maxpat**

[25] It is not an option to begin lines with such semicolons, since, for technical reasons, Max does not allow (unescaped) semicolons in a message box to be placed anywhere except at line endings. This explains the curious look that characterizes the contents of a message box that sends messages to multiple destinations, in which the first semicolon is isolated by itself, and the following ones are fused to the line ends of the text.

Note that in this case we do not use the multichannel system, but a series of separate oscillators. In order to clean the patch up a bit, we have realized a subpatch that is similar to the classic representation of an oscillator, with one inlet for amplitude and one for frequency (as shown in figure 2.27).

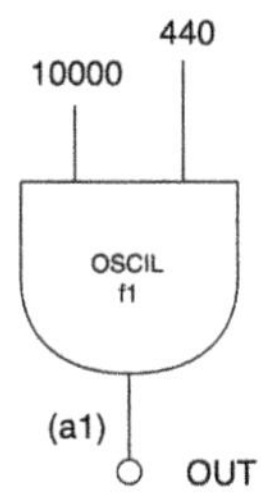

Fig. 2.27 A "classic" oscillator

Figure 2.28 shows the contents of the subpatch named [**p** oscil_var].

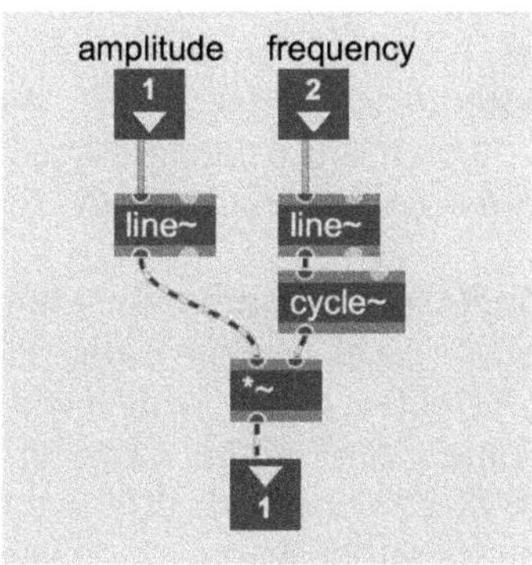

Fig. 2.28 The contents of the [**p** oscil_var] subpatch.

The **inlet** objects for amplitude and frequency are connected directly to two **line~** objects that enable passing lists to the oscillator to define amplitude and frequency envelopes.
Now take a look at the main patch. There are 10 oscillators that receive their amplitude and frequency values via **receive** objects, and return their signals using **send~** objects. Amplitude and frequency will be different for each oscillator, and so the **receive** objects must each possess unique arguments: "env1" and "fr1" correspond to the first oscillator, "env2" and "fr2" to the second, and so forth. Amplitude and frequency values are stored in message boxes that communicate with the **receive** objects, using the same technique as earlier patches. These message boxes can be found inside the [**p** score] subpatch on the right side of the main patch.
If you double click on the subpatch to open it, you can see that there are 6 message boxes, each of which generates a different timbre.

For example, the contents of the first message box are as follows:

description 5 harmonics with different envelopes;
env1 0, 1 1600 0 2400;
env2 0, 1 2200 0 1800;
env3 0, 1 2800 0 1200;
env4 0, 1 3400 0 600;
env5 0, 1 4000 0 10;
fr1 200;
fr2 400;
fr3 600;
fr4 800;
fr5 1000

Recall that the first word of every line is the name of a corresponding **receive** object in the main patch. The first line contains a solitary ';'. The second line sends a comment to the object [**r** description], which displays the message in a message box at the bottom of the patch. Following these two lines comes the data for the envelopes in **line~** format (preceded by the names "env1", "env2", etc.), and for the frequencies ("fr1", "fr2", etc.), which in this case are sent as single values. Clicking on this sizeable message box will send all of its data out to the various **receive** objects simultaneously, thanks to the ';' command.

Let's look at the data-bearing lines one more time and recap their contents. In the third line, we find "env1", which is the name of the **receive** object to which to send the list "0, 1 1600 0 2400", which will be used as an amplitude envelope. On the eighth line, "fr1" is the name of the **receive** object to which the frequency value 200 will be sent. (We would use a list if we needed an envelope for the frequency rather than a single value.)

To try the patch, remember to click on "startwindow", as usual in the main patch and to raise the **gain~** fader. After you've done that, simply click on the message boxes to hear the different timbres! Here are some brief notes about what the configurations stored in the message boxes do:

1) *5 harmonics with different envelopes* – Five partials, at fixed harmonic ratios, reach their maximum amplitude in varying amounts of time, creating a changing sound color.
2) *5 static harmonics and 5 progressively non-harmonic partials (beats)* – The same five partials as in the preceding example have five higher partials added; these become progressively non-harmonic and create beats.
3) *7 harmonics with staggered entrances* – Seven partials enter one after another, with percussive attacks, which create an arpeggio that fuses into a timbre.
4) *non-harmonic spectrum (gong)* – A non-harmonic spectrum with some fixed partials and others that move. The components near each other create beats. There is a percussive envelope.

5) *from unison to harmonic spectrum* – Ten partials all start at 400 Hz and then slide until they create a harmonic spectrum with a fundamental of 150 Hz, passing, during the glissando, through a non-harmonic configuration. During the decay, the components are muted in succession, beginning from the lowest, which creates a gradual change in timbre.
6) *from harmonic spectrum to non-harmonic spectrum (all partials lowered to 260 Hz)* – The components of a harmonic spectrum with a fundamental of 1,000 Hz (1,000 Hz, 2,000 Hz, 3,000 Hz, etc.) are dropped to 260 Hz, which causes a descending glissando and creates a non-harmonic spectrum (760 Hz, 1,760 Hz, 2,760 Hz, etc.). Besides this, the amplitudes are changed, changing the spectral profile of the sound.

These sounds may appear simpler than those created with the patch in figure 2.24a, but they are more difficult to program, owing to the fact that it is very laborious to create envelope lists, and because it takes longer to test the sounds and fix bugs without a graphical UI at your disposal. The primary advantage of this method, as we have mentioned, is the precision with which sonic behaviors can be defined. To realize, for example, a timbre such as that in example 6 would be nearly impossible when using graphical envelopes such as in figure 2.24a. If you find yourself needing to create very specific timing specifications, frequency values, and/or amplitudes for some project, you may very well wish to use the list method shown here. If, on the other hand, you are looking for a particular timbre and need to test various effects "by ear," you will want to use graphical tools.

ATTIVITIES

Using the patch **02_16_addvar_mess.maxpat**, implement the following timbres by adding new message boxes:

- A sound with percussive attack, that begins with a unison at a low frequency, and moves later to a harmonic timbre, after which the components slide, in pairs, to create beats of different speeds.

- A non-harmonic sound whose components have very slow attacks, and whose durations are each different. The maximum amplitude of each component should only be reached at the end of its envelope, after which the decay lasts only 10 milliseconds

- A harmonic sound in which odd harmonics have percussive attacks and slow decays, while even harmonics have slow attacks and sudden decays.

Make a multichannel version of the patch 02_16_addvar_mess.maxpat

USING OSCILLATOR BANKS

We have already spoken about the interesting and complex sonorities that can be obtained by using tens or hundreds of partials. We could of course use the multichannel system to generate hundreds of components, but this means that the multichannel wrapper must generate (behind the scenes) hundreds of separate oscillators, which may soon exhaust all the computing power we have available. Fortunately, Max enables the use of oscillator banks to simplify this process, through the use of the **oscbank~** and **ioscbank~** objects. These objects are basically the same, except that ioscbank~ has better sound quality because its oscillators are interpolated.[26] These oscillator banks, being enclosed in a single MSP object, allow a significant saving of CPU compared to the use of several separate oscillators.
You can explore the ioscbank~ object by building the patch shown in figure 2.29a.

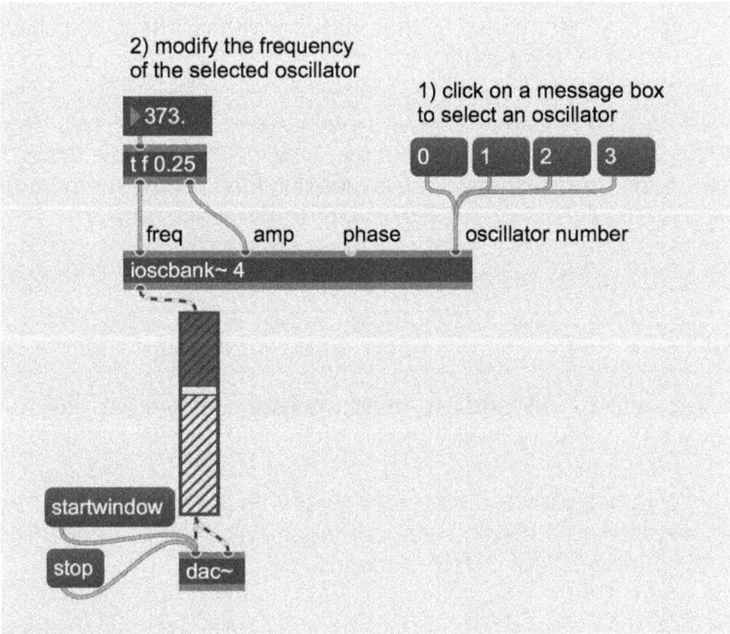

fig. 2.29a An oscillator bank

The ioscbank~ object has four inlets: frequency, amplitude (which in this object is called magnitude), phase, and the index number of the oscillator. This last parameter is a number that is used to select a sine wave oscillator internal to the ioscbank~; the first oscillator has an index of 0, the second 1, the third 2, and so forth. The argument for the object indicates the number of oscillators contained in the bank; in the case of our example patch, the ioscbank~ object contains 4 oscillators. Besides this mandatory first argument, it is possible

26 See Section 2.1T, which is dedicated to interpolation while reading wavetables.

to specify others, which we will detail shortly. As you can see, there are 4 message boxes connected to the right inlet of **ioscbank~**, which is the inlet on which you can specify an index number. A float number box flowing through a **trigger** object with 'f' and 0.25 as arguments is connected to the two leftmost inlets – the left outlet of the **trigger** passes the number from the number box to the frequency inlet of **ioscbank~**, while the right outlet passes the constant 0.25 to the amplitude (magnitude) inlet. Notice that no message is sent to the third inlet of the **ioscbank~** for the control of phase.

Proceeding in order, the first thing to do when working with an oscillator bank is to specify which oscillator you'd like to configure. (By default all of the **ioscbank~** oscillators start with a frequency of 0 Hz and amplitude 0.) In this patch, you select an oscillator by clicking on a message box. Let's say you selected 0: now all messages arriving on the control inlets will be sent to the first oscillator.
Let's set the value of the float number box to 440. Now the first oscillator will have a frequency of 440 Hz and an amplitude of 0.25. Clicking on the "startwindow" message and raising the **gain~** fader, you should be able to hear a sine wave. Click on the message box containing the number 1 and drag the number in the float number box up to 550 using the mouse; you should hear a second sine wave added that rises from 440 to 550 Hz as you manipulate the value in the float number box. Activate the other two oscillators by clicking on the appropriate message boxes and modifying the float number box in a way so that each oscillator has a distinct pitch; playing with the mechanism a bit will help you to understand how it works. Try to create a series of beats with different speeds around 440 Hz and around 880 Hz (you will need to use the oscillators in pairs), and then create some irregular beats around 440 Hz. Try also to increase the number of oscillators by modifying the argument and increasing the number of message boxes used for activating the oscillators. After having experimented with your patch, open the file **02_17_ioscbank.maxpat** (shown in figure 2.29b).

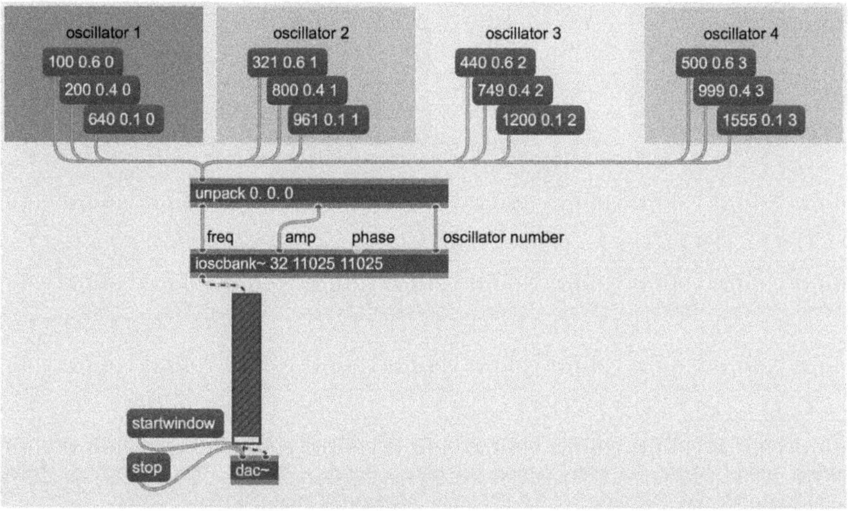

fig. 2.29b: file **02_17_ioscbank.maxpat**

In this patch we have added two additional arguments besides the first (which we know specifies the number of oscillators, which in this case is 32). The two new arguments indicate the time (in samples, not in milliseconds) to spend when moving from one frequency to the next on a given oscillator, or from one amplitude to the next. These two parameters are called ***freqsmooth*** and ***magsmooth***, and can also be changed by sending the object the message *"freqsmooth"* or *"magsmooth"*, followed by a duration in samples.[27]
We can now see that we have a bank of 32 oscillators in this patch, whose frequencies and amplitudes will take 11,025 samples to move from one value to another.[28]
The colored regions of the patch contain message boxes that contain lists of three elements, which we will use to set frequency, amplitude, and oscillator number. (We have omitted phase values, because we don't use them in this patch.) When you click on a message box, the list that it contains is transmitted to the **unpack** object, which separates the three elements from each other. They exit in order from right to left: the first element emitted corresponds to the index of the oscillator and goes to the fourth inlet of **ioscbank~**; amplitude and frequency follow.

In this patch we use only 4 of the 32 oscillators available, and each colored region contains the lists for one of these oscillators (the first region for the first oscillator, the second region for the second oscillator, and so forth). By clicking on the various message boxes, you can obtain different combinations of frequencies. Pay attention to the transition from one frequency to another, which is a glissando whose duration is specified by the second argument to **ioscbank~** (11,025 samples, or 250 milliseconds at 44,100 Hz). You can activate other oscillators by adding other message boxes with other indices.

By using oscillator banks, we can see a way to manage the mass of data necessary to activate the 32 oscillators available. We might, for example, generate sounds with 32 partials randomly selected between a minimum and a maximum.

---

27 The time in samples is naturally dependent on the sampling rate. If, for example, we have a sampling rate of 44,100 Hz, every sample will have a duration of 1/44,100 of a second, or about 0.22 milliseconds. We will take this subject up in more detail in Section 5.1T.

28 At a sampling rate of 44,100 Hz, this is equivalent to a time of about 250 milliseconds.

Open the file **02_18_ioscbankrand.maxpat** (shown in figure 2.30) to see this scenario.

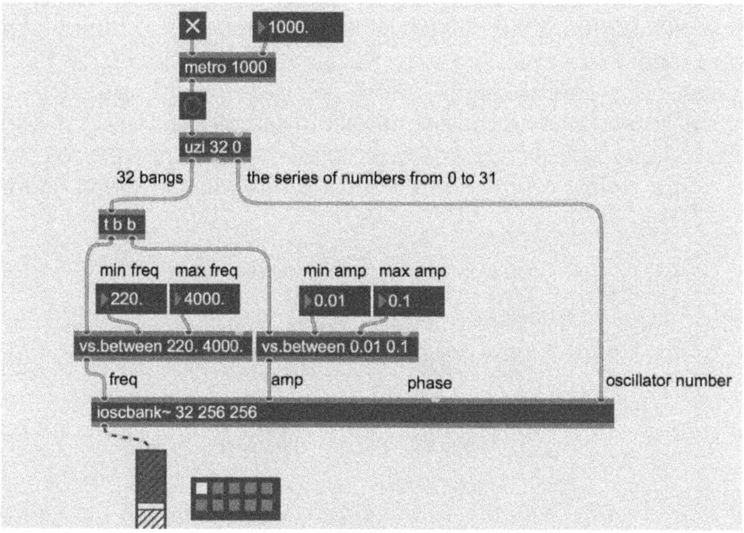

fig. 2.30: The file **02_18_ioscbankrand.maxpat**

In this case, the [**uzi** 32 0] object produces 32 bangs, which emanate from its left outlet whenever it receives a bang. Note that the second argument of this object is equal to 0; this argument sets the starting point for the series of numbers that is generated on the right outlet of **uzi**. (The default series, as we saw in Interlude A, starts at 1, but for this example the series starts at 0 and runs to 31.) Keeping with Max's right-to-left precedence, the number on the right outlet is produced first, followed by the bang on the left, followed by another number on the right, another bang on the left, and so forth. This series of numbers provides a simple way to generate indices for configuring the oscillators in the **ioscbank~** object.
The 32 bangs are passed on as pairs of bangs by a trigger "repeater", and each of the resulting bangs is sent to one of two vs.between random number generators, one that manages frequency, and the other amplitude. The interval in which frequencies are generated ("min freq" to "max freq") is used to create what is called a frequency band in which to generate complex sounds. Every time that uzi receives a bang, a new group of parameters is generated for the 32 oscillators in the **ioscbank~** (oscillator number, amplitude, frequency, oscillator number, amplitude, frequency, etc.) The metronome connected to **uzi** creates a regular "timbral rhythm" for the patch. (Note that we have reduced the *freqsmooth* and *magsmooth* transition values to a snappy 256 samples.) Try the saved presets, and experiment with the behavior of the patch under different parameter settings.

CONVERTING MILLISECONDS TO SAMPLES, AND VICE VERSA

We now talk briefly about a conversion that we will need to use shortly, the conversion of durations expressed in milliseconds into durations specified in samples, and vice versa. These conversions are performed by the objects **sampstoms~** and **mstosamps~**. More precisely, samptoms~ tells us how long a signal composed of a certain number of samples will last in milliseconds, and mstosamps~ tells us how many samples would be needed to compose a signal lasting a certain number of milliseconds (as you can see in figure 2.31).

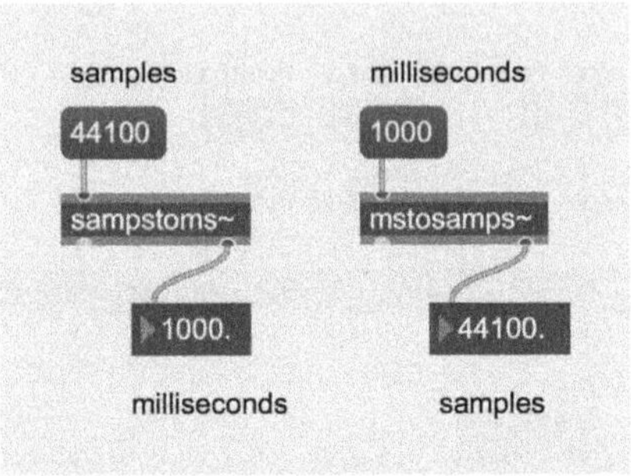

Fig. 2.31 The conversion of samples to milliseconds, and vice versa

Note that we have connected the number box to the right outlets, because the left outlet emits its value as a MSP signal rather than a single Max message. Why do we need these two objects to perform what seems to be a fairly mundane calculation? Because, in reality, the two objects need to have access to an internally variable value: the effective sampling rate of the audio interface. In the case of figure 2.31, the sampling rate is 44,100 Hz, but if the current sampling rate was, instead, 48,000 Hz, we would obtain the results shown in figure 2.32.

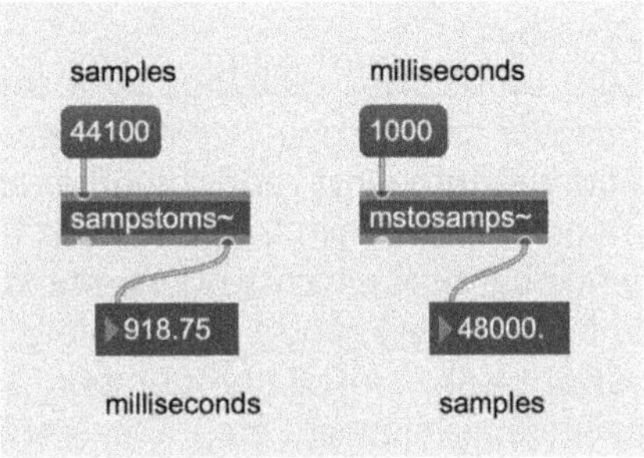

fig. 2.32 Conversion with a sampling rate of 48,000 Hz

We are sure to always obtain the correct conversion, independent of the sampling rate currently being used by our audio interface, by using these objects. In the next section, we will see a practical use for the mstosamps~ object.

VARIABLE SPECTRA AND OSCILLATOR BANKS

We've seen that **ioscbank~** can create very dense and complex component sonorities, but until now, we have not created a sonority with a spectrum that actually changes over time. Every bang produced by the metronome generates 32 components that remain fixed in frequency and amplitude until the next bang.[29] To create a variable spectrum, we might interpolate the frequency and amplitude values found in successive sounds, creating frequency glissandi as well as amplitude crescendos and diminuendos within the components of individual sounds. This kind of interpolation is easy to implement in the patch shown in figure 2.30: all you have to do is modify the transition times between changes in frequency (freqsmooth) and amplitude (magsmooth) in **ioscbank~**, setting them equal to the duration of the beat of the **metro**. Once this is done, sounds pass from one spectrum to the next continuously, and the components of the sounds no longer have fixed spectra.
Try modifying the patch in **02_18_ioscbankrand.maxpat** as shown in figure 2.33.

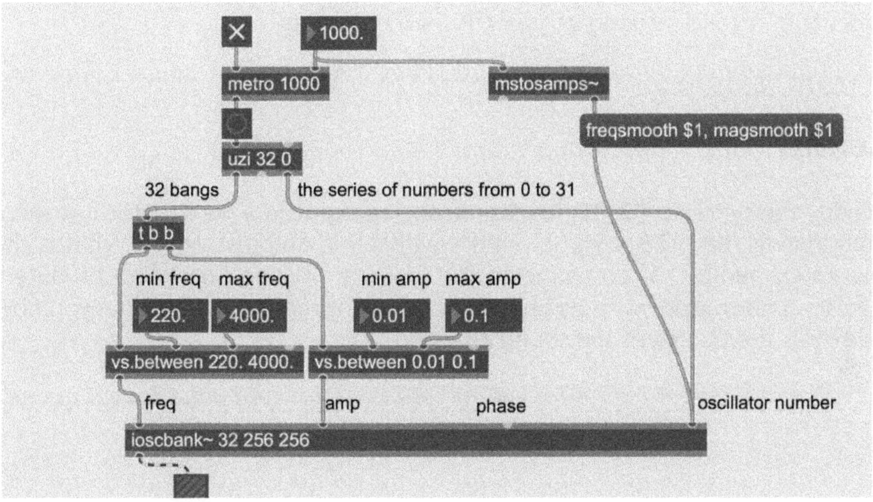

Fig. 2.33 Variable spectra

We have connected the number box that sets the interval of the metronome (in milliseconds) to the **mstosamps~** object, which converts the millisecond setting into a sample count. The converted value is passed, using the right outlet of **mstosamps~**, to the message box that contains the message *"freqsmooth $1"* and *"magsmooth $1"*, separated by a comma.
These two messages, as we know, set the transition time in samples between one frequency and the next, and between one amplitude and the next. The transition times for frequency and amplitude, therefore, are set to match

[29] Of course the frequency and amplitude values are interpolated, and move from one spectrum to the next in an interval of 256 samples. We will concede, therefore, that there is a very short glissando at the beginning of every spectrum.

the beat duration of the metronome through this message box, which is connected to the inlet of the **ioscbank~**.[30]

If you try to select any of the presets after modifying the patch, you will hear obvious glissandi between the components. Create other configurations, greatly slowing the beat duration of the metronome (for example, in the 20,000 to 30,000 millisecond range: 20 to 30 seconds), in a way that generates layers of sound that evolve very slowly, and render the glissandi less evident. Also try a different approach, in which you set frequency bands of various widths. Note that the broader the band, the greater the glissando effect, while a narrower band (from 50 to 500 Hz of difference between the minimum and maximum frequencies) can produce interesting evolutions of irregular beats. Yet another approach is to copy the entire patch, selecting everything (in edit mode, obviously) and dragging while holding the <Alt> key;[31] in this mode, you can create parallel layers, perhaps a low region, for example, with a band from 0 to 400 Hz, that moves quickly, and a higher region, slower, and with a narrower band. And no one is stopping you from making many copies of the patch to execute in parallel, as long as your CPU will cooperate!

ACTIVITY

Modify the patch in **02_18_ioscbankrand.maxpat** in a way that it has more components (64, 128, 256, ...), and create some timbres with it. What is the maximum number of components that you can manage on your computer? Replace **ioscbank~** with **oscbank~**; how many more oscillators can you now add? Has the quality of the sound changed?

[30] We use the right inlet purely to make things go easily – commands that modify the internal parameters of an object (parameters that are usually modified in the Inspector) can often be sent to this inlet.

[31] See the "Survival Manual" in Section 1.1, the section with the title "Selection, Deletion, and Copying".

USING MASKING FOR CONTROL

Another technique to try is called "masking", which was introduced in Section 2.4T and which uses two envelopes to define pitch changes for the lowest and highest frequencies, leaving the other components to fill the intermediate space between these extremes.
With this technique we can easily "draw" sound layers that evolve in time. To implement an algorithm of this type in Max we need to know a little about some new objects. We also need to study up on a property of the **function** object that we haven't yet encountered. The next pages will be dedicated to learning these new things.

We begin with **function**: construct the patch shown in figure 2.34, and create an envelope of some sort – you don't need to create an identical match to the one shown in the figure.[32] The **function** object will define the paths to be taken by the upper and lower components in our mask.

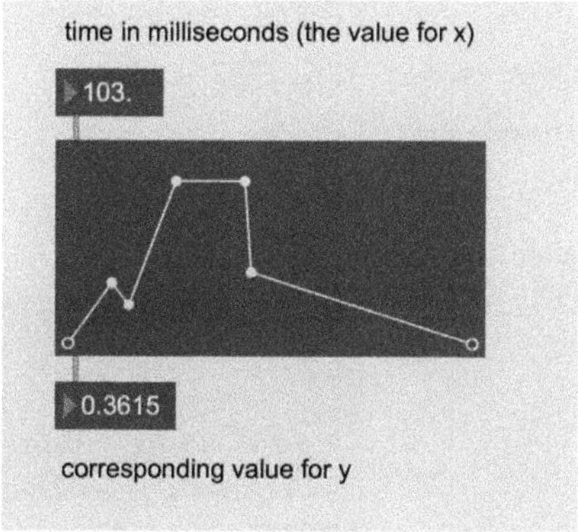

Fig. 2.34 Reading an envelope from function

As you can see, here we are using the first outlet of **function** (up until now we have always used the second, which generates a list to send to **line~**); this outlet generates a number that represents the value of the envelope (the value of the y-axis coordinate) at a specific time (the value of the x-axis coordinate), which we have set using the upper float number box. In the figure, with the particular envelope that is shown, at a coordinate of 103 milliseconds from the beginning of the function, the envelope value returned is 0.3615. If you drag the upper float number box through the range from 0 to 1,000 (across the entire x-axis) you can watch changes in the value of the associated y-axis values, as they change, point-by-point. We have dictated that the **function** object will be used to define changes of frequency for the extremes of the mask.

[32] This "envelope" will not be applied to any particular function, but rather will serve only to illustrate the specific behavior of the **function** object that we are demonstrating. Recall that, by default, the **function** object has a range of values between 0 and 1,000 on the x-axis (values that normally refer to time in milliseconds), and between 0 and 1 in the y-axis.

We will therefore need a way to uniformly scroll through the points on the x-axis in order to obtain their corresponding y-axis values. To do this, we will modify the patch as shown in figure 2.35. Instead of passing values to the inlet of `function` by hand, we will use the uniform periodic signal produced by `phasor~`.
In order to accomplish this, we will need two new objects, **`snapshot~`**, which transforms a MSP signal into a stream of Max numbers, and **`sig~`**, which transforms Max numbers into MSP signals. (In other words, `snapshot~` enables transitions from yellow/black patch cords to grey patch cords, and `sig~` enables transitions from black patch cords to yellow/black patch cords. We will see why we need this in a moment.) Let's follow the algorithm in order to learn how it works: the `phasor~` at the top generates, as we know, ramps ranging from 0 to 1, and in the figure it is set to a frequency of 2 Hz, causing it to generate 2 ramps per second. The signal produced by `phasor~` is transformed via `snapshot~` into a stream of Max numbers.

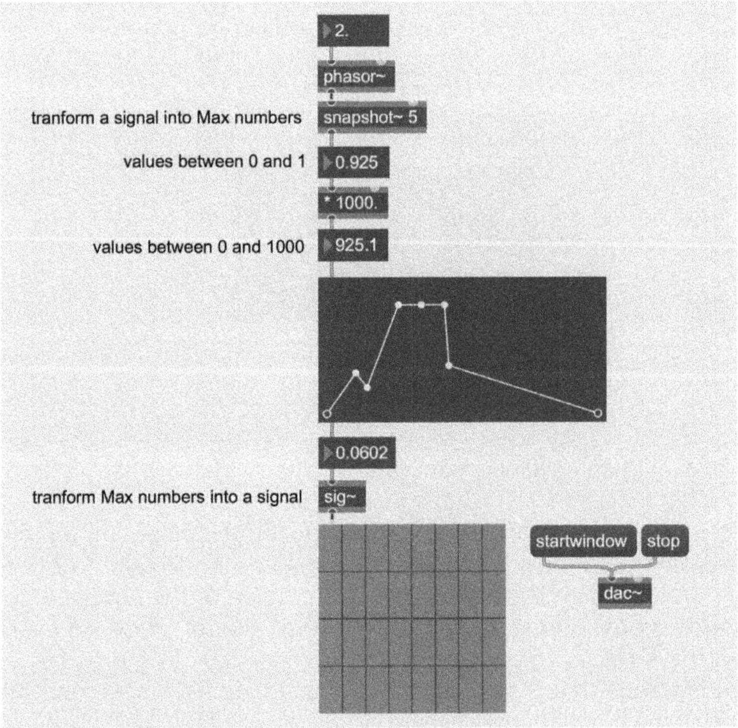

Fig. 2.35 Scanning the `function` object

As you can see, `snapshot~` takes an argument that represents the time, in milliseconds, that should elapse between the generation of one Max number and the next. In this case, the time is set to 5 milliseconds, which means that the object will produce 200 (1000 / 5) numbers per second. Said another way, its sampling frequency is 200 Hz, quite a bit slower than the sampling rate used for signals, which is generally 44,100 Hz or more. In practice, this `snapshot~` object will grab a single sample value every 5 milliseconds, discarding all of the intermediate samples without looking at them.

Why have we transformed the MSP signal produced by **phasor~** into a stream of Max numbers? Because we need to use these numbers with the **function** object, which is not equipped to manage signals as input. After the ramps from 0 to 1 produced by **phasor~** are transformed into Max numbers, they are multiplied by 1,000 (pay attention to the decimal point after the multiplier argument – it needs to be a floating point number!) and we thus obtain ramps (of Max numbers) that run from 0 to 1,000. Using these numbers, we can scroll through the values in the envelope of the **function** object with consistency, as anticipated: the ramps from 0 to 1,000 are sent to **function** in order to extract the corresponding y-axis values for the envelope. Note as well, that the **phasor~** generates its ramps cyclicly (two per second in this case) which means that **function** also generates, as a consequence, two envelopes per second. We are effectively using **function** as a look-up table controlled by **phasor~**, which generates indices (or, if you like, phase values which cycle between 0 and 1,000 rather than between 0 and 1).
Thanks to **sig~** we can create a signal out of the stream of Max numbers, which we can display using a **scope~** object. In the figure, we can see that the envelope has become a waveform that repeats cyclicly. To make the patch work, we must start the DSP engine by clicking on "startwindow"; the patch won't generate any sound, because nothing is connected to the **dac~**, but we can see the cyclic generation of the envelope on the **scope~**.
Practically speaking, you should be able to see that the interval of the x-axis values has no relationship with time in milliseconds, because the passage of time is being completely defined by the frequency of the **phasor~**. Because of this, we can reduce the size of the domain of the **function** to 1, and thus avoid having to multiply the output of **phasor~** by 1,000 (as we did in figure 2.35). Transform your patch to match figure 2.35b.

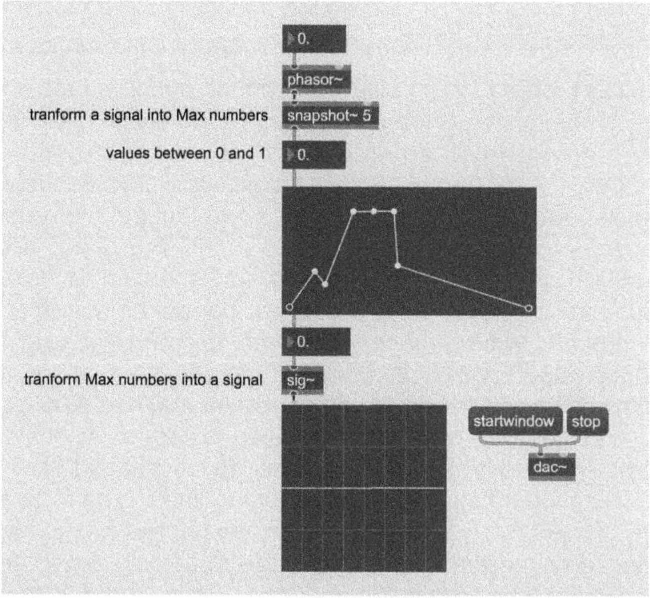

Fig. 2.35b Modification of the domain of the **function** object

In the new version of the patch, we have removed the multiplier after the **snapshot~** object and have connected the number box directly to the **function** object. We must modify the domain of **function** to match: open the Inspector for the object, locate the "Behavior" category, and change the value of the "Hi Domain Display Value" attribute from 1,000 to 1. Now the values on the x-axis will go from 0 to 1, rather than follow the default range of 0 to 1,000. This modification sets the domain of **function** to exactly match that of the **phasor~** object (0 to 1), and because of this, it is no longer necessary to multiply the output from **phasor~** by 1,000.

As we will see shortly, we intend to use the multichannel version of the **function** object to steer the highest and lowest components in our masking patch. But how should we distribute the internal components? Should we divide the space between the outermost components into equal parts, obtaining equidistant frequencies for the other components, or should we use a logarithmic distribution (in which the distances between components get smaller as we go up) or an exponential distribution (in which the distances get bigger)? To implement all of these different approaches, we will use the **vs.explist** object – let's see how this object works by building the patch shown in figure 2.36.

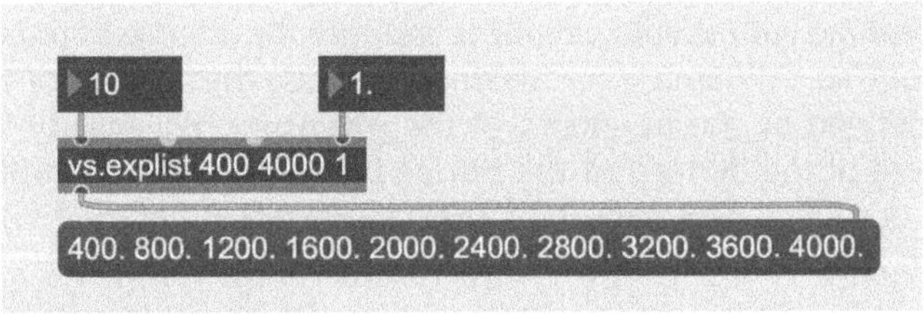

Fig. 2.36 The object **vs.explist**

The **vs.explist** object, as you can tell from its prefix, is part of the Virtual Sound Macros library. It generates a series of numbers that grow from a minimum to a maximum; using its 4 inlets, you can specify the number of elements needed, the minimum value, the maximum value, and how the series should grow (whether it is linear, exponential, or logarithmic – concepts that you will remember from Sections 1.3T and 1.3P). The object accepts three arguments, which are minimum, maximum, and the type of growth to use. The last argument is specified using a number: numbers bigger than 1 indicate exponential growth, while numbers between 0 and 1 indicate logarithmic growth, and the value 1 itself indicates linear growth. In the figure, we see a list of 10 elements being generated, ranging between 400 and 4,000, using linear growth (which means that the distance between successive elements will always be the same). Try modifying values in order to understand how the object functions: analyze what happens when changing linear growth to exponential or logarithmic. (To do this, you need to act on the number box to the right that, as you can see, is connected to a "cold" inlet – to actually trigger the resulting list, you will need to touch the first number box, which specifies the number of elements and which is connected to the "hot" inlet.)

To assign the output list of values to individual components, we will need another object, which is **listfunnel**: modify the previous patch as shown in figure 2.37.

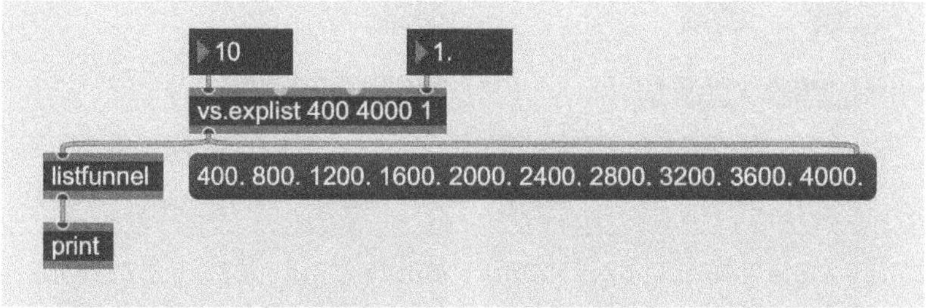

Fig. 2.37 The `listfunnel` object

Here we have connected **vs.explist** to `listfunnel`, and `listfunnel` to **print** so that we can see everything output in the Max Console. The `listfunnel` object, as indicated by the name, is a **funnel** in the loose sense that when it receives a list, the elements of the list "drip" out of its outlet one at a time with index numbers (which by default start at 0) prepended to them. For example, if we were to set the left number box in the figure to 10 (as shown), this is what would be printed in the Max Console:

print: 0 400.
print: 1 800.
print: 2 1200.
print: 3 1600.
print: 4 2000.
print: 5 2400.
print: 6 2800.
print: 7 3200.
print: 8 3600.
print: 9 4000.

All of the elements of the list are produced by separate messages (which is why each appears on its own line) and each is preceded by a number, beginning with 0 and growing to 9. For every element in the list received, a new list of two elements (the index and the value) is output.

We'll now introduce a new object that we need to perform the control by masking: **mc.function**, multichannel version of **function**. Open the **02_18a_mc_function.maxpat** patch (figure 2.38a).

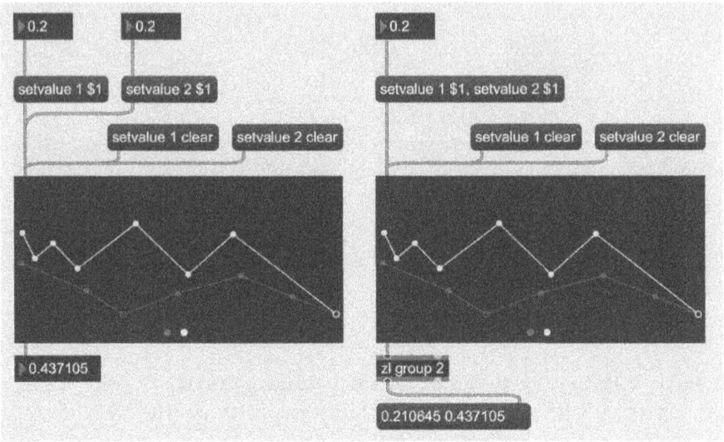

fig. 2.38a: The file **02_18a_mc_function.maxpat**

In this patch we have two **mc.function** objects, each of which contains two instances of **function**. Notice the dots in the lower part of the object, which allow us to select the different instances, just as for the multichannel version of the **scope~** object (see paragraph IA.12, figure IA.74d).
As we already know, in order to send a message to a particular instance of a multichannel object, we must place the "setvalue" command in front of the message followed by the instance number (see also figure 2.24a). So if we want to send the value of the x-axis to the first instance of **mc.function**, we will have to use the message "setvalue 1 $1", and for the second instance "setvalue 2 $1": in response to these messages, the object will send at the output the corresponding y value (see the left part of the figure).
As we will see shortly, for our masking algorithm we need to distinguish the output values of the first instance from those of the second, to send them to two different destinations; but this apparently is not possible because both values come out of the left outlet and there seems to be no way to distinguish them. There are of course many ways to solve this problem and, with the knowledge we have acquired so far, one can use the method shown in the right part of the figure. We consecutively send the messages "setvalue 1 $1" and "setvalue 2 $1" using the same value of x (note that the two messages are inside a single message box separated by a comma), and we group the two output values in a list using the object [**zl** group 2][33]. The first element of the list will be the y value of the first instance; the following element will be the value of the second instance.
Finally, notice that, to delete the contents of an instance of **mc.function**, we must send the "clear" message preceded by "setvalue 1" or "setvalue 2".

[33] We remind you that the characteristics of the zl object have been described in section IA.7.

After studying these new objects, we can move to the patch in file **02_19b_masking.maxpat** (shown in figure 2.38b).

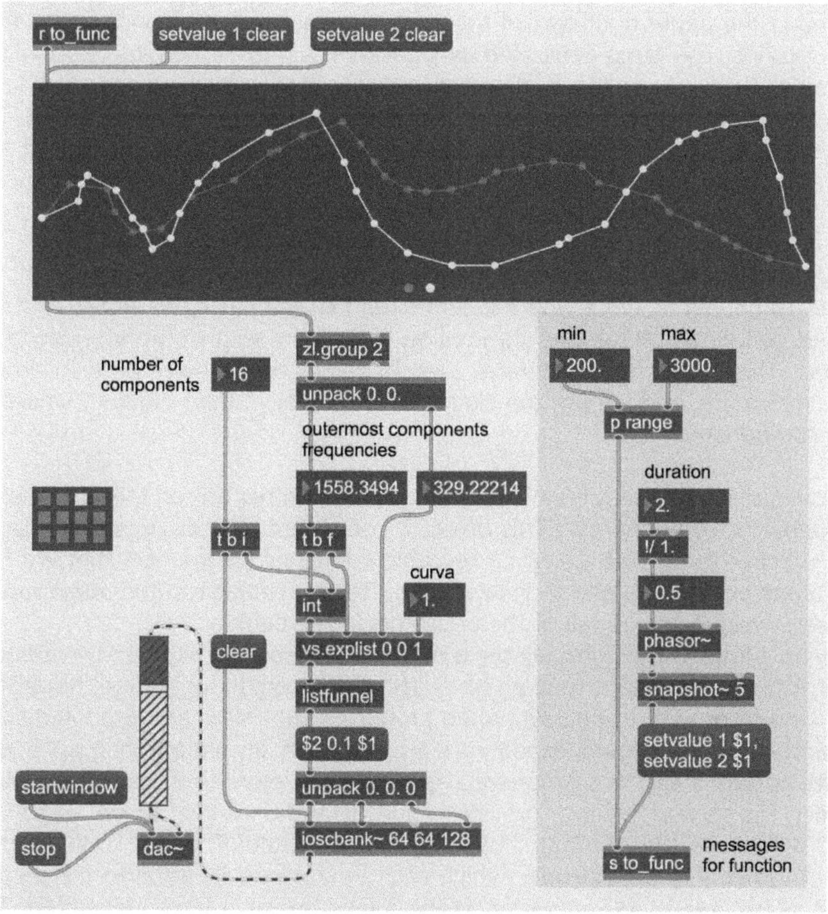

fig. 2.38b: The file **02_19b_masking.maxpat**

Here we have a **mc.function** object with two instances that designate the outermost limits of the mask (as we will see shortly). The **mc.function** object receives messages using [**r** to_func]; these messages are sent by objects that we can find in the bottom right panel, where all of the objects are connected to [**s** to_func]. The two instances contained in **mc.function** have had their domains set using the Inspector so that they run from 0 to 1 rather than the default 0 to 1,000. This change is made to let the domain of the **function** objects match up with the ramps generated by **phasor~**, running from 0 to 1.
In the panel at the lower right we see the subpatch [**p** range], which is identical to a subpatch that was used in the file 02_14_addvar_func.maxpat, which set the minimum and maximum values to be generated by **function**. In the case shown in the figure, the values are 100 and 1,000, which means that y-axis coordinates can take on values between 100 and 1,000, and, as we will see shortly, these values represent the minimum and maximum frequencies that can be set. On

the right of the panel, we have the **phasor~** connected to a **snapshot~** object, which scrolls through the **mc.function** object in the same way that we saw in figure 2.35 and 2.35b. Note that the "length" parameter, which is found in the upper right part of the panel, is expressed in seconds rather than milliseconds. The ramp generated by **phasor~** is transformed into Max values by **snapshot~** and then sent to the message box containing the "setvalue" commands for the two instances, as we have already seen in figure 2.38a. The envelopes designed in the two instances guide the progress of the highest and lowest components. (The two envelopes can also cross, and naturally, if they do, the "high" component becomes the "low" component, and vice versa.)

What is left is to "fill up" the interval between the two envelopes with the other components. Observing the central part of the patch, we notice that the values generated by the two **function** objects are sent to the **vs.explist** object. This object then generates a list of values that grow from a minimum to a maximum, and we use the elements of this list as the frequency values of our components.

Proceeding in an orderly way, let's glance at the number box on the left, labelled "number of components". This object is connected to a **trigger** that saves the number in an **int** object (a reusable container for integers that we first encountered in IA.1), and then sends the "clear" message to the **ioscbank~** object, which zeros out all of the oscillators in the bank.
Moving a little to the right, we see a number box labelled "curve". The number that it produces is sent to the right inlet of **vs.explist**, where it specifies the kind of growth to be used when producing the list: linear, exponential, or logarithmic. (In the figure, exponential is being used, since the setting is 1.5, and anything over 1 specifies exponential growth.) We return to the **mc.function** object: the second instance provides values to the third inlet of **vs.explist** that represents the maximum value to be generated. The first instance provides numbers to a **trigger**, which each time passes its value to the second inlet of **vs.explist**, representing the minimum value to be generated. The **trigger** also sends a bang to the **int** object, which reports the value for the "number of elements" parameter that it is storing. This number is sent to the first inlet of **vs.explist**, which generates a list of frequencies.
The list of frequencies generated by **vs.explist** is sent to **listfunnel**, which divides it into single elements, each preceded by its numerical index (as shown in figure 2.37). We must pass each element to **ioscbank~**, which needs to receive the index values (which correspond to the oscillator numbers) on its right inlet. The **listfunnel** object, however, puts each index value at the beginning of the list it produces, and because of this we will need to rearrange things. Since we need an amplitude value (magnitude) as well, we choose to rearrange the list using a message box that, as you can see, contains [$2 0.1 $1]. This substitution list places the second element in the list into the first spot, puts a constant 0.1 in the second spot, and moves the original first element into the last spot. This new list is given to an **unpack** object, which separates the elements and sends them to **ioscbank~** on the appropriate inlets (corresponding to frequency, magnitude, and oscillator number).

Carefully study all of the presets that we have recorded, seeking to understand how the various parameters influence the sound. In cases of medium complexity such as this patch, it is important to tweak one parameter at a time when experimenting. Try working with them in this order:

- vary the "curve" value, which selects linear, exponential, or logarithmic growth in the list produced by **vs.explist**, for all presets
- vary the number of components (from 1 to 64)
- modify the min/max interval found in the panel, which affects the frequencies outlined by the two instances of the **mc.function** object
- change the length of the mask, by using the "length" parameter in the panel at the lower right

When you have plumbed the depths of the influence that these parameters have on resulting sounds, begin to modify the envelopes or to create new envelopes. (To empty out existing envelopes, click on the "*clear*" messages connected to the **mc.function** object.)
One possible variation on our theme would be to use two independent **phasor~** objects to drive the two envelopes that outline the mask. In this mode, you could give two different lengths to the **phasor~** objects, which would cause continuous variations to be produced. Try modifying the patch in figure 2.38 in this way; delete the **phasor~** block in the panel and then create two independent blocks; send the outputs of the two **snapshots~** to a **pack** object and from there to the message box [setvalue 1 $1, setvalue 2 $2]. In this way the values generated by the two **phasor~** can reach the two instances (Fig. 2.39).

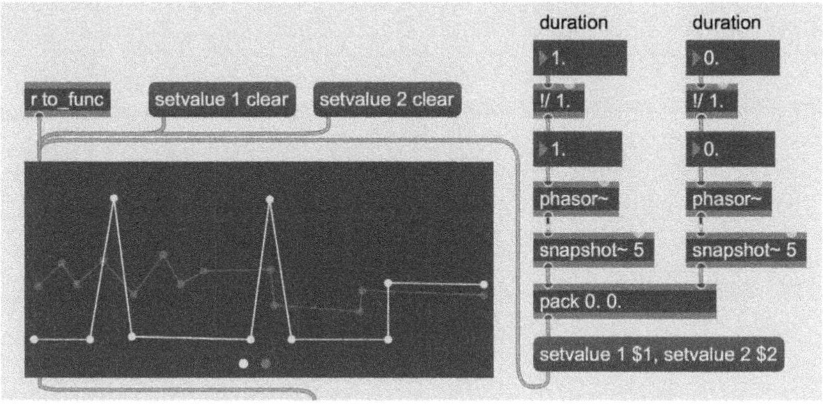

Fig. 2.39 Non-synchronous masking

As you can see in the figure, the length of the first envelope is 1 second and that of the second is 1.1 seconds. This will produce a progressive shifting of the two envelopes against each other, causing the mask to be slightly different in each cycle. The envelopes, in this case, come back into phase every 11 seconds when the first **phasor~** has produced 11 cycles and the second 10 cycles.
Try various combinations of envelopes; try also different lengths, such as 8 seconds for the first and 0.77 for the second.

ACTIVITY – CORRECTING ALGORITHMS

Open the patch contained in **2_Correction.maxpat**.

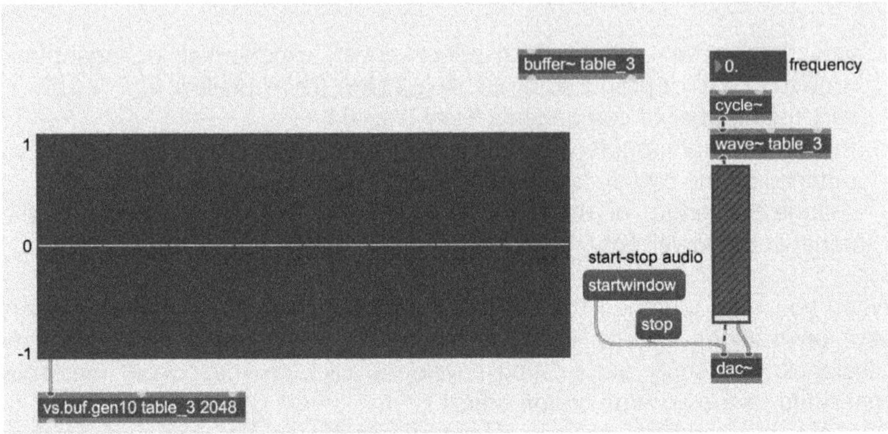

fig. 2.40

We will need to be able to hear the twelfth harmonic of a fundamental set at 80 Hz (which is a pure sound at 960 Hz) on both stereo channels. There is one thing to add to this patch and there are 4 corrections to make.

ACTIVITY – COMPLETING ALGORITHMS

Open the patch contained in **2_Completion.maxpat.**

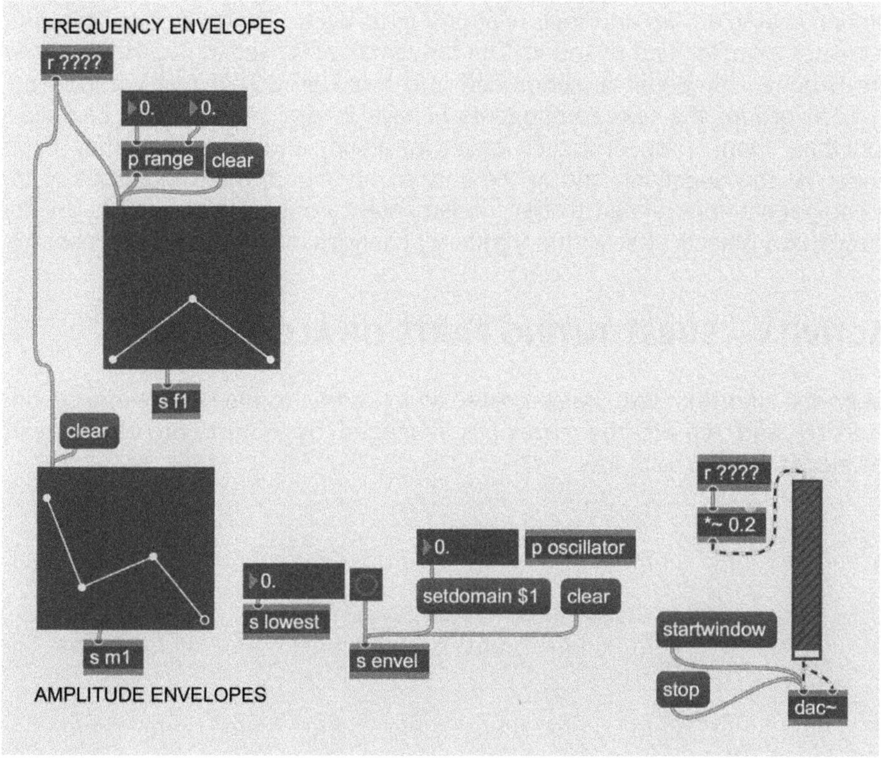

fig. 2.41

This patch is incomplete. To enable the oscillator to function correctly, and to have its amplitude and frequency values controlled by 2 `function` objects, the algorithm needs 5 arguments which have not been called out. Find these 5 missing items (keeping the subpatch in mind as well) and complete the algorithm. Once this is done, explain the logic by which you were operating, step by step.

INTEGRATED CROSS-FUNCTIONAL PROJECT – REVERSE ENGINEERING

Listen carefully and analyze the sound **2_reverse_engine.aif**, describing the timbral characteristics and their relationship to beats. Design an algorithm that recreates a similar kind of sound. The fundamental is fixed at 200 Hz and there are 6 upper components, subdivided into three groups of two components. In each group, the two components behave in similar ways. The pair slides together, then apart, and then together again, and after this, they begin anew. At the beginning and at the end of the sound, the frequencies of the 6 components are related to the fundamental through integer ratios. Use the `function` objects to steer the frequency changes of the various components.

ACTIVITY – SUBSTITUTING PARTS OF ALGORITHMS

Open the algorithm that was prepared as a solution to the reverse engineering exercise, and replace the envelopes managed by `function` objects with envelopes created with lists.

ACTIVITY – ANALYZING ALGORITHMS

This activity is not specific to additive synthesis; it has been designed so that you can discover a different and interesting use of masking, which in this case will apply to the reading of multiple samples sounds. Open the patch contained in **02_analysis.maxpat**, and try the different presets, paying close attention. Note the two subpatches `range` and `8_audiofile`. Now look to understand how this algorithm, which is primarily a variation on the patch in 02_19_masking.maxpat, works, as it is applied to the sound vs_harp_riff.wav.
In particular, describe:

1) the paths that signals follow in the patch and the subpatches

2) the evolution of the sound in each of the presets

3) the way in which the sound is obtained in all of the presets, concentrating on the use of the length parameter, of the minimum and maximum values sent to [`p` range], and on the envelopes for read speed presented by the two `function` objects.

Make a multichannel version of the patch: use the `mc.function` object and modify the subpatch content.

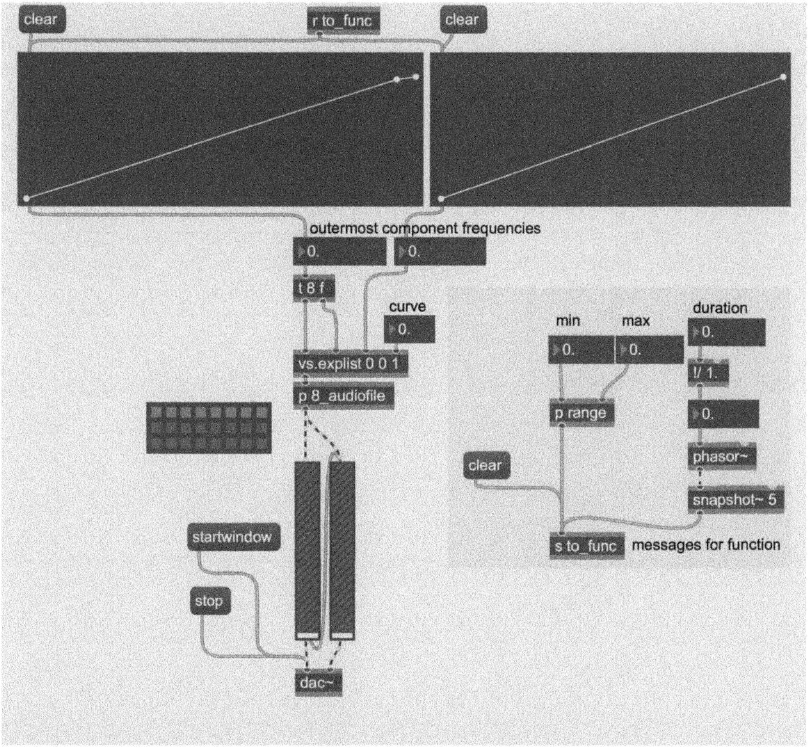

Fig. 2.42 The main window of the file 02_analysis.maxpat

INTEGRATED CROSS-FUNCTIONAL PROJECT – COMPOSING A BRIEF SOUND STUDY (PROJECT A)

Compose a sound study about two minutes long – a brief piece based on the techniques that you have acquired up until now. Save this work in an audio file, and include a text file that details what kinds of operations were used and what kinds of sonic effects you intended to realize. This particular sound study should be based on additive synthesis, and should avoid sampled sounds; compose everything using the addition of single components. In particular, concentrate on the use of glissandi, of beats, of variations in amplitude and frequency envelopes, and in variations to component structure. Use only brief sounds with a percussive character combined with very long sounds (longer than 5 seconds) that have envelopes characterized by a slow attack and a slow decay. Try to take advantage of Max multichannel system.

INTEGRATED CROSS-FUNCTIONAL PROJECT – COMPOSING A BRIEF SOUND STUDY (PROJECT B)

Realize a second sound study based on the techniques above, but controlling the frequency parameters of the components by using the technique of masking, and working only with sounds that have duration of longer than 5 seconds.

LIST OF MAX OBJECTS

abl.dsp.basicshapes~
Band-limited oscillator that can morph between four waveforms: sine, triangular, sawtooth and square.

abl.dsp.swarm~
"Supersaw" oscillator with the ability to change the waveform.

buffer~
An object that manages a memory array in MSP that is called a *buffer*, which can contain a waveform.

ioscbank~
A bank of interpolated oscillators that has four inlets: frequency, amplitude (or magnitude), phase, and an index number for the currently selected oscillator.

jit.cellblock
This object displays a set of values arranged in rows and columns. In the multichannel system it's used to display the values of the signals produced by a multichannel patch cord connected to it.

listfunnel
When this object receives a list, it returns one element of the list at a time, prepending an index number (starting with 0) before each element.

loadmess
This object is similar to `loadbang`, but instead of generating a bang when the patch containing it is loaded, it generates a message based on its argument.

mstosamps~
Convert a duration in milliseconds into a duration expressed as a number of samples.

oscbank~
A non-interpolated bank of oscillators. See **ioscbank~**.

pak
An object similar to **pack**, differing in that all of its inlets are "hot"; a list is generated whenever any of its inlets receive a message.

pictslider
Two-dimensional slider. The name came from the phrase "picture-based slider".

sampstoms~
An object that converts a duration expressed as a number of samples into a duration in milliseconds.

sig~
Transform Max numbers into an MSP signal.

snapshot~
Transform an MSP signal into a stream of Max numbers.

vs.buf.gen10
Fills a wavetable with a waveform calculated as a sum of component harmonics. The amplitude values of the components are given to `vs.buf.gen10` as a numeric list.

vs.explist
Generate a list of numbers that grows from a minimum to a maximum value. It has four inlets: the number of elements to generate, the minimum value, the maximum value, and the type of growth to use in the series.

wave~
Read the contents of a `buffer~` and write them out as a signal. The location to be read is driven by a signal inlet that varies between 0 and 1 (and is often produced by a `phasor~`).

waveform~
Display the contents of a `buffer~`.

MESSAGES, ATTRIBUTES, AND PARAMETERS FOR SPECIFIC MAX OBJECTS

buffer~
- Read (message)
Message for loading a new buffer from an audio file. With the "*read*" message, unlike the "*replace*" message, the buffer is not resized, and therefore if the size of the audio file is bigger than that of the buffer, only the first part of the sound will be loaded.

function
- Setrange (messagge)
Message that sets the minimum and maximum values shown on the y-axis of a `function` object.

ioscbank~
- Freqsmooth (messagge)
- Magsmooth (messagge)
Message that establish the transition time in samples between one frequency and the next, or between one amplitude and the next.

mc wrapper
- deviate (message)
creates a series of random values around a central value.
- harmonic (message)
generates a harmonic series: the first argument is a multiplication factor; the second argument is the fundamental frequency.
- increment (message)
creates a series of values with constant increase.
- setvalue (message)
allows sending messages to individual instances of a multichannel object.

oscbank~
- Freqsmooth (messagge)
- Magsmooth (messagge)
Message that establish the transition time in samples between one frequency and the next, or between one amplitude and the next.

waveform~
- Set (messagge)
Message that assigns a buffer to a **waveform~** object. The name that follows the message must correspond to the name of a **buffer~** object.

GLOSSARY.

;
(Semicolon – Use In A Message Box)
A semicolon inside of a message box enables sending messages to a `receive` object(s) exactly as though they were sent using one or more `send` objects.

Set
A message that has diverse uses, among which is to send internal values to a Max object without triggering output.

3T
NOISE GENERATORS, FILTERS, AND SUBTRACTIVE SYNTHESIS

LEARNING AGENDA

PREREQUISITES FOR THE CHAPTER
- Contents of Chapters 1 and 2 (Theory)

LEARNING OBJECTIVES
Knowledge
- To learn about the theory of subtractive synthesis
- To learn about the theory and use of the main filter parameters
- To learn about the differences between the theory of ideal filters and the actual responses of digital filters
- To learn about the theory and the response of FIR and IIR filters
- To learn how to use filters routed in series or in parallel
- To learn about the theory and use of graphic and parametric equalizers
- To learn how to use filters on different types of signals
- To learn the main elements of a typical subtractive synthesizer

Skills
- To be able to hear the basic effects caused by filters, and to describe their characteristics

CONTENTS
- Subtractive synthesis
- Lowpass, highpass, bandpass, and bandreject filters
- High shelving, low shelving, and peak/notch filters
- The Q factor
- Filter order
- Finite impulse response and infinite impulse response filters
- Graphic and parametric equalization
- Filtering signals produced by noise generators, sampled sounds, and impulses

ACTIVITIES
- Video examples

TESTING
- Questions with short answers
- Listening and analysis

SUPPORTING MATERIALS
- Fundamental concepts
- Glossary
- Discography

3.1 SOUND SOURCES FOR SUBTRACTIVE SYNTHESIS

In this chapter we will discuss *filters*, a fundamental subject in the field of sound design and electronic music, and subtractive synthesis, a widely-used technique that uses filters. A **filter** is a signal processing device that acts selectively on some of the frequencies contained in a signal, applying attenuation or boost to them.[1] The goal of most digital filters is to alter the spectrum of a sound in some way. **Subtractive synthesis** was born from the idea that brand-new sounds can be created by modifying, through the use of filters, the amplitude of some of the spectral components of other sounds.

Any sound can be filtered, but watch out: you can't attenuate or boost components that don't exist in the original sound. For example, it doesn't make sense to use a filter to boost frequencies around 50 Hz when you are filtering the voice of a soprano, since low frequencies are not present in the original sound.

In general, the source sounds used in subtractive synthesis have rich spectra so that there is something to subtract from the sound. We will concentrate on some of these typical source sounds in the first portion of this section, and we will then move on to a discussion of the technical aspects of filters.

Filters are used widely in studio work, and with many different types of sound:

> Sounds being produced by noise generators, by impulse generators, by oscillator banks, or by other kinds of signal generators or synthesis

> Audio files and sampled sounds

> Sounds being produced by live sources in real time (the sound of a musician playing an oboe, captured by a microphone, for example)

NOISE GENERATORS: WHITE NOISE AND PINK NOISE

One of the most commonly used source sounds for subtractive synthesis is **white noise**, a sound that contains all audible frequencies, whose spectrum is essentially flat (the amplitudes of individual frequencies being randomly distributed). This sound is called white noise in reference to optics, where the color white is a combination of all of the colors of the visible spectrum. White noise makes an excellent source sound because it can be meaningfully filtered by any type of filter at any frequency, since all audible frequencies are present. (A typical white noise spectrum is shown in figure 3.1.)

[1] Besides altering the amplitude of a sound, a filter modifies the relative phases of its components.

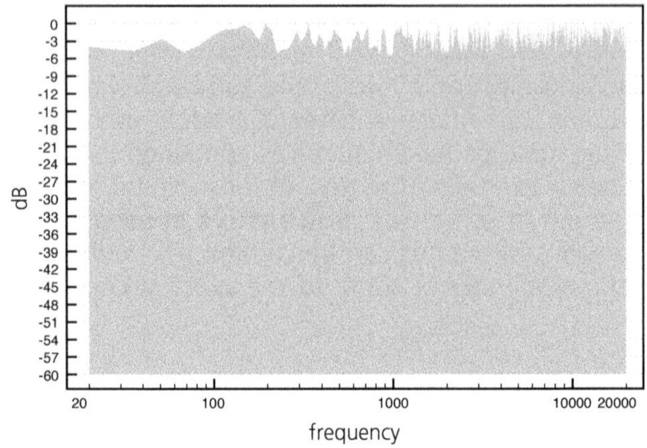

Fig. 3.1 The spectrum of white noise

Another kind of noise that is used in similar ways for subtractive synthesis is **pink noise**. This kind of sound, in contrast to white noise, has a spectrum whose energy drops as frequency rises. More precisely, the attenuation in pink noise is 3 dB per octave;[2] it is also called 1/f noise, to indicate that the spectral energy is proportional to the reciprocal of the frequency. (See figure 3.2.) It is often used, in conjunction with a spectral analyzer, to test the frequency response of a musical venue, in order to correct the response based on some acoustic design.

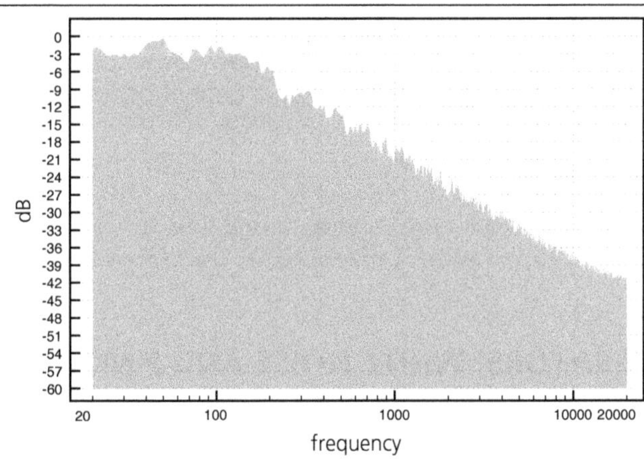

Fig. 3.2 The spectrum of pink noise

[2] Another way to define the difference between white noise and pink noise is this: while the spectrum of white noise has the same energy at all frequencies, the spectrum of pink noise *distributes the same energy across every octave*. A rising octave, designated anywhere in the spectrum, will occupy a raw frequency band that is twice as wide as its predecessor's; pink noise distributes equal amounts of energy across both of these frequency bands, resulting in the constant 3 dB attenuation that is its basic property.

In digital systems, white noise is generally produced using random number generators: the resulting waveform contains all of the reproducible frequencies for the digital system being used. In practice, random number generators use mathematical procedures that are not precisely random: they generate series that repeat after some number of events. For this reason, such generators are called **pseudo-random generators**.

By modifying some of their parameters, these generators can produce different kinds of noise. A white noise generator, for example, generates random samples at the sampling rate. (If the sampling rate is 48,000 Hz, for example, it will generate 48,000 samples per second.) It is possible, however, to modify the frequency at which numbers are generated – a generating frequency equal to 5,000 numbers a second, for example, we would no longer produce white noise, but rather a noise with strongly attenuated high frequencies.

When the frequency at which samples are generated is less than the sampling rate, "filling in the gaps" between one sample and the next becomes a problem, since a DSP system (defined in the glossary for Chapter 1T) must always be able to produce samples at the sampling rate. There are various ways of resolving this problem, including the following three solutions:

> **Simple pseudo-random sample generators**
These generate random values at a given frequency, maintaining a constant value until it is time to generate the next sample. This results in a waveform resembling a step function. In figure 3.3 we see the graph of a 100 Hz noise generator; the random value is repeatedly output for a period equal to 1/100 of a second, after which a new random value is computed. If the sampling rate were 48,000 Hz, for example, each random value would be repeated as a sample 48,000 / 100 = 480 times.

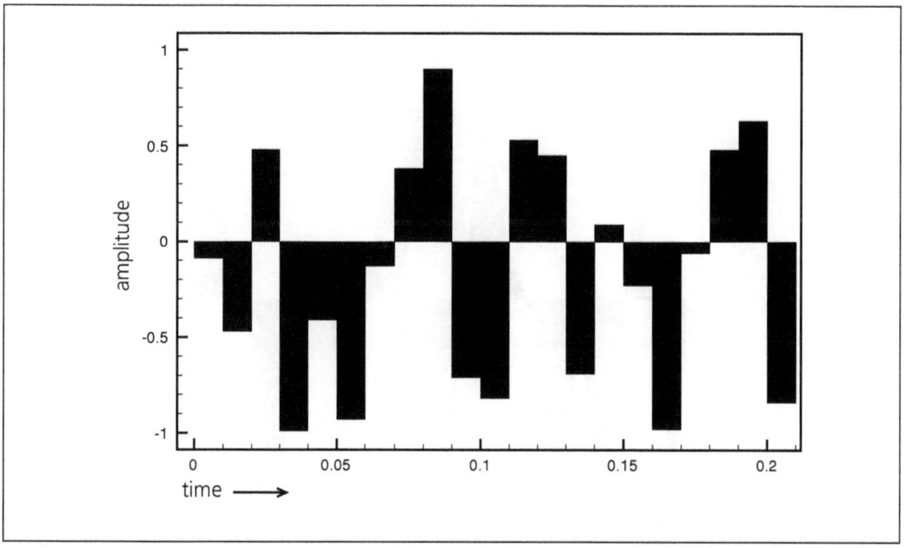

Fig. 3.3 Generation of pseudo-random values

> **Interpolated pseudo-random sample generators**
These generators use interpolation between each random number and the next. (See the section on linear interpolation in Chapter 2.1.) As you can see in figure 3.4, intermediate samples, produced during the gaps between random value computations, follow line segments that move gradually from one value to the next.

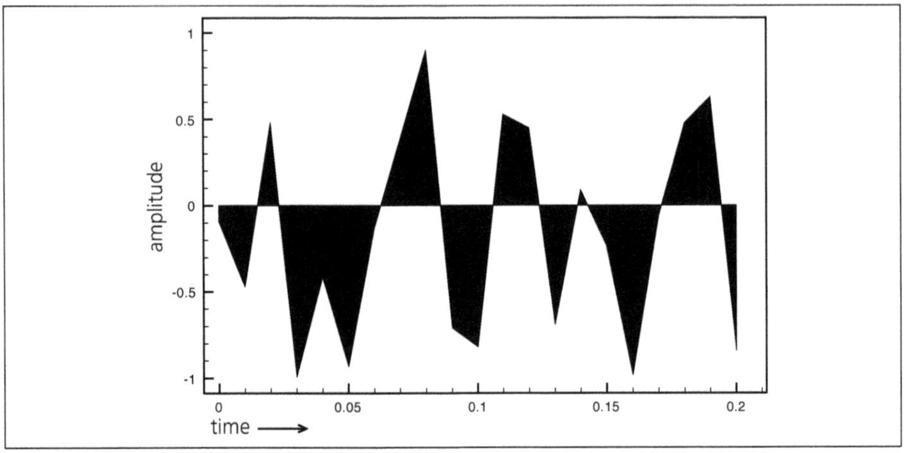

Fig. 3.4 Generation of pseudo-random values with linear interpolation

Interpolation between one value and the next can be linear, as shown in the figure, or polynomial, implemented using polynomial functions to connect the values using curves rather than line segments. (Polynomial interpolation is shown in figure 3.5, however, we will not attempt to explain the details here.) The kinds of polynomial interpolation most common to computer music are quadratic (which use polynomials of the second degree) and cubic (which use polynomials of the third degree). Programming languages for synthesis and signal processing usually have efficient algorithms for using these interpolations built in to their runtimes, ready for use.

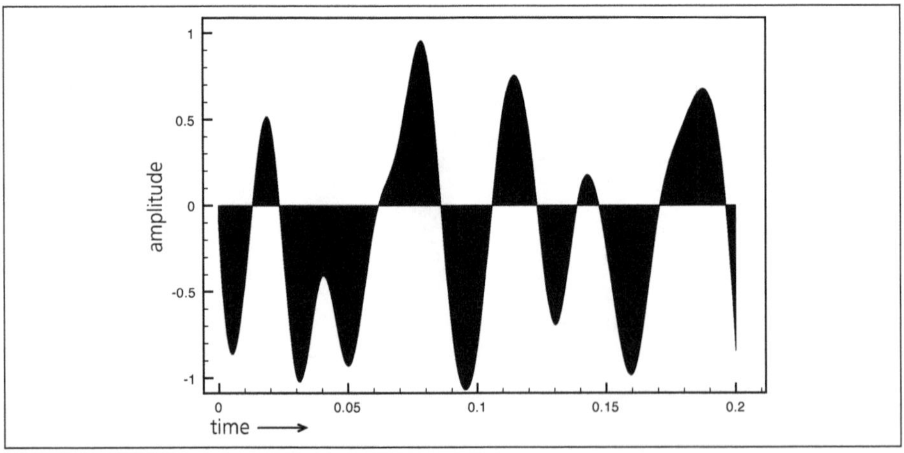

Fig. 3.5 Generation of pseudo-random values with polynomial interpolation

> **Filtered pseudo-random sample generators**
In this kind of approach, the signal produced is filtered using a lowpass filter. We will speak further of this kind of generator in the section dedicated to lowpass filters.

VIDEO EXAMPLE 3A – *NOISE GENERATORS* – PRESETS 1-4

OSCILLATORS AND OTHER SIGNAL GENERATORS

In Section 1.2T, we examined the "classic" waveforms that are often found in synthesizers, such as the square wave, the sawtooth wave, and the triangle wave. Section 2.1T explained how these waveforms, when geometrically perfect (perfect squares, triangles, etc.), contain an infinite number of frequency components. The presence of infinitely large numbers of components, however, causes nasty problems when producing digital sound, since an audio interface cannot reproduce frequencies above half of its sampling rate.[3] (We will discuss this topic in much greater detail in Chapter 5.) When you attempt to digitally reproduce a sound that contains component frequencies above the threshold for a given audio interface, undesired components will appear, which are almost always non-harmonic. To avoid this problem, **band-limited oscillators** are often used in digital music. Such oscillators, which produce the classic waveforms, are built so that their component frequencies never rise above half of the sampling rate. The sounds generated by this kind of oscillator therefore make a good point of departure for creating sonorities appropriate for filtering, and as a result, they are the primary source of sound in synthesizers that focus on subtractive synthesis. In Section 3.5 we will analyze the structure of a typical subtractive synthesizer.

It is, of course, also possible to perform subtractive synthesis using synthetic sounds, rich in partials, that have been realized using other techniques such as non-linear synthesis or physical modeling. We will cover these approaches in following chapters.

FILTERING SAMPLED SOUNDS

Beyond subtractive synthesis, one of the everyday uses of filters and equalizers is to modify sampled sounds. Unlike white noise, which contains all frequencies at a constant amplitude, a sampled sound contains a limited number of frequencies, and the amplitude relationships between components can vary from sound to sound. It is therefore advisable, before filtering, to be conscious of the frequency content of a sound to be processed.

[3] It is for this reason that sampling rate of an audio interface is almost always more than twice the maximum audible frequency for humans.

Remember that *you can only attenuate or boost frequencies that are already present*. This is true for all sounds, sampled or otherwise, including those captured from live sources.

3.2 LOWPASS, HIGHPASS, BANDPASS, AND BANDREJECT FILTERS

It is important to underline the fact that filters, by modifying spectra in the way that we have described, alter the amplitudes and the phases of the components of a sound, while leaving the frequency of the fundamental oscillation of the original signal (and obviously those of its components) unaltered.
To begin our discussion of filters and how they affect spectra, we will choose a sound to modify: this sound will be designated as our input signal. We will define the properties of a given filter, giving particular attention to the frequencies within our *input signal* that will be attenuated, or in some cases boosted. Finally, the action of the filter on our input signal will result in an *output signal*. (This flow can be seen in figure 3.6).

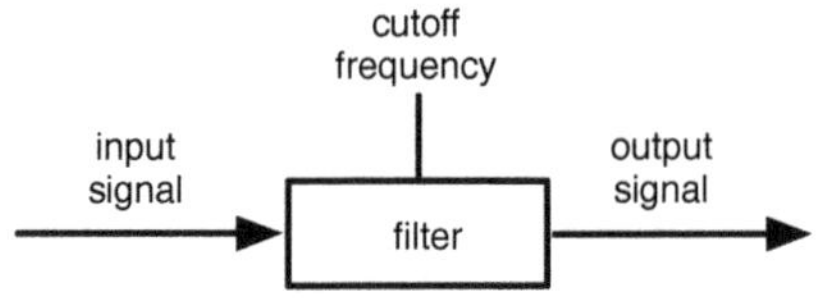

Fig. 3.6 A diagrammatic filter

The most commonly used filters[4] are:

- lowpass filter
- highpass filter
- bandpass filter
- bandreject filter
- high shelving filter
- low shelving filter
- peak/notch shelving filter

For now, we will occupy ourselves with the first four: the lowpass, highpass, bandpass, and bandreject filters.

LOWPASS FILTERING

The **lowpass filter** attenuates all of the frequencies above a cutoff frequency. The term 'lowpass' indicates that our filter will allow low frequencies, those

[4] In addition to the filters that we cover in this chapter, we will consider additional filter-based techniques, spectral analysis and re-synthesis, in Chapter 11.

below the cutoff frequency that we have specified, to pass through to its output, while it will attenuate frequencies above this frequency.

Let's consider the case in which the cutoff frequency is 1,000 Hz (as seen in figure 3.7).

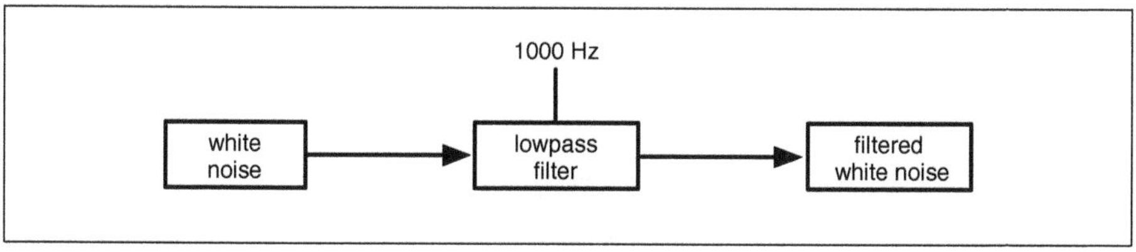

Fig. 3.7 A lowpass filter

The filter attenuates, following some *attenuation curve* (as shown in figure 3.8), the frequencies above 1,000 Hz, leaving frequencies below 1,000 Hz unmodified.

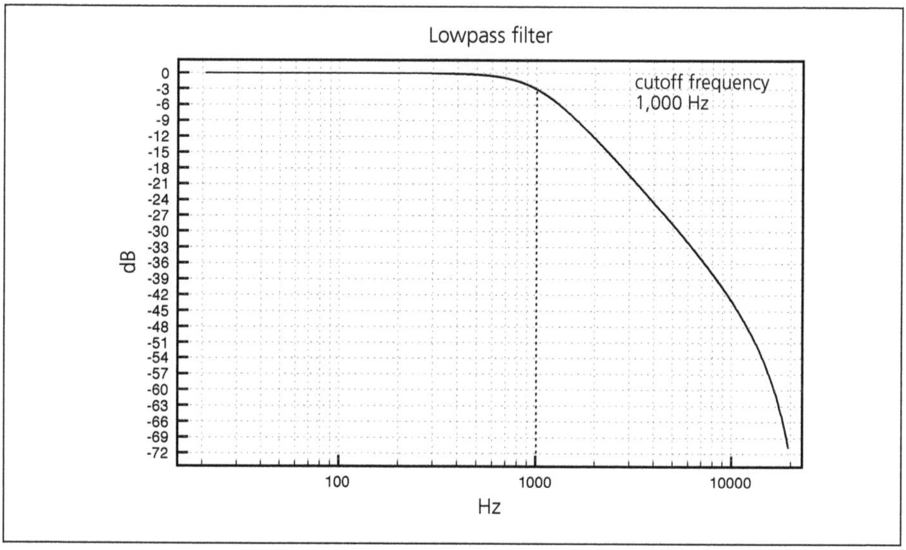

Fig. 3.8 An attenuation curve for a lowpass filter

The sound output by this filter will be more mellow and less brilliant than the input signal, because high frequencies in the resulting sound will be attenuated. Let's listen to some examples of white noise, of sampled sounds, and of a sawtooth wave, all processed by a lowpass filter with various cutoff frequencies.

VIDEO EXAMPLE 3A – *LOWPASS FILTER* - PRESETS 5-14

Another use of lowpass filters is to smooth the sudden changes from one number to the next in pseudo-random number generators (as shown in figure 3.3). When the output signal of such a generator has a lowpass filter applied to it, the graphed values in the resulting signal become visually "rounded". In figure 3.9, you can see four examples in which the transitions from one value to the next become more and more smooth. The original signal is shown at the top of the figure, and the lower graphs show the signal after processing.

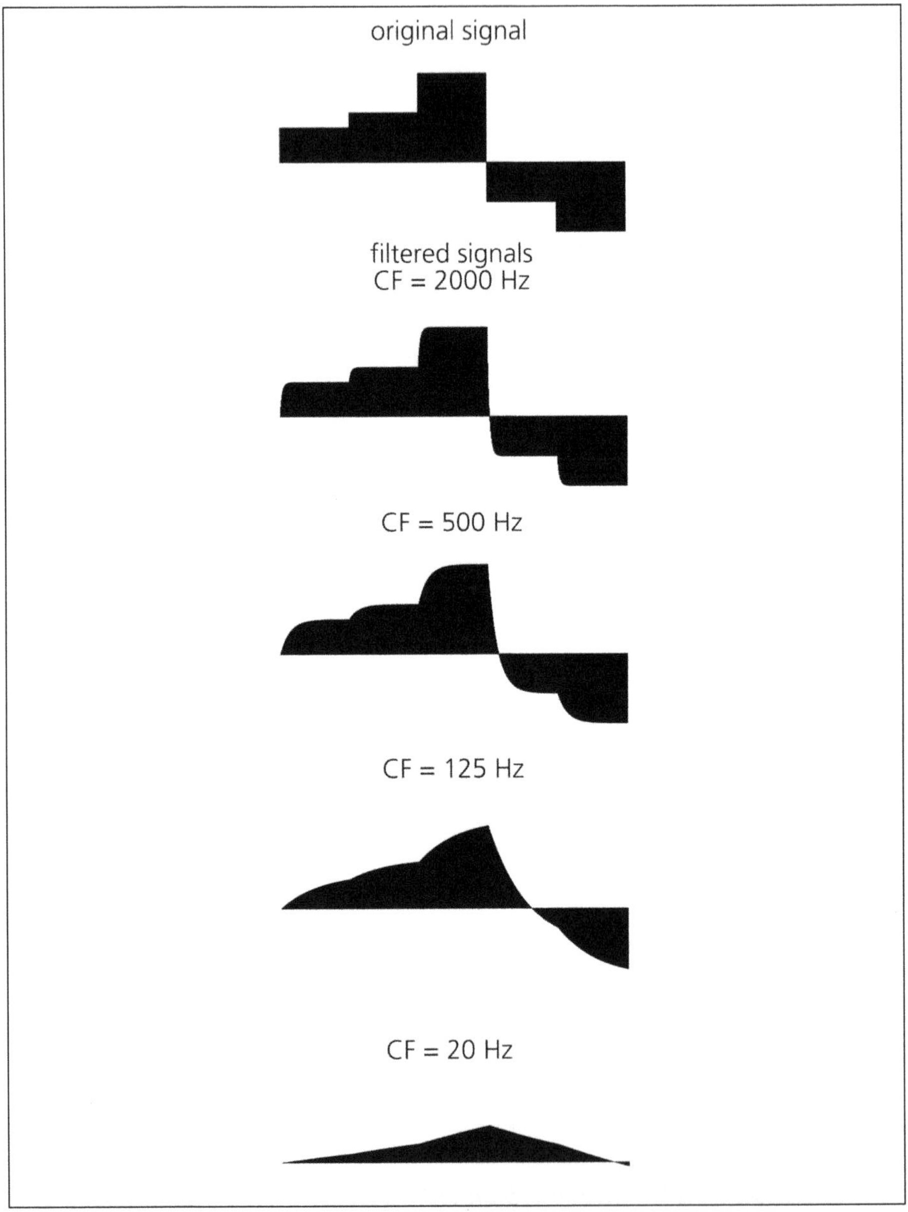

Fig. 3.9 Lowpass filtering of pseudo-random numbers with lower and lower cutoff frequencies

HIGHPASS FILTERING

"A **highpass filter** attenuates all of the frequencies *below* the cutoff frequency. The term 'highpass' indicates that the filter will let frequencies above the cutoff frequency pass, while attenuating the frequencies below it." (Ibid, p. 86.)

If the cutoff frequency for a highpass filter is 1,000 Hz, the filter will attenuate frequencies below 1,000 Hz, according to some curve (as shown in figure 3.10), while leaving the frequencies above this limit unchanged.

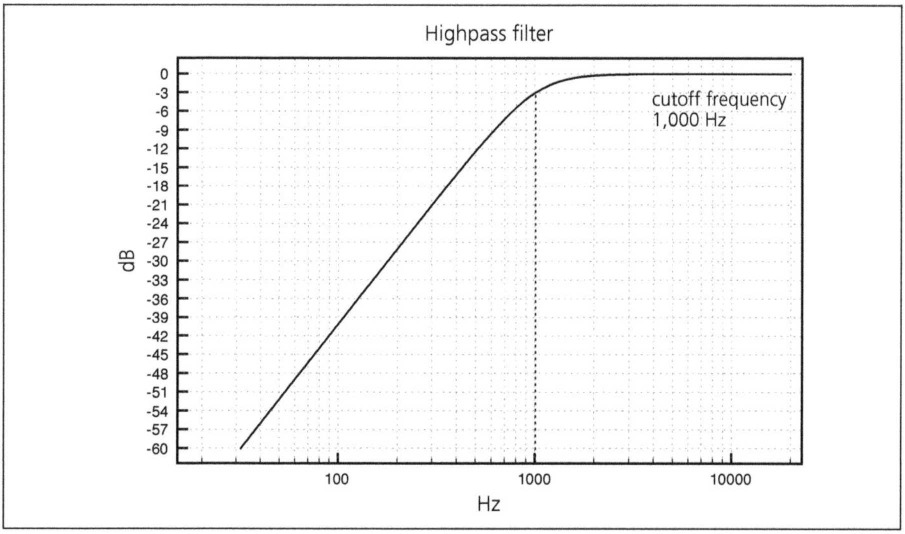

Fig. 3.10 An attenuation curve for a highpass filter

The sound output by a highpass filter will be clearer and more brilliant that the original, because low frequencies are attenuated with respect to the original sound. Listen to some examples of highpass filtering:

VIDEO EXAMPLE 3A – *HIGHPASS FILTERING* – PRESETS 15-24

BANDPASS FILTERING

A **bandpass filter** attenuates the frequencies above and below a certain ***passband***, defined as a continuous zone of frequencies delimited by upper and lower bounds called its **cutoff frequencies**. For example, if we have cutoff frequencies of 1,600 and 2,000 Hz, all of the frequencies above 2,000 Hz and below 1,600 Hz will be attenuated, as shown in figure 3.11. (An unattenuated region of the spectrum is sometimes referred to as a *passband*, while an attenuated region is a *stopband*.)

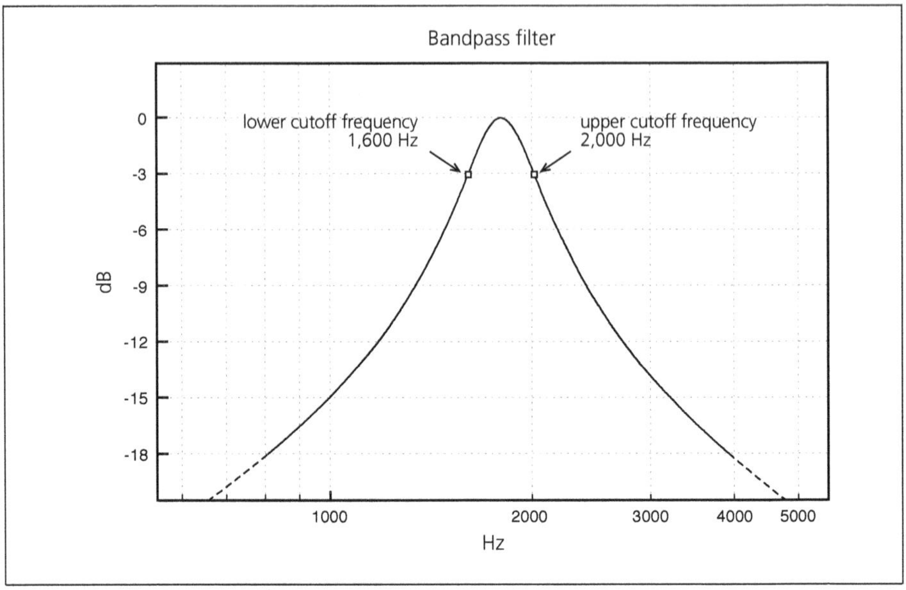

Fig. 3.11 Cutoff frequencies of a bandpass filter

To further help in defining the behavior of a bandpass filter, we can introduce two alternate parameter values that complement the notion of cutoff frequencies: **bandwidth** and **center frequency** (as shown in figure 3.12).

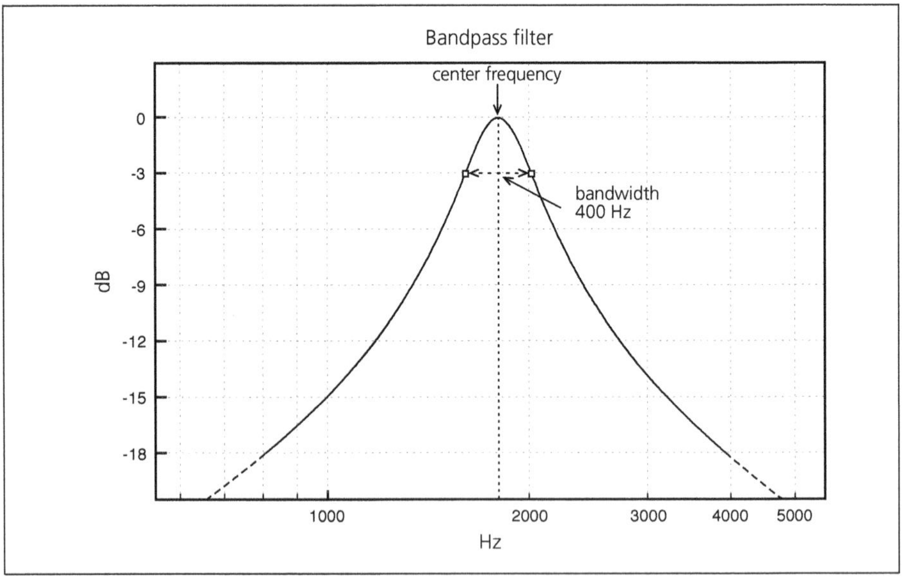

Fig. 3.12 Bandwidth and center frequency of a bandpass filter

If cutoff frequencies are 1,600 and 2,000 Hz, the filter's bandwidth (literally the "width of the passband") will be 400 Hz (between 1,600 and 2,000 Hz), and its center frequency will be located in the vicinity of 1,800 Hz.

What happens if we progressively narrow the bandwidth? The attenuation of the frequencies around the center frequency will become more and more marked, until finally the center frequency alone is audible. By using a very narrow bandwidth in conjunction with an input signal consisting of white noise, we can create a quasi-sinusoidal sound that oscillates at the center frequency of the filter.

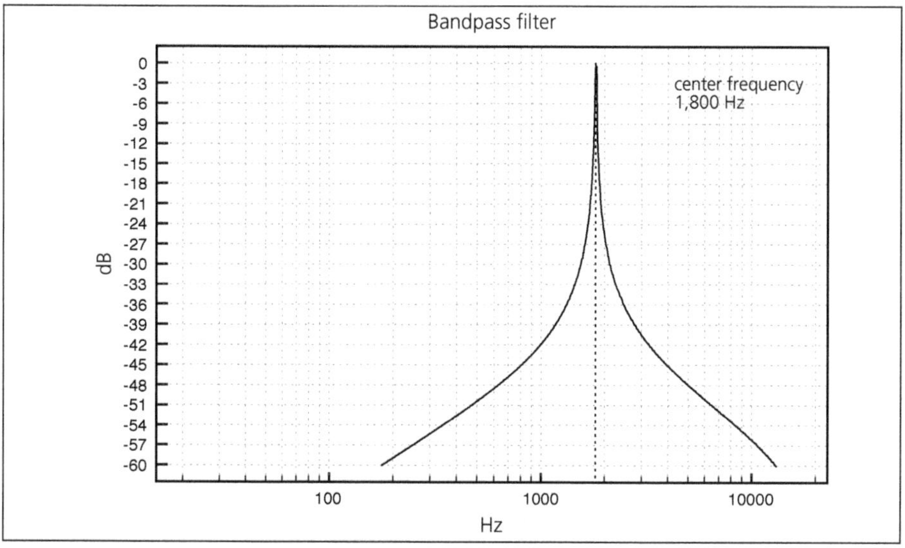

fig. 3.13: A bandpass filter with very narrow bandwidth

Listen to some examples of bandpass filters that have fixed center frequency, but narrower and narrower passbands. (Their bandwidth shrinks from 1,000 Hz to 2 Hz.) After listening to them, try recreating similar effects using a lower center frequency.

VIDEO EXAMPLE 3A – *BANDPASS FILTER* – PRESETS 25-37

VIDEO EXAMPLE 3A – *BANDWIDTH* – PRESETS 38-42

By maintaining a fixed bandwidth for a filter, say 100 Hz, but gradually raising the pitch of its center frequency, you can produce an output signal that sounds higher than the original.

VIDEO EXAMPLE 3A – *CENTER FREQUENCY* – PRESETS 43-55

You probably noticed that at the beginning of this subsection we defined the term "center frequency" using the rather vague expression "in the vicinity of 1,800 Hz", without giving a precise value. To make things easy, the calculation of the center frequency can be approximated as the arithmetic average of the two cutoff frequencies, using the formula:

(lower cutoff + upper cutoff) / 2

For example, (1,600 + 2,000) / 2 = 1,800.

In reality, however, the true center frequency of a filter should be calculated not as an *arithmetic average*, but rather as a *geometric average* of the two cutoff frequencies. This can seem a little complicated, but it really isn't; with the help of a computer (or even a calculator) we can determine the answer in the blink of an eye. The formula is as follows:

$$\sqrt{\text{lower cutoff} \cdot \text{upper cutoff}}$$

For example, 1,600 · 2,000 = 3,200,000, and the square root of this number is 1,788.854.

Therefore, the true center frequency between the two cutoff frequencies of 1,600 and 2,000 Hz is not 1,800 Hz, but instead it is closer to 1,789 Hz.

If the distance between the arithmetic mean and the geometric mean were always small, approximation would not pose much of a problem in many practical applications, especially for higher frequency passbands. After all, if the bandwidth is narrow, the difference between arithmetic and geometric mean is not very significant. But what happens with a wider passband? Let's try an experiment in which our cutoff frequencies are 500 and 5,500 Hz: in this case the arithmetic mean is 3,000 Hz, while the geometric mean is 1,658.312 Hz – a significant difference indeed!

BANDREJECT FILTERING

In a **bandreject** filter the term "bandwidth" refers to a zone of frequencies (sometimes called the *stopband*) to be attenuated rather than passed unaltered. A bandreject filter with cutoff frequencies of 1,600 and 2,000 Hz, for example, will attenuate the frequencies between 1,600 and 2,000 Hz. Both "bandwidth" and "center frequency" remain useful terms in this case: a bandreject filter with cutoff frequencies of 1,900 and 2,000 Hz has a bandwidth of 100 Hz and a center frequency of around 1,950 Hz (as shown in figure 3.14).

The bandreject filter is very useful for eliminating unwanted electronic hum or buzz in recordings, such as the hum of an amplifier. To do this, you need to create a filter with a very narrow bandwidth and a central frequency equal to the frequency of the buzz. It may also be necessary to filter the harmonics of the offending noise. The typical buzz produced by electrical interference has a fundamental of 60 Hz (in the US), and in this case, you might use bandreject filters with frequencies of 60, 120, 180, 240, 300 Hz, etc. Such filters should be connected *in series*, as will be discussed in Section 3.4.

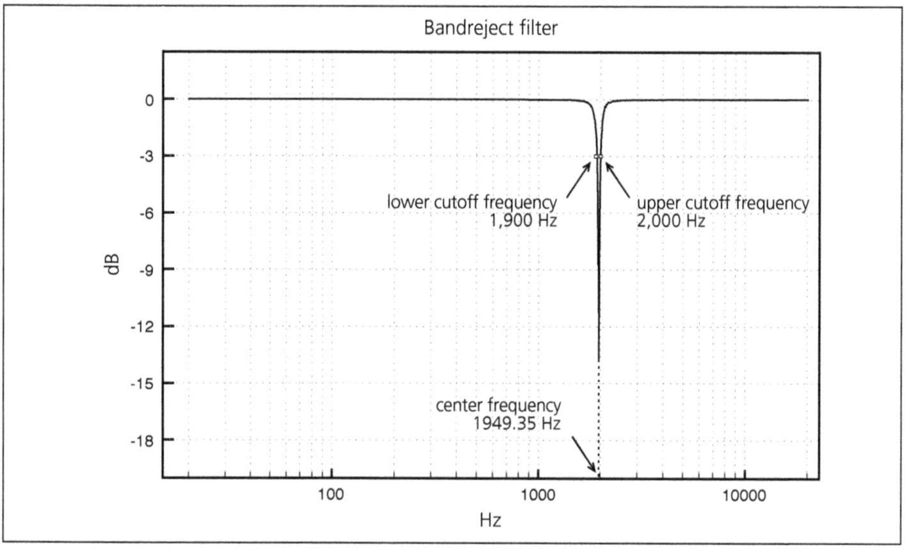

Fig. 3.14 Cutoff frequencies and the center frequency for a bandreject filter

VIDEO EXAMPLE 3A – *BANDREJECT FILTERING* – PRESETS 56-59

TESTING – *QUESTIONS WITH SHORT ANSWERS (30 words maximum)*

1) Why is white noise a signal that is particularly suited to subtractive synthesis?

2) Which frequencies are attenuated when using a highpass filter with a cutoff frequency of 2,000 Hz?

3) Which frequencies are attenuated when using a bandpass filter with a center frequency of 2,000 Hz and a bandwidth of 4 Hz?

4) Which frequencies are attenuated when using a bandreject filter with a center frequency of 2,000 Hz and a stopband that has a bandwidth of 30 Hz?

5) Which frequencies are attenuated when using a lowpass filter with a cutoff frequency of 2,000 Hz?

6) What is the center frequency of a bandpass filter with cutoff frequencies at 300 and 3,000 Hz?

3.3 THE Q FACTOR

In the preceding section, we saw that we could define the properties of a bandpass filter either by specifying its cutoff frequencies, or else its bandwidth and center frequency. A third method exists, in which you specify a center frequency plus a *resonance factor* for the filter (more commonly called a *Q factor*, or just *Q*). The three techniques are equivalent, and you can easily move between them, yet the majority of filters in use today, especially commercial ones, choose to use Q when setting frequency response. For this reason alone, to understand why it is so frequently used, it is important to explain the meaning of Q.

The **Q factor** (*quality factor*) of a filter is defined as:

Q = center frequency / bandwidth

From this, we can derive:

bandwidth = center frequency / Q

As you can see, bandwidth and Q are inversely proportional to each other. If you maintain a fixed center frequency, you must increase the Q in order to *reduce* the bandwidth, boosting the frequencies closest to the center frequency.

Let's take a look at one of the practical advantages that favors the use of Q as a filter parameter. We would like to use parameter values that interact in a simple and consistent way across the entire audible spectrum. But when using bandwidth and center frequency to specify filter behavior, changes to the center frequency can result in radically different filter qualities for the listener, *even when bandwidth remains constant.*
For example, a passband of 300 Hz will sound very wide when the center frequency is 200 Hz, since the cutoff frequencies for this case are 100 and 400 Hz, a full two octaves apart. When the center frequency is 5198 Hz, however, the bandwidth becomes quite narrow, and as a result, the cutoffs of 5050 and 5350 Hz render the passband about a single semitone wide. Clearly the bandwidth of a filter is not very useful knowledge unless we also know its ratio with the center frequency!

VIDEO EXAMPLE 3B – *Q* – PRESETS 1-7

In the two examples cited above, the width of the passband was the same, but the sonic quality of the filters themselves were very different, due to their differences in center frequency. White noise filtered at 200 Hz with a passband that is 300

Hz wide has a Q value of 0.66 (two octaves), while white noise filtered at 5,198 Hz with the same 300 Hz bandwidth results in a Q value of 17.3 (one semitone). Comparing the two Q values, we can understand immediately that the second filter will be much narrower from the psychoacoustic perspective, and that the resonance of the center frequency will be much more marked than that of the first filter, even though the two have the same bandwidth.

The Q factor presents bandwidth *in relation to the center frequency*. If we change the center frequency without changing the Q value, the effect of the filter is consistent from a psychoacoustic point of view. When we maintain a fixed Q, the listener will hear a uniform effect, even when center frequency moves. When holding Q steady, bandwidth varies as a function of the center frequency, and it is the *ratio* between the center frequency and the bandwidth that remains constant.

The term "quality factor" was borrowed from electronics. In that usage, it was said to be a *resonance factor*, because the higher the Q, the narrower the filter's bandwidth, and the more prone it was to begin oscillating (to *resonate*) when excited by a sound whose frequency was close to the center frequency.

We will examine this topic further in Section 3.9, but to start internalizing the concepts, listen to these examples:

> in presets 8 and 9 of the Video Example 3B, the Q is fixed and has a low value (0.66); as a consequence, in both cases, the bandwidth is around *two octaves*.[5]

> in presets 10 and 11 of the Video Example 3B, the Q is fixed at a high value (17.3) and the bandwidth, in both cases, is roughly a *semitone*.

VIDEO EXAMPLE 3B – *THE Q FACTOR* – PRESETS 8-12

Another general characteristic of filters is that they have a response time that is directly proportional to their Q. The narrower the bandwidth (or the greater the Q), the longer the filter will take to respond. A long response time will smooth (or "smear") both the attack and the decay of a filtered sound with respect

[5] Q values can just as well be expressed as musical intervals. For example, the Q value for an interval of a fifth has a value of 2.445, for an octave, 1.414, for a third of an octave, 3.464, and so forth. We will encounter this relationship between bandwidth and musical octaves again, when we examine graphic equalizers (which are filter banks used to correct sound when mixing), which divide their controls according to either full or fractional octaves. (See Section 3.7 for more details.)

to the original input. When working with high Q values, it is also possible to encounter an effect called **ringing**, which is an oscillation produced by **transients**[6] that remains active after the transients have passed. Such an effect, in certain cases, can continue to be heard even after the amplitude of the input signal returns to 0.

VIDEO EXAMPLE 3B – *RESPONSE TIME AND RINGING* – PRESETS 13-15

As a final exercise for this section, let's review the relationships between center frequency, bandwidth, and Q. If f_C is the center frequency and *b* is the bandwidth, they all follow the following relationships:

$Q = f_C / b$
$b = f_C / Q$
$f_C = Q \cdot b$

3.4 FILTER ORDER AND CONNECTION IN SERIES

FILTERS OF THE FIRST ORDER

We have seen how to manage the attenuation of frequency that occurs in various types of filters, but what, exactly, defines the curve with which frequencies are attenuated? This shape of this curve depends heavily upon what is called the *order* of the filter.

To introduce the concept, let's consider a lowpass filter, a hypothetical **first-order filter** with a cutoff frequency of 1,000 Hz. If we introduce a 2,000 Hz sine wave into this filter (one octave above the cutoff), the same sine wave will be output at about half of its original amplitude. A sine wave at 4,000 Hz will have its amplitude reduced to around 1/4 of the original's, and so forth. As a rule, for every doubling of frequency above the cutoff frequency, amplitude will be reduced by half, which is equivalent to an attenuation of about 6 dB per octave. (Section 1.2T contains relevant reference materials.)
Let's now set our hypothetical cutoff frequency at 300 Hz. The amplitude of a 600 Hz sine wave (or a 600 Hz component of a complex input sound) will drop by 6 dB (to 1/2 of the original amplitude), while a sine wave at 1,200 Hz will drop by 12 dB (to 1/4 of the original), and a sine wave at 2,400 Hz will drop

[6] A transient is a brief component that exists during the attack (and sometimes the decay) of a sound that is non-harmonic and differs from the spectral content that defines the stable, later, phase of a sound. An attack transient often produces a short-lived burst of amplitude at some non-harmonic high frequency.

by 18 dB (to 1/8 of the original), and so on. We can see this illustrated in some tables taken from "Virtual Sound" by R. Bianchini and A.Cipriani.[7]

Amplitude	Frequency	Frequency	Frequency	Frequency
0 dB	up to 300 Hz			
-6 dB		600 Hz		
-12 dB			1,200 Hz	
-18 dB				2,400 Hz

Let's now look at a first-order highpass filter.[8] If we hypothesize a cutoff frequency of 1,000 Hz, the amplitude of a sine wave or of a single component at 500 Hz (one octave below the cutoff) will be attenuated by 6 dB (to 1/2 of the original amplitude), a sine wave at 250 Hz will be attenuated by 12 dB (to 1/4 of the original), at 125 Hz will be attenuated by 18 dB (to 1/8 of the original), and so forth. Again in this case, we see a reduction of 6 dB per octave.

Amplitude	Frequency	Frequency	Frequency	Frequency
0 dB				At and above 1,000 Hz
-6 dB			500 Hz	
-12 dB		250 Hz		
-18 dB	125 Hz			

What we have said so far applies to *ideal* filters, but in *digital* filters (such as the filters in Max) the cutoff frequency of a filter, whether lowpass or highpass, isn't exactly 0 dB. Instead, there is a slight attenuation at the cutoff frequency that can be as much as -3 dB.[9] In digital filters the frequency region near the cutoff frequency is called the **transition zone**, and it is marked by roll-off attenuation that can be more or less steep depending on the implementation.
Digital filters, despite these approximated cutoffs, are still characterized by the same rule of doubling found in ideal filters: as the frequency of the

[7] In the tables, 0 dB corresponds to the original amplitude of the sound.
[8] In this section we won't examine bandpass or bandreject filters, because such filters exist only as (yet undefined) second-order filters!
[9] This attenuation occurs in non-resonant filters in general.

cutoff doubles (for highpass filters) or is reduced by half (for lowpass filters), attenuation increases by 6 dB. Likewise, as the frequency quadruples or is quartered, attenuation is 12 db, and so forth, as detailed above. Figure 3.15 is a graph that shows the frequency response[10] of an ideal filter plotted against that of a digital filter. (In the graph, cf stands for cutoff frequency.)

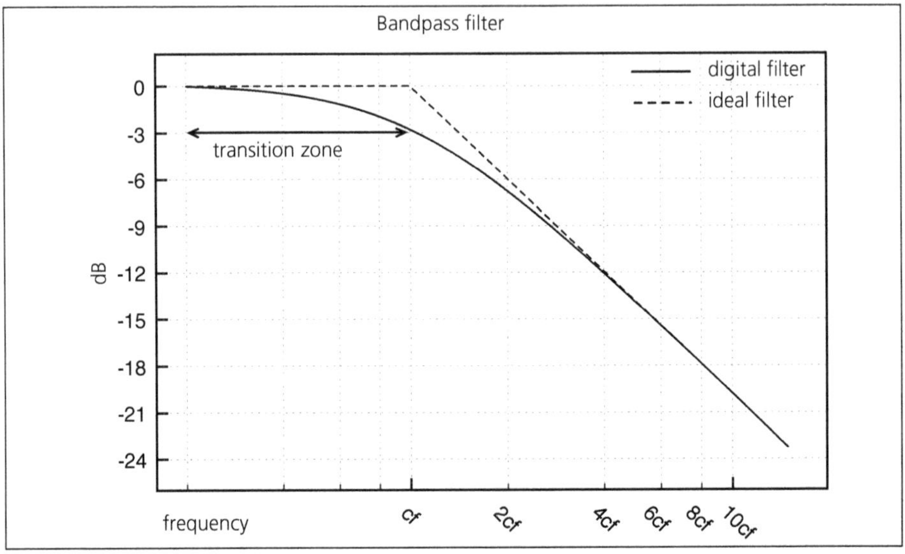

Fig. 3.15 The attenuation curve for a first-order digital filter versus a corresponding ideal filter

First-order filters, in general, are used for specific tasks which we will examine shortly.

SECOND-ORDER FILTERS

We now consider **second-order filters**, which provide twice the attenuation of first-order filters. As a pratical matter, when we filter a sound, we often need more attenuation than first-order filters can produce. For this reason, in the previous practical chapters, we used second-order filters exclusively. The second-order filters that we used in those examples are called **Butterworth filters** (named after Stephen Butterworth, the physicist who first described them).[11]

[10] The frequency response is a measure of the spectrum that is output by a system (in this case a filter), when it is given an input signal that contains all frequencies within the frequency band being measured.

[11] Butterworth filters are second-order IIR ("infinite impulse response") filters, a kind of filter implementation that more closely matches the characteristics of an ideal filter than other popular filter implementation techniques. They are distinguished by flatness in their passband, by very good precision, and by very good attenuation of the frequencies outside of their passband.

If the cutoff frequency of a lowpass second-order filter has a cutoff frequency of 300 Hz, the frequency at 600 Hz (an octave higher) will be attenuated by 12 dB, the frequency of 1,200 Hz will be attenuated by 24 dB, and in general, everything will be double that of a first-order filter.

Amplitude	Frequency	Frequency	Frequency	Frequency
0 dB	up to 300 Hz			
- 6 dB		---		
-12 dB		600 Hz	---	
-18 dB				---
-24 dB			1,200 Hz	
-30 dB				
-36 dB				2,400 Hz

In this table, the symbol --- indicates the level of attenuation attained by a first-order lowpass filter. You can see that the curve of a second-order filter falls off more steeply.

The same things can be said about a second-order highpass filter.

Amplitude	Frequency	Frequency	Frequency	Frequency
0 dB				1,000 Hz and higher
-6 dB			---	
-12 dB		---	500 Hz	
-18 dB	---			
-24 dB		250 Hz		
-30 dB				
-36 dB	125 Hz			

Again, the --- sign indicates the level of attenuation that would be achieved using a first-order highpass filter: once again, the steepness of the second order filter is much greater than that of the first-order filter.

A similar analysis (although more complex) can be made for second-order bandpass filters. In the case of a bandpass filter with cutoff frequencies at 1,600 and 2,000 Hz, when moving beyond the high cutoff frequency of 2,000 Hz the amplitude of the frequency band at every doubling of frequency will drop off at a 12 dB rate of attenuation. Likewise, moving downwards, halving frequencies below the low cutoff frequency of 1,600 Hz will increase the attenuation applied by 12 dB. The following table (ibid, p. 90) illustrates the attenuation of selected frequencies in this kind of filter.

Amplitude	Freq	Freq	Freq	Freq	Freq	Freq	Freq
0 dB				1,789			
-3 dB			1,600		2,000		
-12 dB		800				4,000	
-24 dB	400						8,000

As you can see from the table, frequencies between 1,600 and 2,000 Hz appear to be unaltered. In reality, the only frequency that remains unaltered, maintaining 0 dB, is that of the center frequency. The mathematics of an ideal bandpass filter actually result in amplitudes at the cutoff frequencies that are 3 dB lower than that of the center frequency. In this example, therefore, there is an attenuation curve between 1,789 and 2,000 Hz, as well as an opposite curve between 1,789 and 1,600 Hz. Both of these curves move from 0 dB to -3 dB.

It should be stated that the case under discussion is only accurate for ideal filters. Values for digital bandpass filters, even at two octaves above and below the cutoff frequencies, can be very different from the ideal, sometimes by even more than 6 dB. When evaluating digital filters, you need to take into account not only the transition zone, but also the type of signal being input, the sampling rate, the quality of the filter, and other factors. Ideal values barely describe the situation; they serve only as a point of reference. If you want precise measurements for a given filter, you will need to directly test that specific filter with the sounds that you plan to use.

SECOND-ORDER RESONANT FILTERS

For bandpass filters, the Q factor defines the relationship between center frequency and bandwidth, as discussed in Section 3.3. A particular implementation of this kind of filter that can actually boost the center frequency (thereby *increasing* the amplitude relative to the input signal) by increasing the Q value, is called a *resonant bandpass filter*. In figure 3.16 you can see the difference between the frequency response of a resonant bandpass filter, which boosts the frequencies found in the passband by increasing the Q value, and the frequency response of a standard bandpass filter, which can only attenuate the frequencies found outside the bandwidth.

Resonant lowpass and highpass filters also exist, in which it is possible to specify a Q factor to boost the cutoff frequency and nearby frequencies without otherwise altering the rest of the passed frequencies.[12]

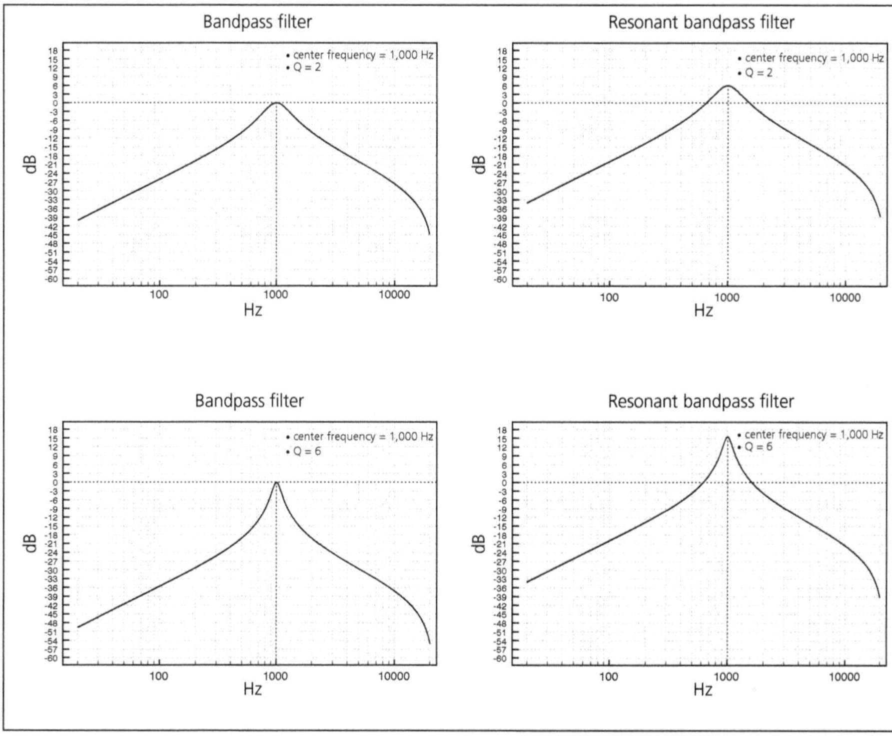

Fig. 3.16 Bandpass and resonant bandpass filters with various Q settings

VIDEO EXAMPLE 3B – *BANDPASS, LOWPASS, AND HIGHPASS RESONANT FILTERS* – PRESETS 16-25

HIGHER ORDER FILTERS: CONNECTING FILTERS IN SERIES

What if we had wanted to re-double the effect of attenuation above and below the passband, to produce an attenuation curve that falls off even more steeply? This can be done; it is enough to place two second-order **filters in series** (or to "cascade" them), each having the same cutoff frequencies, thereby obtaining a much more selective fourth-order filter. Here is how filters can be placed in

[12] We should note in passing that the Butterworth highpass and lowpass filters that we referred to in the previous section do not have a Q factor for resonance.

series in order to implement a fourth-order filter in this way: the input signal enters a filter, and the output of this first filter is used as the input for a second filter, which further attenuates the target frequencies. Note that both filters must have the same cutoff frequency, and that the same scheme will work for both lowpass and highpass filters.

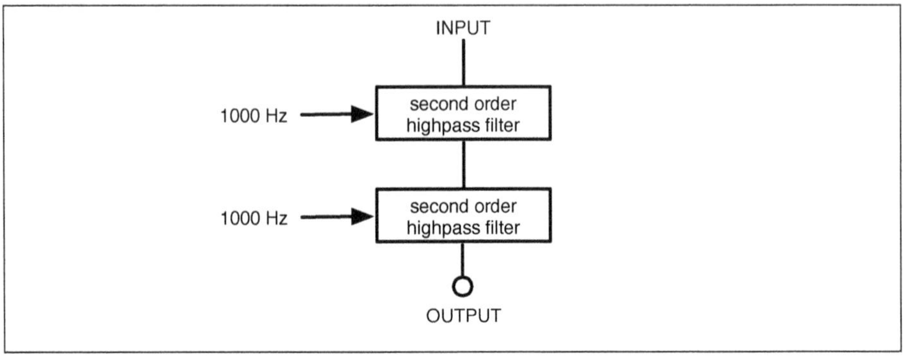

Fig. 3.17a Two second-order filters connected in series

It is possible to construct higher order bandpass and bandreject filters in precisely the same way, sharing center frequencies and the bandwidth settings for filters in series. Let's examine the effect that this has, using a hypothetical fourth-order bandpass filter constructed from two second-order bandpass filters:

Amplitude	Freq	Freq	Freq	Freq	Freq	Freq	Freq
0 dB				1,789			
-3 dB			---		---		
-6 dB			1,600		2,000		
-12 dB		---				---	
-24 dB		800				4,000	
-36 dB	---						---
-48 dB	400						8,000

In this case, the --- signs indicate the attenuation that would have been attained by a second-order filter. You can see that the filter curve for a fourth-order filter falls off more quickly. Moreover, if we remember that the cutoff frequencies for an ideal filter are defined to have 3 dB of attenuation, we can deduce from the table that when using two filters in series, the original cutoff frequencies become attenuated by 6 dB, effectively narrowing the passband by moving the cutoff frequencies closer to the center frequency (as shown in figure 3.17b).

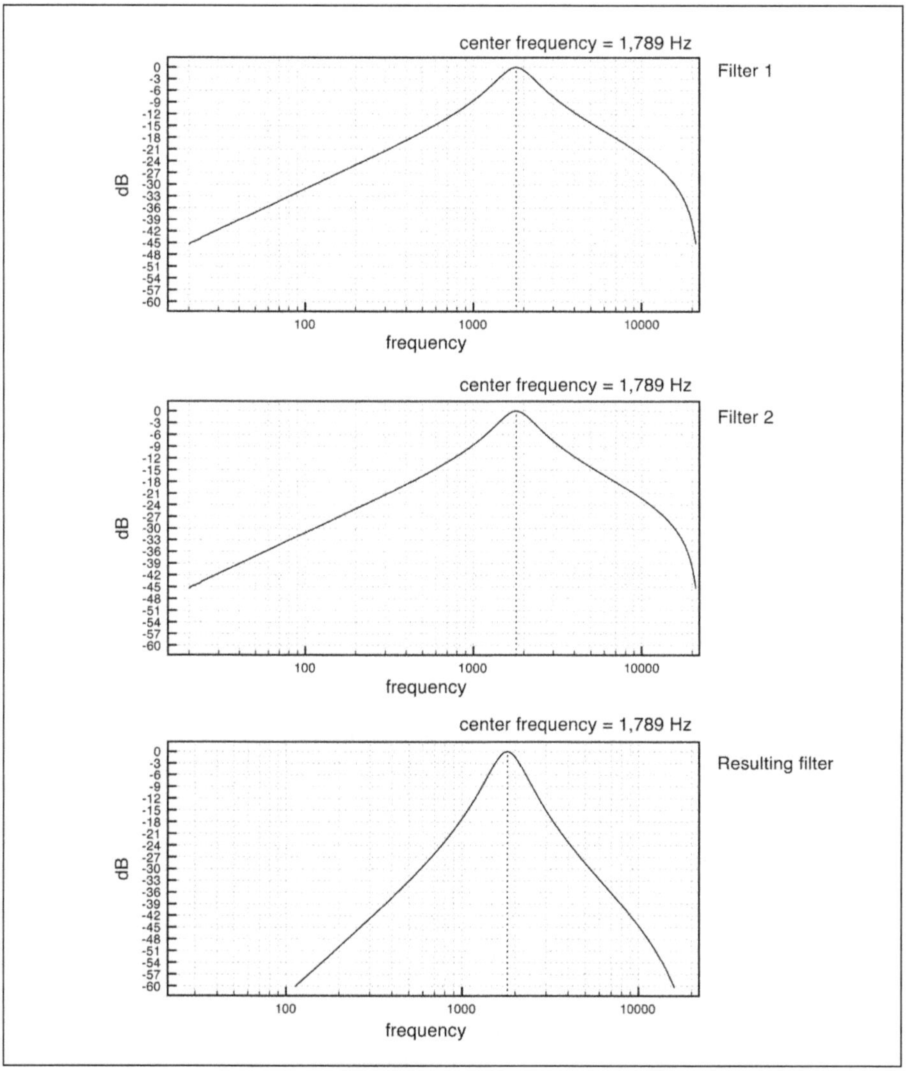

Fig. 3.17b The restriction of the passband caused by increasing a filter's order

VIDEO EXAMPLE 3C – *FILTER ORDER* – PRESETS 1-10

You can use filters connected in series in yet another way: for the purpose of building a filter with a wider passband, but one that has steeper roll-off. All you have to do is to connect two bandpass filters in series with center frequencies that are near each other (but not identical), and that share the same bandwidth settings (as shown in figures 3.18a and 3.18b).

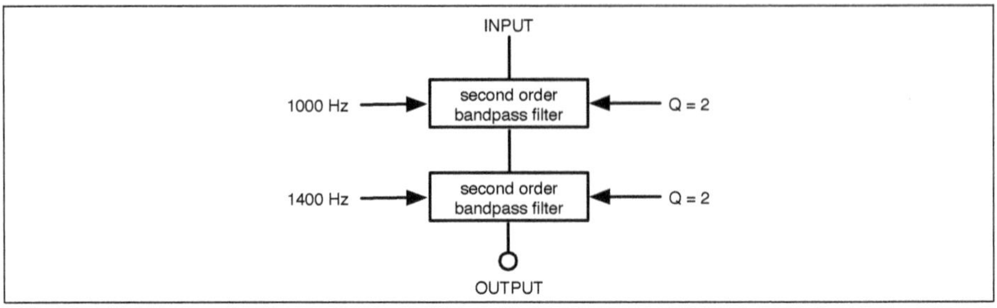

Fig. 3.18a Two bandpass filters in series with center frequencies of 1,000 and 1,400 Hz and a Q of 2

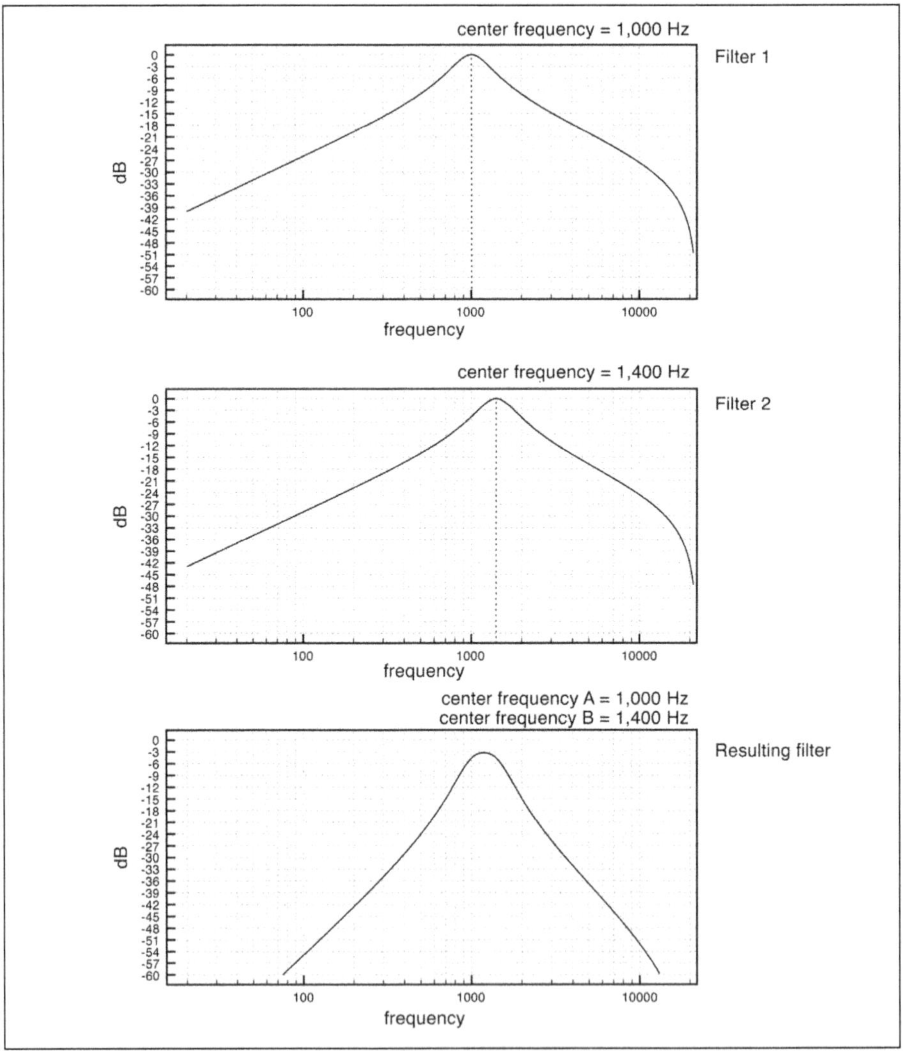

Fig. 3.18b Two cascaded filters with different cutoff frequencies combine to produce a bandpass filter with a wider passband and a steeper attenuation curve

VIDEO EXAMPLE 3C – *CASCADED FILTERS* – PRESETS 11-20

We will see a more complicated use of filters in series in Section 3.8, which is dedicated to parametric equalization.

3.5 SUBTRACTIVE SYNTHESIS

The filtered sounds that you have heard until this point have really had very little to recommend them musically, since we have been concentrating on analysis using static parameter values. But once we start applying dynamic control to the filters, subtractive synthesis offers many sonic possibilities. In the first chapter we saw how to use line segments to vary the amplitude of a sound in time, as envelopes, and to vary the frequency, as glissandi. Nothing should stop you from applying the same idea to the **parameters of a filter**: center frequency (or *cutoff frequency* in the cases of highpass and lowpass filters) and Q.

Varying the cutoff frequency of a lowpass filter, for example, and applying the result to a fixed frequency sawtooth oscillator, enables us to realize a sound that becomes progressively darker or brighter. Furthermore, if the lowpass is a resonant filter and has a Q setting that is sufficiently high, it is possible to isolate the individual harmonics of the sound: if we have a sawtooth at 220 Hz, for example, to which we apply a resonant lowpass filter, varying its cutoff frequency with a segment that slides from 220 Hz to 2,200 Hz, we will hear the first 10 harmonics in succession in a kind of "timbral arpeggio".

VIDEO EXAMPLE 3C – *DYNAMIC VARIATIONS OF CUTOFF FREQUENCY* – PRESETS 21-24

If we vary the Q setting instead, moving between 1 and 100, let's say, for a bandpass filter that has a center frequency of 900 Hz, and if we then apply this to white noise, we produce a sound that passes from unpitched to pitched, and back again.

VIDEO EXAMPLE 3C – *DYNAMIC VARIATIONS OF Q* – PRESETS 25-28

By properly developing the base waveform and the kind of filter to apply, and then by controlling the dynamic evolution of cutoff frequency and Q, we can implement shimmering sounds at low computational cost.

Subtractive synthesis, from the point of view of computer resource usage, is more economical than additive synthesis, in which it is necessary to modify tens or hundreds of parameters just to dynamically vary the spectrum of a single sound. It is thanks to the frugality of the technique that by the mid-1960s the first analog synthesizers had appeared on the market: historical models such as Moog, Buchla, Arp, Oberheim, and after those, products produced by Roland, Korg, and Yamaha, were all based on subtractive synthesis, which could be implemented in a very cost-effective way. Even now, the majority of digital synthesizers, whether packaged as hardware or software, still offer this technique.

ANATOMY OF A SUBTRACTIVE SYNTHESIZER

Subtractive synthesizers are generators of audio signals that can be controlled by a musician using a control panel, a keyboard, or some other device. These synthesizers are driven by one or more oscillators, also called **VCO (Voltage Controlled Oscillators)**,[13] which can produce classic waveforms (sawtooth, square, or triangle), as well as white noise, which is used to create specific effects. The outputs of these oscillators can be mixed together, and can also be slightly detuned in order to create beats.
Most synthesizer hardware is played with a keyboard similar to a piano keyboard, although its range is often limited to 4 or 5 octaves. A synthesizer can be deprived of the keyboard, in which case it may be called an expander or a module. In either case, it can be connected to additional external keyboards or controllers using MIDI (discussed in Chapter 9). Every time that a key is pressed, the oscillators generate a sound at the corresponding frequency. (Of course, triggering of sound can also be done using other inputs.)

The sound produced by the oscillators is processed using an amplitude envelope (**VCA: Voltage Controlled Amplitude**) which defines its attack, decay, sustain, and release. After this, the sound is sent to a lowpass filter (or multiple cascaded filters) whose cutoff frequency depends upon the note played (it might be, for example, a multiple of the fundamental). **Key follow** is the term used for this kind of parameter, whose value tracks the frequency of the key pressed. In a similar vein, the frequency of the filter can also be set to follow the profile of the amplitude envelope, which will result in a more brilliant sound when amplitude is at its maximum and a darker sound when amplitude is at its minimum, mimicking one of the nice characteristics of acoustic instruments. Such a filter may also have its own envelope for cutoff frequency (**VCF: Voltage Controlled Filter**), independent of the key frequency or the amplitude envelope, and Q can also be either set and/or controlled by another envelope.

In short, filter parameters can be controlled by either the note played and/or by amplitude. Sometimes other controllers are also present, such as LFOs (Low Frequency Oscillators), which we will discuss further in the next chapter.

[13] An oscillator controlled by a voltage level, which refers to the control technique that was used in analog synthesizers.

VIDEO EXAMPLE 3D – *SUBTRACTIVE SYNTHESIS* – PRESETS 1-10

Video Example 3D presents a simple subtractive synthesizer. Since it's a complex example, let's examine its architecture in detail. In figure 3.19, you can see a block diagram for this basic synthesizer.

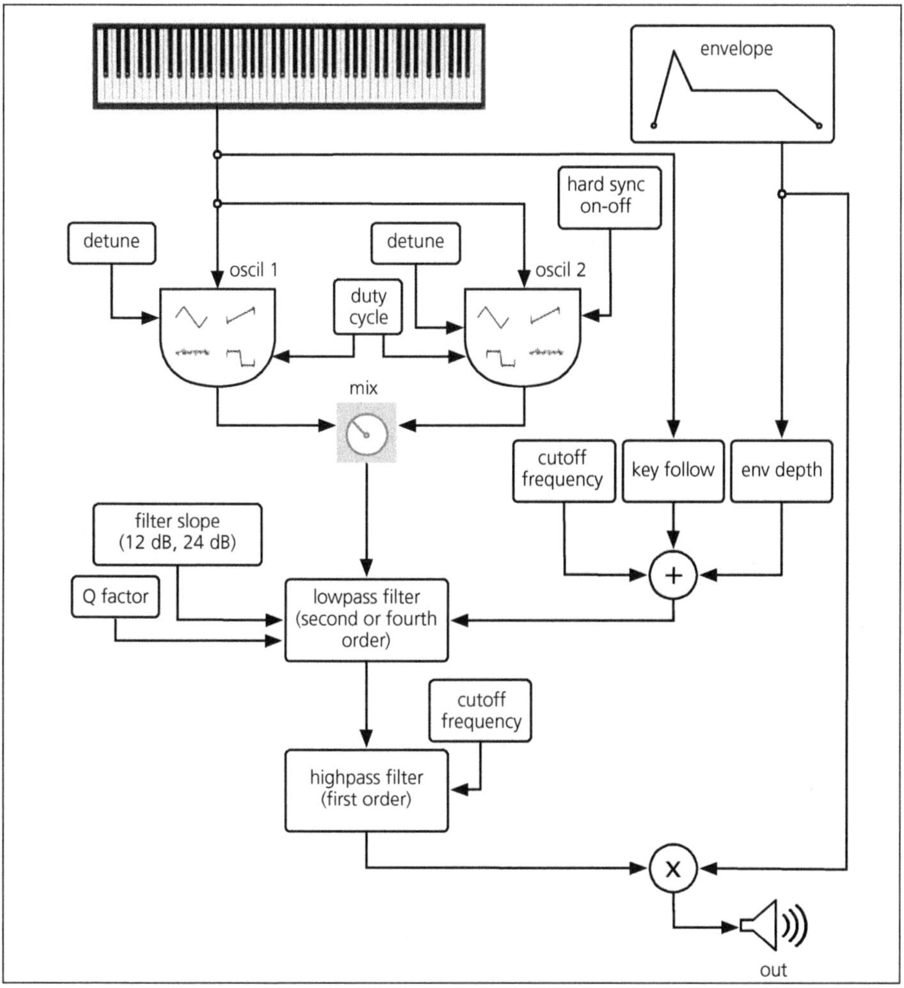

Fig. 3.19 A block diagram for a subtractive synthesizer

Our virtual synthesizer has two oscillators that can produce sawtooth, square, and triangle waves, as well as white noise. It is possible to mix the oscillators together as you wish.

The square wave can be modified by varying the duty cycle in order to produce different harmonic spectra. By detuning, the intonation of the oscillators can be modified in order to produce beats, or to play in parallel intervals such as a fifth or an octave. It is also possible to set **hard sync** between the first and second oscillator; by doing this you get an often-used feature in this kind of synthesizer that synchronizes the cycle of the two oscillators, even when they have different frequencies. When hard sync is active, every time that the first oscillator starts a new cycle, the second oscillator will be forced to restart, independent of its frequency. We'll show an example of this in which the first oscillator (100 Hz) completes a cycle in the same time that the second oscillator (150 Hz) completes one and a half cycle, after which it is forced to restart (as shown in figure 3.20). Needless to say, it is possible to produce spectra in this mode that cannot be realized with classic waveforms!

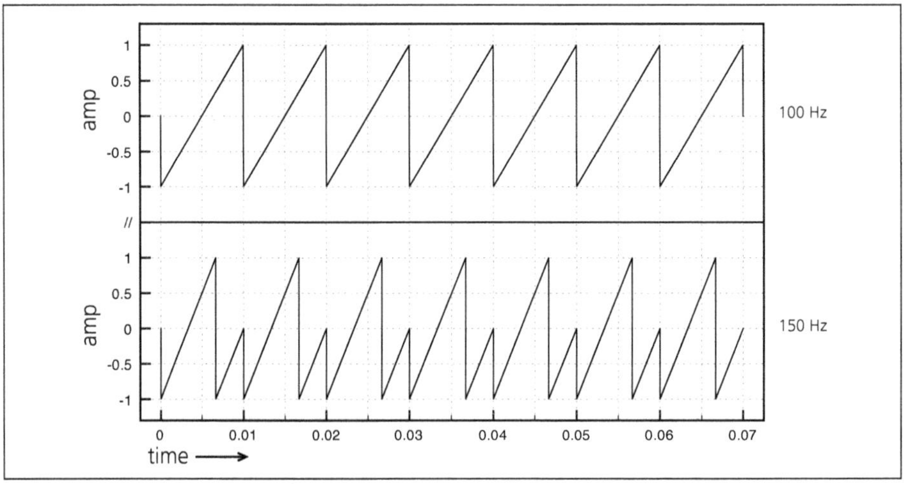

Fig. 3.20 Hard sync between a 100 Hz oscillator and a 150 Hz oscillator

VIDEO EXAMPLE 3D – *HARD SYNC* – PRESETS 11-17

In our synthesizer the sound produced by the generators passes through a classic ADSR envelope and then a lowpass filter that can be switched between second-order (with 12 dB of attenuation per octave) and fourth-order (with 24 dB per octave).

The cutoff frequency of this filter is derived from the sum of three parameters, each of which can be included or excluded at will:

1) a fixed frequency
2) key follow, which is a multiple of the frequency of the played note (if the multiple is equal to 0 the played note doesn't influence the filter)
3) the ADSR envelope, which is multiplied by a "depth" factor (when this factor is 0, the envelope doesn't affect the filter)

There is also a first-order highpass filter that can be set to a fixed frequency, which serves to attenuate the lowest components of the sound. This filter enables you to make sounds less dark or more "subtle" (depending on its setting), and can be very useful for avoiding clashes in the mix, where the sound of the synthesizer overlaps too much with other low sounds (bass, drums, etc.) Finally, the Q for the filter can be set to a fixed value, and gives, along with the other settings, more or less prominence to the components near the cutoff frequency of the filter.

In the video example you can find different examples of timbres made using this simple virtual synthesizer.

3.6 EQUATIONS FOR DIGITAL FILTERS

Now let's examine how the filters that we have talked about in the previous sections can be implemented using a digital system. Digital filters are divided into two categories: FIR (finite impulse response) filters, which operate using what is called *feedforward*, and IIR (infinite impulse response) filters, (called also "recursive filters") which operate using *feedback* coupled with feedforward.

Before defining the advantages and disadvantages of these filter types in more detail, here is what the two new terms mean: when referring to the input and output routings for a filter, you use the term **feedback** when one or more copies of the *output* signal are delayed, then multiplied by a coefficient, and finally combined with the ongoing input signal. The term **feedforward** is used when one or more copies of the *input* signal are delayed, then multiplied by a coefficient, and then combined with the continuing input signal. In the following section, we will examine how filters function, and what part feedback and feedforward play.

FIR filters (which use only feedforward) are characterized by their stability and the fact that they cannot be driven to oscillate, since they don't use a Q factor to produce resonance; they do, however, demand a routing architecture and calculations that are more complex than IIR filters.

IIR filters (which use feedback coupled with feedforward) can be very powerful filters. Although the calculations needed to implement them are simple, they can be subject to several undesirable effects such as *ringing*,[14] phase distortion, and inaccurate propagation of high frequencies and transients.

Each type of filter can be classified by its order. You will recall that the order of a filter corresponds to its capability for boosting or attenuating amplitudes within a frequency band, with more or less roll-off.

---

14 Recall that ringing is caused by resonance, which is caused by transients of a filtered sound remaining active after the point in time that the original sound would have finished its decay.

Until now, we have portrayed a filter as a kind of "black box" that can take an input signal and return it, transformed, as an output signal. Broadly speaking, we can consider a black-box digital filter to be a function that transforms one sequence of numbers into another sequence of numbers. But how are these numbers transformed, exactly? A digital filter carries out three simple operations on the samples that it receives: it multiplies them by given values (called coefficients), it delays them, and it sums them together. The "Technical Details" section that follows immediately will furnish additional information on this subject for you to consider.

TECHNICAL DETAILS – *THE NON-RECURSIVE, OR FIR, FILTER*

We will first describe the algorithm for a *non-recursive filter*, so-called because it needs only input samples to calculate its filtered output signal. We will later see the difference between this type of filter and *recursive filters*.

For each sample generated by a FIR filter, multiplier coefficients are applied to the current sample, as well as to a certain number of the previously processed samples. All of the rescaled samples are then summed together, and the resulting value becomes the new sample output by the filter (as shown in figure 3.21).

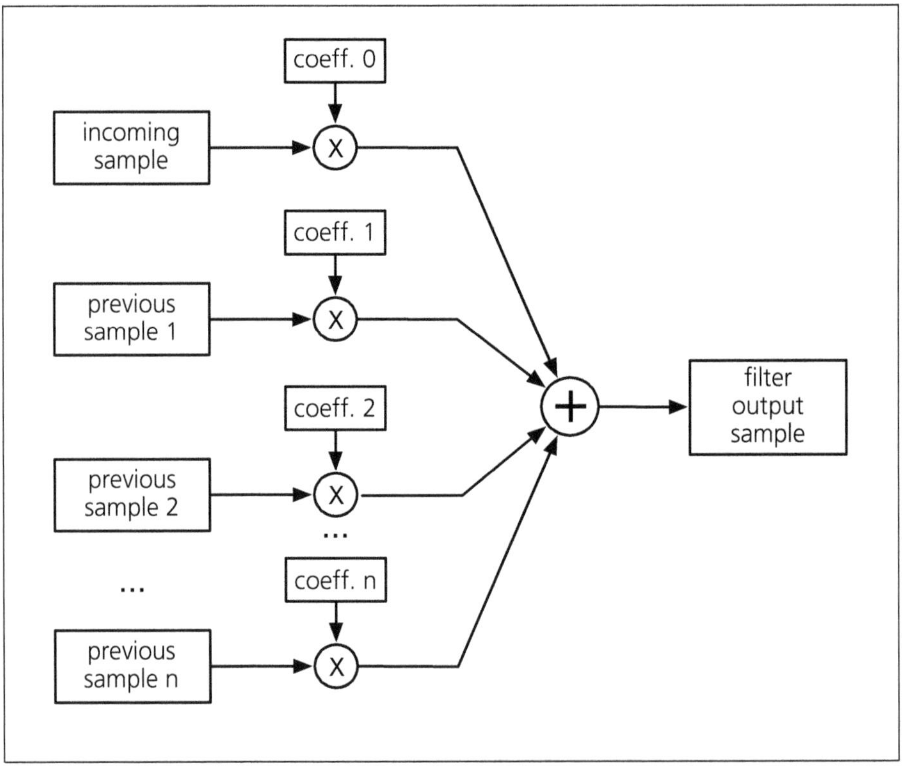

Fig. 3.21 A block diagram of the flow within a FIR filter

How many of the previous samples are taken into consideration? This depends on the order of the filter: a first-order filter will use the current input sample along with the immediately preceding sample, while a second-order filter will use the current sample plus *two* preceding samples. An interesting detail is that any filter of the same order (lowpass, highpass, bandpass, etc.) will use exactly the same algorithm to modify its input signal! The only difference is the coefficients that are used for the multiplication stage (which are contrasted in figure 3.22).

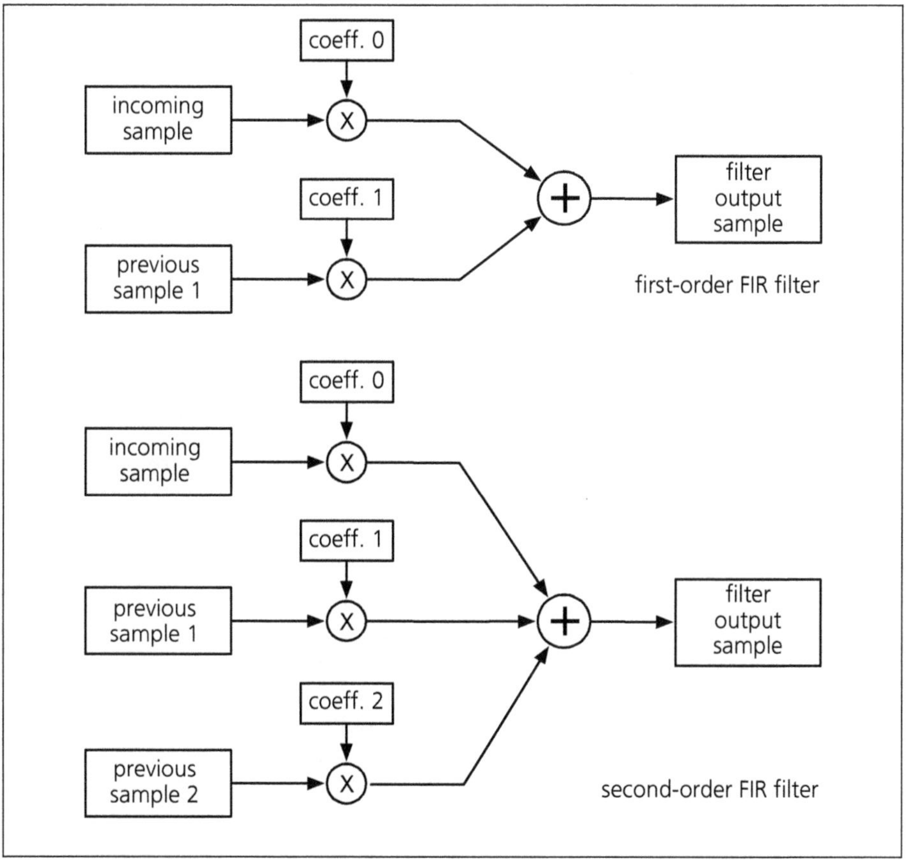

Fig. 3.22 The flow of first and second order FIR filters

We can now see exactly what defines a first-order filter – imagine a series of samples being input and a series of samples being output. Samples are output at the sampling rate, which means that at a rate of 44,100 Hz, for example, a sample is being produced every 1/44,100 of a second, or about every 0.023 milliseconds (a period that we will call the *processing cycle*). For every new sample input, the filter generates a new sample as part of its output signal. The filter needs the previous input sample (the sample that entered the filter during the previous processing cycle) in addition to the current input sample in order to perform its calculations; for this purpose, the sample from the previous processing cycle is stored into a dedicated memory cell, called a **delay line**.

Each time a new sample enters the filter, the "old" input sample is written into the memory cell for the delay line, replacing the one that had come before. A delay line might have more than one cell, of course, and in such a case it would be possible to have a delay of many samples (saving samples from more than one processing cycle). This multi-cell capability is needed when implementing higher order filters.

Returning to our first-order filter, the output sample is conventionally indicated by using the symbol **y(n)**, and the input sample is designated **x(n)**; this style of notation makes it easy to identify the preceding input sample as **x(n-1)**. The two coefficients that multiply the amplitude of the incoming sample and that of its predecessor are designated $\mathbf{a_0}$ and $\mathbf{a_1}$. With these symbols in mind, we can write out the following equation:

$$\mathbf{y(n) = a_0\, x(n) + a_1\, x(n-1)}$$

The equation can be translated as follows: the sample output by the filter, **y(n)**, is defined as the sum of its input sample **x(n)** multiplied by coefficient a_0 and the previous input sample **x(n-1)** multiplied by the coefficient a_1. The behavior of the filter (its cutoff frequency, and whether it is lowpass, highpass, or something else) will depend solely upon the values assigned to a_0 and a_1.

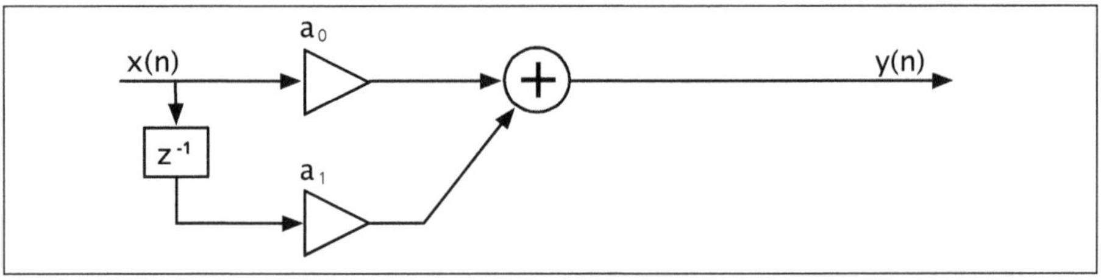

Fig. 3.23 A representation of a first-order digital FIR filter

In figure 3.23, we see a commonly used schematic representation for a digital filter. The symbol $\mathbf{z^{-1}}$ indicates the application of a single sample delay, and the triangular elements represent the multiplication of samples by the coefficient with which they are labeled. The calculation of these coefficients is not a simple thing, and is definitely not within the scope of this book. Fortunately, audio-oriented programming languages such as CSound and Max provide functions that enable their users to calculate filter coefficients in simple ways, using musically relevant quantities such as cutoff frequency, Q, etc. as their input parameters rather than obscure mathematical quantities.

Understanding how filters work can be extremely helpful when trying to follow the progress of a signal. This knowledge will also come in handy when learning about additional ways that filters can be utilized.

Returning to our equation, we assign a_0 and a_1 values of 1/2:

$$\mathbf{y(n) = 1/2\, x(n) + 1/2\, x(n-1)}$$

This equation yields a lowpass filter that has a cutoff frequency of 1/4 of the sampling rate. If the sampling rate is 44,100 Hz, for example, the cutoff frequency for this filter is 11,025 Hz.

VIDEO EXAMPLE 3E – PRESET 1
Two seconds of white noise and two seconds of filtered white noise (first order lowpass filter)

Since our example equation is a filter of the first order, the attenuation of the signal above the cutoff frequency, will be minor.
Making a slight modification, we assign the value of 1/2 to a_0, and change a_1 to be -1/2, as shown:

$$y(n) = 1/2\ x(n) - 1/2\ x(n-1)$$

Now we obtain a highpass filter, whose cutoff frequency is still 1/4 of the sampling rate.

VIDEO EXAMPLE 3E – PRESET 2
Two seconds of white noise and two seconds of filtered white noise (first order highpass filter)

As you can see from the previous equations, a simple relationship does not exist between the coefficient values and the cutoff frequency – the cutoff frequency depends upon the sampling rate. These example equations, for instance, would have different cutoff frequencies at different sampling rates. At a sampling rate of 96,000 Hz, for example, the cutoff would be 24,000 Hz, since 1/4 of 96,000 is 24,000. The art of digital filtering lies in discovering formulas that deliver filter coefficients that result in desirable frequency and resonance characteristics. At the end of this section, we will demonstrate one common series of formulas used to generate coefficients; if you want to learn more, we direct you to the texts listed in the bibliography.
Passing now to equations of the second order, we need not only to consider the input sample, but the two samples preceding it as well. The equation is as follows:

$$y(n) = a_0\ x(n) + a_1\ x(n-1) + a_2\ x(n-2)$$

Here, as before, x(n) is the input sample, x(n-1) is the previous input sample, and x(n-2) is the sample that preceded x(n-1). A block diagram for this equation is shown in figure 3.24.

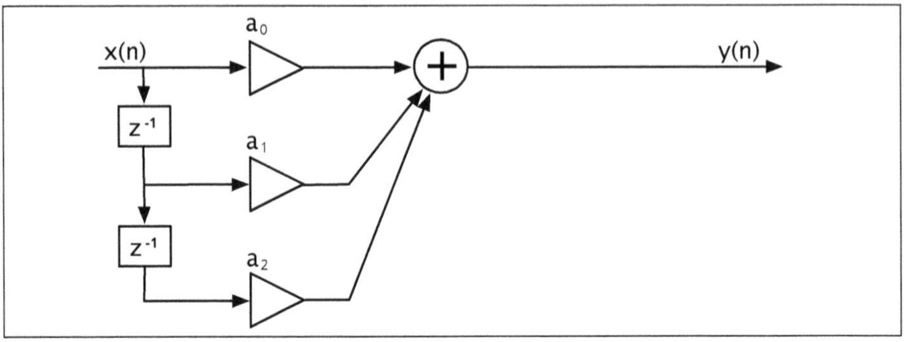

Fig. 3.24 The block diagram for a second-order FIR filter

If we assign the value 1/2 to a_0, 0 to a_1, and -1/2 to a_2, we obtain this equation:

y(n) = 1/2 x(n) - 1/2 x(n-2)

This equation produces a passband filter whose center frequency is 1/4 of the sampling rate; note that the x(n-1) term disappears in this case, because its coefficient is 0.

VIDEO EXAMPLE 3E – PRESET 3
Two seconds of white noise and two seconds of filtered white noise (second order bandpass filter)

The generic operation that we are using – the multiplication of one or more of the input samples of a signal by as many coefficients, and then summing the results – is called *convolution*, and it takes on important roles in many different areas of sound synthesis and signal processing. We will speak more of it in Chapter 12.

TECHNICAL DETAILS – RECURSIVE, OR IIR, FILTERS

All of the equations that we have seen up to this point represent the so-called "non-recursive" filters, which in practice are filters that use input samples alone as input to their calculations.
There is another class of filters, widely used in subtractive synthesis, which are called "recursive filters", and which use saved samples from the *output signal* to calculate the filtered signal in addition to saved input samples. A second-order recursive filter will use its two preceding output samples y(n-1) and y(n-2) in addition to the input samples x(n), x(n-1), and x(n-2), to calculate its current output sample y(n). Such a filter is called *recursive*, because results that have already been calculated and output are reused in the calculation of succeeding results. The symbols a_0, a_1, and a_2 continue to represent the input coefficients,

and now a new set of coefficients, b_1 and b_2, are defined for the newly incorporated output samples. Using these definitions, the equation for a recursive second-order filter is as follows:

$$\mathbf{y(n) = a_0\, x(n) + a_1\, x(n\text{-}1) + a_2\, x(n\text{-}2) - b_1\, y(n\text{-}1) - b_2\, y(n\text{-}2)}$$

You see that while the values derived from the input samples are summed together in this equation, the values derived from output samples are *subtracted*. (Of course, a negative coefficient will change the sign!) See figure 3.25 for the block diagram that accompanies this equation. All of the filters that we discussed in Sections 3.2 and 3.3 are second-order recursive filters, and use this equation.

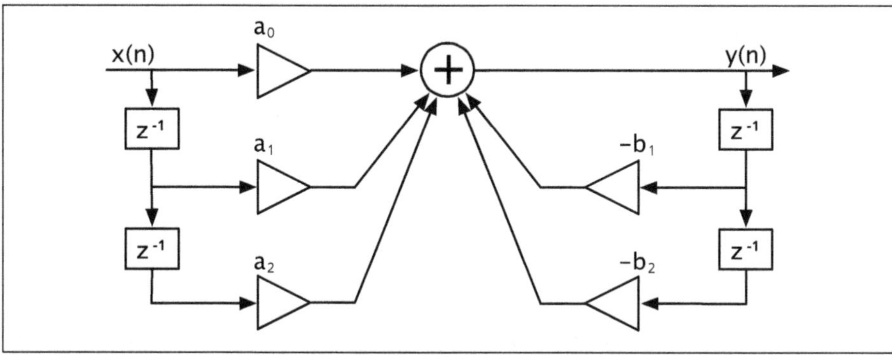

Fig. 3.25 A block diagram for a second-order digital IIR filter

As we already mentioned, calculating the coefficients of this equation in order to obtain a filter with a specific cutoff frequency is not a simple task. We will now give an example of this process, but only to give an idea of the degree of complexity involved in the operation. Let's examine the formulas used to calculate the equation to use for a Butterworth lowpass filter, given some desired cutoff frequency.
If we let $\mathbf{f_s}$ represent the sampling rate and $\mathbf{f_c}$ the cutoff frequency that interests us, we first calculate an intermediate variable **C** in the following way:

$$\mathbf{C} = \frac{1}{\tan\left(\pi \frac{f_c}{f_s}\right)}$$

Using this intermediate variable **C**, we can then calculate the 5 coefficients:

$$a_0 = \frac{1}{1 + \sqrt{2}\,C + C^2}$$

$$a_1 = 2a_0$$

$$a_2 = a_0$$

$$b_1 = 2a_0\left(1 - C^2\right)$$

$$b_2 = a_0\left(1 - \sqrt{2}\,C + C^2\right)$$

If, for example, we would like to create a Butterworth filter that has a cutoff frequency of 1,000 Hz when running at a sampling rate of 44,100 Hz, we would have:

$$\mathbf{C} = \frac{1}{\tan\left(\pi \frac{1000}{44100}\right)} = \mathbf{14.014}$$

$$\mathbf{a_0} = \frac{1}{1 + \sqrt{2}\,C + C^2} = \mathbf{0.0046}$$

$$\mathbf{a_1 = 2a_0 = 0.0092}$$

$$\mathbf{a_2 = a_0 = 0.0046}$$

$$\mathbf{b_1} = 2a_0\left(1 - C^2\right) = \mathbf{-1.7991}$$

$$\mathbf{b_2} = a_0\left(1 - \sqrt{2}\,C + C^2\right) = \mathbf{0.8175}$$

The equation that uses these coefficients values (paying careful attention to the signs of coefficients $\mathbf{b_1}$ and $\mathbf{b_2}$) is therefore:

y(n) = 0.0046 x(n) + 0.0092 x(n-1) + 0.0046 x(n-2) + 1.7791 y(n-1) - 0.8175 y(n-2)

As we have already seen, in programming languages for computer music such as CSound or Max, there are pre-built modules to carry out these calculations for you; these tools can parameterize equations such as this for all cutoff frequencies, liberating us from the toil of calculating the 5 coefficients every time that we need a new cutoff frequency.

TESTING – *QUESTIONS WITH SHORT ANSWERS (30 words maximum)*

7) Why is Q useful as a parameter for bandpass and bandreject filters?

8) In first-order lowpass filters, how attenuated are the frequencies an octave above the cutoff frequency?

9) In second-order highpass filters, how attenuated are the frequencies an octave below the cutoff frequency?

10) Why connect filters in series?

11) Why is it important to consider a filter's transition zone, and what is the difference between an ideal filter and a digital filter with regard to attenuation at the cutoff frequency?

3.7 FILTERS CONNECTED IN PARALLEL, AND GRAPHIC EQUALIZATION

It is both possible and extremely useful to use filters to modify the spectra of more than one frequency band in a signal. One way to do this is to connect additional **filters in parallel**: to simultaneously feed a single input signal to multiple filters, afterwards mixing their outputs into a single output signal.
The goal of this operation is to create a complex spectral envelope[15] with multiple peaks associated and multiple corresponding frequency bands.

VIDEO EXAMPLE 3E – *PARALLEL FILTERS* – PRESETS 4-7

The spectrum output by a bank of filters routed in parallel is the same as the sum of the spectra from the individual filters, unlike the spectrum output by filters routed in series, which equals the product of the individual spectra.[16]
Figure 3.26 shows an example of connecting filters in series, as well as one of connecting filters in parallel.

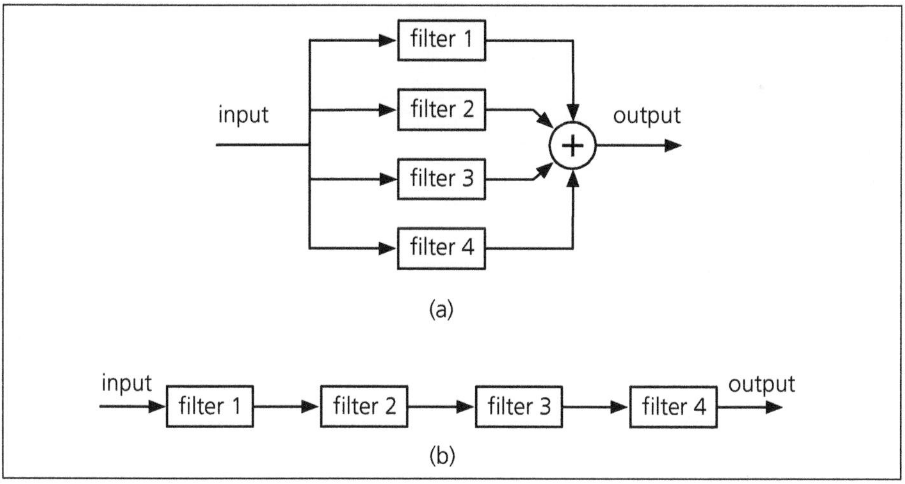

Fig. 3.26 Routing filters (a) in parallel and (b), in series

In this and in the next section, we will examine practical applications in which we can use filters connected both in series and in parallel. As we have seen in preceding sections, it is possible to dynamically shape a sound by varying a

[15] For the definition of spectral envelope, see Section 2.1T, which was dedicated to harmonic and non-harmonic spectra.
[16] We will take up spectral multiplication in more detail in Chapter 12.

center frequency and/or the width of its passband, by applying an amplitude envelope, and by using other techniques. Interactions between multiple sound shaping techniques can be tied to filters routed in parallel to construct interesting dynamic timbres. To demonstrate this, we will develop a progressive series of examples in which we enhance the sounds produced, step-by-step, by adding modules to the algorithm.
We will begin the exercise with a single white noise generator and 4 bandpass filters routed in parallel. Each filter will have a fixed center frequency; the four values will be 40, 80, 120, and 160 Hz. The white noise generator will provide sound events every 0.3 seconds (as the input signal for the 4 filters) that have brief attacks and decays. The signals produced by the 4 filters will then be combined by adding them together, and the result will be sent on as the output signal.

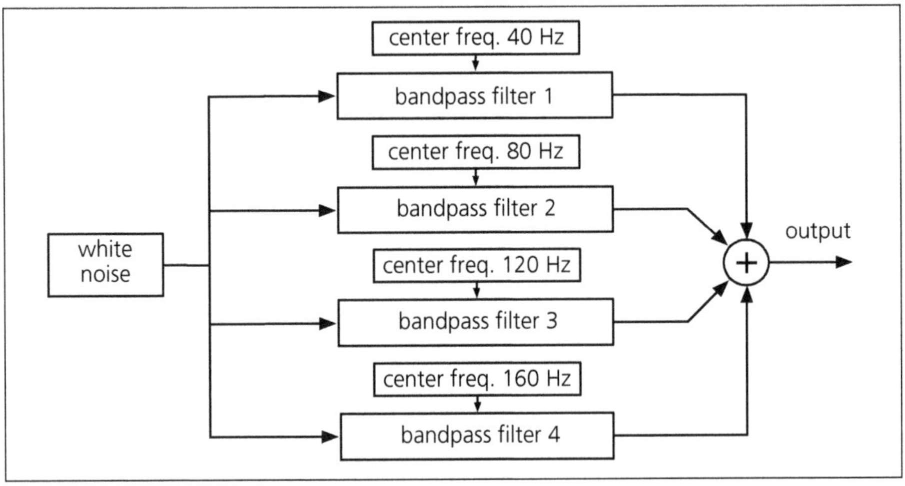

Fig. 3.27 A schematic diagram for the algorithm with 4 parallel filters

We can imagine that one way to make this generator emit sound would be to press a MIDI key[17] connected to the virtual synthesizer. In this particular case, given the unpitched white noise source and the fixed center frequencies of the filters, it would make sense for every key to produce the same sound. As a result, the only way to make output sounds differ, for this first scenario, would be to sound a note with more or less amplitude by pressing more lightly or more firmly on the key. This is what you hear in Video Example 3F, preset 1; in the last part of the example, listen for the sound produced by pressing more firmly on a key.

VIDEO EXAMPLE 3F – PRESET 1
Short sounds with a fixed envelope

[17] For more on the MIDI protocol, see Chapter 9.

At this point in the example, the sounds being produced are somewhat mechanical and are all similar to each other. To begin making them more interesting, we will try sliding the 4 center frequencies away from a single starting frequency. The four glissandi will begin from a single frequency, spreading apart to arrive at 4 final center frequencies (40 Hz for filter 1, 80 for filter 2, 120 for filter 3, and 160 for filter 4). Using this new approach, the keys on the keyboard can now be used meaningfully: each key will start a glissando at a different frequency – the C7 key, for example, will start all 4 glissandi from 4,186.01 Hz (C7) and then proceed as follows:

1) slide the center frequency of the sound to be output by filter 1 from 4,186.01 Hz to 40 Hz
2) slide the center frequency of the sound to be output by filter 2 from 4,186.01 Hz to 80 Hz
3) slide the center frequency of the sound to be output by filter 3 from 4,186.01 Hz to 120 Hz
4) slide the center frequency of the sound to be output by filter 4 from 4,186.01 Hz to 160 Hz

Pressing the Eb3 key (311.12 Hz), on the other hand, will result in the following 4 glissandi:

1) slide the center frequency of the sound to be output by filter 1 from 311.12 Hz to 40 Hz
2) slide the center frequency of the sound to be output by filter 2 from 311.12 Hz to 80 Hz
3) slide the center frequency of the sound to be output by filter 3 from 311.12 Hz to 120 Hz
4) slide the center frequency of the sound to be output by filter 4 from 311.12 Hz to 160 Hz

VIDEO EXAMPLE 3F – PRESET 2
More short sounds, now using an amplitude envelope and single frequency start, with departure frequencies of 4,186.01 and 311.12 Hz

Attempting to make more natural sounds, we will now implement a few more changes. First, we will vary the duration of the glissandi, using longer times for notes starting at higher frequencies. An event triggered by the F7 key (5,587.65 Hz), for example, will have slower glissandi than one triggered by F#1 (92.5 Hz). In addition to this, we will introduce an envelope for the bandwidth of the filters that will narrow the passband as the center frequency approaches its target. Finally, we will modify the evolution of the amplitude envelope, prolonging the sustain phase when the center frequency glissando is slower.

VIDEO EXAMPLE 3F – PRESET 3
More short sounds, now with time-coherent envelopes for amplitude, center frequency, and width of passband

In the last video example, Preset 3, all of the durations, including the sustains in the amplitude envelopes and the time interval used for narrowing the filter bandwidths, are tied to the durations of the center frequency glissandi, which are fixed. Because of this, the parameters move cohesively as they change; all modifications are globally coherent. Time-coherent changes such as this can be effective at creating impact or reinforcing a specific effect, but on the other hand, envelopes whose durations change can create variety. Both approaches are useful.

Returning to the example, we might want to have longer sounds while still maintaining coherence between the three envelopes. We can easily accomplish this by multiplying all of them – the amplitude sustain, the gliss time for the center frequencies, and the time interval for narrowing the bandwidth – by a single value.

VIDEO EXAMPLE 3F – PRESET 4
Medium-length sounds using time-coherent envelopes for amplitude, center frequency, and width of passband

At this point, we will experiment by adding a series of harmonic sounds (with fixed fundamentals) to the white noise that feeds the 4 filters. These harmonic sounds will not depend upon the key pressed for their pitches, and will differ slightly amongst themselves in order to produce beats.[18] The resulting sound, composed of both harmonic and non-harmonic parts, will still be filtered in the same way as Preset 3.

VIDEO EXAMPLE 3F – PRESET 5
Filters applied to a complex sound formed by a series of harmonic sounds and white noise

[18] For the record, the waveform used is an impulse, and the fundamental frequencies are 69, 69.2, 69.4, 70, 70.3, 70.5, 70.8, and 71 Hz.

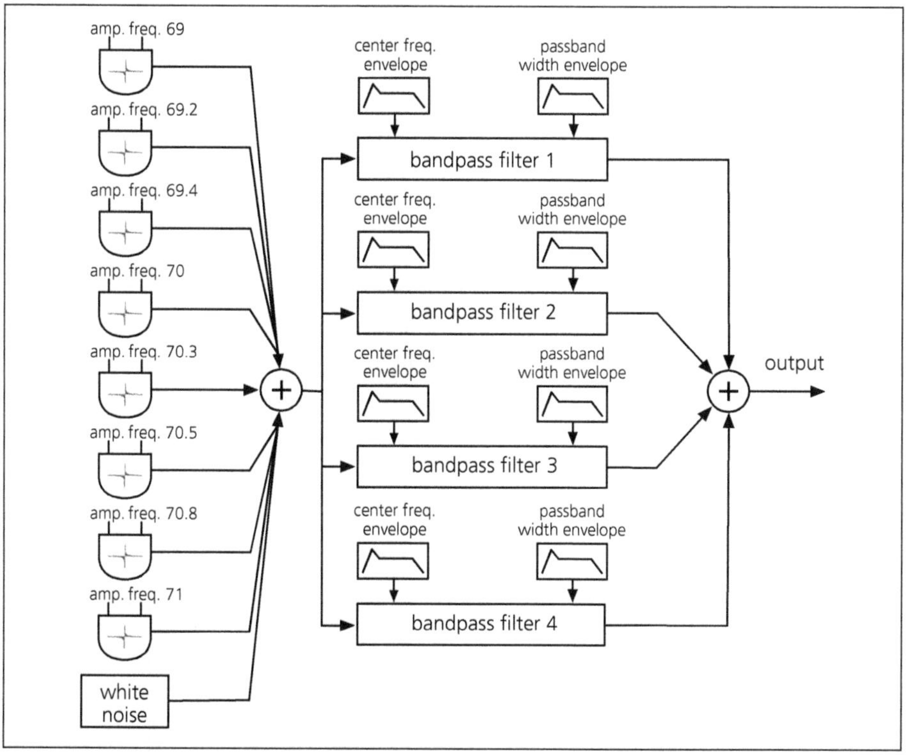

Fig. 3.28 A schematic representation of the algorithm that filters white noise mixed with harmonic sounds

Another technique for developing interesting sounds is to apply dynamic filters to complex sound sources which are recordings of musical instruments. Using an algorithm similar to that in Preset 3, this example simply replaces the white noise of Preset 3 with an orchestral sample. Listen to the sound of the filtered strings.

VIDEO EXAMPLE 3F – PRESET 6
Filters applied to a recorded sound sample

We'll now try a mechanism for decorrelating the durations of the envelopes attached to various parameters. For this example, we will create two separate filter banks. In the first bank, noise will be filtered in parallel by 20 bandpass filters, all set to have very narrow overlapping passbands and fixed center frequencies. These frequencies are organized into 5 grouped clusters, their spectral peaks resembling formants. The frequencies found in these 5 clusters are:

1st group: 308, 309 Hz
2nd group: 400, 401, 402 Hz

3rd group: 897, 898, 900, 902, 903 Hz
4th group: 1498, 1498.5, 1500, 1501.5, 1502 Hz
5th group: 2996, 2998, 3000, 3002, 3004 Hz

After being passed through these filters, the 20 sounds will be filtered again by 20 lowpass filters with envelopes applied to their cutoff frequencies, and after this, by 20 highpass filters with envelopes applied to their cutoff frequencies (which are not correlated time-wise with those of the lowpass filters). The bandpass, lowpass, and highpass filters are routed in series: the output of each of the 20 bandpass filters is connected to the input of one of the lowpass filters, and each lowpass output then enters a corresponding highpass filter. Figure 3.29 shows how this first filter bank is constructed.

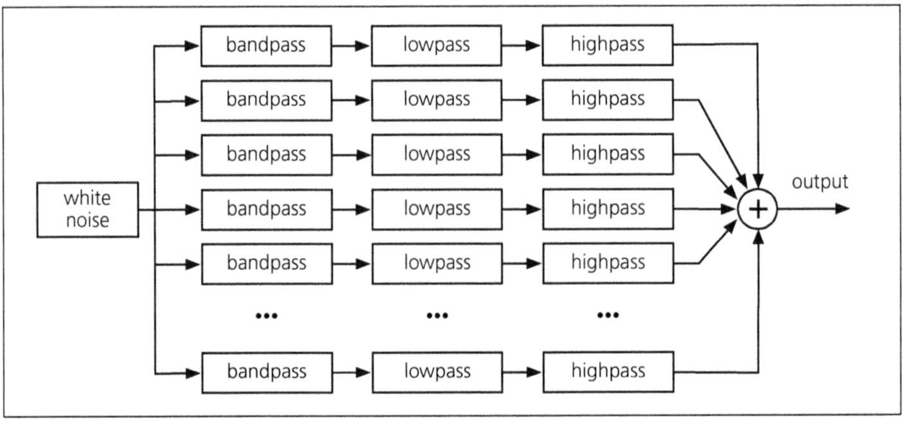

Fig. 3.29 The first filter bank for Preset 7 of Video Example 3F

The bandwidth of all of these filters, initially narrow, is controlled by an envelope that will keep the width of the band stable (somewhere between 2 and 8 Hz) for 14 seconds, after which the width will increase to 200 Hz, which will reveal the non-harmonic nature of the source sound. Finally, the envelope will return to the original, narrower, bandwidths.

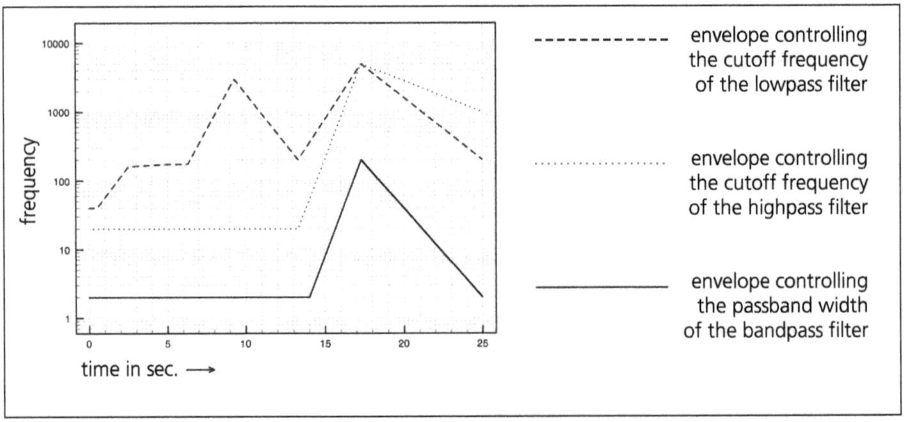

Fig. 3.30 Parameter envelopes for Preset 7 of Video Example 3F

The second filter bank will be comprised of more bandpass filters, and will take as its input the same white noise used by the first filter bank. Unlike the previously described filters, however, the bandpass filters in this second bank will not have fixed center frequencies, but rather, center frequencies that slide continuously. The envelope that controls the bandwidth of these filters will be correlated in time with those of the first bank. And finally, the signal output by these bandpass filters will be routed to as many lowpass filters.

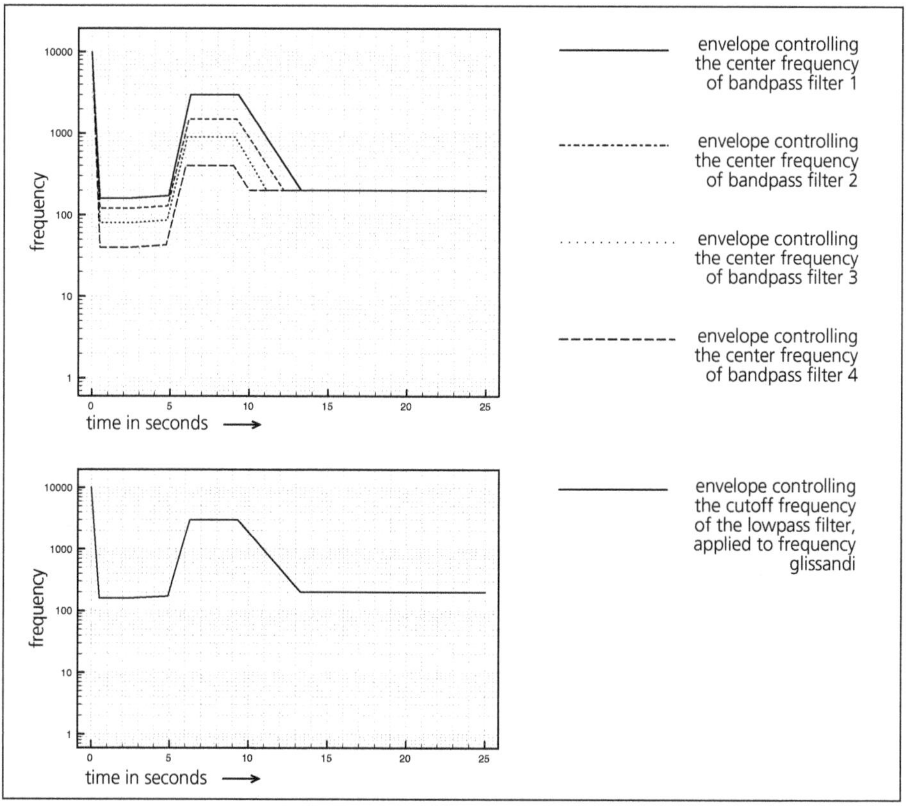

Fig. 3.31 Filter frequency envelopes for Preset 7 of Video Example 3F

VIDEO EXAMPLE 3F – PRESET 7
Filters in series and in parallel with uncorrelated time parameters

GRAPHIC EQUALIZATION

One of the most important configurations for using filters in parallel, although beyond what we typically call subtractive synthesis, is what is commonly called a **graphic equalizer**.

A graphic equalizer is a filter bank composed of bandpass filters that are routed in parallel and that have center frequencies that are separated by a repeated regular interval, such as an octave. Each filter has a constant Q and its own immutable center frequency. Only the *gain* of every band, the amplitude that every band contributes to the overall signal, can be changed. The passbands for adjacent filters overlap in a way that leaves no *empty zones* in the output spectrum.

Graphic equalizers can have a few bands, or many, and this choice determines the number of filters used (which is usually 10, 20, or 30). A graphic equalizer allows independent attenuation or boost to be applied to every frequency band, which enables shaping the overall sound by modifying its spectrum.

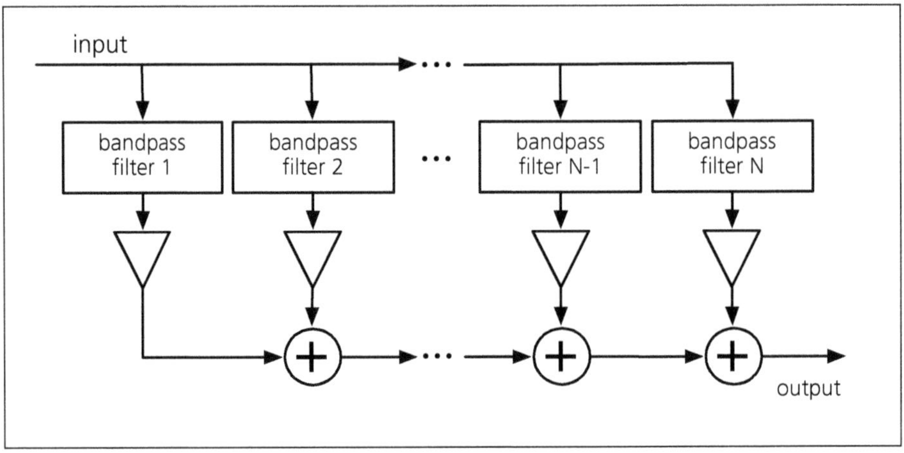

Fig. 3.32 Filters in parallel

In figure 3.32, we see a schematic representation of a graphic equalizer. The triangular elements represent the gain controls for each filter. The filters are laid out in parallel, exactly like those that were shown in figure 3.27, although the illustration technique used in the diagram is different.

The spectrum of audible frequencies in a graphic equalizer is usually divided into 10, 20, or 30 bands. The Q for the equalizer's filters are made to correspond to an octave (in which case there are 10 bands), a half-octave (which results in 20 bands), or a third of an octave (producing 30 bands, and the most accurate control over the spectral envelope). It should be noted that the majority of commercial equalizers do not have a perfectly constant Q; typically, some frequencies are slightly corrected.
The center frequencies for a 30 band graphic equalizer (using 1/3 octave bands) are generally set at 25, 31, 40, 50, 63, 80, 100, 125, 160, 200, 250, 315, 400, 500, 630, 800, 1000, 1200, 1600, 2000, 2500, 3200, 4000, 5000, 6300, 8000, 10000, 12000, 16000, and 20000 Hz. Note that the exact interval of a third of an octave below 1,000 Hz would place the band below at 793.7 Hz, but equalizers commonly correct this to 800 Hz; corrections like this explain how this series was developed.

In the same way, the standard frequencies for a 20 band graphic equalizer (using half-octave bands) are 31, 44, 63, 87, 125, 175, 250, 350, 500, 700, 1000, 1400, 2000, 2800, 4000, 5600, 8000, 11000, 16000, and 20000 Hz. Finally, the frequencies for a 10 band equalizer (using octave bands) are 31, 63, 125, 250, 500, 1000, 2000, 4000, 8000, and 16000 Hz.

VIDEO EXAMPLE 3G – *PRESET 8* – GRAPHIC EQUALIZERS

3.8 OTHER APPLICATIONS OF PARALLEL FILTERS: PARAMETRIC EQ AND SHELVING FILTERS

SHELVING FILTERS

Shelving filters, very commonly found in mixers as internal filters for equalization, are named after the pre-determined parts of the audible spectrum that they control. They are as follows:

> The **high shelving filter** attenuates or boosts high frequencies
> The **low shelving filter** attenuates or boosts low frequencies
> The **peak/notch filter** attenuates or boosts intermediate frequencies

It is very important to remember that, unlike lowpass and highpass filters, the names of the filters ("high" and "low") do not refer to the frequencies that are passed unaltered, but rather to the frequencies whose amplitude is altered.

Let's consider a high shelving filter first (as shown in figure 3.33). All of the frequencies above a certain threshold (the **shelf point**) are subjected to an attenuation (a **cut**), or else to an increase in amplitude (a **boost**). When using a high shelving filter to attenuate components above some frequency, you shouldn't think of the effect as being like a low pass filter. It is substantially different: when using a high shelving filter, all of the frequencies above the shelf point are attenuated equally by some adjustable amount (12 dB, for example, or some other such value), while in a lowpass filter, attenuation increases as frequency moves above and away from the cutoff frequency. In addition, the attenuation produced by a lowpass filter is predetermined by the order of the filter (6 dB for a first-order filter, 12 dB for a second-order filter, etc.), unlike a shelving filter, in which the amount is adjustable.[19]

[19] The term *shelf*, clearly, refers to the shape of the response curve for shelving filters: the boosted or attenuated frequency band is stepped up or down, resulting in flat, shelf-like, response curves.

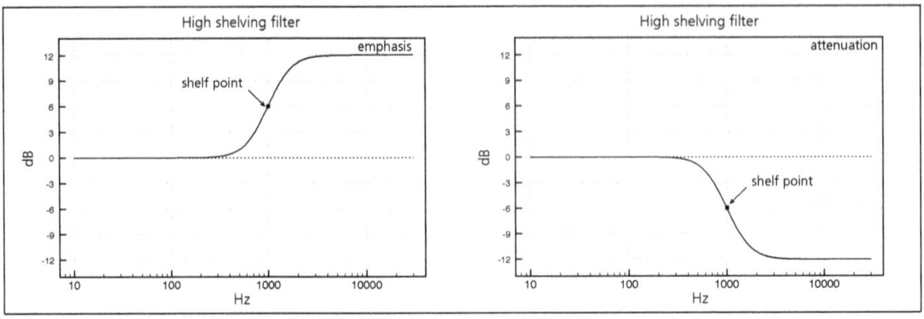

Fig. 3.33 Boost and attenuation of high frequencies using a high shelving filter

A similar description applies to low shelving filters (as seen in figure 3.34): the frequencies that lie under the threshold of a filter are subject to attenuation or boost, applied equally across all of the frequencies below the shelf point. (The attenuation applied by a highpass filter, in contrast, differs for every frequency under the cutoff frequency.)

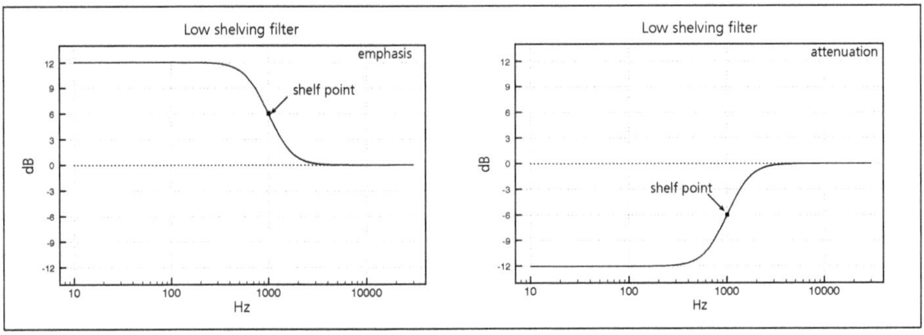

Fig. 3.34 Boost and attenuation of lower frequencies using a low shelving filter

Peak/notch filters have similarities to bandpass and bandreject filters, since both can apply a variable amount of boost or attenuation to a variably wide band of the spectrum. Unlike bandpass filters, however, peak/notch filters leave the frequencies outside of the target region unchanged. (See figure 3.35.)

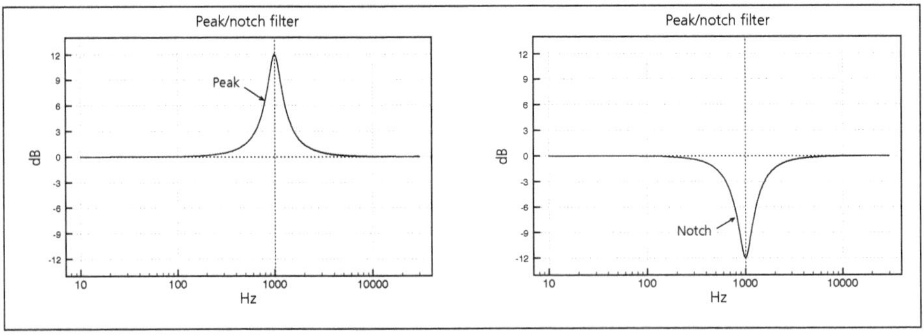

Fig. 3.35 Boost and attenuation of frequencies around 1,000 Hz using peak/ notch filters

Because shelving filters operate strictly on user-defined frequency bands, leaving the remaining input signal spectrum intact, they are ideal for implementing the cascaded filters typical of parametric equalizers (which we will speak of shortly).

The parameters for shelving filters are:

> *cutoff frequency* (*center frequency* in the case of the peak/notch filter)
> *gain*, which determines how much boost or attenuation will be applied to the target frequency band
> **slope**, or roll-off, which is resembles Q, although it functions in a slightly different way

In the case of shelving filters, the transition between unfiltered and filtered frequencies is not sudden, but follows a smooth curve to the point at which the desired level of attenuation or boost is reached. The curve, defined by the slope parameter, controls the way that the response changes within the transition zone. You can see that the slope regulates the width of the band in which this transition happens: the greater the slope, the narrower the band, and the steeper the transition. The right combination of gain and slope can drive a filter into auto-oscillation (when both factors are sufficiently high), just as can happen in resonant filters when you raise the Q.

VIDEO EXAMPLE 3H – *SHELVING FILTERS*

PARAMETRIC EQUALIZATION

When using a **parametric equalizer**, you are typically working with a smaller number of frequency bands than you would be with a graphic equalizer, but controlling a larger number of *parameters* for each band. In addition to setting the amount of attenuation or boost for each band, you can also set its center frequency and its Q, thus determining the frequencies that will be affected. Because of this flexibility, a parametric equalizer doesn't subdivide the sonic spectrum into fixed bands like a graphic equalizer, but rather, it allows parametric variation: center frequency, gain, and the either the width of the band or Q can be changed. Another contrast between these two types of equalizers is that parametric equalizers contain filters that are routed in series, while the filters found in graphic equalizers are routed in parallel.

Many mixers contain parametric equalizers built from shelving filters: typically a low shelf filter for the low region, a high shelf filter for the high region, and a variable number of peak/notch filters for intermediate regions. A construct called a ***semi-parametric equalizer*** also exists, in which it is possible to vary only the gain and the center frequency, but this is typically only found in mixers that are not of professional grade.

Software that allows for programmatic control, such as Max, enables you to construct equalizers with as many bands as you like.

VIDEO EXAMPLE 3I – *PARAMETRIC EQUALIZERS*

3.9 OTHER SOURCES FOR SUBTRACTIVE SYNTHESIS: IMPULSES AND RESONANT BODIES

As we already mentioned in Section 3.3, the response time of a resonant filter is directly proportional to its Q: the higher the Q setting, the slower the response of the filter. In particular, the decay of a sound can suffer a distinct lengthening when filtered in a way that generates a resonant oscillation; this phenomenon is particularly evident in the presence of short sounds with broad spectra, such as percussive sounds. (Listen to Video Example 3B to review this phenomenon.)

When Q is set very high, attacks are also elongated. You can exploit this resonance effect to transform a bandpass filter into a sound generator by feeding it a source that consists of a **unitary impulse**: a signal consisting of a single sample at maximum amplitude, followed by zero-valued samples. This signal contains energy at all frequencies, including, by definition, the center frequency of the passband. Sending a unitary impulse to a filter that has a high enough Q setting will cause the filter to commence **resonance** at its center frequency. The duration of this resonance will depend upon the Q setting; the overall effect is to produce a damped sine wave with a percussive attack and exponential decay.

VIDEO EXAMPLE 3J – *FILTERED UNITARY IMPULSES* – PRESETS 1-2

Using resonance, it is possible to treat bandpass filters as though they were resonant bodies. We mentioned that the duration of a resonant response depends on the Q setting, and it turns out that the value of the Q factor is directly proportional to the number of oscillations to be produced. It follows that the duration of the resonance, given some fixed Q, will diminish as the center frequency rises.
Let's suppose that, given some Q, the resonance produced consists of around 100 oscillations. At a center frequency of 100 Hz, 100 oscillations take one second to occur, since the period of the waveform (the duration of one cycle) is 0.01 seconds. When the center frequency is raised to 1,000 Hz, however, the period drops to 0.001 seconds, causing the same 100 oscillations to last a mere tenth of a second.

A formula that can be used to approximate durations for such resonance (which is designated as D), given Q and a center frequency for a second-order Butterworth filter, is as follows:

$D = 2\,Q / F_C$

This formula calculates the amount of time that needs to elapse for the resonance to drop by 60 dB. For example, a Q of 50 and a center frequency of 100 Hz will yield a duration of 1 second according to the formula, since 50 * 2 / 100 is equal to 1. Likewise, a Q of 50 and a center frequency of 1,000 Hz, will yield a duration of 0.1 seconds.

Furthermore, by multiplying the Q by a factor of 2, we can obtain the number of oscillations completed. With a Q of 50, we have 100 oscillations, lasting a second at 100 Hz and a tenth of a second at 1,000 Hz. We emphasize, however, that although this is a useful rule-of-thumb, it is only an approximation.

If we know the center frequency for a second-order Butterworth filter and want to find how much Q is needed to produce a resonance of a given duration (D), we can approximate the number using the following formula:

$Q = 1 / 2\,F_C \cdot D$

Using N to indicate the number of oscillations, the following formulas are also valid:

$N = Q \cdot 2$ (for example, if Q is 50, the number of oscillations is 100)
$Q = N / 2$ (for example, if the number of oscillations is 100, then the Q is 50)

Note, however, that with other types of second-order filters, the relationship between Q and the durations of resonance events can be very different.

VIDEO EXAMPLE 3J – PRESET 3 – *RESONATING FILTERED UNITARY IMPULSES*

In figure 3.36, the original signal (a brief impulse) is visible at the top, while the bottom shows the same signal, now output by a bandpass filter. Notice that, besides being a pure sine wave, the output signal has a duration that is much longer than the original signal. Besides this, note the very evident exponential decay in the filtered signal, which is caused by the intrinsic properties of the bandpass filter.

The technique of impulse filtering was fully explored by Karlheinz Stockhausen in his electroacoustic pieces for *Gesang der Jünglinge* and *Kontakte*.

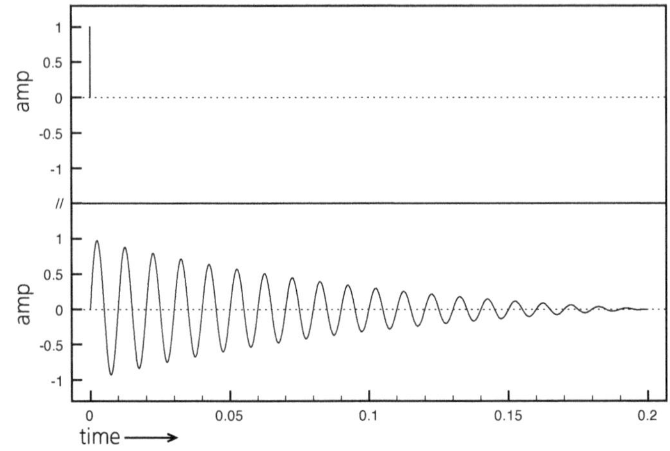

Fig. 3.36 An impulse (above) and a filtered impulse (below)

By sending unitary impulses to a bank of bandpass filters, it is possible to simulate resonant objects made of various materials, such as:

metal, consisting of medium-high frequencies exhibiting long resonance
wood, consisting of medium frequencies exhibiting short resonance
glass, consisting of high frequencies exhibiting medium resonance
skin, consisting of medium-low frequencies exhibiting medium-short resonance

The filterbank technique simulates the vibrations emitted by an object when it is struck, its "modes of vibration", producing multiple frequencies with assorted durations. The spectral distribution of such vibrations and their durations are like a fingerprint; they have a precise relationship to the form, the dimensions, and the material of the struck object.
The quantity of filters used, the amount of harmonicity, and the randomness of the distribution of frequencies and durations all contribute to a faithful simulation. For example, ten filters whose frequencies are randomly distributed between 200 and 2,000 Hz, and whose resonance durations vary between 1 and 10 seconds, can simulate a gong of medium size. Keeping the same frequency band, increasing the number of filters to 40 and reducing the durations of the resonances to a maximum of two seconds will produce a sound more similar to a pot lid struck with a metal tool.

Video Example 3K demonstrates parameter combinations that can be used to simulate various materials, both real and imaginary.

VIDEO EXAMPLE 3K – *RESONANT BODIES*

TECHNICAL DETAILS – *ANALYSIS OF THE BEHAVIOR OF A FILTER: IMPULSE RESPONSE AND FREQUENCY RESPONSE*

In the preceding sections we have outlined the behavior of different types of filters and how they can be effectively used with different kinds of sound sources. But how was this analysis done? To understand the *theoretical* behavior of a filter, it can be useful to analyze how it responds to a well-defined input signal *in practice*. To do this, we need to obtain the *impulse response* and the *frequency response* of the filter.

The **impulse response** is the signal that is output from a system that has been given an impulse as input. By "system" we mean in this case a processing block that, given a sequence of samples at its input, produces a different series of samples on its output. Let's imagine a system that consists of a bandpass filter, whose input signal is an impulse (a signal consisting of one solitary sample at maximum amplitude, as shown in the upper part of figure 3.36). Given that impulses have very wide spectra (the widest possible at a given sampling rate), they are perfect for testing how a system like our filter reacts. We see in the lower part of figure 3.36 the impulse response (in the time domain) of a bandpass filter.

We have not said much until now about the reason for the names IIR (*infinite impulse response*) and FIR (*finite impulse response*), which are given to recursive and non-recursive filters, respectively. In a recursive filter, the impulse response has an infinite duration, because the output signal of the filter, after being multiplied by coefficients as explained in Section 3.6, is re-input to the system, without ever decaying away (in theory) to zero. In a FIR filter, on the other hand, there is no such *feedback*, and so the response to an impulse will always have a finite duration. (The inevitable limits on precision that you encounter when working with digital representations of numbers, however, limit the impulse response of digital IIR filters as well.)

In figure 3.37a, we see an impulse response and two graphs that display its spectrum, beginning with a graph of the amplitude of its components in figure 3.37b, and followed by a graph of the relative phases of the same components in figure 3.37c. Figure 3.37b displays the response curve that amplitude follows at different frequencies and is usually (incorrectly) called the "**frequency response** of a filter". This kind of graph is a summary for a range of frequencies, and clearly shows which frequencies the filter attenuates, which it boosts, and which remain unchanged; it will distinguish, for example, a lowpass from a highpass filter.

Common usage notwithstanding, "frequency response" ought to include not only the amplitude response in relation to frequency, as in figure 3.37b, but also information regarding phase changes across the frequency range, as shown in 3.37c. The graph in figure 3.37b, by itself, actually shows only the *amplitude response* of the filter. Besides boosting or attenuating various frequencies, a filter can and will also delay the phase of a signal by varying amounts at different frequencies, and the modifications to phase are not uniformly tied to frequency in a simple way. The phase alterations produced by filtering are displayed for all of the frequencies in figure 3.37c; such a graph is called the *phase response* of a filter, and complements the amplitude response graph.

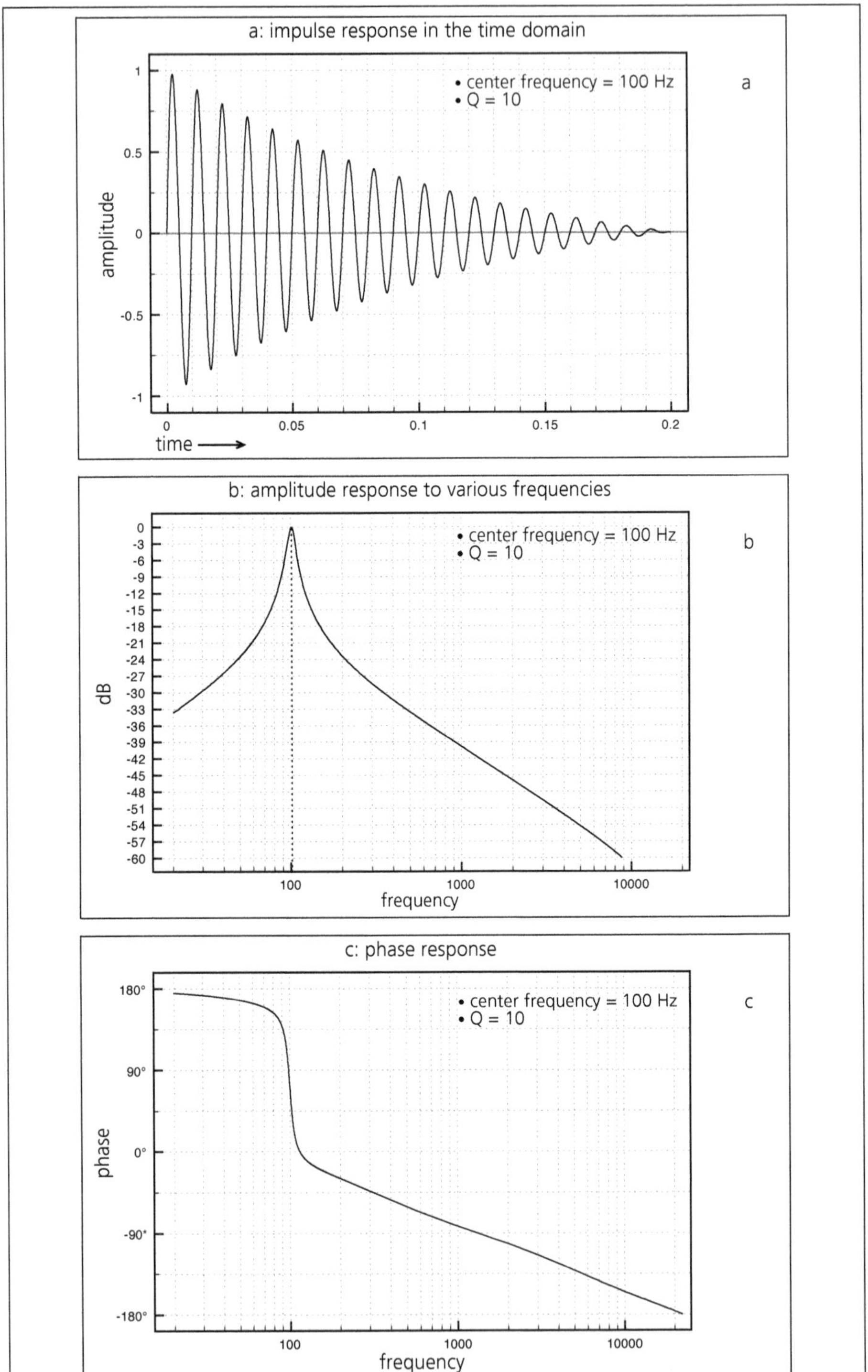

Fig. 3.37 The impulse response in the time domain (a), the amplitude response relative to various frequencies (b), and the phase response (c) of a filter

It is important to underline the fact that shifting phases imply a delay. The introduction of a delay with respect to the input signal is a property common to all filters, and it can be used musically in many ways. We will see in Chapter 6 how to exploit phase shift to implement a *phaser* effect, as well as how to produce fractional delays (which are small delays in the time that elapses between two samples). Another way to obtain the frequency response of a filter is to use, in place of an impulse input signal, a sine wave glissando that covers all of the target frequencies at a constant amplitude. This kind of glissando is called a **sweep**. The amplitude and the phase shifts found in the output signal can be measured, and the corresponding graphs represent the frequency response of the filter.

VIDEO EXAMPLE 3L – *A FILTERED SWEEP AND RELATED GRAPHS OF AMPLITUDE RESPONSE*

TESTING – LISTENING AND ANALYSIS

In Example Sound AA3.1, which parameters are acting on the filter? Which type of filter can be used to control such variations?

In Example Sound AA3.2, which parameters are acting on the filter? Which type of filter can be used to control such variations?

In Example Sound AA3.3, which parameters are acting on the filter? Which type of filter can be used to control such variations?

FUNDAMENTAL CONCEPTS

1) Subtractive synthesis embodies the idea that new sounds can be created by selectively reducing some of the frequency components of other, more complex, sounds through the use of filters.

2) Filters can be used to modify the amplitudes of some of the frequencies present in a complex sound for the purpose of modifying its spectrum and obtaining a different output sound.

3) The sound to be modified becomes the input signal for a filter.

4) The filters most commonly used for this purpose are:
   - lowpass filters
   - highpass filters

- bandpass filters
- bandreject filters
- high shelving filters
- low shelving filters
- peak/notch shelving filters

5) A lowpass filter lets all frequencies below its cutoff frequency pass virtually unaltered, while it attenuates (at an increasing rate which is dependent on the order of the filter) those frequencies above the cutoff frequency.

6) A highpass filter lets all frequencies above its cutoff frequency pass virtually unaltered, while it attenuates (at an increasing rate which is dependent on the order of the filter) those frequencies below the cutoff frequency.

7) Bandpass and bandreject filters, respectively, boost or attenuate the part of the spectrum that falls within a certain band of frequencies. The high and low limits of this band determine its width and center frequency. Subtracting the lower limit from the upper limit, we obtain the bandwidth of the filter, while the geometric mean of the two limits equals its center frequency. The steepness of the attenuation curve depends upon the order of the filter.

8) Using a high shelving filter (alternately, a low shelving filter) all of the frequencies above (below) the shelf point are equally attenuated or boosted (for example, by 12 dB), in contrast to lowpass and highpass filters, which move away from their cutoff frequencies with growing attenuation (6 dB per octave for a first-order filter, 12 dB for a second-order filter, and so on). These characteristics, of course, are for ideal filters; actual digital filters have a transition zone around their cutoff frequencies that is not reflected in the theory.

9) Both peak/notch filters and bandpass/bandreject filters attenuate or boost a region of the spectrum. The difference between these filters is that peak/notch filters leave the frequencies outside of the filtered region unaltered.

10) The Q factor, used to define the bandwidth of a filter as a function of center frequency, is equal to the center frequency / bandwidth.

11) In general, when working in the studio, filters can be used with many kinds of sound:
    - sounds produced by noise generators, by banks of oscillators, or by other signal generators and synthesis algorithms
    - audio files and samples
    - live sounds, played in realtime, such as the sounds of a oboe captured by a microphone
    - impulses

12) Filters of different orders can be constructed by connecting filters in series. Parametric equalizers can be built by routing filters in series, while graphic equalizers can be built by routing filters in parallel.

GLOSSARY

Amplitude response
See *frequency response*

Attenuation curve (Roll-off)
The slope of attenuation in frequencies outside the bandwidth of a filter.

Bandpass filter
A filter that attenuates all of the frequencies above and below a certain frequency band, called the passband. The upper and lower cutoff frequencies of the passband have amplitude values of -3 dB.

Bandwidth
The difference between an upper cutoff frequency and a lower cutoff frequency, expressed in hertz.

Bandreject filter
A filter that attenuates all of the frequencies within a certain frequency band.

Boost
An increase in the amplitude of a signal.

Butterworth filter
A second-order IIR filter characterized by flatness in the passband and reasonably good accuracy.

Center frequency
The center frequency of a filter has different meanings, according to the filter being described: it is the only frequency that is not attenuated in a bandpass filter, the frequency that is maximally attenuated in a notch or bandreject filter, and the frequency that is boosted the most in a peak filter. The center frequency can be derived from low and high cutoff frequencies by calculating their geometric mean.

Cut
A reduction in the amplitude of a signal.

Cutoff frequency
The frequency in a filter above which (or below which) attenuation occurs. Cutoff frequencies are found in pairs in bandpass, bandreject, and peak/notch filters.

Feedback
A technique that stores system output as it is produced so that it can be fed back as input to the same system.

Feedforward
A technique that stores system input so that it can be re-used by being combined with new input.

Filter
A device for modifying the amplitudes and/or phases of the frequencies present in its input signal.

Filter coefficients
Constants used by a digital filter, which multiply the input sample values (and sometimes the stored output values). Coefficients determine the type of a filter (whether it is lowpass, highpass, bandpass, etc.), as well as other properties.

Filter parameters
Values that define the sonic properties of a filter, such as its cutoff frequency, center frequency, Q, etc. Such parameters are defined by the coefficients used to mathematically model the filter.

Filtered pseudo-random sample generator
A pseudo-random sample generator whose output signal is sent to a lowpass filter, which "rounds off" the transitions between one sample value and the next.

Filters in parallel
Connections between filters in which the same input signal is simultaneously sent to multiple filters, whose outputs are then mixed together to form the output signal.

Filters in series
Connections between filters in which the output signal from one filter becomes the input signal for the next.

FIR filter (Finite Impulse Response)
A non-recursive filter based on a delay of one or more copies of the input signal, which are combined with the input signal by means of *feedforward* to produce the output signal.

First-order filter
A filter that produces 6 dB of attenuation per octave.

Frequency response
A description of the output signal of a system, based on a range of input frequencies. The resulting combination of amplitude and phase information is presented as two graphs, one showing relative amplitudes of signal components, and the other showing the relative phases of the same components.

Graphic equalizers
Banks of bandpass filters, routed in parallel, whose center frequencies are spaced uniformly across the spectrum. Each filter has constant Q and a fixed center frequency. The only parameter that can be changed is the gain for each band.

Hard sync
A technique for synchronizing the beginning of each wave cycle for two oscillators whose frequencies differ.

High shelving filter (high shelf filter)
A shelving filter in which all frequencies above a certain threshold frequency, the *shelf point*, are equally attenuated or boosted.

Highpass filter
A filter that attenuates all of the frequencies below a cutoff frequency.

IIR filter (Infinite Impulse Response)
A recursive filter based on a delay of a copy of the output signal, which is combined with the input signal as feedback. IIR filters can also contain feedforward elements.

Interpolated pseudo-random sample generator
A device that generates random samples at a given frequency, and interpolates intermediate values between one generated sample and the next.

Impulse response
The output signal from a system when it is given an impulse as input. An impulse response is graphed in the time domain.

Key follow
A synthesizer setting through which the frequency of a filter (or an oscillator, or some other parameter) is set relative to the keys pressed on a musical keyboard.

Low shelving filter (low shelf filter)
A shelving filter in which all frequencies below a certain threshold frequency, the *shelf point*, are equally attenuated or boosted.

Lowpass filter
A filter that attenuates all of the frequencies above a cutoff frequency.

Notch filter
A filter that attenuates its passband while leaving the frequencies outside of this band unaltered.

Parametric equalizers
Banks of filters, routed in series, which allow the parameters of either Q or bandwidth, of gain, and of center frequency, to be varied for each band.

Passband
The region of the spectrum that is not attenuated by a filter. For filters that have upper and lower cutoff frequencies, the passband is the region between these frequencies.

Peak filter
A filter that boosts its passband while leaving the frequencies outside of this band unaltered.

Peak/notch filter
A filter that boosts or attenuates a region of the spectrum while leaving the frequencies outside of this region unaltered.

Phase response
See *frequency response*

Pink noise
A sound similar to white noise, that is characterized by a spectrum in which energy drops as frequency rises. Pink noise is also called 1/f noise, to indicate that its spectral energy is proportional to the reciprocal of frequency.

Plug-in (or Add-on)
Computer software, typically not in the form of a stand-alone program, designed to add additional capabilities to a host program by integrating with its capabilities and enhancing them.

Q factor (quality factor) (also Resonance factor)
The ratio of center frequency to bandwidth. The Q factor is a filter parameter that links the bandwidth of a filter to its center frequency. When holding Q constant, bandwidth will vary as a function of the center frequency and the ratio of center frequency to bandwidth will remain constant.

Resonance
The effect produced by the tendency of a system to oscillate at a certain frequency (called its *resonant frequency*).

Resonant filter
A filter that boosts the frequencies at its cutoff frequency (or its center frequency), and can create a resonant oscillation at this frequency.

Ringing
Oscillations produced by transients in the input signal of a filter that remain present in the signal after the transients have disappeared.

Second-order filter
A filter that produces 12 dB of attenuation per octave.

Semi-parametric equalizers
Equalizers that are often used in

non-professional mixers, which are similar to parametric equalizers. Only the gain and center frequencies can be changed for each band; there is no Q or bandwidth setting.

Shelf point
In a shelving filter, the threshold that separates the region in which frequencies remain unaltered from the region in which they are either attenuated or boosted.

Simple pseudo-random sample generator
A device that generates random samples at a given frequency, maintaining each sample value until a new sample is generated, thus producing a step-function.

Subtractive synthesis
Synthesis based on modifying the amplitude of components of a sound by using filters.

Subtractive synthesizer
An electronic generator of audio signals that is controlled via a control panel, a keyboard, and/or other devices.

Sweep
A sine wave signal of constant amplitude that slides across all of the frequencies in a given band. It can be used to test the frequency response of a system (for example, a filter).

Transient
A transient is a short region of a signal that represents an unstable and non-harmonic attack portion (or sometimes decay) of a sound.

Transition zone
A frequency band found in digital filters around the cutoff frequency; rather than having an amplitude of 0 dB, signals roll-off in this zone in a way that doesn't match the frequency response predicted by an ideal filter.

Unitary impulse
A signal composed of a single sample at maximum amplitude followed by zero-valued samples.

VCA
(Voltage Controlled Amplitude)
A control envelope for amplitude, which is named after the kind of control that was used in analog synthesizers.

VCF
(Voltage Controlled Filter)
A control envelope for either frequency or Q, which is named after the kind of control that was used in analog synthesizers.

VCO
(Voltage Controlled Oscillator)
A control envelope for oscillator pitch, which is named after the kind of control that was used in analog synthesizers.

White noise
A sound that contains all audible frequencies; the amplitudes of these frequencies are randomly distributed.

DISCOGRAPHY

Karlheinz Stockhausen, *Kontakte* Electronic music CD Stockhausen Verlag #3 1992
György Ligeti, *Glissandi* CD Wergo 60 161-50
Henri Pousseur, *Scambi* CD BVHaast 9010 / Acousmatrix 4
James Tenney, *Analog #1 Noise* Study CD Artifact ART 1007
Wendy Carlos, *Switched on Bach* in *Switched-On Boxed Set* – East Side Digital CD ESD 81422
Morton Subotnick, *Silver Apples of the Moon* CD Wergo 2035

3P
NOISE GENERATORS, FILTERS, AND SUBTRACTIVE SYNTHESIS

LEARNING AGENDA

PREREQUISITES FOR THE CHAPTER
- Contents of Chapters 1 and 2 (Theory and Practice), Chapter 3 (Theory), Interlude A

LEARNING OBJECTIVES
Skills
- To learn how to generate and control different types of complex signals for subtractive synthesis (white noise, pink noise, impulses, etc.)
- To learn how to construct algorithms using lowpass, highpass, bandpass, bandreject, shelving, and resonant filters, and also how to control them using various parameters, Q, and filter order
- To learn how to implement FIR (non-recursive), as well as IIR (recursive), filters
- To learn how to build a simple subtractive synthesizer
- To learn how to write algorithms using filters connected in series and in parallel
- To learn how to build graphic and parametric equalizers

Competence
- To be able to realize a short sound study based on the techniques of subtractive synthesis, and save it to an audio file.

CONTENTS
- Sources for subtractive synthesis
- Lowpass, highpass, bandpass, bandreject, shelving, and resonant filters
- The Q factor and filter order
- Finite impulse response and infinite impulse response filters
- Connecting filters in series and in parallel
- Graphic and parametric equalization

ACTIVITIES
- Replacing parts of algorithms
- Correcting algorithms
- Analyzing algorithms
- Completing algorithms

TESTING
- Integrated cross-functional project: reverse engineering
- Integrated cross-functional project: composing a brief sound study

SUPPORTING MATERIALS
- List of Max objects
- Attributes for specific Max objects

3.1 SOUND SOURCES FOR SUBTRACTIVE SYNTHESIS

As you learned in Section 3.1T, the purpose of a filter is to modify the spectrum of a signal in some manner. In this section, before introducing filtering in Max, we will introduce an object that you can use to display a spectrum: the **spectroscope~** object. This graphical object can be found in the "Audio" category of the Add *palette* (as shown in figure 3.1). As usual, if you can't find it in the Add *palette*, create an object box and type the name "spectroscope~" into it.

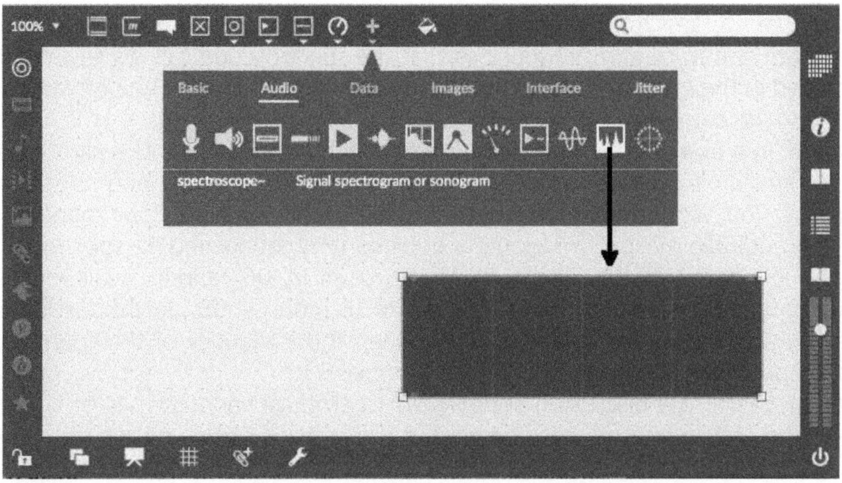

Fig. 3.1 The spectroscope~ object

Open the file **03_01_spectroscope.maxpat** (shown in figure 3.2).

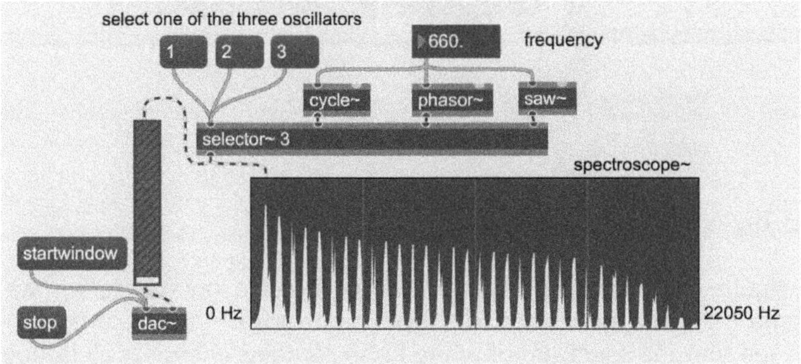

Fig. 3.2 The file 03_01_spectroscope.maxpat

In this patch, we have connected a **selector~** object to the spectroscope so that we can switch between three oscillators, one generating a sine wave (**cycle~**), one generating a non-band-limited sawtooth wave (**phasor~**), and one generating a band-limited sawtooth wave[1] (**saw~**).

1 See Section 1.2.

The three message boxes connected to the left input of the **selector~** object are used to pick one of the three oscillators; by setting the frequency in the float number box and then moving between the three oscillators, you can compare their spectra. Observe that the sine wave has only one component, while the **phasor~**, being a non-band-limited object, has a much richer spectrum.[2]
Make sure to try several frequencies for all of the waveforms, while watching the image being produced by the spectroscope.
As stated, the spectrum of the sound being input is what is being displayed: the components of the sound are distributed from left to right across a frequency band that ranges from 0 to 22,050 Hz by default. These two values, the minimum and maximum frequencies that the spectroscope can display, can be modified in the *Inspector*, using the "Lo and Hi Domain Display Value" attribute in the *Value* category.
Try adding a **spectroscope~** object to a patch that you have already created, so to familiarize yourself with the relationship between sound and its spectral content. You might add the object to the patches found in previous chapters. In 01_14_audiofile.maxpat, for example, you might try connecting the spectroscope to the left outlet of the **sfplay~** object, or in IA_06_random_walk.maxpat, you might try connecting it to the outlet of [**p** monosynth]. (In this last patch, are you able to see the relationship between the frequency of the sound and the shape of the spectrum? Try preset number 5.)
Let's move on to a discussion about ways to produce various types of noise in Max. The first, white noise, is generated using the **noise~** object (as shown in figure 3.3).

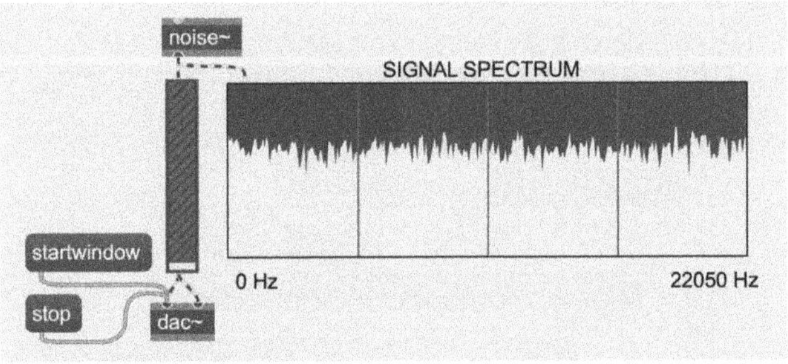

Fig. 3.3 The white noise generator

In the figure (which we encourage you to recreate on your own) we have connected the noise generator to a **spectroscope~** object, through which we can see that the spectrum of white noise contains energy at all frequencies. Unlike the sound generators that we have already encountered, the white noise generator doesn't need any parameters; its function is to generate a signal at the sampling rate consisting of a stream of random values between -1 and 1 (as we discussed in Section 3.1T).

[2] The **spectroscope~** object uses an algorithm for spectral analysis called the Fast Fourier Transform. We already mentioned the Fourier theorem at the end of Chapter 2T, and we will return to a much more detailed discussion of it in the third volume.

The second type of noise generator that is available in Max is the **pink~** object, which, unsurprisingly, generates pink noise (as seen in figure 3.4).

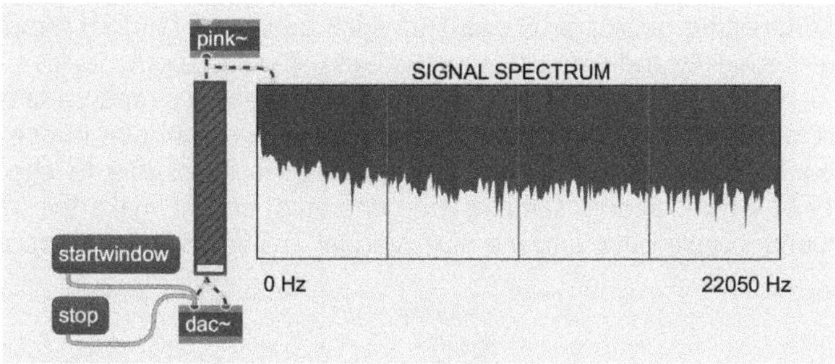

Fig. 3.4 Pink noise

Note that the spectrum of pink noise, unlike white noise, is gradually attenuated as frequencies get higher, and that this attenuation (as we know from Section 3.1T) is 3 dB per octave.
Reconstruct the simple patch shown in the figure and listen carefully to the difference between pink noise and white noise. Which of the two seems more pleasant (or maybe just less unpleasant), and why?
Add an oscilloscope (**scope~**) to the two patches just built, remembering to set the "Calcount - samples per pixel"[3] attributes in the *Value* category of the Inspector, and observe the difference between the waveforms of pink noise and white noise.
In figure 3.5, we see these two waveforms side-by-side.

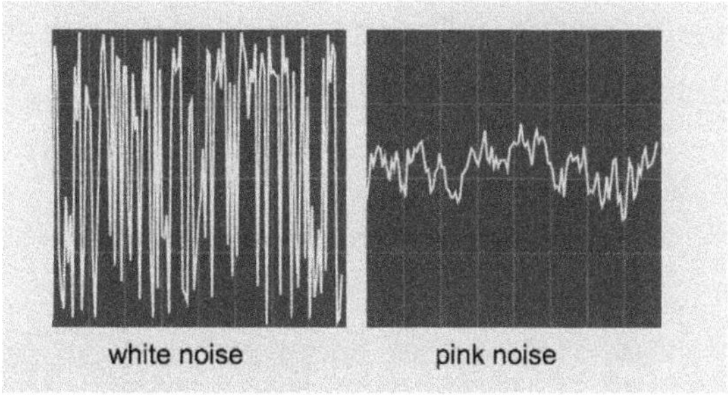

Fig. 3.5 Waveforms of white noise and pink noise

Without bogging down in technical details, you can see that while white noise is basically a stream of random values, pink noise is generated using a more complex algorithm in which a sample, although randomly generated, cannot stray too far from the value of its predecessor. This results in the "serpentine" waveform that we see in the figure. The behavior of the two waveforms demonstrates their spectral content: when the difference between one sample and the next is larger, the energy of the higher frequencies in the signal is

3 We explained this attribute in Section 1.2P.

greater.[4] As you know, white noise has more energy at higher frequencies than pink noise.

Another interesting generator is **rand~**, which generates random samples at a selectable frequency and connects these values using line segments (as shown in figure 3.6). Unlike **noise~** and **pink~**, which each generate random samples on every tick of the DSP "engine" (producing a quantity of samples in one second that is equal to the sampling rate), with **rand~** it is possible to choose the frequency at which random samples are generated, and to make the transition between one sample value and the next gradual, thanks to linear interpolation.

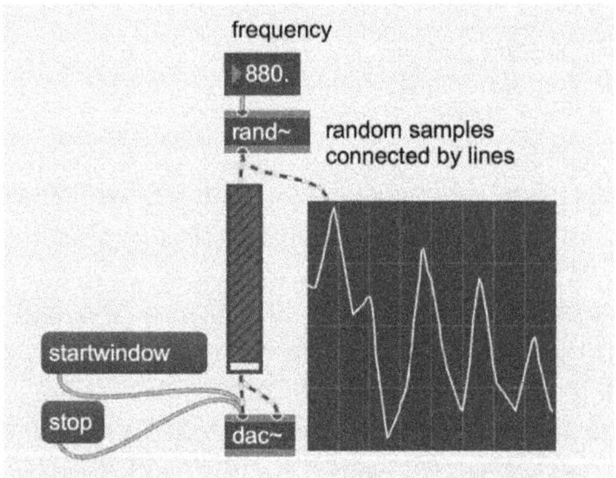

Fig. 3.6 The **rand~** object

Obviously, this generator produces a spectrum that varies according to the frequency setting; it shows a primary band of frequencies that range from 0 Hz up to the frequency setting, followed by additional bands that are gradually attenuated and whose width are also equal to the frequency setting. Figure 3.7 shows this interesting spectrum.

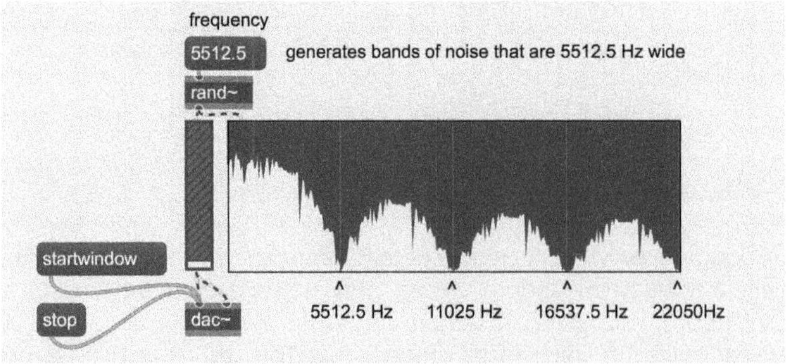

Fig. 3.7 The spectrum generated by the **rand~** object

[4] To understand this assertion, notice that the waveform of a high sound oscillates quickly, while that of a low sound oscillates slowly. At equal amplitudes, the difference between succeeding samples for the high frequency case will be larger, on average, than for the low frequency case.

In the example, we can see that the frequency of the **rand~** object is 5,512.5 Hz (a quarter of the maximum frequency visible in the spectroscope in the figure), and the first band goes from 0 to 5,512.5 Hz. After this come secondary bands, progressively attenuated, all 5,512.5 Hz wide. Changing the frequency of **rand~** changes the width of the bands as well as their number. If you double the frequency to 11,025 Hz, for example, you will see precisely two wide bands, both 11,025 Hz wide.

Another noise generator is **vs.rand0~**[5] (the last character before the tilde is a zero), which generates random samples at a given frequency like **rand~**, but that doesn't interpolate. Instead, it maintains the value of each sample until a new sample is generated, producing stepped changes in value. The spectrum of this object is divided into bands in the same way as that of **rand~** was in figure 3.7, but as you can see in figure 3.8, the attenuation of the secondary bands is much less because of the abrupt changes between sample values.

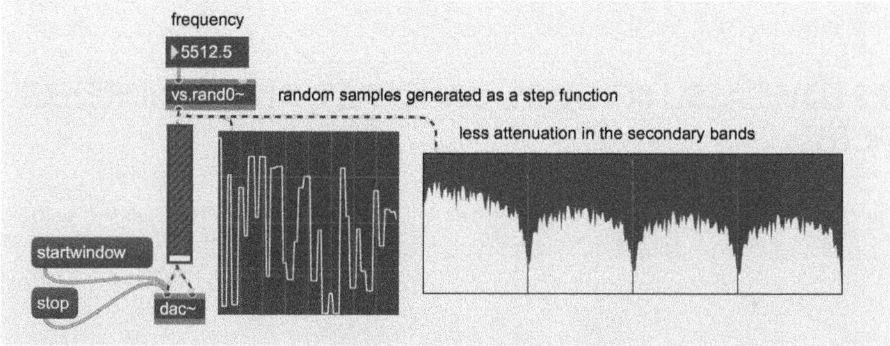

Fig. 3.8 The `vs.rand0~` object

In the *Virtual Sound Macros* library, we also have provided a noise generator that uses cubic interpolation called **vs.rand3~** (as shown in figure 3.9).

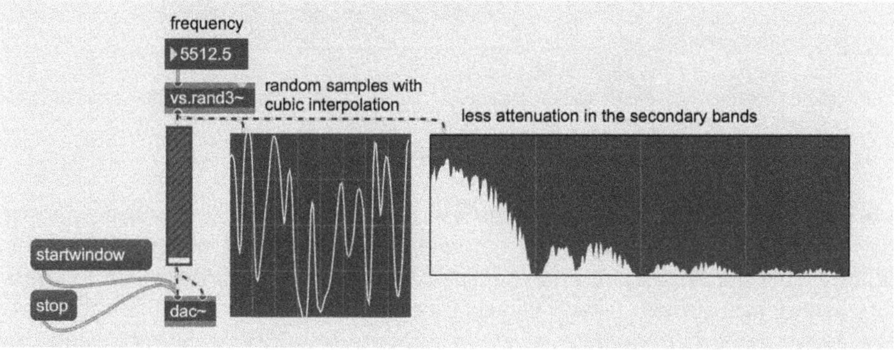

Fig. 3.9 The `vs.rand3~` object

---

5 You should know from preceding chapters that the "vs" at the beginning of this object's name means that it a part of the *Virtual Sound Macros* library.

Thanks to the polynomial interpolation in this object, the transitions between one sample and the next appear smooth, as you can see on the oscilloscope. The transitions form a curve rather than a series of connected line segments, and the resulting effect is a strong attenuation of the secondary bands. Recreate the patches found in figures 3.6 to 3.9 in order to experiment with various noise generators.

"Classic" oscillators – those that produce sawtooth waves, square waves, and triangle waves – are another source of sounds that are rich in components, which makes them effective for use with filters. In Section 1.2, we examined three band-limited oscillators that generate these waves: **saw~**, **rect~**, and **tri~**. Furthermore, in Chapter 2P we saw the complex oscillators **abl.dsp.swarm~** and **abl.dsp.basicshapes~**. We will use these oscillators frequently in the course of this chapter. In Section 3.1T, we also learned about the possibility of filtering sampled sounds. For this reason, we will also give examples in this chapter of filtering sampled sounds, using the **sfplay~** object (first introduced in Section 1.5P).

3.2 LOWPASS, HIGHPASS, BANDPASS, AND BANDREJECT FILTERS

Let's return to the white noise generator and apply a lowpass filter to the signal. (This is shown in figure 3.10, which you should build yourself.)

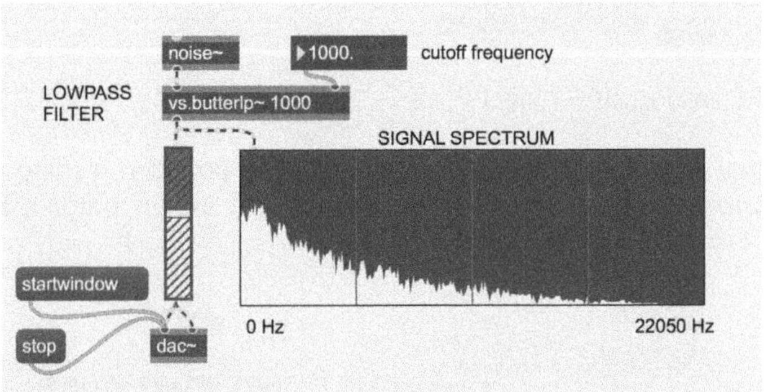

Fig. 3.10 White noise filtered with a lowpass filter

We've inserted a filter with the name **vs.butterlp~** (which is, again, part of the *Virtual Sound Macros* library) between the white noise generator and the output. This name is shorthand that indicates that it is a Butterworth lowpass filter,[6] and its argument, which can be modified at runtime using the right inlet, specifies the cutoff frequency, which in this case is 1,000 Hz. By modifying the cutoff frequency, you can apply effects to the input signal; you can see the impact of such modifications on the signal thanks to the **spectroscope~** object.

[6] Butterworth filters were covered in Sections 3.3T and 3.4T.

Try substituting a highpass filter for the lowpass filter by modifying the last two letters of the filter's name, the name becoming **vs.butterhp~**. By playing with the cutoff frequency, you can familiarize yourself with the effect that it produces.
A bandpass filter needs two parameters: a center frequency and a bandwidth. Modify your patch to look like figure 3.11 in order to try this out.

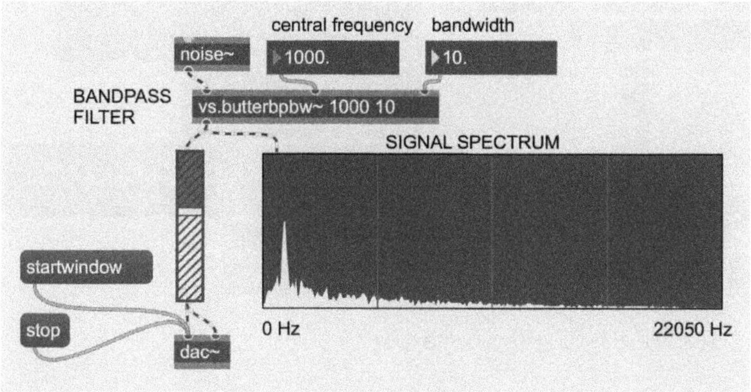

Fig. 3.11 White noise filtered by a bandpass filter

The name of the filter is now **vs.butterbpbw~**; the last letters stand for *BandPass-BandWidth*, which is a way of indicating that the object expects bandwidth as a parameter rather than Q (which is an alternate that we will see in the next section). Experiment with various parameter values on this filter. You should be able to hear that when the bandwidth is set lower, the output intensity is also lower; this is obviously due to the fact that the majority of the components in the input signal are being removed by the filter. We will see in the next section a way to control the intensity of a filter that is independent of the parameter settings.
Now substitute a bandreject filter for the bandpass filter by changing the name to **vs.butterbrbw~** (*BandReject-BandWidth*). Set the volume lower before trying this filter, because it allows all frequencies to pass except the band to be eliminated. Its intensity will therefore be quite a bit greater than that of the bandpass filter.
To verify the efficiency of the bandreject filter, you can swap sine wave input for the white noise, replacing noise~ with cycle~. By setting the frequency of the sine wave to 1,000 Hz and filtering it with a center frequency of 1,000 Hz and an bandwidth of 100 Hz, the sound of the oscillator should be appreciably attenuated.[7]

[7] Also notice that when white noise is used as a source, the bandpass filter will have the largest effect when its passband is narrow (a tenth of the value of the center frequency or less), while the opposite is true for the bandreject filter, which will have its largest effect when the value of its stopband is wider (almost equal to the center frequency).

Let's turn to a more complex example of bandpass filtering, which you can find by opening the file **03_02_bpgliss.maxpat** (which is shown in figure 3.12).

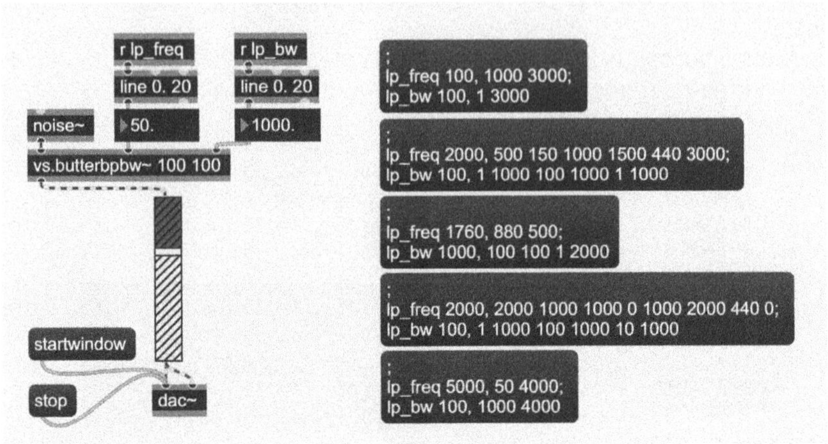

Fig. 3.12 The file 03_02_bpgliss.maxpat

In this example, changing values for the parameters of the bandpass filter are generated using **`line`**. This object is similar to Max's already familiar `line~` object, but it generates Max numbers rather than an MSP signal. The first argument of the object is used to set the initial value and the type of number (integer or floating point) that will be sent; in this example, the values will be floating point numbers because the arguments contain a decimal points. The second argument sets the interval (in milliseconds) that should elapse between each generated number. The two `line` objects are connected to two **`receive`** objects, whose purpose is to receive the lists of parameter values from message boxes on the right side of the patch. We have exploited the multi-target capabilities of these message boxes by using the semicolon prefix, which enables us to bundle related messages together and send them with a single mouse click. (To remind yourself how this approach works, review Section 2.4 as well as the file 02_15_message_send.maxpat.) Clicking on any of the assorted messages will generate "parameter glissandi" that dynamically modify the spectrum of the white noise. Try all of them, seeking to understand the effects that they produce, and after this, add your own sets of parameter changes to the patch so that you can probe the interactions between center frequency and bandwidth.

ACTIVITY

Modify the 03_02_bpgliss.maxpat patch, using two `function` objects in place of the message boxes to create the lists to be transmitted to the two `line` objects. (There is a demonstration of this in Section 1.3, in the file 01_07_envelopes.maxpat.) Don't forget to appropriately modify the duration and the output range of the `function` object by using the *Inspector*, or by using the "*setdomain*" command to set the duration and the "*setrange*" command to set the range of values. We used both of these commands in Section 2.4, but if you don't recall how they are used, you can refresh your memory by looking at figure 3.13.

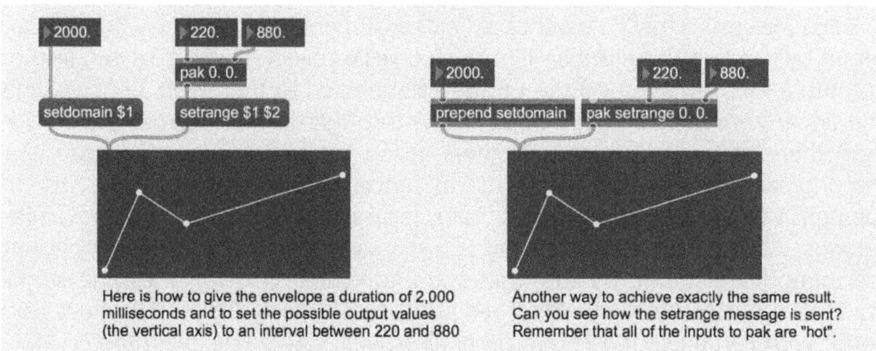

Fig. 3.13 How to set the domain and range of the `function` object

Add a third `function` object to the patch to control the amplitude of the filtered signal, and then create new examples using this parameter. You might want to store these new examples using a `preset` object. If you don't recall how to add an amplitude envelope or how to use `preset`, study Section 1.3.

• •

Now let's look at some applications that use Butterworth filters with sampled sounds. Open the file **03_03_sample_filter.maxpat** (shown in figure 3.14).

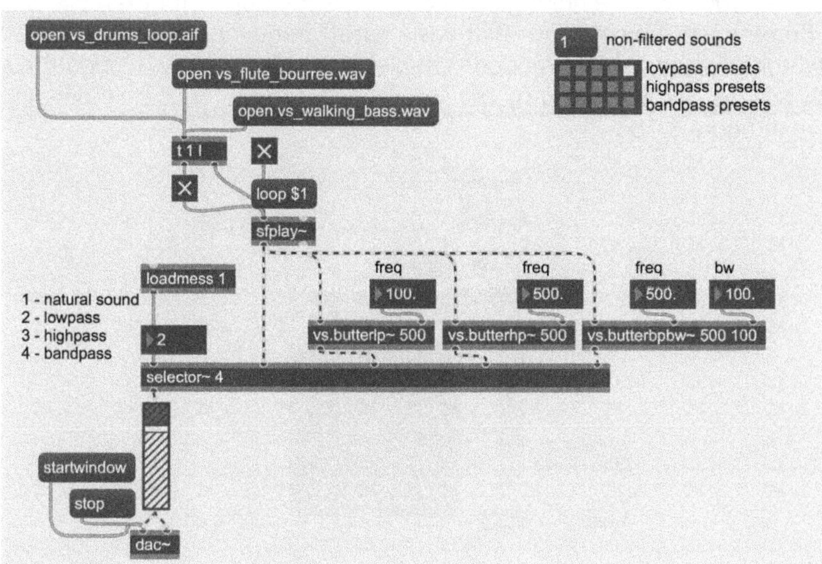

Fig. 3.14 The file 03_03_sample_filter.maxpat

With this patch it is possible to filter sampled sounds using lowpass, highpass, and bandpass Butterworth filters. The patch is quite straightforward – at the top are three messages that will load three different audio files into a **sfplay~** object. (These files can be found in the *Virtual Sound Macros* library.) All three messages are routed to a **trigger** object[8] that will pass an entire messages on to **sfplay~** using the 'l' (lower case "el") argument, and then play the selected sound by sending the number 1 to the **toggle** object. Audio files can also be put into a loop by selecting the **toggle** connected to the "*loop $1*" message. The signal from the **sfplay~** object flows through the **selector~** object and from there to three Butterworth filters; using the **selector~**, you can hear the original sound or else the sound as processed by the three filters. At the top right there is a **preset** object that is pre-loaded with some illustrative filter settings. Above the **preset** object is a message box that enables monitoring the unmodified sound: be sure that you understand why this message works. Try the various presets with the three audio files, noting that some filters work better with certain sounds,[9] and others less well. Can you explain this?

ACTIVITY

Build a patch that varies filter parameters in time, much like the example 03_02_bpgliss.maxpat did, but that uses audio files as its source sounds.

As we mentioned in Section 3.2T, it is possible to use a lowpass filter to smooth the signal produced by a noise generator. If a **rand~** object, for example, is sent to a Butterworth lowpass filter that has a cutoff frequency equal to half of the generator's frequency, the random samples that result follow a smooth curve much like the one produced by the **vs.rand3~** object. (This phenomenon is shown in figure 3.15.)

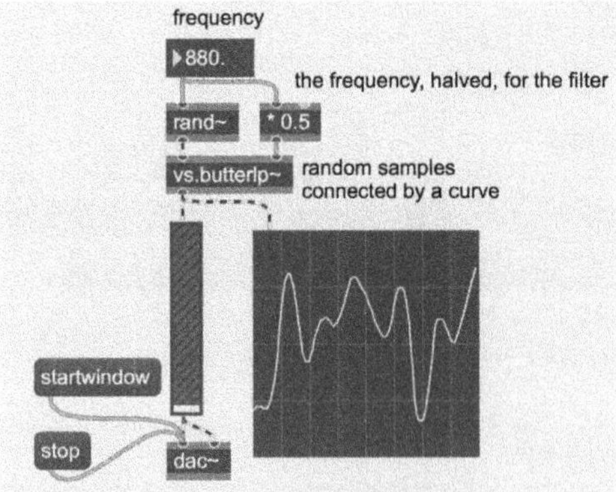

Fig. 3.15 Noise, smoothed by a lowpass filter

[8] We covered the **trigger** object in Section IA.6.

[9] By "work better", we mean to say that they appreciably modify the timbre.

As you can see, the value entered in the float number box is both sent to **rand~** as its generating frequency and reduced by half, after which it is used to set the cutoff frequency for the lowpass filter.
With a highpass filter, you can make an interesting modification that results in a variable frequency noise generator. To do this, filter the uninterpolated noise produced by **vs.rand0~** using a **vs.butterhp~** filter, and assign a cutoff frequency equal to twice the frequency of the noise generator. What results is a generator of random amplitude pseudo-impulses (as shown in figure 3.16.)

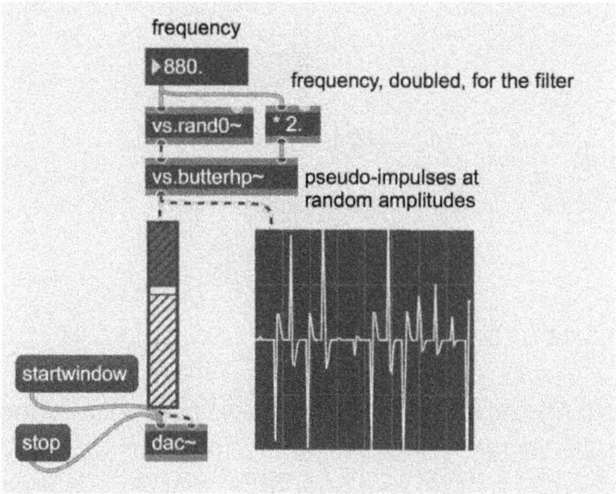

Fig. 3.16 Generation of pseudo-impulses at random amplitudes

Construct the patches shown in figures 3.15 and 3.16, adding a spectroscope to both so that you can observe the evolving spectra of the filtered noise.

3.3 THE Q FACTOR

The **reson~** object, shown in figure 3.17, is a resonant bandpass filter that takes Q as a parameter rather than bandwidth.

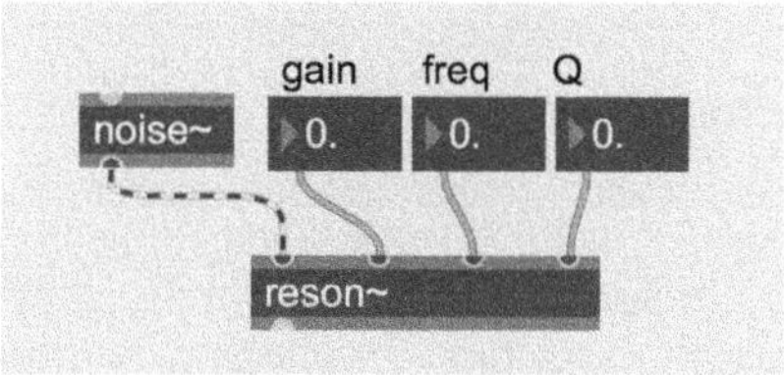

Fig. 3.17 The resonant filter **reson~**

As you can see, **reson~** has four inlets: the first is for the input signal, the second for gain (a multiplication factor that scales the output signal), the third is for center frequency, and the final inlet is for Q. If you build the patch shown in figure 3.17,[10] notice that when you increase the Q, the passband grows increasingly narrow until a point at which you can hear a single frequency over the noise.

10 Adding, of course, the **gain~** and **dac~** objects that you always need to hear the results in Max.

Also in this case, the more the passband is narrowed, the less intensity there is to the output signal, although it is possible to compensate for this attenuation by increasing the gain. An effective solution to this problem is to link the value of Q to the value for gain, after which we can vary the first parameter without suffering the accompanying variation in the other.
Try, for example, taking the Q, calculating its square root (using the **sqrt** object), and then handing the results to the gain parameter (as shown in figure 3.18):

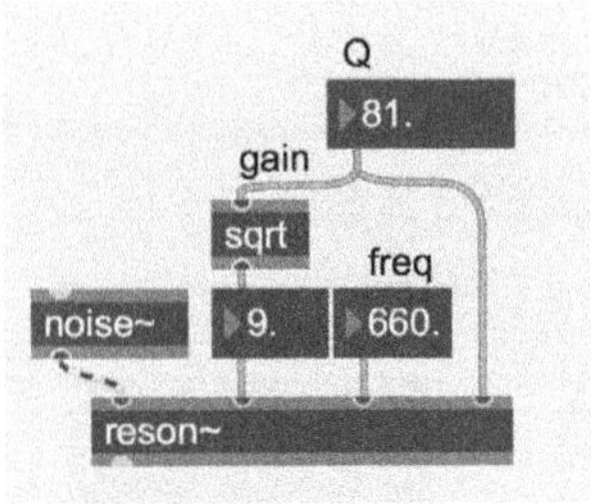

Fig. 3.18 How to link gain to Q

By linking the values, attenuation of the filtered signal is compensated for by increasing the output volume. Construct this patch and try it!
Let's examine the effect that the **reson~** filter has on a periodic signal, such as the **saw~** oscillator, which, as we know, generates a band-limited sawtooth wave.
Recreate the patch shown in figure 3.19 (again, adding **gain~** and **dac~** yourself).

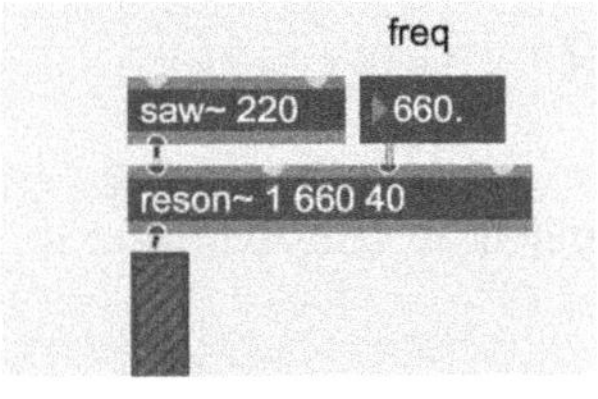

Fig. 3.19 A filtered sawtooth wave

First, we see that **reson~** can take three arguments that correspond to gain, center frequency, and Q, respectively. In this patch, a sawtooth oscillator set to 220 Hz is filtered by a bandpass filter that has a center frequency of 660 Hz and a Q value of 40, which has the effect of focusing the filter on the third harmonic (220 · 3 = 660) of the sound. It is not necessary to increase the gain of the filter in this kind of setup, since the Q value succeeds in boosting the component of a periodic sound much more easily than it does in extracting a sine wave component from white noise.
If we use the mouse to slowly increase the number in the number box connected to the third inlet of **reson~** (the center frequency), we will notice that the amplitude of the signal grows whenever the center frequency touches on one of the component frequencies of the sound (220, 440, 660, and 880 Hz, and so on); it creates an arpeggio out of the harmonics that occur naturally

within the sound. We can make this process automatic by applying a **line~** object to the center frequency, and while we are doing this, we will also add a **spectroscope~** in order to watch the filter modify the spectrum of the sound. (The patch is shown in figure 3.20).

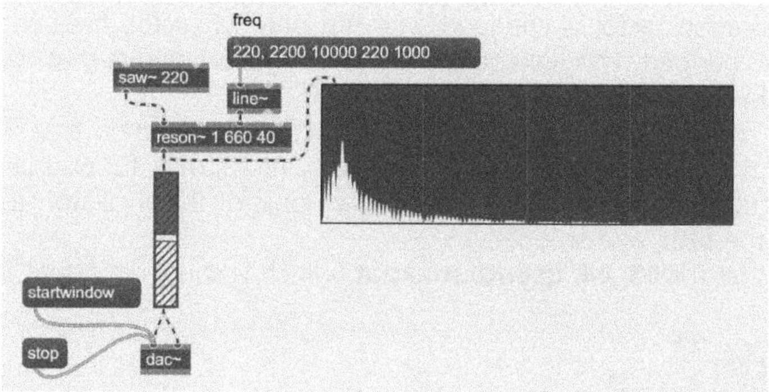

Fig. 3.20 A glissando on the center frequency of **reson~**

After you've modified your own patch to resemble figure 3.20, click on the message box connected to **line~** to start the effect. The center frequency will pass from 220 Hz (the fundamental) to 2,200 Hz (the tenth harmonic) in 10 seconds, after which it will return to 220 Hz in one second. Notice how this allows us to create a sense of motion from a static waveform.
Many lowpass and highpass filters have a Q setting, which represents the amount of boost (or resonance) to be applied in the region around the cutoff frequency. Substitute a lowpass filter for **reson~** in our patch, as shown in figure 3.21, to explore this effect.

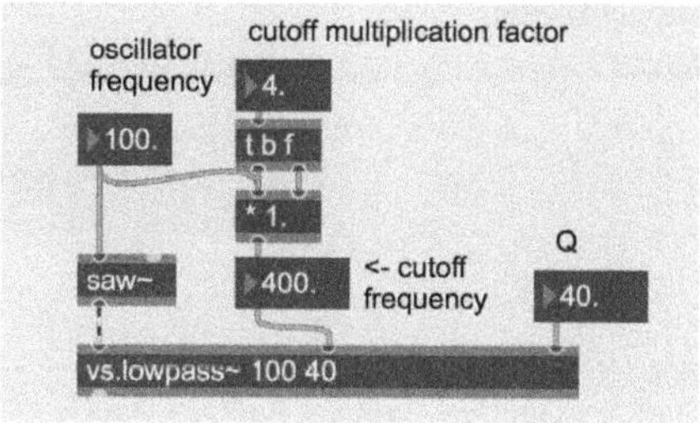

Fig. 3.21 A resonant lowpass filter

The **vs.lowpass~** filter, which is part of the Virtual Sound Macros library (but is actually just a wrapper around a filter that will be discussed in the next section and that is easily created from a pair of standard Max objects) is a lowpass filter with resonance. As you can see, unlike **reson~**, it has no inlet for gain, but only inlets for the input signal, the cutoff frequency, and Q. In the patch, the cutoff frequency depends upon the frequency of the oscillator. We can regulate the cutoff frequency using the "multiplication factor" that is applied to the frequency of the oscillator; in the figure, for example, the oscillator frequency is set to 100 Hz and the multiplication factor is set to 4, resulting in a setting of 400 Hz (100 · 4) for the cutoff frequency. Whenever the oscillator's frequency is changed, the cutoff frequency will also change. Moving the frequency of the oscillator to 200 Hz, for example, will result in a cutoff frequency of 800 Hz (200 · 4); if we then were to change the multiplication factor to 3.5, the cutoff frequency would drop to 700 Hz (200 · 3.5). The **trigger**, taking the arguments "b f", ensures that the calculation of cutoff frequency occurs when the multiplication factor is changed, and not only when the frequency of the oscillator is changed. This linkage is created using a technique that we learned in Section IA.6 of Interlude A.

It is worth noting that the multiplication factor corresponds to a harmonic number of the oscillator when it is an integer. A factor of 4, for example, would place the cutoff frequency at the fourth harmonic of the oscillator, a 5 would place it at the fifth, and so on.

Now open the file **03_04_qsynth.maxpat** (which is shown in figure 3.22).

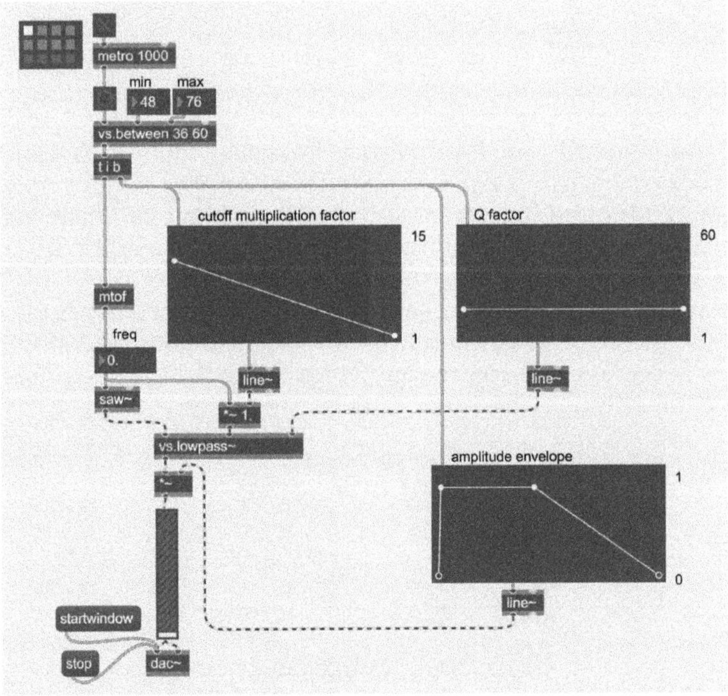

Fig. 3.22 The file 03_04_qsynth.maxpat

This patch links the frequency of the oscillator and the cutoff frequency of the filter, using the same technique that we used in figure 3.21. We have now added envelopes, drawn using the **function** objects, for the cutoff multiplication factor, for Q, and for amplitude. Try the presets that are included with this patch, and carefully study the paths followed by the three envelopes in order to understand how the three parameters interact with each other. Create new presets and add number boxes for modifying the speed of the metronome and the length of the envelopes. (A suggestion: you'll probably want to use the "*setdomain*" message that we introduced in Section IA.8 of Interlude A. See in particular figure IA.65.)

ACTIVITY

Starting with the file 03_04_qsynth.maxpat, (to which you will have added a number box for the **metro** object and a setdomain message for the **function** objects as explained above), create a subpatch [**p** qsynth] similar to the subpatch [**p** monosynth] contained in the file IA_06_random_walk.maxpat (which we examined in Section 5 of Interlude A). The new subpatch should have 5 inlets: MIDI note number, intensity in dB, cutoff frequency envelope (or better, cutoff multiplication factor envelope), Q envelope, and finally, amplitude.
Store various timbres for this synthesizer into presets.
Make a copy of the patch and replace the **saw~** object with the **abl.dsp.basicshapes~** object. Add two floating-point number boxes (limited between 0 and 1) to control the "shape" (second input) and "effect" (third input) parameters, and create new presets.
Now make another copy of the patch and use the **abl.dsp.swarm~** object as the oscillator. The two parameters, normalized between 0 and 1, are "motion" and "spacing". Add an **attrui** to control the "shape" parameter (see Figure 2.15d). Again, create new presets.
In the previous two patches, replace the number boxes that control the normalized parameters of the Ableton oscillators with **line~** objects controlled by **function** objects. Remember to link the **function** objects to the "setdomain" message. Create envelopes for the normalized parameters and save new presets.

Let's now apply a resonant bandpass filter to a sampled sound: open the file **03_05_reson_samples.maxpat** (seen in figure 3.23). As soon as the patch is opened, the audio file vs_harp_riff.wav is loaded into the **sfplay~** object, thanks to the **loadbang** object. The output of **sfplay~** is connected to a **reson~** filter.

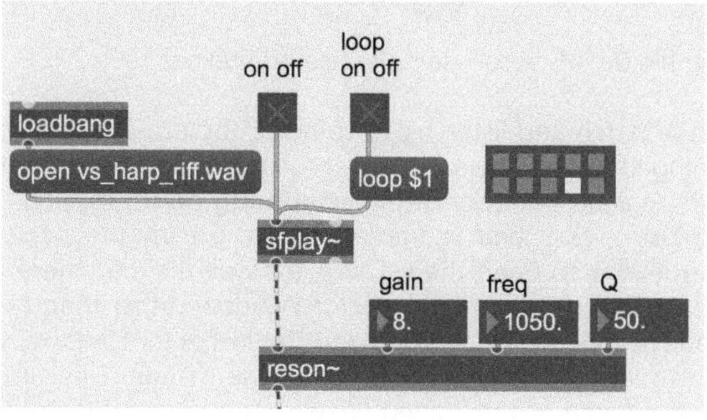

Fig. 3.23 The file 03_05_reson_samples.maxpat

There are saved configurations for this filter in the **preset** object. Try these configurations, listening carefully to how they accentuate some of the partials in the sound and yet attenuate others. After listening, try to create interesting new configurations of your own. Note that when using high Q values, we have raised the gain to compensate. Some of the filtered sounds that result might be considered too poor to use, due to the fact that the resonant bandpass filter eliminates the greater part of their input signal, letting only the frequencies clustered around the center frequency pass. To alleviate this problem, we can mix the original sound with the filtered sound, but in attenuated form. Using this process, we can boost certain frequencies using **`reson~`** without losing the rest. Another variation on the same approach would be to use two filters, one for the right channel and one for the left; by setting various parameters of the two filters, we could alter the stereo image associated with some of the components of the original signal.

Open the file **03_06_reson_samples_stereo.maxpat** (as seen in figure 3.24).

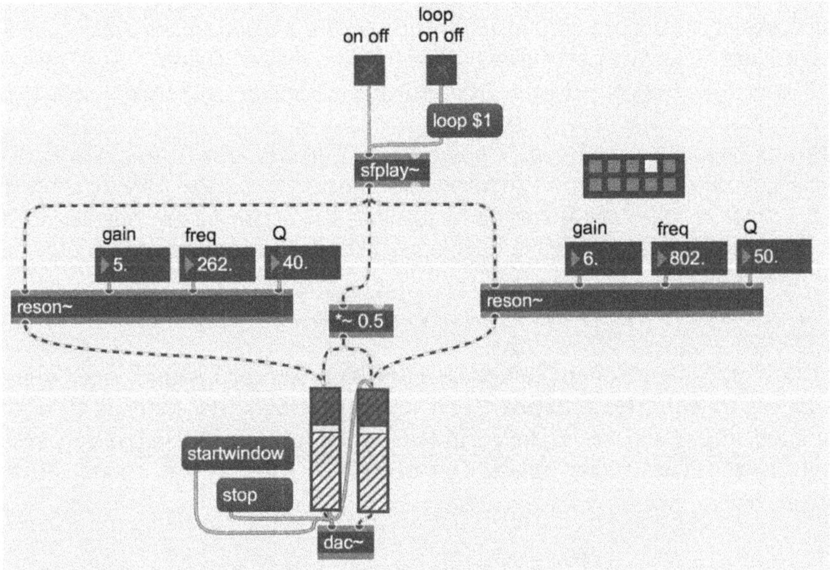

Fig. 3.24 The file 03_06_reson_samples_stereo.maxpat

Try loading the patch and listening to some of the presets. But wait, did you notice anything strange? The sound of the harp is playing, as in the previous patch, but there is no evidence of the **`loadbang`** object that had loaded the file into **`sfplay~`**, as it had in the last patch. Clearly the **`sfplay~`** object received instructions to open the vs_harp_riff.wav file, but these instructions must have been saved using the Inspector Window rather than as part of the Patcher Window. Indeed, when you open the Inspector Window you can see that in the "sfplay~" category there is a single "Audio File" attribute, and following it, the name of the loaded file within braces: {vs_harp_riff.wav}.
It is possible to open and remember an audio file in any **`sfplay~`** object by opening its Inspector and then clicking on the "Choose" button that appears to the right of the attribute; once you've selected a file, you can "freeze" your selection by clicking on the "**Freeze Attribute**" icon, shown graphically as a snowflake, at the bottom of the inspector window.

(This group of icons is called the Inspector Toolbar, and can be seen in fig. 3.25.). After you've frozen an attribute, you can be sure that the value will be remembered whenever the patch is loaded. (However, it should be obvious that you can also change the value at any time, either through the Inspector or with an external command.) Many, but not all, attributes can be frozen in this way in the Inspector. If you later want to "unfreeze" the attribute (to forget the saved value the next time the patch is loaded) you can click again on the snowflake icon..

Continuing with the analysis of the patch, the audio signal output by **sfplay~** is sent to two **reson~** filters, as well as being fed directly to the **gain~** objects (after the amplitude is cut in half). As we said earlier, this allows us to boost some frequencies using the **reson~** filters while not losing the rest of the sound.

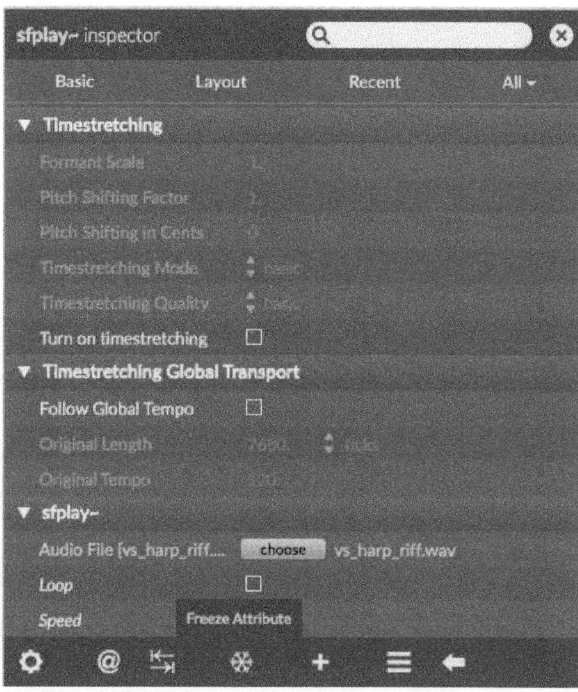

Fig. 3.25 How to freeze an attribute in the Inspector

Examining the two **gain~** objects (one for the right channel and one for the left), we see that they are connected to each other using a Max patch cord (a grey one) that goes from the right outlet of the first **gain~** to the left inlet of the second. The two faders are synchronized, using this connection, as we first saw in Section 1.5; to set the level on both channels, all you have to do is move the left fader.[11]

[11] The **gain~** object sends a numeric value to its left outlet that corresponds to the position of the fader. In the same way, if such a number is received on the left inlet of a **gain~** object, it will position the fader as expected.

Try the various configurations that have been saved in the **preset** object (you might consider using headphones in order to fully appreciate the subtle variations in timbre and spacing), and also create your own new configurations.

ACTIVITY

Replace the fixed values sent to the filters in the patch shown in figure 3.24 with values sent as envelopes, generating these with as many pairs of **function** objects connected to **line** objects as you need (as shown in figure 3.12 above). Save some of the envelope combinations that you develop using the **preset** object.

3.4 FILTER ORDER AND CONNECTION IN SERIES

THE UMENU OBJECT

Before tackling the subject of this section, we will take a moment to introduce an object that will help with many programming tasks, the **umenu** object. This object creates drop-down menus containing whatever items you specify; it can be found in the "Interface" category of the Add *palette* (as shown in figure 3.26).

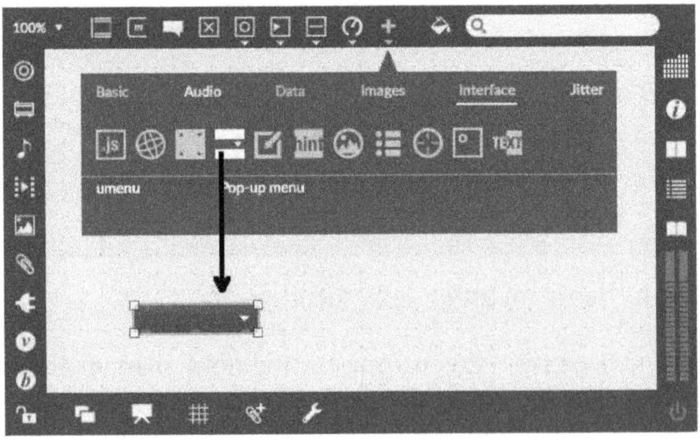

Fig. 3.26 The **umenu** object

Create a **umenu** object and open its Inspector Window, locate the "Items" category and click on the "Edit" button found to the right of the ***Menu Items*** attribute.
You can type menu items into the text field in the window that appears. Try this by typing something like "Blue, Red, Yellow", making sure to separate each item by a comma. This process is illustrated in figure 3.27.

Fig. 3.27 Editing menu items for a **umenu** object

Click on "OK" and close the Inspector; if you go into performance mode, you will see that the object behaves like a normal drop-down menu that enables you to select from the three items that you inserted using the Inspector.Now connect a number box to the first outlet, and a message box to the second outlet, as shown in figure 3.28.

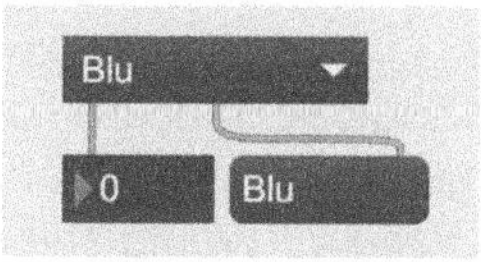

Fig. 3.28 Displaying the selected item of a **umenu** object

As you can see from the figure, the first outlet of **umenu** transmits the number that corresponds to its selected item; the first item is represented by 0, the second by 1, and so on. The second outlet transmits the actual text of the item – you can see that the message box is connected via its right inlet, which displays the incoming message directly.[12]

The **umenu** object is very useful when selecting between multiple options in a patch, or when sending one message selected from many to an object. One possible application can be shown by extending the file 01_05_band_limited.maxpat, which was already used as an example in Section 1.2, and which used a **selector~** to move between the three available band-limited oscillators. Go into edit mode and delete the three message boxes connected to the first inlet of **selector~**, replacing them with a new **umenu** whose left outlet is connected to the left inlet of the **selector~**. Go to the *Items* category of the Inspector for the **umenu**, following the procedure outlined above, and enter four items: "Off, Sawtooth, Triangle, Square", remembering to separate them with commas.

[12] We introduced this message box capability in Section IA.6.

Now return to performance mode and check what happens when items are selected from the **umenu**.
Your patch should now resemble that shown in figure 3.29.

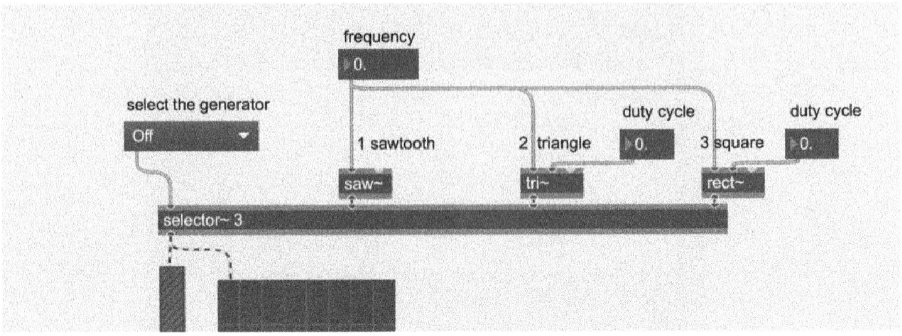

Fig. 3.29 Using a **umenu** with a **selector~**

Set the frequency to somewhere in the audible range, activate the patch, and you should be able to switch between the waveforms, hearing the corresponding sounds. The message path being followed should be clear enough by now: when you select the first item in the **umenu**, "Off", a 0 is sent to the **selector~** which mutes all inputs. The second item, "Sawtooth", sends a 1 to the **selector~**, which routes the signal from **saw~** through to the output. Likewise, the third item sends a 2, routing **tri~** to the output, while the fourth item sends a 3, outputting **rect~**. Note that the text of the items serves only to indicate choices: the ordinal number is what is actually causing the routing to change. You could change the text of the items to anything: "Blue, Red, Green, Yellow" would still yield exactly the same result. Do note, however, that some of the examples to follow will use the text from the second **umenu** outlet directly, rather than having relying upon ordinal item number. Both techniques are useful.

FIRST-ORDER FILTERS

In MSP, a first-order lowpass filter named **onepole~** is available. First-order filters such as this, as you know, have a rather gentle attenuation curve of 6 dB per octave (as demonstrated in figure 3.30).

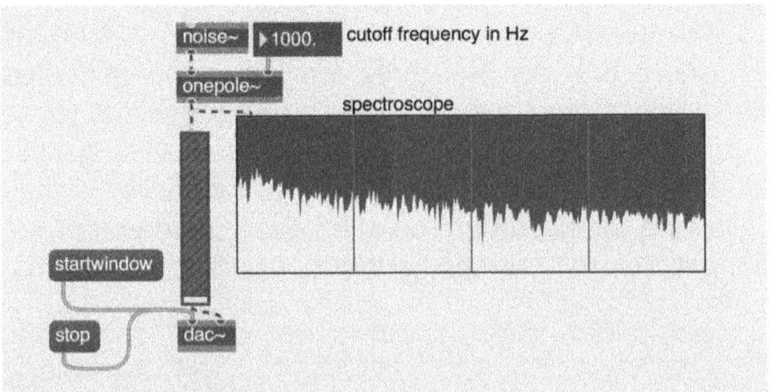

Fig. 3.30 A first-order lowpass filter

This filter is normally not used directly for modifying sounds, as were the filters earlier in the chapter (which, you will remember, were second-order filters). Instead, it is often used to refine a sound before or after other treatments. It might be used, for example, to attenuate high frequency noise in sampled sounds, or to take the edge off of a sound produced using synthesis techniques such as frequency modulation or waveshaping (which we will discuss in upcoming chapters). Another use for it might be for envelope following, which we will cover in Chapter 7.

An analogous first-order highpass filter doesn't exist in MSP, but it is easily obtained by subtracting an unmodified signal from a signal filtered by **onepole~** (as shown in figure 3.31).

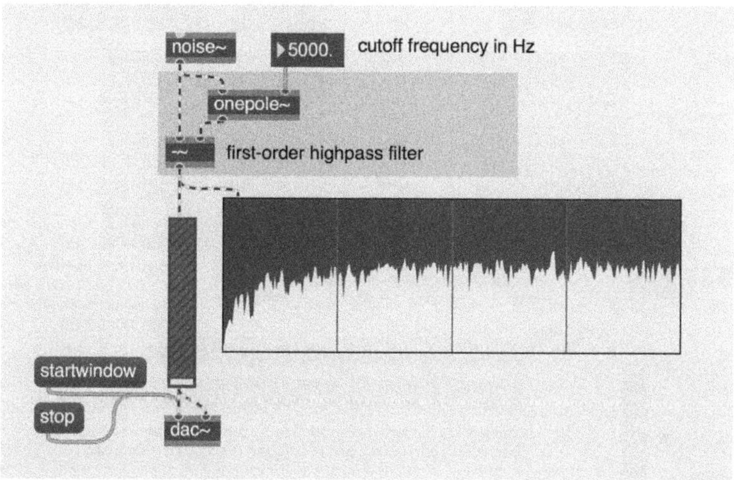

Fig. 3.31 First-order highpass filter obtained by subtracting an unmodified signal from a lowpass filtered signal

Using the **-~** (the object that subtracts one signal from another), we subtract sound filtered by the **onepole~** lowpass filter from the original signal, resulting in a filtered output that is equivalent to the output of a first-order highpass filter.[13]

Such a filter can be used in "special" ways, such as removing DC Offset (which we will take up as a subject in Chapter 5.3T).

SECOND-ORDER FILTERS

Besides the "ready-to-use" second-order filters in MSP, such as **reson~**, which we introduced in the preceding section, there is an object in MSP named **biquad~** that can be used to define second-order filters. This object isn't configured by means of filter control parameters that we've used up until now such as cutoff frequency or Q. Instead, it is controlled by means of a specific

[13] There is an object named **vs.highpass1~** in the *Virtual Sound Macros* library that is a first-order highpass filter that is implemented using exactly this method.

group of 5 *coefficients*, whose inter-relations define the behavior of the filter. In reality, any digital filter needs these coefficients in order to function; objects such as **reson~** have an internal algorithm that translates the values of their control parameters into the correct coefficients for the job. As we learned in Section 3.6T, controlling a filter by manipulating the coefficients directly is a very complicated proposition, but fortunately objects exist in Max that can calculate the coefficients for second-order filters on our behalf, sparing us the effort of performing the calculations ourselves.
Open the file **03_07_biquad_filtergraph.maxpat** (shown in figure 3.32).

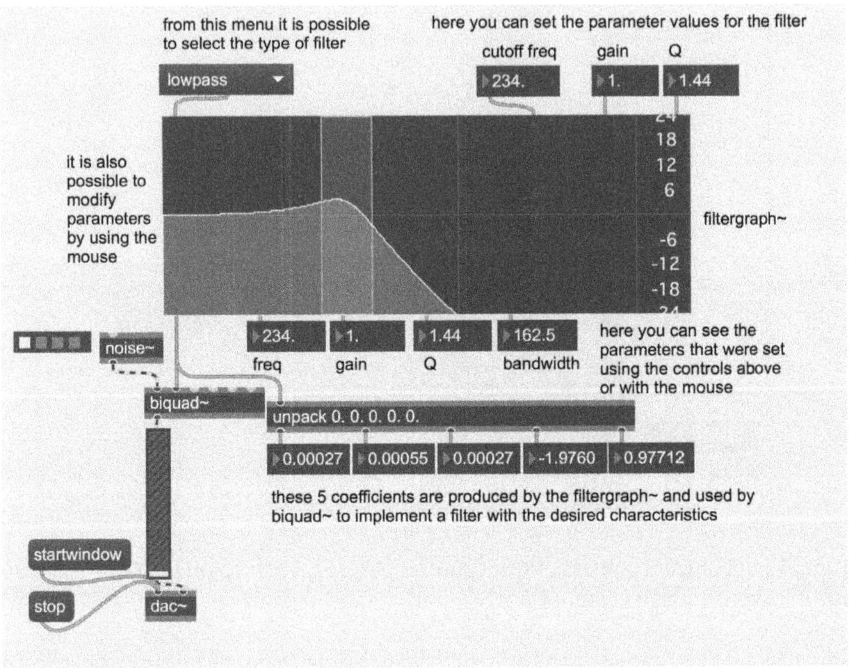

Fig. 3.32 The file 03_07_biquad_filtergraph.maxpat

The graphical object that we see in the upper part of this patch is called a **filtergraph~** and can manage the parameters of different kinds of filters. It is possible to specify the type of filter desired (lowpass, highpass, bandpass, etc.) by sending a message to the left inlet of this object. In the patch, the type of filter is selected by using a drop-down menu that is implemented using a **umenu**.
As you can see, in this example, the second outlet of **umenu** is used to send the text corresponding to the selection directly to the **filtergraph~**.
Every time the **filtergraph~** receives a message from the **umenu** ("lowpass", "highpass" etc.), the internal algorithm for the related filter is selected, which causes coefficients to be generated. (Naturally, the only messages that we have put into the **umenu** are those that correspond to actual filter algorithms implemented by the **filtergraph~** object!)
In the right part of the patch are controls for specifying cutoff frequency, gain, and Q; these filter parameters can also be set graphically using the mouse.

Current values of frequency, gain, Q, and bandwidth are output on four of the outlets of **filtergraph~**, and these are connected to as many float number boxes. The leftmost outlet produces the coefficients that specify the filter shown, which are sent to the **biquad~** object, which is the object performing the actual filtering in this patch. You can see the values of the 5 coefficients in the 5 float number boxes connected to the **unpack** object in the lower part of the patch. You might think that these numbers have no apparent relationship to the parameters set using the **filtergraph~**, but **biquad~** uses them to filter the input signal, as outlined in Section 3.6 of the theory chapter.

You might ask why we would use two objects (**filtergraph~** and **biquad~**) to implement a filter, when there seem to be easier-to-use pre-made objects for every one of the filters in the menu.
The answer is that **biquad~** (an object that can be used with any set of coefficients) can be used to realize any second-order filter, and not just those that can be managed by **filtergraph~**. (Other kinds of second-order filters are possible.) For example, the filters in the *Virtual Sound Macros* library that we have already used, such as the **vs.butterlp~**, and **vs.butterhp~**, use a **biquad~** filter, to which they each send their own specific ranges of coefficients. (Open one or two of these filters by double-clicking on them to see their implementation details.)

For more technical details, fee Section 3.6T and also the upcoming Section 3.6 below.

ACTIVITY

Realize a patch similar to the one in 03_04_qsynth.maxpat, using a **filtergraph~** and a **biquad~** in place of the **vs.lowpass~** filter. Since **filtergraph~** is controlled by Max messages rather than MSP signals, substitute **vs.between** generators for the paired function and **line~** objects, and on each random bang, generate a Q factor and a cutoff multiplier. (For the multiplier, you will need to replace the *~ operator with the Max floating point operator [* 1.].)
Copy the **filtergraph~** object and its menu from 03_07_biquad_filtergraph.maxpat, and for practice, connect it into your patch to try different kinds of filters (highpass, lowpass, bandpass, etc.).

The **filtercoeff~** object is the non-graphical equivalent to **filtergraph~**, and is extremely useful, both because it uses less space on the screen if you don't need to modify parameters graphically, and because it accepts its parameter values as signals rather than as Max messages. Because parameters are provided as signals, it is possible to vary them at the same speed as audio signals; signal input also makes it possible to use objects such as **line~** to provide parameters, as we will see in the next patch.

Open the file named **03_08_filtercoeff.maxpat** (shown in figure 3.33).

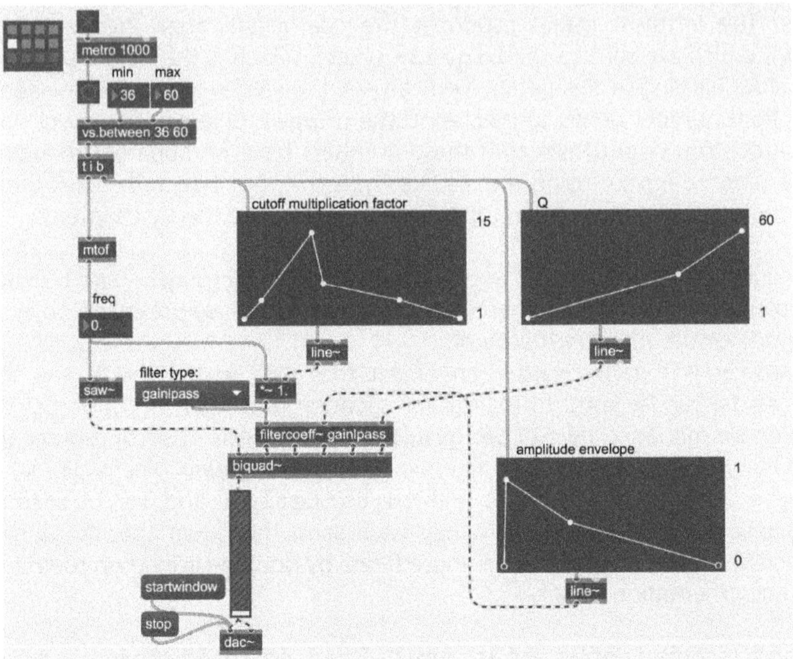

Fig. 3.33 The file 03_08_filtercoeff.maxpat

This patch is similar to the one contained in 03_02_qsynth.maxpat, the difference being that the `vs.lowpass~` filter has been replaced by paired `filtercoeff~` and `biquad~` objects. You can see that `filtercoeff~` accepts an argument for filter type (which is, in the example shown in the figure, "gainlpass", which is short for "lowpass with gain control"). Naturally, it is still possible to modify the filter type using a menu as we did with `filtergraph~`, although a menu for `filtercoeff~` has more options than one for `filtergraph~`, because there are two versions of every base filter: one with and one without gain. In this patch, we have also connected the amplitude envelope to the gain inlet of `filtercoeff~` to act as a multiplier. Try changing the filter type with saved presets, and create your own new configurations, but watch out for changes in output volume! Certain settings for some of the filters can cause the output signal to become considerably more intense.

By regularly varying the cutoff frequency of a lowpass filter at each repeating time interval, you can duplicate a well-known subtractive synthesis control effect: **sample and hold**[14] filtering. To try it, build the patch shown in figure 3.34:

14 "Sample and hold" refers to a technique in which you sample the output of a sound generator at regular intervals and use the resulting sample value to control a processing parameter, such as the cutoff frequency of a filter. In this example, we have used a slightly different implementation, but we have kept the name because the resulting effect is identical.

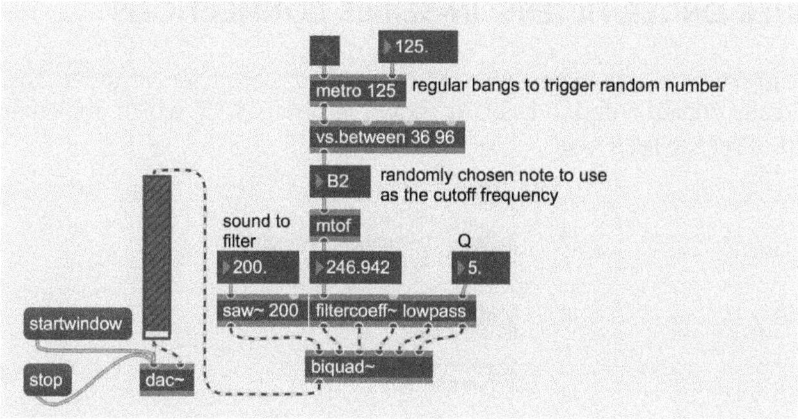

Fig. 3.34 Sample and hold filtering

In this patch, the sound of a fixed-frequency oscillator is filtered by a lowpass filter whose frequency changes every 125 milliseconds. A rhythmic sound characterized by a regular timbral pulse is the result.

ACTIVITIES

Here are some possible variations to the patch shown in figure 3.34:

- Add a random note generator connected to a **metro** to vary the frequency of the oscillator at a slower rate than the one used for filter modifications.

- Starting with the patch implemented for the preceding exercise, bind the pulse durations of the two (filter and oscillator frequency) **metro** objects together so that every change in pitch will result in 8 changes in cutoff frequency. You will need to control that any modification to the speed of pitch changes will automatically update the filter **metro** to run 8 times faster than the pitch **metro**. Add an amplitude envelope for the oscillator as well.

- Find a general way to set up a ratio between the speed of note changes on the oscillator and the speed of cutoff frequencies changes. You should make it possible to have 8 changes per note change (as we did in the preceding exercise), or 4, or 5, or any other number.

- Make the generation of random frequencies for the filter dependent upon the frequency of the oscillator, by generating a series of random numbers whenever the MIDI note changes, which can then be used to drive the cutoff frequencies.

HIGHER ORDER FILTERS: IN-SERIES CONNECTIONS

You can create higher-order filters by connecting more filters in series. This can be directly implemented in MSP, as shown in figure 3.35, which implements a fourth-order lowpass filter.

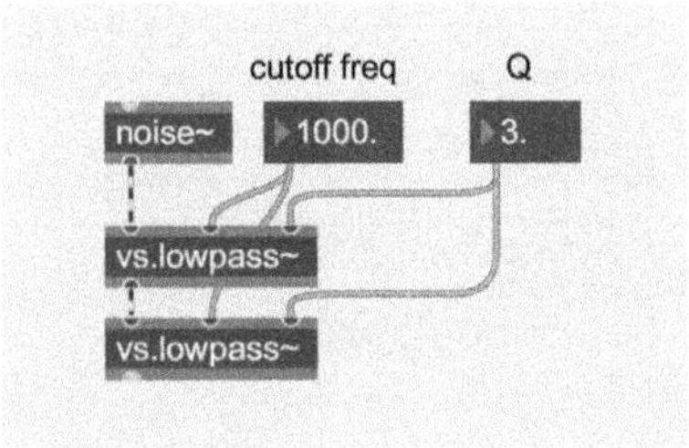

Fig. 3.35 A fourth-order lowpass filter

Figure 3.36 shows an eighth-order highpass filter:

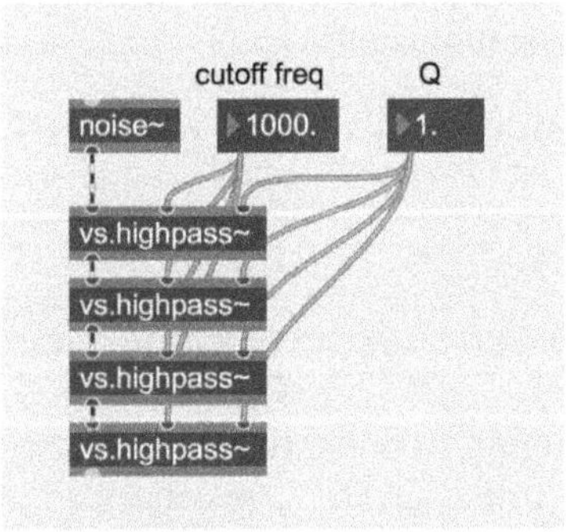

Fig. 3.36 An eighth-order highpass filter

Build these patches in order to hear how they sound, and take care to keep the Q factor low, because the resonance of these filters accumulates and can easily exceed the maximum amplitude capability of Max.

It is also possible to create higher-order filters by using first-order filters; you could, for example, connect 5 `onepole~` filters in order to create a fifth-order lowpass filter.
It is interesting to note that composing filters of the same type and the same order, but realized using different algorithms, will give divergent results, even though ideally the filters ought to have the same effect on the sound.
For example, consider the two fourth-order lowpass filters illustrated in figure 3.37:

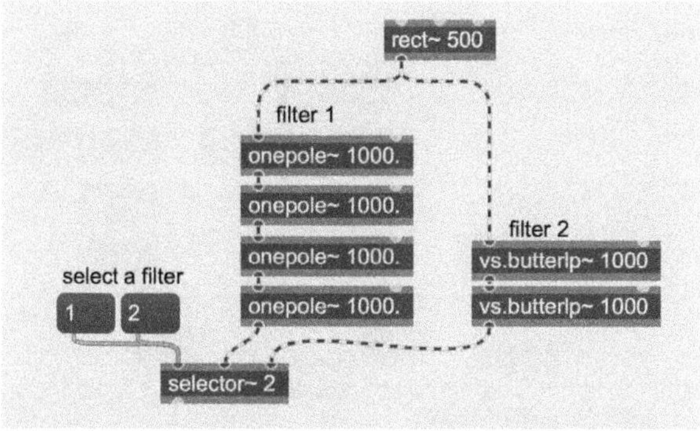

Fig. 3.37 Two different fourth-order filters

If you build this patch, notice that the two filters each have a different effect on the sound. In particular, the second filter, constructed using Butterworth filters, tends to boost the frequencies near the cutoff frequency. This is due to the fact that the implementations of the filters are pretty far away from the theoretical properties of ideal filters, as explained in Section 3.4T.
It is also possible to construct particular filters by connecting filters that differ from each other in series. For example, using resonant lowpass and highpass filters in series, it is possible to create a bandpass with two resonance frequencies. (See figure 3.38.)

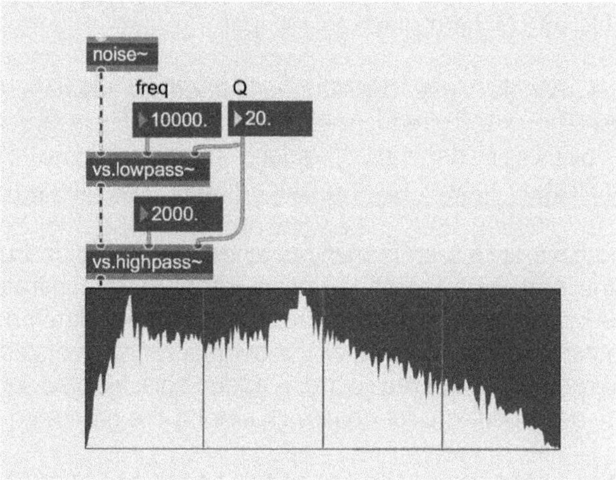

Fig. 3.38 A bandpass filter with two resonance frequencies

Notice that the cutoff frequency of the lowpass filter (`vs.lowpass~`) must be higher than that of the highpass filter (`vs.highpass~`). Do you understand why?

Taking our cue from the last example, here are some exercises that might be more musically interesting. Open the file **03_09_harmonicwalk.maxpat** (which is shown in figure 3.39).

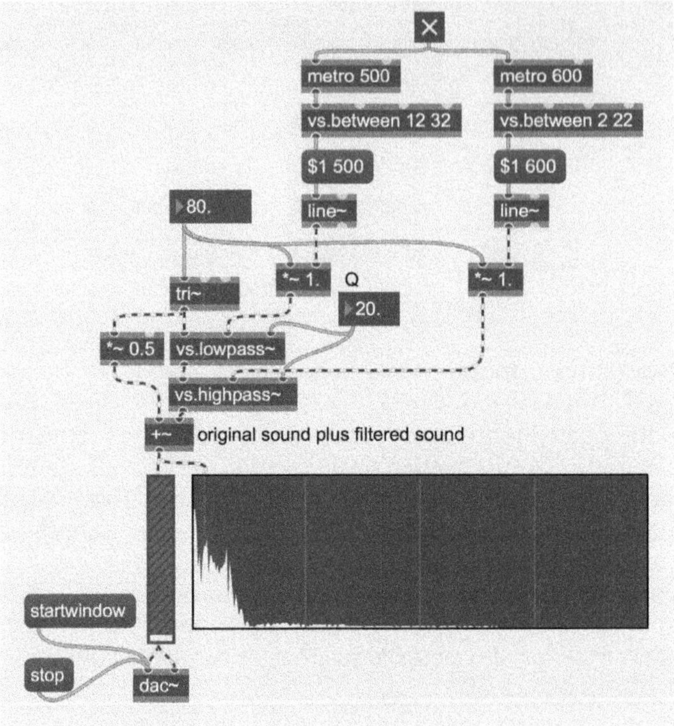

Fig. 3.39 The file 03_09_harmonicwalk.maxpat

In this patch a triangle wave oscillator is filtered by lowpass and highpass filters in series. The cutoff frequencies for the two filters are controlled by a pair of `vs.between` generators, guided by two `metro` objects, which generate multiplication factors for the fundamental. The filters, thanks to their Q, emphasize the shifting harmonics using the technique that we first saw in figure 3.21 and have since seen in many patches. The transition from one cutoff frequency to the next is navigated by means of glissandi generated by `line~` objects; the `metro` speeds that drive these glissandi are different for the two independent parameter paths. Some of the original sound, reduced in amplitude so as not to overpower the filtered sound, is added back into the sound obtained, which might be described as a random walk among the harmonics of a sound.

ACTIVITIES

Here are some potential extensions to the 03_09_harmonicwalk.maxpat patch:
- Add a random frequency generator connected to a `metro` that will vary the frequency of the oscillator between 50 and 200 Hz at a slow tempo (such as one bang per 3,000 milliseconds).

- Tie the `metro` tempos together (the principal pulse becoming the oscillator's frequency, acting as a master for those of the two cutoff frequencies) in the following way: for every note generated, the filters change 5 and 6 times, respectively. This ratio should remain constant, even when the tempo of the principal **metro** is changed. Pay attention to the second elements of the messages that are sent to the **line~** objects!

- Add two amplitude envelopes: one for the original sound and one for the filtered sound. Also try other waveforms. Save the interesting timbres that you create as a result into presets.

3.5 SUBTRACTIVE SYNTHESIS

In Section 3.5T, we described the internals of a modest virtual synthesizer that could exploit the techniques of subtractive synthesis. This synthesizer, which was used to create some of the interactive examples found at www.virtual-sound.com/cmsupport, was implemented in Max. We will spend this entire section analyzing its operation and architecture.
The patch containing this synthesizer is more intricate and is also much bigger than any other patch that we have discussed to this point. None of its subsections, taken alone, is particularly complex, but to get a clear overall vision of how they fit together into the patch, a certain amount of concentration will be necessary. We therefore advise you to work on this section when your mind is fresh, and also not to try to read it in a single gulp. Instead, you might benefit from breaking your study into manageable chunks. Above all, make sure that you have a firm grasp of the Max programming techniques that have already been presented.

"WIRELESS" COMMUNICATIONS: THE PVAR OBJECT

Speaking of programming technique, our first step in this analysis will be to introduce an object that makes managing a Max interface (the ensemble of number boxes, faders, buttons, and other graphical objects used to set parameter values for a given patch) much easier: **pvar**.
To see how this object works, implement the simple patch shown in figure 3.40:

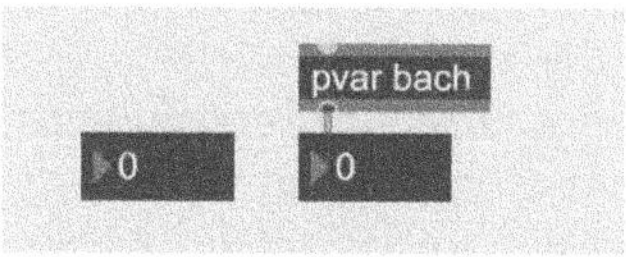

Fig. 3.40 The **pvar** object

We have two number boxes in this somewhat mysterious patch, the second of which is connected to a **pvar** object with the argument "bach". If you modify the contents of the two number boxes in performance mode, nothing unusual happens at all, since the outputs of the number boxes are not connected to other objects; input to them triggers no actions.

However, try the following: return to edit mode and open the Inspector for the number box that is not connected to the **pvar** object. Locate the "Name" category and double-click on the space to the right of the ***Scripting Name*** attribute, where a text field will appear into which you can type "bach" (as shown in figure 3.41).

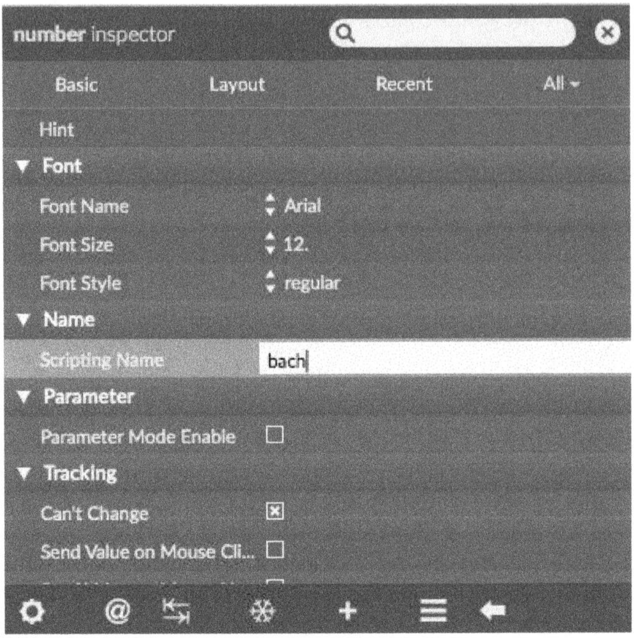

Fig. 3.41 Naming an object in the Inspector

When you close the Inspector, you have given a unique name to the number box. No other object within the same patch can have the same name, and if you now return to performance mode and modify the value of the number box named "bach", you will see the **pvar** object forward your input to the other, unnamed, number box.
When a **pvar** object has an argument that matches the name of another object, it automatically receives messages from that named object and forwards them to its own outlet. The **pvar** object resembles a **receive** object in that it can receive messages from other objects without being connected to them. There are differences however; the **pvar** object receives messages directly from the named object for which it is a proxy, and communication can occur only within a single patch. (Recall that **send** objects can send messages to matching **receive** objects even when they are in another patch.) As we will soon see, **pvar** objects are very useful for constructing user interfaces without patch-cord clutter.

MULTIPLE CHOICES: THE RADIOGROUP OBJECT

Before diving into synthesizer details, there is another object that we need to explain: the **radiogroup** object. This object is used as part of a user interface, and represents a group of options from which an element can be chosen. It is found in the "Buttons" *palette*, and consists of a set of buttons. The number of buttons in the group can be defined by the user. (See figure 3.42.)

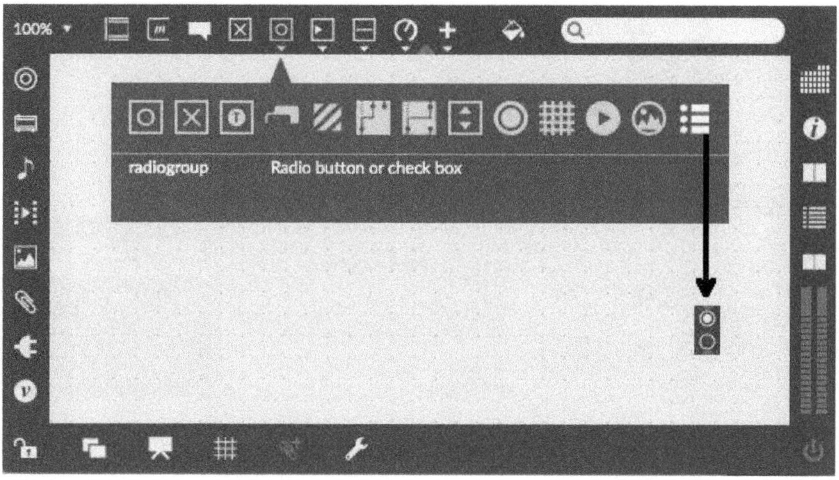

Fig. 3.42 The **radiogroup** object

By default, a **radiogroup** contains two buttons, but this number can be changed by setting the ***Number of Items*** attribute in the *Value* category of the Inspector. Create a **radiogroup** with 4 buttons, using the Inspector, and connect a number box to its outlet. When you click on the various buttons in performance mode, you will see that each button has been given a number: the first button is numbered 0, the second 1, and so on (as shown in figure 3.43).

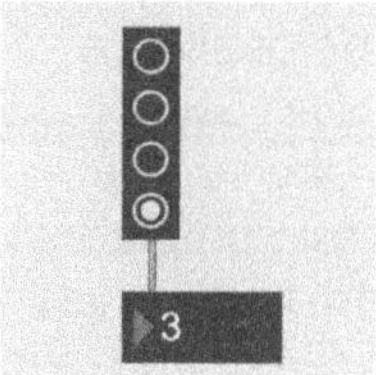

Fig. 3.43 A **radiogroup** with 4 buttons

This object makes it easy to select one option from among a group of options, using an approach that is similar to that of **umenu**. Because of their similarities, it would be straightforward to replace the **umenu** in figure 3.29, for example, with a **radiogroup**: in this example, you would add a comment box next to each button containing the name of the waveform represented by the button.

ANATOMY OF A SUBTRACTIVE SYNTHESIZER

Now we can begin the actual dissection of our virtual synthesizer. If you have not already done it, re-read Section 3.5 of the theory chapter. We are not going to expound on the synthesis techniques here, only on the Max implementation itself.

Open the file **03_10_subsynth.maxpat**. In figure 3.44, we see the synthesizer's interface, which makes up the upper part of this patch.

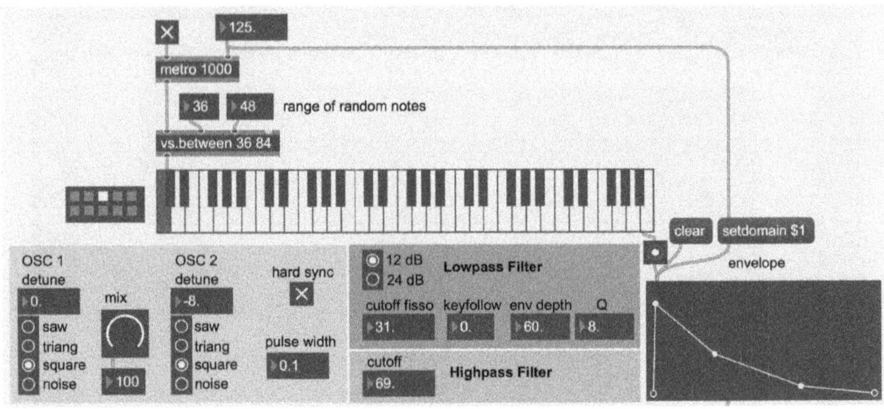

Fig. 3.44 The synthesizer interface found in the file 03_10_subsynth.maxpat

The region at the lower left contains parameters for the two oscillators. The waveform for each can be selected using a radiogroup, and above these `radiogroup` objects are two number boxes that change the tuning of the oscillators, in fractions of a semitone. In the center part of the panel, under the "mix" label, is a **`dial`** object (the rotational equivalent of the slider object introduced in Section 1.6) that ranges from 0 to 100 and mixes the outputs of the two oscillators. When its value is 0, only the oscillator on the left can be heard, and when its value is 100, only the oscillator on the right can be heard. Any other number causes the outputs to be mixed proportionately; a value of 50, for example, causes the oscillators to be mixed in equal proportions. A `toggle` labeled "hard sync" (see Section 3.5T to review the theory behind this control), and a number box labeled "pulse width" that is used to control the duty cycle of the square waves, complete this region of the interface.
Moving to the right, we find two panels, one above the other. The upper panel controls the lowpass filter, and enables setting the roll-off, using a `radiogroup`, to 12 or 24 dB per octave (a choice between a second-order or a fourth-order filter). There are also number boxes for setting the cutoff frequency, the key follow factor, the depth at which the envelope will affect the filter's cutoff, and the filter Q. The lower panel contains nothing but a number box for setting the fixed cutoff frequency of the highpass filter.
To the right of the two filter panels is a `function` object that is used to draw the synthesizer's amplitude envelope (which also can affect the cutoff frequency for the lowpass filter, using a technique that we discussed in Section 3.5T). In the upper part of the interface is a random note generator, similar to those we've seen in other patches. Note that the interval between pulses for its `metro` object is also used to set the duration of the envelope, thanks to the "*setdomain*" technique that we developed in Section IA.8 in Interlude A. (See figure IA.65 for details.)
The majority of the objects in the interface have been given names, so that each can communicate with corresponding `pvar` objects in the lower half of

the patch. To make these **pvar** objects stand out in the patch, we have colored their borders, using the Inspector; each is also connected to a number box so that you can easily track their values. Try changing the parameters in the upper interface with the metronome off, and confirm that the values change below. For example, you might click on one of the keys of the **kslider** object – there are two different **pvar** objects that receive the resulting message. Are you able to pick them out?
We move now to an analysis of the "engine" that drives this synthesizer, beginning with the section that generates sound, which can be found at the bottom left of the patch (shown in figure 3.45).

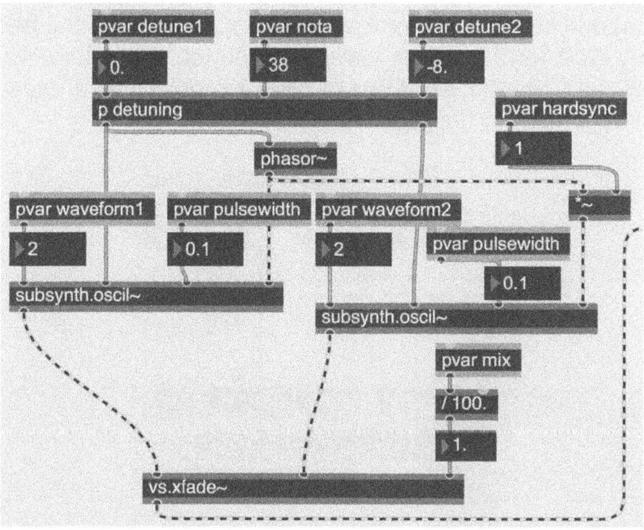

Fig. 3.45 The oscillator section of the patch found in 03_10_subsynth.maxpat

In the upper part of this section, there are three **pvar** objects that receive the note number for the randomly generated MIDI note and two *detuning* factors. These three values are sent to the [**p** detuning] subpatch, which you can open for inspection using a double-click (and which is shown in figure 3.46).

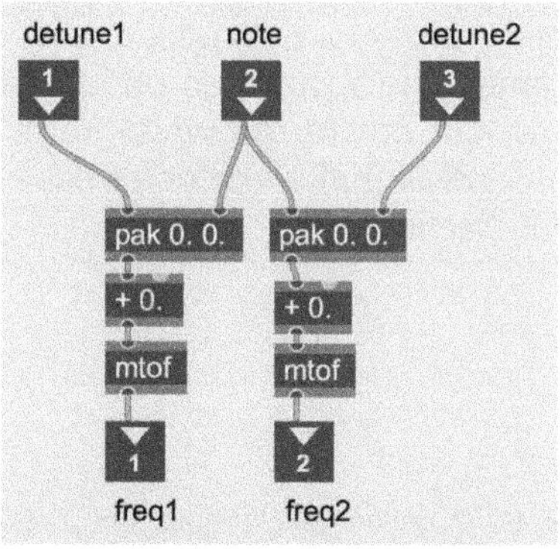

Fig. 3.46 The contents of the [**p** detuning] subpatch

Within the subpatch, the note and the detuning factors are summed,[15] and the two results are converted into hertz by two **mtof** objects. The two frequencies thus obtained are sent to the outlet of the subpatch.

Returning to the main patch of figure 3.45, we see that the first frequency drives a **phasor~** (which we will discuss in a moment) as well as a **subsynth.oscil~**, and the second frequency also drives its own **subsynth.oscil~**.
If you have not heard us mention the **subsynth.oscil~** object before, don't fret: it is, in fact, an abstraction, created out of other Max objects specifically for this patch. (The relevant file, which contains the implementation and can be found in the same folder as the main patch, is named subsynth.oscil~.maxpat.) The object has 4 inlets: the first for the waveform, the second the frequency, the third the duty cycle for the square wave, and the fourth the hard sync setting. By double-clicking on the **subsynth.oscil~** object, you can open it for examination (as shown in figure 3.47).

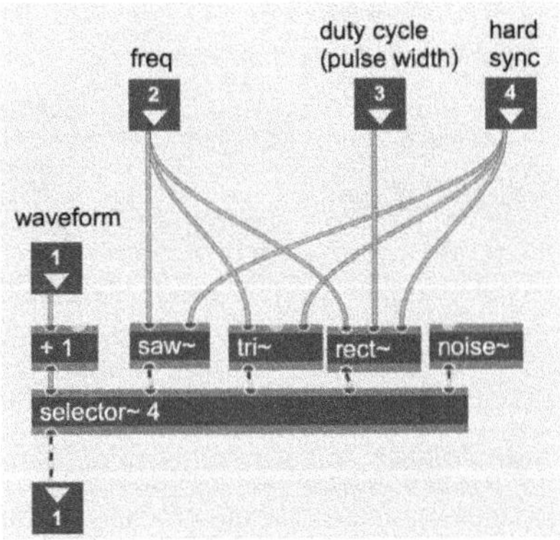

Fig. 3.47 The internals of the **subsynth.oscil~** abstraction

As you can see, the patch is quite simple; a **selector~** enables choosing either white noise or one of three band-limited waveforms (sawtooth, triangle, and square). The choice is made using a **radiogroup** in the interface, and arrives as an integer at the first inlet of the abstraction, which is labeled "waveform". This value is incremented by 1 before being used as the input to the **selector~** object; do you understand why this is necessary? The frequency value, which enters the abstraction on its second inlet, is sent to the three periodic waveforms, but not to the white noise generator, for reasons that are hopefully obvious: recall that white noise has no need for a frequency parameter (as discussed in Section 3.1).

15 The values are sent to **pak**, which generates a list each time it receives a message on any of its inlets (as discussed in Section 2.4). In this case, the **pak** object sends the list to a summation object (+) that executes the operation. (To review the behavior of lists sent to operators, see section IA.1.)

The **rect~** object, which we use to produce square waves, accepts the value for duty cycle that enters on the third inlet (details of duty cycle can be found in Section 1.2, both theory and practice), while the fourth and final inlet, labeled "hard sync", is connected to the rightmost inlet of each of the band-limited oscillators. When these oscillators receive a signal on their rightmost inlet that passes from a value less than 0.5 to a value greater than 0.5, the cycle of the waveform will begin again, no matter what point had been being sampled. This means that connecting a **phasor~** to this input will force the oscillator to reset its cycle every time that the **phasor~** rises above the halfway point in its ramp. Figure 3.48 shows a patch that illustrates this mechanism: the **phasor~** object has a frequency of 100 Hz and is connected to the rightmost inlet of a **saw~** object, which has a frequency of 150 Hz. The **saw~** object is repeatedly "forced" to return to the beginning of its cycle after completing one and a half cycles.

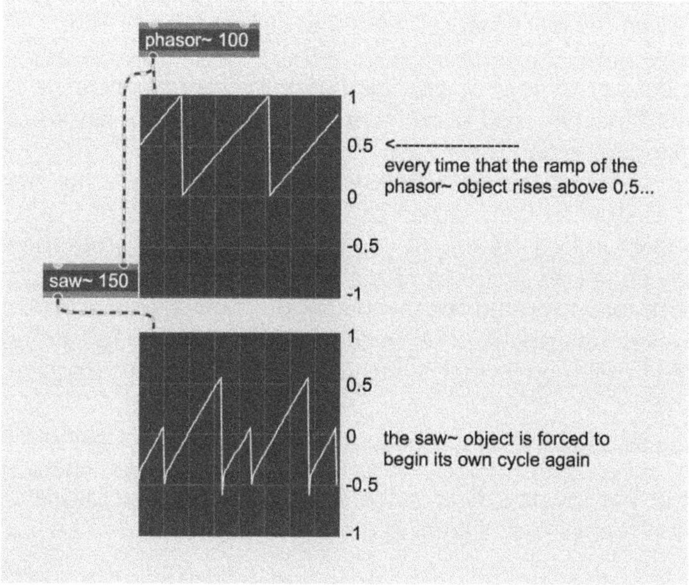

Fig. 3.48 The hard sync mechanism

Returning to the main patch of figure 3.45, let's occupy ourselves with the **phasor~** object for a moment. This object receives the same value for its frequency from [**p** detuning] as the left oscillator does. As you can see, the outlet of the **phasor~** is connected to a ***~** multiplier; each time that the **toggle** in the interface labeled "hard sync" is clicked, a 0 or a 1 is sent to the [**pvar** hardsync] object, and this number is continuously multiplied with the **phasor~** signal. Multiplying by 1 allows the ramp to pass, while multiplying by 0 zeroes the signal out, which cancels its effect. The output from the multiplier is routed to the fourth inlet of the right **subsynth.oscil~** object; since the **phasor~** has the same frequency as the left oscillator, when hard sync is selected, the oscillator on the right becomes a slave to the one on the left.

Notice that the **phasor~** signal is also sent directly to the fourth inlet of the oscillator on the left, which might seem like a pointless thing to do, since this oscillator already shares the same frequency as the **phasor~** and therefore would seem not to need the synchronization signal. But in actuality, the presence of this signal guarantees that both oscillators will be perfectly synchronized; when hard sync is active, both oscillators start their cycles at precisely the same moment.

The signals emerging from the two oscillators are sent to the **vs.xfade~** object, part of the *Virtual Sound Macros* library, which takes the signals and mixes them based on the parameter value that it receives on its third inlet. A 0 will emit the first signal alone, a 1 the second signal alone, and any other number between 0 and 1 will produce a proportional mix of the two signals. The value for the mix parameter arrives from the **dial** labeled "mix" by way of the [**pvar** mix] object. When it is received, it is divided by 100 in order to rescale the input, since the dial produces a number between 0 and 100.

This concludes our somewhat detailed tour of the sound generation facilities of our virtual synthesizer. You might consider taking a break before continuing, since the filtering section is even more intricate!
The output signal of the **vs.xfade~** object, which mixes the signals from the two oscillators, is then routed to the filtering section of the synthesizer, which is shown in figure 3.49. As you can see, the signal from the oscillators immediately enters the first inlet of the **subsynth.filter~** object, which is another abstraction created for this patch. But before taking this abstraction apart, however, let's analyze the function of the subpatch [**p** calc_lpfreq] that you can see in the upper right, which calculates the cutoff frequency for the lowpass filter.

As you will recall from reading Section 3.5 of the theory chapter, the cutoff frequency of our lowpass filter is the result of a series of calculations. More precisely, it is the result of summing three parameters:

1) a fixed frequency
2) a multiple of the frequency of the sounding note (key follow)
3) the current value of the amplitude envelope, multiplied by a depth factor

In figure 3.49 we see that the [**p** calc_lpfreq] object has five inlets: the first receives randomly generated MIDI note numbers, the second, the fixed value for the cutoff frequency, the third, the key follow factor, the fourth, the depth factor for the envelope, and the fifth, the signal generated by the **line~** object for the envelope.

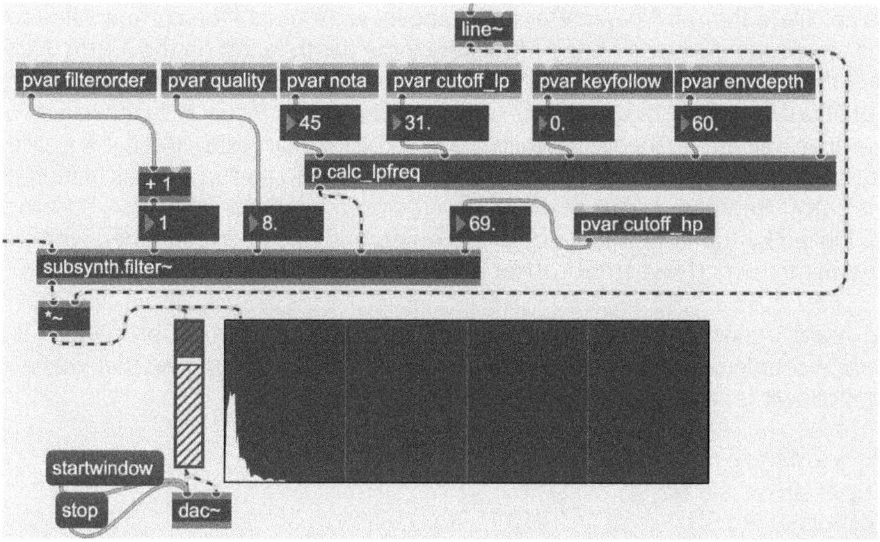

Fig. 3.49 The filter section of the patch found in 03_10_subsynth.maxpat

Double-click on [p calc_lpfreq] in order to open it (as shown in figure 3.50).

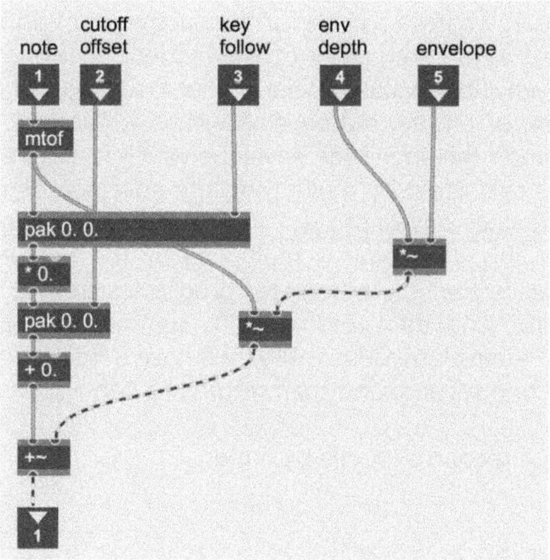

Fig. 3.50 The contents of the [p calc_lpfreq] subpatch

You can see that the MIDI note number from the first inlet is immediately converted to a frequency and multiplied by the key follow factor received on the third inlet: when this factor equals 1, the parameter is the same as the frequency of the note, if the factor is 2, the frequency is doubled, an so forth. Naturally, when the factor is equal to 0, the key follow parameter is disabled. To the key follow value thus calculated, the fixed cutoff offset frequency from the second inlet is added.

To calculate the third parameter listed above, we multiply the current value for the amplitude envelope on the fifth inlet by the depth factor on the fourth. Note that the multiplier is an MSP object (marked by the tilde), since the envelope is a signal rather than a Max message. Again, if the depth factor is 1, the values of the envelope are unchanged, while if it is 2, they are doubled, and if it is 0, they are completely zeroed out (and the envelope plays no part in the calculation of the cutoff frequency). The envelope signal, scaled by the depth factor, is further multiplied by the note frequency at this point, and finally, it is summed with the two parameters (fixed cutoff offset and key follow) previously calculated.

To really understand how processing of the cutoff frequency proceeds, let's trace a couple of practice calculations, by hand. First, let's suppose that we have the following parameter values:

Note = 440 Hz
Cutoff offset = 0 Hz
Key follow = 1
Env depth = 1

Let's also suppose that the amplitude envelope is triangular, and proceeds from 0 to 1 over 1 second, returning to 0 in 1 second.

Since key follow is 1, we have a value for the parameter of 440 (440 · 1 = 440), to which the fixed cutoff frequency of 0 is added. To those values, we also need to add the envelope value. While the first two values remain fixed for the entire duration of a note, the envelope value is dynamic, varying in time, since it depends upon the amplitude envelope which is a signal that varies over time. The value is calculated by multiplying the envelope depth parameter by the envelope, and since env depth is 1 in our example, the envelope remains unchanged. After this, the result is multiplied by the frequency of the note (440 Hz). This means that the parameter progresses from 0 to 440 over the period of a second, and then returns to 0. Summing the three parameters together (440 + 0 + envelope value · 440), we have a frequency that goes from 440 to 880 Hz in one second, and then returns to 440 Hz in one second.

Working through a second example by hand:

Note = 220 Hz
Cutoff offset = 100 Hz
Key follow = 2
Env depth = 0.5

We will use the same envelope as we did in the previous example, a triangular envelope that goes from 0 to 1 in 1 second, and returns to 0 in 1 second.
The frequency value 220 · 2 (key follow) yields 440, to which we add 100 for the cutoff offset, producing a final parameter value of 540. We now multiply envelope depth, which is 0.5, times the envelope, and further multiply this by the frequency of the note (220 Hz). The result is a value that goes from 0 to 110 over

one second, and then returns to 0 over one second. Summing all parameters (540 + envelope · 0.5 · 220) we obtain a cutoff frequency that goes from 540 Hz to 650 Hz over one second, and then returns to 540 Hz in one second.

Returning to the main patch (figure 3.49), you can see that the cutoff value thus calculated by the [**p** calc_lpfreq] subpatch is submitted to the fourth inlet of the **subsynth.filter~** object. But before opening this object, let's examine the data sent to each of its five inlets.
As mentioned earlier, the signal produced by the oscillators and mixed by **vs.xfade~** is routed to the first inlet. A value that establishes whether the lowpass filter will be a second-order (with 12 dB of attenuation) or a fourth-order one (with 24 dB of attenuation) is sent to the second inlet; when a value is received by [**pvar** filterorder] (whose input comes from the **radiogroup** in the center panel of the interface, as seen in figure 3.44), this value (either 0 or 1, depending on whether the button labeled "12 dB" or "24 dB" was pressed) is incremented by 1 before being transmitted to the second input of **subsynth.filter~**.The value for Q is sent to the third inlet, the lowpass filter cutoff frequency signal calculated by the subpatch that we just analyzed is sent to the fourth inlet, and finally, the cutoff frequency for the highpass filter, which is a fixed number, is sent to the fifth inlet.
With that information in mind, double-click on the **subsynth.filter~** object to open it (as shown in figure 3.51).

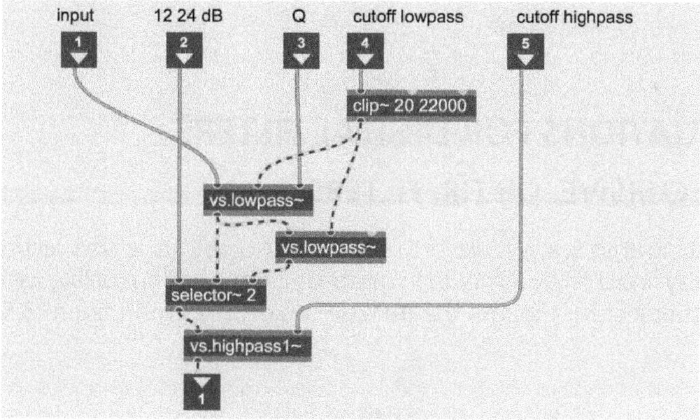

Fig. 3.51 The internals of the **subsynth.filter~** object

As you see in the figure, the audio signal arriving on the first **inlet** is sent to a lowpass filter that is connected in cascade to a second lowpass filter. The output signals of both filters are connected to the inlets of a **selector~** object; incoming data from the second **inlet** is also connected to the first inlet of this object, and the value received on it, 1 or 2, determines whether the filter will have a roll-off of 12 or 24 dB. (If the **selector~** receives a 1, it routes the output from the first filter to its own output, but if it receives a 2, the output from the second filter is chosen, which is cascaded with the output of the first filter in order to implement a fourth order filter.) The third **inlet** has the Q setting, which is applied to the first lowpass filter, but not to the second (which, as a consequence, has a default Q value of 1). Sending Q to both filters would create excessive boost around the cutoff frequency.

The cutoff frequency for the lowpass filter, in the form of a signal, is received on the fourth **inlet**. This signal is made to pass through a **clip~** object before anything else, which forces the sample values of the signal to comply with the fixed limits defined by its two arguments; in this case, in order to avoid unstable filter behavior, **clip~** ensures that the cutoff frequency never goes lower than 20 Hz, and never goes higher than 22,000 Hz. These limits are based on a sampling rate of 44,100 Hz, and if your audio interface uses a higher sampling rate, you can change the upper limit of **clip~** in the patch. (However, the upper limit should never exceed half of the sampling rate; we will cover this in Chapter 5.) The outlet of **clip~** is connected to the second inlets for both lowpass filters, and finally, the cutoff frequency for the first-order highpass filter, implemented using **vs.highpass1~**, is passed in using the fifth **inlet**. The input signal for this filter comes from the output of the **selector~** object, and the output signal becomes the output signal for the entire abstraction.

Returning one final time to the main patch of figure 3.49, you can see that the output from **subsynth.filter~** is multiplied by the envelope generated by the **line~** object, which itself is connected to the graphical **function** object. The signal, after envelope processing, is handed to a spectrum analyzer and, thanks to **gain~** and **dac~**, to the audio interface, where it is finally transformed into audible sound.[16]

3.6 EQUATIONS FOR DIGITAL FILTERS

NON-RECURSIVE, OR FIR, FILTERS

The first thing that we will do in this section is construct a non-recursive filter, using a delay line directly rather than pre-built filters. Without delay, we introduce the perfect object for the job: the **delay~** object (shown in figure 3.52).

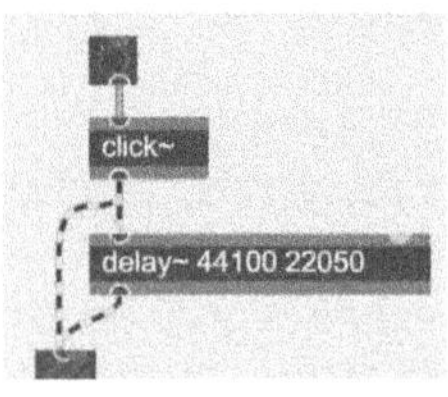

Fig. 3.52 The **delay~** object

[16] We also suggest you take a look at the **abl.device.drift** object, a very interesting subtractive synthesizer with two oscillators and parameter modulation via LFO (see chapter 4). The object is very complex and has dozens of parameters, for its use you can check the help patch. You can also find a full explanation of the instrument's behavior in the Live manual, which is available online at ableton.com. Look for the reference to the "Drift" device in the manual.

The **delay~** object takes two arguments, both expressed as a number of samples: the first indicates the maximum possible delay, and the second the *effective delay*. The object in the figure, for example, will have a maximum delay of 44,100 samples (one second at a sampling rate of 44,100 Hz) and an effective delay of 22,050 samples (half a second). The second parameter can be modified dynamically by sending a numeric value to the right inlet, but the number should never exceed the maximum value. The **click~** object connected to **delay~** in the figure is an audio click generator; every time that it receives a bang it emits a single sample with an amplitude of 1, followed by a series of zeros. If you construct this patch, you'll hear a click when you press the button, and another click when half a second has elapsed.

Now let's implement the first filter described in Section 3.6 of the theory chapter. To do this, build the patch shown in figure 3.53:

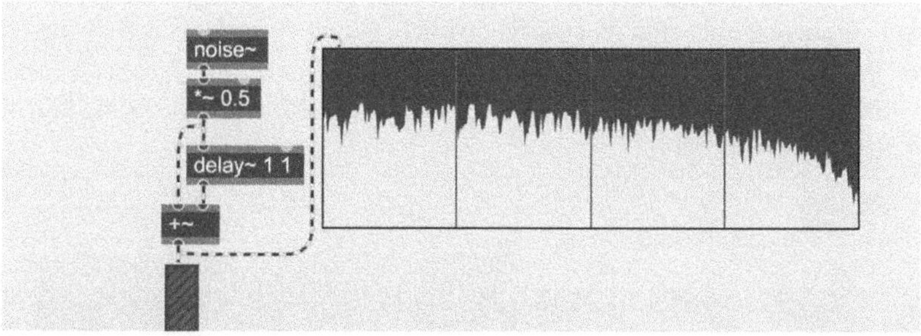

Fig. 3.53 A FIR lowpass filter

This filter directly reflects the equation y(n) = 1/2 x(n) + 1/2 x(n-1). We multiply the signal by 0.5, cutting it in half. We then split the signal, delaying one branch by a single sample (with **delay~**), and then adding the delayed signal to the original signal. The resulting filter is a lowpass filter that has a cutoff frequency equal to a quarter of the sampling rate. (For example, a sampling rate of 44,100 Hz will produce a filter with a cutoff frequency of 11,025 Hz.)

In figure 3.54, we see a filter implementation that reflects the equation y(n) = 1/2 x(n) - 1/2 x(n-1).

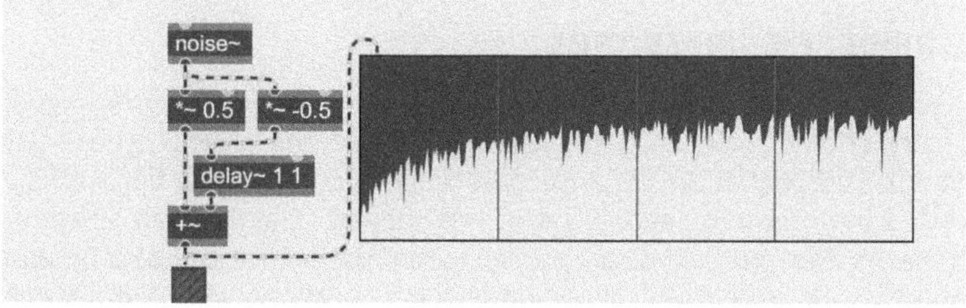

Fig. 3.54 A FIR highpass filter

This equation results in a highpass filter with a cutoff frequency of a quarter of the sampling rate. We leave it to you to analyze the patch; once you've done this, you can move directly to constructing a bandpass filter using the equation y(n) = 1/2 x(n) - 1/2 x(n-2), which is shown in figure 3.55:

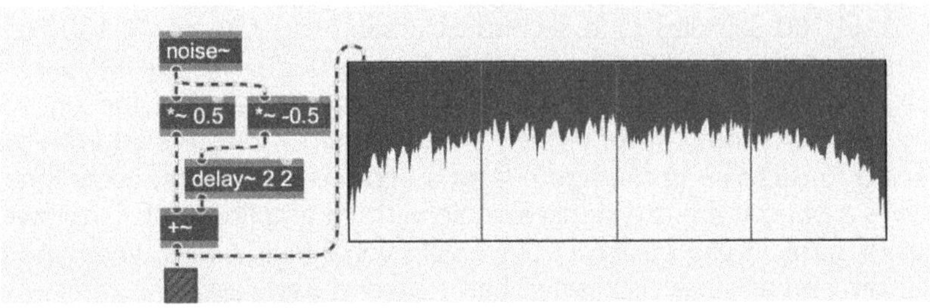

Fig. 3.55 A FIR bandpass filter

As you can see, to build this filter you need to increase the delay to two samples in order to reflect the x(n-2) term. At the same time, the signal delayed by one sample is now absent since its coefficient is 0. (Review Section 3.6 in the theory chapter if you aren't following this.)
We will now experiment with generic FIR filters of the second-order. Our patch is shown in figure 3.56:

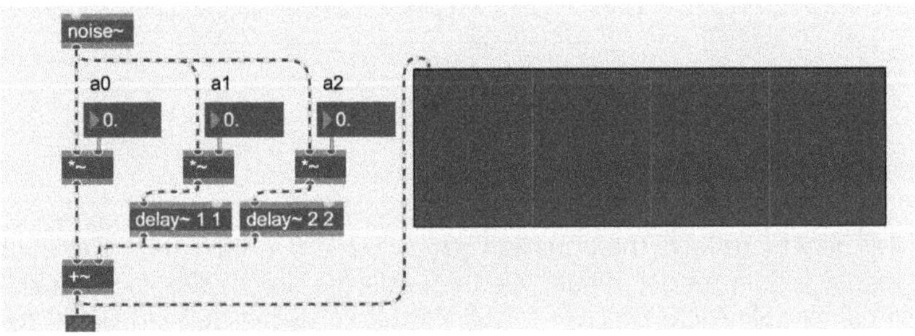

Fig. 3.56 A generic second-order FIR filter

The three float number boxes contain the values of the coefficients a_0, a_1 and a_2, which can be freely varied to try various combinations. Try, for example, $a_0 = 0.5$, $a_1 = 0$ and $a_2 = 0.5$. What type of filter does this produce? Using the same configuration, try moving a_1 between -1 and 1.

RECURSIVE, OR IIR, FILTERS

Since you've already read the section that corresponds to this section in the theory chapter, you probably recognized that the MSP **biquad~** object implements the equation of a second-order recursive (IIR) filter when we introduced the object in Section 3.4 of this chapter. The five right inlets of the object are for the coefficients a_0, a_1, a_2, b_1 and b_2, which can also be entered as arguments. Because of this, if we enter the 5 coefficients used in our analysis of the Butterworth filter in section 3.6 of the theory chapter as arguments of **biquad~**, we should obtain a lowpass filter with a cutoff frequency of 1,000 Hz (assuming a sampling rate of 44,100 Hz!).

Build the patch in figure 3.57 to try this:

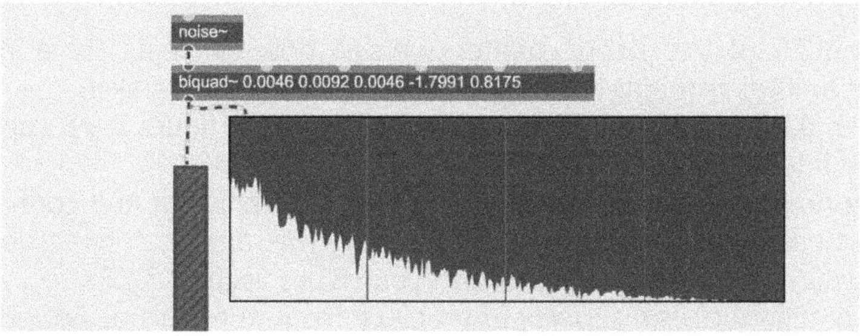

Fig. 3.57 A second-order IIR filter

The **vs.butterlp~** filter in the *Virtual Sound Macros* library contains a module that calculates this kind of filter exactly as we described in the theory section. If you open a **vs.butterlp~** object by double-clicking on it, you can see the objects that it contains, which, besides a **biquad~**, include the module **vs.butterlpc** (which stands for *Butterworth LowPass Coefficients*). This module produces a list of the 5 coefficients for a given cutoff frequency. If you build the patch shown in 3.58, you can observe how the coefficients vary with changes in the cutoff frequency.

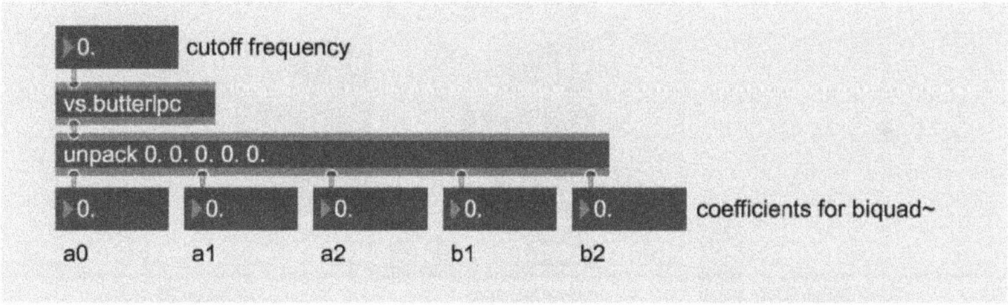

Fig. 3.58 Examining the coefficients produced by **vs.butterlpc**

When you open **vs.butterlpc** with a double-click, you will see a calculation of some complexity, which will probably make more sense once you've studied the **expr** object in Interlude B. Even with this handicap, however, it shouldn't be too difficult to analyze the patch and to see the equations that we derived in Section 3.6 of the theory chapter. Obviously, other objects also exist that implement Butterworth highpass, bandpass, and bandreject filters, and that contain the appropriate coefficient calculations for each (see the glossary). The **filtergraph~** and **filtercoeff~** objects work in a similar way, but since they are externals that were compiled in the C programming language, it is unfortunately not possible to double-click and trace their calculations visually.
If, in the future, you find the equation for some interesting filter that you would like to experiment with in a textbook, you can build it using a patch similar to that shown above for the Butterworth filter, and then connect it to a **biquad~** object. In Interlude B, in the section dedicated to the **expr** object, we will see how such a series of formulas for calculating the coefficients of a filter can be implemented in a subpatch using **biquad~**.

3.7 FILTERS CONNECTED IN PARALLEL, AND GRAPHIC EQUALIZATION

In Section 3.7 of the theory chapter, we saw how to create some interesting dynamic timbres through the use of filters connected in parallel.
The patch **03_11_parallel_filters.maxpat**, shown in figure 3.59, captures the sound of Interactive Example 3E2.
Let's see how it works. Before anything else, try the patch and confirm that it produces a sequence similar to, but not exactly the same as, Interactive Example 3F2. (If you don't remember it, refresh yourself in Section 3.7T.)
In this patch, we use a pertinent object from the Virtual Sound Macros library, **vs.choose**, that, every time it receives a list, randomly chooses an element and sends it to its left outlet. As you can see, there are two message boxes that send their lists to matching **vs.choose** objects every time that they receive a bang from the **metro** object. The random choice on the left falls into the range between 63 and 108, which corresponds to MIDI note numbers Eb3 to C7, while the choice on the right falls between the values 0.5 to 1, which will be used as amplitude values.

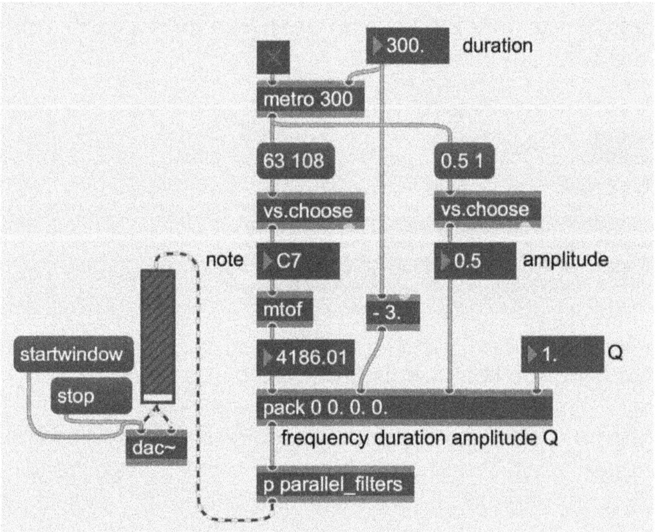

Fig. 3.59 The file 03_11_parallel_filters.maxpat

You can see that every bang generated by the **metro** object generates a list of four values that correspond to frequency, duration, amplitude, and Q. Frequency is the randomly selected MIDI value (converted to frequency by **mtof**), while amplitude is the unmodified result of the random choice. The duration, initially 300 ms, is reduced by 3 milliseconds before being included in the list, and the Q value is fixed at 1. The four values, packaged as a list using **pack**, are then sent on to the subpatch [**p** parallel_filters], which is shown in figure 3.60.

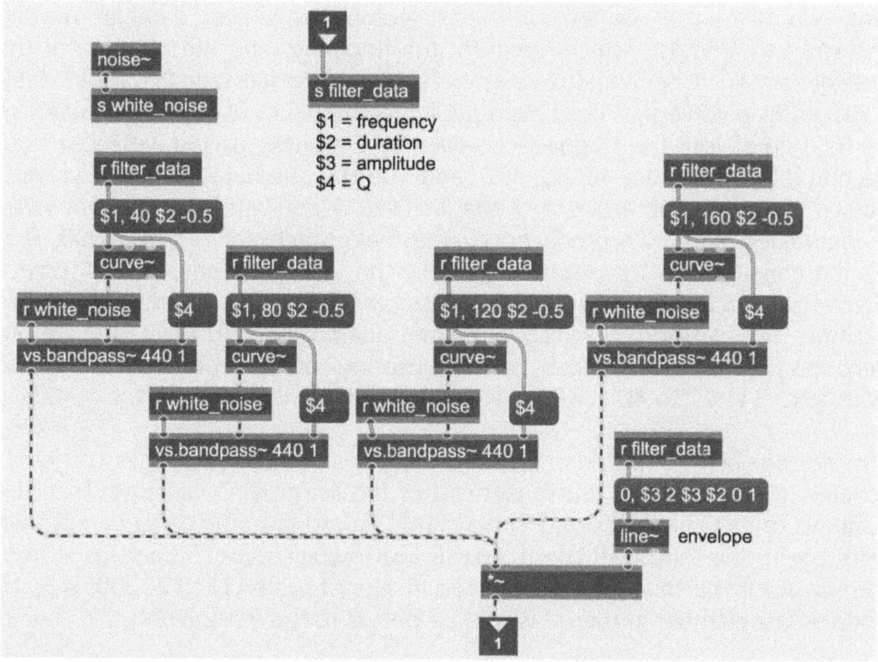

Fig. 3.60 The contents of the subpatch [p parallel_filters]

There are four bandpass filters, all implemented using **vs.bandpass~**, that filter a white noise source (**noise~**) and are multiplied by the envelope generated by the **line~** object. Recall that the first inlet of the **vs.bandpass~** object takes the signal to be filtered, the second the center frequency (which in this case is a value dynamically generated by the **curve~** object,[17] using a curvature factor of -0.5), and the third the Q.

We leave it to the reader to complete the analysis of this subpatch, which, notwithstanding its appearance, is pretty simple. We will, however, take a moment to speak about how the variable arguments ($ arguments) are used by the numerous message boxes in this patch. As you know, the elements packed into a list by the **pack** object in the main patch (figure 3.59) match up with $ variable arguments used in the various message boxes. This list is distributed to the message boxes using the [**s** filter_data] object to send and the [**r** filter_data] object to receive. Recall that the list contains values for initial frequency, glissando duration, amplitude, and Q. These values, when sent to any of the message boxes, always correspond to the variable names **$1**, **$2**, **$3**, and **$4**, when they appear in the receiving message boxes (The variables and their corresponding parameter names are shown as text in figure 3.60, near the [**s** filter_data] object at the top.)
To illustrate, look at the leftmost message box connected to a **curve~** object, which contains the message [$1,40 $2 -0.5].

---

17 To review the **curve~** object, see Section 1.3.

Only two of the four elements in the list received by [`r` filter_data] are used in this case: `$1` and `$2`, which represent the frequency and the duration of the note generated. When the `curve~` object receives the message [$1, 40 $2 -0.5], it generates a curve that goes from the initial frequency (`$1`) to a frequency of 40 Hz (one of four fixed frequencies used by the filters, as you will recall from Section 3.7T, which are 40, 80, 120, and 160 Hz); the duration of the curve is passed as the second element of the list (`$2`). A concrete example may help: if the values in the list produced by the main patch are [311.12, 300, 0.5, 1], the message box for `curve~` will take the first two elements and replace the variables `$1` and `$2` with their values, which are 311.12 and 300 in this example. The message contained in the message box, [$1, 40 $2 -0.5], therefore becomes [311.12, 40 300 -0.5], and the `curve~` object produces a curve that goes from 311.12 to 40 in 300 milliseconds, using a curvature factor of -0.5.

The message box connected to the third inlet of `vs.bandpass~` uses a different scheme, taking only the fourth element of the list as its Q value. (In fact, the contents of its message box are simply [$4].) Referring to the concrete example once again, the third inlet of `vs.bandpass~` would accept the value 1 from the list, since the four values contained in the list were [311.12, 300, 0.5, 1], and the last element in the list would be bound to the variable `$4`.

Can you see why the amplitude envelope generated by `line~` uses the elements `$2` and `$3`? And why `$3` is used twice in the message box connected to `line~`? Which values correspond to these elements? Can you explain why the duration of the note is reduced by 3 milliseconds in the main patch, by examining the message that generates the envelope?

ACTIVITY

Following the explanation given in Section 3.7T, try to modify the patch shown in figure 3.59 to obtain sounds similar to those in Interactive Examples 3F3-3F5.

USING A PARALLEL FILTERBANK

The MSP object of choice for implementing filters in parallel is called **`fffb~`**, which implements a filterbank of bandpass filters that are each equivalent to the `reson~` filter that we have already used. (The name stands for *Fast Fixed Filter Bank*.)
This object can take a variable number of arguments: the first argument, the only one strictly required, specifies the number of filters to be provided and consequently the number of outputs (one for each filter). A second argument provides a frequency for the lowest filter, the third, a ratio with which to separate filter frequencies (a value of 2, for example, would imply that the frequencies of succeeding filters double), and the fourth, a value for Q.

Take a look at figure 3.61:

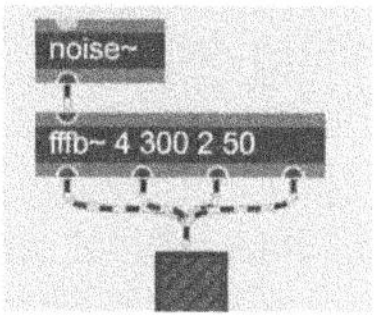

Fig. 3.61 The **fffb~** object

Here we have a bank of four filters, whose frequencies are 300, 600, 1,200, and 2,400 Hz: the ratio between the frequencies is 2 and therefore each doubles the frequency that came before, beginning with 300. The fixed Q value used for these filters is 50. Notice that the outputs of the object are 4, corresponding to the number of filters.
It is also possible to specify the frequency, Q, and gain for every filter in the filterbank dynamically, by sending parameter values as lists that use the keys "freq", "Q", and "gain". To construct these lists, you first enter a key, and then specify the number of the filter (the first filter should be designated as 0), followed by one or more values. The values in the list are sent to the filter specified and the filters that immediately follow it. For example, a message list formatted as [**freq** 0 100 150 225] would set the frequency of the first three filters in a bank to be 100, 150, and 225 Hz. Likewise, a message looking like [**Q** 2 7.5] would change the Q value of filter number 2 (which is the third filter!) to 7.5. To try an example, build the patch shown in figure 3.62.

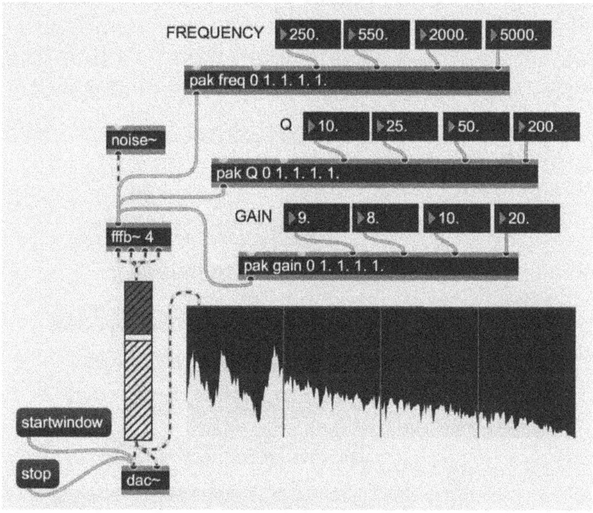

Fig. 3.62 Messages for the **fffb~** object

As you can see, in this patch, the **fffb~** object has only one argument, which establishes the number of filters to be included in the filterbank.
The use of **pak** objects in this patch (which, you recall, is like a **pack** object whose inlets are all "hot", generating a list every time a message arrives on any of the inlets as a result) is worth noting. The first **pak** object has 6

arguments [**freq** 0 1. 1. 1. 1.], and consequently has 6 inlets, each of which corresponds to one of the arguments. As you know, a message sent to any of the inlets replaces the corresponding argument value; a message to the fourth inlet, for example, will replace the fourth argument (which in the figure would cause the value 1 to be replaced by the value 550). Since no message is ever sent to the first two inlets of this **pak** object, the lists that it generates always begin with the elements '**freq**' and '**0**', followed by 4 variable values. By building lists in this way, we can easily change the four frequency values for the filterbank created by **fffb~**.
The other two **pak** objects also have 6 arguments, and each is constructed to have 2 fixed arguments (*Q* 0 and *gain* 0). This allows us to change the Q and amplitude values for the filters in the filterbank using the same mechanism.
Try setting the parameter values as illustrated in the figure, and then create other sonorities.

As we have seen, the **fffb~** object has the same number of outputs as the number of filters it contains: this means that with 8 filters it would have 8 outputs, with 16 filters, 16 outputs and so on. This is certainly useful when we intend to send the different outputs to different destinations, but very often we need a single signal containing the sum of all the filters (such as in Figs. 3.61 and 3.62, where we have summed the **fffb~** outputs by sending them all to the same **gain~**).
If we want to avoid adding all the outputs manually, we can use a variant of the multichannel system available for some objects, including **fffb~**. In this variant, identified by the prefix "mcs" instead of "mc", only one instance of the object is generated, but all the audio inputs and all the audio outputs are grouped into a single multichannel input and a single multichannel output respectively. The object [**mcs.fffb~** 4], therefore, will have a single multichannel output that contains 4 signals corresponding to the 4 filters. Modify the previous patch as shown in figure 3.62b.

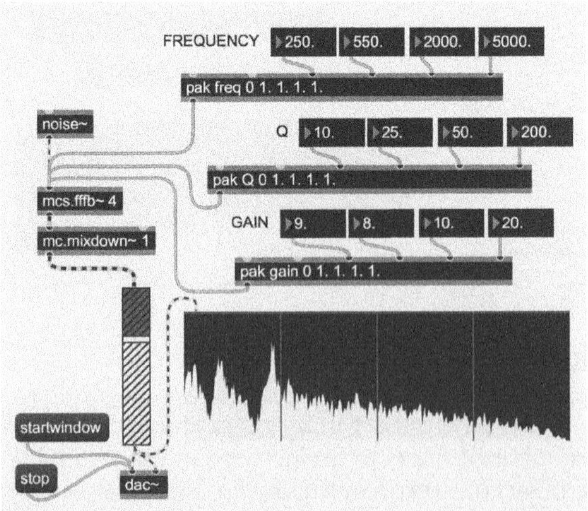

fig. 3.62b: the **mcs.fffb~** object

As you can see, in order to hear the sound produced by the four filters, we need to reduce the four channels to a single channel via [**mc.mixdown~** 1] before sending the signal to the **gain~** object.

GRAPHIC EQUALIZERS

Here is one possible implementation of a graphic equalizer, that is contained in the file **03_12_graphic_eq.maxpat**.

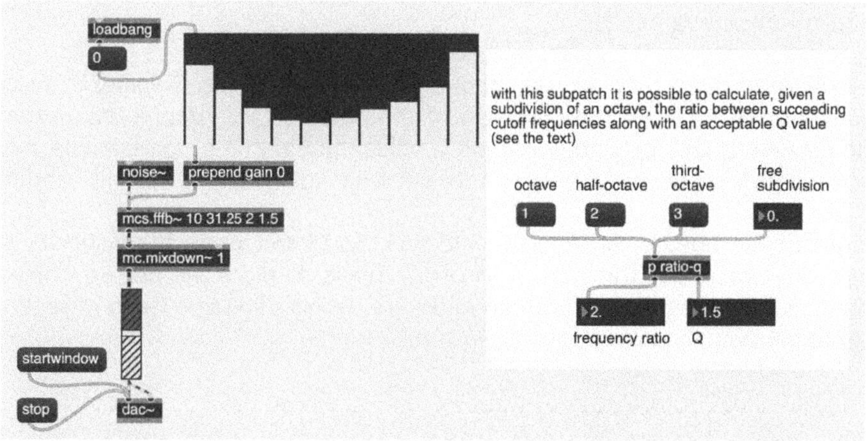

Fig. 3.63 The file 03_12_graphic_eq.maxpat

In this patch, we find a 10 band equalizer with one-octave bands. The **mcs.fffb~** object has 4 arguments: the number of filters (10), the starting frequency (31.25 Hz), the ratio between filters (a doubling factor, which makes the distance an octave), and the Q (1.5). Let us spend a couple of moments on the Q factor selected: there is a lot of discretion in how much Q to use, because its effect is linked to both the audio material being filtered and to the definition that we want to hear between the bands. One possible way to go is to make the upper limits of the passband coincide with the lower limits of the passband of the next filter, so that the bands "touch". A Q of 1.5 has exactly this characteristic when working with bands of one octave. Listening to the results, you can decide for yourself whether to narrow the bands (increasing the Q) or to make them wider (by reducing the Q).
In the right part of the patch you will find an algorithm that, given a subdivision of the octave, will calculate the ratio by which the frequencies of the filters should be separated (that can be used as the third argument to **mcs.fffb~**), and its related Q factor (used for the fourth argument), defined so that the confines of the bands will just coincide. You can use this algorithm to construct your own custom equalizers. We won't explain how the subpatch **ratio-q** works, because it contains still-unknown objects; if you'd like, you can look it over after completing Interlude B (however, be warned that there are calculations in it that are complex enough to fall outside the scope of this book).

We have added a **multislider** into the patch with which you can change the gain for individual filters.

ACTIVITIES

Starting with the examples that were furnished as part of Section 3.7T, implement a graphic equalizer with 20 half-octave bands, and one with 30 third-of-an-octave bands.

Calculate the ratio between the frequencies, as well as the Q value, by using the algorithm found in the right part of the patch 03_12_graphic_eq.maxpat, and try slightly changing the resulting Q value (multiplying it, for example, by a factor slightly lower or higher than 1) to get what you believe is optimal filtering.

Augment the number of sliders in the **multislider** using the Inspector so that you can control the gain of all of the filters. Replace the **noise~** object acting as the sound source with an audio file, using **sfplay~** (seen in Section 1.6) to do this.

3.8 OTHER APPLICATIONS OF CONNECTION IN SERIES: PARAMETRIC EQ AND SHELVING FILTERS

If you have played with the `filtergraph~` object in the 03_07_biquad_filtergraph.maxpat patch, you surely noticed the presence of the shelving filters "lowshelf", "highshelf", and "peaknotch" – let's revisit them now in the patch contained in **03_13_shelving.maxpat** (shown in 3.64).
We are now better equipped to experiment with the effect of these filters, now that we understand the theory. The high shelf filter acts on the high part of the spectrum, leaving other frequencies unchanged, while the low shelf filter acts only on the low part, and the peak/notch filter acts only on a given frequency band, the other regions remaining unchanged. Boost and attenuation of the frequencies are given by a gain parameter: when it is between 0 and 1, the signal is attenuated, and when the value is over 1, the signal is boosted.

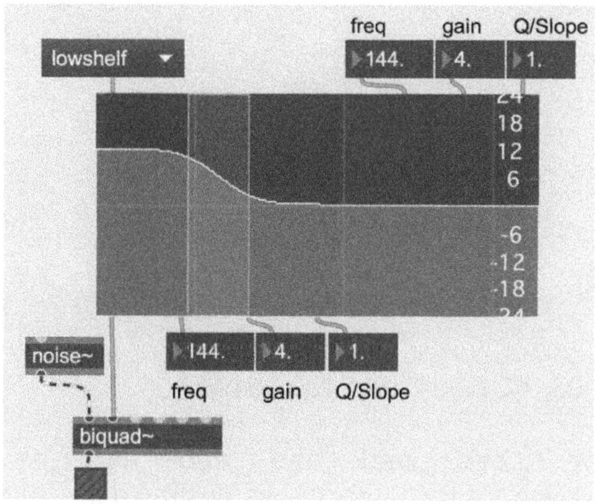

Fig. 3.64 The file 03_13_shelving.maxpat

Besides the frequency and gain parameters, there is a third, dually named, parameter, which is called "Q" in the case of the "peaknotch" filter and "slope" in the case of the "highshelf" and "lowshelf" filters. When the Q/Slope parameter increases, the cutoff frequency is boosted, even to the point of resonance.
Thanks to the flatness that characterizes frequency regions that are not part of the target band around the center frequency, the peak/notch filter can be connected very effectively in series. It is exactly that kind of configuration that we will examine in the next section, which is dedicated to parametric equalization.

PARAMETRIC EQUALIZATION

When we need to connect many filters in series (such as when we are building a parametric equalizer), we can use the **`cascade~`** object[18] in place of many objects connected in series. This object allows us to specify the number of filters

[18] Filters connected in series are also said to be "cascaded".

to be connected together, taking a list of coefficients, and activating enough filters to use the coefficients provided. (The number of coefficients must be divisible by 5, since there are 5 coefficients per filter. 5 coefficients = 1 filter, 10 coefficients = 2 filters, and so on.) Because we are using grouped coefficients, we can use the `filtergraph~` object to manage more than one filter at a time. Open the file **03_14_parametric_eq.maxpat** (shown in figure 3.65) to see this in action.

In this patch, we find a parametric equalizer implemented using the `cascade~` object, and made up of one low shelf, one high shelf, and three peak/notch filters. The `filtergraph~` object allows us to set parameter values for all of the five of the filters from a single graphical object.

Varying the parameters from within the `filtergraph~` will cause the object to produce a list of 25 coefficients for the use of `cascade~`.

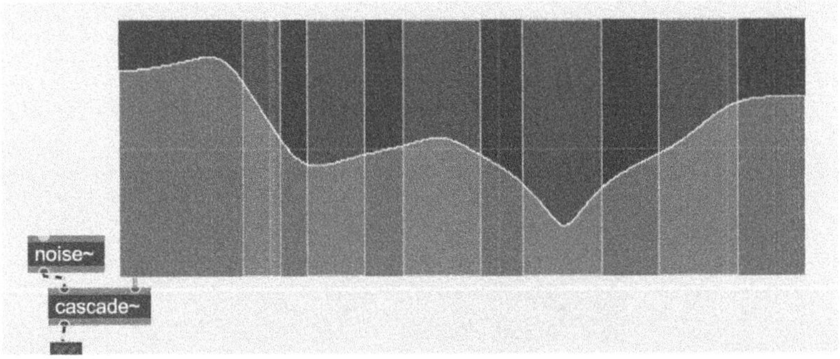

Fig. 3.65 The file 03_14_parametric_eq.maxpat

How do you give `filtergraph~` the number and type of filters to be managed? This is a job for the Inspector, as illustrated in figure 3.65b.

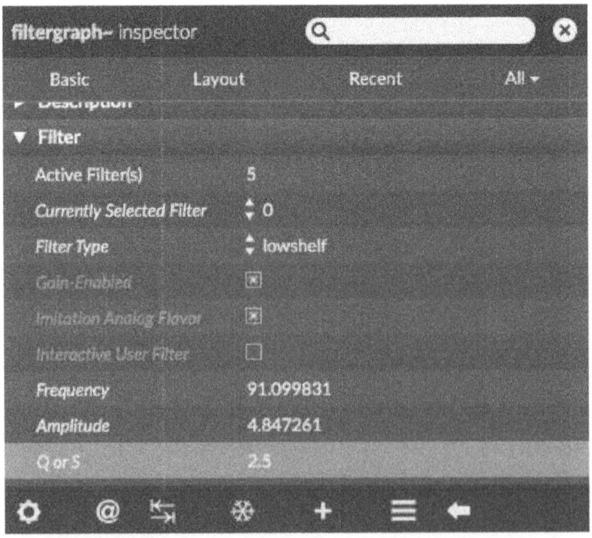

Fig. 3.65b The `filtergraph~` inspector

Locate the "Filter" category: the first item that you see in the panel is the ***Active Filters*** attribute, which you can use to set the number of active filters (the number of filters to be managed by **filtergraph~**). With the next attribute, ***Currently Selected Filter***, you can select the filter to be configured by using the menu found next to its name. Once a filter is selected, you can set its type by using ***Filter Type***. If you select the five filters in the patch, one after another, you can confirm that there are exactly one "lowshelf", three "peaknotch", and one "highshelf" filters in the patch.

ACTIVITIES

- Replace the low shelf and the high shelf, respectively, with a highpass and a lowpass (in that order!), and notice the differences in terms of equalization.
- Use an audio file in place of white noise.
- Implement a parametric filter using 10 filters: a low shelf, a high shelf, and 8 peak/notch filters.

There is a three-band semi-parametric equalizer in the Ableton library: **abl.device.channeleq~**. Note that the name contains the term "device" and not "dsp," indicating that this is a complete Live effect and not a module inside a device. Let's see how it works, open the patch **03_14b_abl.device.channeleq.maxpat** (Figure 3.66).

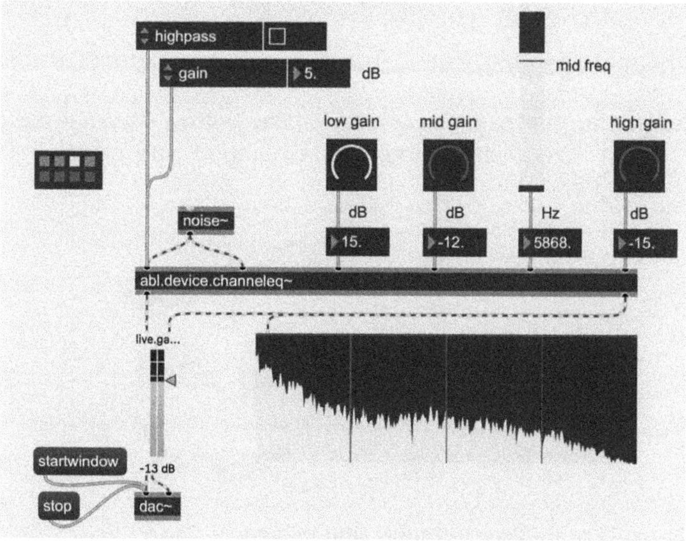

Fig. 3.66: patch **03_14b_abl.device.channeleq.maxpat**

It is a three-band equalizer with the following settings: the gain of the low band (-15 to 15 dB), the mid band (-12 to 12 dB) and the high band (-15 to

15 dB), the center frequency of the mid band (120 to 7500 Hz), the output gain (-12 to 12 dB) and the activation of an optional high-pass filter at 80 Hz, which serves to attenuate any booming of the sound material. The object has a stereo input and output and four inputs for band-related parameters. We added two attrui objects to control the overall gain and the activation of the high-pass filter. Try changing the parameters to hear how the sound is equalized: as you will notice, the limitation of the parameter range prevents us from "abusing" the effect with extreme values.[19]

3.9 OTHER SOURCES FOR SUBTRACTIVE SYNTHESIS: IMPULSES AND RESONANT BODIES

In Section 3.9 of the theory chapter, we spoke about the resonance that you can obtain from a bandpass filter when the Q factor is high and, as a consequence, the passband is narrow. As we've also seen, sending a unitary impulse to the input of a filter for which the Q is sufficiently high, can be used to obtain a damped sine wave pitched at the center frequency of the filter. In MSP, it is possible to create a unitary impulse by using a **click~** object, which, as we see in figure 3.67, generates an impulse every time it receives a bang.

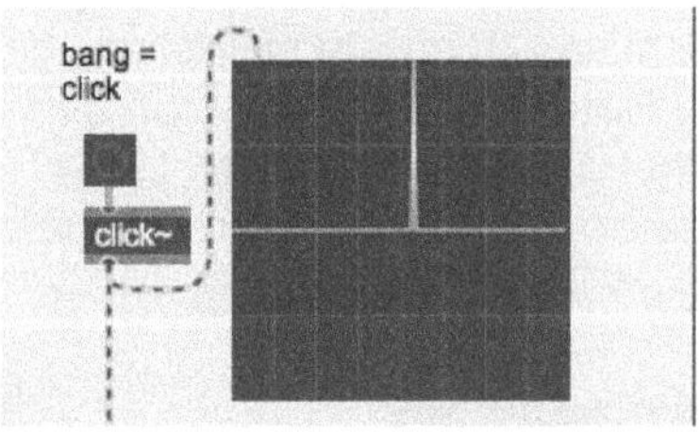

Fig. 3.67 The **click~** object

Let's implement a little patch in which a filter with a very narrow passband generates, when it receives an impulse, a damped sine wave. This patch is shown in figure 3.68.

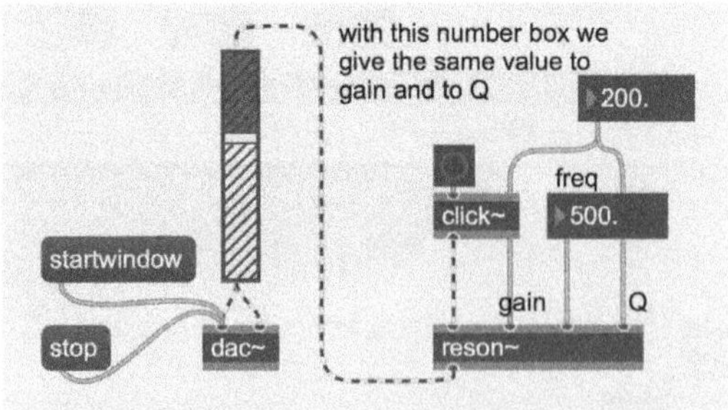

Fig. 3.68 How to produce a damped sine wave

[19] A full explanation of the effect's behavior can be found in the Live manual, available online at ableton.com. Look for a reference to the "Channel EQ" device in the manual.

On every click of the **button**, a unitary impulse is filtered by **reson~**. Since increasing the Q narrows the passband, the resulting sound will always be weaker. To do this in a way that keeps the amplitude of the sound constant, you need to change the Q and the gain proportionately, which is why we use the same number box to control both parameters.

Another thing that we learned in Section 3.9T was that, in the case of unitary impulses, the Q is directly proportional to the number of cycles generated in the damped sine wave produced by the filter. The **reson~** filter, for example, produces a sine wave that drops by 60 dB after having produced a number of cycles that is slightly bigger than the Q value. If the Q is 50, for example, the filter produces a sine wave whose amplitude drops by 60 dB in a little more than 50 cycles. With a Q of 100, it will produce a little more than 100 cycles, and so on.[20]
Of course, if the sine wave has a frequency of 100 Hz, it oscillates 100 times per second, producing 100 cycles, while a frequency of 200 Hz will reduce this to a half a second, and so on. This means that, given the same Q, increasing the center frequency of the filter will reduce the duration of the resonance. There is, however, a way to link the Q setting to the center frequency of the frequency, allowing us to set the duration directly in seconds. This is shown in figure 3.69.

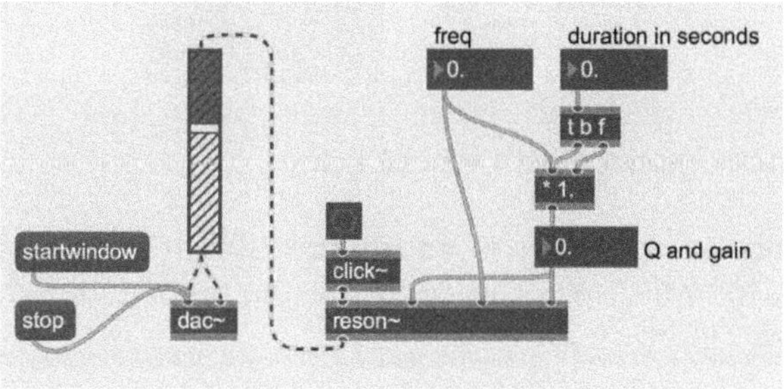

Fig. 3.69 How to set the duration of a resonance response

For simplicity, we have considered any resonance to be "done"[21] once the number of cycles exactly equals the Q value. To obtain the Q necessary to sustain a certain duration, the center frequency must be multiplied by the number of seconds desired. In the figure, we see a resonance at 500 Hz that is meant to last 3 seconds: by multiplying the frequency by the duration, we obtain the number of cycles to be completed before finishing (500 · 3 = 1500), and this number is used as the Q.
Notice the **trigger** in this patch with the arguments 'b' and 'f'; this is used to make the right inlet of the multiplication object "hot" (as originally demonstrated in Section IA.6).

[20] The **reson~** filter produces, when driven at the same Q, half of the cycles produced by a Butterworth bandpass filter (which was examined in Section 3.9 of the theory text).
[21] In reality, it drops by around 60 dB; at this level, the amplitude is one-thousandth of the original amplitude.

Build the patch and confirm that the algorithm effectively sets the duration of a resonance, whatever frequency is set.

To ease using this filtering technique, there are two utility impulse generators in the Virtual Sound Macros library: the first of these is **vs.click~**, which generates a "click train" of unitary impulses at a given frequency (as shown in figure 3.70).

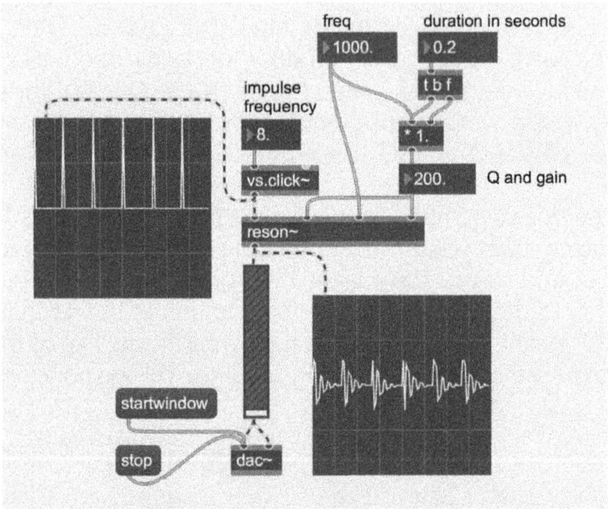

Fig. 3.70 Resonant impulses with `vs.click~`

The second impulse generator is **vs.dust~**, which generates a "dust" of irregular clicks, for which you can designate the average density of clicks per second (as shown in figure 3.71).

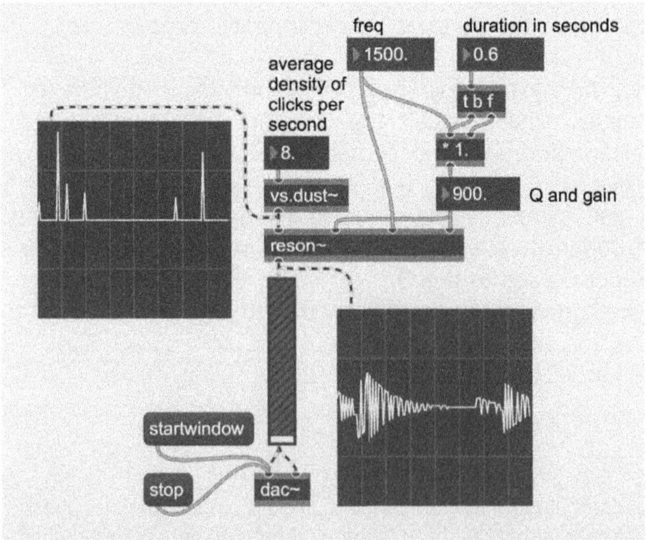

Fig. 3.71 Resonant impulses with `vs.dust~`

We encourage you to create the patches shown in these two figures and to experiment with various parameter settings. Also try creating additional generators based on resonant impulses, each with different settings; we've shown one possible way to do this in figure 3.72. (Notice the use of **send** and **receive**, which enable us to avoid excessive cable clutter. The different signals received on [**r** resbodies] are summed "automatically" by Max, as would normally happen when multiple signals enter a single inlet, as first discussed in Section 1.3).

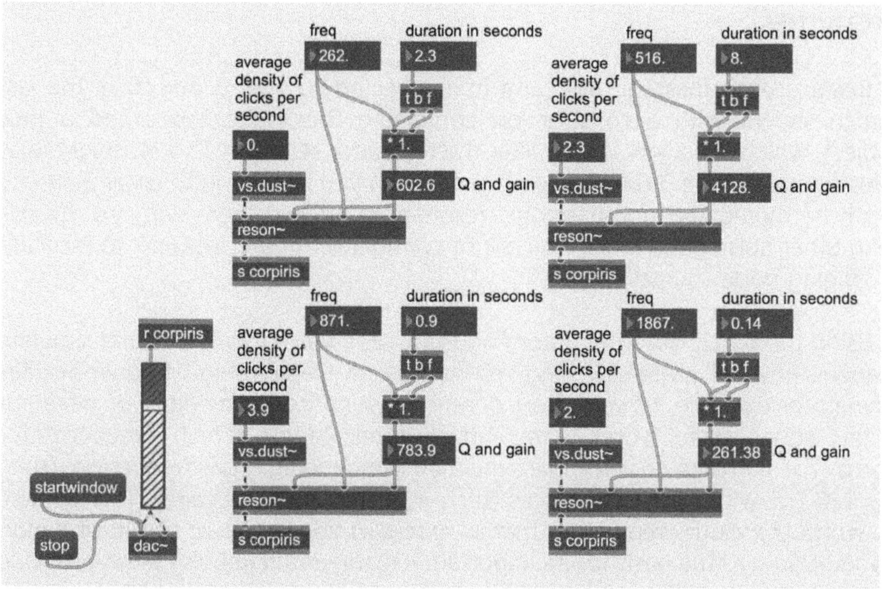

Fig. 3.72 Polyphonic resonant impulses

Using the **mcs.fffb~** object, it is also possible to create some complex resonances by setting values for multiple filters in parallel (as shown in figure 3.73).

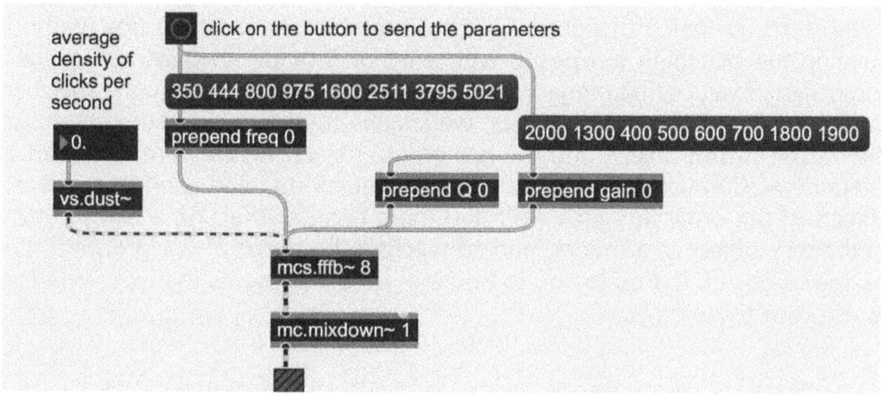

Fig. 3.73 Resonant impulses in parallel

In this patch, we have created a filterbank containing 8 filters that produce a metallic resonance. After building the patch yourself and experimenting with parameter settings, try replacing **vs.dust~** with other noise generators, such as **noise~**, **pink~**, **rand~**, and **vs.rand0~**, the last two at various frequencies. Watch out, though – lower the volume first!

ACTIVITIES

- Replace each message box (and its connected **prepend** object) in the last patch shown with a construction combining 8 number boxes and a **pak** object, which will allow you to alter the resonator settings. (This technique was illustrated in figure 3.62.) Based on that which you learned in Chapter 2, create both harmonic and non-harmonic resonances, driving them with **vs.dust~** and other noise generators. You might consider using **selector~** to facilitate changing noise sources.

- Using the patch from the preceding exercise, create resonances that simulate various physical materials: long resonances of medium-high frequencies for metal, for example, or very short duration resonances at medium or medium-high frequencies for wood, or medium-short resonances at high frequencies for glass. The skin on a drum can be simulated using medium-low frequencies (such as 120 Hz) with short resonances (such as 3 tenths of a second). This exercise is worth the pain – remember that a three-part concatenated sound of metal-wood-skin was the basis for an important experiment in impulse filtration made by Karlheinz Stockhausen for his piece Kontakte at the end of 1950.

ACTIVITY – *REPLACING PARTS OF ALGORITHMS*

- Return to the patch of figure 3.73 and replace each message box (without deleting the matching **prepend**) with a list of 8 randomly generated values, comprised of values that range from some specified minimum to some specified maximum. To implement such lists, we suggest that you use the **uzi** object, the **vs.between** object, and the [**zl** group] object, which were discussed in Interlude A. Can you build the patch? We suggest that you connect the three objects in the order in which we listed them here, connecting a bang button to the **uzi** object as a trigger, and connecting the outlet of [**zl** group] to the **prepend** object. It is up to you to figure out the arguments that you will need to use with these objects...

ACTIVITY – *CORRECTING ALGORITHMS*

Open the patch contained in **3_Correction.maxpat.**

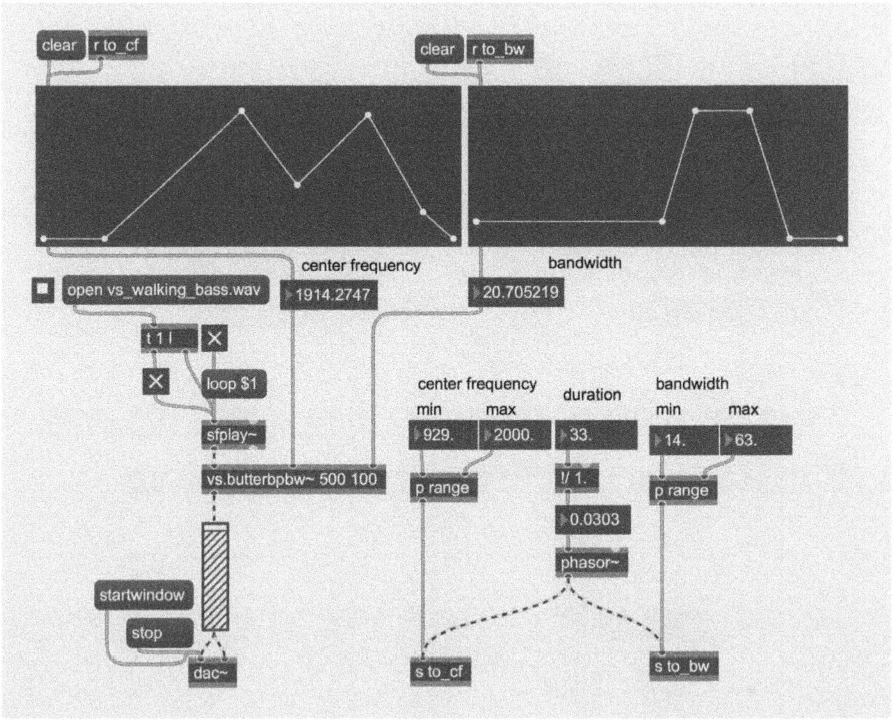

Fig. 3.74

There is something that prevents the two **`function`** objects from working correctly. Corrections should be made so that the cycle of parameter variations to the center frequency (the left **`function`** object) and the bandwidth (the right **`function`** object) are completed in 33 seconds.
The file vs_walking_bass.wav should also playback an octave lower than the original recording.

ACTIVITY – *ANALYZING ALGORITHMS*

Open the patch contained in **3_analysis.maxpat.**

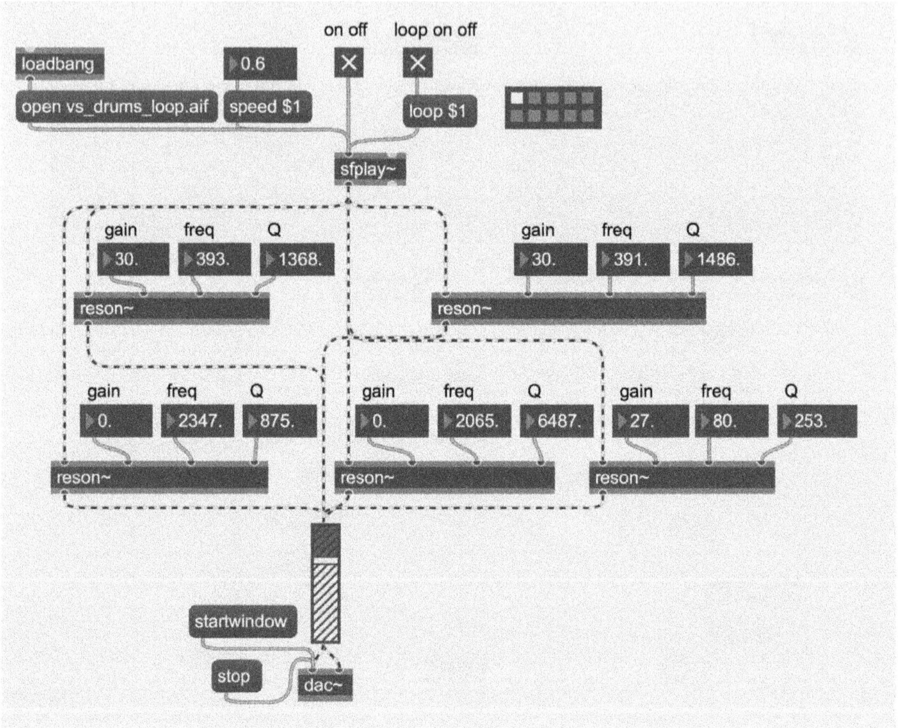

Fig. 3.75

Listen to all of the presets, and describe:

- how the algorithm functions, including the way in which the file vs_drums_loop.aif is loaded
- the way in which sounds occur separately, with different pitches (yet connected to the bass drum, to the snare, and to accented snare shots), when a single audio file is playing
- the parameters that remain unchanged, and those that change, when the speed of `sfplay~` is modified.

ACTIVITY – *COMPLETING ALGORITHMS*

Open the patch contained in **3_Completion.maxpat.**

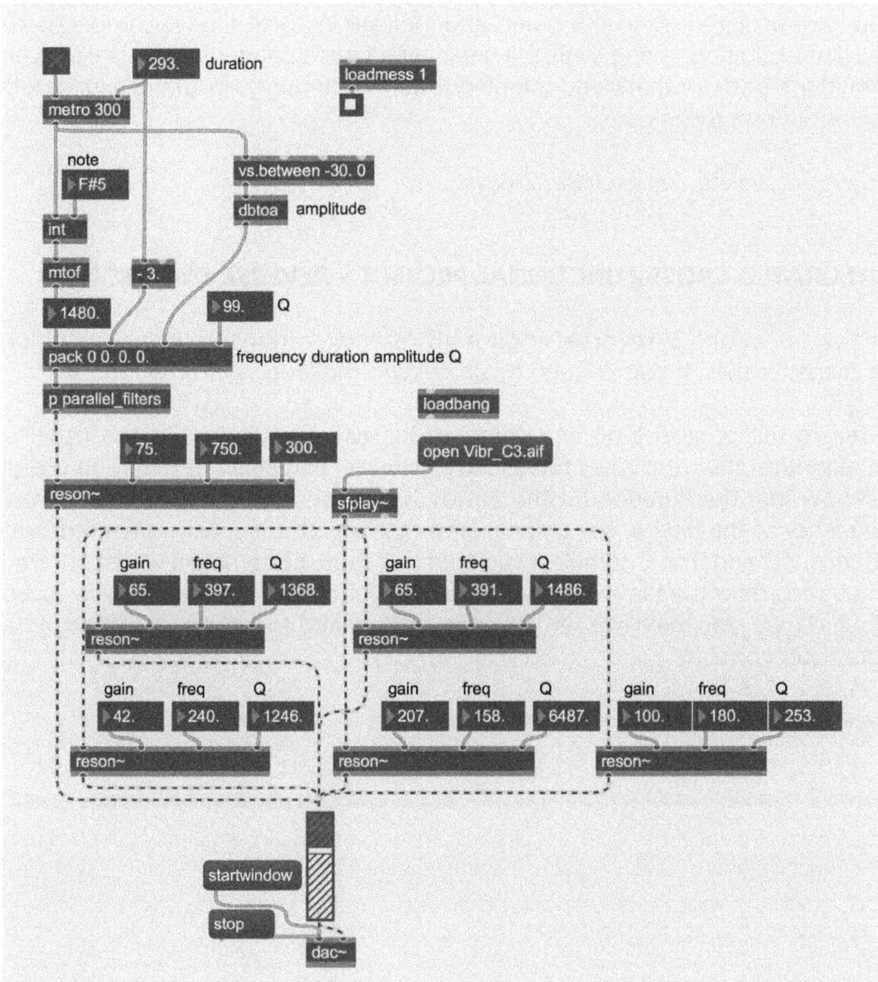

Fig. 3.76

This patch is incomplete: the goal is to trigger the sound synthesis using the pulse of the `metro` object. Bangs that arrive from the `metro` should alternately start and stop the `sfplay~` object (which should play the file Vibr_C3.aif). Effectively, on every beat of the synthetic noise-based sound, we should also hear a sampled sound.
After the correction, make a multichannel version of the patch, transforming the 5 `reson~` in a single `mc.reson~`.

INTEGRATED CROSS-FUNCTIONAL PROJECT – *COMPOSING A BRIEF SOUND STUDY*

Realize a short sound study of about two minutes, based on techniques that you have acquired up to this point, and indicate in a text file which operations you are exploiting, along with the sonic directions intended. In particular, you should use both synthetic and sampled sound in combination, along with ample use of filtering techniques.

Time to complete this exercise: 2 days.

INTEGRATED CROSS-FUNCTIONAL PROJECT – *REVERSE ENGINEERING*

Analyze the sound **3_reverse_engine.aif**, listening carefully to it and describing its characteristics. It was created by processing the loop vs_drums_loop.aif.

Listen to the original loop and compare the two sounds before constructing an algorithm that re-creates the sound 3_reverse_engine.aif. It might be useful to know that the duration for the `function` object that controlled the center frequency of the filter in the original (and that was continuously reiterated) was 20 seconds, and that 3 complete cycles of this `function` object were captured when recording the file (which is 60 seconds long). Pay attention to the speed at which you play the file vs_drums_loop.aif, and also to setting your bandwidth parameter correctly.

Time for implementation: 1 hour.

LIST OF MAX OBJECTS

abl.device.channeleq~
Three-band semi-parametric equalizer.

abl.device.drift~
Subtractive synthesizer with two oscillators and modulation via LFO.

biquad~
This object enables you to define any second-order filter. In place of the parameters normally used to control filters, such as cutoff frequency or Q, this object takes 5 filter coefficients.
These coefficients can be supplied by the **filtercoeff~** or **filtergraph~** objects.

cascade~
A container object that can hold a variable number of cascaded second-order filters. It takes a list of coefficients as input, and internally creates one second-order filter for every 5 coefficients it receives.

click~
A generator of audio clicks. Every time that this object receives a bang as input, it emits a single sample with an amplitude of 1. At all other times, it emits a stream of samples with an amplitude of 0.

clip~
Forces the sample values in a signal to remain between the upper and a lower limits fixed by its arguments.

delay~
A delay line, which takes two arguments, the first which indicates the maximum delay possible, and the second which indicates the effective current delay. Both arguments are specified in numbers of samples.

dial
A graphical object in the form of a knob, which produces values that reflect its current rotation.

fffb~
A filterbank consisting of a variable number of resonant bandpass filters, similar to **reson~**.
Its first argument specifies the number of filters to create.

filtercoeff~
An object that takes high-level filter parameter values as input signals and turns them into 5 signals containing second-order filter coefficients; it can be connected to a **biquad~** object, which will use the 5 output coefficients as a specification of its filter behavior.

filtergraph~
The graphical equivalent to **filtercoeff~**.

line
An object that generates sequences of Max numbers, connecting them through linear interpolation. It is the Max equivalent of **line~**.

noise~
A white noise generator.

onepole~
A first-order lowpass filter.

pink~
A pink noise generator.

pvar
An object that receives messages "remotely" from another named object in the same patch. Any object will forward the messages to one or more **pvar** objects, as long as their arguments match its scripting name and it is in the same patch.

radiogroup
A container object that holds a programmer-defined number of related buttons.

rand~
A random noise generator (that connects one value to the next by means of linear interpolation) with a settable operating frequency.

reson~
A resonant bandpass filter.

spectroscope~
A graphical object that displays the representation of a spectrum.

umenu
An object that creates drop-down menus with programmer-defined menu items.

vs.bandpass~
A second-order bandpass filter, that is part of the Virtual Sound Macros library.

vs.butterbpbw~
A Butterworth bandpass filter, controlled using a bandwidth parameter, that is part of the Virtual Sound Macros library. An object named **vs.butterbp~** (a bandpass filter controlled using a Q parameter) is also available.

vs.butterbrbw~
A Butterworth bandreject filter, controlled using a bandwidth parameter, that is part of the Virtual Sound Macros library. An object named **vs.butterbr~** (a bandreject filter controlled using a Q parameter) is also available

vs.butterhp~
A Butterworth highpass filter that is part of the Virtual Sound Macros library.

vs.butterlp~
A Butterworth lowpass filter that is part of the Virtual Sound Macros library.

vs.butterlpc
An internal module in the Virtual Sound Macros library that accepts cutoff frequency as input and produces a list of 5 coefficients that can be given to **biquad~** to use as a Butterworth lowpass filter implementation. (The corresponding objects for generating other Butterworth filter coefficients also exist: **vs.butterhpc**, **vs.butterbpc**, and **vs.butterbrc**.)

vs.choose
An object that randomly chooses one element from the list that it receives as input and returns it. This object is part of the Virtual Sound Macros library.

vs.click~
An impulse generator that is part of the Virtual Sound Macros library, which produces a train of unitary impulses at a given frequency.

vs.dust~
An impulse generator that is part of the Virtual Sound Macros library, which produces a "dust" of unitary impulses that is specified by the average density of clicks per second.

vs.highpass~
A resonant highpass filter that is part of the Virtual Sound Macros library.

vs.highpass1~
A first-order highpass filter that is part of the Virtual Sound Macros library.

vs.lowpass~
A lowpass resonant filter that is part of the Virtual Sound Macros library.

vs.rand0~
A noise generator with a variable frequency that generates random samples without interpolation, thus producing a step-function. It is part of the Virtual Sound Macros library.

vs.rand3~
A noise generator with a variable frequency and cubic interpolation, that is part of the Virtual Sound Macros library.

vs.xfade~
An object that takes two signals as input and mixes them together proportionately, based on a parameter value between 0 and 1. It is part of the Virtual Sound Macros library.

ATTRIBUTES FOR SPECIFIC MAX OBJECTS

All Objects
- Freeze/Unfreeze (Inspector Toolbar)
The *Freeze Attribute* option enables attribute values to be stored into a patch and then retrieved whenever the patch is loaded. The *Unfreeze Attribute* option releases a frozen attribute, eliminating the stored value and returning the attribute value to its default the next time that the patch is loaded.

- Scripting name (attribute)
this attribute, which is present in all Max objects, is used to name the object. A named object can be used to transmit messages to **pvar** objects without the use of patch cords, among other things.

filtergraph~
- Active filter(s) (attribute)
An attribute that configures the number of filters to be controlled by a **filtergraph~.**

- Filter type (attribute)
An attribute that decides the type of the current filter in the **filtergraph~** Inspector.

radiogroup
- Number of items (attribute)
This attribute specifies the number of buttons to be included in a **radiogroup**.

umenu
- Menu items (attribute)
an attribute that contains the editable set of menu items for a given **umenu**.

GLOSSARY

Inspector toolbar
The icons found at the bottom of the inspector window that can be used to issue common inspector commands.

Interlude B
ADDITIONAL ELEMENTS OF PROGRAMMING WITH MAX

LEARNING AGENDA

PREREQUISITES FOR THE CHAPTER

- Contents of Chapters 1, 2 and 3 (Theory and Practice), Interlude A

LEARNING OBJECTIVES

Skills

- To learn how to use simple MIDI objects and signals
- To learn how to implement recursive operations in Max
- To learn how to use Max's conversion operators
- To learn how to build an arpeggiator that exploits probabilistically generated intervals
- To learn how to route signals and messages to switched inlets and outlets
- To learn how to compare values using relational operators
- To learn how to take apart lists of data
- To learn how to program repeating sequences using iterative structures
- To learn how to generate random lists for simulating resonant bodies
- To learn how to implement Shepard tone, or "infinite glissando"

CONTENTS

- Basic use of the MIDI protocol
- Recursive operations and repeating sequences
- Arpeggiators and probabilistic intervals
- Comparing and converting values, and routing signals and messages
- Taking lists apart, and generating random lists
- Shepard tones

ACTIVITIES

- Replacing parts of algorithms
- Correcting algorithms
- Analyzing algorithms
- Completing algorithms
- Constructing new algorithms

TESTING

- Integrated cross-functional project: reverse engineering

SUPPORTING MATERIALS

- List of Max objects
- Messages, and attributes for specific Max objects
- Glossary

IB.1 INTRODUCTION TO MIDI

MIDI is a protocol for communicating between electronic and/or digital musical instruments and computers. Using a physical MIDI cable, it is possible to connect a synthesizer to a computer, enabling the computer to "play" synthesizer, for example. Using the MIDI protocol, the computer sends notes to the synthesizer along with the intensity with which they should be played, their durations, and other information.
MIDI instruments do not need to exist in physical form: they can also run as "virtual" instruments, which are computer applications that simulate the behavior of real instruments and produce sound through audio interfaces. Such digital instruments can communicate via MIDI, just as real-world instruments do. Programs like Max can send MIDI commands directly to a receiving program such as a virtual instrument. Indeed, Max has many objects that exploit the MIDI protocol, as we will learn in more detail in Chapter 9, but for the moment, we will stick to a basic subset that is used to manage MIDI messages.
Open the file **IB_01_MIDI_note.maxpat**; figure IB.1 shows the upper part of the Patcher Window.

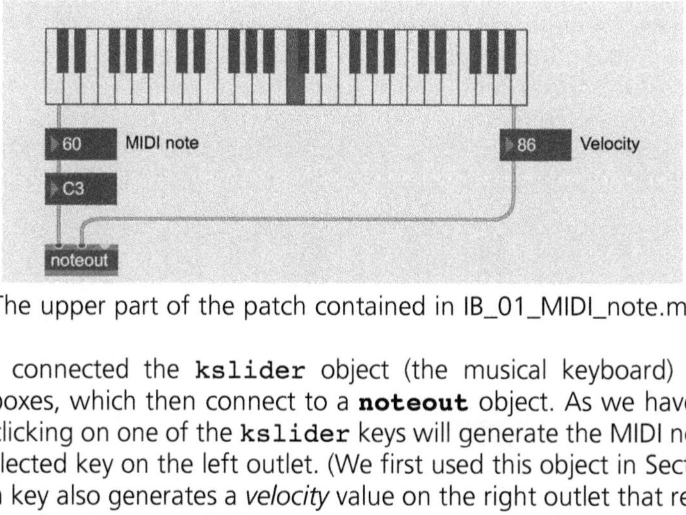

Fig. IB.1 The upper part of the patch contained in IB_01_MIDI_note.maxpat

We have connected the **kslider** object (the musical keyboard) to some number boxes, which then connect to a **noteout** object. As we have already learned, clicking on one of the **kslider** keys will generate the MIDI note value for the selected key on the left outlet. (We first used this object in Section 1.4.) Pressing a key also generates a *velocity* value on the right outlet that represents an intensity for the note; clicking on the upper part of the key will produce a higher velocity value, while clicking on the lower part will produce a lower value. (On physical keyboards, velocity actually reflects the velocity with which the key is pressed, hence the origin of the term.) Values for velocity can vary between 1 and 127 in MIDI.

Note and velocity values are sent to the left and center inlets of a **noteout** object, which then sends the appropriate command to any MIDI instruments (real or virtual) that are connected to it.[1] In the MIDI protocol, this message is

[1] The right inlet of the noteout object is used to set the MIDI channel, which we don't need at the moment. The details of this will be forthcoming in Chapter 9.

defined to be the "***note-on***" command. When you click close to the top of a **kslider** key, generating a high enough velocity value (let's say above 90), you should hear the sound of a piano. This sound is not coming from Max, but instead, it is generated by a virtual instrument that is part of the operating system of your computer, which, by default, plays MIDI notes using the sound of a piano. If you try playing more notes, you will realize that **noteout** plays a sound for every new note that it receives, without interrupting or stopping the notes previously played. A slight problem remains: using noteout, we have told the virtual instrument when to begin playing, without telling it when to stop.
To interrupt a note and solve this problem, we will need to send another MIDI command: a matching MIDI note with a velocity equal to 0, which is called the "***note-off***" command. (A kind of "remove finger from key" command.)

One way to properly "extinguish" a MIDI note generated by **kslider** is to change the way that the object manages MIDI notes. In edit mode, call up the Inspector for the upper **kslider**, in the "Value" category change the ***Display Mode*** parameter value from "**Monophonic**" to "**Polyphonic**". Then return to performance mode. The first time that you click on a **kslider** key, the note will sound at the velocity chosen, and the second time that you click on the same key, the note will be triggered again, but this time with a velocity of 0, which will make the sound stop: try this. Besides adding the handy note-stopping feature, this also now enables you to activate more than one note at the same time: the performance capability has become polyphonic.
Now turn your attention to the lower half of the patch in **IB_01_MIDI_note.maxpat.**

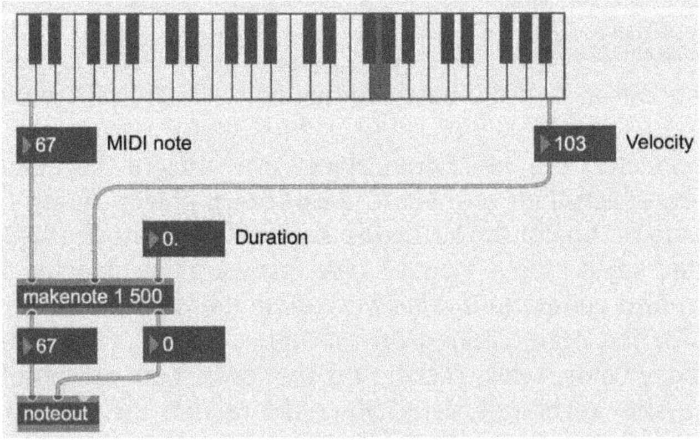

Fig. IB.2 The lower part of the patch in IB_01_MIDI_note.maxpat

We have connected the **kslider** object (in monophonic mode) to the **makenote** object, which generates a MIDI *note-on/note-off* command pair. Every time this object receives a *note-on*, it generates a *note-off* after a configurable length of time has elapsed. The object has three inlets, one for MIDI note number, one for velocity, and one for the duration in milliseconds (which is, of course, the amount of time to pass before the *note-off* command is sent). It has two outlets, one for MIDI note number and the other for velocity.

There are two arguments associated with **makenote**, a velocity and a duration in milliseconds. In the patch, we have set velocity equal to 1 (a placeholder, as we will see), and duration equal to 500 milliseconds (or half a second). When the object receives a *note-on*, it will send the pitch and velocity of the *note-on* directly to its outlets, where, after the prescribed duration (500 milliseconds in this example) a *note-off* is also sent. Note that the velocity sent by the **kslider** (which in the example shown in the figure is a value of 103) overrides the value of 1 that had been provided as an argument. We don't need to use the first argument, and so we will simply provide a placeholder for its value. The second argument, the duration, can also be modified by sending a value to the right inlet, which will replace the value originally specified in the second argument.
Try playing some notes and changing the duration: observe how velocity values first reflect the value generated by **kslider**, and then, after the time specified by the duration parameter, they change to 0.

Now add an addition object to the lower part of the patch as shown in figure IB.3:

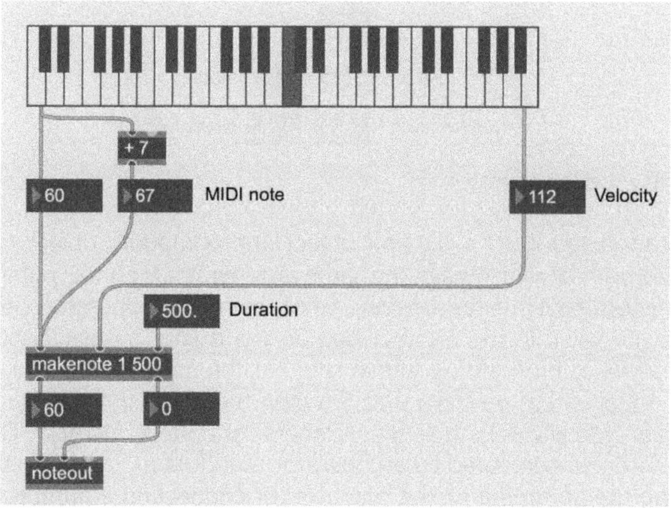

Fig. IB.3 Transposing MIDI notes

This patch is similar to the one in the file IA_01_transposition.maxpat, which we examined in the first section of Interlude A. In this case, every key pressed on the keyboard generates two notes simultaneously, separated by a distance of 7 semitones: the interval of a fifth. Every time that a **kslider** key is pressed, in fact, the value of the MIDI note number is sent to the **makenote** object and also to the addition object that adds 7 to the first note number and then sends its output to **makenote**. To create these note pairs, we didn't need to repeat velocity and duration values, since these values are sent to "cold" inlets of the **makenote** object, which are stored as internal variables (the contents of internal variables are re-used every time that a new value arrives at the "hot" inlet). In the figure, for example, both notes (the middle C and the G above it) will have a velocity of 112 and a duration of 500 milliseconds.

From this example, you can see that Max's rule about "hot" inlets being on the left is complementary with right-to-left execution, as discussed in Section 1.7. The first messages to be processed are those on the right, and processing these "cold" inlets initializes the internal variables in the object (such as the value for velocity used by **makenote**); the last message to be processed is to the "hot" inlet on the left, which causes output to occur only after internal variables have been set up.

IB.2 THE MODULO OPERATOR AND RECURSION

Let's return to the discussion of binary operators that we began in Section IA.1, and present the **modulo operator**, which is represented by the percentage symbol: %.
Modulo is defined as the remainder of a division operation. If, for example, you divide 20 by 6, you get 3 as the result, with a remainder of 2 (since 6 · 3 = 18, and 2 is the quantity that remains). To better understand this function, build the patch shown in figure IB.4.

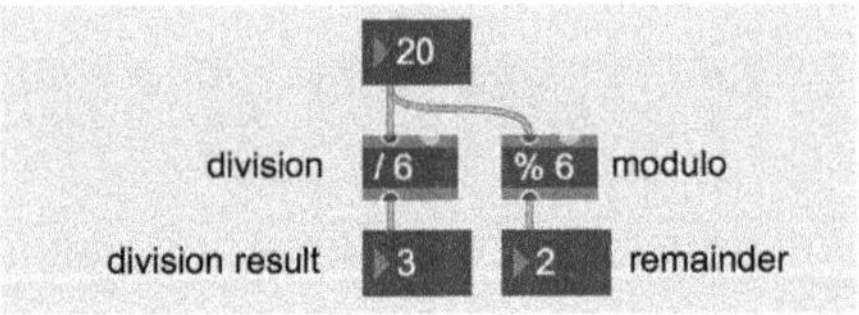

Fig. IB.4 The modulo operator

We have connected both a division object and a modulo object to a single number box, both of which have the same argument. Using this patch, you can see both the results of integer division and of the modulo operator, side-by-side. If you slide the value in the number box up using your mouse (generating an increasing series of numbers), you can see that the modulo operator generates a series of integers that go from 0 to 5 (when the argument is 6) and that this series repeats cyclically as long as the numbers continue to increase. (Try it!) The rule is that integers generated by an operator "modulo n" range from 0 to n-1. Try replacing the argument of the operator (or connecting a number box to its right inlet) and testing its behavior with various arguments.
We mentioned that modulo is the remainder of a division operation, which implies that the results of division are always integers. (If they weren't, there would be no remainder!) This doesn't stop us from doing division with floating point numbers, however. Try changing the patch from figure IB.4 as shown in figure IB.5:

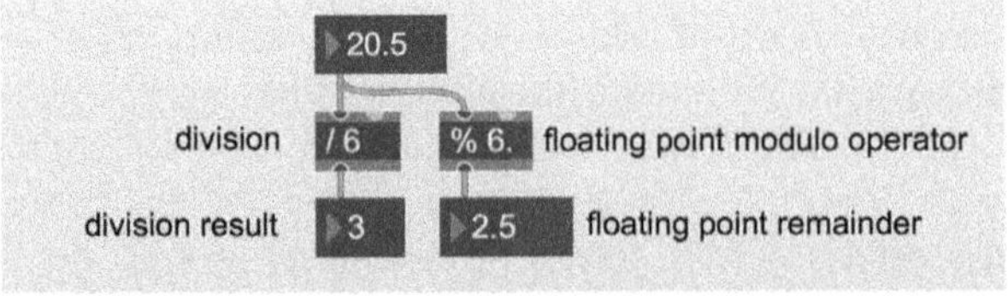

Fig. IB.5 The fractional modulo operation

We've replaced the number box at the top with a float number box, we have added a decimal point to the number that is the argument of the modulo operator. Finally, we have connected the output of the modulo operator to another float number box. In this configuration, the % operation returns the remainder from division operation while maintaining any decimal part. In the example shown in the figure, 20.5 is divided by 6, resulting in the integer result 3, plus a remainder of 2.5. (6 • 3 = 18, which is indeed 20.5 when you add 2.5.)

Among other things, by using the floating point capabilities, % can be used to separate the decimal portion of a number, as you can see in figure IB.6.

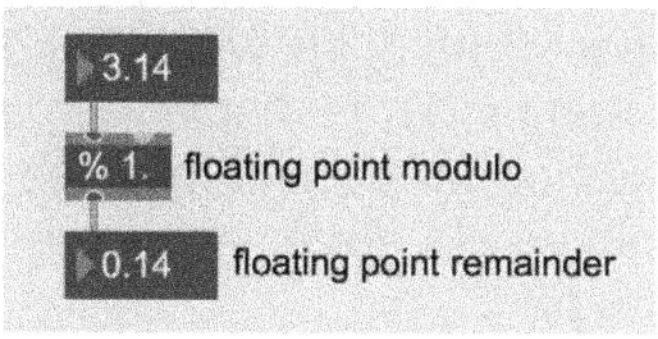

Fig. IB.6 Extracting the decimal part of a number

In this figure, we see that when we calculate a decimal remainder for division by 1, the decimal part of the number is separated from its integer part. Looking at the example shown in figure IB.6, the integer result of "dividing" 3.14 by 1 is obviously 3, while the remainder is 0.14, which is the decimal portion of the original number.

As with other operators, there is an MSP version of the object, %~ (pronounced modulo tilde), which performs modulus arithmetic on a signal. We will use this object in Section IB.9.

RECURSION

By exploiting the "cold" inlets of an operator, we can execute **recursive operations**, which are sequences of operations in which the result is obtained by using previous results. Build the patch in figure IB.7 to try this.

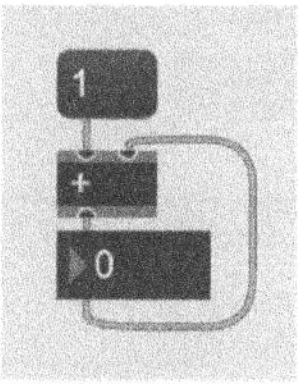

Fig. IB.7 A recursive sum

The patch shows a message box containing the number 1 connected to an addition operator whose outlet is connected to a number box. The outlet of the number box goes back again to the "cold" inlet of the addition operator. If you click repeatedly on the message box, you will see the result of the summation increase constantly by 1. The result of all sums, in fact, becomes an addend for the next sum (the other addend being the 1 contained in the message box), and the sequence of resulting operations is this:

hot inlet		cold inlet		result
1	+	0	=	1
1	+	1	=	2
1	+	2	=	3
1	+	3	=	4
etc.				

The "cold" inlet, as you see, always stores the result of the previous operation. If we want to restart the series from 0, we would need to send the right inlet of the addition operator the number -1, perhaps using a second message box. In this way, after having clicked on the second message box, the internal variable of the right inlet would contain -1, which, when summed with a 1 sent to the left inlet, would yield a sum of 0.
It should be obvious that recursion can be used with all operators. Sending a "2" to a multiplier (the object *) with an argument of "1" would double the results on every repetition, for example. Alternatively, sending a "2" to an "inverse" division operator !/, with an argument of "1.", would halve its result on every repetition.

CONSTRUCTING AN ARPEGGIATOR

We now want to show how to build a simple arpeggiator, using only objects illustrated thus far. For starters, we will exploit the patch in IB.7 to generate a chromatic scale[2] with help from a **metro** object and from the MIDI objects that we learned about in the previous section. Build the patch shown in figure IB.8.

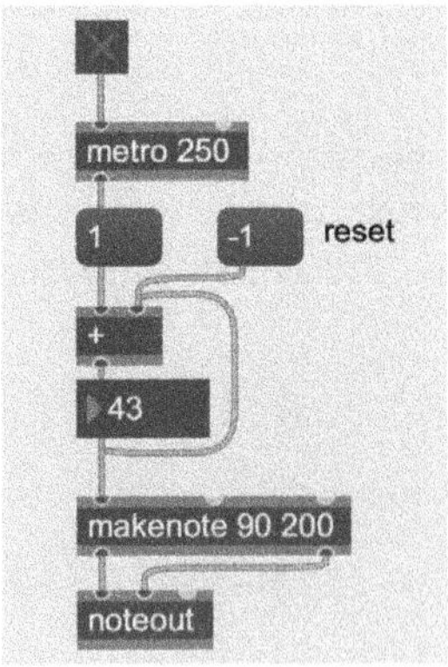

Fig. IB.8 A chromatic scale

This patch produces consecutive MIDI notes one after another, every 250 milliseconds. The notes, created by the **makenote** object, each have a velocity

[2] To review the concept of a chromatic scale, revisit Section 1.4T.

of 90 and a duration of 200 milliseconds. Every time that the "*reset*" message box on the right is clicked, the sequence will begin again at 0, but since the note represented by MIDI note number 0 and its successors are decidedly too low to be heard, we need to add a fixed number to the sequence, in order to raise the pitch. This is what is shown in figure IB.9 (which you should build yourself).

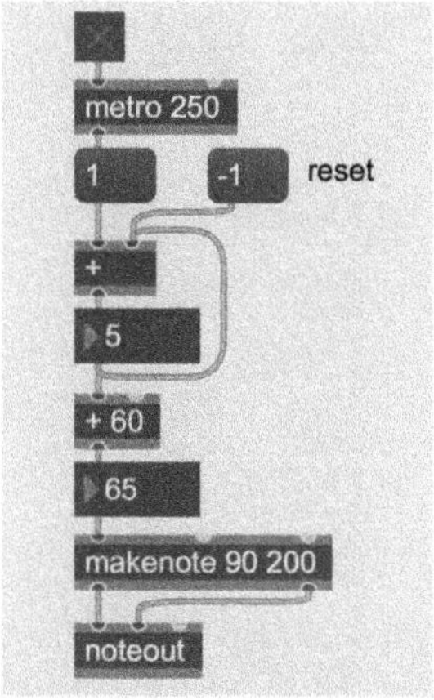

Fig. IB.9 Transposing a chromatic scale

Here, after the recursive addition, we have inserted an addition object with an argument of 60. In this new version, the scale will begin at MIDI note 60 (middle C) rather than 0 when the sequence is restarted.
The value 60, added to the chromatic scale that is produced by the recursive summation, is called an **offset**, a term defined as a fixed value (60 in this example) that is added to a series of values (which in our example is the recursive sum) for the purpose of shifting the starting point of the series (which in our example moves from 0 to 60). Another problem with this patch is that the chromatic scale rises in an unrestricted way, quickly reaching the limits of the MIDI specification (which defines note numbers as being always between 1 and 127). Our first try at a solution to this is to add two messages boxes, the first containing the value 1 and the second containing the value -1 (see figure IB.10), and to connect them to the "cold" inlet of the first message box in the patch. With this change in place, you can reverse the direction of the scale, toggling between an ascending and a descending scale at will.

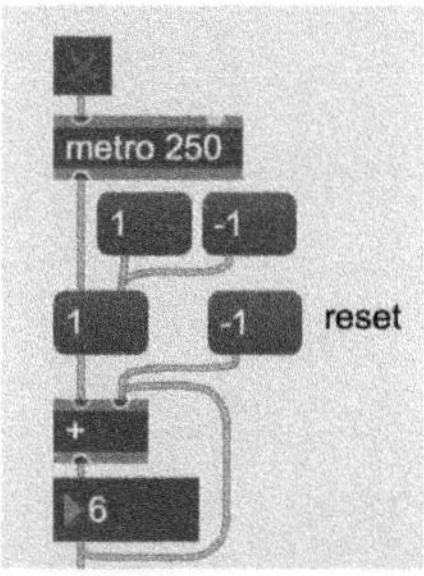

Fig. IB.10 Ascending versus descending chromatic scales

Another possible fix is shown in figure IB.11 (which you should try building), in which we limit the rising chromatic scale to an octave.

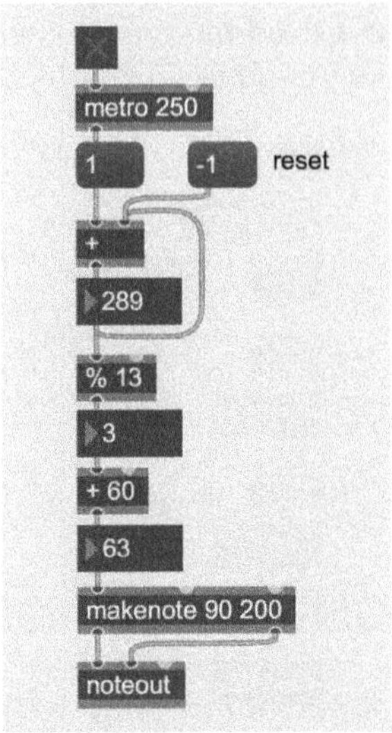

Fig. IB.11 Generating a chromatic octave

We have now inserted a modulo operator with an argument of 13 between the recursive addition and the offset. By doing this, the limitless chromatic sequence is transformed into a sequence that constantly cycles between 0 and 12. (Recall that a modulo operation always varies between 0 and n-1.)
Moving to a slightly more complex example, let's see how to generate a sequence that proceeds in minor thirds rather than semitones.
Add to the patch the changes shown in figure IB.12.

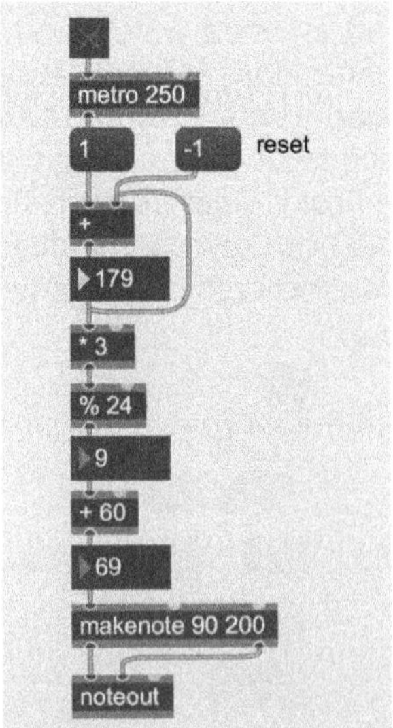

Fig. IB.12 An arpeggio of minor thirds

We have inserted a multiplication operator with an argument of 3 immediately after the recursive addition operation, which transforms the series 0, 1, 2, 3... into the series 0, 3, 6, 9... When applied to MIDI notes, this change converts what was a chromatic scale into an arpeggio[3] of minor thirds. The modulo argument has also been changed to 24, enabling arpeggios that span two octaves rather than one.
The recursion in this example is cyclic; the numbers output by modulo always equal 0, 3, 6, 9, 12, 15, 18, 21... (24 % 24 is, of course, 0 – dividing 24 by 24 yields 1 with a remainder of 0.) You will hear the same 8 notes repeated over and over for this sequence. To generate numbers for a longer cycle, you can use a number that is not an exact multiple of the increment as an argument to modulo. We have done this in figure IB.13, where the multiplier remains 3, but the argument to the modulo operator becomes 25 rather than 24. Using this scheme, we see that the output from the modulo operator follows the same sequence as the original example, diverging after the number 21 to produce the number 24, and, after that: 2, 5, 8, 11, 14, 17, 20, 23, 1, 4, 7, 10, 13, 16, 19, 22, 0, 3, etc.
With this simple change, the patch produces 3 different arpeggios rather than a single static arpeggio of 8 notes. Each of the new arpeggios varies by a semitone from its predecessor, and 2 of them are made up of 8 notes while the other is made up of 9 notes; the difference in length creates an interesting sense of rhythmic phasing, which you will hear when you try the patch.

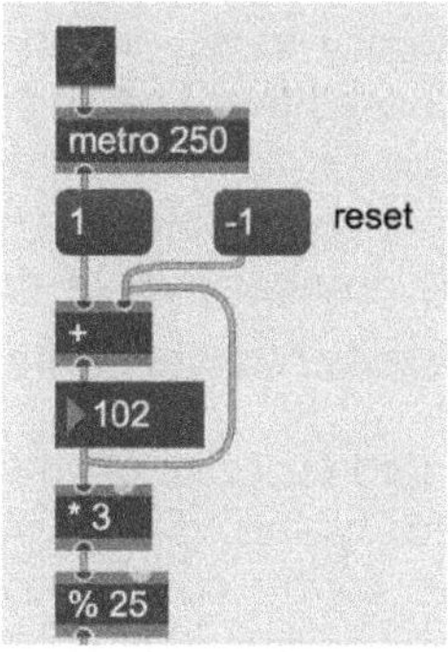

Fig. IB.13 A minor-third arpeggio with variations

You can also vary the value of the multiplier and of other parameters, rather than just the modulo argument.

[3] An arpeggio is an ascending or descending sequence of notes that are members of a musical chord.

We explore these variations in the next patch, which you can see when you open the file **IB_02_arpeggiator.maxpat** (shown in figure IB.14).

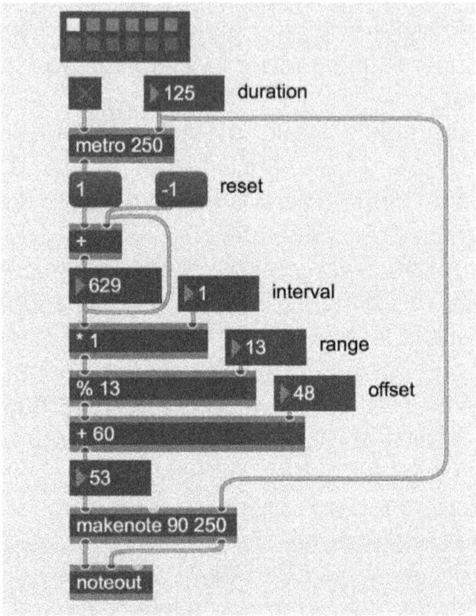

fig. IB.14 File IB_02_arpeggiatore.maxpat

This arpeggiator patch is very similar to the one that we constructed above, with the addition of some number boxes that enable changing the interval between notes, the range of the arpeggio (in number of semitones), the offset, and the duration of the note. The duration parameter is shared by the `metro` object and the `makenote` object; a single number box, at the upper right, sends its value to the right inlets of both objects. Configurations of this patch can be saved into the `preset` object at the top.
Recall that clicking on the darker cells of the `preset` object will recall configurations previously saved; typing <Shift-Click> enables you to save new configurations for the first time. Try the configurations that we have provided in the first row, observing how the parameters change. After this, make up your own new configurations and store them into the second row of presets.

We see now more "variations on a theme": open the file **IB_03_random_arpeggiator.maxpat** to see the patch shown in figure IB.15.

In all of the arpeggiators we have seen until now, the note increment was implemented by using a recursive sum with a fixed increment (which was 1). In this patch, we have added a random generator (immediately under the `metro` object) that adds a variable amount to the increment, which is then summed into the fixed amount using the + object directly under it. In the example shown in the figure, the random generator has an argument of 2 and generates random numbers between 0 and 1 (producing, obviously, a 0 or a 1), and the fixed increment to be added is 1. This results in a sum that will be either be 1 or 2, since the random number, a 0 or a 1, is added to the fixed number 1.

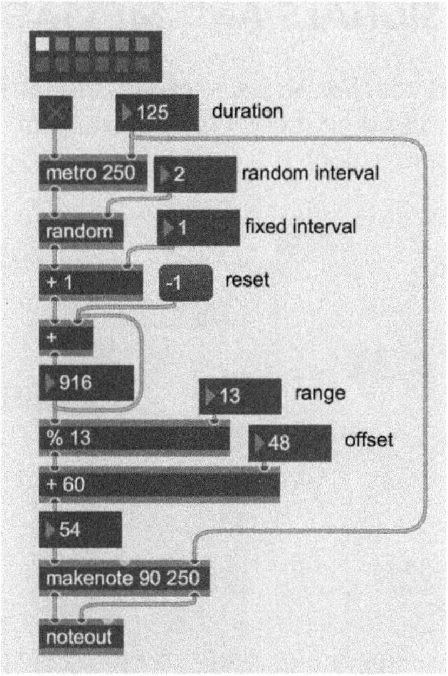

Fig. IB.15 The file IB_03_random_arpeggiator.maxpat

Notice that we have eliminated the multiplication object that was found in the previous version after the recursive sum, which determined the fixed interval to be used between notes of the arpeggio. In the new version, the interval (which varies) is given by the randomized process detailed above. Also note that there are more presets to try; use them to understand the relationship between the random and the fixed components of the increment, and how they influence the patterns of the arpeggios.

Of course, nothing should stop you from using the arpeggiators from this section with sound generators from previous chapters. Try replacing the random sequence generator in the file 03_10_subsynth.maxpat with an arpeggiator, for example.

IB.3 ROUTING SIGNALS AND MESSAGES

We have already used the **`selector~`** object several times, an object that enables you to switch between members of a group of source signals. Figure IB.16 shows this object in action.

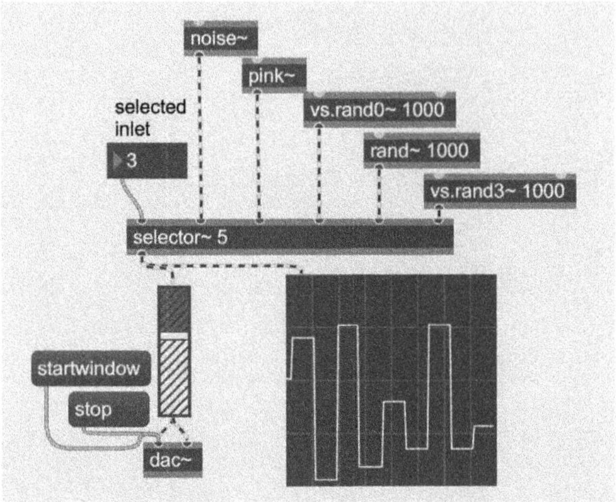

Fig. IB.16 The `selector~` object

The **`gate~`** object which enables you to send an incoming signal to one of several selectable outlets, is similar. Its argument specifies how many outlets it should have. Figure IB.17 shows one possible use: a white noise generator whose output can be routed, using the outputs of a `gate~` object, to one of three filters.

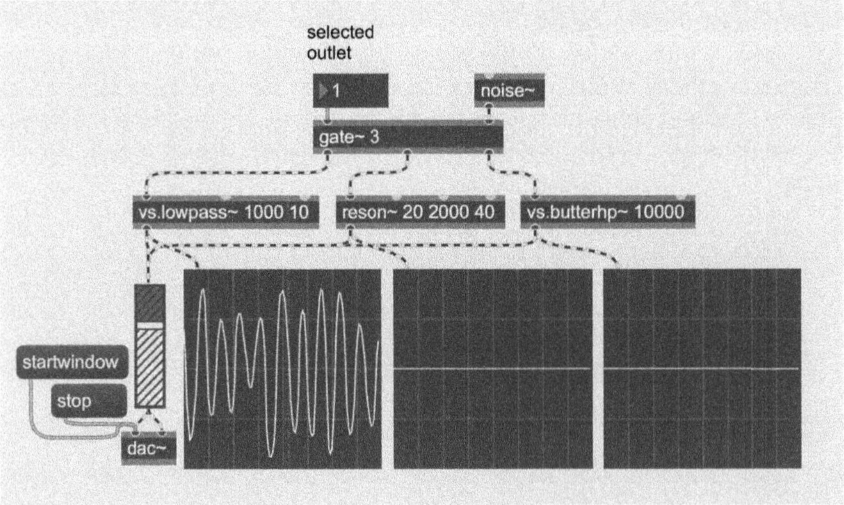

Fig. IB.17 The `gate~` object

As with `selector~`, a 0 on the left inlet mutes all output, while an integer corresponding to an outlet causes the input signal to be routed to that outlet.

In the example, a 1 would route white noise through the lowpass filter, a 2 through the resonant bandpass filter, and a 3 though the highpass filter.
The **selector~** and **gate~** objects in MSP have equivalents in Max, which route messages instead of signals. These are **switch** and **gate**, both shown in figure IB.18.

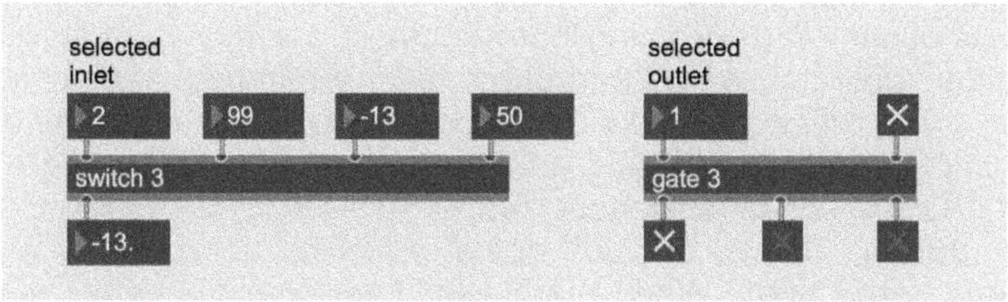

Fig. IB.18 The **switch** and **gate** objects

To demonstrate the **gate** object in action, we will modify the patch originally shown in IB_02_arpeggiator.maxpat (which is shown in figure IB.14) so that it can produce arpeggios with more than one note sounding at once; the new patch will be able to produce arpeggios that play one, two, or three sounds at once. Modify the patch as shown in figure IB.19, and then save it to disk, since we will continue modifying it several times in the following section.

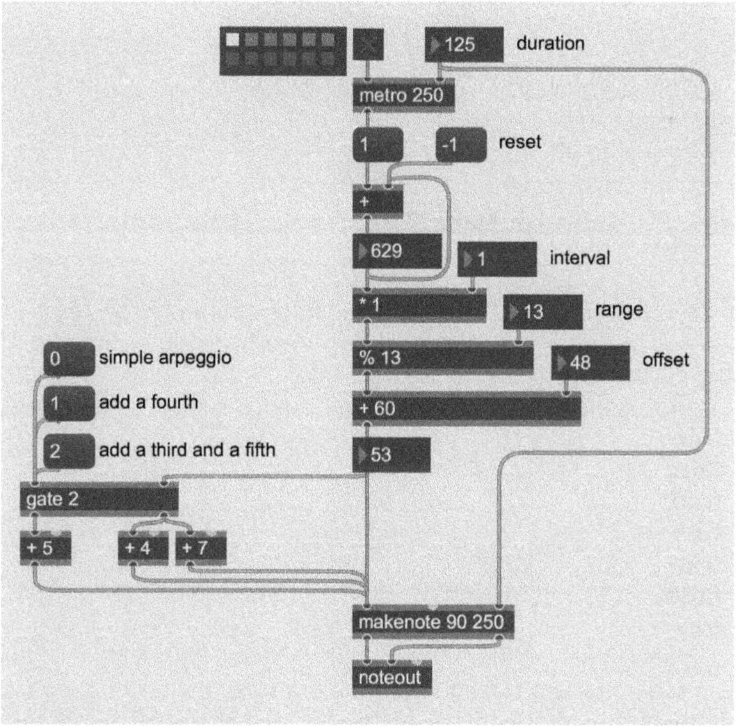

Fig. IB.19 Parallel arpeggiation

MIDI note numbers generated by the algorithm, besides being sent to `makenote`, are also sent to a `gate` object, where there are three possibilities. Selecting the message box containing '0' shuts the `gate` object off, which causes us to hear only the note sent directly to `makenote` (an option that sounds the same as the original patch).
Selecting the message box containing '1' "opens" the first outlet of the `gate` object, and incoming note numbers are then sent through to an addition operator which transposes by 5 semitones, after which the numbers are processed by `makenote`, sounding a fourth above the original note (which is also played) and producing an arpeggio that proceeds in parallel fourths. In an analogous fashion, selecting '2' sends the note number through to two addition operators which transpose by 4 and 7 semitones, respectively. When these two notes sound together with the original, an arpeggio of major triads is the result.

IB.4 THE RELATIONAL OPERATORS AND THE SELECT OBJECT

Let's take up the subject of relational operators, which are operators that compare two values in order to establish a relationship between them.
Here are some examples of this kind of operator for two numbers, designated x and y. Each operator answers a specific question:

x > y is x greater than y?
x < y is x less than y?
x == y is x equal to y?
x != y is x not equal to y?
x >= y is x greater than or equal to y?
x <= y is x less than or equal to y?

For each of these relations, there is a separate operator. The result of these operations will be "true" or "false", determined by whether the two numbers satisfy the relation. For example:

5 > 2 true
4 < 4 false
7 != 8 true
3 == 3 true
3 <= 3 true
3 <= 2 false
3 <= 4 true

As you can see in the last three lines of the example, the relation <= is satisfied when x is equal to y, or when x is less than y (and the same is true, of course, when the terms are inverted with the >= relation). In Max, the result "true" is represented by the value 1 and "false" by the value 0.

Which for our example means:

5 > 2 = 1
4 < 4 = 0
7 != 8 = 1
3 == 3 = 1
3 <= 3 = 1
3 <= 2 = 0
3 <= 4 = 1

Look at the fourth line in the example, and notice the single equal sign that precedes the result versus the double equal sign that indicates the relation to be tested; it is important to understand that the two signs are different, and that they have different uses.

To try Max's relational operators, build the patch shown in figure IB.20.

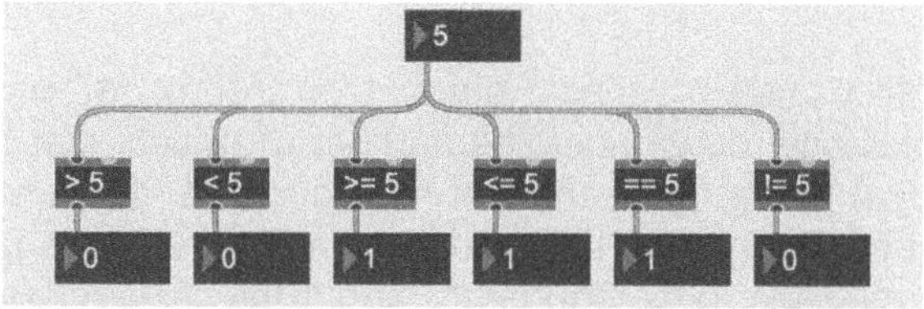

Fig. IB.20 The relational operators

First, check the correctness of the relations shown in the figure, and then try different values in the number box, observing how they change the results. (As with all operators, the right inlet can be used to modify the argument.)
Try building the simple patch in figure IB.21, which tests a stream of random numbers using a relational operator.

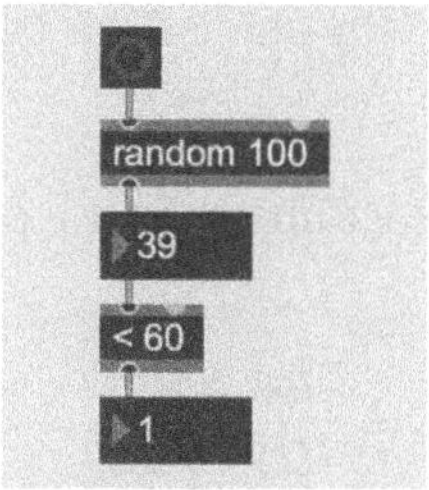

Fig. IB.21 Testing random numbers

You can see how this patch works: a random number generator with an argument of 100 produces random numbers between 0 and 99, and these numbers are tested using the < operator to see whether they are less than 60. As a consequence, values between 0 and 59 (60 numbers in all) will produce a value one, while values between 60 and 99 (40 numbers) will produce a value zero. In other words, given that the numbers between 0 and 99 have an equal probability of being generated, the relational operator will produce a value one 60% of the time, and a value zero 40%. By changing the argument of the < object, it is possible to change the percentage of ones and zeros that are produced. We will shortly see an interesting way to use this simple algorithm.

THE SELECT OBJECT

The **select** object is similar to the relational operators, since it performs a comparison between the value sent to its inlet and the values of its arguments. To see how this object works, build the patch in figure IB.22.

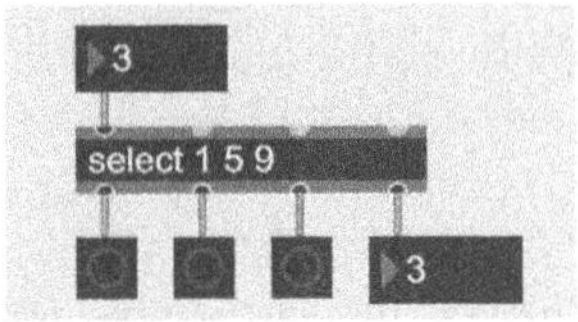

Fig. IB.22 The select object

The select object takes a variable number of arguments, and the number of arguments, plus one, determines the number of outlets that will appear. In the example shown in the figure there are 3 arguments; as a result, the object displays four outlets. Every time that select receives a message, it compares the value of the message to its arguments, and if the value received is equal to one of the arguments, a bang is generated on the corresponding outlet (if the received value matches the first argument, for example, a bang is issued on the first outlet). If the incoming message is not equal to any of the arguments, the unmatched message (and *not* a bang) is forwarded to the last outlet.
Referring to the figure, when select receives a 1, it generates a bang on the first outlet. If it receives a 5, it generates a bang on the second outlet, and if it receives a 9, a bang goes out on the third outlet. All other messages will be forwarded to the fourth outlet and sent on. In the example shown in the figure, we have sent a 3, which does not generate a bang, but instead, is forwarded to the last outlet.

In figure IB.23, we apply the select object to the patch originally shown in IB.21.

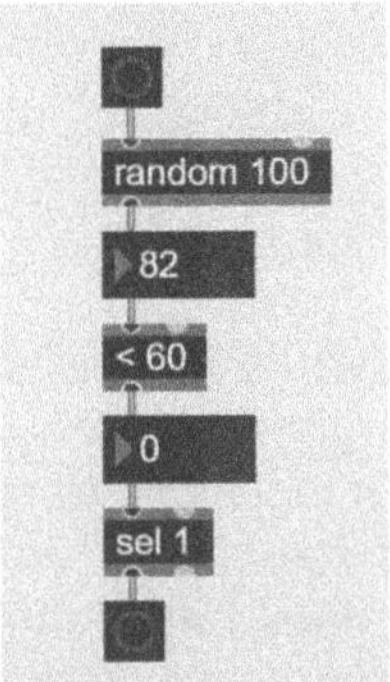

Fig. IB.23 Generating probabilistic bangs

We've added a **select** object with an argument of 1 to the bottom of the patch (abbreviated as **sel**, as you can see). This object is connected to a button on its first outlet, and as a consequence, every time that it receives a 1, it generates a visible bang on the lower button. Alternatively, every time it receives a 0, nothing visible happens, since nothing is connected to the last outlet. In this patch 60% of the bangs produced by the upper button are allowed to pass. It is possible to change the percentage of bangs by changing the argument of the relational operator.

A PROBABILISTIC METRONOME

Now build the patch shown in figure IB.24.

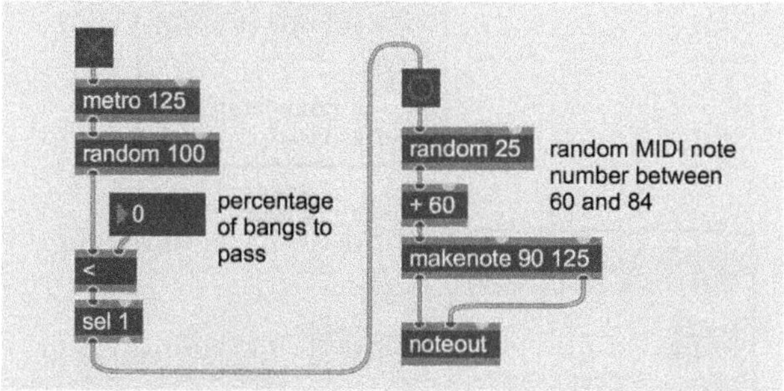

Fig. IB.24 A probabilistic metronome

Here we have connected a metronome to the patch of figure IB.23, generating a stream of intermittent bangs that in turn trigger a random sequence of MIDI notes according to the probability given in the number box. By varying the percentage setting, and thus modifying the argument to the < object, you can obtain sequences of notes that are more or less "gappy".
Try using this algorithm with the arpeggiator that was shown in figure IB.19 – our own implementation is shown in figure IB.25.

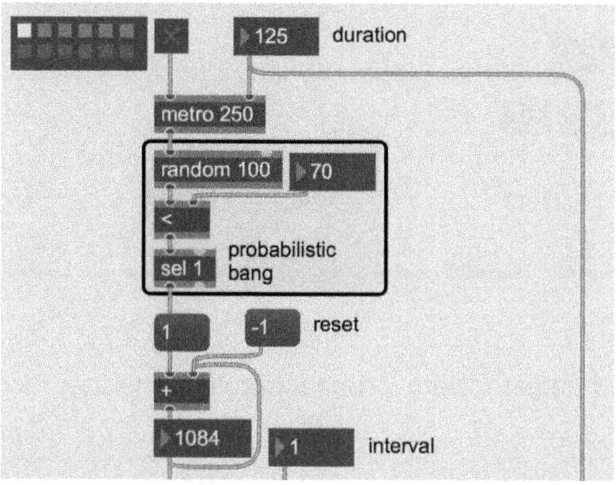

Fig. IB.25 A probabilistic arpeggiator

With this modification, the patch also sometimes pauses between one note and the next based on the probability percentage, rather than continuously arpeggiating. Going one step further, a final modification enables additional notes to be tacked onto some, but not all, of the notes that are part of these arpeggios (refer to the parallel intervals described in figure IB.19).

See figure IB.26 for the details of this finishing touch to the patch.

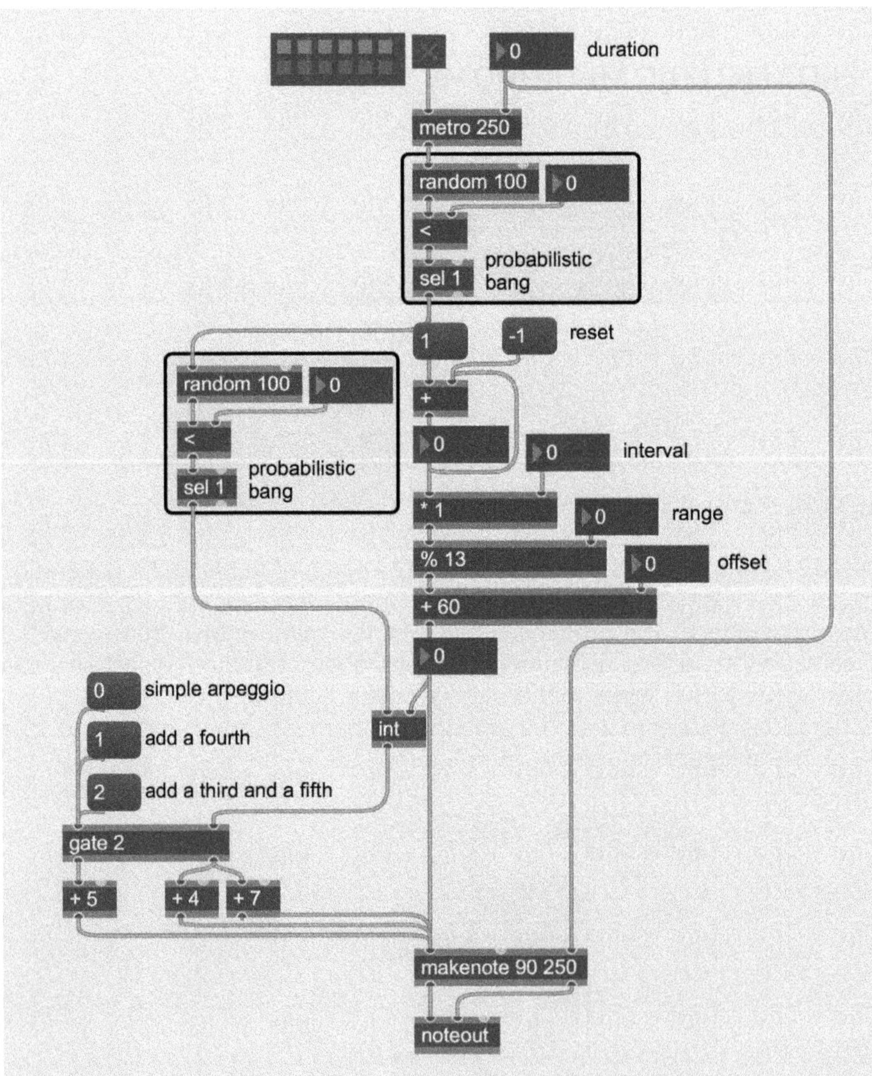

Fig. IB.26 An arpeggiator with probabilistically generated notes and parallel intervals

There is now a probability assigned to whether a note will be generated for the arpeggio, and a different probability assigned to whether the note generated will be accompanied by additional notes. Probabilities are set using the message boxes connected to `gate`. In the example shown in the figure, for each bang there is a 70% chance that a note will be generated for the arpeggio, and when such notes are generated, there is a 50% chance that they will be accompanied by additional notes.
Notice that we have added an `int` object (which we first encountered in Section IA.1 of Interlude A) in the lower part of this patch, which is connected to the right inlet of `gate`.

Do you know why this is needed? What would happen in the absence of this object?

IB.5 REDUCING A LIST TO ITS PARTS: THE ITER OBJECT

We now will discuss the **`iter`** object: an object that can be used to reduce a list to its elements. (See figure IB.27.)

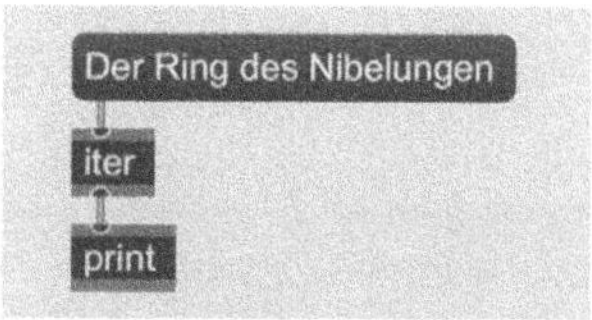

Fig. IB.27 The `iter` object

Build the patch shown and click on the message box to see the individual words that compose the phrase "Der Ring des Nibelungen" displayed, each on its own line, in the Max window. The `iter` object has separated the elements of the list, which is why each has its own line.
To what use is an object like this? One simple thing that we could do with it is to play chords; construct the patch shown in figure IB.28 to try this approach.

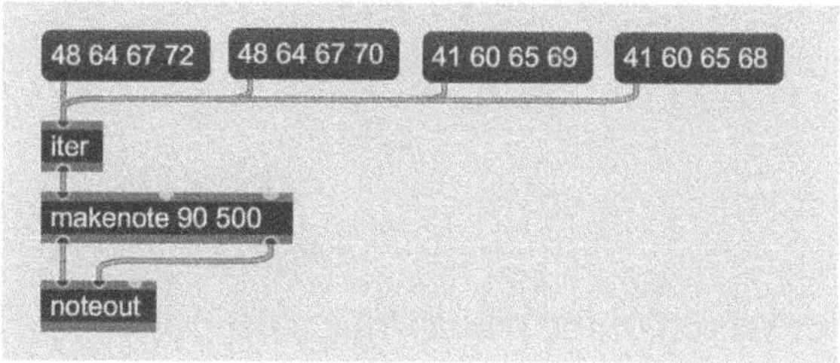

Fig. IB.28 Sounding chords with `iter`

Every time that you click on a message box, the `iter` object reduces the list to single elements, sending each of them in turn to **`makenote`**, which then uses each as a MIDI note value. (Velocity and duration are based on the values given by the arguments, which are 90 and 500.)

The **iter** object generates the elements in quick succession,[4] and because of this, the sounds of the notes occur practically simultaneously.

Despite our perception that the four notes are simultaneous, it is important to underline the fact that the **iter** object sends four separate messages to **makenote**. What would happen if there were no **iter** object between the message boxes and the **makenote** object? The **makenote** object would use the first three values in the list to populate its internal variables for note, velocity, and duration, and would discard the fourth value. Clicking on the first message box (if it were not connected to **iter**) would produce MIDI note 48 with a velocity of 64 and a duration of 67 milliseconds. This would happen because, as we covered in Section IA.1 (see figure IA.5), many Max object will distribute the elements of a list that they receive to their internal variables. Of course, objects that explicitly manage lists, such as **iter** or **zl** (discussed elsewhere) do not behave in this way.

Let's exploit the **iter** object to implement an even more baroque version of our arpeggiator; return to the patch of figure IB.19, and modify it as shown in figure IB.29.

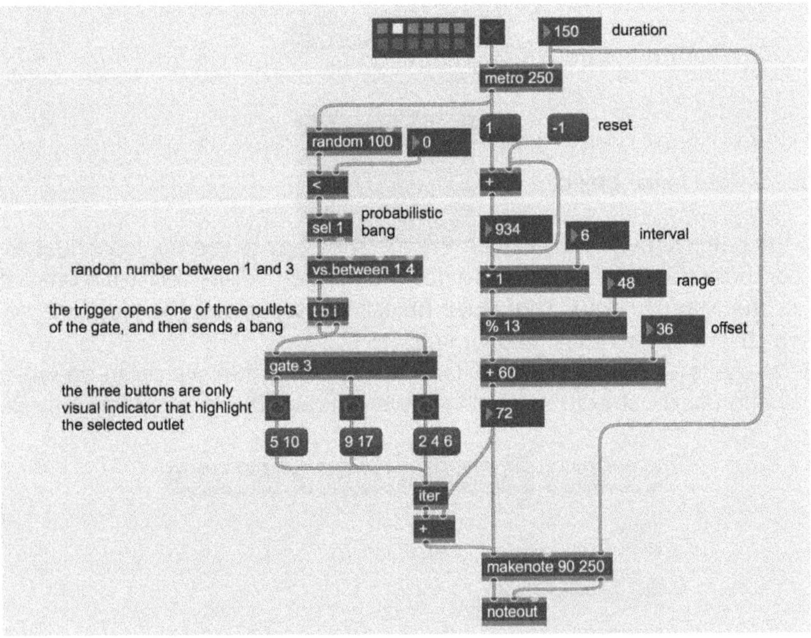

Fig. IB.29 Another version of the probabilistic arpeggiator

[4] In some ideal sense, we can say that the elements generated are simultaneous, but in reality, they are produced in sequence. The time interval that separates two outgoing messages on the outlet, from the design perspective of the executing patch, is zero (exactly as it is with consecutive bangs produced by **uzi**).

Unlike the example shown in figure IB.26, the notes of the arpeggio in this new case are generated on every bang of the **metro** (without probabilistic gaps), and each note may be accompanied by additional notes according to a probability given in the number box. You can see that the **vs.between** object is connected to the outlet of a "probabilistic bang" (in the upper left), which generates random numbers between 1 and 3.[5] The numbers generated open one of the three outlets of the **gate** object below, allowing the bang to pass to one of the three message boxes containing lists of numbers.
The list in the message box thus "struck by a bang" is sent to the **iter** object, which separates it into its elements, which are added to the notes of the arpeggio, and finally dispatched to **makenote**.

Try modifying the intervals in the message boxes, and then adding other intervals (after incrementing the argument of **gate** and the maximum value of the **vs.between** object!).

[5] Recall that with integer arguments, **vs.between** generates random numbers between the minimum and the maximum, minus 1.

IB.6 ITERATIVE STRUCTURES

One of the many things that programming has in common with music composition is the productive use of repetitive sequences. Whoever has used a programming language has encountered an **iterative structure** (or **looping structure**), in which a pre-determined procedure is repeatedly applied to a sequence of data. In the same way, anyone who has composed music has used repeating drum patterns, or musical forms such as the passacaglia or the chaconne, which employ a "bass ostinato" that repeats (with variations) over and over in the course of a piece. Other examples of looped musical patterns are the gradually evolving repetitive sequences used in minimalist music, or the looped sound samples and MIDI patterns that repeat in an uninterrupted fashion in some electronic music.

We will see in a moment how to generate a repetitive sequence in Max, but first we need to introduce a capability of `multislider` that we haven't yet discussed. The `multislider` object, as you already know, can be used to generate lists of values graphically, using the mouse. Although we have only used the output to generate complete lists until now, it is also possible to extract the values one-by-one. A single value of the list can be procured with the "***fetch n***" message (in which n is an index for the internal list); the message "*fetch 1*", for example, would extract the value of the first element, "*fetch 2*" the value of the second, and so on. By connecting a message box containing the message "*fetch $1*" to the outlet of a number box, you can extract elements at will, in whatever order you choose, as shown in figure IB.30.

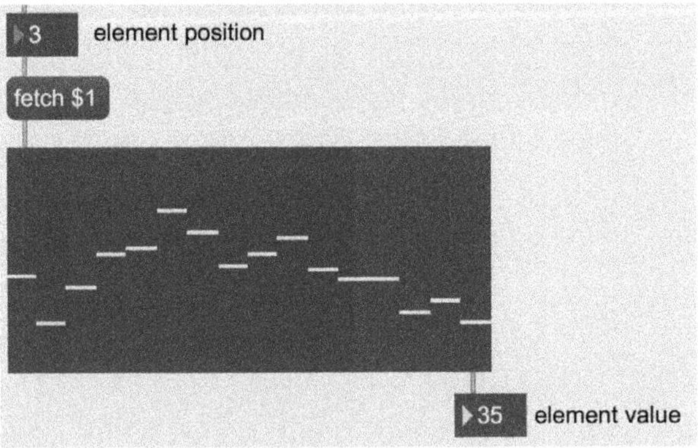

Fig. IB.30 Extracting individual element values from a `multislider`

Notice that as individual elements are extracted, they are emitted on the right outlet rather than the left; the left outlet is reserved for emitting the entire list.

Before proceeding, let's also briefly take a look at a new object, the **counter** object, which is shown in the little patch in figure IB.31.

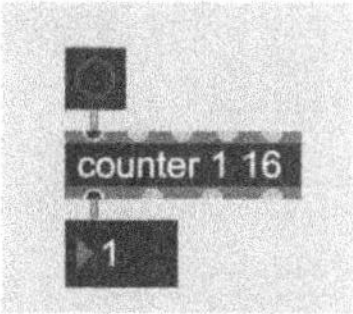

Fig. IB.31 The **counter** object

The **counter** object generates a consecutive series of numbers, one per bang.[6] In our patch, there are two arguments, 1 and 16, which specify the minimum and maximum numbers for the series. Try clicking repetitively on the **button** and watching the series repeat cyclicly; every time that it reaches the number 16, it returns to 1 on the next bang. By connecting the **counter** object to the message box of figure IB.30 and putting a **metro** into the patch to generate a regular set of bangs, we produce the patch shown in figure IB.32.

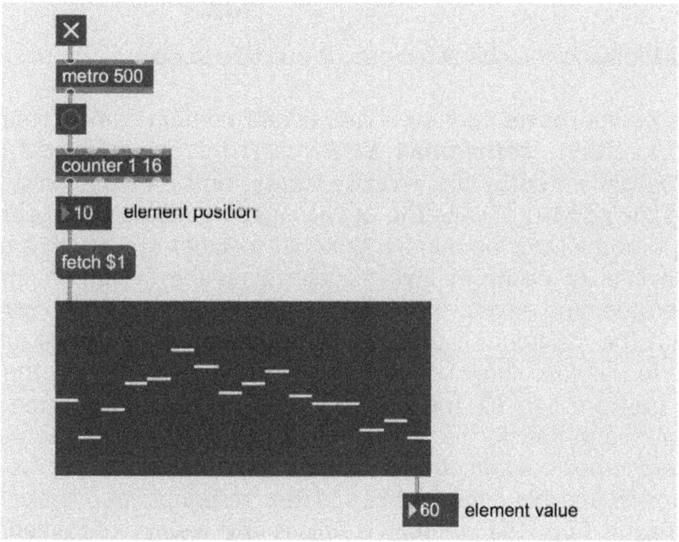

Fig. IB.32 A repetitive sequence

In this simple patch, we have created a repeating sequence of 16 **multislider** values that are produced with a regular cadence. Notice that it is possible to modify the contents of the **multislider** while the sequence is playing. You can also modify the message-sending behavior of the **multislider** while the sequence is playing, without having to resort to the Inspector.

[6] The **uzi** object, as you know, also generates a series of consecutive numbers from its right outlet; in the case of counter, it is necessary to send a bang for each successive number, unlike **uzi**, which will generate an entire series with a single bang.

To try this, modify the patch as illustrated in figure IB.33.

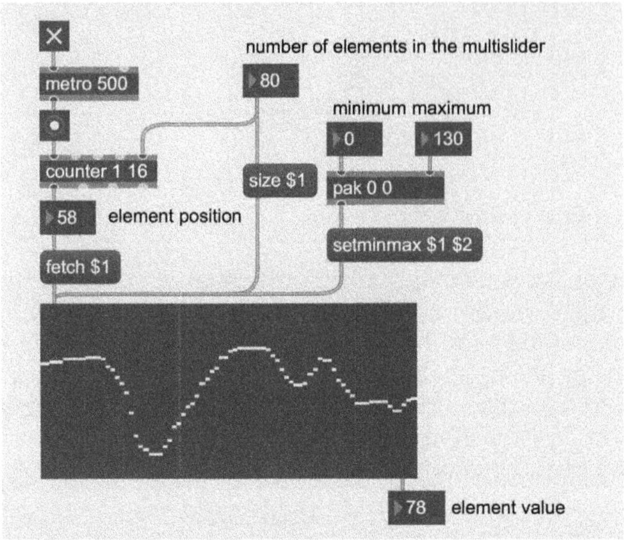

Fig. IB.33 Modifying the characteristics of `multislider`

The two message boxes that we have added contain some commands for the `multislider`: "***setminmax** $1 $2*" sets the minimum and maximum values to be generated by the `multislider`, and the command "*size $1*" determines the number of values to be managed by the `multislider` (which is the length of the list). The number box that specifies this length is connected to the fifth inlet of `counter`, which determines the maximum limit for the series generated, and also to the "***size** $1*" message box. In this way, we can be sure that the maximum is used for both the length of the list and for the `counter`. In the case shown in the figure, the limit is 80, and the numbers generated go from 1 to 80. The `pak` object on the right collects the minimum and maximum and transforms them into a list of two elements, which is given to the message box containing the message [setminmax $1 $2]. Try changing these values to see how the `multislider` responds; also make sure that you understand how the generated values are always contained between minimums and maximums set with the command "*setminmax*".

Now open the file **IB_04_sequence.maxpat** (shown in figure IB.34). This file contains a patch similar to that in the file IA_06_random_walk.maxpat, but the sequence of notes that had previously been generated randomly is now replaced by a sequence generated by the `multislider`.
You can see the section of the patch that generates the sequence on the left side of figure IB.34. We have basically copied the patch shown in figure IB.33; the length of the list contained in the `multislider` corresponds to the length of the loop, and the minimum and maximum values correspond to the range of the notes of the sequence. The single elements of the sequence are emitted by the right outlet of `multislider`, and this outlet is the one that we connect to the `monosynth`.

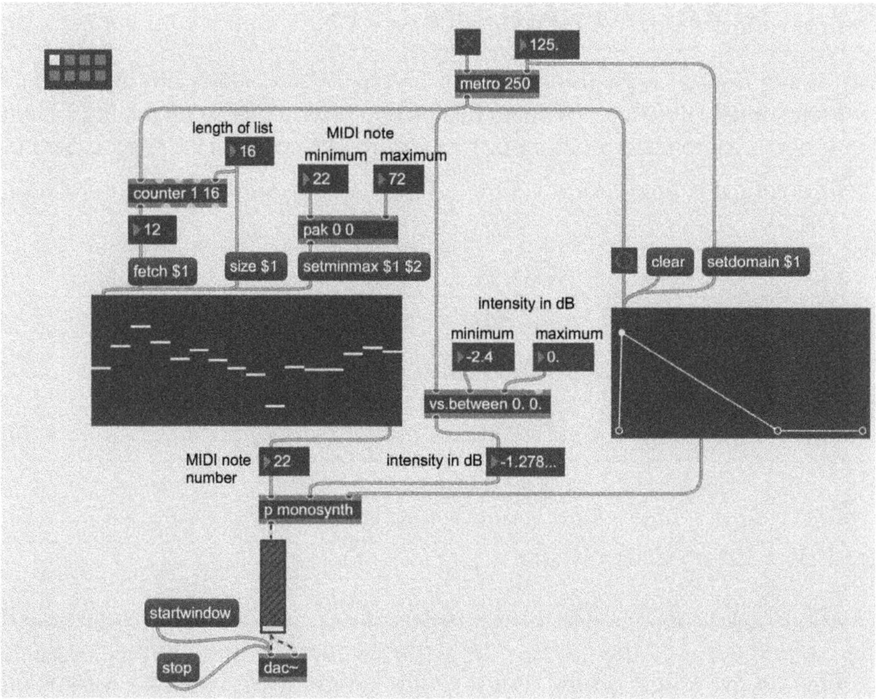

Fig. IB.34 The file IB_04_sequence.maxpat

ACTIVITY

Try the various presets saved in the final patch of this section, and modify them, replacing the random intensity generator with a sequence generated by another new `multislider`.
Try setting lengths for the sequence of notes and the sequence of intensities that differ (12 notes versus 11 intensities, for example).

IB.7 GENERATING RANDOM LISTS

You should now analyze and construct the patch shown in figure IB.35, which generates a list of random values. In this patch we have used the **zl** object; if you don't remember much about it, you might consider rereading Section IA.7.

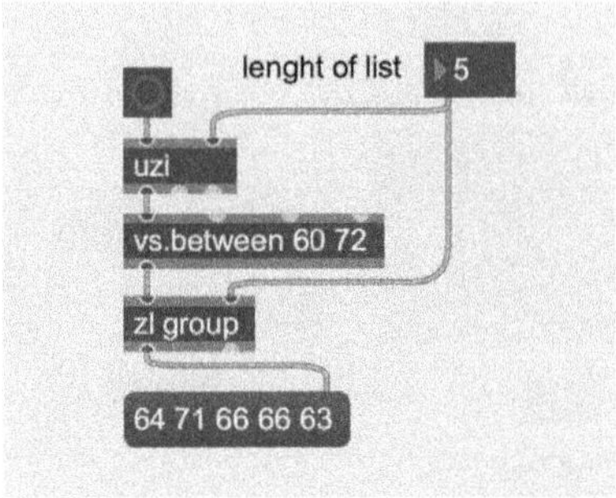

Fig. IB.35 A list of random values

A number box is connected to the right inlets of **uzi** and [**zl** group] in this patch. The **uzi** object uses this number as a specification for the number of bangs to generate, while [**zl** group] uses it as the length of the list to be assembled. Clicking on the button, five bangs are transmitted by **uzi** to **vs.between**, which generates 5 random numbers. These numbers are received by [**zl** group], which assembles them into a list of 5 elements. By changing the number in the number box, it is possible to generate lists of any size, and if we connect the outlet of [**zl** group] to the inlet of the **multislider** in figure IB.34, we can generate random lists of notes in the loop. Try it! [7]

At the end of Section 3.9, we suggested that you might generate random lists to send to the **mc.fffb~** object for simulating resonant bodies (refer to figure 3.73 and the text after it: "Replacing Parts of Algorithms"). The method for doing this could be exactly what we have shown in figure IB.35.

And while we are on resonant bodies, let's look at an interesting variation on this theme: open the file **IB_05_bounce.maxpat** (as shown in figure IB.36). Every time that you click on the button at the top of this patch, you will hear a resonant body that "bounces" on a surface. We aren't going to explain how it works, instead, we will leave this as an exercise.

Remember that the **vs.click~** object (which we first saw in Section 3.9) generates a train of unitary impulses at a given frequency.

[7] As we have pointed out, you are connecting [**zl** group] output to a **multislider**, rather than the message box below, which is used only for the visualization of the list.

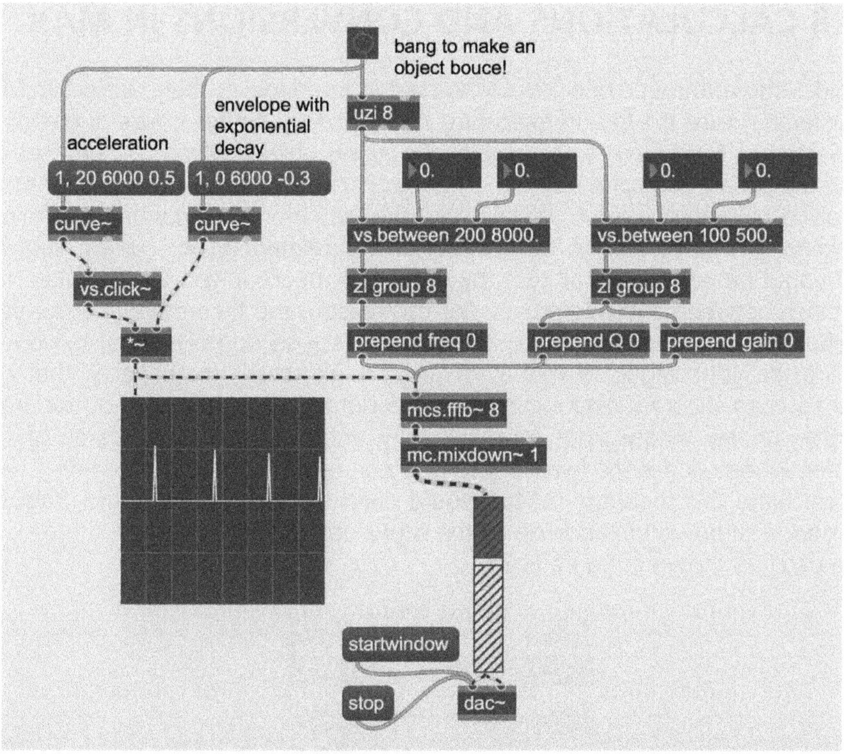

Fig. IB.36 The file IB_05_bounce.maxpat

IB.8 CALCULATIONS AND CONVERSIONS IN MAX

Besides the arithmetic operators discussed in Interlude A, there are other Max objects that ease the task of executing calculations, whether simple or complex. In Section 1.6 we saw, for example, the `sqrt` object, which can be used to take the square root of a number. This object can also be used as part of more involved calculations, such as, let's say, the Pythagorean theorem. You might imagine such theorems to be abstract and unrelated to our current subject, but you'd be wrong! Recall that, by using this theorem, you can calculate the distance between any two points. For this reason, the theorem will prove very useful when we discuss sound spatialization in the second volume of this book. Calling on your vague memories of junior high school math, recall that the Pythagorean theorem establishes that, in a right triangle, the sum of the areas of the squares whose sides form the right angle is equal to the area of the square whose side is the hypotenuse (the side opposite the right angle).
To calculate this theorem in Max, you'd need the **pow** object (which raises a number to a power) in addition to the `sqrt` object.[8]
The patch is shown in figure IB.37.

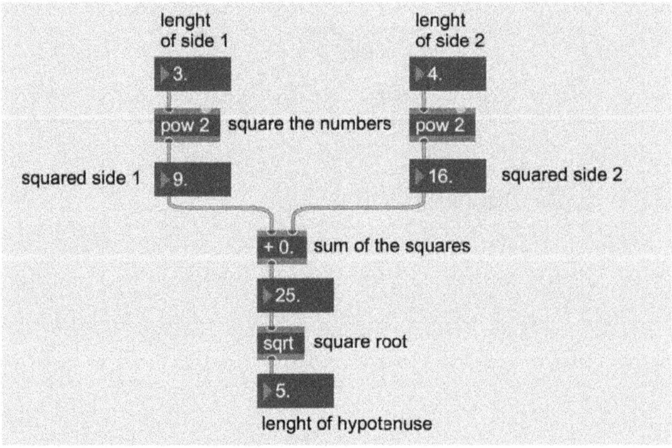

fig. IB.37 Calculating the Pythagorean theorem

As you see, the **pow** object takes an argument that represents its exponent; incoming numbers will be raised to this power. (A 2 will square the number, a 3 will cube it, 4 will raise it to the fourth, and so on.) When entering values in this patch, remember to enter the number in the float number box on the right (side 2) before the number on the left (side 1), since the number on the left triggers the addition operator. Can you think of a way to make the operation of the patch less brittle, that would enable these numbers to be entered in either order?

---

[8] A note for readers who are more advanced in mathematics: there is an object in Max called **cartopol** that performs a conversion between Cartesian coordinates and polar coordinates. This object clearly provides direct access to the Pythagorean theorem, but in this section, we are interested in using the intermediate calculations for teaching purposes. For the readers less familiar with math: if you haven't followed one word of this footnote, don't worry about it. Carry on!

THE EXPR OBJECT

For this calculation, which is still relatively simple, we had to add 4 objects into our network of float number boxes and comments: two **pow** objects, an addition object, and the **sqrt** object. It is clear that when doing calculations, the more complex the formula, the more objects (and connections between objects) will be needed. It is also clear that this could quickly become a problem. Fortunately, the **expr** object enables us to construct complex mathematical expressions from its text argument; the argument can combine numbers, variables, operators, and functions directly, without requiring any other objects. Let's illustrate this object by creating a simple example: let's calculate the sum of three numbers, as in figure IB.38.
You can see how the syntax of **expr** works: for every value that you use, you need a corresponding embedded dollar variable. What this means for this example is that in order to sum three numbers, three dollar variables are needed.

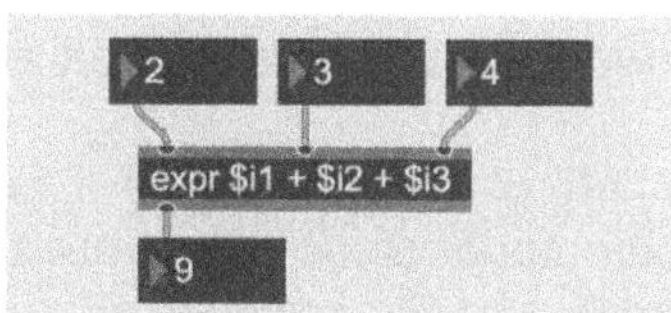

Fig. IB.38 The **expr** object

Take care, though, as these variables differ slightly from those that we've seen for message box – in this case, it is necessary to indicate the *type* of value represented by the dollar variable by inserting a letter between the dollar sign and the number following it. (An 'i' indicates an integer, while an 'f' indicates a floating point number.) In the example shown, $i1, $i2, and $i3 indicate three integer variables; the fact that these variables are integers also means that if we send floating point numbers to the **expr** object shown in figure IB.38, they will be converted into integers before the calculation is performed, and any portion of the numbers found after the decimal point will be discarded.

Besides operators, it is also possible to insert various functions into the **expr** object. Figure IB.39 shows how to calculate the square root of a number in order to illustrate this capability.

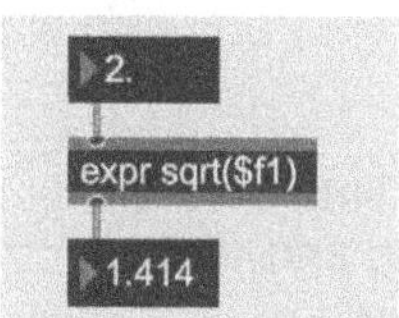

Fig. IB.39 Calculating a square root with the **expr** object

In the **expr** object a function is followed by the parenthesized values necessary to complete its calculation. This syntax is common to many programming languages, including the C language. (For those who will benefit from the knowledge, we will mention that the functions available within the **expr**

object are shared with the C language. We'll shortly see some examples of this.) Returning to figure IB.39, the *sqrt* function needs a value for which to calculate a square root. This value is represented by "$f1", which will be, as you can see, a floating point number.
In figure IB.40 we see how to use the function *pow* to raise a number to a specified power.

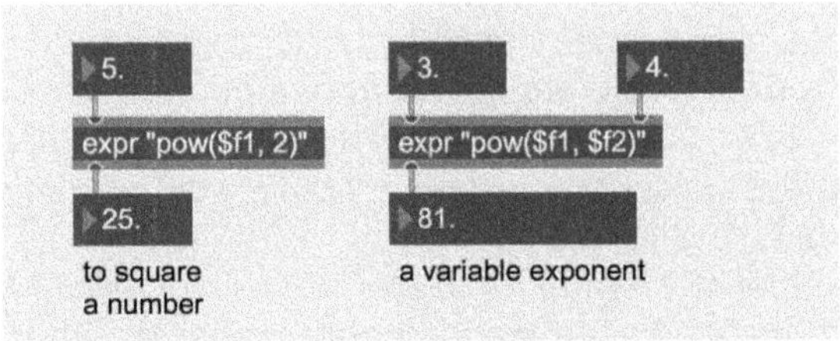

Fig. IB.40 The *pow* function

The *pow* function takes two values, a base and an *exponent*, which must be separated by a comma.
The **expr** object on the left of the figure has a fixed exponent of 2, and calculates the square of the number on its inlet, while that on the right has both a variable base and exponent, and can calculate any power.
With this background, let's now look at how to calculate the Pythagorean theorem with the **expr** object. (See figure IB.41.)

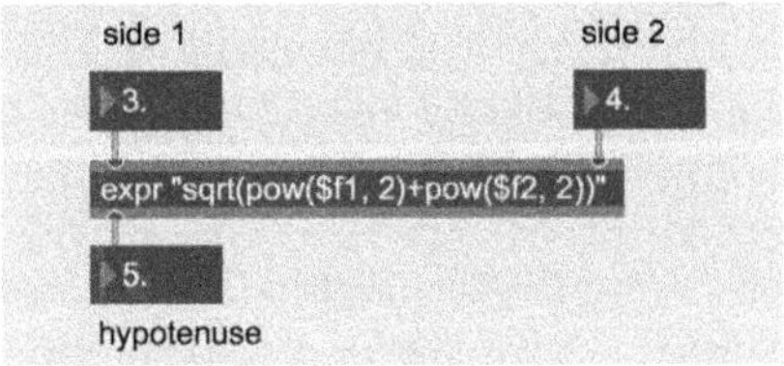

Fig. IB.41 Calculating the Pythagorean theorem using the **expr** object

The variables "$f1" and "$f2" correspond to the lengths of the two sides that contain the right angle, and furnish bases for calls to the *pow()* function that, summed, then furnish the value given to the *sqrt()* function used to calculate the square root.
Besides the *pow()* and *sqrt()* functions, **expr** has many other functions available, including:

log10	: base 10 logarithm
sin, cos, tan	: sine, cosine, and tangent
random	: random number

For a complete list, consult the help pages for the **expr** object.

Some of the objects that we've seen previously for converting values from one scale to another, such as **mtof** or **dbtoa**, could easily be replaced by analogous expressions in an **expr** object, as shown in figure IB.42:

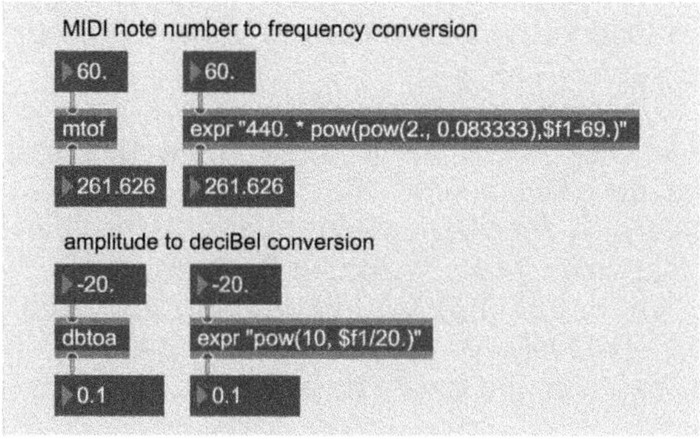

Fig. IB.42 Conversions done with the **expr** object

We won't go into the details of the calculations shown in IB.42, although you should be able to follow them; it is enough to know that inside "magic" objects such as **mtof** or **dbtoa** one actually finds normal mathematical expressions.
In Section 3.6, we pointed out the fact that the Butterworth filters found in the Virtual Sound Macros library contain an algorithm for calculating coefficients. In figure IB.43, as an example of this, we see the contents of the **vs.butterlpc** object, which calculates the coefficients of a lowpass Butterworth filter.

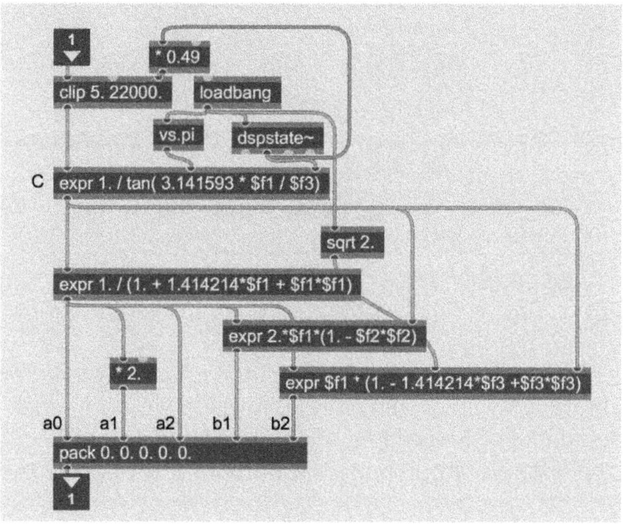

Fig. IB.43 The contents of the **vs.butterlpc** object

The **vs.butterlpc** object receives the desired cutoff frequency on its inlet, and generates on its outlet a list of 5 coefficients. Besides the **expr** object, this algorithm uses other objects that we have not encountered. The **vs.pi** object found under the **loadbang** returns the constant π when it receives a bang;

the **dspstate~** object to the right of **vs.pi** sends the current sampling rate to the second outlet,[9] and finally, the **clip** object under the inlet limits the numbers on the inlet to lie between a minimum and a maximum that can be set by the programmer. (In this case, the cutoff frequency of the filter is limited to lie between 5 Hz and the Nyquist frequency, half of the sampling rate, which we will discuss further in Chapter 5.)

We won't analyze the calculations involved in **vs.butterlpc** in detail, because they are definitely beyond the scope of this book. Adventurous readers, however, should definitely attempt to decode the patch with the help of the formulas that were shown in Section 3.6T. Recall also that the objects **vs.butterhpc**, **vs.butterbpc**, and **vs.butterbrc**, used for calculating the coefficients, respectively, of the Butterworth highpass, bandpass, and bandreject filters, also exist and can be dissected in similar fashion.

CONVERTING INTERVALS AND SIGNALS

We should now take up a discussion about some of the objects that enable you to convert one numeric interval into another; the first of these is **scale**. This object takes four arguments: the first two are the endpoints of a range to convert, and the last two are endpoints of the target range. In figure IB.44, we show a practical example that should help to clarify what this object does. Build the patch and test it.

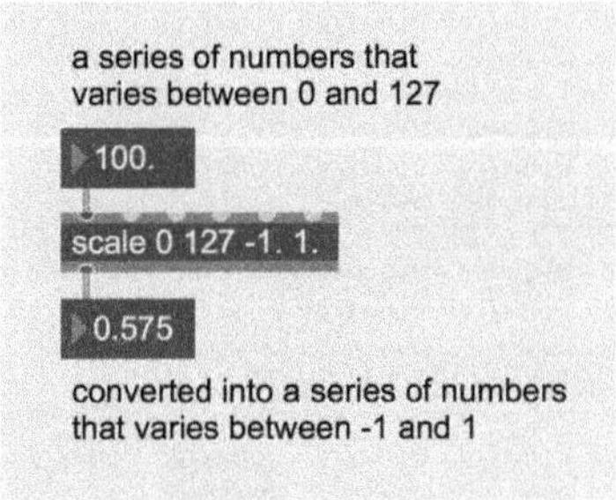

Fig. IB.44 The **scale** object

You can see from the figure that the 4 arguments are 0, 127, -1.0 and 1.0 – the last two of these arguments have decimal points, which indicate that the output should be a floating point range, rather than an integer range.[10] The first two arguments in the example, the input range, signify numbers between 0 and 127; the last two arguments, the output range, signify the range to be

[9] The **dspstate~** object, on which we will return in Chapter 5, furnishes information about the DSP system in Max. The first outlet produces a 1 or a 0 according to whether the DSP engine is active or inactive. The second outlet, as you know, furnishes the sampling rate, the third and fourth furnish the values of two parameters that we will cover in Chapter 5 (*I/O Vector Size* and *Signal Vector Size*).
[10] If any argument of the **scale** object has a decimal point, the output will be a floating point number, but if all four arguments are integers, the output will be an integer.

covered, which is -1.0 to 1.0 in this case. The **scale** object will map the values from 0 to 127 into floating point values between -1.0 and 1.0. (The value 0 will become -1.0, for example, and 127 will become 1.0; a value of 63.5, lying halfway between 0 and 127, will result in the value 0.0, and intermediate values will be scaled accordingly.)
Numbers to be converted are input to the first inlet of the **scale** object, and the four inlets that follow it allow the arguments to be modified. The last inlet is for generating exponential conversions.

Figure IB.45 shows a small patch that you should build that uses the **scale** object and also brings back some of the converters that we've already encountered.

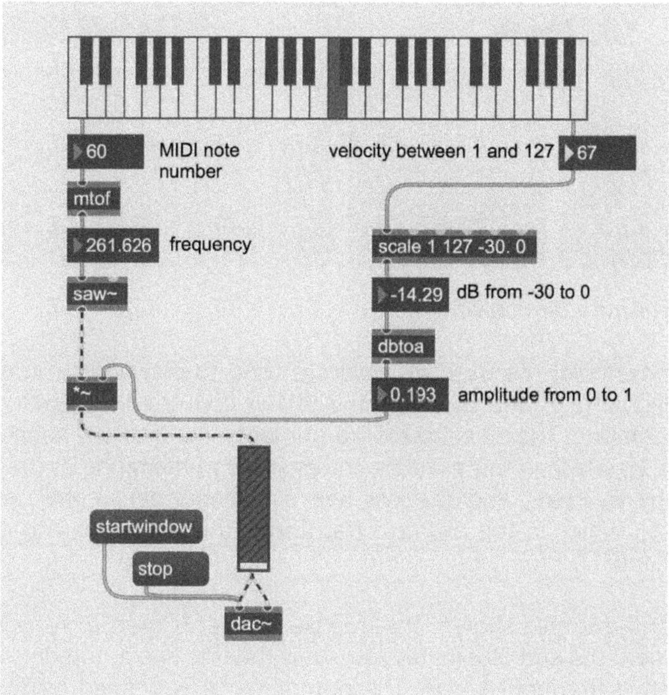

Fig. IB.45 Various conversions

On the left we have the conversion of MIDI note numbers to frequency, and on the right we have a conversion from velocity to amplitude.
Velocity is defined as having logarithmic growth like intensity in deciBels, but we can't use the values directly as dB, because they vary between 1 and 127,[11] and 127 dB is way above our maximum conventional dB value of 0.[12]

[11] The value 0 is reserved for MIDI note-off messages.

[12] For a discussion of this topic, see Chapter 5.1T.

To solve this scaling problem, we first use **scale** to convert velocity values between 1 and 127 into a range between -30 and 0; this is a more limited dynamic range, which corresponds to a typical keyboard instrument. We then convert the resulting number into an amplitude value using **dbtoa**, and we are done.

We will conclude this section by introducing the **scale~** object (the MSP equivalent to **scale**), which enables us to map one range of values onto another range.
We first see two examples of the use of **scale~** in figure IB.46.

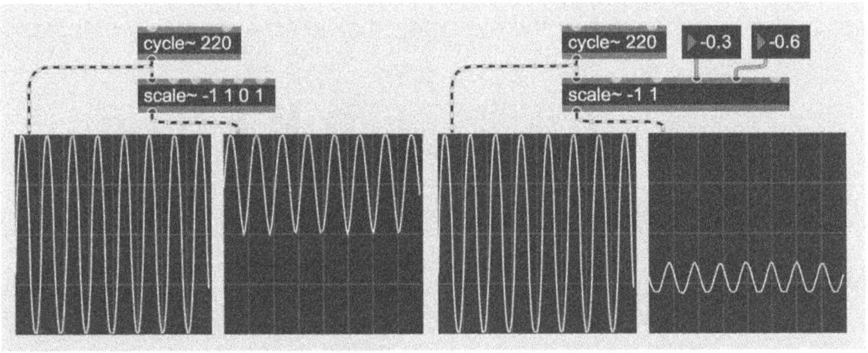

Fig. IB.46 The **scale~** object

In the first example, the **scale~** object is used to convert the interval [-1,1] into the interval [0,1] and by doing this, it has converted a bipolar sine wave into a unipolar one. The object takes 4 arguments: the first two define the input interval, [-1,1], which in this example corresponds to the range of the oscillation produced by **cycle~**, and the last two arguments define the range to be output, [0,1], which in this example transforms the sine wave into oscillations between 0 and 1.

In the second example shown, the **scale~** object is used to rescale the sine wave between -0.3 and 0.6. In this case, only the first two arguments have been used to define the input range. The output range is defined using two float number boxes connected to the fourth and fifth inlet of **scale~**.

The **scale~** object can also receive signals on its inlets that define the input and/or output ranges, as you can see in the example in figure IB.47.
In figure IB.47, we have once again defined the input range as [-1,1], using two arguments. The minimum value of the output signal has been given as -0.2, using a float number box, while the maximum value has been given by a **phasor~** object that generates a ramp between 0 and 1 continuously. The maximum value, therefore, varies between 0 and 1, following the progress of the **phasor~**. Notice in the figure that the oscilloscope on the right that shows the ramp generated by **phasor~**, and the center oscilloscope shows how the sine wave sent to **scale~** is continuously rescaled: the minimum value remains fixed at -0.2 (set by the float number box), while the maximum value is guided by the signal produced by **phasor~**.

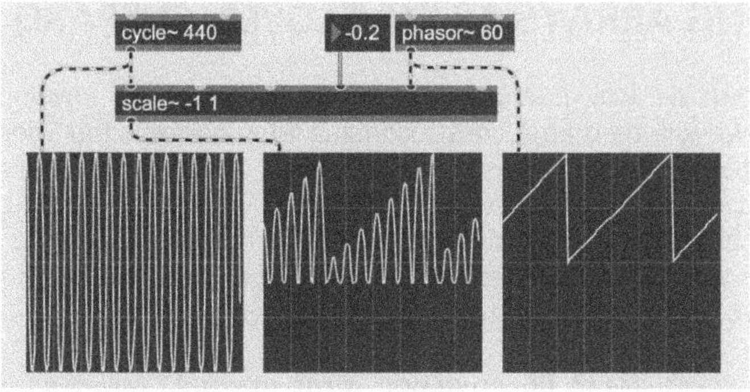

Fig. IB.47 Defining the output range with a signal

This concludes the section, and might be a good moment to pause, relax, and review the concepts that you've acquired, because in the final section of this chapter, we will take up a fairly rigorous topic...

IB.9 USING ARRAYS AS ENVELOPES: SHEPARD TONES

In this section we will describe a technique for saving an envelope into an array, and we will then apply this technique to implement the Shepard/Risset infinite glissando that was described in Section 2.3T. Up until now we have used the `line~` and `curve~` objects (discussed in Section 1.3) for generating envelopes, but now we will demonstrate how to use an array to apply any arbitrary sequence of numbers as an envelope, not limiting ourselves to straight lines, exponential, and logarithmic curves.

To begin, open the file **IB_06_envelope_array.maxpat** (shown in figure IB.48).

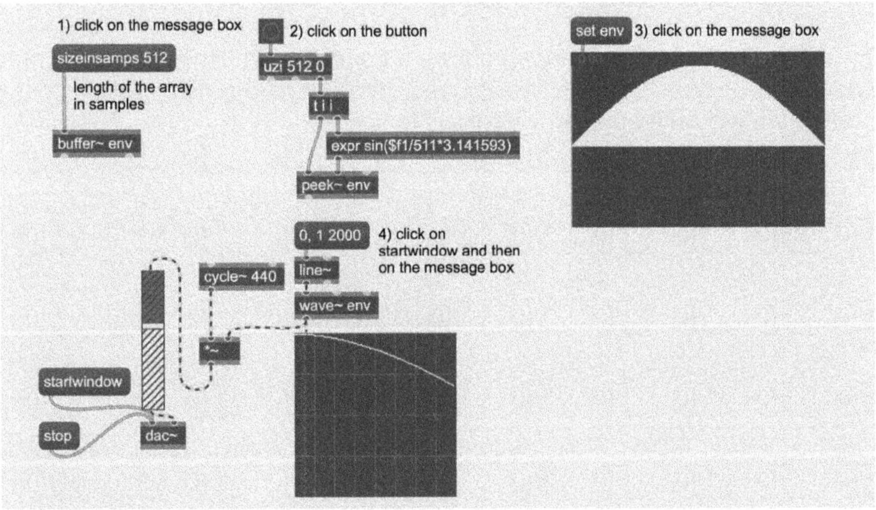

Fig. IB.48 The file IB_06_envelope_array.maxpat

Take a careful look at this patch, because it contains many new items. We've divided it into four parts, each of which can be considered a patch in its own right. In the upper left, is a `buffer~` with the name "env" (standing for "envelope"), which is used to save the array containing the envelope. Clicking on the message box containing the message "***sizeinsamps** 512*" dimensions the array, giving it a size of 512 samples; we hope that it is obvious that "*sizeinsamps*" is a command that sets the size of the `buffer~` in samples.[13]

In the central upper part of the patch, we introduce a new object: **`peek~`**. This object enables reading and writing single values into a `buffer~`, and takes, as an argument, the name of the `buffer~` to which it will refer. The center inlet of the object receives a value to write, and the left inlet is an index into the array indicating where to write the value. If you sent a value of -0.3 to the

[13] There is also a "***size***" command which will dimension an array in milliseconds; a command of [size 1000], for example, would set the array to a duration of 1000 milliseconds, or 1 second, which at a sampling rate of 44,100 Hz would be 44100 samples.

center inlet, for example, and then a 100 to the left inlet, **peek~** would write -0.3 at position 100, writing over any value that had been there previously in the process. As you can see, every time that we want to write a new value into the array, we need to first introduce the value to the center inlet and then send the index to the "hot" left inlet.[14]

The top center part of the patch generates the half of a sine wave cycle that we will use as an envelope. Here is how this part of the patch works, in detail: when you click on the button, the **uzi** object (introduced in Section IA.9) generates 512 bangs on its left outlet (which we don't use) and 512 consecutively rising integers on its right outlet. Its first argument (512) sets the number of bangs/numbers to generate. The second argument (0) sets the value for the initial integer in the series, which as a consequence runs from 0 to 511; we will specify the indexes of the array using this number, which is why we choose to start at 0. The elements of the series are cloned by the **trigger** object; each incoming number is emitted by both **trigger** outlets, first on the right and then on the left, according the Max rules of precedence.

You can see what happens to the right output of **trigger**: each element of the series is sent to an **expr** object with the argument "sin($f1/511 · 3.141593)" as it is generated (recall that those elements are generated one by one, rather than as a list). The **expr** object is calculating the sine function using the values being sent to it by **uzi** (and being passed via the $f1 variable), which are first being divided by 511 and multiplied by π (3.141593). Dividing a series of numbers that run from 0 to 511 by 511 yields a series of floating point numbers that runs from 0 to 1. This new (rescaled) series of numbers are then being multiplied by an approximation for π (3.141593), resulting in yet another series, which now runs from 0 to π. These values are used by the *sin* function to calculate the sine of an angle expressed in radians, and the results are sent, one value at a time, to the center inlet of **peek~**; since the values the we are using with *sin* run from 0 to π, the object will generate a half of a sine wave cycle. (A full cycle of a sine wave would run from 0 to 2π radians).

Returning to the **trigger** object, after each number in the series from 0 to 511 is emitted on the right outlet, an identical number is emitted on the left outlet. This number goes to the left inlet of **peek~** and is used as an index value into the array contained in the **buffer~** named "env". For every value generated by **expr**, a matching index is generated. In this way, the 512 values of the sine half-cycle are saved into the array.[15]

[14] An alternative approach would be to send the left inlet a list containing two elements, the first of which is the index and the second of which is the value to be written. (For our example, the list would be [100 -0.3].) This kind of compound-message-in-a-list is a common capability of many Max objects, as you learned in Section IA.1 of Interlude A.

[15] There are also commands for the **buffer~** object that allow us to fill the table with various functions, including the sine function. We will talk about it in the chapter on granular synthesis in the third volume. Here we wanted to explain a technique that allows us to generate arbitrary functions: we will use this technique for the realization of the "Shepard tone".

In the upper right part of the patch is a **waveform~** object, which you should already be familiar with. A click on the message *"set env"* enables us to display the waveform, which you can see in the figure is exactly a half-cycle of a sine wave. This wave form will be used as our envelope, and note well that it could not have been produced using either the **line~** or the **curve~** objects.

In the lower part of the patch, the array that we have compiled is used as an envelope for sounds produced by the **cycle~** object. As you know, an envelope describes variations to be made to a sound's amplitude over time, and in Max it is applied through the use of a multiplication operator. Because of this, we need to multiply the values coming from the **cycle~** oscillator by the "env" array; we do this using a **wave~** object, which produces its cycle, as you already know, guided by a ramp that changes from 0 to 1.[16]

In preceding parts of the book, we have used **phasor~** objects to produce a series of ramps to control the phase of **wave~**, but this time we need only a single ramp to generate the sine half-cycle envelope. Such a ramp can be produced using the **line~** object: the message [0, 1 2000] that is connected to **line~** in the example produces a ramp from 0 to 1 over 2,000 milliseconds (2 seconds). This ramp guides a single cycling of the **wave~** object (which itself contains only a half-cycle!), thus describing a curve that starts at 0, rises to 1 at the center, and then descends to 0. Click on the message box and hear how the amplitude of the sound produced by **cycle~** follows the curve that you can see on the oscilloscope at the bottom. We have successfully created an amplitude envelope using an array.

REPEATING ARRAY-BASED ENVELOPES

There is nothing stopping you, of course, from generating a repeating series of envelopes using a **phasor~**. To do this, modify the lower part of the patch in the way shown in figure IB.49:

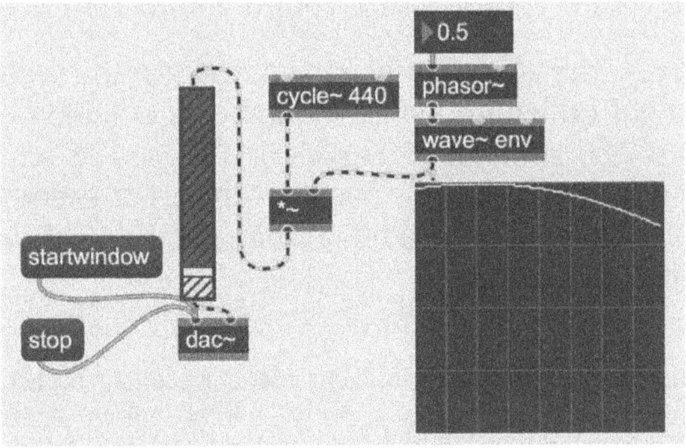

Fig. IB.49 Repeating envelopes

[16] See Section 2.1, "Using Wavetables with Oscillators".

Here, in place of the **line~** object, we have a **phasor~** that oscillates at 0.5 Hz, taking two seconds to complete a cycle. The duration of the envelope therefore remains the same, but we now have an uninterrupted series of envelopes. If you try increasing the frequency to make shorter envelopes, note that the timbre of the sound changes at a certain point because you are generating what is called "amplitude modulation", and which we will cover in more detail in the third volume. For now, keep the frequency over 10 Hz to avoid generating these effects, which for the moment we'd rather not explain in detail.

Controlling the duration of the envelope by changing the frequency of the **phasor~** seems a bit complicated; wouldn't it be better to directly set the duration and have Max calculate the necessary frequency? Since we know that period is the inverse of frequency, the solution is very easy – transform the patch as shown in figure IB.50.

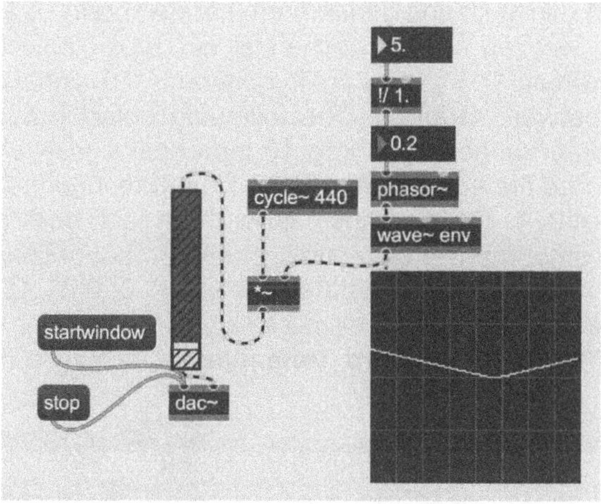

Fig. IB.50 Transforming a period into a frequency

Using the [**!** / 1.] operator, you can obtain the inverse of a number. When doing this, if you specify the duration in seconds (NOT in milliseconds), the operator will calculate relative frequency. In the example shown in the figure, we see that a duration of 5 seconds corresponds to a frequency of 0.2 (1/5) Hz.

SHEPARD TONES

Before dealing with the Shepard Tones, let's introduce a new message that generates a series of values in the multichannel system: "spread". Recreate the patch in figure IB.51.

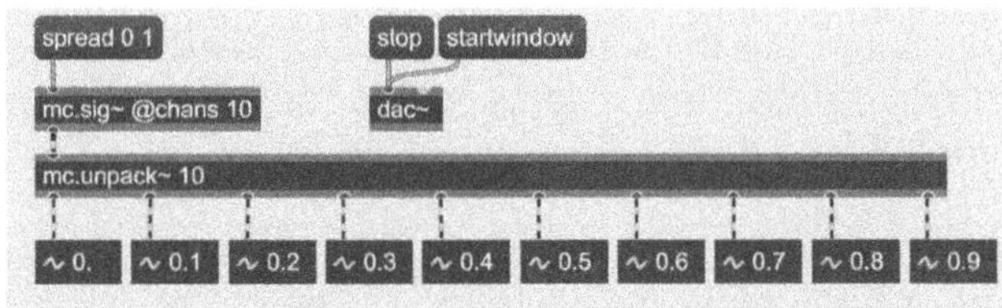

fig. IB.51: the "spread" message

This message is part of the same family of "generators" we have already discussed in paragraphs 2.1P and 2.2P.[17] In particular, "spread" generates a linear series of values between a minimum and a maximum that we specify as arguments.
In Figure IB.51 we can see a 10-channel **mc.sig~** object that receives the message "spread 0 1", and so it generates 10 signals whose values are comprised between 0 and 1. The following object [**mc.unpack~** 10] separates the multichannel signal into 10 individual signals. As you can see, the values produced are equidistant and go from 0 to 1, with the exclusion of the maximum value 1. The message "spread", in fact, does not include the maximum value among those generated: if the number of channels had been 4, for example, it would have generated the values 0, 0.25, 0.5 and 0.75.[18]
At this point, we have all of the tools necessary to realize Shepard tones; open the patch in the file **IB_07_shepard_tone.maxpat** (shown in figure IB.52).

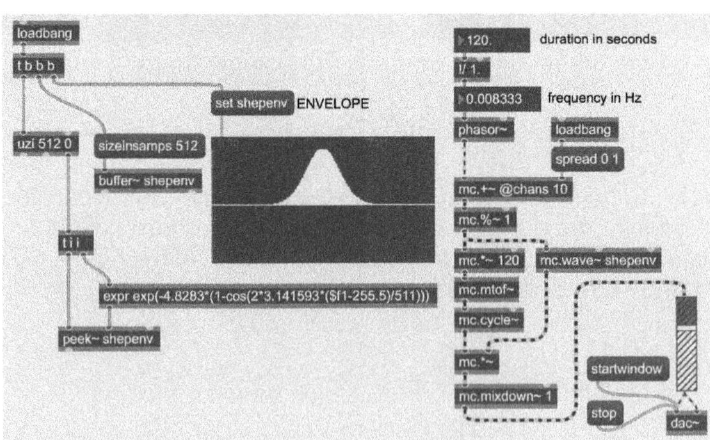

Fig. IB. 52 The file IB_07_shepard_tone.maxpat

[17] As you may remember, we talked about the "harmonic", "increment" and "deviate" messages.
[18] There are, however, other variations of "spread" for all combinations of inclusion and exclusion of the minimum and maximum value.

By clicking on *"startwindow"* and raising the **gain~** fader, you can hear a typical Shepard tone effect. This patch is based on an implementation by Risset described in Dodge-Jerse (1997), and generates an infinite glissando over 10 octaves, using 10 parallel oscillators, each of which is separated by an octave from its neighbors. The first thing to look at in this patch is the envelope, which is saved in a **buffer~** with the name "shepenv", and which is applied to each oscillator for the duration of the entire cycle of the glissando.

The formula that Risset provided to realize the 512 elements of the envelope's array is:

$y = \exp(-4.8283 \cdot (1-\cos(2\pi \cdot (x-255.5)/511)))$

We won't explain the formula in detail; it is enough to understand that for every value of *x* (which varies between 0 and 511) we can obtain the related value of *y* by calculating the right part of the equation after substituting the *x* value. For example, for *x* = 0, we obtain:

$\exp(-4.8283 \cdot (1-\cos(2\pi \cdot (\boldsymbol{0} -255.5)/511)))$

for *x* = 1:

$\exp(-4.8283 \cdot (1-\cos(2\pi \cdot (\boldsymbol{1} -255.5)/511)))$

for *x* = 2:

$\exp(-4.8283 \cdot (1-\cos(2\pi \cdot (\boldsymbol{2} -255.5)/511)))$

You get the idea. For our Max implementation, we use the same system that we did in the patch of figure IB.48, replacing the formula in the **expr** object that had calculated the sine half-cycle with Risset's formula. Examining the left side of the patch, notice the **loadbang** connected to a **trigger**, which takes care of associating the graphical **waveform~** object with the "shapeenv" array containing the envelope, then gives the array a size of 512 elements, and finally calculates the actual values to fill the array. Fortunately, the **expr** object has a syntax very similar to the one used by Risset, and so all we need to do is replace *x* with the symbol $f1. The symmetrical envelope that results, as you can see, has very low values in its first and last thirds, which are nearly zero; it rises to its maximum in the central part of the curve, dropping off in a matching fashion – such an envelope will fade oscillators in and out almost imperceptibly.
To the right, you can see a **phasor~** (the cycle of which is expressed in seconds, using the same approach that we used in figure IB.50) that controls the glissando envelope which will be applied to all of the oscillators, as we will see shortly. The duration of one cycle of this **phasor~** is quite long: 120 seconds, which translates to a frequency of 0.008333 Hz.

The output of the **phasor~** object is connected to a 10-channel **mc.+~** adder[19], whose second operand is the series of values produced by the message "spread 0 1". The message, as we know (see figure IB.51), produces the values 0, 0.1, 0.2 and so on, up to 0.9: this means that a constant value, different for each channel, is added to the ramps produced by **phasor~**. In this way the ramps of the first channel go from 0 to 1, those of the second from 0.1 to 1.1, those of the third from 0.2 to 1.2, etc. The ramps are then reset to the interval 0-1 by the modulo operator **mc.%~**. As a result, the ramps produced by each channel are phase shifted by 1/10 with respect to the previous channel. In fact, when the first ramp is at the beginning of the cycle, i.e. at 0, the second one is at 0.1, the third at 0.2 and so on. Every time a ramp reaches and exceeds the value 1 it is reset to 0 by the module operator, and this happens at a distance of one-tenth of a cycle between a signal and the following one.
The ramps are immediately routed to two different objects, a signal multiplier and a **mc.wave~** object. The **mc.wave~** object contains the envelope that we calculated from the Risset formula, and guided by the **phasor~,** it generates a 2 minute envelope (120 seconds) that rescales (that is, is multiplied by) the output of the **mc.cycle~** oscillator. Meanwhile, the signal multiplier [**mc.*~** 120] multiplies the ramp by 120, transforming it into a ramp that goes from 0 to 120, which becomes our glissando of 10 octaves expressed in semitones (because 120 semitones is 10 octaves of 12 notes – in MIDI, 0 to 120 corresponds to the C five octaves below middle C to the C five octaves above). The glissando is converted into frequencies by the **mc.mtof~** object (which produces a linear glissando from a pitch perception perspective, as we learned in Section 1.4), and then drives the oscillator. The glissando of 10 octaves and the envelope cycle are completed at the same time. Every 120 seconds the **phasor~** generates a new ramp, and therefore a new glissando and a new envelope. The glissando covers 120 semitones in 120 seconds, which is the same as 1 semitone a second, or one octave every 12 seconds (1/10th of an envelope cycle). Since, as we know, the ramps are out of phase by one tenth of a cycle, the glissandos are out of phase by 12 seconds. That means that each glissando is one octave away from the previous one (given that, as we have just said, the glissando covers an octave in 12 seconds).
When the glissando/envelope cycle lasts 120 seconds (or more), the infinite glissando is a pretty good illusion, but if you reduce the length of the cycle (by increasing the frequency of the **phasor~**) the "trick" becomes obvious: try this!
If you want a descending glissando (as in Risset's original demonstration) you will need to set a negative duration (-120, for example) which will become a negative frequency (-0.0083333 Hz) that will reverse the direction of the **phasor~** object, producing a descending ramp.[20]

---

[19] Note that when we send a single signal to a multichannel object, the signal is duplicated in all channels. That is because the "replicate" attribute of multichannel objects is active by default. This attribute is found in the inspector under the "Wrapper" category and, if the incoming channels are less than the channels of the receiving object, it replicates the signals as many times as necessary to compensate for the difference.
[20] There is also an **abl.dsp.shepard~** object that simulates a shepard tone different from the one illustrated here.

ACTIVITY – *ANALYSING ALGORITHMS*

Open the file **IB_analysis.maxpat** (shown in figure IB.53).

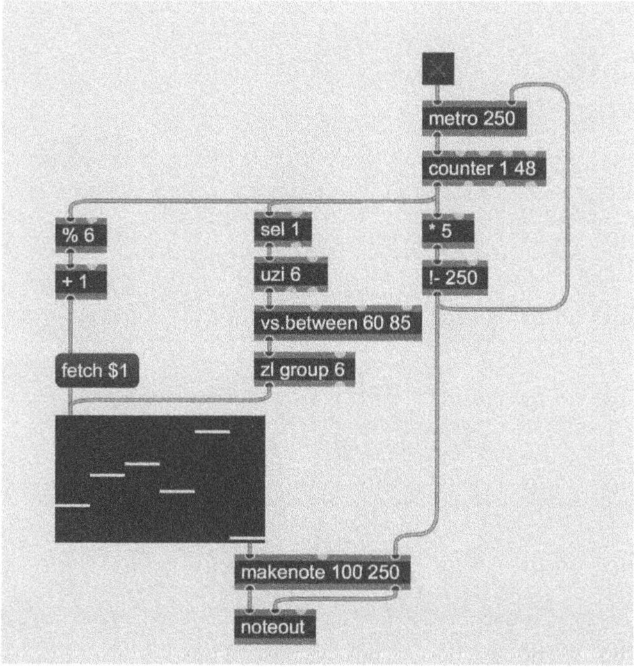

Fig. IB.53

Activate the `metro` object and listen carefully to the sound produced.

The pulse produced by the `metro` isn't regular: can you hear how it evolves? Can you see how it was implemented? Notice the connection that routes the output of the `!-` object to the right inlet of `metro`.

The contents of the `multislider` change regularly. According to what criteria? How was this implemented?

What is the purpose of the modulo (`%`) operator in the patch? Why is 1 added to the results of this operation?

To help you respond to these questions, we suggest that you connect number boxes and/or message boxes to various objects in order to display intermediate calculations and outputs.

ACTIVITY – *COMPLETING ALGORITHMS*

Open the patch in **IB_completion.maxpat** (shown in figure IB.54).

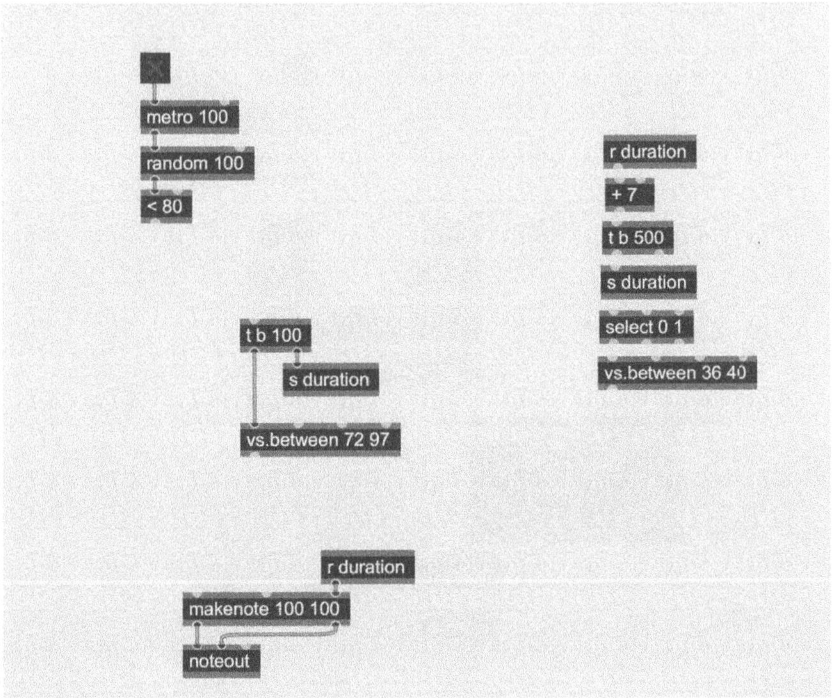

Fig. IB.54

The patch presented on the left side of the figure is incomplete: there are six object on the right side that need to be correctly inserted in order to make it work. The patch is a random note generator that should produce a 100 millisecond note 80% of the time, whose MIDI note number is between 72 and 96; the other 20% of the time, it should produce an interval of a fifth, whose duration is 500 milliseconds, and in which the fundamental lies between MIDI note 36 and note 39. The metronome pulse should equal the lengths of the notes (using a technique similar to that shown in the patch in figure IB.53, but executed in this case by using `send` and `receive` objects).

ACTIVITY – *REPLACING PARTS OF ALGORITHMS*

Open the patch in **IB_substitution.maxpat** (shown in figure IB.55).

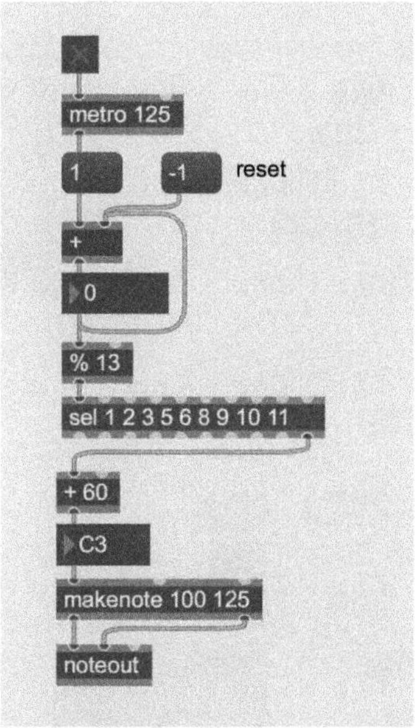

Fig. IB.55

This patch plays a C major arpeggio (C3, E3, G3, C4); do you understand how it works? Why is the rhythm of the arpeggio not uniform? Modify the patch in such a way that it plays a C minor arpeggio (C3, Eb3, G3, C4), a C major scale (C3, D3, E3, F3, G3, A3, B3, C4), and a C natural minor scale (C3, D3, Eb3, F3, G3, Ab3, Bb3, C4).

ACTIVITY – *CORRECTING ALGORITHMS*

Open the file **IB_correction.maxpat** (shown in figure IB.56).

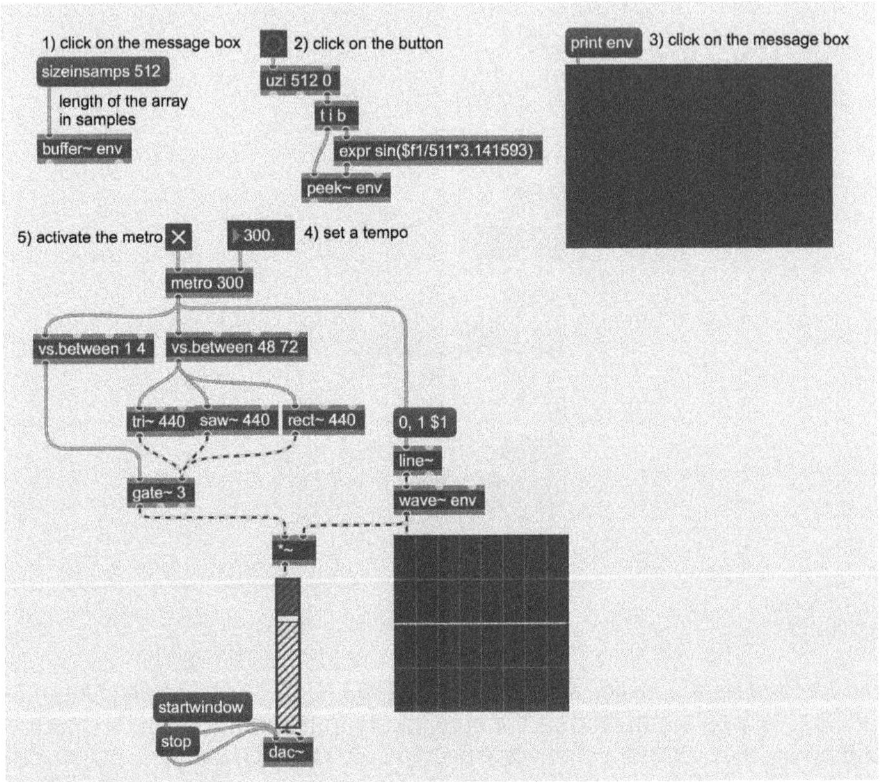

Fig. IB.56

This patch would, given debugging, generate sounds with frequencies from a tempered scale ranging from one octave below middle C to one octave above. The waveform would be band-limited and chosen at random from a selection of triangle, sawtooth, and square wave, the envelope would be found in the "env" buffer, and the duration of the envelope would be equal to the pulse duration of the **metro** object. The patch contains some errors that would need to be corrected before these statements would become true and the patch could function. There is a messaging bug, an object with an error in one of its arguments, a missing connection, a mistaken object, and an object to be added.

INTEGRATED CROSS-FUNCTIONAL PROJECT – *REVERSE ENGINEERING*

Listen to the audio file IB_reverse_engine.aif and try to reconstruct the patch that generated it. (It is based on one of the patches presented in this chapter.) The audio file is 40 seconds long and contains two complete cycles in the evolution of its sound.

LIST OF MAX OBJECTS

% (Max object)
%~ (MSP object)
The modulo operator, which returns the remainder from a division operation.

>
<
==
!=
>=
<=
(relational operators)
The relational operators compare two values in order to establish their relation to each other. More exactly, given two numbers x and y, we can find the following:

>	greater than
<	less than
==	equal to
!=	not equal to
>=	greater than or equal to
<=	less than or equal to

clip
Limits the numbers that it receives to falling within the range between its settable minimum and maximum value.

counter
Generates a series of consecutive numbers, one per input bang, starting from a minimum number (set using the first argument), rising to a maximum number (set with the second argument), and then cycling.

dspstate~
An object that furnishes realtime information about the DSP system running Max.

expr
An object that interprets text-based mathematical expressions, constructed from operators, functions, numbers, and variables. The argument of this object is the expression to be calculated.

gate
Routes its incoming messages to an outlet selected from several possible choices.

gate~
Routes its incoming signal to an outlet selected from several possible choices.

iter
Reduces a list to its component elements and sends them to its outlet in sequence.

makenote
Upon receiving a MIDI note number, sends a MIDI *note-on* command to its outlet, and generates a matching *note-off* command after a configurable amount of time has elapsed.

noteout
Sends MIDI *note-on* and *note-off* commands to connected MIDI instruments or virtual instruments.

peek~
Writes and reads single values to and from a **buffer~** object.

pow
Raises a number to some power. Used to square numbers in this chapter.

scale
Converts one numeric range into another, by relative position. The object has configurable input (1st and 2nd argument) and output ranges (3rd and 4th argument). These ranges are used to calculate a ratio that is used to convert incoming numbers (found in the input range) into outgoing numbers occupying the same relative position in the output range.

scale~
An MSP version of **scale**, which operates on signals.

select
Compares an input message with its arguments. If the input equals one of the arguments, it generates a bang on a corresponding outlet, otherwise it forwards the input message (not a bang!) to its last outlet.

switch
A Max object that permits incoming messages from one of its inlets to flow through, based on an inlet selector.

vs.pi
Emits the constant π when it is sent a bang.

MESSAGES, AND ATTRIBUTES FOR SPECIFIC MAX OBJECTS

buffer~

- Sizeinsamps (message)

Assigns a **buffer~** object a size in samples. For example, the message "*sizeinsamps 512*" will yield an array of 512 samples.

kslider

- Display mode (attribute)

This attribute can take on one of two values: Monophonic or Polyphonic.
In Monophonic mode, *note-on* messages a
re produced by clicking on **kslider** keys. In Polyphonic mode, the first click on a key generates a *note-on* command, and the next a *note-off* command, and multiple keys can be "pressed" at one time.

mc wrapper

- spread (message)

generates a series of equidistant values between a minimum and a maximum.

multislider

- Fetch (message)

Extracts the value of one element of a **multislider** object from the right outlet of the **multislider**. The elements are indexed starting with 1; the message "*fetch 1*" will recover the first value, "*fetch 2*" the second, and so on.

- Size (message)

Sets the number of elements in a **multislider**. For example, the message "*size 8*" will produce 8 sliders within the **multislider**.

GLOSSARY

Iterative structure
A cyclic sequence of operations that is repeated as part of an algorithm.

Looping structure
see *Iterative Structure*

Modulo operator
an operator that returns the remainder from a division operation.

Note-off
a MIDI command that ends the playing of a note.

Note-on
a MIDI command that begins the playing of a note.

Offset
A fixed value that is added to a changing series of numbers to displace their range.

Recursive operation
an operation in which the result is obtained by using previous results of the same operation.

Recursion
see *Recursive Operation.*

Velocity
indicates the intensity of the note indicated within a MIDI note-on command. The term originated as a reference to the speed with which a key was pressed on a physical MIDI keyboard.

4T
CONTROL SIGNALS

LEARNING AGENDA

PREREQUISITES FOR THE CHAPTER
- Contents of Chapters 1, 2, and 3 (Theory)

LEARNING OBJECTIVES
Knowledge
- To learn about the theory and practice of low frequency oscillators
- To learn about the use of DC Offset with LFOs
- To learn about the use of frequency modulation for vibrato
- To learn about the use of amplitude modulation for tremolo
- To learn about the use of pulse-width modulation
- To learn how to use LFOs to control filters
- To learn about the use of pseudo-random signal generators for control
- To learn how to use LFOs to control location in stereo and multichannel systems

Skills
- To be able to hear and describe LFO-controlled modulations of basic parameters

CONTENTS
- Low frequency oscillators: depth, rate, and delay
- Managing LFO parameters and using DC offset
- Managing vibrato, tremolo, and PWM using LFOs
- Managing filter parameters using LFOs
- Positioning and moving sound in stereo and multichannel systems
- Modulating control oscillators with pseudo-random LFOs

ACTIVITIES
- Video examples

TESTING
- Questions with short answers
- Listening and analysis

SUPPORTING MATERIALS
- Fundamental concepts
- Glossary

4.1 CONTROL SIGNALS: STEREO PANNING

As we have seen throughout this book, envelope generators can be used to vary the parameters of a sound, such as frequency or amplitude, in time. Signals that come from envelope generators – signals that are expressly produced to vary parameter values rather than to produce sound – are called **control signals**.

To this point, we have used line segments and exponential curves to describe control signals. These techniques are efficient because they require only a few values to describe parameter changes; think of the four segments that we use for ADSR envelopes, or of the numbers that define an exponential curve, which can completely describe a glissando. Other control signals, however, may need to vary in more complex ways. Take the vibrato associated with a string instrument as an example: there is a continuous change in the frequency of a note played with vibrato that can best be described as an oscillation around a central pitch. To simulate such a vibration using an envelope, we might need to use tens, or even hundreds, of line segments, which would be both tedious and impractical. Instead of resorting to such primitive methods, we might instead choose to use a **control oscillator**, an oscillator whose output is produced for the sole purpose of providing parameter values to *audio oscillators* or other parameterized devices used in sound synthesis and signal processing.

Control oscillators are usually **Low Frequency Oscillators (LFOs)**; their frequency is usually below 30 Hz. They produce continuously changing control values that trace waveforms in the same way that audio oscillators do. Every instantaneous amplitude of a wave generated by a control oscillator corresponds to a numeric value that can be applied to audio parameters as needed.

Here is an example demonstrating the use of an LFO: in Figure 4.1, you see a graphic representation of an LFO controlling the position of a sound in space. This LFO generates a sine wave that oscillates between MIN (representing its minimum value) and MAX (its maximum value).

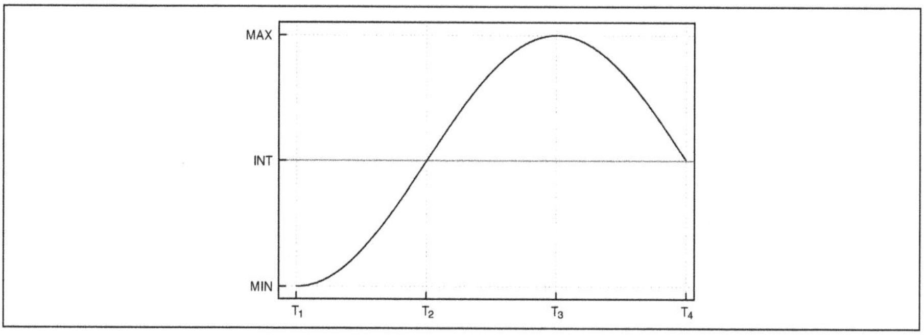

Fig. 4.1 An LFO for controlling the position of a sound in space

The minimum and maximum values, or the **depth** of the oscillator, define the limits of the amplitude values being produced, while the **rate** of the oscillator is a value that defines its frequency.

In the example, the instantaneous amplitude values of the sine wave generated by the LFO is used as input to two multipliers that inversely scale the amplitude of an audio oscillator on two output channels. Whenever the control signal reaches MIN (its minimum value), the sound is panned completely left, and whenever it reaches MAX (its maximum value), the sound is panned completely right. While intermediate values are being produced (represented in the figure by the central value INT), the sound is smoothly mixed between the two channels.

It should be obvious that it would be possible to use other waveforms (triangle, random, etc.) to control parameter values in the same way; a square wave, for example, could control the location of a sound bouncing between left and right channels without intermediate positions. In this case, there would be no continuous change, as there is when using a sine wave; the values would simply alternate between MIN and MAX.

VIDEO EXAMPLE 4A • *Panning using different LFO waveforms*

The rate with which values change depends on the frequency assigned to a given control oscillator. If you use a frequency of 1 Hz, you will move from MAX to MIN and back again in one second; if you use a frequency of .2 Hz, you will have 1 complete oscillation in 5 seconds. What if you use a frequency of 220? In this case, the 220 oscillations per second would be too fast to allow us to hear the location moving between left and right; this frequency would instead enter the audio range and would generate new components in the spectrum of the resulting sound. We will cover this phenomenon, *amplitude modulation*, in Chapter 10.

VIDEO EXAMPLE 4B • *Panning using a sine wave LFO at various frequencies*

By using control oscillators, we can control the depth and the rate of a vibrato, of a tremolo, or of variations in filter parameters, all of which we will cover in the following sections.

4.2 DC OFFSET

To sum up the first section: you can use a control oscillator, an LFO, to produce values that alternate between a minimum and a maximum at some given rate, and these values can be supplied to multipliers in order to modify the

amplitudes of the output levels of two channels. Using this technique, you can create a continuous movement of sound between one side of a stereo image and the other.
But before diving into the details of LFO usage, we need to clarify which kinds of signals are appropriate for use as control oscillators. For example, if you need the amplitude values for an LFO to fall between 0.5 and -0.5, you need to create a sine wave that has an amplitude of 0.5. This is no problem. However, if you need the values need to fall into the range of 0 to 1, as we did for the stereo example, you need to shift all of the sine wave values into positive territory in such a way that the central value of the oscillation becomes 0.5. In this situation, you need to add a fixed quantity called a **DC Offset** to all of the sample values of the sine wave. (The term was originally used with analog synthesizers – DC refers to "direct current".)

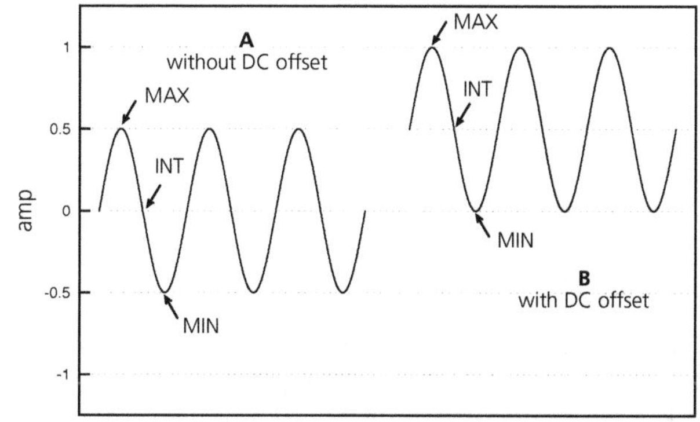

Fig. 4.2 Using a DC offset

Let's refer to the sine wave with an amplitude of 0.5, oscillating between 0.5 and -0.5, as A. We are trying to create a sine wave that will oscillate between 1 and 0, never dropping into negative values; we will refer to this wave as B. By adding a fixed quantity of 0.5 to all of the amplitude values in A, the value of MAX becomes 1 (0.5 + 0.5 = 1), MIN becomes 0 (-0.5 + 0.5 = 0), and the central value INT – the value around which the sine wave oscillates – moves from 0 in A to 0.5 in B. All other instantaneous amplitude values of B also have their value increased by 0.5, and therefore the entire sine wave takes on positive values, due to the DC offset.
Figure 4.2 shows the sine wave A without DC Offset on the left, symmetrically oscillating around the horizontal axis, while on the right you can see the sine wave B after the addition of DC offset. Every point described by the second wave has had the value 0.5 added to it, which has the consequence of moving the entire waveform "up" to sit on and above the horizontal axis.

An alternate way to think about DC offset is to view it as a fixed signal. As a fixed signal, it doesn't oscillate, and because of this, its frequency is 0 Hz. This is less abstract than you might think! In Chapter 5 we will see how it is possible to eliminate DC offset through the use of a highpass filter. We will also use DC offset in the third volume, in the section dedicated to amplitude modulation.

4.3 CONTROL SIGNALS FOR FREQUENCY

VIBRATO

Imagine a violinist playing an A440 (the note A above middle C) while holding the finger of her left hand perfectly still on the third string and moving only her right hand, which holds the bow. The resulting sound would have a stable frequency of 440 Hz. If the violinist begins to make small oscillations by moving her left hand, which causes her fingertip to move up and down the string above and below its original position, she achieves an effect called **vibrato**, which is defined as a small oscillatory variation around a central pitch. Vibrato is a common musical technique, and is often used when playing acoustic instruments or singing.

DEPTH OF VIBRATO

The more the fingertip of our violinist moves away from the central position of 440 Hz, the wider the movement, and the wider the deviation in the frequency of the note. This vibrato "amplitude" (that is, the extent of frequency variation) is referred to as the *depth* of the vibrato.

RATE OF VIBRATO

How many oscillations does the fingertip of our violinist complete per second? It might be 4, 5, or even more (Vibrato typically varies slightly more or less around 5 Hz.) This number, the frequency with which the pitch rises, returns, falls, and returns again to the center, is referred to as the *rate* of the vibrato.

We can simulate the playing of our violinist by using an audio oscillator to simulate the effect of the bow on the string, and by using a control oscillator to simulate the movement of the fingertip on the string.

VIDEO EXAMPLE 4C • *Variations in vibrato depth*

In the video example, the "virtual violinist" is playing an A440 note, and at the same time deviating from the pitch with vibrato caused by fingertip oscillations. The bigger the amplitude of this secondary oscillation, the bigger the deviation from the base frequency of 440 Hz, and the wider the vibrato.

To have a sound that vibrates between 436 and 444 Hz, the amplitude of the control oscillator (the ***modulator***), needs to be 4, which results in an oscillation between 4 and -4, which when added the audio oscillator's center frequency (the *carrier*) and results in the vibrato that we seek. How fast is such vibrato? The number of cycles per second completed by the fingertip in Video Example

4C was 5 cycles per second, which means that the virtual violinist was playing in a way that moved the pitch from 440 to 444, back to 440, to 436, and finally back to 440 Hz again, five times a second.

In the following example, we hear vibratos played at various rates.

VIDEO EXAMPLE 4D • *Variations in vibrato rate*

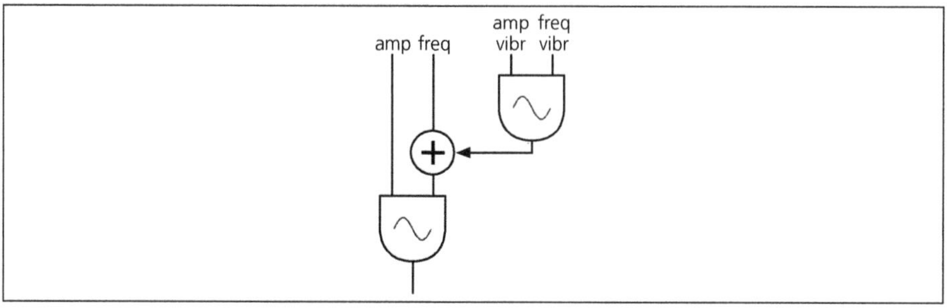

Fig. 4.3 Frequency modulation

In Figure 4.3, you see the "carrier", which is the audio oscillator producing sound, in the lower left. The value of "amp" determines the absolute amplitude of the output signal, and the "freq" value determines the frequency of the output signal before this central frequency value is continuously modified by the modulating oscillator. The values being produced by the modulating oscillator to control the carrier's frequency continuously change, but by how much? How wide is the oscillation of the modulating LFO that determines the vibrato? Its amplitude value, or *depth*, is given by the "amp vibr" setting in the figure, and the number of oscillations in the vibrato per second, the *rate*, is given by the "freq vibr" setting. Some video examples may help to make this clear:

VIDEO EXAMPLE 4E • *A vibrato, applied to multiple carrier frequencies*

In the video example, you can hear that the amplitude given to the modulating oscillator doesn't have the same effect on all carrier frequencies. For example, the note whose frequency is 880 Hz sounds very different with a 2 Hz vibrato applied to it than the note whose frequency is 220 Hz. In the first case, there is a pitch deviation of around 0.23%, while in the second case, the percentage value of the deviation is 0.9%. This means that you can hear a wider vibrato in the second example than in the first.

To make these vibratos sound similar, you would need to make the *percentage* of deviation from the carrier frequency constant, rather than using a fixed amplitude value. Let's try this, using the following simple algorithm (which is more consistent with our auditory expectations): in place of a frequency, add 1 to the values produced by the modulating oscillator and multiply the result by the base frequency of the carrier.
Adding 1 to the values produced by a modulating oscillator with an amplitude of 0.009 would result in values that oscillate between 1.009 and 0.991. Multiplying these values by the frequency of the carrier, say 100 Hz, we obtain a modulating frequency that oscillates between 100.9 and 99.1 Hz, which is a pitch deviation of 0.9% with respect to the carrier's base frequency. If, on the other hand, we imagine a carrier of 1,000 Hz, multiplying by the same modulating values results in frequency modulation that oscillates between 1,009 Hz and 991 Hz, which is also a pitch deviation of 0.9% of the base frequency. This algorithm will achieve a uniform vibrato, since the pitch deviation remains stable at 0.9%, independent of the frequency of the carrier.

VIDEO EXAMPLE 4F • *A vibrato with relative deviation, applied to multiple carrier frequencies*

4.4 CONTROL SIGNALS FOR AMPLITUDE

By changing the amplitude of a carrier signal rather than its frequency, we can achieve a different effect, which is called **tremolo**. In the case of tremolo, values output by the modulating oscillator are multiplied with the amplitude of the carrier, rather than the frequency. For example, a modulator oscillating between 0.6 and 1.0, when applied to a carrier with an amplitude of 0.5, will produce an output signal whose amplitude oscillates between 0.3 (0.5 · 0.6) and 0.5 (0.5 · 1.0). The small cyclic variation that you hear in the amplitude of the output is the tremolo. When the rate of the modulating signal (its frequency) is two cycles per second, the period of the audible tremolo will be 1/2 second. To actually generate modulating values that vary between 0.6 and 1.0, of course, you need to add DC offset, as shown in Figure 4.4.

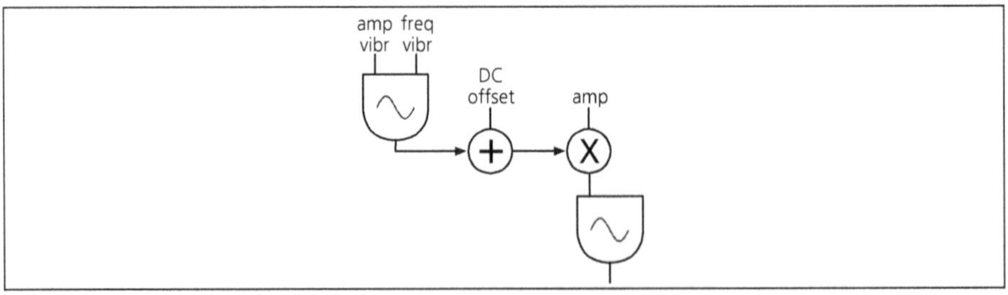

Fig. 4.4 Amplitude modulation

VIDEO EXAMPLE 4G • *Tremolo*

Besides depth and rate, you may also encounter a parameter for use with control oscillators named *delay*. Unrelated to the delayed repetition of a sound (which we will discuss in Chapter 6), **LFO delay** refers only to a delay in the activation of the control oscillator: the time that it takes for the LFO to be fully working. If an LFO delay were to be 3 seconds, you would hear the tremolo fully in place after 3 seconds, and the sound would start with no tremolo. (In practice, this is implemented by using an amplitude envelope on the LFO in question that starts with an amplitude value of 0.)

VIDEO EXAMPLE 4H • *Variations in depth, rate, and delay for a tremolo*

Vibrato is implemented as frequency modulation in our examples, while tremolo is implemented as amplitude modulation. These modulation techniques can be used for other purposes: we will see how to use them for modifying the spectral contents of a sound in volume three.

4.5 VARYING THE DUTY CYCLE (PULSE-WIDTH MODULATION)

We saw in Section 1.2 that the timbre of a square wave can be modified by varying the ratio between the time within each cycle of the waveform that is positive and the time that is negative. You'll remember that the parameter that controls this ratio is called the *duty cycle*, and is normally expressed as a numeric value between 0 and 1. When the duty cycle is 0.5, which means that half the cycle is positive and half the cycle is negative, you have a square wave. When it is 0.25, 1/4 of the cycle has positive amplitude values versus the 3/4 that has negative values, etc. It is possible to control this duty cycle using an LFO, which creates continuous variations in timbre. (The resulting sound is similar to the *chorus* effect, which we discuss in Chapter 6.)
One way to actually apply an LFO to the duty cycle would be to start with a DC offset of 0.5, which would adjust the central axis for the square wave control oscillator, shifting its amplitude values into the positive realm, and then to add a bipolar LFO, whose amplitudes vary between 0 and 0.5, to the shifted square wave. Set to a maximum amplitude of 0.5, the LFO would produce values between -0.5 and 0.5, which, after adding the fixed DC offset of 0.5, would result in oscillation values appropriate for duty cycle modulation, with values ranging from 0 to 1. At an amplitude less than 0.5, the LFO would produce proportionately smaller oscillations, with a central value of 0.5.

A slightly more complex implementation might use a configurable DC offset between 0 and 1, to which would be added a bipolar LFO whose amplitude, when summed with the DC offset, would never exceed the limits of 0 and 1 (the minimum and maximum values that can be meaningfully assigned to the duty cycle parameter).
The duty cycle is also sometimes referred to as the *pulse width* of the wave, and changing this parameter by using an oscillator is called **pulse-width modulation**.

VIDEO EXAMPLE 4I • *preset 1 • Pulse-Width Modulation*

4.6 CONTROL SIGNALS FOR FILTERS

Control signals can be used to control timbral processing of sounds by filters. One example would be oscillating bandpass filtration, which produces the familiar *wah-wah* effect: the modulating oscillator acts as a control signal for filter parameters. In the *wah-wah* case, a single modulating oscillator dictates both the depth and the rate of variations around the center frequency of a bandpass filter.

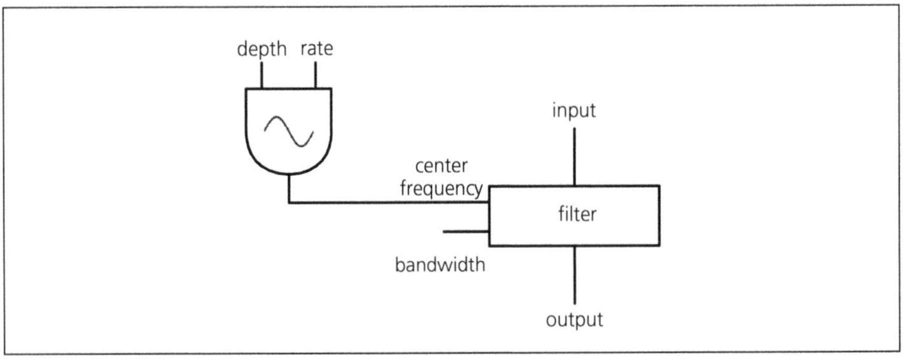

Fig. 4.5 Controlling a filter's center frequency with an oscillator

Let's listen to an example:

VIDEO EXAMPLE 4I • *preset 2 • Oscillations in a filter's center frequency*

In the second preset of Video Example 4I, we hear white noise being filtered by a bandpass filter whose center frequency is moving between 100 and 2,100

Hz. The movement is guided by an LFO whose signal, varies between the values 100 and 2,100. This LFO is controlling the center frequency parameter of the bandpass filter; since it is guiding the center frequency of a bandpass filter, we will refer to its output values in hertz.

To produce control values that range between 100 and 2,100 Hz:

> Determine the amplitude for the oscillator by subtracting minimum from maximum, and then dividing the result by two, which in this case would be (2,100 - 100)/2 = 1,000
> Assign an amplitude of 1,000 to the oscillator, which will then move between -1,000 and 1,000
> Add a DC offset of 1,100 to the output, which shifts the oscillation to the desired range of 100 to 2,100 Hz

In general, to calculate the amplitude needed for a bipolar modulation oscillator, subtract the minimum value desired from the maximum value desired, and divide by two. For the example just shown, this results in (2,100 - 100) / 2, which is 1,000. To then find the right DC offset, subtract that amplitude from the maximum value desired. Using the example again, 2,100 - 1,000 = 1,100, which is the DC offset needed.

Amplitude = (Maximum - Minimum) / 2
DC Offset = Maximum - Amplitude

In the third preset of Video Example 4I, the control oscillator's amplitude values vary between -200 and 200. Adding a constant quantity of 210 to this bipolar signal, we obtain a unipolar control signal that varies between 10 and 410. This signal is used to control the bandwidth of a bandpass filter.

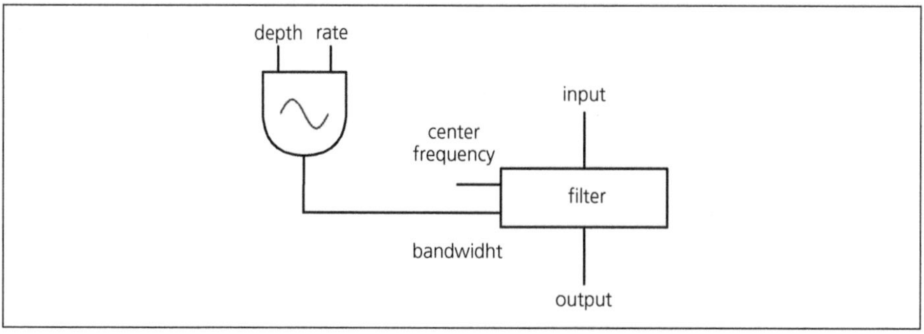

Fig. 4.6 Controlling a filter's bandwidth with an oscillator

VIDEO EXAMPLE 4I • *preset 3 • Oscillating filter bandwidth*

TESTING • *QUESTIONS WITH SHORT ANSWERS*

1) What do control signals do?

2) By modifying what parameter can you realize an increase in *depth*?

3) By modifying what parameter can you realize an increase in *rate*?

4) By modifying what parameter can you realize an increase in the *delay* of a modulation?

5) To create an LFO that emits amplitude values between 3.5 and 2,003.5, what amplitude and DC offset settings would you need to apply to the control oscillator?

6) What is DC offset used for, in general, when controlling stereo spatialization?

7) If you wish to reduce the speed of a vibrato when using an audio oscillator controlled by an LFO, which parameter of which oscillator do you need to act upon?

8) If you wish to increase the amplitude of a tremolo when using an audio oscillator controlled by an LFO, which parameter of which oscillator do you need to act upon?

9) If you want to reduce the Q of a bandpass filter that is being controlled by an LFO, which parameter of the oscillator do you need to act upon and how would you achieve the reduction?

10) What operations would you use, given certain desired amplitude values, to determine the base amplitude for an LFO, to which DC offset would then be added?

11) What operations would you use, given a base amplitude setting and certain desired amplitude values, to determine the correct DC offset for an LFO?

12) Given an LFO controlling an audio oscillator, which parameter of which oscillator would you act upon in order to raise and lower the rate of the oscillation in a periodic way?

4.7 OTHER GENERATORS OF CONTROL SIGNALS

Up until now, we have primarily used sine waves as control signals, but it is certainly possible to use other wave forms, including square waves, sawtooth waves, or any other periodic shape. They can be applied effectively as control signals for the parameters of oscillators or filters, and can produce musical effects that are distinct from the vibrato and tremolo that we've already heard.

Aleatoric signals, based on pseudo-random oscillators, can also be used like LFOs. In fact, aleatoric control signals often help to avoid the sense of artificiality that characterizes much music produced by synthetic means. We covered pseudo-random generators, which generate unpredictable sequences of numbers between some minimum and some maximum value, in Section 3.1. When using aleatoric control signals to dictate parameters values in a pseudo-random way, low frequencies (below 30 Hz) are the norm.[1] Recall that pseudo-random generators can take three forms: simple, interpolated, or lowpass filtered. Using the first of these, a simple generator without interpolation, you can implement what is called **sample and hold** control. The name comes from the early days of analog synthesis, when an analog electrical signal was "sampled" at regular intervals and "held" at a constant level until the next sample was taken.[2] The result was the transformation of the original signal into a step function. In particular, the technique that eventually became synonymous with the term "sample and hold" consisted of sampling a noise source at regular intervals and to using the resulting series of steps to control the center (or cutoff) frequency of a filter. A filtered signal produced in this way changes timbre with a regular rhythm corresponding to the rate at which the random steps change. The term *sample-and-hold* today remains current, and indicates the use of a pseudo-random, non-interpolated, noise generator as a control signal.

VIDEO EXAMPLE 4J • Pseudo-random control signals

CONTROLLING A SUBTRACTIVE SYNTHESIZER WITH AN LFO

In order to create Video Example 4K, we augmented the capabilities of the subtractive synthesizer that was previously analyzed in Section 3.5. Specifically, we added an LFO that can modulate the frequencies and the amplitudes of the oscillators (to generate vibrato and tremolo), their duty cycles (for pulse-width modulation), as well as the cutoff frequency and/or the Q of the lowpass filter.

VIDEO EXAMPLE 4K • *A synthesizer with LFO control*

[1] You will recall that higher frequencies are used with pseudo-random oscillators in subtractive synthesis, where they are used to produce audible sound.

[2] We are speaking of analog sampling here, not digital.

You can select the waveform to be used for this LFO, choosing from sine, sawtooth, square, or pseudo-random; its rate, which can be set from 0.01 to 32 Hz; and its delay time in seconds. The four synthesis parameters that the LFO can control, which are frequency, amplitude, cutoff frequency, and Q, each has an "LFO depth" control that can vary between 0 and 100, which establish the depth of the modulation to be applied to these parameters by the control signal. Let's examine exactly how this works for each type of modulation:

> Oscillator frequency: In this case, the LFO causes the **pitch** to oscillate around the sounding note. The variance of the note is calculated in semitones rather than in hertz in a way that maintains a proportional vibrato at all frequencies. With an "LFO depth" of 100, the pitch will vary by four octaves above and four octaves below the given frequency; a depth of 50 creates an oscillation of two octaves above and below; a depth of 25 causes an oscillation of one octave above and below; and a depth of around 2 causes one semitone of variance above and below. (Also note that it is possible, and in fact common, to use depth values between 0 and 1.)

> Amplitude: The depth value indicates the percentage of amplitude to be modulated. If, for example, the amplitude of an oscillator at a given time is 1 (the maximum), and the depth setting has a value of 100 (the maximum possible percentage), the modulated amplitude will oscillate between 0 and 1. A depth of 50 will result in oscillations between 0.5 and 1.0, a depth of 25 between 0.75 and 1.0, and so forth.

> Pulse-width Modulation: This effect works only with the pulse width of the square wave, of course. The value of the depth setting indicates the amplitude of the LFO that is summed with the fixed *pulse-width* parameter (see Section 4.5 for details on this). When depth equals 100, the amplitude of the LFO is 0.5; when it is 50, the amplitude of the LFO is 0.25, etc. To avoid exceeding the limits of 0 and 1, the summed parameter values are clipped to remain between 0 and 1.

> Filter cutoff frequency: Here, the depth setting indicates the width of a frequency band. This band is a percentage of the frequency calculated from the *key follow* and *env depth* parameters described in Section 3.5. If, for example, the cutoff frequency is 500 Hz and the depth is 100%, the cutoff frequency will oscillate between 1,000 Hz (500 + 500) and 0 Hz (500 - 500). If the depth is 50%, the frequency will oscillate between 750 Hz (500 + 250) and 250 Hz (500 - 250). If the depth is 10%, the frequency will oscillate between 550 Hz (500 + 50) and 450 Hz (500 - 50), and so on. The fixed value for the *cutoff* parameter is added to the resulting signal before the filter is applied.

> Q factor: In this case, the depth setting simply represents the quantity to add to the Q setting. If, for example, the Q is set to 10 and the depth is set to 5, the resulting oscillation in Q will range from 10 to 15.

As you can see, the control signal acts on each parameter in a different way, so to create the most effective variations of the parameter in question. Pay attention to the presets in Video Example 4K, where you will be able to listen to some of the many ways that an LFO can control synthesis parameters.

4.8 CONTROL SIGNALS: MULTICHANNEL PANNING

Until now, we have located sounds within a sonic field produced using only one or two channels (see sections 1.5 and 4.1), but it is possible to position sounds across a field formed by an arbitrary number of channels. In such a case, you might want to use an LFO as a control signal to enable rotations or other movements around these channels. We will refer to such a setup as **multichannel panning**. (We use this term rather than spatialization; true spatialization will be covered in volume three, along with reverb.)

When panning within a stereo field, you need to implement a crossfade between the left and the right channels in order to pass a sound from the left to the right. In the case of multichannel panning, such a crossfade can proceed from one channel to the next, producing a rotation around the field when the speakers form a circle. (The crossfade graph for moving a sound around a system with 8 channels would look like this: ch1→2, 2→3, 3→4, 4→5, 5→6, 6→7, 7→8, 8→1.) It is just as valid, however, to crossfade between a channel and any other channel; the type of movement desired determines the panning rule.

Let's consider how you might use LFOs in a quadraphonic system, for example, to cause other kinds of movement, such as alternation between non-adjacent channels. (This could be represented by a pattern such as ch. 1→3→1→3, etc.) This kind of pattern could be implemented by using a square wave LFO (slightly smoothed to avoid unwanted clicks) to control channel assignment.

A single LFO could, of course, control two different parameters, as we saw with the synthesizer implementation in Section 4.7. Our square wave LFO, besides moving sounds between channels 1 and 3, might control other parameters in sync with this panning operation; for example, when the sound is on channel 1, it might be filtered with a center frequency of 300 Hz, and when it is on channel 3, it might be filtered with a center frequency of 2,000 Hz. In the video example, we simulate on two channels what channels 1 and 3 would sound like in this hypothetical example.

VIDEO EXAMPLE 4L • Control of multiple parameters with a single LFO

But there is a problem with implementing this scenario: how can a single oscillator generate multiple parameter values at once? For our example, we would need values switching between 300 and 2,000 to control the filter, and at the same time, numbers switching between 0 and 1 for use as amplitude multipliers. There are different ways to solve this problem, as you will find out in the practical section of this chapter; the most common solution is to split the output signal from the LFO before changing its amplitude and its DC offset. One LFO is used to produce two synchronized output signals.

Consider a different routing scenario: one LFO controlling another LFO.Extending the example given previously, we might want to transform the 1→3→1→3 channel oscillation gradually into a 2→4→2→4 oscillation; the signal being filtered with a center frequency of 300 Hz that appears and disappears on channel 1 would gradually start to appear and disappear on channel 2, and at the same time, the filtered signal with a center frequency of 2,000 Hz that appears and disappears on channel 3 would gradually start to appear and disappear on channel 4.

VIDEO EXAMPLE 4M • *An LFO controlling another LFO*

To implement this algorithm we used a triangle wave to control variations in DC offset for the square wave oscillator that is controlling panning. The triangle wave oscillator oscillates between 0 and some value *x*. When the value of the amplitude of the triangle wave oscillator is 0, the DC offset of the square wave is in its first position, cycling sound between channels 1 and 3. When the amplitude of the triangle wave oscillator is *x*, the DC offset of the square wave changes, and the sound cycles between channels 2 and 4. In all of the intermediate stages between 0 and *x*, there is a proportionate crossfade between one type of oscillation and the other.

You can also implement other symmetric patterns, such as the one shown in this example:

300 Hz ch1	/	2,000 Hz ch3
300 Hz ch3	/	2,000 Hz ch2
300 Hz ch2	/	2,000 Hz ch4
300 Hz ch4	/	2,000 Hz ch1
300 Hz ch1	/	2,000 Hz ch3

This pattern repeats, and it too can be produced by using a secondary LFO to control the DC offset of a square wave LFO, as you will see in Section 4.8 of the practical chapter. The secondary LFO in this example uses a sawtooth waveform, rather than the triangular waveform of the previous example.

FUNDAMENTAL CONCEPTS

abc

1) Control oscillators are low-frequency oscillators (LFOs) that generally operate at frequencies below 30 Hz. Their purpose is not to produce sound, but instead, to produce values that follow the shape of some waveform, and that are intended for the continuous control of parameters. Every instantaneous amplitude value of a wave generated by a control oscillator is meant to be used directly as the value of one or more audio parameters.

2) Numeric control values can be used as parameters for audio oscillators, for filters, for spatialization, or for any other parameter-driven item.

3) The rate with which a stream of control values oscillates depends upon the frequency assigned to its control oscillator

4) If a stream of values produced by the control oscillator needs to oscillate around a value other than zero, it is necessary to add a fixed quantity, a DC offset, to every value being output by the control oscillator.

5) When synthesizing sound, vibrato is implemented by using frequency modulation. The amplitude of the frequency deviations in a vibrato depend on the amplitude of the control oscillator, and the speed of the vibrato depends on the frequency of the control oscillator.

6) When synthesizing sound, tremolo is implemented by using amplitude modulation. The deviations of amplitude in a tremolo depend on the amplitude of the control oscillator, and the speed of the tremolo depends on the frequency of the control oscillator.

7) The parameters of a filter, its center (or cutoff) frequency and its Q, can be controlled using an LFO. In this case, as in the case of vibrato and tremolo, the deviation of the parameters depend on the amplitude of the control oscillator, and the speed depends upon the frequency of the control oscillator.

8) To implement an LFO that oscillates between two arbitrary values, you can calculate the necessary amplitude for the underlying bipolar modulating oscillator by subtracting the minimum value from the maximum value and dividing by two. To then find the right DC offset, subtract that amplitude from the maximum value desired.

9) There are various type of pseudo-random generators, including simple pseudo-random number generators, interpolated pseudo-random number generators, and lowpass filtered pseudo-random number generators. It is possible to use them as low-frequency control oscillators.

10 It is possible to use LFOs to control other LFOs. This combination might be used to control the movement of sound between various loudspeakers in a multichannel system, for example, resulting in a variable-speed circular motion of a sound in space.

TESTING • *LISTENING AND ANALYSIS*

Which parameter is the control oscillator acting on in Sound AA4.1?

Which parameter is the control oscillator acting on in Sound AA4.2?

Which parameter is the control oscillator acting on in Sound AA4.3?

Which parameter is the control oscillator acting on in Sound AA4.4?

What waveform does the LFO have in sound AA4.5?

What waveform does the LFO have in sound AA4.6?

What waveform does the LFO that modulates the first LFO have in sound AA4.7? And what parameter does it control?

What waveform does the LFO that modulates the first LFO have in sound AA4.8? And what parameter does it control?

GLOSSARY

Aleatoric
Dependent on chance.

Carrier signal
A signal that is modulated by a control signal.

Control oscillator
a low-frequency oscillator that isn't used to produce sound, but rather, that produces continuously changing values that follow the path of a certain waveform.

Control signal
A signal that doesn't generate sound, but rather guides changes in the parameter values of another signal.

Dc offset (for LFOs)
A fixed value that is added to every sample in the output signal of a control oscillator.

Depth
An amplitude value for an LFO that controls the size of the deviation of a control parameter.

Lfo
(Low frequency oscillator)
An oscillator whose frequency is usually below 30 Hz, generally used to modulate parameter values as part of an algorithm.

Lfo delay
a delay in the start of an LFO, such that LFO processing has fully begun after this period has elapsed. Not to be confused with the delay effects used in signal processing and filter theory.

Modulation
the process of controlling parameters in an oscillator or a filter with a control signal.

Modulator
see *Control Signal*

Multichannel panning
the location and movement of sound in a space created by more than two channels.

Pulse-width modulation
variation in the width of the positive/negative parts of a rectangular waveform (duty cycle) caused by a control oscillator.

Rate (of an LFO)
The frequency value of an LFO which controls the speed at which the value of a controlled parameter oscillates.

Sample and hold
transformation of a signal into a stepped control signal by holding its values at a constant level for a specified period of time.

Spatialization
a term used to indicate the spatial movement of a signal and the technique for controlling it.

Tremolo
a small oscillation in the amplitude of a sound.

Vibrato
A small oscillation in the frequency of a sound

4P
CONTROL SIGNALS

LEARNING AGENDA

PREREQUISITES FOR THE CHAPTER
- Contents of Chapters 1, 2, and 3 (Theory and Practice), Chapter 4 (Theory), Interludes A & B

LEARNING OBJECTIVES
Skills
- To learn how to move a sound within a stereo field
- To learn how to implement vibrato
- To learn how to simulate instruments whose frequency is controlled, such as a theremin
- To learn how to implement tremolo
- To learn how to build pulse width modulation algorithms
- To learn how to vary cutoff frequency, center frequency, and Q of filters using oscillating control signals
- To learn how to use pseudo-random signal generators for control
- To learn how to locate and move sounds in a system of 4 or more channels using control signals

Competence
- To be able to create a short sound study based on the technique of controlling parameters using LFOs

CONTENTS
- Low frequency oscillators: depth, rate, and delay
- Managing LFO parameters and using DC offset
- Managing vibrato, tremolo, and pulse width modulation using LFOs
- Managing filter parameters using LFOs
- Positioning and moving sound in stereo and multichannel systems
- Modulating control oscillators with pseudo-random LFOs

ACTIVITIES
- Replacing parts of algorithms
- Correcting algorithms
- Analyzing algorithms
- Completing algorithms
- Constructing new algorithms

TESTING
- Integrated cross-functional project: reverse engineering
- Integrated cross-functional project: composing a brief sound study

SUPPORTING MATERIALS
- List of Max objects
- Attributes for specific Max objects
- Glossary

4.1 CONTROL SIGNALS: STEREO PANNING

You can use the output of a normal **cycle~** object as a sine wave control signal for positioning a signal within a stereo field, as described in Section 4.1T. The frequency of the **cycle~** object, in this case, should be low enough to be below the threshold of human hearing. You learned how to parameterize stereo position in Section 1.6,[1] and you can begin your work here by extracting the algorithm for positioning a sound in a stereo field from the file 01_18_pan_function.maxpat. (You'll wind up with the parts of the original patch that were connected to the **line~** object, as shown in Figure 4.1.)

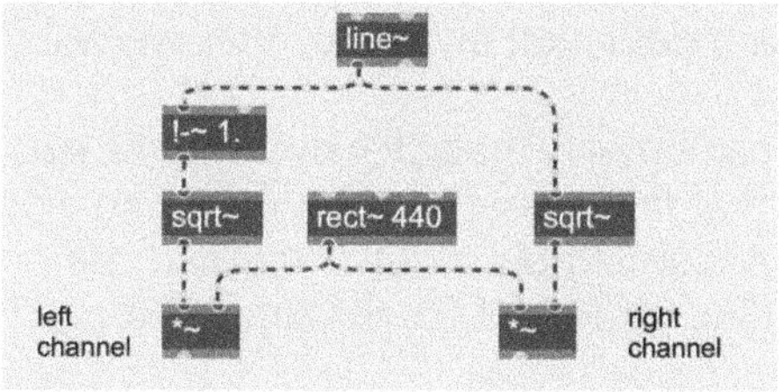

Fig. 4.1 A panning algorithm

You need to replace the **line~** object from the original patch (which modulated the position of the sound in space by using line segments) with a sine wave generator oscillating between 0 and 1. (A value of 0 will pan the sound left, while a value of 1 will pan the sound right.) The **cycle~** object, however, generates a sine wave that oscillates between -1 and 1. You could modify this oscillation interval by using the pair of simple calculations that you learned about in the theory chapter, but this will be the subject of the next section. For now, employ the **scale~** object, introduced in Section IB.8, to rescale the signal, completing the patch as shown in Figure 4.2.

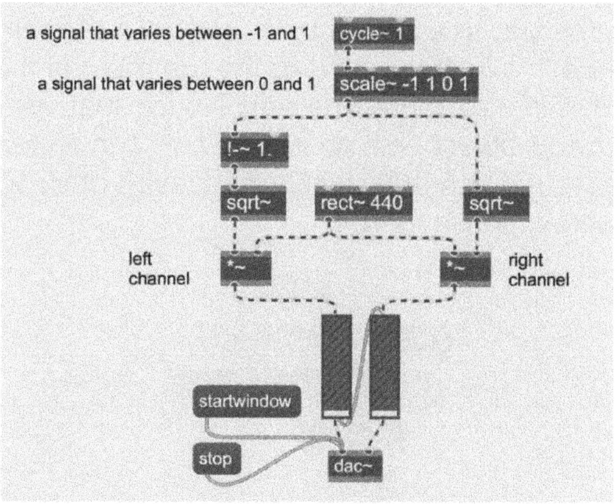

Fig. 4.2 Stereo panning controlled by an LFO

[1] If you don't remember how to do this, refresh your memory by rereading the relevant sections of both theory and practice.

In this patch, the **line~** object has been replaced by the **scale~** object, and a **cycle~** object has been connected to it. As you know, the **scale~** object takes four arguments, the first two specifying the range of the input signal, and the last two specifying the desired range of the output signal. In our case, the arguments [-1 1 0 1] indicate that we will be feeding the object an input signal that ranges from -1 to 1, and that we want to rescale this input to fit a signal that ranges from 0 to 1. The **cycle~** object itself is set to generate a control signal of 1 Hz, which will make the sound travel from the left to the right and back again over the period of one second; by connecting a float number box to the **cycle~** object, you can change the oscillation frequency.Try the patch with various frequencies, but stay below 20 Hz; higher frequencies will generate interesting audible modulation anomalies that we will take up in Chapter 10.

At this point, you can simplify the patch by using the **mc.stereo~** multichannel object, an object that implements a stereo panning algorithm; the object takes the sound to be positioned on its left inlet, and the positioning control signal on its right inlet. (See Figure 4.3 for the simplified patch.)

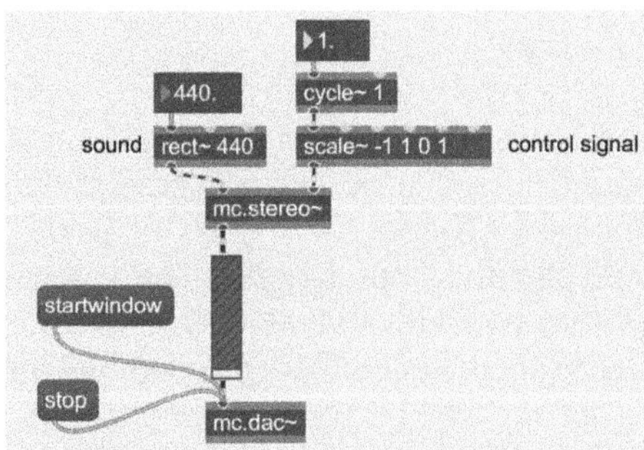

Fig. 4.3 Stereo panning using the **mc.stereo~** object

You can see that the **mc.stereo~** object performs the same function as the algorithm in Figure 4.1. We are using it to free up room in the graphical display of our patch, and it is also more efficient. Notice that we replaced the two **gains~** and the **dac~** object with an **mc.gain~** and an **mc.dac~**.
Try this patch, substituting control signals made with other waveforms, such as the square wave shown in Figure 4.4.

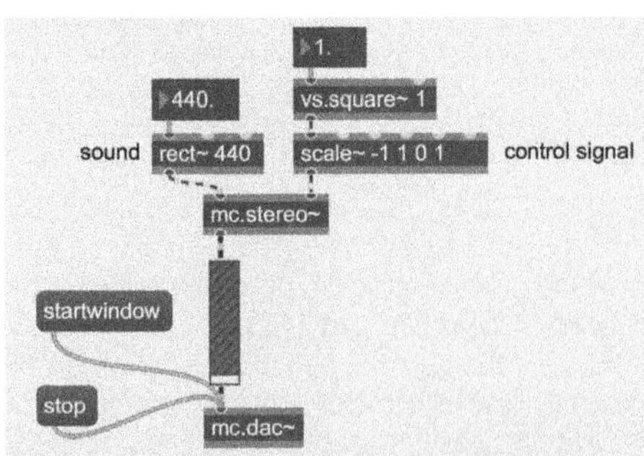

Fig. 4.4 Controlling panning with a square wave LFO

Under the control of a square wave, the sound moves from channel to channel without passing through intermediate positions. The sudden discontinuity, however, generates an undesirable click in the output signal. Fortunately, this can be eliminated by filtering the control signal with a lowpass filter, which smooths the sharp corners of the square wave. (See Figure 4.5 for this modification.)

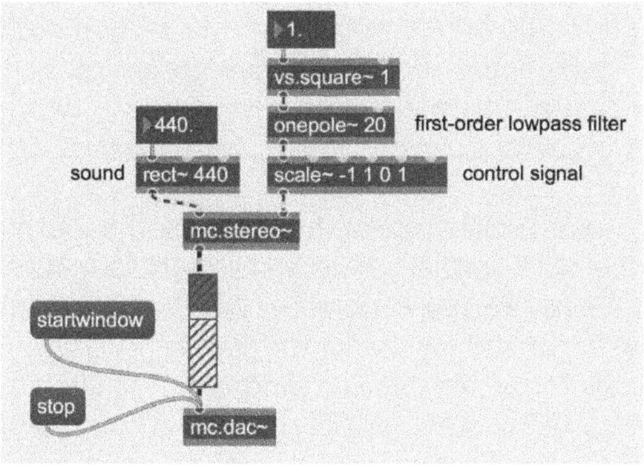

Fig. 4.5 Filtering an LFO

In this patch, we have set a cutoff frequency of 20 Hz, which means that the control signal can't jump from one value to the other faster than 20 times a second. Try changing the cutoff frequency for the filter to better understand how it influences the path of the sound; the lower the cutoff frequency, the smoother the transitions between channels will be.

We conclude this section with an object from the Ableton library that allows us to move sound along the stereophonic front using different trajectories. Load the patch **04_01a_abl.dsp.stereolfo.maxpat** (fig. 4.5b).

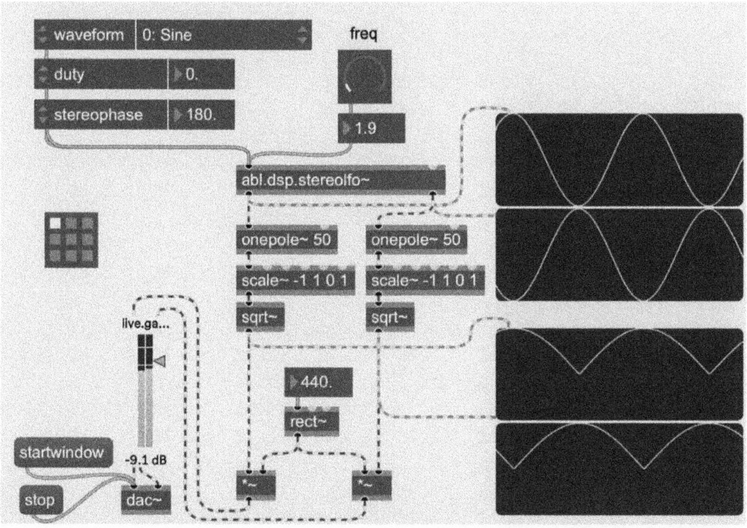

Fig. 4.5b: patch **04_01a_abl.dsp.stereolfo.maxpat**

The object **abl.dsp.stereolfo~**, shown at the top of the figure, is a waveform generator that can be used as an LFO. The object has two outputs that produce the same signal; you can change the phase of the right signal, for example, and put the two signals in phase opposition.
At the top left we see three **attrui** objects that allow us to change the waveform (there are nine possible shapes), the duty cycle, which deforms the wave by changing the ratio between the first and second part of the cycle, and the "stereophase" parameter, which changes the phase of the right channel in degrees. In the figure, this parameter is set to 180, which means that the two outputs are in phase opposition. Finally, we have a **dial** that changes the frequency.
On the right are four oscilloscopes showing us the output signals, which are bipolar, and the same signals after some transformations. Note that the oscilloscopes are **live.scope~** objects, which by default have a signal scrolling mode that is particularly useful for displaying LFOs.
As we said, the waveforms are bipolar, and we first filter the signal with an **onepole~** object to eliminate the click due to any discontinuities, then we make the signal unipolar with the **scale~** object, and finally we calculate the square root of the signal to make sure that the power of the sound produced is uniform along the entire stereophonic front (see sections 1.6T and 1.6P). Finally, we multiply the audio signal by the two signals generated by **abl.dsp.stereolfo~** and send the two products to the two stereophonic channels.
Try the different presets and then create other configurations. Observe the behavior of the different waveforms and listen carefully to what happens to the sound trajectories when you change the duty cycle and phase.

4.2 DC OFFSET

If you didn't have the **scale~** object at your disposal you could easily transform the standard bipolar signal emitted by the **cycle~** object, which moves between -1 and 1, into a unipolar signal that moves between 0 to 1. As you learned in Section 4.2T, only a few calculations are necessary. The first step is to reduce the range of the oscillations from [MIN -1, MAX 1] to [MIN -0.5, MAX 0.5], in order to obtain a sine wave identical to the one shown in Figure 4.2 of the theory chapter. You can accomplish this by multiplying the signal by 0.5. After doing this, transform the resulting bipolar sine wave, now oscillating between -0.5 and 0.5, into the desired unipolar signal by adding a DC offset of 0.5. The steps taken in this calculation, including the final output of [MIN 0, MAX 1], are shown visually in Figure 4.6.

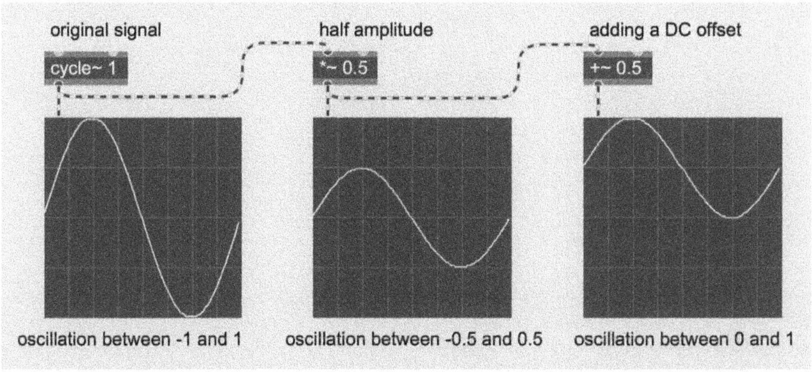

Fig. 4.6 Transforming a bipolar wave into a unipolar wave

Try building the patch, and then use it to replace the **scale~** object in the previous patch, connecting the outlet of the **+~** object to the control inlet of the panning object to verify that the results sound the same.

4.3 CONTROL SIGNALS FOR FREQUENCY

Following the approach that was diagrammed in Figure 4.3 of the theory chapter, you should now create the patch shown in Figure 4.7 that produces a sound with vibrato.

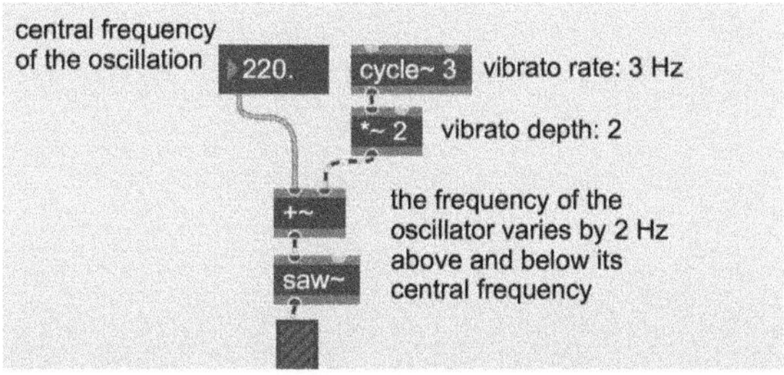

Fig. 4.7 Controlling frequency to produce vibrato

Listen to the vibrato applied to a frequency of 220 Hz, and then to a frequency of 880 Hz. The same amount of vibrato has a more marked effect on the 220 Hz sound than it does on the 880 Hz sound. As you know, this is because the sensation of vibrato is based on the depth of the vibrato relative to the central frequency; given constant vibrato settings, the higher the pitch, the narrower the vibrato will sound.

Modify the preceding patch to produce a vibrato that is proportional to the frequency of the oscillator, as we have done in Figure 4.8.

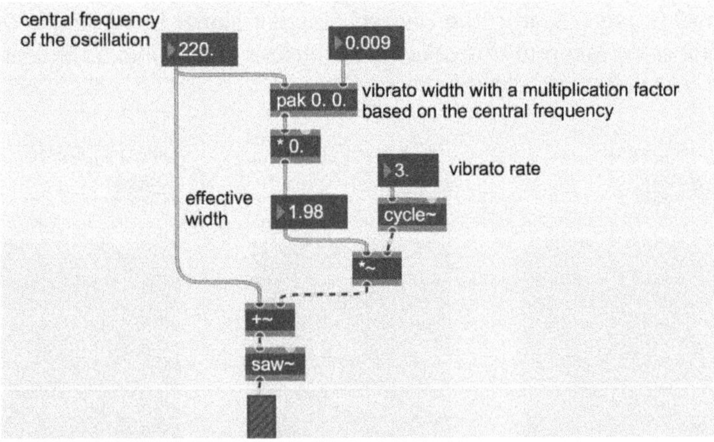

Fig. 4.8 Proportional control of vibrato

For a vibrato amplitude of 0.009, applied to a frequency of 220 Hz (as shown in the example in the figure), the absolute multiplication factor will be 1.98. Changing the frequency of the oscillator to 880 Hz will change this absolute factor to 7.92, but the vibrato effect itself will sound unchanged, since its amplitude to frequency ratio is a constant 0.009.

Try changing the multiplication factor and the rate of the vibrato: which settings sound the most realistic to you? At what point does the vibrato become a glissando?

SIMULATING A THEREMIN

The **Theremin** is one of the oldest electronic instruments, and it is still played and enjoyed by a significant number of enthusiasts. It is played by moving your hands in the vicinity of two antennas, a vertical one that controls pitch, and a horizontal one that controls the amplitude of the sound. The hand movements, almost dancelike motions by the player that serve to place the hands closer to or further away from the antennas, generate continuous changes in frequency and amplitude. The sound that emerges slides from one note to another, and is characterized by a vibrato that is controlled by rapid hand fluttering. It might remind you of a stringed instrument or of a human voice.

Let's attempt to construct a simulation of a Theremin. We will begin by modifying the patch from Figure 4.8, making the changes shown in Figure 4.9.

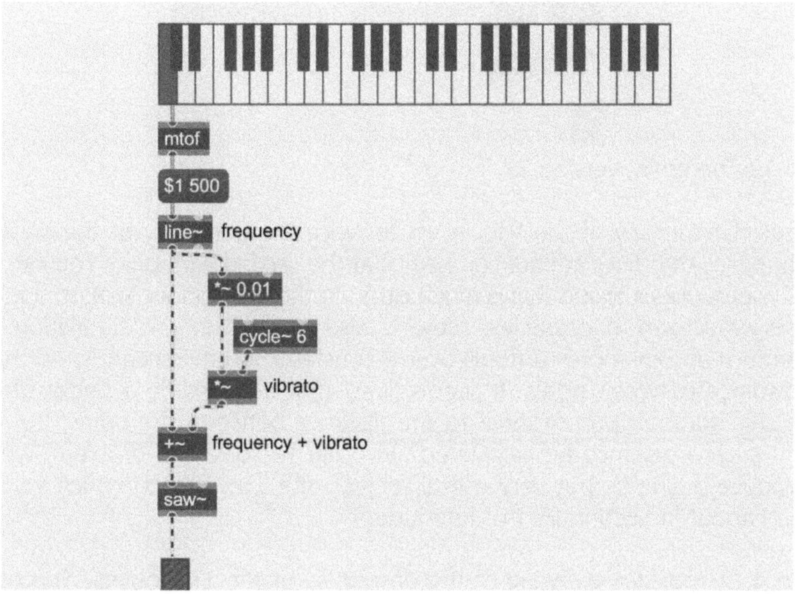

Fig. 4.9 Theremin, version 1

A **kslider** is used to generate a MIDI note number every time that one of its keys is pressed, and the note number is converted into a frequency using **mtof**. The resulting frequency is not immediately played, however; it becomes the endpoint of a glissando, which is reached, with the help of a **line~** object, after half a second, via a slide from the previous note. Vibrato is added to the note at a rate of 6 Hz with a width equal to 1% of the frequency. (These values have been selected to mimic the values used by actual Theremin players.) All of this frequency information is then applied to a **saw~** sawtooth oscillator.
Try building the patch and listening to the sound, which is still a long way from being a decent simulation. If you have heard a Theremin before, the first thing that you might notice is that the timbre of the oscillator is too harmonically rich; perhaps we need to apply a lowpass filter as shown in Figure 4.10.

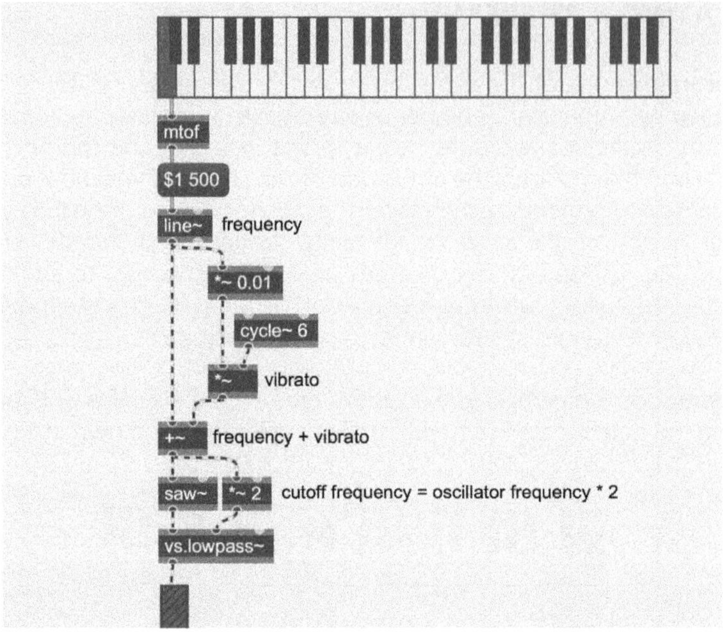

Fig. 4.10 Theremin, version 2

The cutoff frequency of the filter is set to twice the frequency of the oscillator, which means that filter attenuation begins at the second harmonic. You can hear that this produces a sound that is much closer to the one that we seek to simulate. Besides waveform inaccuracies, there is also a glitch in the simulation. The glissando that joins notes unfolds over a constant 500 milliseconds, no matter the distance between notes. It seems likely that it might be a better idea to make this duration proportional to the distance between the notes, but how should such a distance be calculated? In order to solve this problem, we will reintroduce a simple, but very useful, object: the `int` object, which you first learned about in Section IA.1 of Interlude A.

Figure 4.11 provides a review of the properties of the `int` object. This object acts like a memory "cell" that contains a single integer. (Remember that there is also a corresponding float object for handling floating point numbers.) As you see in the figure, the object can take an argument to initialize its value.

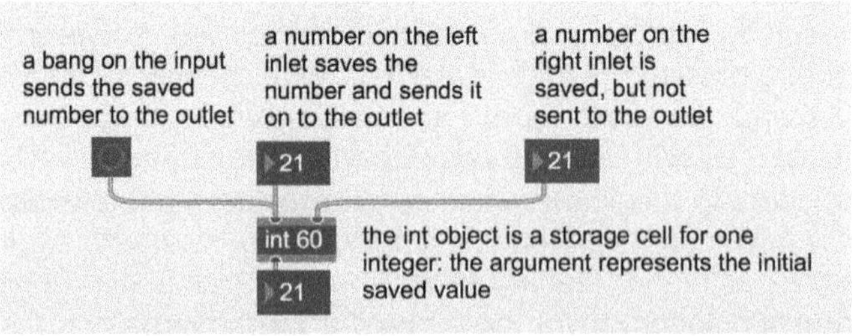

Fig. 4.11 The `int` object

Looking at Figure 4.12 should help you understand how it can be used to calculate the interval between two successive (integer) MIDI notes. Build and analyze this patch.

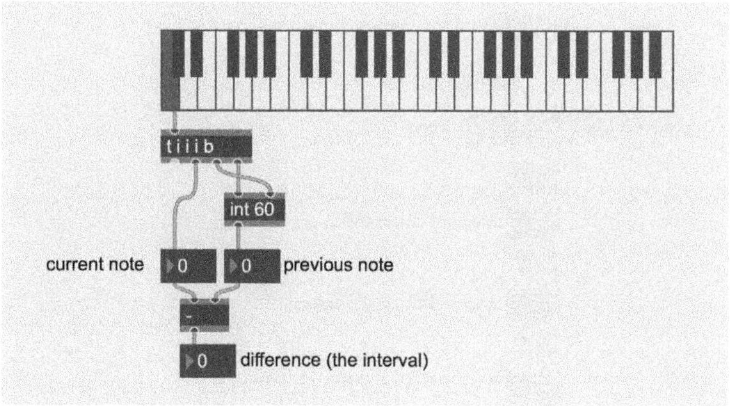

Fig. 4.12 Calculating an interval

The first time that you click on a **kslider** key, the MIDI note number that is produced passes through a **trigger** with the arguments "i i b" (a bang followed by two copies of the integer value on the inlet). The bang, which is emitted before anything else, is sent to the **int** object, which holds the number 60 to start; this number goes to the right inlet of a subtraction operator. After this, a copy of the number produced by **kslider** is sent by the **trigger** to the right inlet of the **int** object, replacing the previous value but not sending it on. A second copy of the number produced by **kslider** is then sent to the left inlet of the subtraction operator, causing the actual subtraction to occur. What is actually calculated in this first click scenario is the difference between the number produced by the **kslider** and the default initial default MIDI note value for the patch: the number 60.
The next click of a key generates a new MIDI note number, which is again sent to **trigger**, which emits a new bang, causing the **int** object to emit the saved value of the previous MIDI note, which is sent to the right inlet of the subtraction operator. In practice, every time that you click on a key, the previous note number is sent from the **int** object to the subtraction operator, where it is subtracted from the current MIDI note number; the difference calculated is the interval in semitones between the two notes.[2]

Now we can use this mechanism to constrain the duration of the glissando in our main patch to be proportional to the interval. If, for example, we decide that the distance of a semitone should be covered in 20 milliseconds, all we have to do is multiply the interval by 20, as shown in Figure 4.13.

---

[2] Those who know Max might have used a **bucket** object rather than an **int** for saving the preceding note, but we prefer to introduce the concept of a "memory cell" at this point, by which we can save a number for use at a future time.

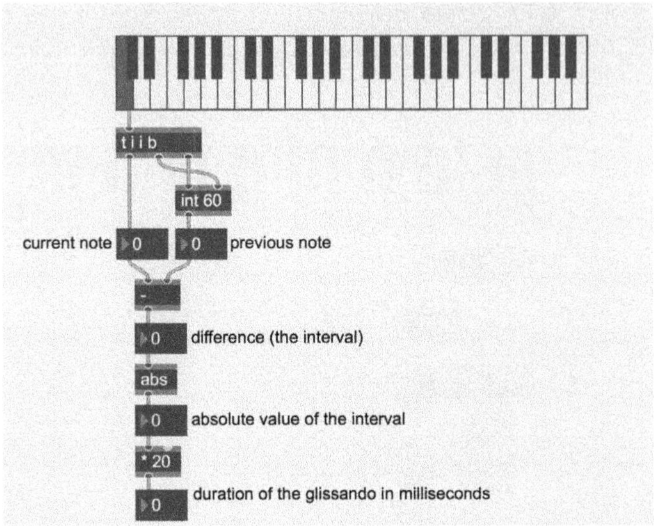

Fig. 4.13 The duration of the glissando is proportional to the interval

Before calculating the duration of the glissando, we have extracted the absolute value of the number using the **abs** object in order to avoid the negative numbers that are produced by descending intervals (as you can see in the figure). Connecting the patch in Figure 4.13 to our simulated Theremin, we get the patch shown in Figure 4.14.

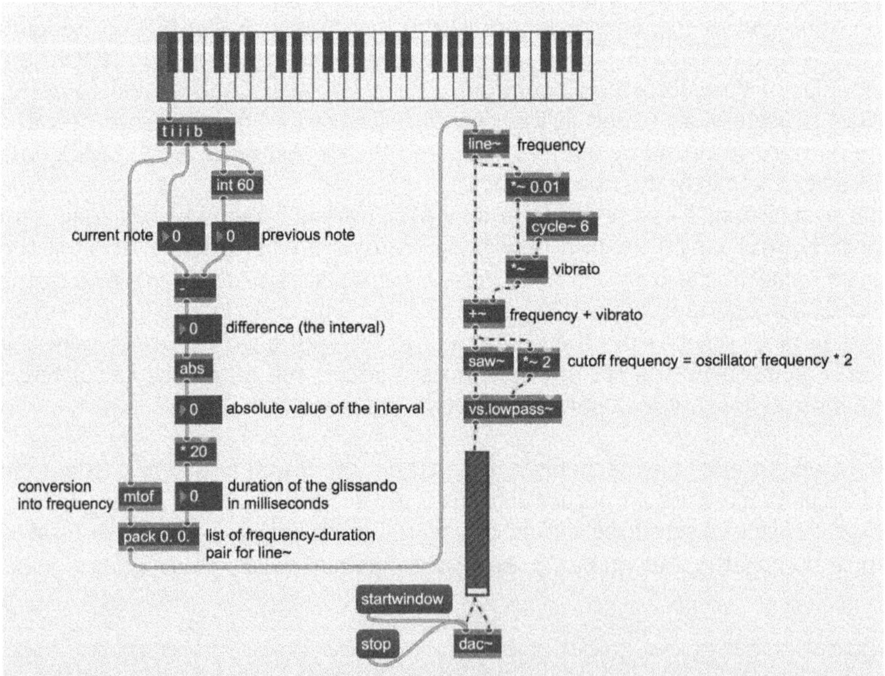

Fig. 4.14 Theremin, version 3

Note that we have added an outlet to the **trigger** object that is connected to the **kslider** in order to provide a note value for the **mtof** conversion object. At this point, we can add control over amplitude to our simulation, by using the velocity value provided by the right outlet of the **kslider** (as shown in Figure 4.14b).

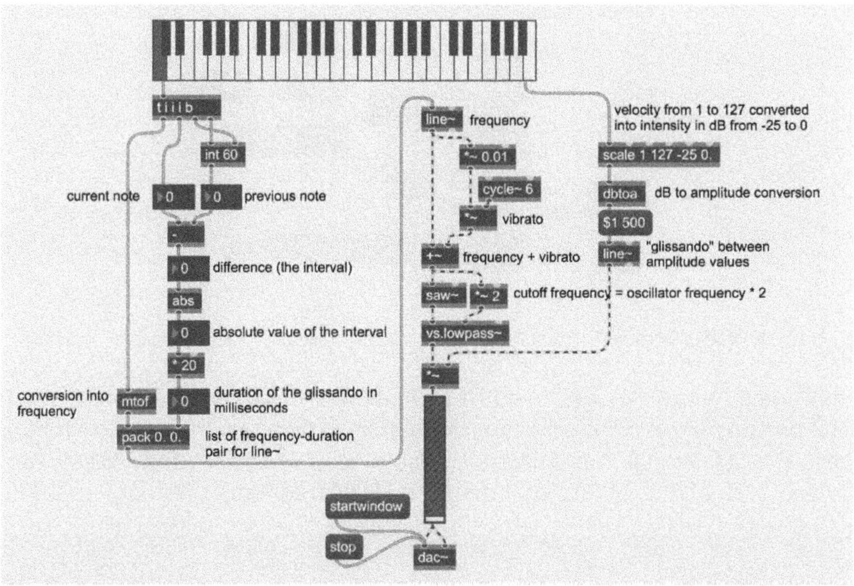

Fig. 4.14b Theremin, version 4

The velocity is sent to a **scale** object (introduced in Section IB.8), which scales the incoming values of 1 to 127 into values between -25 and 0, exactly as the object **scale~** would do for signals. (The **scale~** object, in fact, is nothing more that a MSP version of the **scale** object.) When, as in this case, none of the numbers input to the **scale** object has a decimal point, the output will be an integer. The values thus output in dB are converted into amplitudes, and the results are sent to the signal multiplier ***~**, which rescales the signal. Note that the transitions from one amplitude to the next are rendered less abrupt by using a **line~** object to interpolate from one value to the next over a 500 millisecond interval.

ACTIVITY

Add velocity-based control over frequency and amplitude oscillations to the Theremin simulation patch, using **scale** and **line~** objects as part of the implementation. Vibrato rates should range from a minimum of 5 Hz to a maximum of 7.5 Hz, and amplitude values (or better, the amplitude multiplication factor that was previously fixed at 0.01) should vary between 0.005 and 0.015. Input will need to be rescaled from velocity's range (1 to 127) to other intervals.

So far, we have applied vibrato to oscillators by changing the frequency parameter; we can do the same with sampled sounds by varying the readout speed, for example with **groove~** (Figure 4.15).

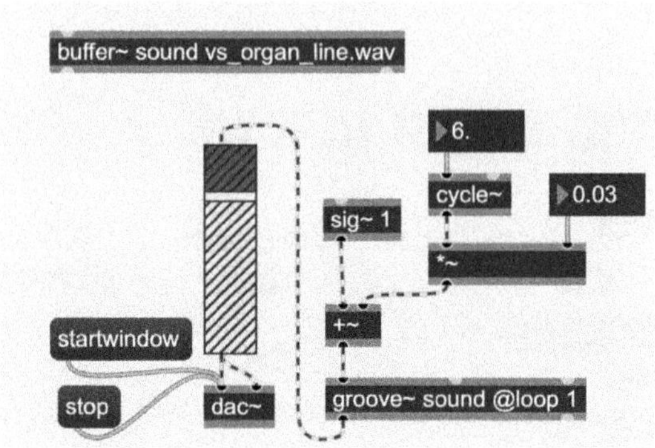

fig. 4.15: vibrato of a sampled sound

In this patch, which we invite you to recreate, we have added a low frequency (6 Hz) sine oscillator to the constant signal that determines the groove~ readout speed; the LFO signal is multiplied by 0.03, so that the readout speed varies between 0.97 and 1.03. Try changing the LFO's frequency and amplitude.

4.4 CONTROL SIGNALS FOR AMPLITUDE

Recreate the patch in Figure 4.16, which produces a tremolo.

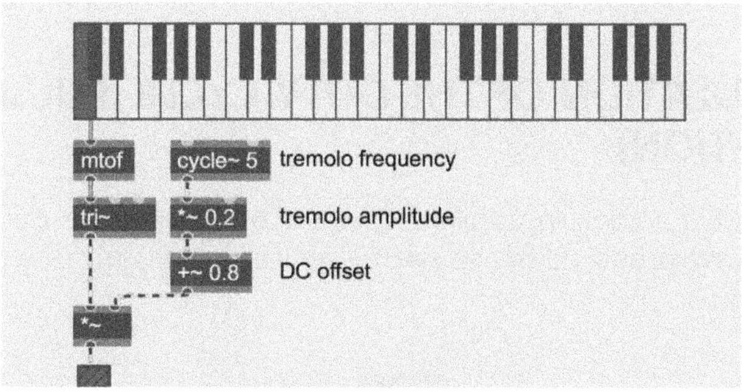

Fig. 4.16 Controlling amplitude to produce tremolo

The amplitude of the **tri~** oscillator in this patch is modulated by a sine wave coming from **cycle~** which has a frequency of 5 Hz and an amplitude of 0.2. The sine wave oscillator is therefore producing a waveform whose amplitude cycles from -0.2 to 0.2. By adding a DC offset of 0.8 to this signal, we shift it to produce an oscillation whose amplitude ranges between 0.6 and 1, and which is used as input to the amplitude multiplier.
Adding an envelope enables us to define a delay for the start of the tremolo, as shown in Figure 4.17.

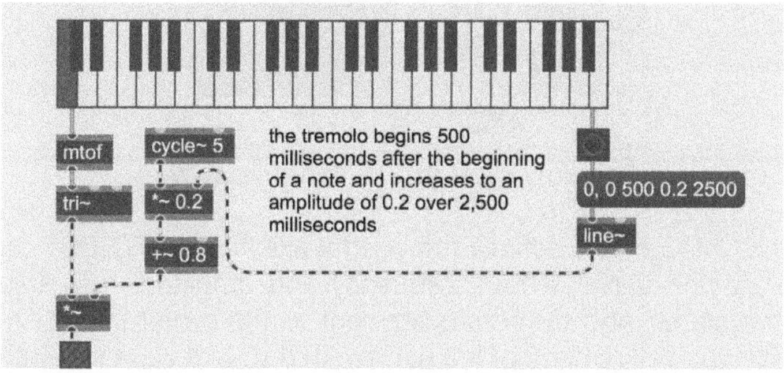

Fig. 4.17 Adding delay to the tremolo effect

In this patch, every time that a new note sounds, the amplitude of the tremolo goes to zero. After a half-second, it begins to increase until it reaches a value of 0.2 after two-and-a-half seconds.

ACTIVITIES

Replace the message box connected to the **line~** object with a **function** object, and create various envelopes to control the tremolo amplitude (remembering to set a range of between 0 and 0.2 using the *Inspector* for **function**).

As in the exercise for the preceding section, add velocity-based control over the intensity of the sound and the frequency of the tremolo oscillator.

4.5 MODULATION OF THE DUTY CYCLE (PULSE WIDTH MODULATION)

To understand the sonic possibilities created by varying the duty cycle of a rectangular wave produced by the **rect~** oscillator, construct the patch shown in Figure 4.18.

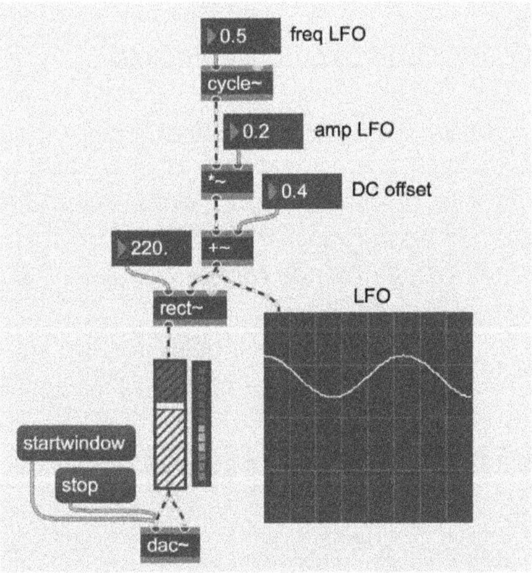

Fig. 4.18 Controlling the duty cycle of a rectangular wave

In this patch, a DC offset defines the central axis for an LFO that controls the duty cycle. A sine wave, whose frequency and amplitude are adjustable, is added to this signal, and the results are sent to the center inlet of the **rect~** object (which you will remember is a bandlimited square wave generator). In the example shown in the figure, the LFO moves the duty cycle parameter values between 0.2 and 0.6 at a rate of 0.5 Hz.

We use the **clip~** object to avoid producing parameter values that exceed the limits of 0 and 1. This object is the MSP version of the **clip** object (no tilde), which was introduced in Section IB.8. The object takes two arguments, a minimum and a maximum, and constrains the input signal to lie between these values. You can see it in action in Figure 4.19.

As you see in the figure, the **clip~** object, with arguments of 0 and 1, has been inserted between the LFO and the rectangular wave oscillator. The arguments set the limits for the signal to stay between 0 and 1. Without these limits, the parameters as shown in the figure would cause the LFO to oscillate between -0.3

and 0.5; with the **clip~** object in place, the negative part of the wave is clipped to the value 0, as you can see on the oscilloscope display. An interesting side-effect of this technique is that the sine wave of the LFO is deformed. If you try the patch with parameters set as shown, you can hear that the effect produced by this clipped sine wave is a sort of intermittent pulsation. You could also send the product of **cycle~** to a **scale~** object, exactly as we did in the stereo panning example in Chapter 4.1, to avoid clipping. We leave this as an exercise.

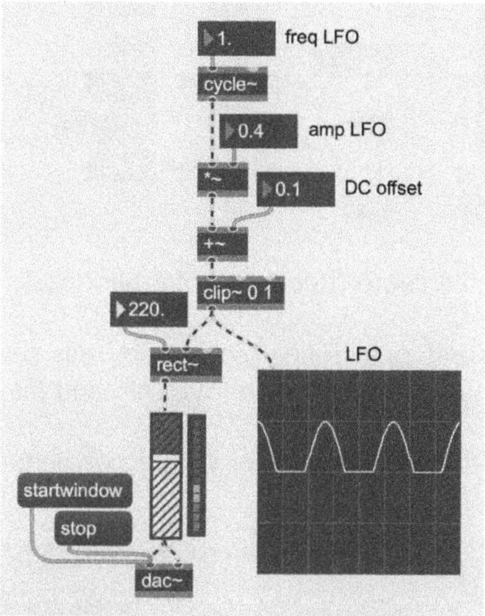

Fig. 4.19 Using **clip~** when controlling the duty cycle

4.6 CONTROL SIGNALS FOR FILTERS

We will now implement the configuration described in Section 4.6 of the theory chapter, where we discussed an algorithm for filtering white noise that used a bandpass filter with a center frequency oscillating between 100 and 2,100 Hz. The algorithm transforms an oscillation ranging between -1 and 1 into an oscillation ranging between arbitrary minimum and maximum values.

For reference, we will reiterate the two steps of this algorithm here:

> Subtract the minimum from maximum, and then divide the result by two, yielding a quantity we will call *X*.
> Multiply the amplitude by *X*.
> Add a DC offset equal to the maximum minus *X*.

For the example values, this algorithm would proceed as follows:

> *X* = (2,100 - 100) / 2 = 1,000
> After the multiplication the oscillation will move between -1,000 and 1,000
> DC Offset: 2,100 - 1,000 = 1,100

In Figure 4.20, you can see a patch that implements this algorithm. Construct it yourself.[3]

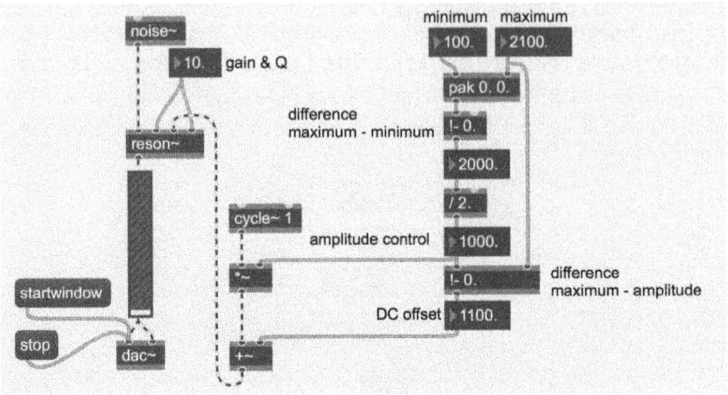

Fig. 4.20 Controlling the center frequency of a bandpass filter with an LFO

To hear the various sonic possibilities provided by this patch, try changing the minimum and maximum, the frequency of **cycle~**, and the Q setting of the filter.

We will now replace the noise generator with an oscillator. (See Figure 4.21.)

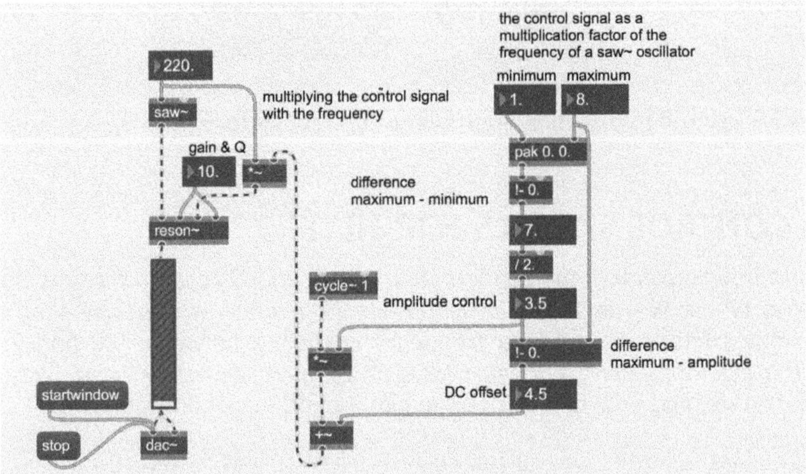

Fig. 4.21 Controlling the frequency of a filtered source with an LFO

The frequency of the filter in this case depends upon the frequency of the oscillator, multiplied by the control signal. In the example shown in the figure, the control signal varies from 1 to 8, and as a consequence, the frequency of the filter varies between 220 · 1 and 220 · 8, or put another way, between the first and the eighth harmonics of the **saw~** object.

[3] The algorithm illustrated could be replaced by a **scale~** object. We have not used this approach here, since we want to demonstrate the calculations explicitly.

Of course, we could also manipulate Q with a control signal (as shown in Figure 4.22).

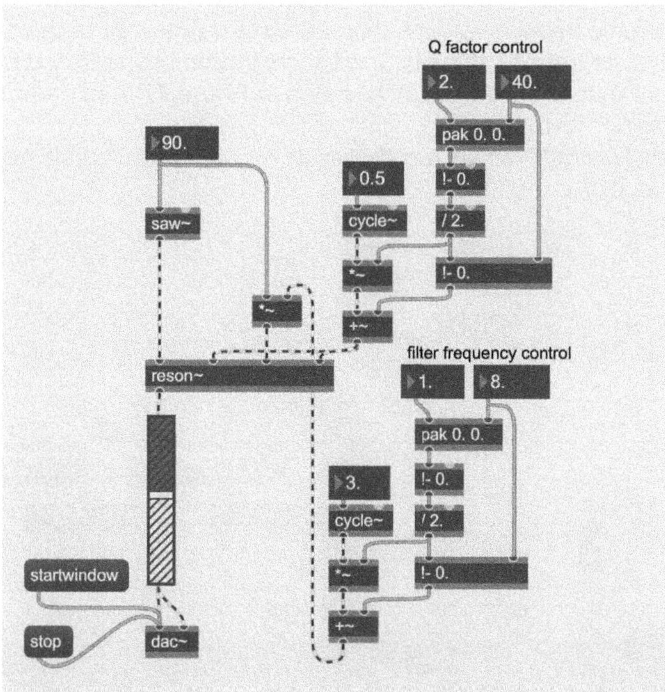

Fig. 4.22 Controlling Q in a bandpass filter with an LFO

We encourage you, as always, to vary the control parameters to find interesting sonorities.[4]

ACTIVITY

Re-open the patch from the previous chapter found in 03_04_qsynth.maxpat, and replace the envelopes that control the cutoff frequency and the Q factor with sine wave control signals. To define the amplitude of the LFO and the value of the DC offset, use the technique that we demonstrated in this section.

[4] We also encourage you to take a look at the **abl.device.autofilter~** object, which contains an internal LFO that is applied to the filter frequency.

4.7 OTHER GENERATORS OF CONTROL SIGNALS

You already know about the **rand~** signal generator from chapter 3; now we will use it at subsonic frequencies (less than 20 Hz) to control all of the parameters that we have seen up to this point: frequency (vibrato), amplitude (tremolo), and spectrum (filter). Build the patch shown in Figure 4.23, in order to explore these possibilities further.
In this patch, we once again use the **scale~** object to control tremolo and cutoff frequency for the filter.

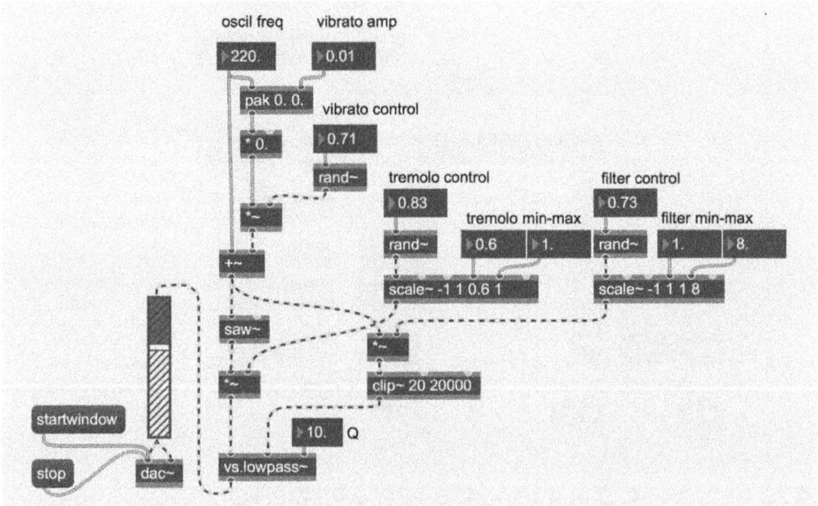

Fig. 4.23 A noise generator as an LFO

The cutoff frequency is scaled, as in the previous section, by multiplying the control signal by the frequency of the oscillator, but in this case, the oscillator itself is also modulated by a control signal, producing vibrato. To avoid having the filter "blow up" by producing values that are either too high or too low, we have inserted a **clip~** object (explained in Section 4.5) with the arguments 20 and 20,000; as a consequence, the cutoff frequency of the filter will never stray above 20,000 Hz or below 20 Hz.

Build the patch and try varying all of the parameters. You don't always have to hear all of the control signals as part of the output signal, since you can selectively eliminate them. Vibrato, for example, can have its amplitude set to 0. To eliminate tremolo or filter frequency modulation, you can set the minimum and maximum of the corresponding **scale~** to matching values.

ACTIVITY

Add a random signal to the patch in Figure 4.23 that controls Q.

Now let us look at an interesting object in the Ableton library that generates random LFOs: load the patch **04_01b_abl.dsp.wander.maxpat** (Figure 4.23b).

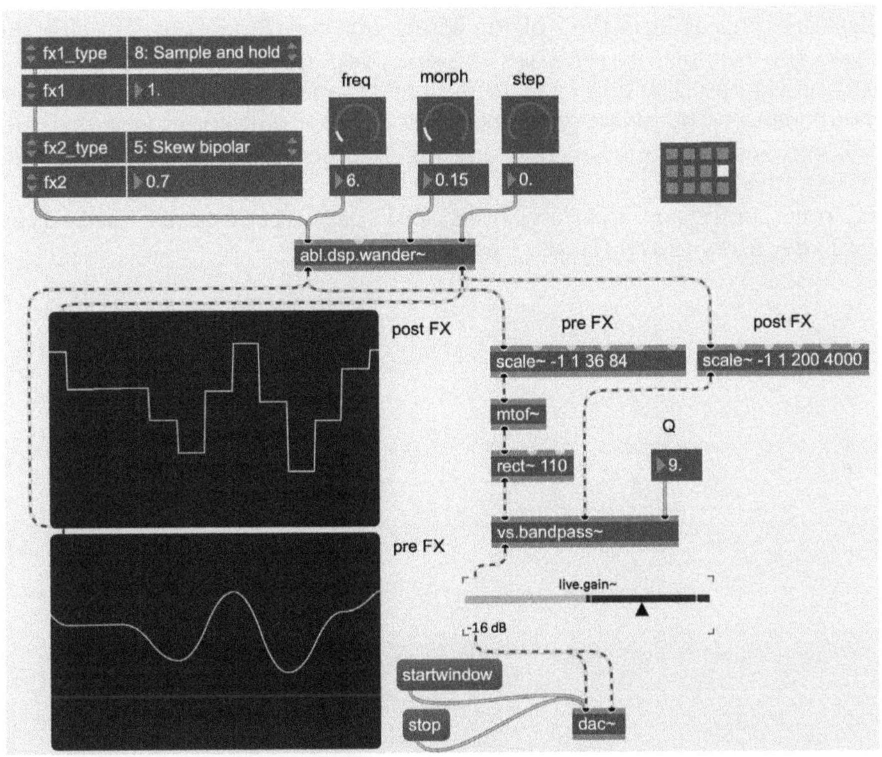

fig. 4.23b: patch **04_01b_abl.dsp.wander.maxpat**

The **`abl.dsp.wander~`** object, visible at the top of the image, generates random "paths" with variable frequency. The parameters we can set with the three dials are the frequency, the "morph" parameter, normalized between 0 and 1, which changes the type of pattern generated, and the "step" parameter (0 to 1), which performs a quantization of the signal over 8 amplitude levels.
An interesting feature of this object is the possibility of modifying the signal through a chain of two functions ("fx1" and "fx2") that can be selected from the 16 available. In the upper left part of the patch, we have created four `attrui` objects with which we can select the functions and the relative value (normalized between 0 and 1). The modified signal ("post FX") comes out of the second output, while the original signal ("pre FX") comes out of the first. In the figure, the first function is "Sample and Hold", which samples and holds the value produced by the signal at regular intervals, while the second function, "Skew bipolar", distorts the positive and negative values of the signal symmetrically.
Observe through the `attrui` objects the behavior of the different functions, and of course listen to all the presets in the patch.

We have applied the "pre FX" signal to the frequency of the oscillator **rect~**, while the "post FX" signal is used to change the center frequency of the filter **vs.bandpass~**.
There are other LFOs in the Ableton library with these functions that alter the signal. For example, try replacing the **abl.dsp.modulator~** object in the patch in Figure 4.23b and listen to the presets again (you may need to lower the frequency). This object generates the four classic waveforms (sine, triangle, sawtooth and square) as an LFO, and the "morph" parameter creates a fade between the waveforms.
The other objects in this family are: **abl.dsp.alternate~**, **abl.dsp.euclid~**, **abl.dsp.pulsate~** e **abl.dsp.ramp~**.[5]

[5] All these LFOs come from the Meld synthesizer, which is part of Ableton Live's native Virtual Instruments.

THE MODULATION MATRIX

Let's examine how to build patches that can apply control signals to parameters dynamically, using a mechanism called a *control matrix*. To facilitate this, we need to introduce a very important ingredient, the **matrix~** object, before doing anything else. This object takes two arguments, which are required, and which indicate the number of inlets and outlets, respectively. By using appropriate messages, it is possible to connect any inlet to any outlet; the object is essentially a kind of mixer.
Open the file **04_02_matrix.maxpat**, whose contents are shown in Figure 4.24.

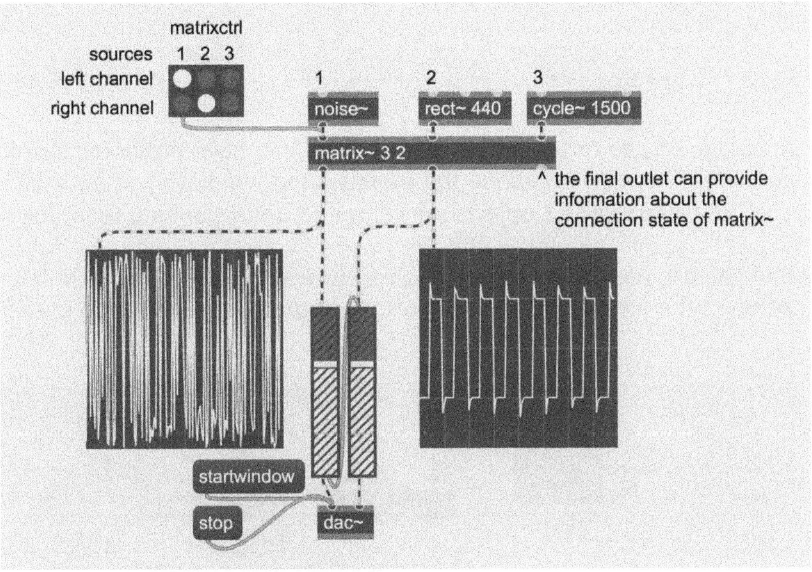

Fig. 4.24 The file 04_02_matrix.maxpat

In this patch, there is a `matrix~` object with 3 inlets and 2 outlets. Each inlet has a sound generator connected to it: one has a noise generator, one has a square wave, and the last has a sine wave. The two outlets are connected to the two channels of the audio interface's stereo output device. A graphical device, called a **matrixctrl** object, is connected to the first inlet of the `matrix~` object. This object can be found in the "Buttons" *palette*, and is used to facilitate connecting the inlets of a `matrix~` to its outlets; it presents a grid that can be arbitrarily sized using the *Inspector*, and whose columns and rows represent `matrix~` inlets and outlets. You can connect and disconnect an inlet and an outlet by clicking on their row/column crossing; the presence of a connection is indicated by a small red dot on the `matrixctrl`.

Try making various connections between the inlets and outlets of the patch to see what they do. We recommend that at first you try a single connection at a time (shown by a single red dot); making a single connection at a time will make it easier to verify that the connection you've established matches what you expect to hear.

ACTIVITIES

Working in the patch for this section, set the number of inlets of the **`matrix~`** object to 5, and add a triangle wave (**`tri~`**) and a sawtooth wave (**`saw~`**), each with a different frequency. Modify the **`matrixctrl`** object so that its grid has 5 columns, shown as 5 vertical lines. To resize the **`matrixctrl`** object, you can go to the "Behavior" category of the *Inspector* and modify the values of the *Number of Columns* and *Number of Rows* attributes.
Add a third outlet to the **`matrix~,`** to be used as a "center channel". Multiply this outlet by 0.707 and connect it to both **`gain~`** objects (which are the faders connected to the **`dac~`**).[6] You will obviously need to modify the **`matrixctrl`** as well.

• •

We encourage you to not continue reading until you have thoroughly explored the patch in Figure 4.24 and done the exercises that we have just outlined. The **`matrix~`** and **`matrixctl`** objects are central to understanding what follows.

Now that you can use the **`matrix~`** and **`matrixctrl`** objects with confidence, you can open the file **04_03_matrixmod.maxpat** (as shown in Figure 4.25).

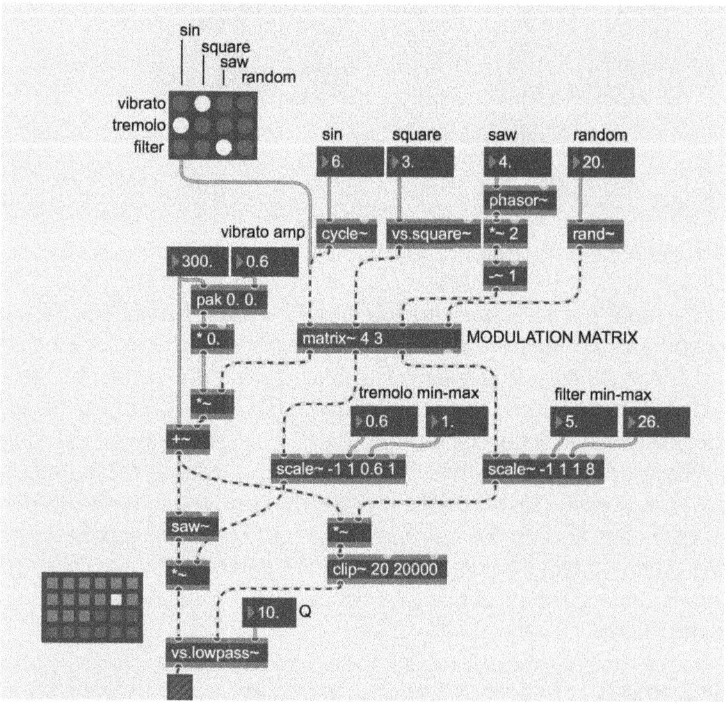

Fig. 4.25 The file 04_03_matrixmod.maxpat

6 Do you understand why we need to multiply by 0.707 rather than 0.5?

In this patch, which is evolved from the one shown in Figure 4.23, there is a **matrix~** object that has 4 inlets and 3 outlets. The inlets are a sine wave, a square wave, a sawtooth wave,[7] and an interpolated random noise generator. The outlets respectively modulate the frequency of an oscillator (producing vibrato), the amplitude of an oscillator (producing tremolo), and filter frequency. Using the *Inspector*, we have configured the **matrixctrl** to allow only one connection per row, so that every parameter can be connected to no more than one modulating signal at a time. (This is done by using the *One Non-Zero Cell Per Row* attribute in the "Behavior" tab.) Note, however, that it is possible to use a single modulator simultaneously on multiple parameters.
Study the presets that have been saved into the patch carefully, making sure that you understand how they work.

ACTIVITY

Continue to work on the same patch, change the number of inlets for the **matrix~** object to 6, and the number of outlets to 4. Connect two new control signals, a triangle wave and the non-interpolated noise generator **vs.rand0~** to the new inlets, and connect the fourth outlet (after passing it through a **scale~** object) to the Q inlet of the bandpass filter. Resize the **matrixctrl** object appropriately, and try out new configurations. What do you need to do, in particular, to obtain a "classic" sample-and-hold effect?

[7] The sawtooth waveform is implemented using a **phasor~** object, which emits a unipolar signal (a signal that ranges between 0 and 1). Because of this, it is necessary to multiply by 2 and add a DC offset of -1.

4.8 CONTROL SIGNALS: MULTICHANNEL PANNING

In this section, we will occupy ourselves by building an algorithm that will rotate sounds in space, using signals to control location within a field of 4 or more audio channels. In other words, we will implement LFO control over multichannel panning. You can configure the **mc.mixdown~** object to easily perform multichannel panning, but for a better understanding of the problems related to this type of algorithm, let's see first how you can achieve panning using Max basic objects.
In the case of stereo panning, we saw that if you want to make a sound move from left to right, for example, you essentially need to perform a crossfade between the volume of the left channel and that of the right channel. Imagine now that we have a system with 4 channels, in which the speakers are positioned in the corners of the room, as shown in Figure 4.26.

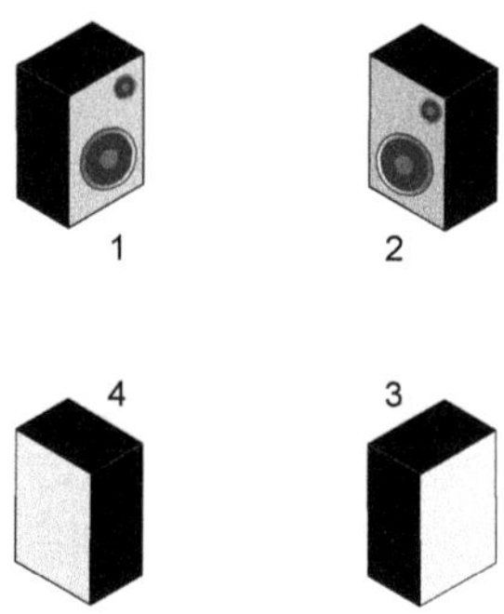

Fig. 4.26 A quadraphonic system

If you want to have a sound circle the room, starting with speaker number 1, you need to perform successive crossfades between channel 1 and 2, 2 and 3, 3 and 4, and finally between 4 and 1, which closes the circle. If you want to control this rotation with a control signal that moves between the values 0 and 1, this implies a relationship between the signal and the panning:

Control signal	Channel crossfade
0 to 0.25	1 to 2
0.25 to 0.5	2 to 3
0.5 to 0.75	3 to 4
0.75 to 1.0	4 to 1

In practice, you would like the volume of channel 1 to drop from 1 to 0 when the control signal goes from 0 to 0.25, while that of channel 2 would rise from 0 to 1. Likewise, when going from 0.25 to 0.5, the volume of channel 2 would drop from 1 to 0, while that of channel 3 would rise from 0 to 1. The same relationships would hold for the other two crossfades.

Dividing the problem into simpler parts, let's occupy ourselves with channel 2 to start. The volume of this channel should rise from 0 to 1 when the control signal goes from 0 to 0.25, and then drop back to 0 when the control signal goes from 0.25 to 0.5. The volume should then remains at 0 for the rest of the control signal's range. Figure 4.27 shows one way to link such a control signal to volume – try building the patch.

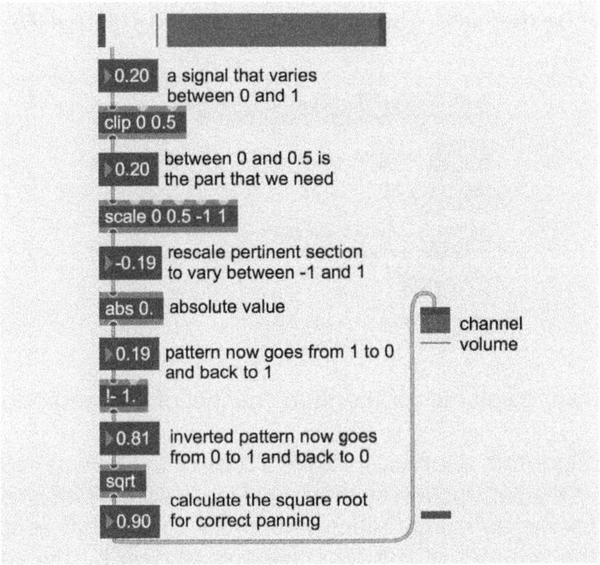

Fig. 4.27 Calculating volume for the second channel of a quadraphonic system

We have created a simulation of the second channel in Max. First, with a horizontal slider,[8] we generate a decimal value[9] between 0 and 1 that represents the value of the control signal. We then use a **clip** object (the Max version of the **clip~** object) to isolate the part of the signal between 0 and 0.5, and rescale it so that it ranges from -1 to 1. When the **scale** input value runs from 0 to 0.5, the value output will run from -1 to 1. By taking the absolute value of the generated interval, we transform the negative portion of the range into positive numbers: the original values -1, 0, 1 become 1, 0, 1. We then invert this range by using the !- operator, which causes 1 to become 0, 0 to become 1, and all numbers in between to likewise flip. The progression of 1, 0, 1, therefore, becomes 0, 1, 0, which is exactly what we are after. Finally, we calculate the square root of these values, so that the intensity of the signal behaves correctly (as described in Section 1.5T).

Channel 3 works in the same way, the sole difference being that the pertinent "live" portion of the control signal lies between 0.25 and 0.75, rather than between 0 and 0.5. When the signal goes from 0.25 to 0.5, the volume of channel 3 goes from 0 to 1, and when the control signal goes from 0.5 to 0.75, the volume goes from 1 to 0. The volume then remains at 0 for the rest of the control signal's range.

---

[8] The slider object is vertical by default: remember that you can cause it to become horizontal by grabbing the small square in its lower right corner and resizing it.

[9] To generate decimal values, open the Inspector for the slider, set the "Range" attribute to 1, and then activate the "Float Output" attribute on the Value category by clicking on the checkbox.

Rather than building an entirely new patch, we can reuse the patch that we just made, subtracting 0.25 from the control signal rather than modifying the calculations in the patch. By subtracting 0.25 from the control signal, the interval from 0.25 to 0.75 is converted into the interval from 0 to 0.5, and the patch need not be modified. This approach is seen in Figure 4.28

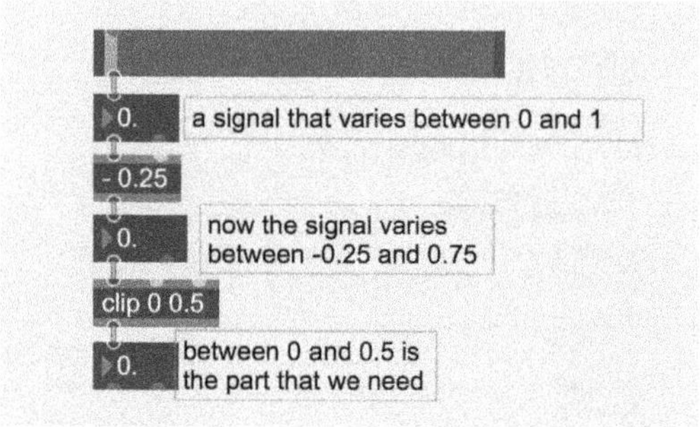

Fig. 4.28 Calculating volume for the third channel of a quadraphonic system

The rest of the algorithm is identical. Make a copy of the objects in the preceding patch and insert the subtraction as shown in Figure 4.28. Then connect the two patches to the same horizontal slider, and check to see that as the horizontal slider moves, the volumes of the two channels (shown by the vertical sliders) move so as to simulate a crossfade.

For channel 4, the same discussion applies, except that we subtract 0.5 from the control signal rather than 0.25.

Channel 1 is slightly more complex, since the volume goes from 1 to 0 when the control signal goes from 0 to 0.25, and from 0 to 1 when the control signal goes from 0.75 to 1. There is a hole in the middle of the range! To solve this problem, we need to add 0.25 to the control signal, which will then range from 0.25 to 1.25, and after this calculate the remainder by using the modulo operator with a base of 1 (which we outlined in Section IB.2), which causes the values to fall between 0 and 1. As a result, control values that go from 1 to 1.25 are transformed into values that go from 0 to 0.25, and the rest of the control values are unchanged:

original interval	modulo
0.25 - 1	0.25 - 1 (unchanged)
1 - 1.25	0 - 0.25

We thus reduce the values for channel 1 to the interval 0-0.5, which is what we needed in order to reuse the algorithm.

Figure 4.29 shows the complete algorithm in MSP, which, as always, we encourage you to build.

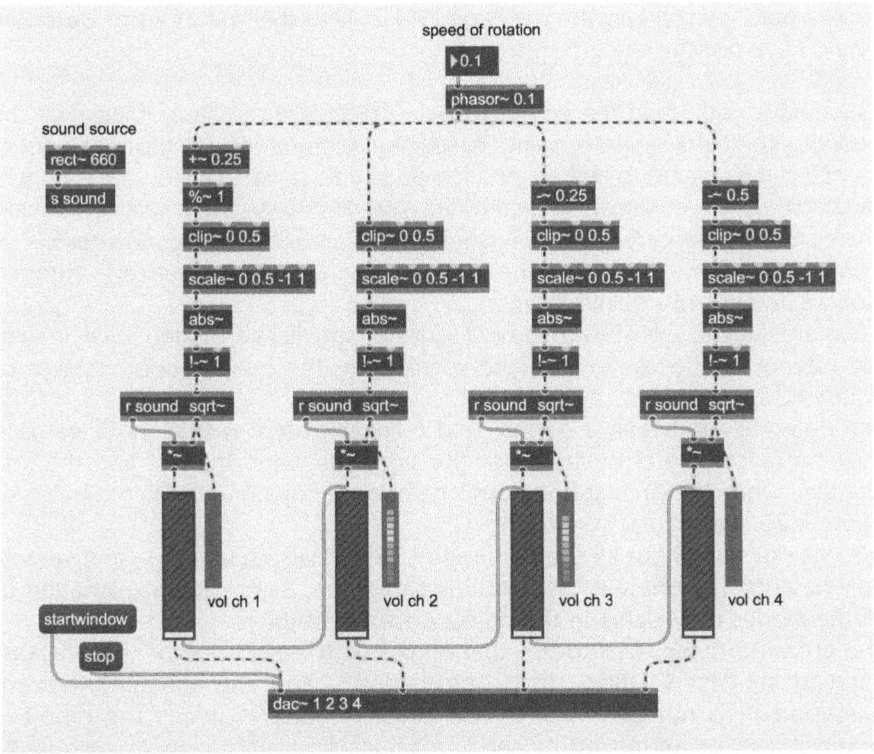

Fig. 4.29 Panning on four channels

Note that the **dac~** object in this patch takes 4 arguments, one for each channel that we want to use on the audio interface. The numbers represent the outlets: if for any reason the 3 and 4 speakers were physically reversed with respect to the configuration shown in Figure 4.24, you could invert the order of the last two arguments ([**dac~** 1 2 4 3]), in order to obtain the correct rotation. Alternatively, it is possible to send a message [**set** channel_number] to one of the inlets of the **dac~** to modify its output outlets. Figure 4.29b shows how you might invert channels 2 and 3 in a quadraphonic system, for example.

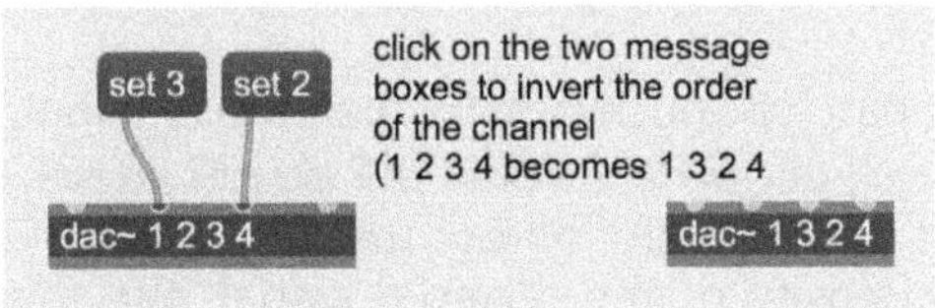

Fig. 4.29b How to reorder output channels

This technique can be very useful when you need to quickly change from one configuration to another. The change shown in Figure 4.29b, for example, enables changing a rotating movement (as in Fig. 4.29) into an "X" type movement. (Refer to the speaker diagram in Figure 4.26 to visualize the path of the signal.) It is also possible to send a list with the desired channels order:

for example, by sending the message [1 3 2 4] to the first input of **dac~** we would have got the same result.

As we have said, using the **mc.mixdown~** object, we can easily implement the algorithm for multichannel panning. By sending a control value to the right input of the object it is possible to redirect the incoming audio signal to the output channels, crossfading between signals when they are placed between two adjacent channels. There are 4 different multichannel panning modes available in **mc.mixdown~**:
- two of these are linear, i.e. they require a series of loudspeakers arranged along a line in front of the listener
- two are circular, i.e. they assume a series of speakers arranged in circle with the listener at the center (like the speakers in the quadraphonic system of figure 4.26).
The difference between a circular and a linear system is that the linear one does not allow the cross-fading of the signal between the last and the first channel, while the circular one does (the one we implemented in the patch of figure 4.29 is a circular system).[10]
We will not talk about all the panning modes of **mc.mixdown~**, and we will only describe the one we need for this paragraph; a complete explanation of all the modes is available in the object documentation.
The attribute of **mc.mixdown~** that allows us to select one of the available panning modes is called "pancontrolmode", and the modality we are interested in is number 3. That is a circular mode in which the different channels can be addressed by sending values from 1 to n (with n equal to number of speakers) to the right inlet of the object.
In a quadraphonic system, therefore, the values from 1 to 4 identify the four channels. Values that are not integers put the signal between the channels: by gradually passing from the value 2 to the value 3, for example, a crossfade is achieved between the second and the third channel.
The values of the channels are repeated cyclically; in other words, considering a 4-channel system, the value 5 corresponds to channel 1, the value 6 to channel 2 and so on. In general, if we want to make a cross-fade between the last and the first channel in a system with n channels, it is sufficient to pass gradually from the value n to the value n + 1 (i.e. from the value 4 to the value 5 in a quadraphonic system)
Now open the patch **04_04_mc_panning.maxpat** (figure 4.30).

As you can see, the patch is much simpler than the one in figure 4.29, because the calculations are all performed inside the **mc.mixdown~** object.
The graphic object to the right of **mc.gain~** is called **meter~**. It allows us to display the intensity of the received signal: the four columns we see correspond to the 4 channels generated by **mc.mixdown~**. Notice the attribute "@pancontrolmode 3" in **mc.mixdown~**, which allows us to use the circular panning system we described above.

---

[10] Actually the **mc.stereo~** object we introduced in section 4.1 is, under another name, a two-channel **mc.mixdown~** with linear panning.

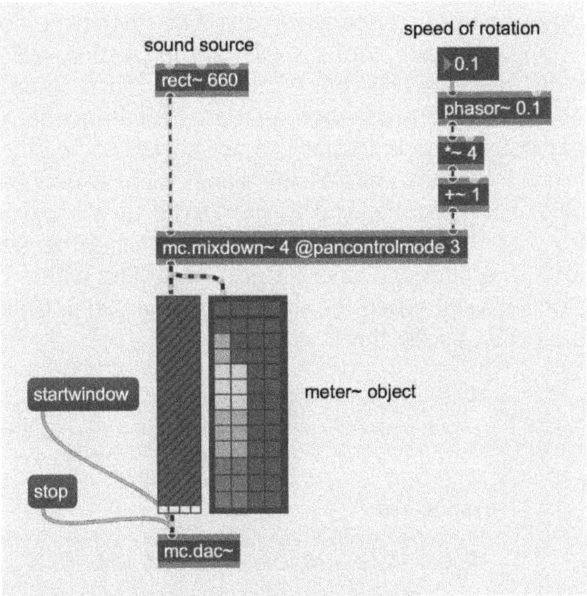

fig. 4.30: the **04_04_mc_panning.maxpat** patch

Let's see how the signal that controls the rotation of the source sound is generated in the quadraphonic system: the signal produced by the **phasor~** on the right is multiplied by 4, thus obtaining a ramp that goes from 0 to 4. The next object [+~ 1] moves the ramp values between 1 and 5. In this way, the source sound cyclically passes through all the channels of the system, and when the ramp reaches the value 5, the source sound returns, as we know, to channel 1. Notice that the abrupt passage of the ramp from 5 to 1 at the end of the cycle does not generate any discontinuity in the rotation of the sound because both values correspond to the first audio channel.
Keep in mind that if you run this patch with a stereo system, you will hear the sound only when it is routed to channels 1 and 2, i.e. only when the first two columns of the **meter~** display a signal.

ACTIVITIES

Replace the **phasor~** with another control signal such as **rand~**. Recall that you will need to transform bipolar signals into unipolar signals.

Implement a panning algorithm for 6 or 8 channels. You will need to modify the control signal appropriately.

Besides rotary movement, it is certainly possible to think of other panning motions for a signal in space. And as we saw in Section 4.8 of the theory chapter, we might use the LFO that is modifying the position of the signal to also alter other characteristics, such as the cutoff frequency of a filter, for example. To demonstrate these possibilities, we have modified the patch shown in Figure 4.30 in a way that enables the signal to pass between channels 1 and 3 with almost no crossfade, and to be filtered by a lowpass filter whose cutoff frequency is controlled by the same LFO. Recalling the example used in the theory chapter, the filter will have a cutoff of 300 Hz when the signal is on channel 1, and of 2,000 Hz when the signal is on channel 3. Change the patch as shown in figure 4.31 to see this in action.

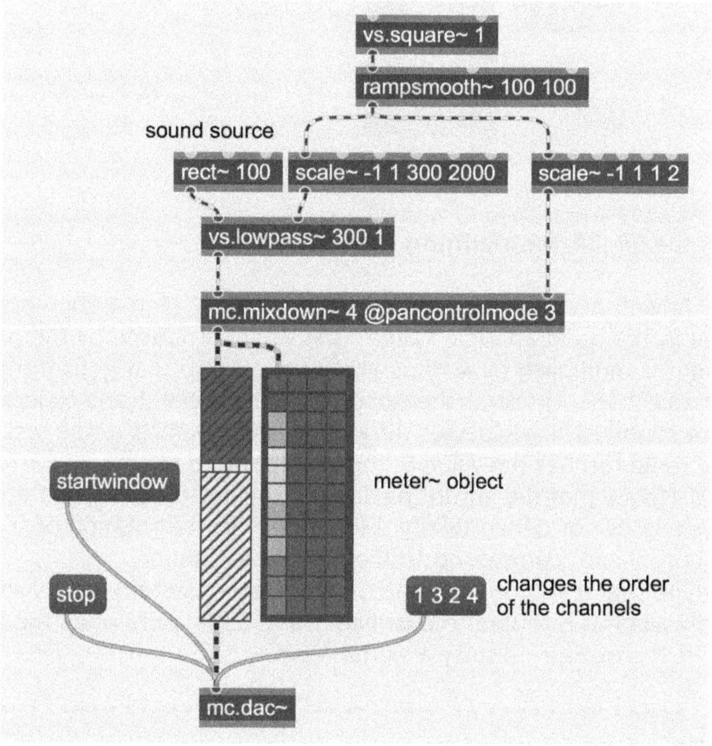

Fig. 4.31 Alternating between two channels

Looking at the lower part of the figure, you can see that, before anything else, we have exploited the ability of the **mc.dac~** object to change channel order, swapping channels 2 and 3 to set up an overall pattern that moves the sound from 1 to 3 to 2 to 4, rather than from 1 to 2 to 3 to 4. By doing this, we reduce the number of modifications needed to the original patch of Figure 4.29.

Looking at the upper part of the patch, you'll see that we've replaced the sawtooth LFO (the **phasor~**) with the non-bandlimited square wave generator **vs.square~**. This generator, which is given the frequency of 1 Hz, controls the position of the signal, as well as the frequency of the lowpass filter's cutoff.

To avoid clicks caused by sudden parameter changes, we've routed the output of **vs.square~** to a new object: **rampsmooth~**.
The **rampsmooth~** object smooths jumps that can be present in a signal. To do this, the object implements linear interpolation between two successive values of its input signal. The arguments indicate the number of samples to employ for the interpolation; more precisely, the first argument indicates the number of samples to use when the signal is rising, and the second argument indicates the number to use when the signal is falling. In the example in Figure 4.31, this means that when the signal produced by the square wave generator passes from -1 to 1 with an upward jump, the **rampsmooth~** object transforms this discontinuity into a rising ramp of 100 samples (since its first argument is 100). Since the second argument is also 100, there will also be an interpolation of 100 samples when the square wave drops from 1 to -1. The **rampsmooth~** object is functionally similar to the **onepole~** object shown in Figure 4.5 of Section 4.1. The difference between them is precision: we can establish an exact number of samples to use in the interpolation with the **rampsmooth~** object, and we can also differentiate between rising discontinuities and falling ones.

Returning to Figure 4.31, we see that the outlet of **rampsmooth~** is sent to two **scale~** objects. The left object transforms the bipolar oscillations of the square wave into a smoothed oscillation between the values 300 and 2,000, which are used as the cutoff frequency for the resonant lowpass filter that is filtering the bandlimited square wave emitted by the **rect~** object. The right scale~ object rescales the LFO to the interval of 1 to 2. Those numbers are sent to the right mc.mixdown~ input. This LFO limits the quadraphonic panning algorithm to its first two channels;; because we have modified the order of the channels, the pan moves the sound from channel 1 to channel 3 and back, as we showed in Section 4.8 of the theory chapter.

In Figure 4.32, you can see how to move sound from channels 1 and 3 to channels 2 and 4 through the addition of a second LFO.

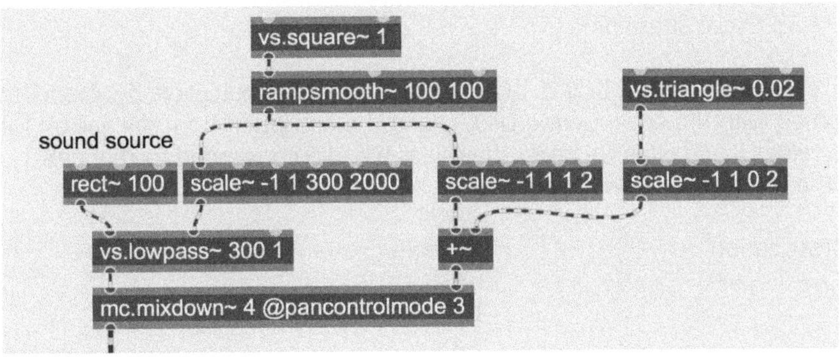

Fig. 4.32 Using two LFOs

In this example, a triangle wave LFO, with a frequency of 0.02 Hz (a period of 50 seconds) is rescaled between 0 and 2, and is summed with the square wave LFO. This summation causes the peak values of the oscillation of the square wave LFO to gradually move from the values 1 and 2 to the values 3 and 4 and back. Because we have modified the channel order to 1 3 2 4, the signal passes gradually from alternating between channels 1 and 3 to alternating between channels 2 and 4. (See also the description of the algorithm in Section 4.8T.)

As a final example, we will implement the following cyclic pattern:

300 Hz		2,000 Hz
ch1	|	ch3
ch3	|	ch2
ch2	|	ch4
ch4	|	ch1
ch1	|	ch3
...	|	...

We briefly introduced this pattern in Section 4.8 of the theory chapter. Figure 4.33 shows how the previous example can be used to implement this pattern by replacing the triangle wave LFO with a **phasor~**.

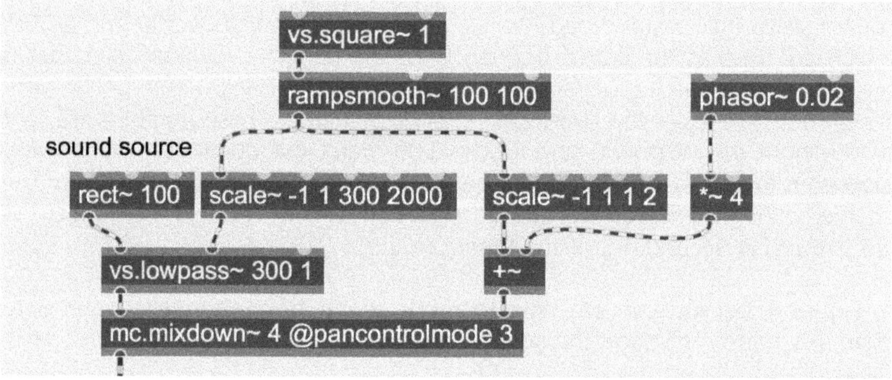

Fig. 4.33 Cyclic alternation

The **phasor~**, generating a ramp from 0 to 1, is multiplied by 4 and then summed with the square wave LFO, taking the oscillation from the values 1 and 2 to values 5 and 6 (as we know the values 5 and 6 correspond to channels 1 and 2.) The result is this alternation:

LFO oscillation	Alternating channels
1-2	1-3
2-3	3-2
3-4	2-4
4-5	4-1
5-6	1-3

Although more complex, this pattern is still cyclic; it repeats indefinitely.

ACTIVITIES

In the patches of Figure 4.31, 4.32, and 4.33, replace the **`vs.square~`** LFO with another control signal, such as **`rand~`**. Besides this, modify the order of the output channels in order to try out different "geometric movements" of the audio signal.

Transform the quadraphonic algorithms of Figure 4.31, 4.32, and 4.33 into algorithms for 6 or 8 channels.

ACTIVITY – *ANALYSING ALGORITHMS*

Open the patch contained in **04_analysis.maxpat**.

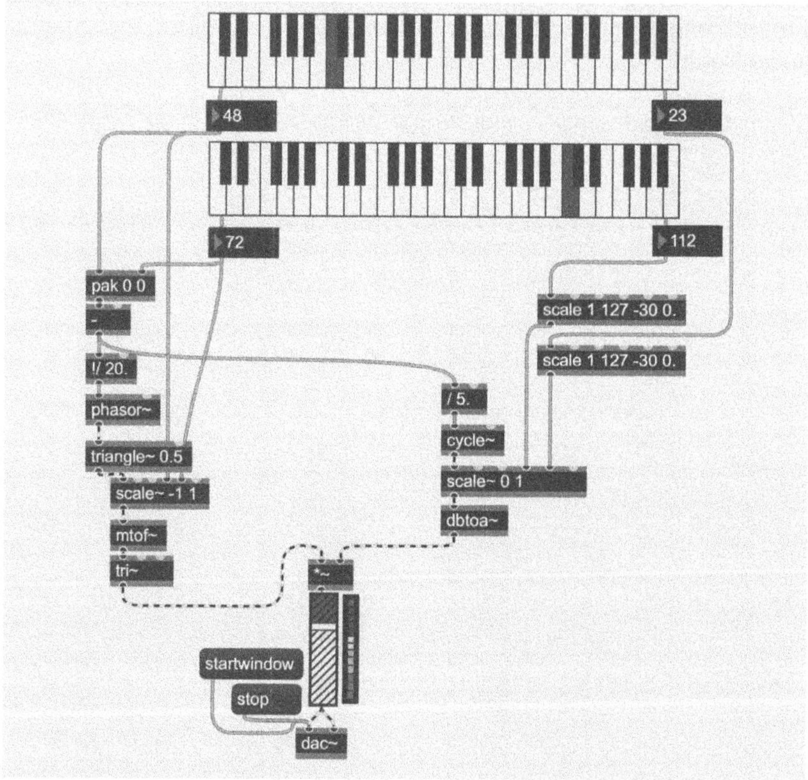

Fig. 4.34 The file 04_analysis.maxpat

Generating MIDI note values and velocities with two **kslider** objects, this patch produces a sound that has a triangular waveform, that is also supplied with vibrato (frequency oscillations) and tremolo (amplitude oscillations).
How are the control signals linked to the pitch and to the velocity of the two MIDI notes?

ACTIVITY – *COMPLETING ALGORITHMS – ACTIVITY A*

Return to the file 02_11_crossfading.maxpat, which we first analyzed in Section 2.3, and which covered wavetables and vector synthesis. Add an LFO to this patch that will control the crossfade between the two waveforms. Use a **cycle~** oscillator with a frequency of 1 Hz, which, of course, you will need to convert to be unipolar. The outlet of the LFO should be routed to the third inlet of the subpatch [**p** x_dissolve], replacing the message generated by the slider and the objects connected to it. The [**p** x_dissolve] subpatch will need to be slightly modified, because the third inlet expects to receive a list of two values rather than a signal. Can you see what this modification will look like? (Suggestion: it is enough to delete an object within the subpatch and to re-establish the connections.) After testing the patch to make sure that the new functionality is working properly, try modifying the frequency and the waveform of the LFO.

ACTIVITY – *COMPLETING ALGORITHMS – ACTIVITY B*

Return to the file 02_13_vectors.maxpat, which we first analyzed in Section 2.3, and add two LFOs to control the crossfade between tables. The two LFOs will replace the values generated by **pictslider** and the objects connected to it. Use two unipolar sine wave oscillators, each set to a slightly different frequency (perhaps 1 Hz and 0.9 Hz, for example). Port the modification that you made to the three [**p** x_dissolve] subpatches in Activity A into this patch, because you will need it. After testing the patch to make sure that it is working properly, try changing the frequencies and the waveforms of the LFOs. With this technique, it is possible to implement very interesting evolving timbres.

ACTIVITY – *COMPLETING ALGORITHMS – ACTIVITY C*

Return to the file 03_10_subsynth.maxpat, which we first analyzed in Section 3.5, and add an LFO to the synthesizer that can take on the waveform of a sine wave, a sawtooth wave, a square wave, or non-interpolated random noise generator. (Suggestion: use four generators corresponding to the waveforms indicated, and connect them to a **selector~** with 4 audio inlets that can be used to choose between them.) This LFO should be able to influence the frequency of the audio generators (producing vibrato), their amplitude (producing tremolo), the center frequency and the Q of the lowpass filter, and/or the duty cycle of the audio oscillator (when the audio oscillator is a square wave). Video Example 4L was created with exactly this synthesizer: refer to the description that we provided in Section 4.7 of the theory chapter for more information. This is a difficult exercise, but if you have followed attentively up to this point, you should surely be able to pull it off!

ACTIVITY – *REPLACING PARTS OF ALGORITHMS*

Return to the file 04_03_matrixmod.maxpat, which was shown in Figure 4.25, and replace the bandlimited sound generator with a **`groove~`** object playing the audio file vs_drums_loop.aif, in order to create new presets that function well with percussion sounds. Change the control signal for vibrato to alter the speed of the playback, remembering that the vibrato setting also affects the cutoff frequency of the filter. Try playing the file in reverse, while avoiding a negative cutoff frequency for the filter.

ACTIVITY – *CORRECTING ALGORITHMS*

Open the file **04_correction.maxpat**.

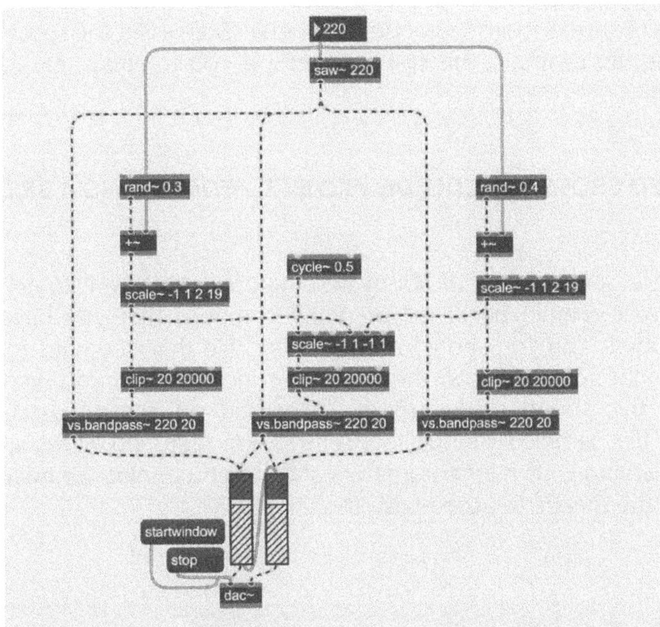

Fig. 4.35 The file 04_correction.maxpat

If you activate this patch, all that you hear is the sound of a bandlimited sawtooth waveform: the number box at the top can be used to change the frequency of the oscillator, but the timbre remains mostly fixed.

Here is what you *want* to be able to hear:

1) On the left channel: a bandpass filtered sound whose center frequency changes in a random way at a frequency of 0.3 Hz, so as to shift between the 2nd and the 19th harmonics of the sound produced by the oscillator.
2) On the right channel: the same type of setup as described for the left channel, with the only difference being that the random LFO has a frequency of 0.4 Hz.
3) On the center channel (and therefore on both channels): a bandpass filtered sound whose center frequency oscillates in a sinusoidal manner at a rate of 0.5 Hz. The extreme values of this oscillation correspond to the frequency values being generated by the two random LFOs.

In the patch, there are 3 object mistakes that must be corrected, and in addition, the position of two pairs of objects is inverted.

INTEGRATED CROSS-FUNCTIONAL PROJECT – *REVERSE ENGINEERING*

Listen to the audio file 04_reverse_engine.aiff. How was this sound created? Notice that the frequency of the LFO used in its synthesis varies in time, and that this LFO controls more than one parameter. Examining the spectrum of the sound (using, for example, the `spectroscope~` object) may help your reverse engineering.

INTEGRATED CROSS-FUNCTIONAL PROJECT – *COMPOSING A BRIEF SOUND STUDY*

Realize a short sound study of about two minutes and save it to an audio file. The brief piece should be based on the techniques that you have acquired up to this point, and you should include a text file that describes the kinds of operations that you used and the kinds of sonorities that you were working with. For this sound study, which is focused on control oscillators, you should also use sampled sounds. Concentrate on featuring vibratos, tremolos, oscillating variations of filter parameters and stereo panning (or quadraphonic, if you have the means to accomplish this).

LIST OF MAX OBJECTS

`abl.dsp.modulator~`
Low-frequency classic waveform generator.

`abl.dsp.stereolfo~`
Stereophonic LFO with phase and duty cycle control.

`abl.dsp.wander~`
Low-frequency random path generator.

`abs`
Returns the absolute value of a number (removing any negative signs).

`matrixctrl`
Graphical object used to establish and break connections between the inlets and the outlets of a `matrix~` object.

`matrix~`
A signal mixer object that can be equipped with a freely settable number of signal inlets and outlets. It is possible to connect any inlet to any outlet by using appropriate messages or by using a `matrixctrl` object.

`mc.stereo~`
An object that implements stereo panning. It positions the signal received on its left inlet in the stereo field, under the control of the signal received on its right inlet.

`rampsmooth~`
An object that smooths any jumps that may appear in a signal, by applying linear interpolation to the samples on its inlet.

ATTRIBUTES FOR SPECIFIC MAX OBJECTS

matrixctrl
- Number of columns (Inspector attribute)
The number of columns in the object

- Number of rows (Inspector attribute)
The number of rows in the object

- One non-zero cell per row (Inspector attribute)
When this attribute is checked, only one connection is permitted per row: only one outlet can be connected to a given inlet (although one inlet can still be connected to many outlets).

GLOSSARY

Theremin
An electronic instrument that is played by changing the distance between the player's hands and two antennas, one of which controls the frequency and the other of which controls the amplitude of the sound.

REFERENCES

The decision was made to limit the bibliography in this book to a list of only the most absolutely essential reference works, and, of course, a list of the books and articles cited in the text. A more comprehensive bibliography is available online.

CITED REFERENCES

Bianchini, R. 2003. *Acustica*. Unpublished.

Bianchini, R. and Cipriani, A. 2001. *Il Suono Virtuale*. Roma: ConTempoNet

Casati, R. and Dokic, J. (1994), *La Philosophie du Son*. Nîmes: Chambon

Dodge, C. and Jerse, T.A. (1997), *Computer Music: Synthesis, Composition, and Performance*. 2nd Ed. New York, NY: Schirmer

Frova, A. (1999), *Fisica nella Musica*. Bologna: Zanichelli.

Grey, J.M. (1975), *An exploration of Musical Timbre*. Doctoral dissertation. Stanford, CA: Stanford University

Grey, J.M. (1977), "Multidimensional Perceptual Scaling of Musical Timbre" *Journal of the Acoustical Society of America* 61: 1270-1277

Rossing, T. D. (1990, *The Science of Sound*. London: Addison-Wesley

Shepard, R.N. (2024), "Circularity in Judgments of Relative Pitch". *Journal of Acoustic Society of America* 36: pp.2406-2371

OTHER LITERATURE

Alton Everest, F. and Ken Pohlmann. 2009. *Master Handbook of Acoustics*. New York, NY: McGraw-Hill/TAB Electronics

Bianchini, R. and Cipriani, A. 2000. *Virtual Sound*. Rome: ConTempoNet

Boulanger, R. (ed.). 1999. *The Csound Book. Perspectives in Software Synthesis, Sound Design, Signal Processing and Programming*. Cambridge, MA: MIT Press

Chadabe, J. 1997. *Electric Sound. The Past and Promise of Electronic Music*. Upper Saddle River, NJ: Prentice Hall

Cook, P. R. 1999. *Music, Cognition, and Computerized Sound*. Cambridge, MA: MIT Press

Miranda, Eduardo. (2002). *Computer Sound Design: Synthesis Techniques and Programming*. Oxford: Focal Press

Moore, F.R. 1990. *Elements of Computer Music*. Englewood Cliffs, NJ: Prentice-Hall

Puckette, M. 2007. *Theory and Techniques of Electronic Music*: World Scientific Publishing

Roads, C. 1996. *Computer Music Tutorial*. Cambridge, MA: MIT Press

Rocchesso, D. 2004. *Introduction to Sound Processing*. Firenze: Mondo Estremo

Uncini, A. 2006. *Audio Digitale*. Milano: McGraw-Hill

Wishart, T. 1994. *Audible Design*. York: Orpheus the Pantomime Ltd.

INDEX

The page numbers printed using a plain font refer to definitions embedded in the text, while numbers printed in italics refer to definitions contained in lists or glossaries at the end of the chapters.

Z

www.ingramcontent.com/pod-product-compliance
Ingram Content Group UK Ltd.
Pitfield, Milton Keynes, MK11 3LW, UK
UKHW020129290926
15471UKWH00003B/381

9 788899 212285